SAFETY SYMBOLS

SAFETY SYMBOLS	HAZARD	PRECAUTION	REMEDY
Disposal	Special disposal required	Dispose of wastes as directed by your teacher.	Ask your teacher how to dispose of laboratory materials.
Biological	Organisms that can harm humans	Avoid breathing in or skin contact with organisms. Wear dust mask or gloves. Wash hands thoroughly.	Notify your teacher if you suspect contact.
Extreme Temperature	Objects that can burn skin by being too cold or too hot	Use proper protection when handling.	Go to your teacher for first aid.
Sharp Object	Use of tools or glassware that can easily puncture or slice skin	Practice common sense behavior and follow guidelines for use of the tool.	Go to your teacher for first aid.
Fumes	Potential danger from smelling fumes	Must have good ventilation and never smell fumes directly.	Leave foul area and notify your teacher immediately.
Electrical	Possible danger from electrical shock or burn	Double-check setup with instructor. Check condition of wires and apparatus.	Do not attempt to fix electrical problems. Notify your teacher immediately.
Irritant	Substances that can irritate your skin or mucous membranes	Wear dust mask or gloves. Practice extra care when handling these materials.	Go to your teacher for first aid.
Chemical	Substances (acids and bases) that can react with and destroy tissue and other materials	Wear goggles and an apron.	Immediately flush with water and notify your teacher.
Toxic	Poisonous substance	Follow your teacher's instructions. Always wash hands thoroughly after use.	Go to your teacher for first aid.
Fire	Flammable and combustible materials may burn if exposed to an open flame or spark	Avoid flames and heat sources. Be aware of locations of fire safety equipment.	Notify your teacher immediately. Use fire safety equipment if necessary.

Eye Safety
This symbol appears when a danger to eyes exists.

Clothing Protection
This symbol appears when substances could stain or burn clothing.

Animal Safety
This symbol appears whenever live animals are studied and the safety of the animals and students must be ensured.

GLENCOE

California Edition

SCIENCE VOYAGES
LIFE
SCIENCE

NATIONAL
GEOGRAPHIC
SOCIETY

Glencoe
McGraw-Hill

New York, New York   Columbus, Ohio   Woodland Hills, California   Peoria, Illinois

A Glencoe Program

California Edition

Glencoe Science Voyages

California Student Edition
California Teacher Wraparound Edition
Assessment
    Chapter Review
    California Science Content Standards Practice
     Questions
    Performance Assessment
    Assessment—Chapter and Unit Tests
    ExamView Test Bank Software
    Performance Assessment in the Science
     Classroom
    Alternate Assessment in the Science Classroom
Study Guide for Content Mastery, SE and TE
Chapter Overview Study Guide, SE and TE
Reinforcement
Enrichment
Critical Thinking/Problem Solving
Multicultural Connections

Activity Worksheets
Laboratory Manual, SE and TE
Science Inquiry Activities, SE and TE
California Home Involvement
Teaching Transparencies
Section Focus Transparencies
Science Integration Transparencies
Spanish Resources
California Lesson Plans
Lab and Safety Skills in the Science Classroom
Cooperative Learning in the Science Classroom
Exploring Environmental Issues
MindJogger Videoquizzes and Teacher Guide
English/Spanish Audiocassettes
Interactive Lesson Planner CD-ROM
Interactive CD-ROM
Internet Site
Using the Internet in the Science Classroom

THE PRINCETON REVIEW

The "Test-Taking Tip" and "Test Practice" features in this book were written by The Princeton Review, the nation's leader in test preparation. Through its association with McGraw-Hill, The Princeton Review offers the best way to help students excel on standardized assessments.

The Princeton Review is not affiliated with Princeton University or Educational Testing Service.

Glencoe/McGraw-Hill

A Division of The McGraw·Hill Companies

Send all inquiries to:
Glencoe/McGraw-Hill
8787 Orion Place
Columbus, OH 43240

ISBN 0-07-823989-3
Printed in the United States of America.
3 4 5 6 7 8 9 10 071/043 06 05 04 03 02 01

Series Authors

Alton Biggs
Biology Instructor
Allen High School
Allen, Texas

John Eric Burns
Science Teacher
Ramona Jr. High School
Chino, California

Lucy Daniel, Ph.D.
Teacher, Consultant
Rutherford County Schools
Rutherfordton, North Carolina

Cathy Ezrailson
Science Department Head
Oak Ridge High School
Conroe, Texas

Ralph Feather, Jr., Ph.D.
Science Department Chair
Derry Area School District
Derry, Pennsylvania

Patricia Horton
Math and Science Teacher
Summit Intermediate School
Etiwanda, California

Thomas McCarthy, Ph.D.
Science Department Chair
St. Edwards School
Vero Beach, Florida

Ed Ortleb
Science Consultant
St. Louis Public Schools
St. Louis, Missouri

Susan Leach Snyder
Science Department Chair
Jones Middle School
Upper Arlington, Ohio

Eric Werwa, Ph.D.
Department of Physics and Astronomy
Otterbein College
Westerville, Ohio

National Geographic Society
Educational Division
Washington D.C.

Contributing Authors

Al Janulaw
Science Teacher
Creekside Middle School
Rohnert Park, California

Penny Parsekian
Science Writer for
The National Geographic Society
New London, Connecticut

Gerry Madrazo, Ph.D.
Mathematics and Science Education
 Network
University of North Carolina, Chapel Hill
Chapel Hill, North Carolina

Contents in Brief

GRADE SEVEN: FOCUS ON LIFE SCIENCE

What are science content standards and why does California have them? Standards are guidelines for schools, students, and parents that describe the essential science concepts and skills for understanding the world in which we live. In 1999, The California State Board of Education established science content standards, and these standards will be the basis for state assessments that measure student achievement in science.

ADDITIONAL CONTENT STANDARDS FOR GRADE 7

- California Science Standards and Case Studies, found at the back of the book
- California Science Content Standards Assessment Practice booklets
- Chapter Assessments at the end of each chapter
- Science Voyages Website at www.glencoe.com/sec/science/ca

Cell Biology

1. All living organisms are composed of cells, from just one to many trillions, whose details usually are viible only through a microscope.. As the basis for understanding this concept, students know:

   a. cells function similarly in all living organisms
   Sections 2-1, 2-2, 3-1, 3-2, 3-3, 4-1, 4.-2, page 628

   b. the characteristics that distinguish plant cells from animal cells, chloroplasts and cell walls.
   Sections 2.2, 4-1, page 629

   c. the nucleus is the repository for genetic information in plant and animal cells.
   Sections 4-1, 4-3, page 630

   d. mitochondria liberate energy for the work that cells do, and chloroplasts capture sunlight energy for photosynthesis.
   Sections 2-2, 3-3, page 631, 632

   e. cells divide to increase their numbers through a process of mitosis, which results in two daughte5r cells with identical sets of chromosomes.
   Sections 4-1, 5-1, page 632

   f. as multicellular organisms develop, their cells differentiate.
   Sections 2-2, 21-2, page 633

Genetics

2. A typical cell of any organism contains genetic instructions that specify its traits. Those traits may be modified by environmental influences. As the basis for understanding this concept, students know:

   a. the differences between the life cycles and reproduction of sexual and asexual organisms.
   Sections 4-1, 4-2, page 634

   b. sexual reproduction produces offspring that inherit half their genes from each parent.
   Sections 4-1, 4-2, 5-1, 6-1, page 634

   c. an inherited trait can be determined by one or more genes.
   Sections 4-3, 6-1, 6-2, 6-3, pages 634

   d. plant and animal cells contain many thousands of different genes, and typically have two copies of every gene. The two copies (or alleles) of the gene may or may not be identical, and one may be dominating in determining the phenotype while the other is recessive.
   Sections 6-2, 6-2, 6-3, page 635

   e. DNA is the genetic material of living organisms, and is located in the chromosomes of each cell.
   Sections 2-2, 4-3, 6-1, 6-2, page 635

Evolution

3. Biological evolution accounts for the diversity of species developed through gradual processes over many generations. As a basis for understanding this concept, students know:

   a. both genetic variation and environmental factors are causes of evolution and diversity of organisms.
   Sections 7-1, 30-1, 30-2, 30.3, page 638

   b. the reasoning used by Darwin in making his conclusion that natural selectin is the mechanism of evolution.
   Sections 7-1, page 639

   c. how independent lines of evidence from geology, fossils, and comparative anatomy provide a basis for the theory of evolution.
   Sections 7-1, 7-2, 7-3, 29-1, 29-2, 30-1, 30-2, 30-3, page 639

   d. how to construct a simple branching diagram to classify living groups of organisms by shared derived characteristics, and expand the diagram to include fossil organisms.
   Sections 7-1, 7-3, page 640

   e. extinction of a species occurs when the enviromnent changes and the adaptive characteristics of a species are insufficient for its survival.
   Sections 30-1, 30-2, 30-3, page 640

Earth and Life History (Earth Science)

4. Evidence from rocks allows us to understand the evolution of life on Earth. As a basis for understanding this concept, students know:

   a. Earth processes today are similar to those that occurred in the past and slow geologic processes have large cumulative effects over long periods of time.
   Sections 27-1, 27-2, 27-3, 27-4, 29-3, page 643

   b. the history of life on Earth has been disrupted by major catastrophic events, such as major volcanic eruptions or the impact of an asteroid.
   Sections 29-2, pages 643, 646

   c. the rock cycle includes the formation of new sediment and rocks. Rocks are often found in layers with the oldest generally on the bottom.
   Sections 7-2, 27-1, 27-2, 27-3, 27-4, 29-2, pages 643 - 644

   d. evidence from geologic layers and radioactive dating indicate the

Earth is approximately 4.6 billion years old, and that life has existed for more than 3 billion years.
Sections 7-2, 29-3, page 634

e. fossils provide evidence of how life and environmental conditions have changed.
Sections 7-2, 29-1, 29-2, 30-1, 30-2 30-3 , page 634

f. how movements of the Earth's continental and oceanic plates through time, with associated changes in climate and geographical connections, have affected the past and present dirtribution of organisms.
Sections 30-1, 30-2, 30-3, page 645

g. how to explain significant developments and extinctions of plant and animal life on the geologic time scale.
Sections 30-1, 30-2, 30-3, page 645

Structure and Function in Living Systems

5. The anatomy and physiology of plants and animals illustrate the complementary nature of structure and function. As a basis for understanding this concept, students know:

a. plants and animals have levels of organizati9on for structure and function, including cells, tissues, organs, organ systems, and the whole organism.
Sections 2-1, 2-2, 5-1, 17-2, 18-1, 18-2, 18-3, 19-1, 19-2, 20-1, 20-2, 20-3, 21-1, 21-2, 21-3, 22-1, 22-2, 22-3, 27-1, page 648

b. organ systems function because of the contributions of individual organs, tissues, and cells, tissues, and cells. The failure of any part can affect the entire system.
Sections 13-2, 13-3, 17-2, 18-1, 18-2, 18-3, 19-1, 19-2, 22-2, 22-3, pages 649, 653

c. how bones and muscles work together to provide a structural framework for movement.
Sections 13-1, 13-2, page 649

d. how the reproductive organs of the human female and male generate eggs and sperm, and how sexual activity may lead to fertilization and pregnancy.
Sections 21-1, 21-2, page 650

e. the number and types of organisms an ecosystem can support depends on the resources available and abiotic factors, such as quantity of light and water, range of temperatures, and soil composition.

Sections 21-2, page 651

f. the structures and processes by which flowering plants generate pollen and ovules, seeds, and fruit.
Section 5-2, page 650

g. how to relate the structures of the eye and ear to their functions.
Section 20-2, page 651

Physical Principles in Living Systems (Physical Science)

6. Physical principles underlie biological structures and functions. As a basis for understanding this concept, students know:

a. visible light is a small band within a very broad electromagnetic spectrum.
Section 23-1, page 654

b. for an object to be seen, light emitted by or scattered from it must enter the eye.
Sections 23-1, 23-2, page 654

c. light travels in straight lines except when the medium it travels through changes.
Sections 20-2, 23-3, page 654

d. how simple lenses are used in a magnifying glass, the eye, camera, telescope, and microscope.
Sections 2-1, 23-3, 23-4, pages 654 - 655

e. white light is a mixture of many wavelengths (colors), and that retinal cells react differently with different wavelengths.
Sections 20-2, 23-1, page 655

f. light interacts with matter by transmission (including refraction), absorption, or scattering (including reflection).
Sections 23-1, 23-2, 23-3, page 655

g. the angle of reflection of a light beam is equal to the angle of incidence.
Section 23-2, page 656

h. how to compare joints in the body (wrist, shoulder, thigh) with structures used in machines and simple devices (hinge, ball-and-socket, and sliding joints).
Section 13-1, page 656

i. how levers confer mechanical advantage and how the application of this principle applies to the musculoskeletal system.
Sections 13-2, 25-2, page 656

j. contractions of the heart generate blood pressure, and heart valves prevent backflow of blood in the

circulatory system.
Section 18-1, page 657

Investigation and Experimentation

7. Scientific progress is made by asking meaningful questions and conducting careful investigations. As a basis for understanding this concept, and to address the content the other three strands, students should develop their own questions and perform investigations. Students will:

a. select and use appropriate tools and technology (including calculators, computers, balances, spring scales, microscopes, and binoculars) to perform tests, collect data, and display data.
Sections 1-1, 1-2, 1-3, 2-1, 2-3, 6-3, 7-1, 13-2, 17-1, 18-2, 19-2, 23-3, 24-3, 25-1, 25-2, pages 628, 638, 655

b. utilize a variety of print and electronic resources (including the World Wide Web) to collect information as evidence as part of a research project.
Sections 1-1, 2-3, 3-1, 3-2, 4-1, 4-3, 5-1, 5-2, 6-1, 6-3, 7-1, 7-2, 13-1, 17-1, 18-1, 18-2, 19-1, 19-2, 20-1, 20-3, 21-1, 21-2, 21-3, 22-2, 22-3, 23-4, 24-2, 24-3, 25-2, 26-2, 28-2, 28-3, 29-2, 29-3, 30-1, 30-2, 30-3, pages 630, 634, 637, 638, 639, 642, 644, 645, 649, 653, 655

c. communicate the logical connection among hypothesis, science concepts, tests conducted, data collected, and conclusions drawn from the scientific evidence.
Sections 1-2, 2-1, 5-2, 7-1, 17-2, 19-1, 20-2, 22-2, 25-2, pages 630, 635, 637, 638, 639, 650, 657

d. construct scale models, maps and appropriately labeled diagrams to communicate scientific knowledge (e.g., motion of Earth's plates and cell structure).
Sections 1-2, 4-3, 6-1, 6-2, 7-1, 15-1, 15-2, 21-3, 26-2, 30-2, 30-3, pages 630, 631, 635, 638, 639, 643

e. communicate the steps and results from an investigation in written reports and verbal presentations.
Sections 2-1, 2-2, 3-2, 5-2, 6-2, 13-2, 17-2, 18-3, 19-1, 21-2, 23-1, 24-2, 25-2, 26-2, 27-1, 29-1, 30-1, pages 69, 95, 121, 463, 519, 571, 628, 633, 635, 647, 651, 656, 785, 817, 847, 907, 971

Contents

Contents

Contents

Contents

Contents

UNIT 4   **The Human Body**   **436**

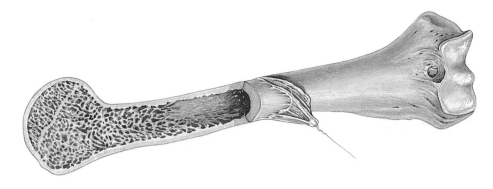

Contents

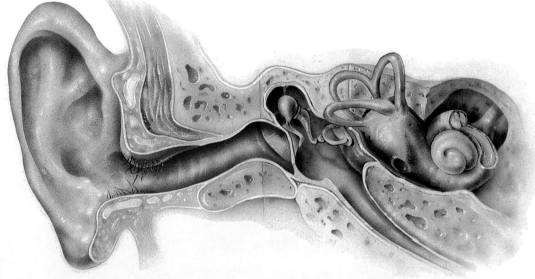

Contents

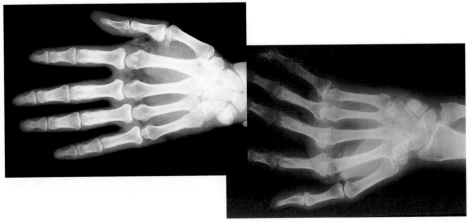

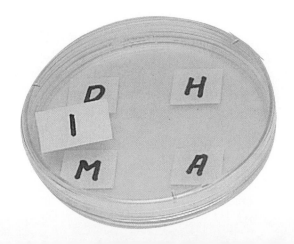

Contents

Science Connections

Activities

Activities

Mini Lab

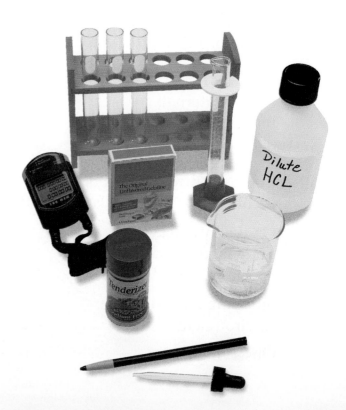

Whorl

Arch

Loop

Explore Activities

Problem Solving

Skill Builders

Skill Activities

Interactions in the Living World

What's Happening Here?

The world within the living cell can be filled with deception, intrigue, and deadly conflict. These jumbled rods (left, magnified 34 000 times) are particles of a tobacco mosaic virus that has taken over a cell of a tobacco plant. So, instead of following its own genetic code, the plant cell has been tricked into helping the virus multiply. Eventually, the plant will weaken or die. Trickery in the living world can also be beneficial. Without asking, some plants get help to spread their seeds. How? The seeds of the strawberry plant dot the surface of its delicious, juicy fruit (below). Animals eat the strawberries and deposit the seeds in new places. In this unit, you will explore the dynamic world within the cell and the processes by which cells multiply and change into various parts of complete living things. You will also learn some of the ways plants populate Earth.

interNET CONNECTION

Explore the Glencoe Science Web Site at **www.glencoe.com/ sec/science/ca** to find out more about topics found in this unit.

The Nature of Science

Chapter Preview

Skills Preview

Skill Builders
- Communicate
- Hypothesize

Activities
- Design an Experiment
- Make and Use a Table

MiniLabs
- Compare and Contrast
- Observe and Infer

Reading Check ✔

As you read about the nature of science, use the headings and subheadings to make an outline. Under each subheading, write a few important points.

Explore Activity

You are painting your bedroom. You decide to paint the room green, but when you get to the paint store, you see different shades of green. Which shade will go best with the other things in your room? To match the color, you take paint samples home. You hold the samples next to curtains, blankets, and other decorations. The paint samples are a tool you use to solve your problem. You use the samples to accurately "measure" the shade of green. Tools and measuring are all parts of science. To learn more about the importance of tools, complete the following Explore Activity.

Use Tools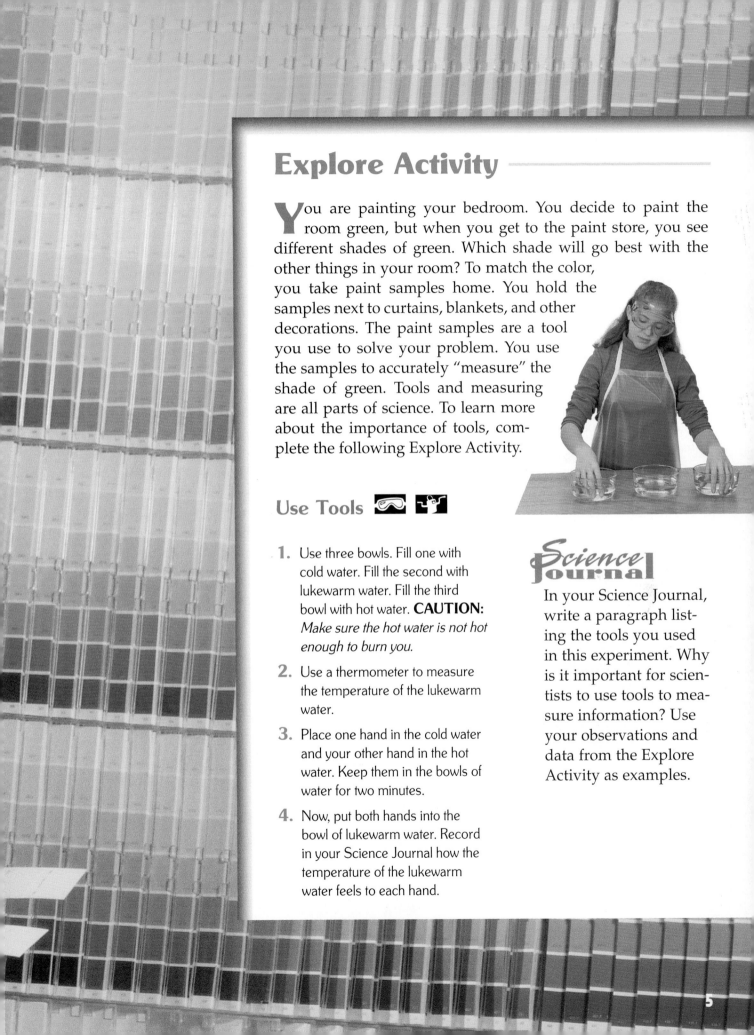

1. Use three bowls. Fill one with cold water. Fill the second with lukewarm water. Fill the third bowl with hot water. **CAUTION:** *Make sure the hot water is not hot enough to burn you.*

2. Use a thermometer to measure the temperature of the lukewarm water.

3. Place one hand in the cold water and your other hand in the hot water. Keep them in the bowls of water for two minutes.

4. Now, put both hands into the bowl of lukewarm water. Record in your Science Journal how the temperature of the lukewarm water feels to each hand.

Science Journal

In your Science Journal, write a paragraph listing the tools you used in this experiment. Why is it important for scientists to use tools to measure information? Use your observations and data from the Explore Activity as examples.

1•1 What is science?

Science in Society

What You'll Learn

▶ How science is a part of your everyday life
▶ What skills are used in science

Vocabulary
science
technology

Why It's Important

▶ What and how you learn in science class can be applied to other areas of your life.

Science. When you hear this word, do you think it has little to do with what's important in your life? You go to science class. You have a science teacher. You learn science terms and facts. But, what is the connection between sitting in the class and the rest of your daily life? Science is more than just terms or facts. You and other people are curious about what is happening in the world. You may have problems to solve or questions that need answers, as illustrated in **Figure 1-1. Science** is a way or a process used to investigate what is happening around us. It provides some possible answers.

Science is not new. Throughout history, people have tried to find answers to questions about what was happening around them. Many used observations to find the answers. These observations were based on using their senses of sight, touch, smell, taste, and hearing. They made up stories based on their observations. From the Explore Activity, you know that only using your senses can't answer all questions. Seeing is not always believing. Cold may feel hot. Tools such as thermometers are needed to make mathematical measurements. Numbers can be used to describe observations. Scientists use both observations and experiments to find answers. Let's see how science can be useful to you.

Figure 1-1 Science is used every day as you make decisions.

Science as a Tool

As Luis and Midori walked into science class, they were still talking about their new history assignment. Mr. Johnson overheard them and asked what they were all excited about.

"We have a special assignment celebrating the founding of our town 200 years ago," answered Luis. "We need to do a project tying together a past event with something now going on in the community. We need to demonstrate the similarities and the differences in the two events."

Mr. Johnson put down his pencil and responded. "That sounds like a big undertaking. Have you chosen the two events yet?"

"We were looking through some old newspaper articles and came across several stories about a cholera epidemic that killed ten people and made more than 50 others ill. It happened in 1871—right after the Civil War. Midori and I think that it's like the *E. coli* outbreak going on now in our town," replied Luis.

"What do you know about outbreaks of the disease cholera and problems caused by *E. coli*, Luis?"

"Well, Mr. Johnson, cholera is a disease caused by a bacterium that is found in contaminated bodies of water," Luis replied. "People who eat seafood from this water or drink this water get really sick. They have bad cases of diarrhea and may become badly dehydrated, which can lead to death. *E. coli* is another type of bacterium that causes similar intestinal problems when polluted food and water are consumed."

"In fact," added Midori, "one of the workers at my dad's store is just getting over being sick. We hope no one else in his family gets it. Anyway, Mr. Johnson, we want to know if you can help us with the project. We want to compare how people tracked down the source of the cholera in 1871 with how they are now tracking down the source of the *E. coli*."

Figure 1-2 Newspapers, magazines, books, and the Internet are all good sources of information.

Reducing Water Pollution
The U.S. Congress has helped reduce water pollution by passing several laws. The 1986 Safe Drinking Water Act is a law to ensure that drinking water in our country is safe. The 1987 Clean Water Act gives money to the states for building sewage- and wastewater-treatment facilities.

Figure 1-3 Scientists are like detectives, making conclusions based on clues. Such skills can be practiced by playing board games and solving puzzles.

A Puzzles require such skills as observing and inferring. **What other skills may be involved?**

B Board games often include skills such as communicating and sequencing. **What are some other skills involved in playing such games?**

Using Science Every Day

"I'll be glad to help," grinned Mr. Johnson. "This sounds like a great way to show how science is a part of everyone's life. In fact, you are acting like scientists right now."

Luis had a puzzled look on his face. "What do you mean? How can we be doing science? This is really a history project."

"Well, you're acting like a detective right now. You have a problem to solve. You and Midori are looking for clues that show how the two events are similar and different. As you complete the project, you will use several skills and tools to find the clues. You will then follow the clues to determine the similarities and differences. These things will help you solve your problem."

Mr. Johnson continued, "In many ways, scientists do the same thing. People in 1871 followed clues to track the source of the cholera epidemic and solve their problem. Scientists are doing the same now by finding and following clues to track the source of the *E. coli.*"

Using Prior Knowledge

Mr. Johnson continued talking as he walked over to the chalkboard. "Let's look at another way that your history project is like science. Luis, how do you know what is needed to complete the project?"

Luis thought for a minute before responding. "The report must be at least three pages long and have maps, pictures, or charts and graphs. Our teacher, Miss Hernandez, also said that we had to use several different sources for our information. These could be newspaper or magazine articles, letters, videotapes of educational programs, the Internet, or government documents. I also know that it must be handed in on time and that correct spelling and grammar count."

"Did Miss Hernandez actually talk about correct spelling and grammar?" asked Mr. Johnson.

At this point, Midori quickly responded, "No, she didn't have to. Everyone knows that Miss Hernandez counts off for incorrect spelling or grammar. I certainly learned that with my last report. I forgot to check my spelling and I got a whole point taken off."

"Ah-ha! That's where your project is like science," exclaimed Mr. Johnson. "You know from experience what will happen. Each time you don't follow her rule, your grade is lowered. You can predict, or make an educated guess, that Miss Hernandez will react the same way with future reports."

Mr. Johnson continued, "Scientists also use prior experience to predict what will happen under certain circumstances. If the results support their prediction, they continue to follow the same procedure. If the results change or don't support their prediction, they must change their predictions."

Figure 1-4 It is important to discover background information about any problem you are attempting to solve. Different sources of information can provide such information. **How would you find information on a specific topic? What sources of information would you use?**

Using Science Technology and Skills

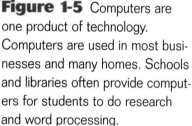

interNET CONNECTION

Visit the Glencoe Science Web Site at **www.glencoe.com/sec/science/ca** for more information about how to do research on the Internet.

Figure 1-5 Computers are one product of technology. Computers are used in most businesses and many homes. Schools and libraries often provide computers for students to do research and word processing.

"Midori, you said that you want to compare the tracking of the two diseases. I said that, like scientists, you will use some skills and tools to find the similarities and differences." Mr. Johnson then pointed to Luis. "You listed a variety of resource materials that can be used to find out the information. How will you know which materials will be useful?"

"We'll go to the library and use the computer." Luis smiled as he pointed to the library book in his hand. "We can use the computer to find which books, magazines, newspapers, or videos have information we need."

"We also can use the computer to get on the Internet and find different Web pages or links that might help us," added Midori.

"Exactly," said Mr. Johnson. "And, that's another way that you are acting like scientists. The computer is one tool that modern scientists use to find and analyze data. The computer is a product of technology. Remember that **technology** is the application of science to make products or tools that people can use. In fact, I'm sure that one of the big differences you will find between the way diseases were tracked in 1871 and how they are tracked now is the result of new technology."

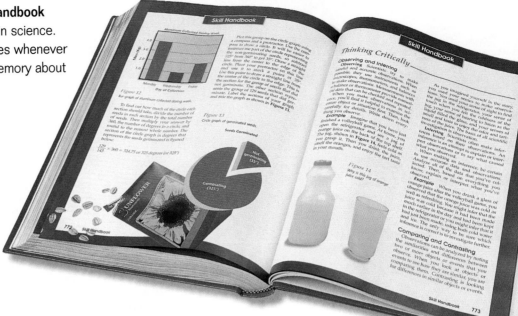

Figure 1-6 The **Skill Handbook** describes many skills used in science. You may refer to these pages whenever you need to refresh your memory about scientific methods.

Science Skills

"Perhaps one of the similarities between the two time periods will be some of the skills used to track the disease," continued Mr. Johnson. "Today's doctors and scientists might have new technological gadgets to use, but they still practice the same skills such as observing, classifying, and interpreting data. In fact, you might want to review the science skills we've talked about in class. That way, you'll be able to identify how they were used during the cholera outbreak and how they are still used today."

Luis and Midori had a lot to think about during the next few days as they started working on their project. They began by following Mr. Johnson's suggestion to review the science skills. The skills used by scientists are described in the **Skill Handbook,** shown in **Figure 1-6** and found at the back of this book. The more you practice these skills, the more comfortable you will become using them.

Think about the Explore Activity at the beginning of this chapter. Observing, measuring, and comparing and contrasting are three skills you used to complete the activity. Scientists probably use these skills more than any others. But, you will learn that sometimes observation alone does not provide a complete picture of what is actually happening. In addition to making careful observations, you must provide other information such as precise measurements to have the best data possible. ✓

Luis and Midori want to find the similarities and differences between the disease-tracking techniques of the late 1800s and today. They will be using the skill of comparing and contrasting. They will compare the techniques available when they look for similarities. They will contrast the techniques when they look for differences.

Reading Check ✓

List three common skills used in science.

Picture 1

Picture 2

Mini Lab

Inferring from Pictures

Procedure

1. In your Science Journal, copy the following table.

Observations and Inferences		
Picture	Observations	Inferences
1		
2		

2. Study the two pictures on this page. Write down all your observations in the table.

3. Make inferences based on your observations. Record your inferences.

4. Share your inferences with others in your class.

Analysis

1. Analyze the inferences that you made. Are there other explanations for what you observed?

2. Why must you be careful when making inferences?

3. Create your own picture and description. Have other students make inferences based on the picture and description.

Communication in Science

What do scientists do with their findings? The results of their observations, experiments, and hard work will not be of use to the rest of the world unless they are shared. Scientists use several methods to communicate their observations.

Results and conclusions of experiments are often reported in scientific journals or magazines, where other scientists can read of their work. Hundreds of scientific journals are published weekly or monthly. In fact, scientists often spend a large part of their time reading journal articles in an effort to keep up with new information being reported.

Another method of maintaining records is to keep a Science Journal or log. Descriptions of experiments with step-by-step procedures, listings of materials, and drawings of how equipment is set up may be in a log or journal, as well as specific results. The journal may include descriptions of all of their observations and mathematical measurements or formulas.

Additional questions that come up during experiments also can be recorded. Problems that occur also are noted, along with possible solutions. Data may be recorded or summarized in the form of tables, charts, or graphs, or it may just be recorded in a paragraph. Remember, it's important to use correct spelling.

You will be able to use your Science Journal to communicate your observations, questions, thoughts, and ideas as you work in science class, as illustrated in **Figure 1-7.** You will practice many of the science skills and become better at identifying problems and planning ways to solve these problems. At the same time, you will gain more scientific knowledge. In the next section, follow Luis and Midori as they continue to research their project. You will have a chance to practice some science skills as you solve problems.

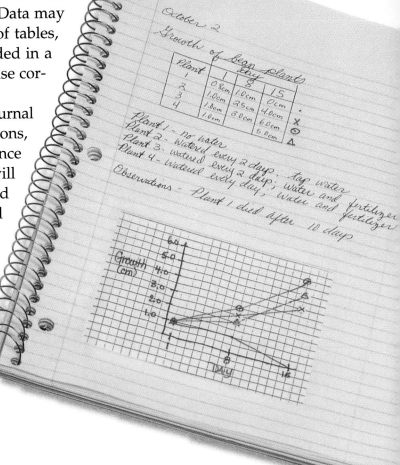

Figure 1-7 Science Journals are used to communicate scientific observations, questions, thoughts, and ideas. They may include graphs, tables, and illustrations.

Section Assessment

1. Why do scientists use tools, such as thermometers and rulers, when they make observations?

2. How are scientists like detectives?

3. What are some skills used in science?

4. **Think Critically:** What is the difference between science and technology?

5.  **Skill Builder**
   Communicating In your Science Journal, draw a shape that includes angles, curves, and straight lines. Find a partner, but do not show this shape to your partner. Describe this shape and have your partner try to reproduce it. If you need help, refer to Communicating in the **Skill Handbook** on page 677.

*inter***NET**
CONNECTION

Visit the Glencoe Science Web Site at **www.glencoe.com/ sec/science/ca** for more information about disease control. In your Science Journal, report two different diseases that the Centers for Disease Control and Prevention (CDC) has tracked down and identified in the past.

1·2 Doing Science

Solving Problems

Midori and Luis spent several more minutes discussing their project with Mr. Johnson. As they talked, it became apparent that they had different ideas about how to complete the project. After listening to them, Mr. Johnson commented, "You both have some good ideas. How about a friendly suggestion before you get started. Even though you are working on a history project, I think you might find some helpful ideas written on the science poster that's hanging on the wall. Scientists know that there is more than one way to solve a problem. There are usually several scientific methods that can be used, or sometimes one method is used more than another. **Scientific methods** are approaches taken to try to solve a problem. The poster shows one method. Come back on Monday and let me know if it has helped."

Getting Organized

Midori and Luis are learning what scientists already know. The quality of a solution to a problem depends on how well the entire project is planned and carried out. They are finding out that preparation is as important as any of the other steps of the problem-solving method presented in **Figure 1-8.**

You can't solve a problem if you haven't identified the problem. Before scientists move on to the other steps of the method, they make sure that everyone working on the problem has a clear understanding of what needs to be solved. Sometimes, the problem is easy to identify. Sometimes, scientists find out that they are dealing with more than one problem. There may be several problems to be solved. For example, a scientist trying to find the source of a disease might first have to make sure of the correct identification of the disease.

What You'll Learn

▶ The steps scientists follow to solve problems
▶ How a well-designed experiment is developed

Vocabulary
scientific methods
model
hypothesis
independent variable
dependent variable
constant
control

Why It's Important

▶ Using step-by-step methods and carefully thought-out experiments can help you solve problems.

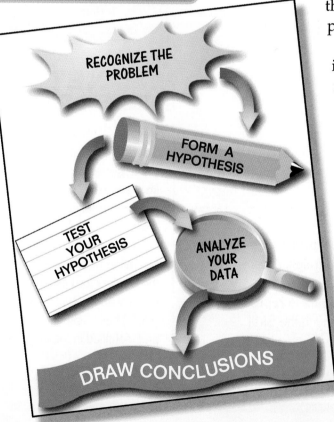

RECOGNIZE THE PROBLEM

FORM A HYPOTHESIS

TEST YOUR HYPOTHESIS

ANALYZE YOUR DATA

DRAW CONCLUSIONS

Figure 1-8 This poster shows one way to solve problems using scientific skills.

Making Plans

Once the problem is identified, a detailed plan is developed that includes possible ways to solve the problem. Part of the plan includes listing what is already known about the problem. For the doctors working on tracking the source of the 1871 cholera outbreak, part of their prior knowledge would be based on what was learned during the cholera epidemic that spread across the United States in 1866.

This would include being able to identify cholera as the disease causing the deaths. They also knew that cholera is spread in unclean water. They might have known that boiling the water kills whatever causes cholera. However, they would not know the actual bacterium that caused the disease.

Another part of the plan includes carefully studying the problem. Maybe more than one problem needs to be solved. Or, maybe a large problem needs to be broken down into smaller problems. If this occurs, a decision is made on which problem should be solved first. Suppose people in your school are getting sick with an infectious disease. Identifying the disease is the first problem to solve. This may be difficult if two diseases share the same symptoms but are caused by different sources of contamination. For example, two diseases might cause high fever, a similar rash, and coughing. Bacteria released into the air might cause one. The other might be spread only by direct physical contact with the infected person. Once the disease is identified, a plan can be made to stop its spread.

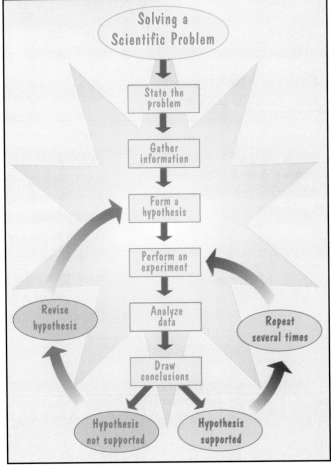

Figure 1-9 The steps in solving a problem in science are a series of procedures called scientific methods.

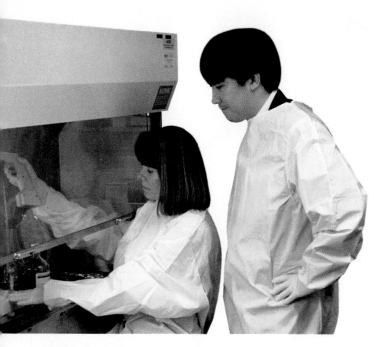

Carrying Out the Plan

Once a plan is made, the next step is to carry it out. Perhaps only one scientist is needed to complete the plan. However, in today's society, it is normal for several different scientists or teams to work on solving different parts of a problem, as illustrated in **Figure 1-10**. In the case of an *E. coli* outbreak, some scientists will work to identify the bacterium, and some will survey the victims affected by the disease (including age, sex, ethnic group, occupation, and where they live). Other scientists will test the many possible sources of contamination for the presence of the bacterium.

Figure 1-10 It takes many different people to solve major medical problems such as AIDS and other epidemics. The technician here is filling a container with a drug discovered by the onlooking medical student. This drug helps fight AIDS.

Using Models

A part of carrying out the plan might include making models. In science, a **model** is a mathematical equation or physical object that is used to think about things that happen too slowly, too quickly, or are too big or small to observe directly. Models are also useful in situations where observation would be too dangerous or expensive. Scientists in 1871 could make a model of the town by using a map.

In 1854, Dr. Snow made a model of the cholera outbreak that took place in London. He plotted the location of the cholera victims on a map, as illustrated in **Figure 1-11.** He knew that the most likely source of the disease would be in the area

Problem Solving

Using Flex Your Brain

All reliable problem-solving methods begin with a plan. Some plans are easy enough to be stored in your mind. More complicated plans need to be written down. *Flex Your Brain* is a process that will help you organize a plan to solve a problem. This process is shown in the chart.

Think Critically: Use the *Flex Your Brain* chart to explore information about cholera. How does *Flex Your Brain* help you organize your search?

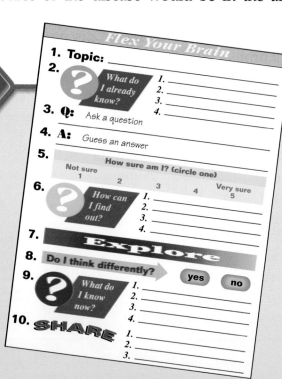

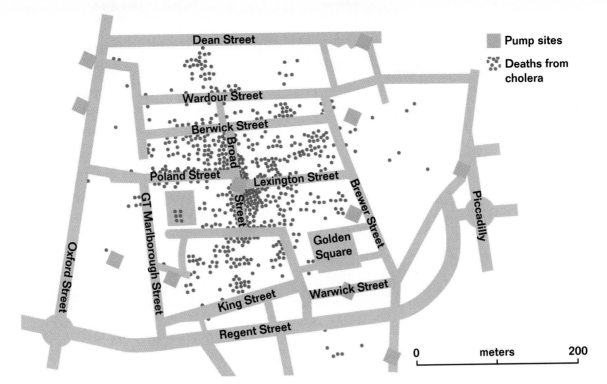

Figure 1-11 Dr. Snow plotted the distribution of deaths in London on a map. He determined that an unusually high number of deaths were taking place near a water pump on Broad Street.

where the most victims were located. The source of cholera in the map he made appeared to be a contaminated water pump.

Today, many people in different careers use models to complete projects. Computers are used to make many kinds of these models. For example, computers can analyze information and predict how far and how quickly the spruce beetle will spread across an area. Scientists will then have a prediction of how many spruce trees may be killed by the beetle within the next five years. Computers can produce three-dimensional models of a microscopic bacterium or a huge asteroid. They are used to design safer airplanes and office buildings. All kinds of models save time and money by testing ideas that otherwise are too small, too large, or take too long to build. Luis and Midori know that computer modeling is an important part of modern scientists' work as they try to track diseases affecting current societies.

Planning an Experiment

Even with their increased role in science, computers cannot provide all of the answers. Experiments often are needed. Scientists continue to include experiments as part of their plans to solve problems. Luis and Midori learned that doctors in the 1800s often used trial-and-error techniques to treat patients. These treatments were not planned experiments and often led to more problems when patients did not respond well. Modern science and medicine use carefully planned experiments to provide solutions. Activities in this book give you the opportunity to design your own experiments.

Recognize the Problem

Recall how important it is for scientists to know exactly what question needs to be answered or which problem needs to be solved. Your first step in designing your experiment is to be sure about what you want to find out. Some helpful information can be found in the activity's introductory statement. Additional information might come from material presented earlier in the chapter or that you already have learned in other science classes.

Form a Hypothesis

Use your prior knowledge, new information, and any previous observations to form a hypothesis (hi PAH thuh sus). A **hypothesis** is a prediction or statement that can be tested. You learned that the doctor in London used a map to plot cholera deaths. He used the information from the map to make a hypothesis, or prediction. He hypothesized that a particular water pump was the source of the cholera contamination, as illustrated in **Figure 1-12**. He then needed to test his hypothesis. To test it, he convinced the town authorities to close down the water pump by removing its handle. If no new cases of the disease appeared, then his hypothesis was supported. The water pump was the source of contamination. However, if the disease continued to strike new victims, the hypothesis was not supported and a different hypothesis would have to be developed and tested.

You form your hypothesis based on information you already know. However, part of your plan to test the hypothesis might include continuing to gather more information. Sometimes, background information and suggestions for types of experiments can be found in science literature at your local library. The World Wide Web and information stored on computer CDs or disks are additional sources of information.

Figure 1-12 Suspecting the Broad Street water pump (A) as the source of the cholera, Dr. Snow had the water pump handle removed and thus ended the epidemic. *Vibrio cholerae* (B) is the microorganism responsible for causing cholera in people.

A

B *Vibrio cholerae*

Magnification: 6000✕

Plan the Experiment

It is important to design your experiment carefully. Suppose, instead of tracking the source of a disease, you want to test the effectiveness of antibiotics in killing the bacteria that cause the disease. Let's look at how each condition might influence the results.

Variables and Controls

In well-planned experiments, variables are tested. Experiments are reliable only if the variables are controlled. This means that only one factor, or variable, is changed at a time. The variable that is changed is called the **independent variable.** A **dependent variable** is the factor being measured.

To test which of two antibiotics will kill a type of bacterium, you must make sure that every variable but the type of antibiotic remains the same. The variables that stay the same are called **constants.** For example, you cannot run the experiments at two different room temperatures, with different amounts of antibiotics, with applications made at different times, or with different types of bacteria. If you are going to test two antibiotics, then everything else about your experiment must be the same. If you change any of the variables, you will not be sure if it is one of the antibiotics alone that killed the bacteria, one of the other variables, or a combination of the factors.

Your experiment will not be valid unless a control is used. A **control** is a sample that is treated exactly like the other experimental groups except that the independant variable is not applied to it. In the experiment described above, your control will be a culture of bacteria that is not treated with either antibiotic. The control shows how the bacteria grow when left untreated by one of the antibiotics. **Figure 1-13** gives another example of a well-planned experiment.

Figure 1-13 In this experiment, a student wanted to test the effect of sunlight on the growth of radish plants. The amount of sunlight received by the radish plants is the independent variable.

A At the beginning of the experiment, radish seeds received the same amount of water. One group of seeds was kept in the sunlight and another group of radish seeds was grown in a dark area.

 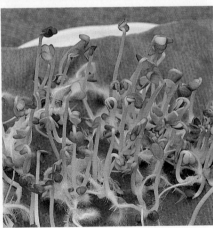

B The photos above show the young radish plants after being grown for the same period of time. All factors were kept constant with the exception of the amount of sunlight. **Based on these photographs, what would you conclude about the effects of sunlight on radish plants?**

Mini Lab

Comparing Paper Towels

Procedure

1. Make a data table similar to the data table in **Figure 1-14.**
2. Cut a 5 cm by 5 cm square from each of three brands of paper towel. Lay each piece on a smooth, level, waterproof surface.
3. Add one drop of water to each square.
4. Continue to add drops until the piece of paper towel can no longer absorb the water.
5. Record your observations in your data table and graph your results.

Analysis

1. Did all the squares of paper towels absorb equal amounts of water?
2. If one brand of paper towel absorbs more water than the others, can you conclude that it is the towel you should buy? Explain.
3. Which scientific methods did you use to answer the question of which paper towel is more absorbent?

Number of Trials

Experiments do not always have the same results. To make sure that your results are valid, you need to conduct several trials of your experiment. Multiple trials mean that an unusual occurrence, which changes the outcome of the experiment, won't be considered the true result. For example, if another substance is accidentally spilled on one of the containers with an antibiotic, that substance might kill the bacteria. Without results from other trials to use as comparisons, you might think that the antibiotic killed the bacteria. Errors in labeling or measuring or timing can occur at any time. The more trials you do using the exact same methods, the more likely it is that your results will be reliable and repeatable.

The actual number of trials you choose to do will vary with each experiment, but the more trials completed, the more reliable the results will be. Your decision will be based on how much time you have to complete the experiment. It also will depend on the cost of running each trial, the availability of materials, or possibly the amount of space you have to set up the trials.

Selecting Your Materials

Scientists try to use the most up-to-date materials they can find. If possible, you should use balances, spring scales, microscopes, and metric measurements when performing experiments and gathering data. These tools will help to

Figure 1-14 Data tables help you organize your observations and test results.

A Most tables have a title that tells you, at a glance, what the table is about.

B A table is divided into columns and rows. The items to be compared are listed in columns—different brands of paper towels.

C The first column lists the trials or characteristics to be compared across in rows.

Paper Towel Absorbency (drops of water/sheet)			
Trial	**Brand A**	**Brand B**	**Brand C**
1			
2			
3			
4			

make your data more accurate. Calculators and computers can be helpful in evaluating the data or for visually displaying it. However, remember that you don't have to have the latest or most expensive materials and tools to conduct good experiments. Your experiments can be successful with materials found in your home or classroom. Paper, colored pencils, or markers work well for displaying your data. An organized presentation of data done neatly is as effective as a computer graphic.

Safety

Forming a hypothesis will be one important part of your science experiences. Once you have developed your own hypothesis, your next goal is to design an experiment that will test the hypothesis. As you design the experiment, you need to be aware of any possible safety issues that might occur as you complete your work. Some good safety habits include the following suggestions. Always check with your teacher at several times in the planning stage and while doing your experiment to make sure your actions and materials are safe. Remember to use safety goggles and always wash your hands after working with materials. **Figure 1-15** lists several safety rules. Safety symbols are listed inside the front cover of this book.

Designing Your Data Tables

A well-thought-out experiment includes a way to accurately record results and observations. Data tables are one way to organize and record your results and observations.

Most tables have a title that tells you, at a glance, what the table is about. It is divided into columns and rows. The items to be compared are listed in columns, and the first column lists the trials or characteristics to be compared across in rows.

As you complete the data table, you will know that you have the information you need to accurately analyze the results of the experiment. It is wise to make all of your data tables before beginning the experiment. That way, you will have a place for all of your data as soon as they become available. You also save time by not having to go back and organize the data or trying to decide where it goes at a later date.

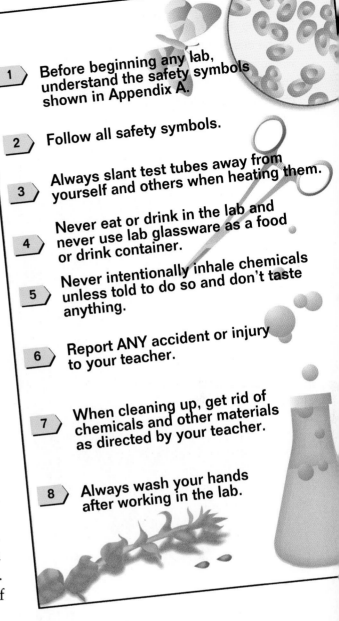

1 ⟩ Before beginning any lab, understand the safety symbols shown in Appendix A.

2 ⟩ Follow all safety symbols.

3 ⟩ Always slant test tubes away from yourself and others when heating them.

4 ⟩ Never eat or drink in the lab and never use lab glassware as a food or drink container.

5 ⟩ Never intentionally inhale chemicals unless told to do so and don't taste anything.

6 ⟩ Report ANY accident or injury to your teacher.

7 ⟩ When cleaning up, get rid of chemicals and other materials as directed by your teacher.

8 ⟩ Always wash your hands after working in the lab.

Figure 1-15 Here are a few safety rules you should follow when you are doing an experiment.

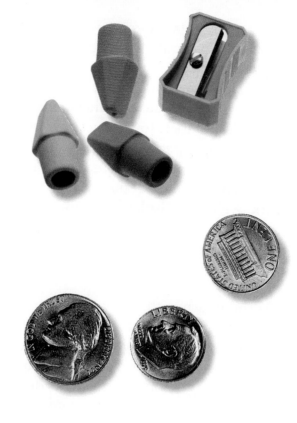

Figure 1-16 Items can be described by using words and numbers. **How could you describe these objects using both of these methods?**

Eliminating Bias

It's a Saturday afternoon. You want to see a certain movie, but your friends are not interested in seeing it. To sway them to your way of thinking, you tell them about a part of the show that you know will interest them. You slant the information you give them so they will make the choice you want. Similarly, scientists may want or simply expect that the results of experiments will come out a certain way. However, good experiments are set up to avoid bias. One way to avoid bias is to take measurements of all the results. Numerical measurements provide quantitative data. They are more precise than descriptions. Saying that a plant grew 12 cm in a day is more precise than saying the plant grew a lot. Twelve centimeters means the same for every person reading the results. The phrase "a lot" means different amounts to different people. How would you describe the objects in **Figure 1-16?**

Another type of bias may occur in surveys or groups that are chosen for experiments. Suppose you need to find out what the students want as a theme for the next school dance. You might choose to have only girls answer your questions. However, any conclusion you reach will not accurately reflect the opinions of the whole school. To get a more accurate result, you need to take a random sample. In this case, you might ask every fifth student entering the cafeteria for lunch to make a suggestion.

Do the Experiment

You have formed your hypothesis and planned your experiment. Before you actually begin the experiment, you will give a copy of it to your teacher. Your teacher must give approval to begin. He or she must know that all of your materials are safe to use and that your plans are safe to follow. This is also a good way to find out if any problems exist in how you plan to set up the experiment. Potential problems might include length of time to complete the experiment and the cost or availability of materials. You might also need to figure out how to keep an experiment running over a holiday period or where to set up a large experiment in a classroom.

Once you begin the experiment, make sure to carry it out as planned. Don't skip steps or change your plans in the middle of the process. If you skip steps or change procedures, you will have to begin the experiment again. Also, record your observations and complete your data tables in a timely manner. Incomplete observations and data reports mean that it is difficult to analyze the data. This threatens the accuracy of your conclusions.

Figure 1-17 Safety is important when doing a laboratory experiment. The safety symbols used throughout this book can be found at the front of the book. **Can you tell which safety cautions are being followed in this picture?**

Table 1-1

Common SI Measurements			
Measurement	**Unit**	**Symbol**	**Equal to**
Length	1 millimeter	mm	0.001 (1/1000) m
	1 centimeter	cm	0.01 (1/100) m
	1 meter	m	1 m
	1 kilometer	km	1000 m
Volume	1 milliliter	mL	1 cm^3
	1 liter	L	1000 mL
Mass	1 gram	g	1000 mg
	1 kilogram	kg	1000 g
	1 metric ton	t	1000 kg = 1 metric ton

International System of Units (SI)

Scientists use a system of measurements to make observations. Scientists around the world have agreed to use the International System of Units, or SI. SI is based on certain metric units. Using the same system gives scientists a common language. They can understand each other's research and compare results. Most of the units you will use in science are shown in **Table 1-1.** Because you may be used to using the English system of pounds, ounces, and inches, see Appendix B to help you convert English units to SI.

SI is based on units of ten. Multiplying or dividing by ten makes calculations easy to do. Prefixes are used with units to change them to larger or smaller units. **Figure 1-18** shows equipment used for measuring in SI.

Figure 1-18 Some of the equipment used by scientists is shown here.

A The amount of space occupied by an object is its volume. Liquid volumes are found using a graduated cylinder.

B Mass is the amount of matter in an object. Mass is measured with a balance.

C Scientists often use a thermometer with the Celsius scale to measure temperature. On the Celsius scale, water freezes at 0°C and boils at 100°C.

D A microscope is used to observe items that cannot be seen easily.

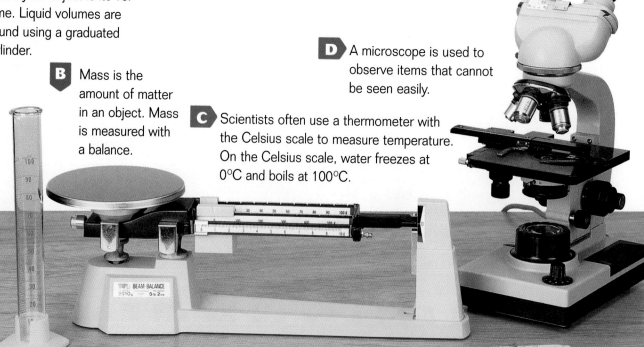

Analyze Your Data

Your experiment is over. You breathe a sigh of relief. Now, you have to figure out what your results mean. You have to analyze your data. To do this, you have to review all of the observations and measurements you recorded. You have to organize the data in an orderly fashion. Charts and graphs are excellent ways to organize data. You can draw the charts and graphs or use a computer to make them.

Draw Conclusions

Once you have organized your data, you are ready to draw a conclusion based on the data. Do the data allow you to make a conclusion that supports your hypothesis? Sometimes they will, but sometimes they won't support the hypothesis. You may be concerned if your data don't support your hypothesis. You may think that your hypothesis is wrong. But, this is not true. There are no wrong hypotheses—just results that don't support your hypothesis. Scientists know that it is important to learn if something doesn't work. In looking for an antibiotic to kill bacteria, scientists spend years finding out which antibiotics will work and which won't. Each time they find one that doesn't work, they learn some new information. They use this information to help make other antibiotics that have a better chance of working. A successful experiment is not always the one that comes out the way you originally wanted it to end.

Communicating the Results

Every experiment begins because there is a problem to solve. Analyzing data and drawing conclusions are the end of the experiment. However, they are not the end of the work a scientist does. Usually, scientists communicate their results to other scientists, government agencies, private industries, or the public. To do this, they write reports and give presentations. The reports and presentations provide details on how experiments were carried out, summaries of the data, and final conclusions. They may include recommendations on what direction further research should take. They may also include a recommendation to try a specific course of action as a way of solving the original problem. Charts, graphs, tables, posters, and models are included with both the written reports and verbal presentations as **Figure 1-19** demonstrates.

Figure 1-19 Communication is important in science. Giving talks, writing papers, and presenting information on the Internet are just a few ways of communicating science.

Just as scientists communicate their findings, you will have the chance to communicate your findings to other members of your science class. You may not give an oral presentation after each of your experiments, but you will have the chance to talk with other students or your teacher. You will share with other groups the charts, tables, and graphs that show your data. Other students will share their work with you, too. Sharing experimental data, like the students in **Figure 1-20,** is an important part of scientific experimentation. In the next section, you will learn some other ways that science is a part of your real world.

Figure 1-20 Communicating laboratory results to your classmates is an important part of the laboratory experience. Results are shared and better conclusions are made.

Section Assessment

1. Why do scientists use models?
2. What is a hypothesis?
3. Name the three steps scientists might use when designing an experiment to solve a problem.
4. **Think Critically:** The data gathered during an experiment do not support your original hypothesis. Explain why the experiment is not a failure.
5. **Skill Builder**
   Measuring in SI Measurements are one way to communicate experimental results. Do the **Chapter 1 Skill Activity** on page 706 to discover what units are most useful for measuring various lengths.

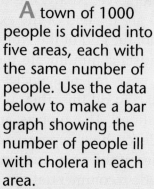

Using Math

A town of 1000 people is divided into five areas, each with the same number of people. Use the data below to make a bar graph showing the number of people ill with cholera in each area.

Area A–50%; Area B–5%; Area C–10%; Area D–16%; Area E–35%

Science & Math

Using a Scale Drawing

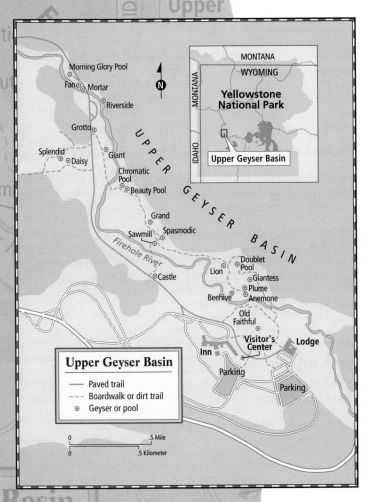

Upper Geyser Basin

Using a scale drawing of an area helps you know how far it is from one place to another. A scale drawing shows the area as it appears but makes it look smaller. The scale gives the relationship between actual distances and distances on the drawing.

   Look at the map of Upper Geyser Basin in Yellowstone National Park. The scale used is 2 cm = 0.5 km. That means that 2 cm on the map represent a distance of 0.5 km on Earth. Follow these steps to find out how far it is in a straight line from Old Faithful geyser to Castle geyser.

Solution

1. With a metric ruler, measure the distance between those two places on the map.
2. Compare scale distances to actual distances and write a proportion.

Let d represent the distance from Old Faithful to Castle geyser.

Scale Distances	Distances from Old Faithful to Castle geyser
map distance →	2 cm = 3.1 cm ← map distance
actual distance →	0.5 km = d ← actual distance

$2 \times d = 0.5 \times 3.1$ *Find the cross products*

$2d = 1.55$ *Multiply*

$\dfrac{2d}{2} = \dfrac{1.55}{2}$ *Divide each side by 2*

$0.775 = d$

The distance from Old Faithful to Castle geyser is 0.775 km or 775 m.

Practice PROBLEMS

1. **What is the actual distance between Grand geyser and Daisy geyser?**

2. **How far is it along the path shown from the Visitor Center to Morning Glory Pool?**

Using Scientific Methods

Possible Materials

- Widemouthed, 0.5-L containers (3)
  *clear plastic cups (3)
- Brine shrimp eggs
- Wooden splint
- Distilled water (500 mL)
- Weak salt solution (500 mL)
- Strong salt solution (500 mL)
- Wax pencil
  *labels (3)
- Hand lens
  *Alternate Materials

You are to use scientific methods to determine how salt affects the growth of brine shrimp. Brine shrimp are tiny organisms that live in the ocean. How can you find out why they live where they do?

Recognize the Problem

How can you use scientific methods to determine how salt affects the hatching and growth of brine shrimp?

Form a Hypothesis

Based on your observations, make a hypothesis about how salt affects the hatching and growth of brine shrimp.

Goals

- **Design and carry out an experiment** using scientific methods.
- **Infer** why brine shrimp live in the ocean.

Safety Precautions

Protect clothing and eyes. Be careful when working with live organisms.

Test Your Hypothesis

Plan

1. As a group, agree upon and **write out** the hypothesis statement.

2. **List** the steps that you need to take to test your hypothesis. Be specific. **Describe** exactly what you will do at each step. **List** your materials.

3. How will you know whether brine shrimp hatch and grow?

4. **Decide** what data you need to collect during the experiment. **Design** a data table in your Science Journal to **record** your observations.

5. **Identify** the steps in solving a problem that each of your actions presents. For example, what action have you taken that represents stating the problem or gathering information? Make sure you include all the steps needed to reach a conclusion.

6. **Read** over your entire experiment to make sure that all steps are in logical order.

7. **Identify** any constants, variables, and controls of the experiment.

8. Can you explain what variable you are testing?

9. **Decide** whether you need to run your tests more than once. Can your data be summarized in a graph?

Do

1. Make sure your teacher approves your plan before you proceed.

2. **Carry out** the experiment as planned.

3. While the experiment is going on, **write down** any observations that you make and complete the data table in your Science Journal.

Analyze Your Data

1. **Compare** your results with those of other groups.

2. Was your hypothesis supported by your data? **Explain** your answer.

Draw Conclusions

1. **Describe** how the physical conditions in the container in which the brine shrimp hatched and grew best are similar to those in the ocean.

2. How did you use scientific methods to solve this problem? Give examples from this activity.

Science and Technology

What You'll Learn

▶ How science and technology influence your life
▶ How modern technology has led to a globalization of science

Why It's Important

▶ Due to modern communications systems, scientific information is discovered by and shared with people all over the world.

Science in Your Daily Life

You have learned how to do science. How is this useful and meaningful to your daily life? The most obvious answer is that it helps you succeed in science class. Remember that doing science means more than just completing a science activity or reading a science chapter. Doing science is not following just one method to find answers. **Figure 1-21** illustrates some aspects of science.

Scientific Discoveries

Besides being a way of thinking, science is meaningful in your everyday life in other ways. New discoveries are constantly incorporated into products that influence your style of

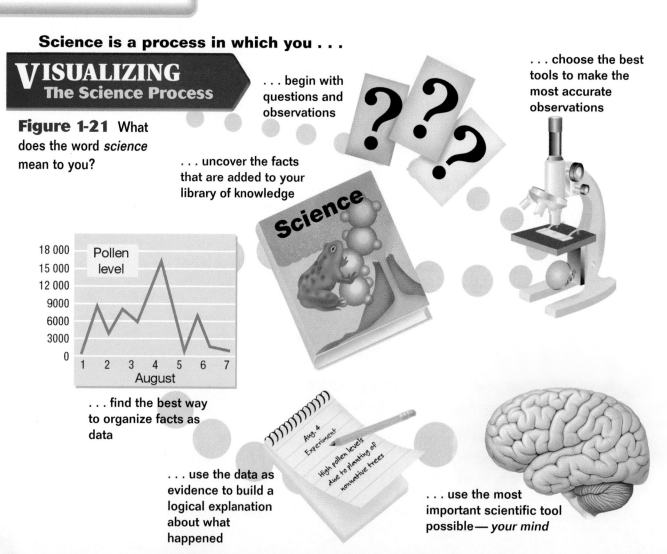

Science is a process in which you . . .

VISUALIZING The Science Process

Figure 1-21 What does the word *science* mean to you?

. . . begin with questions and observations

. . . uncover the facts that are added to your library of knowledge

. . . choose the best tools to make the most accurate observations

. . . find the best way to organize facts as data

. . . use the data as evidence to build a logical explanation about what happened

Aug. 4
Experiment
High pollen levels
due to planting of
nonnative trees

. . . use the most important scientific tool possible— *your mind*

living, such as those shown in **Figure 1-22.** For example, in the last 100 years, technological advances have allowed entertainment to move from live stage shows to large movie screens. Movies that once were shown only in theaters are now seen on television sets in the home and you don't even have to get up to adjust the volume, thanks to the remote control. Videotapes allow viewers to watch shows whenever they please on their television sets. And now, DVDs allow computer users to choose a variety of options while viewing a movie on their computer monitor. Do you want to hear English dialogue with French subtitles or Spanish dialogue with English subtitles? Do you want to change the ending?

Technology also makes your life more convenient. Watches and clock faces glow in the dark for easier reading. Small calculators fit in a wallet or checkbook cover. Laptop computers can be carried in a briefcase. Foods can be prepared in minutes in the microwave, and hydraulic tools (running on compressed air) make construction work faster. Pagers make communication easier and garage-door openers save time. A satellite tracking system can even give you verbal and visual directions to a destination as you drive your car in an unfamiliar city.

New discoveries influence other areas of your daily life, including your health. A disease may be controlled because a skin patch releases a constant dose of medicine into your body. Miniature instruments allow doctors to operate on unborn children and save their lives. Bacteria is even being used to make important drugs such as insulin for people with diabetes. ☑

Figure 1-22 Technology has become part of our everyday lives.

Reading Check ☑

What scientific discovery have you used?

B Garrett A. Morgan invented an early traffic signal in 1923.

C Flossie Wong-Staal is involved in AIDS research.

A Rita Levi-Montalciniv won the 1986 Nobel Prize in medicine for her discovery of nerve growth factors.

Figure 1-23 Science and technology are the results of many people's efforts.

inter**NET**
CONNECTION

Visit the Glencoe Science Web Site at **www.glencoe.com/ sec/science/ca** for more information about different inventions.

Science—The Product of Many

Scientific knowledge also can mean that old ways of thinking or doing things are challenged. Aristotle, an ancient Greek philosopher, classified living organisms into plants and animals. This system worked until new tools, such as the microscope, produced new information that challenged the two-kingdom classification system. The new information changed how scientists viewed the living world. The current six-kingdom classification system will be used only as long as it continues to answer questions scientists have or until a new discovery allows them to look at information in a different way.

Scientific discoveries have never been limited to one race, sex, culture, or time period, as illustrated in **Figure 1-23**. As in the past, people all over the world are making discoveries. These people are not always professional scientists. Often, discoveries are made by people pursuing a hobby. In fact, students your age have made some important discoveries.

Advances in Technology

Information about new discoveries is not limited to pure science, either. The modern electronic communications network quickly spreads word of new discoveries throughout the world. New knowledge and technology brought about by these discoveries are shared by people in all countries.

Science can provide information that people use to make decisions. A new car can be designed. A new drug can be found. A new way to produce electricity can be developed. However, science cannot decide if the information is good or harmful, moral or immoral. People decide if the information is used to help or to harm the world and its inhabitants.

E Albert Einstein, a physicist, studied the motion of atoms, gravity, and the space-time continuum.

D Eloy Rodriguez makes substances in the lab that occur naturally in plants. Some may cure human diseases.

F Mae Jemison was a Space Shuttle astronaut on the *Endeavor* in 1992.

Looking to the Future

Midori and Luis discovered that several of these factors have changed how modern scientists track the source of a disease. New information about bacteria and modern tools, such as the electron microscope, mean they can identify specific strains of these organisms. Computers are used to model how the toxins kill healthy cells or which part of a population the bacteria will infect. Today's scientists use cellular phones and computers to communicate with each other even when they are in remote parts of the world. This information technology has led to the globalization, or worldwide distribution, of information.

Section Assessment

1. What is the most important tool scientists use?

2. What will cause scientists to change a theory they have believed in for more than 100 years?

3. **Think Critically:** Explain why modern communications systems are important to scientists.

4. **Skill Builder**
   Comparing and Contrasting
   Make a drawing showing how a modern scientist and one from the 1800s communicated their data with other scientists of their time. If you need help, refer to Comparing and Contrasting in the **Skill Handbook** on page 684.

Using Computers

Word Processing Research the life of a famous scientist. Find at least two sources for your information. Take notes on ten facts and use them to write a short biography of the scientist on a word processor. If you need help, refer to page 696.

For a **preview** of this chapter, study this Reviewing Main Ideas before you read the chapter. After you have studied this chapter, you can use the Reviewing Main Ideas to **review** the chapter.

The Glencoe MindJogger, Audiocassettes, and CD-ROM provide additional opportunities for review.

Section 1-1 WHAT IS SCIENCE?

Science is a process that can be used to solve problems or answer questions about what is happening in the world. Scientists use tools to make accurate mathematical measurements that quantify or put a numerical value on observations. Observations are clues to help solve problems. Scientists hypothesize based on prior experiences. These hypotheses will change procedures they follow if responses change. The **Skill Handbook** lists skills scientists use to solve problems. Computers are a valuable technological tool. Communication is an important part of all aspects of science. *What are some skills scientists use to solve problems?*

Section 1-2 DOING SCIENCE

No single **scientific method** is used to solve all problems. Organization and careful planning are important in solving problems. The first step is to make sure that everyone has clearly identified the problem. Models save time and money by testing ideas that are too difficult to build or do. Computers are used to make models, and experiments are needed to solve problems. The steps of a well-designed experiment include: recognize the problem, form a **hypothesis,** test the hypothesis, do the experiment, analyze the data, and draw conclusions. *What is the next step after scientists have analyzed data and drawn conclusions?*

Reading Check ✓

Find three or four words in this chapter that are new to you, but not on the vocabulary list. Write these words and their definitions.

Section 1-3 SCIENCE AND TECHNOLOGY

Science is part of everyone's daily lives. New discoveries lead to new technology and products. Science continues to challenge old knowledge and ways of doing things. Old ideas are kept until new discoveries prove them wrong. People of all races, ages, sexes, cultures, and professions practice science. Modern communication assures that scientific information is spread around the world. *A new discovery is made in a South American rain forest. How can a scientist in Chicago find out about the data?*

Career CONNECTION

Dr. Enriquetta Barrera, Geochemist

Enriquetta Barrera studies the chemistry of rocks, which hold clues to Earth's past. Enriquetta loves her job but admits that the job is not easy. Scientific research involves careful observations and analyses to formulate hypotheses. As she practices science, Enriquetta is constantly revising her ideas and learning about her field. It takes years of hard work to become established in a field of research. Why is it important to be able to revise your ideas?

Chapter 1 Assessment

Using Vocabulary

a. constant
b. control
c. dependent variable
d. hypothesis
e. independent variable
f. model
g. science
h. scientific methods
i. technology

Match each phrase with the correct term from the list of Vocabulary words.

1. the factor being measured in an experiment
2. a statement that can be tested
3. use of knowledge to make products
4. sample treated like other experimental groups except variable is not applied
5. way of thinking to solve a problem

Checking Concepts

Choose the word or phrase that best answers the question.

6. To make sure an experiment's results are valid, you must complete which of the following tasks?
A) conduct multiple trials
B) pick your hypothesis
C) add bias
D) communicate the results

7. In an experiment on bacteria, using different amounts of antibiotics is an example of which of the following?
A) control
B) hypothesis
C) bias
D) variable

8. Computers are used in science to do which of the following processes?
A) analyze data
B) make models
C) communicate with other scientists
D) all of the above

9. Which of the following skills is being used by scientists when they interpret an observation?
A) hypothesizing
B) inferring
C) taking measurements
D) making models

10. Using a computer to make a three-dimensional picture of a building is a type of which of the following?
A) model
B) hypothesis
C) control
D) variable

11. Which of the following provides access to the Internet?
A) variable
B) hypothesis
C) control
D) computer

12. Which of the following is the first step toward finding a solution?
A) analyze data
B) draw a conclusion
C) identify the problem
D) test the hypothesis

13. Predictions about what will happen can be based on which of the following?
A) controls
B) prior knowledge
C) technology
D) number of trials

14. Which of the following terms describes a variable that stays the same throughout an experiment?
A) hypothesis
B) dependent variable
C) constant
D) independent variable

15. Which of the following is a prediction that can be tested?
A) conclusion
B) data table
C) observation
D) hypothesis

Thinking Critically

16. What is the advantage of eliminating bias in experiments?

17. Why is it important to record data as they are collected?

18. What is the difference between analyzing data and drawing conclusions?

19. How is a Science Journal a valuable tool for scientists?

20. When solving a problem, why do scientists have to make a list of what is already known?

Developing Skills

If you need help, refer to the Skill Handbook.

21. Recognizing Cause and Effect: If three variables were changed at one time, what would happen to the accuracy of the conclusions made for an experiment?

22. Making and Using Graphs: Scientists recorded the following data about victims of a disease. Prepare a bar graph of the number of people in each age group that contracted the disease.

Which age group appears to be the most likely to get the disease? Do adults have to worry about getting the disease? Why or why not?

Disease Victims	
Age Group	**Number of People**
0-1 yr.	10
1-5 yr.	27
5-10 yr.	20
10-15 yr.	2
20-20 yr.	1
20-25 yr.	0
over 25 yr.	0

23. Forming a Hypothesis: Basketball practice is scheduled for two hours after school every Tuesday through Friday. Your friend goes home sick every Tuesday. Form a hypothesis about why your friend gets sick. How can the hypothesis be tested?

THE PRINCETON REVIEW

Test-Taking Tip

Words Are Easy to Learn Make a huge stack of vocabulary flash cards and study them. Use your new words in daily conversation. The great thing about learning new words is the ability to express yourself more specifically.

Test Practice

Use these questions to test your Science Proficiency.

1. In an experiment using bean plants, all the variables were kept constant except for the amount of fertilizer given to the different plants. Which of the following describes the fertilizer in this experiment?
A) constant
B) control
C) independent variable
D) dependent variable

2. In the experiment described above in question 1, the measured growth indicated how the fertilizer affects plants. Which of the following terms describes growth in this experiment?
A) constant
B) control
C) independent variable
D) dependent variable

3. Which of the following is **NOT** an example of technology?
A) wagon
B) copper
C) braces on teeth
D) bicycle

The Structure of Organisms

Chapter Preview

Skills Preview

Skill Builders
- Map Concepts
- Interpret Scientific Illustrations

Activities
- Compare and Contrast
- Use Numbers

MiniLabs
- Observe and Infer
- Make a Model

Reading Check ✔

Different types of microscopes are presented at the beginning of this chapter. As you read, think about how these inventions helped scientists separate fact from fiction. Why was this important?

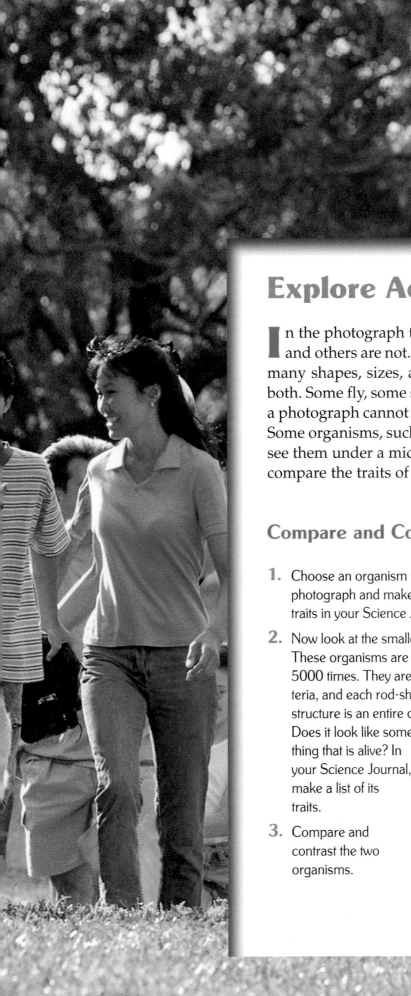

Explore Activity

In the photograph to the left are many things. Some are alive, and others are not. Living things are called organisms and are many shapes, sizes, and colors. They live on land, in water, or both. Some fly, some swim—others move fast, or just creep. But, a photograph cannot show all the organisms in an environment. Some organisms, such as bacteria, are so small that you can only see them under a microscope. In the following activity, you will compare the traits of two organisms.

Compare and Contrast Two Organisms

1. Choose an organism in the large photograph and make a list of its traits in your Science Journal.

2. Now look at the smaller photo. These organisms are magnified 5000 times. They are soil bacteria, and each rod-shaped structure is an entire organism. Does it look like something that is alive? In your Science Journal, make a list of its traits.

3. Compare and contrast the two organisms.

Infer why you and something as small as a bacterium are both considered organisms.

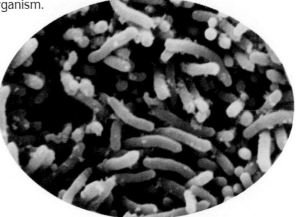

Magnification: 5000×

2•1 Cells—The Units of Life

The Microscope

The number of living things in your environment that you can't see is much greater than those that you can see. Many of these things are just one cell in size. Larger living things are made of many cells. We need to use a magnifying glass or a microscope to see most of these cells.

Trying to see separate cells in a leaf, like one in **Figure 2-1,** is like trying to see individual bricks in a wall from three blocks away. If you start to walk toward the wall, it becomes easier to see individual bricks. When you get right up to the wall, you can see each brick in detail and many of the small features of each brick. A microscope performs a similar function. A microscope has one or more lenses that make an enlarged image of an object. Through these lenses, the leaf is brought closer to you, and you see the individual cells that carry on life processes.

Magnification: 500×

Figure 2-1 Individual cells become visible when the ivy leaf is viewed with a microscope.

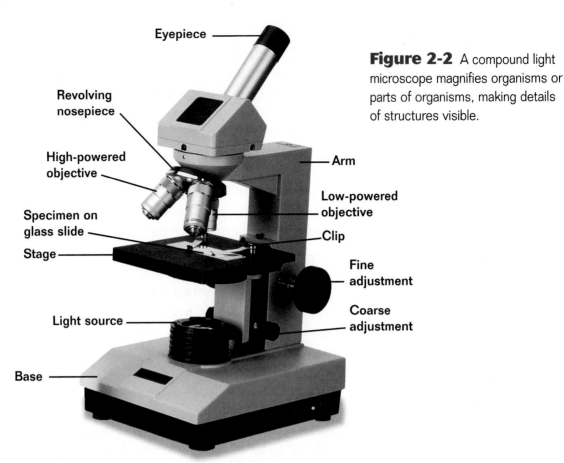

Eyepiece

Revolving nosepiece

High-powered objective

Specimen on glass slide

Stage

Light source

Base

Arm

Low-powered objective

Clip

Fine adjustment

Coarse adjustment

Figure 2-2 A compound light microscope magnifies organisms or parts of organisms, making details of structures visible.

Early Microscopes

Microscopes are simple or compound, depending on how many lenses they contain. A simple microscope is similar to a magnifying glass. It has only one lens. In 1590, a Dutch maker of reading glasses, Zacharias Janssen, put two magnifying glasses together in a tube. The result was the first crude compound microscope. By combining two lenses, he got an image that was larger than an image made by only one lens. These early compound microscopes weren't satisfactory, however. The lenses would make an image larger, but it wasn't always sharp or clear.

In the mid 1600s, Anton Van Leeuwenhoek, a Dutch fabric merchant, made a simple microscope with a tiny glass bead for a lens. With it, he reported seeing things in pond water that no one had ever imagined before. His microscope could magnify up to 270 times. Another way to say this is that his microscope could make the image of an object 270 times larger than its actual size. Today, we would say his lens had a power of 270×.

The Compound Light Microscope

The microscope you will use in studying life science is a compound light microscope similar to the one in **Figure 2-2.** In a **compound light microscope,** light passes through and around an object and then through two or more lenses.

PHYSICS
INTEGRATION

Convex Lenses
A magnifying glass is a convex lens. All microscopes use one or more convex lenses. In your Science Journal, diagram a convex lens and describe its shape. Use the illustration to explain how it magnifies.

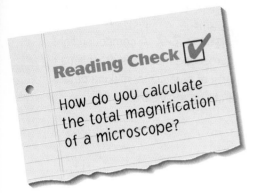

Reading Check ☑

How do you calculate the total magnification of a microscope?

Lenses enlarge the image and bend the light toward your eye. It has an eyepiece lens and objective lenses. An eyepiece lens usually has a power of 10×. An objective lens may have a power of 43×. Together, they have a total magnification of 430× (10× times 43×). Some compound microscopes have more powerful lenses that can magnify an object up to 2000 times (2000×) its original size. ☑

The Stereomicroscope

Your classroom may have stereoscopic (stereo) light microscopes. Stereomicroscopes have lenses for each eye that give you a three-dimensional image of an object. They are used to look at objects that are too thick for light to pass through or too large to fit in the stage of a compound light microscope. You may look at whole insects, leaves, or your fingertips with a stereomicroscope.

Electron Microscopes

Things that are too small to be seen with a light microscope can be viewed with an electron microscope. Instead of using lenses to bend beams of light, an **electron microscope** uses a magnetic field to bend beams of electrons. Electron microscopes can magnify images up to 1 million times. **Figure 2-3** shows the kind of detail that can be seen with an electron microscope. Electron microscope images must be photographed or electronically produced.

There are several kinds of electron microscopes. One is the transmission electron microscope (TEM), which is used to study parts inside a cell. The object has to be sliced thin and placed in a vacuum. A vacuum has no air. As a result, only dead cells and tissues can be observed this way. A scanning electron microscope (SEM) is used to see the surfaces

PHYSICS
INTEGRATION ▶

Figure 2-3 Electron microscopes reveal details that cannot be seen using a compound light microscope.

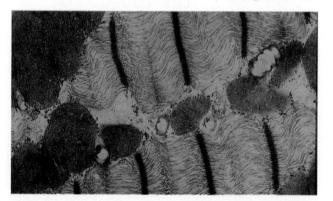

Magnification: 75 625×

A Transmission electron microscopes (TEM) provide images that show great detail. This TEM image shows a thin cross section of a bee's skeletal muscle.

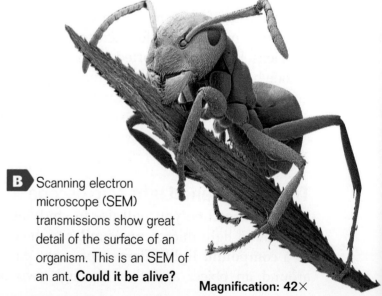

B Scanning electron microscope (SEM) transmissions show great detail of the surface of an organism. This is an SEM of an ant. **Could it be alive?**

Magnification: 42×

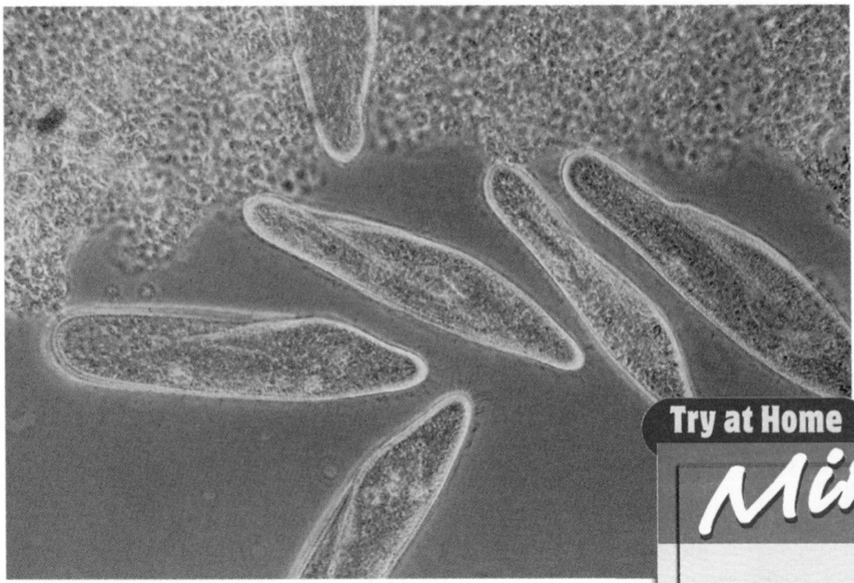

Figure 2-4 This is an image of *paramecia*—one-celled organisms found in pond water.

Magnification: 98×

of whole objects. An SEM called the Environmental SEM allows images of some living things to be produced. From the time of Van Leeuwenhoek until the present, the microscope has been a valuable tool for studying cells. You will see how it was used to develop the cell theory.

The Cell Theory

During the seventeenth century, when explorers were discovering new lands, scientists were discovering the microscopic world. They examined blood and scrapings from their own teeth. In mud from ponds and drops of rainwater, they discovered organisms like the ones in **Figure 2-4.**

Cells weren't discovered until the microscope was improved. In 1665, Robert Hooke, an English scientist, cut a thin slice of cork and looked at it under his microscope. To Hooke, the cork seemed to be made up of little empty boxes, which he called cells. **Figure 2-5** is an image of cells observed and sketched by Robert Hooke more than 300 years ago. Actually, Hooke was not aware of the importance of what he was seeing.

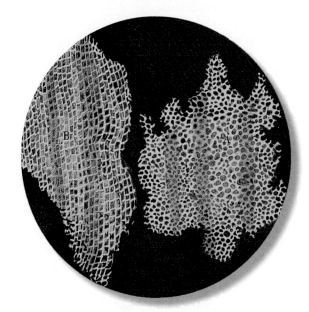

Figure 2-5 Robert Hooke made these drawings of cork cells.

Development of the Cell Theory

In the 1830s, Matthias Schleiden, a German scientist, used a microscope to study plant parts. He concluded that all plants are made of cells. Just a year later, another German scientist, Theodor Schwann, after observing many different animal cells, concluded that all animals are made up of cells. Together, they became convinced that all living things are made of cells.

Figure 2-6 The observations and conclusions of many scientists became known as the cell theory. The major ideas of the cell theory are as follows:

The Cell Theory

1. All organisms are made up of one or more cells.

2. Cells are the basic units of structure and function in all organisms.

3. All cells come from cells that already exist.

Several years later, a German doctor, Rudolf Virchow, hypothesized that new cells don't form on their own. Instead, cells divide to form new cells. This was a startling idea. Remember that at that time people thought earthworms fell from the sky when it rained. People thought that life came about spontaneously. What Virchow said was that every cell that is or ever has been came from a cell that already existed.

The **cell theory** is one of the major theories in science. It is not based on the hypotheses and observations of only one person, but results from the discoveries of many scientists. Today, it serves as the basis for scientists who study the parts of cells, how cells are organized, and how cells and organisms reproduce and change through time. The cell theory is summarized in **Figure 2-6.**

Section Assessment

1. Explain why the invention of the microscope was important in the study of cells.

2. Why is the cell theory important?

3. What is the difference between a simple and a compound light microscope?

4. **Think Critically:** Why would it be better to look at living cells rather than dead cells?

5. **Skill Builder**
   Concept Mapping Using a network tree concept map, show the differences between compound light microscopes and electron microscopes. If you need help, refer to Concept Mapping in the **Skill Handbook** on page 678.

Using Math

Calculate the total low-power and high-power magnification of a microscope that has an 8× eyepiece, a 10× objective, and a 40× high-power objective.

Practice
PROBLEMS

1. Suppose you are 150 cm tall. A particular alga is about 0.0001 cm in length. How many of these algae could be placed end-to-end to span your height?

2. A certain bacterium with a length of about 0.00015 mm is the smallest known living organism. In a book, a picture of this bacterium measures 2.4 cm. How many times has the picture been magnified?

Using Decimals in Division

Problem

Decimal division can help you better visualize the size of small cells and organisms seen through a microscope. A red blood cell (like those magnified at left) is about seven ten-thousandths of a centimeter (0.0007) in diameter. How many red blood cells could be placed across the diameter of a dime?

Solution

1. Measure the diameter of a dime in centimeters. It should be about 1.8 cm.

2. To find how many red blood cells will fit across a dime, divide the diameter of the dime by the diameter of one red blood cell.

$$1.8 \text{ cm} \div 0.0007 \text{ cm}$$

3. In order to do this division, the divisor (the number you divide by) must be a whole number. The divisor in this problem is 0.0007. To make it a whole number, move the decimal point to the right four places. The divisor now equals 7. Moving the decimal point four places to the right is the same as multiplying by 10 000. In division problems, whatever you do to the divisor must also be done to the dividend (the number you divide into). So, you multiply 1.8 by 10 000 to get 18 000. The problem becomes 18 000 cm ÷ 7 cm or

```
       2571
    7)18000
       14
       40
       35
       50
       49
       10
        7
        3
```

Because the remainder of 3 is less than half the divisor of 7, do not round the quotient up to 2572. Thus, the answer to the problem is that you could place about 2571 red blood cells across the diameter of a dime.

Design Your Own Experiment

Activity 2•1

Comparing Light Microscopes

Possible Materials

- A compound light microscope
- A stereoscopic light microscope
- Any 8 items from the classroom; include some living or once-living items
- Microscope slides and coverslips
- Plastic petri dishes
- Distilled water
- Dropper

You're a technician in a police forensic laboratory. You use stereoscopic and compound light microscopes in the laboratory. A detective just returned from a crime scene with bags of evidence. You must examine each piece of evidence under a microscope. How do you decide which microscope is the best tool to use?

Recognize the Problem

Microscopes are useful tools for scientists. Stereoscopic and compound light microscopes are used for many tasks. What things are better viewed with a compound light microscope? What things are better viewed with a stereoscopic microscope?

Form a Hypothesis

Compare the items to be examined under the microscopes. Which microscope will be used for each item?

Goals

- **Learn** how to use a stereoscopic microscope and a compound light microscope.
- **Compare** the uses of the stereoscopic and compound light microscopes.

Safety Precautions

Thoroughly wash your hands when you have completed this experiment.

Test Your Hypothesis

Plan

1. As a group, **decide** how you will test your hypothesis.

2. **List** the steps that you will need to complete this experiment. Be specific, describing exactly what you will do at each step. Make sure the steps are in a logical order. Remember that you must place an item in the bottom of a plastic petri dish to **examine** it under the stereoscopic microscope. You must **make a wet mount** of any item to be examined under the compound light microscope.

3. If you need a data or observation table, **design** one in your Science Journal.

Do

1. Make sure your teacher approves the objects you'll examine, your plan, and data table before you proceed.

2. **Carry out** the experiment as planned.

3. While doing the experiment, **record** your observations and **complete** the data table.

Analyze Your Data

1. **Compare** the items you examined with those of your classmates.

2. Based on this experiment, **classify** the eight items you observed.

Draw Conclusions

1. **Infer** which microscope a scientist might use to examine a blood sample, fibers, and live snails.

2. If you examined an item under both microscopes, how would the images differ?

3. **List** five careers that require people to use a stereomicroscope. **List** five careers that require people to use a compound light microscope. Enter the lists in your Science Journal.

2·2 Cell Organization

An Overview of Cells

In contrast to the dry cork boxes that Hooke saw, living cells are dynamic and have several things in common. They all have a membrane and a gel-like material called cytoplasm inside the membrane. In addition, they all have hereditary material that controls the life of the cell.

How Cells Differ

Cells come in a variety of sizes. A single nerve cell in your leg may be a meter in length. A human egg cell, on the other hand, is no bigger than a dot on this i. Going a step further, a human red blood cell is about one-tenth the size of a human egg cell.

The shape of a cell may also tell you something about the job the cell does. The nerve cell in **Figure 2-7** with its fine extensions sends impulses through your body. Look at its shape in contrast to the white blood cell, which can change shape. Some cells in plant stems are long and hollow with holes. They transport food and water through the plant. Human red blood cells, on the other hand, are disk-shaped and have to be small and flexible enough to move through tiny blood vessels.

What **You'll Learn**

► The names and functions of each part of a plant cell and an animal cell
► How important a nucleus is in a cell
► What tissues, organs, and organ systems are and how they compare

Vocabulary

cell	Golgi body
membrane	mitochondria
nucleus	lysosome
chromatin	cell wall
cytoplasm	chloroplast
organelle	tissue
endoplasmic	organ
reticulum	
ribosome	

Why **It's Important**

► If you know how your cells work, it's easier to understand how you can do what you do.

Figure 2-7 Often, the shape of a cell tells you something about the job it performs.

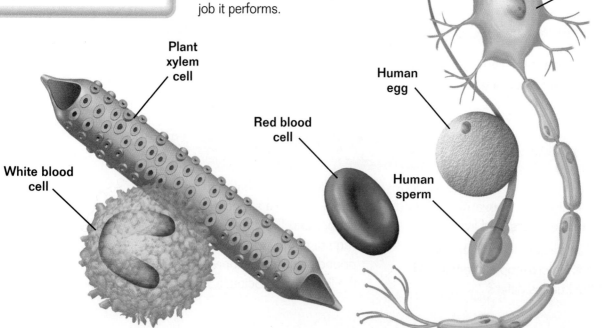

Plant xylem cell

Nerve cell

Human egg

Red blood cell

Human sperm

White blood cell

Figure 2-8 Pond scum is made up of prokaryotic cells. **Where do most of its chemical reactions take place?**

Magnification: 1000×

Cell Types

Scientists have found that there are two basic types of cells. Cells that have no membrane around their hereditary material are prokaryotic cells. Bacteria and cells that form pond scum, like those in **Figure 2-8,** are prokaryotic cells. A eukaryotic cell has a nucleus, which is hereditary material surrounded by a membrane. The animal and plant cells in this chapter are eukaryotic cells.

Bacterial Cells

Bacteria, such as those in **Figure 2-9,** and other prokaryotes exist as one-celled organisms. Most prokaryotes have an outer, protective cell wall. Inside the cell wall is the cell membrane. The cell membrane forms a container for the gelatin-like cytoplasm. The hereditary material and other cell substances are in the cytoplasm. Most of the chemical reactions that the cell needs to survive happen in the cytoplasm.

Magnification: 11 408×

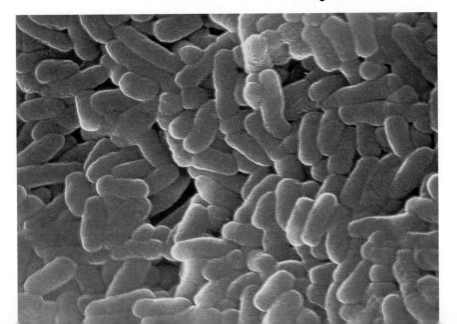

Figure 2-9 A bacterial cell is a one-celled organism. It does not have a membrane around its nucleus. These bacteria cause tuberculosis in humans.

Figure 2-10 Animal cells are typical eukaryotic cells. Refer to this diagram as you read about cell parts and their jobs.

A The cell membrane is made up of a double layer of phospholipids, which are fatlike molecules.

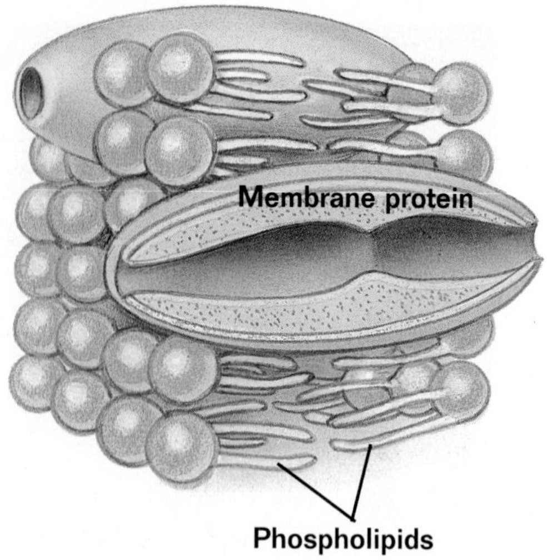

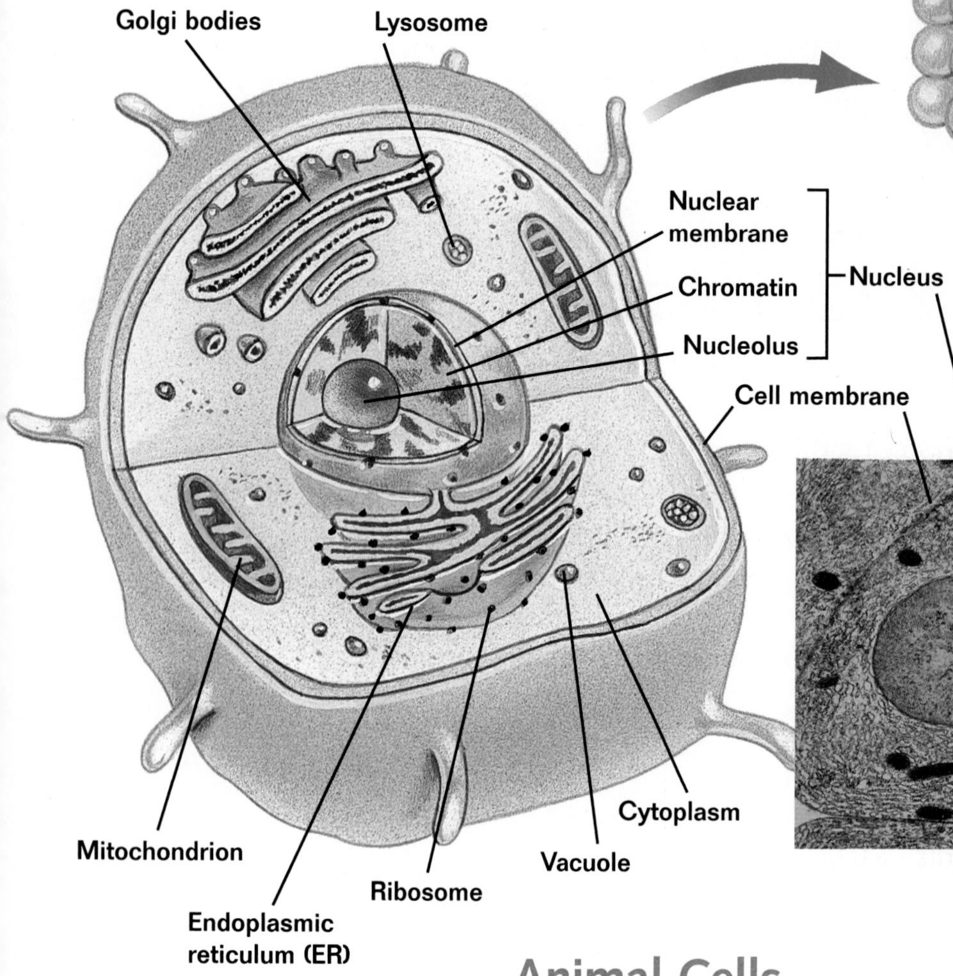

Membrane protein

Golgi bodies

Lysosome

Nuclear membrane

Chromatin — Nucleus

Nucleolus

Phospholipids

Cell membrane

B Below is the image of an animal cell. The parts of the cell are labeled in the diagram to the left.

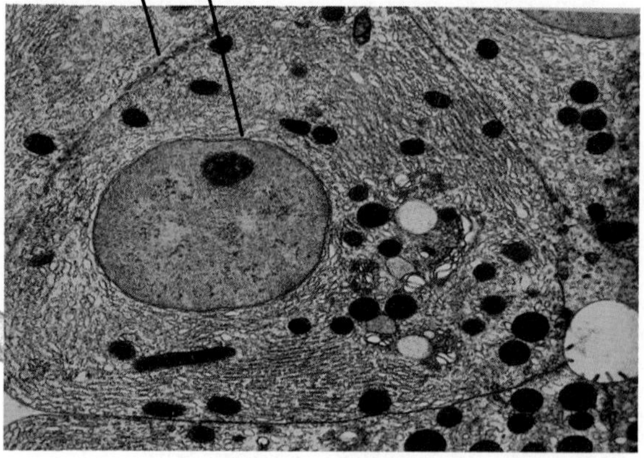

Nucleus

Cytoplasm

Mitochondrion

Vacuole

Ribosome

Endoplasmic reticulum (ER)

Magnification: 1875×

Animal Cells

Each cell in your body is constantly active and has a specific job to do. The activities in your cells might be compared to a business that operates 24 hours a day making dozens of different products. A business operates inside a building. A cell is similar. It functions inside a structure called the cell membrane. Materials that are needed to make specific products are brought into the building. Finished products are shipped out. Similarly, substances move into a cell and products and wastes move out.

Cell Membrane

The **cell membrane** is a structure that forms the outer boundary of the cell and allows only certain materials to move into and out of the cell. The membrane, as shown in **Figure 2-10**, is flexible. It is made up of a double layer of molecules with some proteins and other large molecules scattered throughout. The cell membrane helps to maintain a chemical balance between materials inside and outside the cell. Food and oxygen move into the cell through the membrane. Waste products also leave through the membrane. Many substances enter and leave the cell in different ways.

Nucleus

The largest structure in the cytoplasm of a eukaryotic cell is the nucleus. The **nucleus** directs all the activities of the cell. The nucleus, shown in **Figure 2-11,** is like a manager who directs everyday business for a company and passes on information to employees. A nucleus is separated from the cytoplasm by a nuclear membrane. Materials enter and leave the nucleus through openings in the membrane. The nucleus contains the instructions that direct all of the cell's functions. These instructions are found on long threadlike chromatin. **Chromatin** is a form of hereditary material. It is made of proteins and DNA. DNA is the chemical that is the blueprint for the cell's structure and activities. When a cell begins to divide, the chromatin tightly coils and takes on the form of chromosomes, which are easier to see. A structure called a nucleolus is also found in the nucleus.

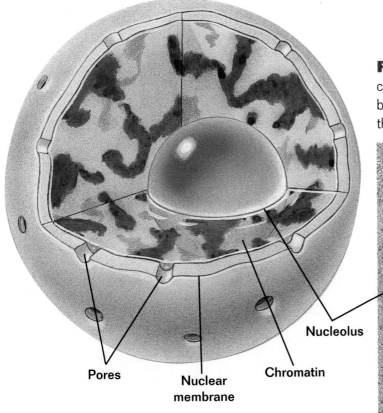

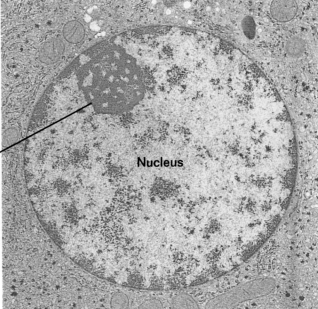

Figure 2-11 The nucleus of a cell is surrounded by a double membrane. DNA in the nucleus controls the activities in the cell. **Magnification: 20 500×**

Nucleus

Nucleolus

Pores

Chromatin

Nuclear membrane

Cytoplasm

Cytoplasm is the gelatinlike mixture inside the cell membrane. Cytoplasm contains many chemicals including a large amount of water. Within the cytoplasm are structures that carry out the life processes for the cell. Cytoplasm constantly moves or streams.

The structures within the cytoplasm of eukaryotic cells are **organelles.** Each one has a specific job or jobs. Some organelles break down food molecules. Others move wastes to be expelled from the cell. Still others store materials. Most organelles are surrounded by membranes. The nucleus is an organelle

Organelles in the Cytoplasm

The **endoplasmic reticulum (ER),** illustrated in **Figure 2-12,** is a folded membrane that moves materials around in the cell. The ER extends from the nucleus to the cell membrane and takes up a lot of space in some cells. The ER is like a system of conveyor belts in a business along which materials are moved from one place to another.

One chemical that takes part in nearly every cell activity is protein. Proteins are part of cell membranes. Other proteins are needed for chemical reactions that take place in the cytoplasm. Cells make their own proteins on small, two-part structures

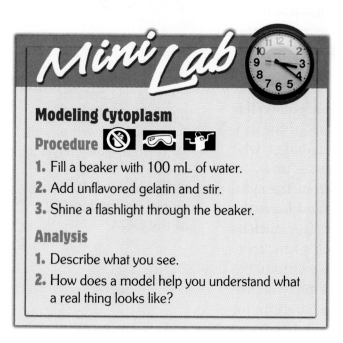

Figure 2-12 Endoplasmic reticulum (ER) is a complex series of membranes in the cytoplasm of the cell. If ribosomes are present on the endoplasmic reticulum, then the endoplasmic reticulum is referred to as *rough ER*. Proteins are made on these ribosomes. **What would smooth ER look like?**

Magnification: 63 548×

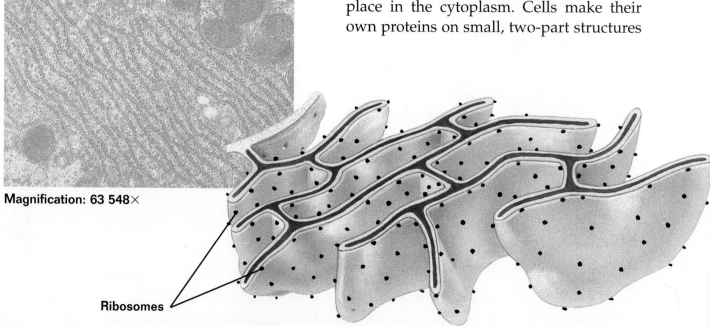

Ribosomes

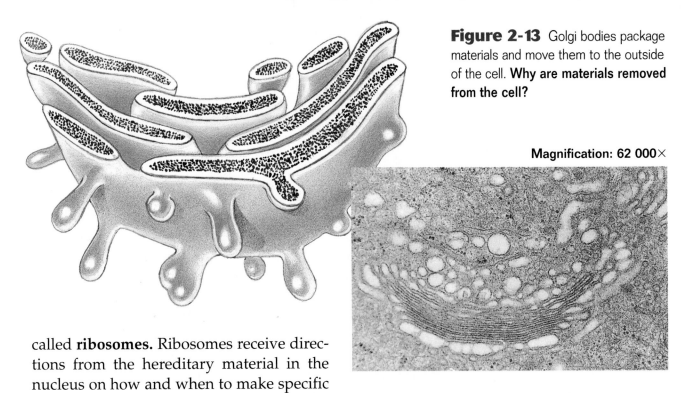

Figure 2-13 Golgi bodies package materials and move them to the outside of the cell. **Why are materials removed from the cell?**

Magnification: 62 000×

called **ribosomes.** Ribosomes receive directions from the hereditary material in the nucleus on how and when to make specific proteins. Some ribosomes are scattered in the cytoplasm. Others are attached to the ER. Ribosome parts are made in the nucleolus.

In a business, products are made, packaged, and moved to loading docks to be carried away. In cells, stacks of membrane-covered sacs called **Golgi bodies** package cell products to be moved outside of the cell. When something is moved to the outside of a cell, the cell secretes it. **Figure 2-13** illustrates Golgi bodies.

Cells require a continuous supply of energy. Energy is stored in molecules that can power cell reactions. Just as a power plant supplies energy to a business, mitochondria

Figure 2-14 Mitochondria are known as the "powerhouses of the cell." In these organelles, food molecules are broken down, and energy is released. **What types of cells may contain many mitochondria?**

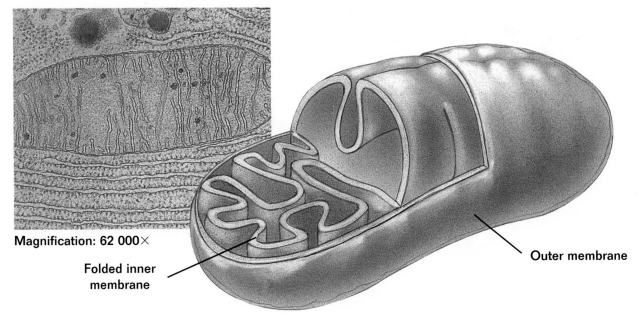

Magnification: 62 000×

Folded inner membrane

Outer membrane

release energy for the cell. **Mitochondria,** such as the one pictured in **Figure 2-14,** are organelles where food molecules are broken down and energy is released. Some types of cells are more active than others. Muscle cells, which are always moving in some way, have large numbers of mitochondria. Why would active cells have more or larger mitochondria? ☑

An active cell constantly breaks down and recycles substances. In animal cells, organelles called **lysosomes** contain digestive chemicals that break down food molecules, cell wastes, and worn out cell parts. In a healthy animal cell, chemicals are released only when needed. When a cell dies, a lysosome's membrane disintegrates. This releases digestive chemicals that quickly break down the cell's contents for reuse by the organism. In plant cells, digestive chemicals and many other substances are in the central vacuole.

Vacuoles and vesicles are storage organelles in cells. Vacuoles are larger than vesicles. Either structure may store water, waste products, food, and other cellular materials. In plant cells, the vacuole may take up most of the cell's volume.

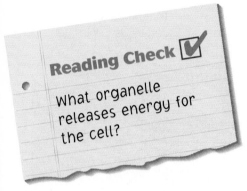

Reading Check ☑

What organelle releases energy for the cell?

Problem Solving

Using Numbers to Find the Surface Area and Volume of Cells

The cells in mice, elephants, and humans are about the same size. More than 10 trillion cells make up the human body. If 1000 of these cells were lined up, they would total less than 2 cm in length—about the width of a thumbnail.

Why are most cells microscopic? In order to survive, a cell must take in nutrients and remove wastes. Substances move into and out of a cell by passing through the cell membrane. This fact limits the size to which a cell can grow. Why?

Solve the Problem

1. Assume that a cell is like a cube.

2. Find the surface area of each cube illustrated below. Surface area is width × length × 6. (A cube has six faces.)

3. Calculate the volume of each cube. The volume of a cube is length × width × height.

4. Find the ratio of surface area to volume for each cube by dividing the surface area by the volume.

Think Critically

1. What happens to the surface area-to-volume ratio as the size of the cube increases?

2. If a cell doubled its volume, how much bigger would its cell membrane be?

3. How can a large cell solve its low surface area-to-volume ratio?

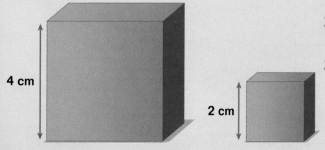

4 cm

2 cm

1 cm

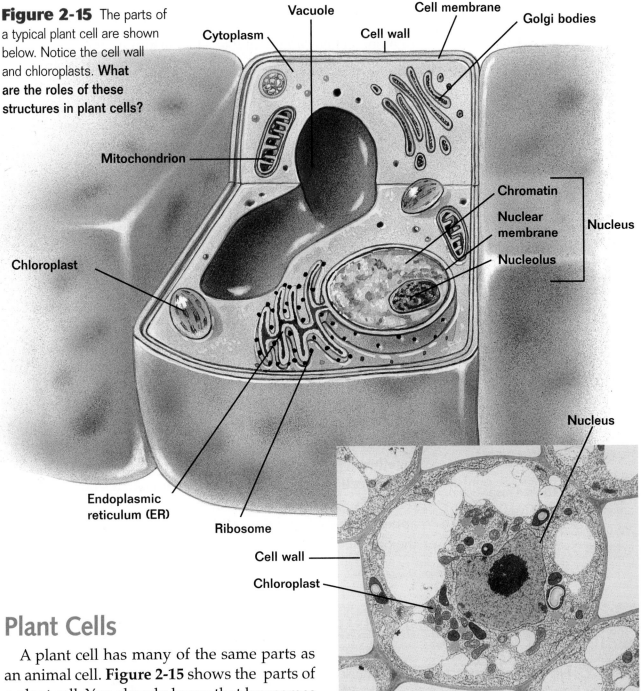

Figure 2-15 The parts of a typical plant cell are shown below. Notice the cell wall and chloroplasts. **What are the roles of these structures in plant cells?**

Vacuole

Cytoplasm

Cell membrane

Cell wall

Golgi bodies

Mitochondrion

Chloroplast

Chromatin

Nuclear membrane

Nucleolus

Nucleus

Endoplasmic reticulum (ER)

Ribosome

Nucleus

Cell wall

Chloroplast

Magnification: 1750×

Plant Cells

A plant cell has many of the same parts as an animal cell. **Figure 2-15** shows the parts of a plant cell. You already know that lysosomes are found only in animal cells. Another difference between a plant cell and an animal cell is that a plant cell has a cell wall outside the cell membrane. The **cell wall** is a rigid structure that supports and protects the plant cell and is made of bundles of tough cellulose fibers. Sometimes, other substances made by the cell are part of the cell wall.

Unlike animal cells, many plant cells have the ability to make their own food, a sugar. It is made in the **chloroplasts,** the green organelles found in the cytoplasm. Chloroplasts contain chlorophyll, a green pigment that traps light energy. As a result of many chemical reactions, light energy is changed into chemical energy and stored in sugar molecules.

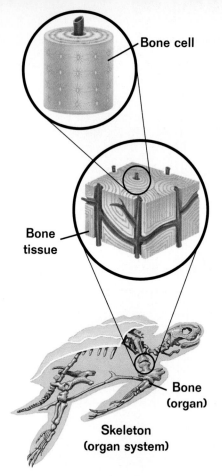

Bone cell

Bone tissue

Bone (organ)

Skeleton (organ system)

Turtle (organism)

Figure 2-16 In a many-celled organism, different types of tissues are organized into organs and systems.

Organizing Cells

A one-celled organism like a bacterium may perform all its life functions by itself. Cells in a many-celled organism, however, do not work alone. Instead, each cell depends in some way on other cells as the organism carries out its functions. This interaction helps the whole organism stay alive.

In **Figure 2-16,** you can see a single bone cell. You also see a group of the same type of bone cells that together form a tissue. In many-celled organisms, cells are organized into **tissues,** which are groups of similar cells that work together to do one job. Each tissue cell does its part to keep the tissue alive.

Tissues are organized into organs. An **organ** is a structure made up of different types of tissues that work together to do a particular job. Your heart is an organ made up of muscle, nerve, and blood tissues. Several different tissues make up a plant leaf, an organ of the plant in which food is made.

A group of organs working together to do a certain job is an organ system. Your heart and blood vessels make up your cardiovascular system. What other systems can you think of?

In a many-celled organism, several systems work together. Roots, stems, and leaves in a plant work together to keep the plant alive. Name three systems in your body that work together.

Each cell in a many-celled organism carries on its own life functions. Although cells in an organism may differ in appearance and function, all the cells working together keep the organism alive.

Section Assessment

1. Explain the importance of the cell nucleus in the life of a cell.

2. Give an example of an organ system in an animal and name the parts that make up the organ system.

3. **Think Critically:** How is the cell of a one-celled organism different from the cells in many-celled organisms?

4. **Skill Builder**
   Interpreting Scientific Illustrations
   Illustrations provide the reader with important information. Do the **Chapter 2 Skill Activity** on page 707 to learn about cells and cell organelles by interpreting the scientific illustrations.

Science Journal

Your textbook compared cell functions to that of a business. In your Science Journal, write an essay that explains how a cell is like your school or town.

Comparing Plant and Animal Cells

Materials

- Microscope
- Microscope slide
- Coverslip
- Forceps
- Dropper
- *Elodea* plant
- Prepared slide of human cheek cells

If you were to compare a goldfish to a rose bush, you would find the two to be very different. However, when the individual cells of these organisms are compared, will they be so different? Try this activity to see how plant and animal cells compare.

What You'll Investigate

In this exercise, you will observe an animal cell, a human cheek cell, and a plant cell, *Elodea*, under a compound light microscope.

Goals

- **Compare and contrast** an animal cell and a plant cell.

Procedure

1. **Copy** the data table in your Science Journal. Check off the cell parts as you observe them.

2. Follow the directions for using low- and high-power objectives on your microscope and for making a wet-mount slide.

3. Using forceps, **make** a wet-mount slide of a young leaf from the tip of an *Elodea* plant.

4. **Observe** the leaf on low power. Focus on the top layer of cells. Carefully focus down through the top layer of cells to observe other layers of cells.

5. Switch to high power and focus on one cell. Does the center of the cell appear empty? This is the central vacuole that contains water and stores cell products. **Observe** the chloroplasts in the cytoplasm, which are the green disk-shaped objects moving around the central vacuole. Try to find the cell nucleus. It looks like a clear ball.

6. Make a drawing of the *Elodea* cell. **Label** the cell wall, cytoplasm, chloroplasts, central

vacuole, and nucleus. Return to low power and remove the slide.

7. Place a prepared slide of cheek cells on the microscope stage. Locate the cells under low power.

8. Switch to high power and **observe** the cell nucleus. **Draw and label** the cell membrane, cytoplasm, and nucleus.

Conclude and Apply

1. How many cell layers could you see in the *Elodea* leaf?

2. **Compare and contrast** the shape of the cheek cell and the *Elodea* cell.

3. What can you conclude about the differences between plant and animal cells?

Cell Observations		
Cell Part	*Elodea*	**Cheek**
cytoplasm		
nucleus		
chloroplasts		
cell wall		
cell membrane		

2·3 Viruses

Characteristics of Viruses

Imagine something that doesn't grow or eat, yet reproduces. This something is a virus. A **virus** is nonliving and consists of a core of hereditary material surrounded by a protein coat. Viruses are so small that scientists must use extremely powerful microscopes to see them.

Viruses are unlike living things. They can reproduce only inside a living cell. Some viruses can be made into crystals and stored in a jar on a shelf for years. Then, if they enter an organism, they may quickly reproduce. This may cause new infections and damage the organism. Viruses, therefore, have the potential to greatly impact the living world.

What You'll Learn

► The structure of a virus and how viruses reproduce and cause disease
► The benefits of vaccines
► Some helpful uses of viruses

Vocabulary
virus
host cell
vaccine

Why It's Important

► Viruses affect nearly all organisms.

Figure 2-17 Viruses, from a Latin word for *poison*, come in a variety of shapes and are responsible for many diseases. On these pages are photos and computer models of several types of viruses.

Magnification: 20 000×

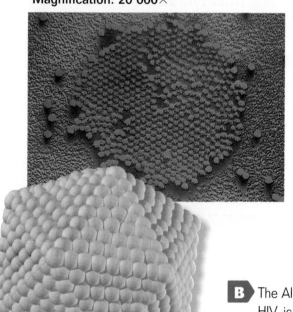

A The polio virus is many-sided and looks like a small crystal when magnified 20 000 times.

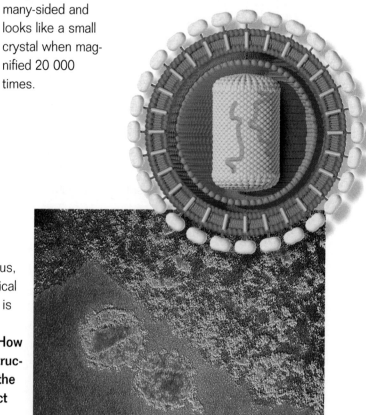

B The AIDS virus, HIV, is spherical in shape and is studded with projections. **How might this structure enable the virus to infect cells?**

Magnification: 46 000×

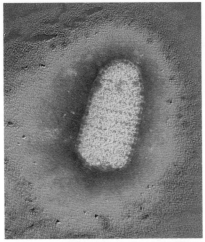

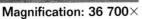
Magnification: 36 700×

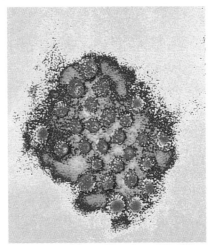
Magnification: 35 000×

Figure 2-18 Many viruses are named for the disease they cause or where they were first found. The rabies virus, shown on the left, is named for the disease it causes in animals. The virus on the right is named for where it was first found. It is the Norwalk virus named for Norwalk, Ohio.

Classification of Viruses

Viruses, as illustrated in **Figure 2-17,** may be classified by their shape, the kind of hereditary material they have, the kind of organism they infect, or their method of reproduction. The protein coat of a virus gives it its shape. As shown in **Figure 2-18,** viruses are often named for the diseases they cause, such as the polio virus; the organ or tissue they infect; or where they were first found.

Magnification: 95 000×

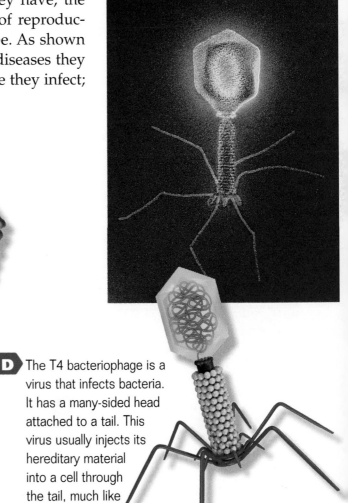

C The tobacco-mosaic virus is rod shaped and has a coat of proteins that spiral around a single strand of hereditary material. It causes tobacco plants to become stunted and the leaves to become discolored and blotchy.

D The T4 bacteriophage is a virus that infects bacteria. It has a many-sided head attached to a tail. This virus usually injects its hereditary material into a cell through the tail, much like a hypodermic needle.

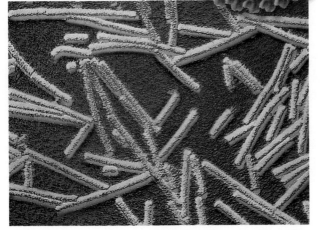
Magnification: 220 000×

Reproduction of Viruses

When most people hear the word *virus*, they relate it to a cold sore, a cold, or HIV, the virus that causes AIDS. Mumps, measles, and chicken pox are also diseases caused by viruses. A virus must be inside a living cell to reproduce. The cell in which a virus reproduces is called a **host cell.** Once a virus is in a host cell, the virus can act in two ways. It can either be active, as shown below, or it can become latent, an inactive stage.

Active Viruses

When a virus enters a cell and is active, it causes the host cell to make new viruses, which destroy the host cell. Follow the steps in **Figure 2-19** to see how an active virus reproduces itself inside a bacterial cell.

VISUALIZING
An Active Virus

Figure 2-19 An active virus, such as a bacteriophage, reproduces and destroys the cell it attacks.

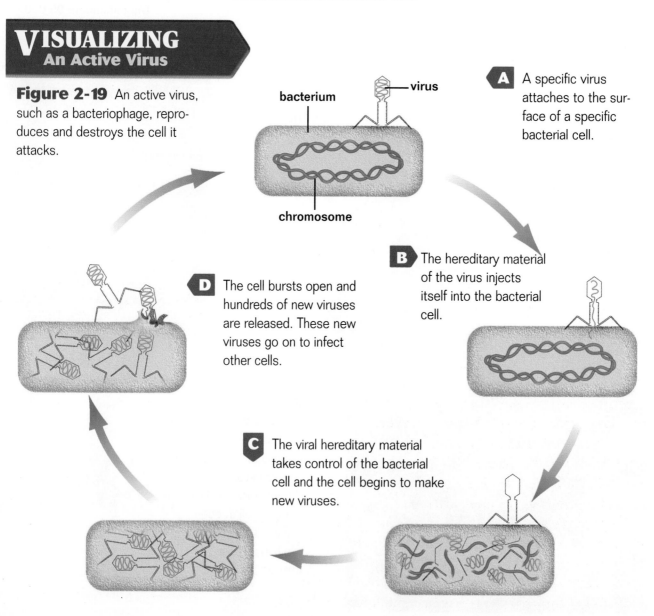

A A specific virus attaches to the surface of a specific bacterial cell.

B The hereditary material of the virus injects itself into the bacterial cell.

C The viral hereditary material takes control of the bacterial cell and the cell begins to make new viruses.

D The cell bursts open and hundreds of new viruses are released. These new viruses go on to infect other cells.

bacterium

virus

chromosome

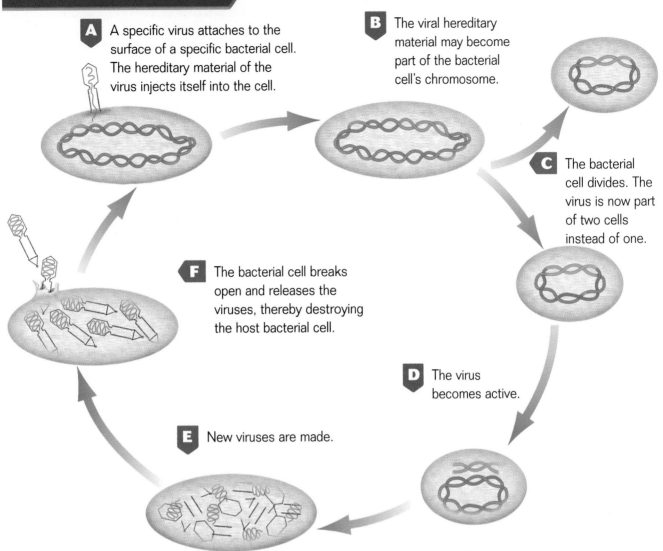

A A specific virus attaches to the surface of a specific bacterial cell. The hereditary material of the virus injects itself into the cell.

B The viral hereditary material may become part of the bacterial cell's chromosome.

C The bacterial cell divides. The virus is now part of two cells instead of one.

F The bacterial cell breaks open and releases the viruses, thereby destroying the host bacterial cell.

D The virus becomes active.

E New viruses are made.

Figure 2-20 A latent virus may not immediately destroy the cell it attacks.

Latent Viruses

Some viruses may be latent viruses. A latent virus enters a cell and its hereditary material may become part of the cell's hereditary material. It does not immediately destroy the cell or make new viruses. Latent viruses may appear to hide inside host cells for many years. Then, at any time, the virus can become active. Stress, or too much sun or cold, may cause a virus to become active. Follow **Figure 2-20** as it outlines the reproduction cycle of latent viruses. ☑

If you have ever had a cold sore, you've been infected by a virus that has gone from its latent phase into its active phase. The appearance of a cold sore on your lip is a sign that the virus is active and destroying cells in your lip. When the cold sore disappears, the virus has become latent again. The virus is still in your body's cells, but you just don't realize it.

Reading Check ☑
What is a latent virus?

Table 2-1

Viral Diseases in Humans		
Disease	Caused By	Vaccine
AIDS	HIV	No
Chicken pox	*Varicella zoster*	Yes
Common cold	more than 200 rhinoviruses	No
Influenza	flu types A, B, and C	Yes
Measles	rubella—*Rubivirus* rubeola—paramyxovirus	Yes
Mumps	paramyxovirus	Yes
Polio	*Poliovirus hominis*	Yes
Rabies	rhabdovirus	Yes
Smallpox	orthopoxvirus	Yes

Viral Diseases

Viruses may cause diseases in plants, animals, fungi, bacteria, and protists. There are no antibiotic medications to *cure* viral diseases. But some viral diseases can be *prevented* by vaccines. A **vaccine** is made from damaged virus particles that can't cause disease anymore. **Table 2-1** lists many viral diseases found in humans. The availability of vaccines to fight such infections is also indicated.

Vaccines

Edward Jenner, an English doctor, is credited with developing a vaccine in 1796. Jenner developed a vaccine for smallpox, a disease that was greatly feared even into the twentieth century. Jenner noticed that people who milked cows and came down with a disease called cowpox didn't get smallpox. He prepared a vaccine from the sores of milkmaids who had cowpox. When injected into healthy people, the cowpox vaccine seemed to protect them from smallpox. Did Jenner know he was fighting a virus? No. At that time, no one understood what caused disease or how the body fought disease.

Figure 2-21 Modern vaccination procedures help prevent many childhood and adult diseases. **What other common vaccinations are given?**

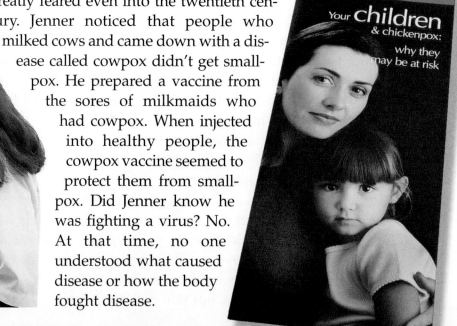

Your **children** & chickenpox: why they may be at risk

Vaccinations are an important step in maintaining health. **Figure 2-21** shows a child receiving a vaccination by receiving a shot.

Studies Using Viruses

Most of what you hear about viruses might make you think that viruses always act in a harmful way. However, there are some cases where, through research, scientists are discovering uses for viruses that may make them helpful.

One experimental method, called gene therapy, involves substituting normal hereditary material for a cell's defective hereditary material. The normal hereditary material is enclosed in a virus. The virus may then "infect" targeted cells, taking the new strand of hereditary material into the cells to replace the defective hereditary material.

Using gene therapy, scientists hope to help people with genetic disorders. For example, some people have the genetic disorder sickle-cell anemia. Because of a defective gene, abnormal hemoglobin causes changes in red blood cells. They cannot function normally, which causes many problems. With the help of a virus, a repaired gene was allowed to infect blood cells in a mouse, and the mouse blood cells began to produce the correct substance. Researchers are hoping to use similar techniques for humans with sickle-cell disease or cancer.

interNET CONNECTION

Scientists have determined that Marburg virus, Ebola Zaire, and Ebola Reston all belong to the virus family *Filoviridae*. Visit the Glencoe Science Web Site at **www.glencoe. com/sec/science/ca** for more information about the Marburg and Ebola viruses.

Section Assessment

1. Describe the structure of viruses and explain how viruses reproduce.

2. How are vaccines beneficial?

3. How may some viruses be helpful?

4. **Think Critically:** Explain why a doctor might not give you any medication if you had a viral disease.

5. **Skill Builder**
   Concept Mapping Make an events-chain concept map to show what happens when a latent virus becomes active. If you need help, refer to Concept Mapping in the **Skill Handbook** on page 678.

Using Computers

Spreadsheet Enter the following data in a spreadsheet and make a line graph. How does temperature affect viruses?
At 36.9°C, there are 1.0 million viruses; at 37.2°C, 1.0 million; at 37.5°C, 0.5 million; at 37.8°C, 0.25 million; at 38.3°C, 0.10 million; and at 38.9°C, 0.05 million. If you need help, refer to page 702.

For a **preview** of this chapter, study this Reviewing Main Ideas before you read the chapter. After you have studied this chapter, you can use the Reviewing Main Ideas to **review** the chapter.

The Glencoe MindJogger, Audiocassettes, and CD-ROM provide additional opportunities for review.

Section 2-1 CELLS—THE UNITS OF LIFE

The first compound microscope was made in 1590. In the mid 1600s, a simple microscope was developed that could make an image of an object 270 times larger than the actual size of the object. As scientists learned more about lenses, **compound light microscopes** were made. Compound light microscopes use light and lenses to make images. Things that are too small to be seen with a light microscope can be viewed with an **electron microscope.** An electron microscope bends beams of electrons in a magnetic field. Images can be seen only when they are photographically or electronically produced.

With the help of the microscope, scientists concluded that all living things were made of cells. According to the cell theory, the cell is the basic unit of life. Organisms are made of one or more cells, and all cells come from other cells.

What are the similarities and differences between a compound light microscope and an electron microscope?

2-2 CELL ORGANIZATION

There are two basic types of cells, prokaryotic cells and eukaryotic cells. A prokaryotic cell has no membrane around its hereditary material. A eukaryotic cell has a **nucleus,** hereditary material surrounded by a membrane. In both cell types, the hereditary material controls all cell functions. All cells are surrounded by a **cell membrane.** Inside the cell membrane is a gelatinlike mixture called **cytoplasm.** The hereditary material is in the cytoplasm along with other cell structures. Eukaryotic cells have structures called **organelles** that do specific jobs. All cell parts work together to keep a cell alive. There are differences among animal, plant, and bacterial cells. Animal cells do not have cell walls. Plant cells have cell walls and chloroplasts. Bacteria have no membrane-covered organelles.

Many-celled organisms are organized to perform all the jobs necessary to keep them alive. Most have tissues, organs, and organ systems. *What feature distinguishes a prokaryotic cell from a eukaryotic cell?*

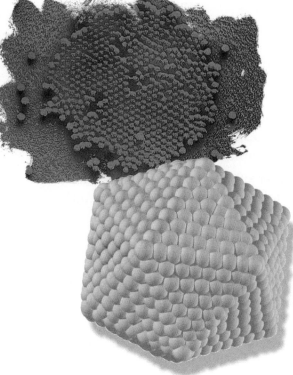

Section

2-3 VIRUSES

A virus is a structure containing hereditary material surrounded by a protein coat. It can only reproduce when inside a living host cell. An active virus enters a cell, reproduces, and then destroys the cell. A latent virus enters a cell and may become a part of the cell's hereditary material. Latent viruses may hide inside host cells for many years before becoming active. Viruses cause diseases in animals, plants, fungi, and bacteria. Vaccines prevent some viral diseases. *Why don't scientists consider viruses living organisms?*

Chapter 2 Assessment

Using Vocabulary

a. cell membrane
b. cell theory
c. cell wall
d. chloroplast
e. chromatin
f. compound light microscope
g. cytoplasm
h. electron microscope
i. endoplasmic reticulum
j. Golgi body
k. host cell
l. lysosome
m. mitochondria
n. nucleus
o. organ
p. organelle
q. ribosome
r. tissue
s. vaccine
t. virus

Using the vocabulary words, give two examples of each of the following.

1. a tool to view cells and microorganisms
2. made from more than one cell
3. an organelle where energy is converted
4. part of all cells
5. involved in moving cellular products

Checking Concepts

Choose the word or phrase that best completes the sentence.

6. Which of the following is a viral disease?
   A) tuberculosis   C) smallpox
   B) anthrax   D) tetanus
7. Which microscope uses lenses to magnify?
   A) compound light microscope
   B) scanning electron microscope
   C) transmission electron microscope
   D) atomic force microscope
8. Which microscope magnifies up to 1 million times or more?
   A) compound light microscope
   B) stereoscopic microscope
   C) transmission electron microscope
   D) atomic force microscope

9. Which scientist gave the name *cells* to structures he viewed?
   A) Hooke   C) Schleiden
   B) Schwann   D) Virchow
10. What organelle helps to recycle old cell parts?
    A) chloroplast   C) lysosome
    B) centriole   D) cell wall
11. What structure allows only certain things to pass in and out of the cell?
    A) cytoplasm   C) cell wall
    B) cell membrane   D) nuclear envelope
12. What are structures in the cytoplasm of the eukaryotic cell called?
    A) organs   C) organ systems
    B) organelles   D) tissues
13. What is made of folded membranes that move materials around inside the cell?
    A) chromatin   C) Golgi body
    B) cytoplasm   D) endoplasmic reticulum
14. Which of the following is part of a bacterial cell?
    A) a cell wall   C) mitochondria
    B) lysosomes   D) a nucleus
15. What do groups of different tissues form (such as the heart)?
    A) organ   C) organ system
    B) organelle   D) organism

Thinking Critically

16. Why is it difficult to get rid of viruses?
17. What type of microscope would be best to use to look at a piece of moldy bread? Give reasons to support your choice.
18. What would happen to a plant cell that suddenly lost its chloroplasts?
19. What would happen to an animal cell if it didn't have ribosomes?
20. How would you decide whether an unknown cell was an animal cell, a plant cell, or a bacterial cell?

Developing Skills

If you need help, refer to the **Skill Handbook.**

21. **Interpreting Scientific Illustrations:** Use the illustrations of cells in Section 2-2 to describe how the shape of a cell may be related to its function.

22. **Concept Mapping:** Complete the following concept map of the basic units of life.

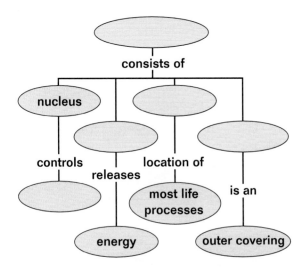

23. **Sequencing:** Sequence the following from simple to complex: *small intestine, circular muscle cell, human,* and *digestive system.*

24. **Making and Using Tables:** List the cell structures and their functions in a table.

25. **Comparing and Contrasting:** In a table, compare and contrast the structures of a virus, a bacterial cell, and a eukaryotic cell.

26. **Making a Model:** Make a timeline to show the development of the cell theory. Begin with the development of the microscope in 1590 and end with Virchow's statement in the 1850s. Include the contributions of Van Leeuwenhoek, Hooke, Schleiden, and Schwann.

Test-Taking Tip

Plan Your Work and Work Your Plan
Set up a study schedule for yourself well in advance of your test. Plan your workload so that you do a little each day rather than a lot all at once. The key to retaining information is to repeatedly review and practice it.

Test Practice

Use these questions to test your Science Proficiency.

1. A cell wall is found in plant cells but not in animal cells. Which of the following statements would indicate the presence of a cell wall in plant cells?
   A) Plant fibers are used for weaving fabrics like cotton and linen.
   B) Plants are food producers.
   C) Plants and plant products are often used as medicines.
   D) Crushed leaves, stems, and other plant parts may be used as dyes.

2. Mitochondria are more numerous in active cells like liver cells and muscle cells. Which of the following explains why these cells need more mitochondria?
   A) Mitochondria are surrounded by two membranes.
   B) Mitochondria have their own DNA.
   C) Mitochondria are sites where food molecules are broken down and energy is released.
   D) New mitochondria are produced only when existing ones grow and divide.

3. What is the cell structure that acts as the control center of a eukaryotic cell?
   A) cell membrane   C) mitochondrion
   B) chloroplast   D) nucleus

Cell Processes

Chapter Preview

Skills Preview

Skill Builders
- Use Numbers
- Map Concepts

Activities
- Measure in SI
- Conclude

MiniLabs
- Infer
- Observe

Reading Check ✔

As you read this chapter about cell processes, compare the use of the word *compound* to its use in other subject areas. What are the similarities and differences?

Explore Activity

Have you ever forgotten to water a plant and remembered when the plant began to wilt? After you watered the plant, it probably straightened up and looked healthier. What caused the plant to straighten? How long does it take for a wilted plant to return to normal? Why does this happen? In the following activity, find out about water entering and leaving plant cells.

Observe Cell Processes

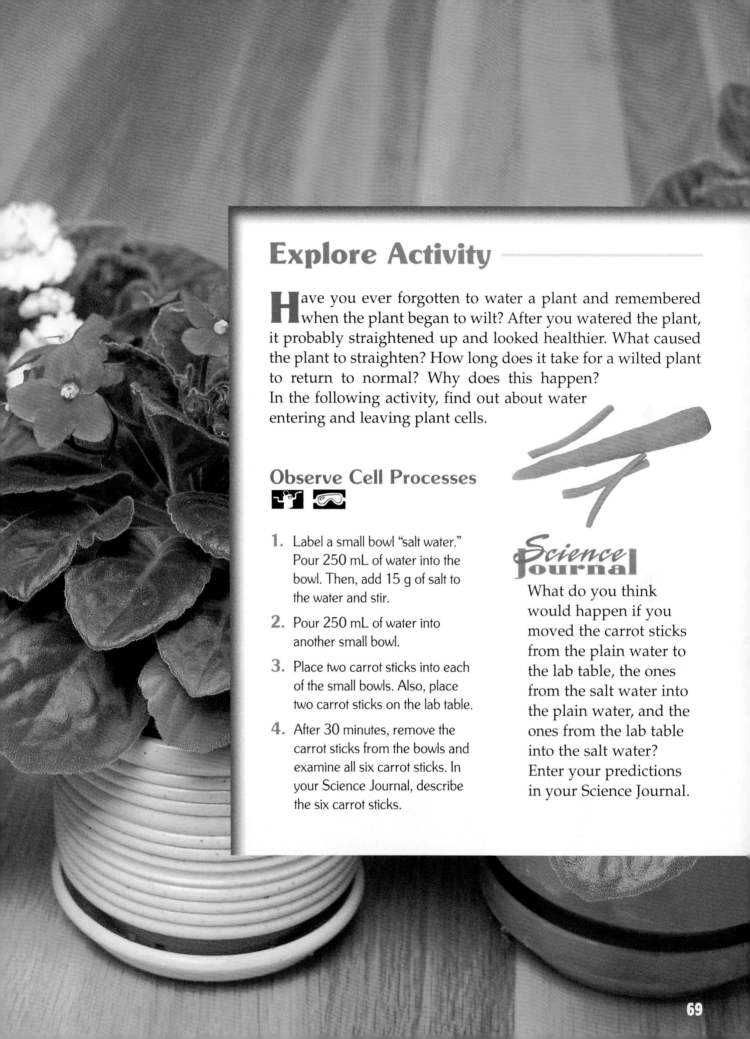

1. Label a small bowl "salt water." Pour 250 mL of water into the bowl. Then, add 15 g of salt to the water and stir.

2. Pour 250 mL of water into another small bowl.

3. Place two carrot sticks into each of the small bowls. Also, place two carrot sticks on the lab table.

4. After 30 minutes, remove the carrot sticks from the bowls and examine all six carrot sticks. In your Science Journal, describe the six carrot sticks.

Science Journal

What do you think would happen if you moved the carrot sticks from the plain water to the lab table, the ones from the salt water into the plain water, and the ones from the lab table into the salt water? Enter your predictions in your Science Journal.

Chemistry of Living Things

What You'll Learn

► The differences among atoms, elements, molecules, and compounds
► How to recognize the relationship between chemistry and life science
► The differences and similarities between inorganic and organic compounds

Vocabulary
mixture
organic compound
enzyme
inorganic compound

Why It's Important

► You grow because of chemical reactions in your body.

The Nature of Matter

Do you know what makes up Earth? If you ask someone, he or she may answer "matter and energy." Matter is anything that has mass and takes up space. How many things can you think of that fit that category?

Atoms

Everything in your environment, including you, is made of matter. Matter is made of atoms. **Figure 3-1** shows a model of an oxygen atom. At the center of an atom is a nucleus. A nucleus contains protons and neutrons. A proton has a positive charge, a neutron has no charge, and they have nearly equal masses. Outside the nucleus are electrons. An electron has a negative charge. About 1837 electrons equal the mass of one proton.

But, what about energy in your environment? Sunlight and electricity are forms of energy. Energy holds the parts of an atom together. One form of energy, called chemical energy, bonds groups of atoms together. To release or transfer this energy, a chemical reaction must occur. In a chemical reaction, chemical bonds break, new bonds form, and atoms are rearranged. The substances produced are different from those that began the chemical reaction. As shown in **Figure 3-2,** chemical reactions take place in living organisms.

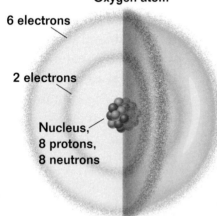

Oxygen atom

6 electrons

2 electrons

Nucleus,
8 protons,
8 neutrons

Figure 3-1 An oxygen atom model shows the placement of electrons, protons, and neutrons.

Figure 3-2 When fireflies blink and shine in the dark, energy is released in the form of light as chemical bonds are broken and new ones are formed.

Table 3-1

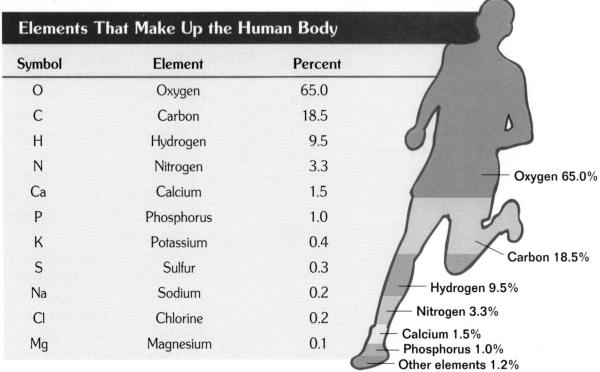

Elements That Make Up the Human Body		
Symbol	**Element**	**Percent**
O	Oxygen	65.0
C	Carbon	18.5
H	Hydrogen	9.5
N	Nitrogen	3.3
Ca	Calcium	1.5
P	Phosphorus	1.0
K	Potassium	0.4
S	Sulfur	0.3
Na	Sodium	0.2
Cl	Chlorine	0.2
Mg	Magnesium	0.1

Oxygen 65.0%
Carbon 18.5%
Hydrogen 9.5%
Nitrogen 3.3%
Calcium 1.5%
Phosphorus 1.0%
Other elements 1.2%

Elements

When something is made up of only one kind of atom, it is called an element. An element can't be broken down into a simpler form by ordinary chemical reactions. The element oxygen is made up of only oxygen atoms, and hydrogen is made up of only hydrogen atoms. Each element has its own symbol. Ninety elements occur naturally on Earth. Everything, including you, is made of one, or a combination of, these elements. **Table 3-1** lists elements as they occur in the human body. What two elements make up most of your body?

How Atoms Combine

Suppose you've just eaten an apple, such as the one in **Figure 3-3.** Did you know that the apple contains a sugar made of the elements carbon, oxygen, and hydrogen? The water in the apple contains both oxygen and hydrogen. Notice that the apple and water both contain oxygen. Yet, in one case, oxygen is part of a colorless, tasteless liquid—water. Oxygen is also part of a colorful solid—the apple. How can one element be part of two materials that are so different? The atoms of elements combine chemically to form new substances called compounds.

CHEMISTRY INTEGRATION

Periodic Table of Elements
All elements are arranged in a chart known as the periodic table of elements. What information does it provide for each element?

Hydrogen	Carbon	Nitrogen	Oxygen
1	6	7	8
H	**C**	**N**	**O**
1.008	12.011	14.007	15.999

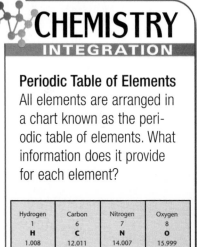

Figure 3-3
An apple is made up of mostly carbon, oxygen, and hydrogen.

Figure 3-4 The chemical formula for a water molecule is H₂O.

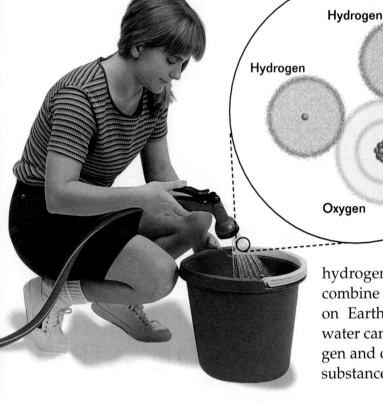

Hydrogen

Hydrogen

Oxygen

Glucose, an energy-storing sugar in plant cells, is a compound. It is made of the elements carbon, hydrogen, and oxygen and has the chemical formula $C_6H_{12}O_6$. When elements form a compound, the properties of the individual elements change. How does this happen?

One way that atoms combine is by sharing their outermost electrons. The combined atoms form a molecule. For example, two atoms of hydrogen can share electrons with one atom of oxygen to form one molecule of water as illustrated in **Figure 3-4.** Water is a compound composed of molecules. The properties of hydrogen and oxygen are changed when they combine to form water. Under normal conditions on Earth, oxygen and hydrogen are gases. Yet, water can be a liquid, a solid, or a gas. When hydrogen and oxygen combine, changes occur and a new substance forms. ☑

Ions

Some atoms combine by sharing electrons. But, atoms also combine because they've become positively or negatively charged.

Atoms are usually neutral. They have no overall electric charge. Under certain conditions, however, atoms can lose or gain electrons. When an atom loses electrons, it has more protons than electrons so the atom is positively charged. When an atom gains electrons, it has more electrons than protons so the atom is negatively charged. Electrically charged atoms—positive or negative—are called ions.

Ions are attracted to one another when they have opposite charges. Oppositely charged ions join to form electrically neutral compounds. Table salt is made of sodium (Na) and chlorine (Cl) ions. As shown in **Figure 3-5,** a chlorine atom captures an electron of a sodium atom. The chlorine becomes a negatively charged ion, and the sodium a positively charged ion. These oppositely charged ions are attracted to each other and form the compound sodium chloride, NaCl.

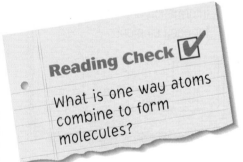

Reading Check ☑

What is one way atoms combine to form molecules?

Mixtures

Many times, two substances can be mixed together without combining chemically. A **mixture** is a combination of substances in which individual substances retain their own properties. For example, if you mix sugar and salt together, neither substance changes, nor do they combine chemically. Mixtures can be solids, liquids, gases, or any combination of them.

Solutions and Suspensions

Why are molecules important? In living organisms, cell membranes, cytoplasm, and other substances are all in the form of molecules. During its lifetime, a cell will make and break apart many molecules for growth, repair, and energy. Many of these molecules are found dissolved in the cytoplasm, forming a solution. A solution is a mixture in which two or more substances are mixed evenly.

*inter*NET
CONNECTION

Air is a mixture of many things. Weather forecasts often include information about *air quality.* Visit the Glencoe Science Web Site at **www.glencoe. com/sec/science/ca** for more information about air quality.

VISUALIZING Ions

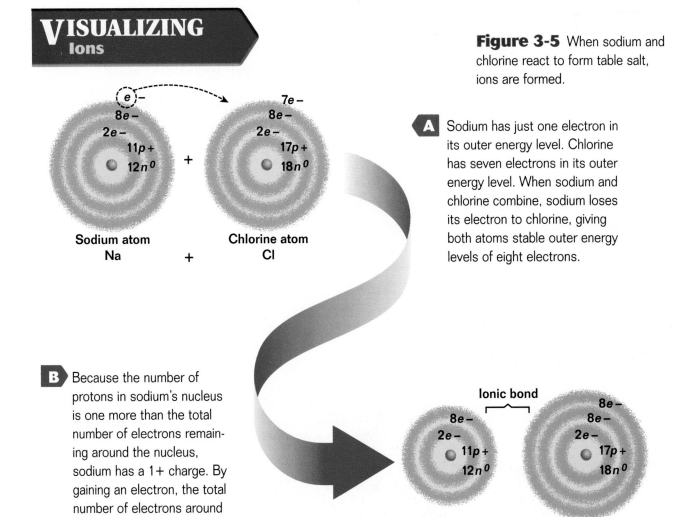

Figure 3-5 When sodium and chlorine react to form table salt, ions are formed.

A Sodium has just one electron in its outer energy level. Chlorine has seven electrons in its outer energy level. When sodium and chlorine combine, sodium loses its electron to chlorine, giving both atoms stable outer energy levels of eight electrons.

B Because the number of protons in sodium's nucleus is one more than the total number of electrons remaining around the nucleus, sodium has a 1+ charge. By gaining an electron, the total number of electrons around chlorine's nucleus is one more than than the number of protons in its nucleus, so chlorine has a 1– charge.

When you dissolve salt in water, you get a salt solution. You've probably noticed the taste of salt when you perspire. That's because your cells are surrounded by a salt solution. Living organisms also contain suspensions. A suspension is a mixture in which substances are evenly spread through a liquid or gas. Unlike solutions, the particles in a suspension eventually sink to the bottom. Blood, shown in **Figure 3-6,** is an example of a suspension. If a test tube of blood is left undisturbed, the red blood cells and white blood cells will gradually sink to the bottom. Because your blood is constantly moved by the pumping action of your heart, the cells remain suspended.

Figure 3-6 When a test tube of whole blood (right test tube) is left standing, the blood cells and the plasma separate, (left test tube).

Organic Compounds

Compounds in living organisms may be classified as either organic or inorganic. Most compounds containing carbon are **organic compounds. Table 3-2** compares the four groups of organic compounds that make up all living things—carbohydrates, lipids, proteins, and nucleic acids.

Problem Solving

Examining the Properties of Ice

Have you ever noticed that as water freezes, ice forms on the surface first, not at the bottom? When you place ice cubes in a glass of water, they float. This difference between water and ice is important in nature.

Think Critically

1. When a lake or pond freezes over, what happens to the living organisms in it?
2. Predict what would happen to the living organisms in a lake or pond if freezing occurred from the bottom up.
3. Does ice provide living organisms protection from cold temperatures? Explain.

Table 3-2

Organic Compounds That Make Up Life				
	Carbohydrate	**Lipid**	**Protein**	**Nucleic Acid**
Elements	carbon, hydrogen, and oxygen	carbon, hydrogen, and oxygen	carbon, hydrogen, oxygen, nitrogen, and sulfur	carbon, hydrogen, oxygen, nitrogen, and phosphorus
Unit	simple sugar	fatty acid	amino acid	nucleotide
Examples	sugars, starch, and cellulose	fats, oils, and waxes	enzymes, skin, hair	DNA, RNA
Function	supply energy for cell processes; form plant structures	store large amounts of energy long term	regulate cell processes and build cell structures	carry hereditary information
Location	cell membranes, cytoplasm, and plant cell walls	cell membranes and plant cell walls	throughout cells and cell membranes	nucleus, mitochondria, ribosomes, and chloroplasts

Carbohydrates are organic compounds made up of carbon, hydrogen, and oxygen. Carbohydrates supply energy for cell processes. Lipids, commonly called fats and oils, are organic compounds that store and release even larger amounts of energy than carbohydrates.

Proteins are the building blocks of many structural components of organisms. They are scattered throughout cell membranes and are made up of smaller molecules called amino acids. Certain proteins called **enzymes** regulate nearly all chemical reactions in cells without being changed.

Nucleic acids are large organic molecules that store important coded information in cells. One nucleic acid, DNA, is found in the nucleus, in chromosomes, in mitochondria, and in chloroplasts. It carries information that directs each cell's activities. Another nucleic acid, RNA, carries the information required to make proteins and enzymes.

Mini Lab

Determining How Enzymes Work

Procedure

1. Make a mark on one of two clean test tubes. Place them in a test-tube rack then fill each halfway with milk.
2. Place a tablet of rennin, an enzyme, in a small plastic bowl. Crush the tablet using the back of a metal spoon. Add the crushed tablet to the marked test tube.
3. Let both test tubes stand undisturbed during your class period.
4. Observe what happens to the milk.

Analysis

1. What effect did the rennin have on the milk?
2. Predict what would eventually happen to the milk without rennin.
3. Infer how rennin's effect on milk might be useful to the dairy industry.

Figure 3-7 All organisms depend on water for life.

Inorganic Compounds

Most **inorganic compounds** are made from elements other than carbon. Water, an inorganic compound shown in **Figure 3-7,** makes up a large part of living matter. It is one of the most important compounds in living things. Substances used in cells must be dissolved in water. Nutrients and waste materials are carried throughout your body in solution form.

Section Assessment

1. How are atoms different from molecules?
2. What is the difference between organic and inorganic compounds?
3. What are the four groups of organic compounds that make up all living things?
4. **Think Critically:** If you mix salt, sand, and sugar with water in a small jar, will the result be a suspension, a solution, or both?
5. **Skill Builder**
   Using Numbers Chemical equations consist of letters and numbers. The letters represent elements, and the numbers are used to represent atoms and molecules. Do the **Chapter 3 Skill Activity** on page 708 to learn how numbers are used in chemical equations.

Using Computers

Spreadsheet Find the percentage of elements that make up Earth's crust. Make a spreadsheet that includes this information and the information in **Table 3-1.** Create a circle graph for each set of percentages. What five elements have the total highest percentages? If you need help, refer to page 702.

Cell Transport

Control of Materials by Cells

Cells obtain food, oxygen, and other substances from their environment. They also release waste materials into their environment. If a cell has a membrane around it, how do these things move into and out of the cell? How does the cell control what enters and leaves?

Do you enjoy opening a window to allow fresh air into a room? How do you prevent unwanted things like insects, birds, or leaves from coming through the window? As seen in **Figure 3-8,** a window screen provides the protection needed to keep unwanted things outside. It also allows some things to pass from the room to the outside like air, unpleasant odors, or smoke. A cell membrane performs in a similar way for the cell. It allows some things to enter or leave the cell while keeping other things outside or inside the cell. When membranes function this way, they are called selectively permeable. The window screen is selectively permeable based on the size of the wire grid.

Diffusion

Molecules in solids, liquids, and gases constantly and randomly move. When molecules move from areas where there are more of them, into areas where there are fewer of them, it is called **diffusion.**

What You'll Learn

▶ The function of a selectively permeable membrane
▶ The processes of diffusion and osmosis
▶ The differences between passive transport and active transport

Vocabulary

diffusion   active
equilibrium   transport
osmosis   endocytosis
passive   exocytosis
  transport

Why It's Important

▶ Substances move in your body by entering and leaving cells.

Figure 3-8 A cell membrane, like a screen, will let some things through more easily than others. Air gets through, but insects are kept out.

Figure 3-9 Diffusion happens because molecules are in constant motion.

A Blue crystals were added to a beaker of water. In a few minutes, the blue-colored ions of the dissolving compound have partially diffused throughout the water.

B After two days, diffusion is greater.

C Complete diffusion can take months or even years if the water is left undisturbed and covered.

Mini Lab

Observing the Rate of Diffusion

Procedure

1. Use two beakers of equal size. Label one "hot," then fill it halfway with hot water. Label the other "cold," then fill it halfway with cold water. **CAUTION:** *Do not spill hot water on your skin.*

2. Add one drop of food coloring to each beaker. Carefully release the drop just above the water's surface to avoid splashing and disturbing the water.

3. Observe the beakers and record your observations. Repeat your observations after 10 minutes and record them again.

Analysis

1. Describe what happens when food coloring is added to each beaker.

2. How does temperature affect the rate of diffusion?

The random movement of molecules or particles is why diffusion happens.

Particles diffuse in liquids and in gases. **Figure 3-9** illustrates the diffusion of a blue compound in a beaker of water. You experience the effects of diffusion when someone opens a bottle of perfume in a closed room.

Drop a sugar cube into a glass of water and taste the water. Then, taste it again in three or four hours. At first, the sugar molecules are concentrated near the sugar cube in the bottom of the glass. Then, slowly, the sugar molecules diffuse throughout the water until they are more evenly distributed. When the molecules of one substance are spread evenly throughout another substance, a state of **equilibrium** occurs. Molecules don't stop moving when equilibrium is reached. They continue to move and maintain equilibrium.

Osmosis—The Diffusion of Water

You may remember that water makes up a large part of living matter. The diffusion of water through a cell membrane is called **osmosis.** Osmosis is important to cells because they contain water molecules and most cells are surrounded by water molecules. If cells aren't surrounded by relatively pure water, water will diffuse out of them. This is why water left the carrot cells in the Explore Activity at the beginning of the chapter. Because there were relatively fewer water molecules in the salt solution around the carrot cells than in the carrot cells, water moved out of the cells into the salt solution. Losing water from inside a plant cell causes the cell to shrink, pulling the cell membrane away from the cell wall, as seen in **Figure 3-10A.** This reduces the pressure against the cell wall and the plant cell becomes limp. If the carrot sticks were taken out of the salt water and put in pure water, the water around the cells would move into the cells. The cells would expand, pressing their cell membranes against their cell walls, as in **Figure 3-10B.** Pressure would increase and the plant cells would become firm. That is why the carrot sticks would be crisp again. ☑

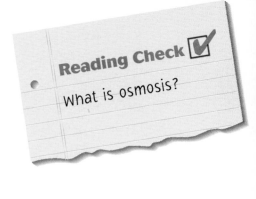

Reading Check ☑

What is osmosis?

Figure 3-10 Cells respond differently depending on whether the concentration of water inside the cell is equal to, greater than, or less than the water concentrations in the environment.

B Equilibrium occurs when water leaves and enters the cells at the same rate.

A Wilting occurs when more water leaves the cells than enters them.

Types of Transport

Cells take in many substances. Some substances pass easily through the cell membrane by diffusion. Other substances, such as glucose molecules, are so large that they enter the cell only with the help of transport protein molecules in the cell membrane. This process is known as *facilitated diffusion*. Transport proteins allow needed substances or wastes to move through the cell membrane. Diffusion and facilitated diffusion are types of passive transport. **Passive transport** is the movement of substances through the cell membrane without the use of cellular energy.

Active Transport

Sometimes, a substance is needed in a cell even though the amount of that substance inside the cell is already greater than the amount outside the cell. For example, root cells require minerals from the soil. The roots may already may contain more of those minerals than the surrounding soil. In this case, the minerals cannot move into the root cells by diffusion or facilitated diffusion. In order for the minerals to enter the root cells, cellular energy must be used. When energy is required to move materials through a cell membrane, **active transport** takes place in the cell membrane.

Active transport involves transport proteins. In active transport, a transport protein binds with the needed particle and uses cellular energy to move it through the cell membrane, as illustrated in **Figure 3-11.** When the particle is released, the transport protein is ready to move another needed particle.

*inter***NET**
C O N N E C T I O N

Active transport plays an important role in moving nutrients into our bodies during digestion. Visit the Glencoe Science Web Site at **www.glencoe. com/sec/science/ca** for more information about the transport of materials in cells.

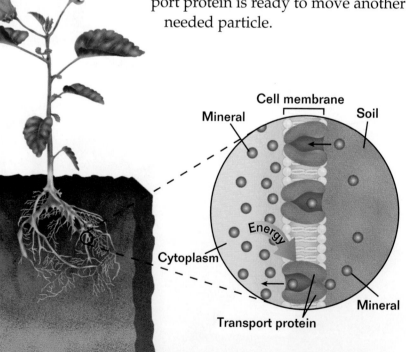

Figure 3-11 Plant root cells use active transport to take in minerals from the surrounding soil.

Cell membrane

Mineral

Soil

Energy

Cytoplasm

Transport protein

Mineral

Endocytosis and Exocytosis

Large protein molecules and bacteria may enter a cell when they are surrounded by the cell membrane. The cell membrane folds in on itself, enclosing the item in a sphere. The sphere pinches off, and the resulting vacuole enters the cytoplasm. This process is called **endocytosis** (en duh sy TOH sus). Some one-celled organisms, such as amoebas, take in food this way.

Vesicles and vacuoles are transport and storage structures in a cell's cytoplasm. They release their contents outside the cell by a process called **exocytosis** (ek soh sy TOH sus). Exocytosis happens in the opposite way that endocytosis happens. The membrane of the vesicle or vacuole fuses with the cell's membrane, and the vesicle's or vacuole's contents are released. Endocytosis and exocytosis are illustrated in **Figure 3-12.**

Figure 3-12 Substances that are too large to pass through cell membranes by passive or active transport enter and leave cells by endocytosis and exocytosis.

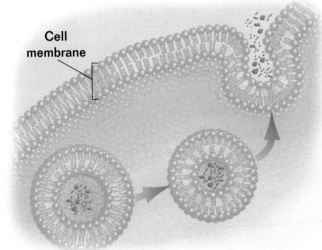

Cell membrane

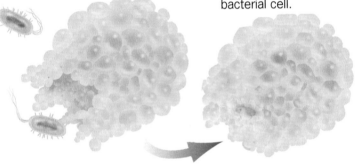

A A white blood cell uses endocytosis to engulf a bacterial cell.

B In exocytosis, substances in vacuoles or vesicles are released at the cell membrane.

Section Assessment

1. In what way are cell membranes selectively permeable?

2. Compare and contrast osmosis and diffusion.

3. Identify the molecules that help substances move through the cell membrane.

4. **Think Critically:** Why are fresh fruits and vegetables sprinkled with water in produce markets?

5.  **Skill Builder**
   Concept Mapping Make a network tree concept map to use as a study guide to help you tell the difference between passive transport and active transport. Begin with the phrase *Transport through membranes.* If you need help, refer to Concept Mapping in the **Skill Handbook** on page 678.

Science Journal Seawater has a higher concentration of salts than plain water. In your Science Journal, explain why drinking large amounts of seawater would be dangerous to humans.

Observing Osmosis

Materials

- Egg
- containers (500 mL) with covers (2)
- White vinegar (250 mL)
- Light corn syrup (250 mL)
- Graduated cylinder (100 mL)
- Labels (A and B)
- Small bowl
- Spoon

It is difficult to see osmosis occurring in cells because most cells are so small. However, a few cells can be seen without the aid of a microscope. Try this activity to see how osmosis occurs in a large cell.

What You'll Investigate

How does osmosis occur in an egg cell?

Goals

- **Observe** osmosis in an egg cell.
- **Determine** what affects osmosis.

Procedure 🥽 👐 🚫

1. **Copy** the tables below and use them to record your data and observations.

2. **Place** label A on one of the 500-mL containers and label B on the other. **Pour** the vinegar into container A and the syrup into container B. **Record** these data on the table. **Cover** container B.

3. **Place** the egg in container A and **cover** the container.

4. **Observe** the egg after 30 minutes, then again in two days. After each observation, **record** the egg's appearance on the table.

5. After the second observation, **remove** container A's cover. Carefully **remove** the egg from the liquid with a spoon and gently **rinse** the egg in a slow stream of cool tap water.

6. **Remove** the cover from container B. Carefully **place** the egg in the syrup and replace the cover.

7. **Measure** the volume of liquid in container A and **record** on the table.

8. **Observe** the egg the next day and **record** its appearance on the table.

9. **Remove** container B's cover. Gently remove the egg and allow the syrup to drain back into container B. Then, place the egg in the small bowl. **Measure** the volume of syrup and **record** on the table.

Conclude and Apply

1. What caused the change in volume of container A and container B?

2. Calculate the amount of water that moved into and out of the egg.

3. **Infer** what part of the egg controlled what moved into and out of the cell.

Volume Data

	Beginning volume	Ending volume
Vinegar		
Syrup		

Egg Observations

After 30 minutes	
After 2 days	
After 3 days	

Energy in Cells

Trapping Energy for Life

Think of all the energy players use in a basketball game. Where does that energy come from? The simplest answer is "from the food they eat." Cells take chemical energy stored in food and change it into forms needed to perform all the activities necessary for life. In every cell, these activities begin as chemical reactions. The total of all chemical reactions in an organism is called **metabolism.**

Living things are divided into two groups—producers and consumers—based on how they obtain their food energy. Organisms that make their own food, such as plants, are called **producers.** Organisms that can't make their own food are **consumers.**

Photosynthesis

Most producers use photosynthesis to produce food that has energy stored in its chemical bonds. The energy in sunlight triggers the chemical reactions of photosynthesis. Water and carbon dioxide (CO_2) are combined, producing sugar and giving off oxygen as a by-product. The chemical bonds, which hold the sugar molecules together, store energy. In plants and other photosynthetic producers, pigments capture sunlight's energy. Chlorophyll, a green pigment, is found in the chloroplasts where photosynthesis occurs. During photosynthesis, more sugar is made than the plant needs for survival. Excess sugar is changed and stored as starches and other carbohydrates. **Figure 3-13** illustrates the products of photosynthesis such as trees, grass, and apples.

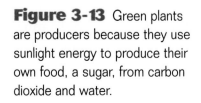

Figure 3-13 Green plants are producers because they use sunlight energy to produce their own food, a sugar, from carbon dioxide and water.

What You'll Learn

► The differences between producers and consumers
► The processes of photosynthesis and respiration
► How cells get energy from glucose through fermentation

Vocabulary
metabolism   consumer
producer   fermentation

Why It's Important

► Because of photosynthesis and respiration, energy gets from the sun to you.

Do you eat vegetables? Have you ever watched sheep graze or a bird catch a worm? People, sheep, and birds are examples of consumers. Consumers take in energy by eating producers or other consumers. These relationships form food chains. Producers are the first link in any food chain.

Releasing Energy for Life

To release and use the energy stored in food molecules, all organisms, both producers and consumers, must break down food molecules. For most cells, glucose is the food that is broken down. To break down glucose, many processes must happen. The final breakdown and energy release is called cellular respiration. This process usually requires the presence of oxygen. For some cells, it takes place in the mitochondria.

What happens in respiration?

Before respiration begins, glucose molecules in the cytoplasm are broken down into simpler substances. These substances enter the mitochondria where their stored energy is released in a series of chemical reactions called respiration. The final products of respiration are carbon dioxide, water vapor, and energy. Some of the energy released by respiration is used to produce high-energy molecules, and some is lost as heat.

Photosynthesis

$$6CO_2 + 6H_2O + \text{light energy} \xrightarrow{\text{chlorophyll}} C_6H_{12}O_6 + 6O_2$$

carbon dioxide · water · · · sugar · oxygen

Respiration

$$C_6H_{12}O_6 + 6O_2 \longrightarrow 6CO_2 + 6H_2O + \text{energy}$$

sugar · oxygen · · · carbon dioxide · water

Fermentation

During periods of vigorous activity, your muscles need more and more energy. You begin to breathe harder to supply the oxygen needed for respiration and the release of energy. If you are unable to supply enough oxygen, your muscles can use a process called fermentation to release energy. **Fermentation** is a form of respiration that releases energy from glucose when oxygen is not available. But, fermentation releases a smaller amount of energy than respiration that uses oxygen. In muscle cells, lactic acid is produced during fermentation. The presence of lactic acid is why your muscles may become stiff and sore after you use them too much.

CHEMISTRY
INTEGRATION ▶

Fermentation takes place in the cytoplasm of cells, not in the mitochondria. Similar to respiration with oxygen, molecules of glucose are changed to simpler substances before fermentation begins. Prokaryotic organisms, one-celled organisms without a nucleus or other membrane-surrounded structures in the cytoplasm, may use fermentation to release energy from food molecules. Some organisms, such as yeast and some bacteria, use a form of fermentation called alcohol fermentation to release energy and carbon dioxide (CO_2). **Figure 3-14** discusses the role of yeast in making the types of bread shown in the photograph. ☑

Photosynthesis and respiration are alike because both involve complex sets of reactions. Both occur in specific organelles, involve energy, and require enzymes. In many ways, photosynthesis is the opposite of respiration. The end products of respiration are the starting materials of photosynthesis. In summary, producers capture the sun's energy and store it in the form of food. Consumers eat producers. Cells use the glucose made by producers for energy. **Figure 3-15** shows the relationship between photosynthesis and respiration.

Figure 3-14 Yeast is an organism that breaks down the glucose in bread dough to produce carbon dioxide and alcohol. The bubbles of carbon dioxide cause the dough to rise. Baking the bread evaporates the alcohol.

Reading Check ☑

Where in a cell does fermentation take place?

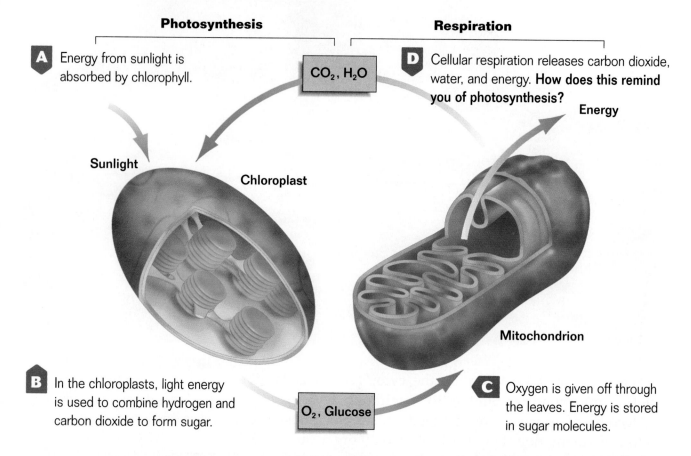

VISUALIZING
Photosynthesis and Respiration

Figure 3-15 Photosynthesis and respiration are related because the products of one may become the starting materials for the other.

Photosynthesis

A Energy from sunlight is absorbed by chlorophyll.

CO₂, H₂O

Sunlight

Chloroplast

B In the chloroplasts, light energy is used to combine hydrogen and carbon dioxide to form sugar.

O₂, Glucose

Respiration

D Cellular respiration releases carbon dioxide, water, and energy. **How does this remind you of photosynthesis?**

Energy

Mitochondrion

C Oxygen is given off through the leaves. Energy is stored in sugar molecules.

Section Assessment

1. Explain the difference between producers and consumers.

2. Explain how the energy used by all living things on Earth can be traced back to sunlight.

3. Compare the amount of energy released by respiration, which uses oxygen, to the amount of energy released by fermentation.

4. **Think Critically:** How can indoor plants help purify the air in a room?

5. **Skill Builder**
   Comparing and Contrasting Make a table that compares and contrasts respiration and fermentation. If you need help, refer to Comparing and Contrasting in the **Skill Handbook** on page 684.

Using Math

Refer to the chemical equation for respiration. Calculate the number of carbon, hydrogen, and oxygen atoms before and after respiration. How do they compare?

Bioreactors—
Harvesting Cell By-Products

Microscopic Workforce

Q: "What's that microorganism doing in the bread dough?"
A: "Its job!"

For centuries, people unknowingly used microorganisms to make bread rise and to ferment wine and beer. Microorganisms and their by-products and processes remained a mystery until the middle of the nineteenth century. Since that time, scientists have learned a lot about the structure, processes, and uses of microorganisms. They have developed new technologies for growing microorganisms and harvesting their by-products to use in a wide variety of products.

Bioreactors

The cultivation of large quantities of microorganisms and their by-products is done in bioreactors—giant, sterile, stainless-steel vats that hold 945 000 L or more (see inset). If growing conditions are right, less than 30 g of bacteria may become a mass of nearly 3 metric tons in just one day. Growing conditions inside the vats are carefully controlled and electronically monitored. Under different growing conditions, microorganisms produce different substances. For example, when the nitrogen in its environment is below a certain level, the mold *Penicillium* (seen at far left) makes the antibiotic penicillin.

Cellular By-Products

Today, microorganisms and their by-products are cultivated in bioreactors to make medicines, vitamins, alcohol, food thickeners, and other substances. Often, the microorganism itself is the desired product. For instance, the bacterium *Bacillus thuringensis* is grown for use as a natural pesticide to kill caterpillars that damage vegetable crops.

interNET CONNECTION

Visit the Glencoe Science Web Site at **www.glencoe.com/sec/science/ca** to learn more about microorganisms. In your Science Journal, list six products that are made using this technology.

Materials

- Test tubes,
  16 mm × 150 mm
  with stoppers (4)
  *small, clear-glass baby
  food jars with lids (4)
- Test-tube rack
- Stirring rod
- Balance scale
- Scissors
- Carbonated water
- Bromothymol blue solution in dropping bottle
- Aged tap water
  *distilled water
- Pieces of *Elodea* (2)
  *other water plants

  *Alternate Materials

Photosynthesis and Respiration

Every living cell carries on many chemical processes. Two important chemical processes are respiration and photosynthesis. Every cell, including the ones in your body, carries on respiration. But, some plant cells, unlike your cells, carry on both. In this experiment, you will investigate when these processes occur in plant cells.

What You'll Investigate

When do plants carry on photosynthesis and respiration?

Goals

- **Observe** green water plants in the light and dark.
- **Determine** whether green plants carry on both photosynthesis and respiration.

Safety Precautions

Protect clothing and eyes and be careful using chemicals.
CAUTION: *Do not get chemicals on your skin.*

Procedure

1. **Label** each test tube using the numbers 1, 2, 3, and 4. **Pour** 5 mL aged tap water into each test tube.

2. **Add** 10 drops of carbonated water to test tubes 1 and 2.

3. **Add** 10 drops of bromothyol blue to each test tube. Bromothyol blue turns green to yellow in the presence of an acid.

4. **Cut** two 10-cm pieces of *Elodea.* **Place** one piece of *Elodea* in the liquid in test tube 1 and one piece in the liquid in test tube 3. Stopper all test tubes.

5. Copy the Test Tube Data Table in your Science Journal. **Record** the color of the solution in each of the four test tubes.

6. **Place** test tubes 1 and 2 in bright light. Place tubes 3 and 4 in the dark. Observe the test tubes for 30 minutes or until there is a color change. Record the colors.

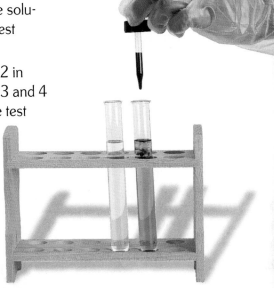

Conclude and Apply

1. What is indicated by the color of the water in all four test tubes at the start of the activity?

2. Infer what happened in the test tube or tubes that changed color after 30 minutes.

3. What can you conclude about the test tube or tubes that didn't change color after 30 minutes?

4. Describe the purpose of test tubes 2 and 4.

5. Does this experiment show that both photosynthesis and respiration occur in plants? Explain.

Test Tube Data Table		
Test tube	**Color at start**	**Color after 30 minutes**
1		
2		
3		
4		

For a **preview** of this chapter, study this Reviewing Main Ideas before you read the chapter. After you have studied this chapter, you can use the Reviewing Main Ideas to **review** the chapter.

GLENCOE TECHNOLOGY

The Glencoe MindJogger, Audiocassettes, and CD-ROM provide additional opportunities for review.

Section
3-1 CHEMISTRY OF LIVING THINGS

Matter is anything that has mass and takes up space. Atoms are the basic building blocks of matter. Energy in matter is in the chemical bonds that hold atoms together. Matter made of only one kind of atom is an element. Elements combine chemically to form compounds. The properties of the compound are different from those of the elements that made it. In a **mixture,** another form of matter, each substance retains its own properties. All **organic compounds** contain the element carbon. The organic compounds in living things are carbohydrates, lipids, proteins, and nucleic acids. Most **inorganic compounds,** such as water, do not contain carbon. Both organic and inorganic compounds are important to living things. *What is the relationship between matter and energy?*

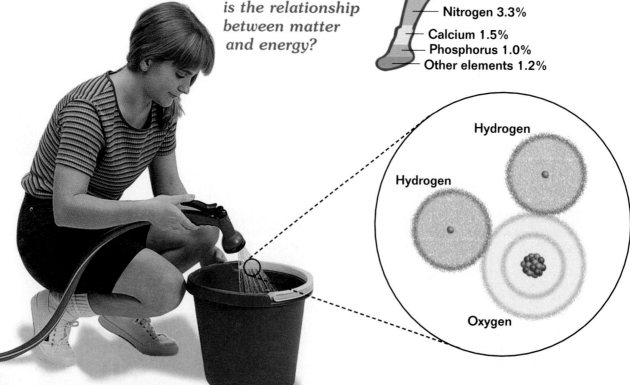

Oxygen 65.0%

Carbon 18.5%

Hydrogen 9.5%

Nitrogen 3.3%

Calcium 1.5%

Phosphorus 1.0%

Other elements 1.2%

Hydrogen

Hydrogen

Oxygen

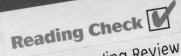

Reading Check ✓

Without reading Review Main Ideas, write a three to five sentence summary for one section of this chapter. Reread the section if necessary.

Section

3-2 CELL TRANSPORT

Particles of matter are in constant, random motion. **Diffusion** is the movement of particles from areas where they are more numerous to areas where they are less numerous. **Osmosis** is the diffusion of water through a membrane. The cell membrane controls what enters and leaves a cell. Diffusion and osmosis are forms of **passive transport,** which is the movement of particles across a cell membrane that requires no cellular energy. When a transport protein in the cell membrane uses energy to move particles across the cell membrane, it is called **active transport.** Large particles may enter a cell by **endocytosis** and leave by **exocytosis.** *Using the concept of osmosis, explain why people with sore throats often gargle with salt water.*

Section

3-3 ENERGY IN CELLS

Photosynthesis is the process by which some **producers** change light energy into chemical energy. Chlorophyll, in the chloroplasts of a green plant's cells, traps light energy for photosynthesis. Plants use some of the sugars they make as energy for other cellular functions. Excess sugar is stored as starch or other carbohydrates. Cells release stored energy from food molecules by respiration. Respiration that uses oxygen releases all of the energy in the food molecules and gives off carbon dioxide and water vapor as by-products. Respiration without oxygen is called **fermentation.** Fermentation releases only part of the energy in food molecules. *How are photosynthesis and respiration important to living things?*

Using Vocabulary

a. active transport
b. consumer
c. diffusion
d. endocytosis
e. enzyme
f. equilibrium
g. exocytosis
h. fermentation
i. inorganic compound
j. metabolism
k. mixture
l. organic compound
m. osmosis
n. passive transport
o. producer

Using the list of Vocabulary words, give two examples for each statement.

1. categories for the movement of materials through the cell membrane
2. classifications for substances in living organisms
3. organisms in a food chain
4. how large food particles enter and large waste particles leave an amoeba
5. types of passive transport

Checking Concepts

Choose the word or phrase that answers the question.

6. What is it called when energy is used to move molecules?
   A) diffusion   C) active transport
   B) osmosis   D) passive transport

7. How may bacteria be taken into cells?
   A) osmosis   C) exocytosis
   B) endocytosis   D) diffusion

8. What occurs when molecules are evenly distributed through a solid, liquid, or gas?
   A) equilibrium   C) fermentation
   B) metabolism   D) cellular respiration

9. Which of the following is an example of a carbohydrate?
   A) enzymes   C) waxes
   B) sugars   D) proteins

10. What are chromosomes made of?
    A) carbohydrates   C) lipids
    B) water molecules   D) nucleic acids

11. What organic molecule releases the greatest amount of energy?
    A) carbohydrate   C) lipid
    B) water   D) nucleic acid

12. What kind of molecule is water?
    A) organic   C) carbohydrate
    B) lipid   D) inorganic

13. Which of these is an example of an organic compound?
    A) $C_6H_{12}O_6$ C) H_2O
    B) NO_2 D) O_2

14. What are organisms that can't make their own food called?
    A) biodegradables   C) consumers
    B) producers   D) enzymes

15. What process requires chlorophyll?
    A) fermentation   C) diffusion
    B) endocytosis   D) photosynthesis

Thinking Critically

16. If you could place one red blood cell in distilled water, what would you see happen to the cell? Explain.

17. In snowy places, salt is used to melt ice on the roads. Explain what may happen to many roadside plants as a result.

18. Why does sugar dissolve faster in hot tea than in iced tea?

19. What would happen to the consumers in a lake if all the producers died?

20. Meat tenderizers contain protein enzymes. How do these enzymes affect meat?

Developing Skills

If you need help, refer to the **Skill Handbook.**

21. **Interpreting Data:** Water plants were placed at different distances from a light source. Bubbles coming from the plants were counted to measure the rate of photosynthesis. What can you say about how light affected the rate?

Photosynthesis in Water Plants		
Beaker number	Distance from light	Bubbles per minute
1	10 cm	45
2	30 cm	30
3	50 cm	19
4	70 cm	6
5	100 cm	1

22. **Making and Using Graphs:** Using the data from question 21, make a line graph that shows the relationship between the rate of photosynthesis and the distance from light.

23. **Concept Mapping:** Complete the events chain concept map to sequence the parts of matter from smallest to largest: *element, atom,* and *compound.*

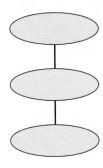

24. **Hypothesizing:** Make a hypothesis about what will happen to wilted celery when placed into a glass of plain water.

THE PRINCETON REVIEW

Test-Taking Tip

If It Looks Too Good to Be True . . .
Beware of answer choices that seem obvious. Remember that only one answer choice is correct of the several that you're offered for each question. Check each answer choice carefully before selecting one.

Test Practice

Use these questions to test your Science Proficiency.

$$6CO_2 + 6H_2O + \text{light energy} \xrightarrow{\text{chlorophyll}} C_6H_{12}O_6 + 6O_2\uparrow$$

1. The equation above is a summary of photosynthesis. According to the equation, what is one product of photosynthesis?
   A) water
   B) chlorophyll
   C) carbon dioxide
   D) oxygen

2. What type of molecule are enzymes?
   A) carbohydrate
   B) lipid
   C) protein
   D) nucleic acid

3. What process keeps some raw vegetables crisp in cool water?
   A) endocytosis   C) exocytosis
   B) diffusion   D) transpiration

4. Which of these statements is **NOT** true for respiration with oxygen?
   A) It is a simple chemical reaction.
   B) Energy is released.
   C) It happens in mitochondria.
   D) Water and carbon dioxide are by-products.

Cell Reproduction

Chapter Preview

Skills Preview

Skill Builders
- Sequence Events
- Map Concepts

Activities
- Observe and Infer
- Compare and Contrast

MiniLabs
- Make a Model

Reading Check ✓

As you read about cell reproduction, outline meiosis I and meiosis II. Then, write a description of meiosis in your own words.

Explore Activity

Would you believe that the image to the left is part of a complicated set of coded messages found in every cell? The messages called DNA contain the instructions and information needed for the cell and the organism it is part of to survive. In the following activity, see what information is in the cells of seeds.

Observe Seeds

1. Carefully split open a bean seed that has soaked in water overnight.

2. Observe both halves of the seed. Record your observations.

3. Place four other bean seeds in a moist paper towel in a self-sealing, plastic bag.

4. Make observations for a few days.

Science Journal

In your Science Journal, describe what happened to the seeds. From your observations, hypothesize about the messages in the seed's cells.

4•1 Cell Growth and Division

What You'll Learn

► Why mitosis is important
► How mitosis compares in plant and animal cells
► Two examples of asexual reproduction

Vocabulary
mitosis
chromosome
asexual reproduction

Why It's Important

► Many cells in your body grow and divide every day.

Why do cells divide?

It's likely that each time you go to the doctor, someone measures your height and weight. Similar data collected from thousands of people over the years, shows how people grow. The main reason you grow is because the number of cells in your body increases.

Constant Change

You are constantly changing. You aren't the same now as you were a year ago or even a few hours ago. At this very moment, as you read this page, groups of cells throughout your body are growing, dividing, and dying. Worn-out cells on the palms of your hands are being replaced. Cuts and bruises are healing. Red blood cells are being produced in your bones at a rate of 10 to 15 million per second to replace those that wear out. Muscle cells that you exercise are getting larger. Other organisms undergo similar processes. New organisms are created, like the protist in **Figure 4-1A.** Other organisms, like the plant in **Figure 4-1B,** can grow because new cells are formed. How do cells increase in number?

Figure 4-1 Cell division occurs in all organisms.

A A one-celled organism, such as this amoeba, reaches a certain size and then reproduces.

Magnification: 150×

B Many-celled organisms, such as the tomato plant, grow by increasing the numbers of cells.

Figure 4-2 An organism undergoes many changes as it develops. Below are a few stages of an oak tree's development.

The Cell Cycle

A living organism, such as the oak in **Figure 4-2,** has a life cycle. A life cycle begins with the organism's formation, is followed by growth and development, and finally, ends in death. Right now, you are in a stage of your life cycle called adolescence, a period of active growth and development. A cell also has a life cycle. Most of the life of any eukaryotic cell, a cell with a nucleus, is spent in a period of growth and development called *interphase.* During interphase, a cell grows, makes a copy of its hereditary material, and prepares for cell division. In cell division, the nucleus divides, and then the cytoplasm separates to form two new cells. Cell division is a continuous process. The cell cycle, as shown in **Figure 4-3,** is a series of events that takes place in a cell from one division to the next. The cycle is constantly repeated by cells, like skin and bone cells, that are needed for repair, growth, or replacement. Cells in your body that no longer divide, such as nerve and muscle cells, are always in interphase.

Figure 4-3 Cell division is a continuous process. **When do chromosomes duplicate?**

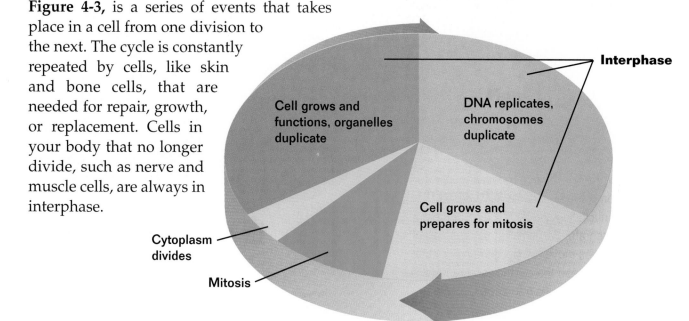

Interphase

Cell grows and functions, organelles duplicate

DNA replicates, chromosomes duplicate

Cell grows and prepares for mitosis

Cytoplasm divides

Mitosis

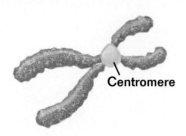

Figure 4-4 A duplicated chromosome is two identical DNA molecules that are held together at a region called the centromere.

Centromere

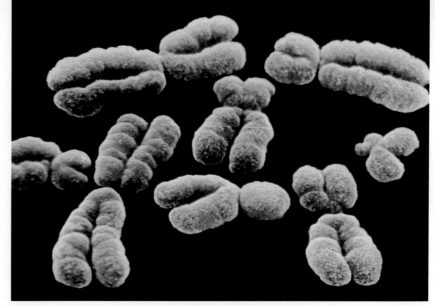

Magnification: 18 000×

Mitosis

Cells divide in two steps. First, the nucleus of the cell divides, and then the cytoplasm divides. **Mitosis** (mi TOH sus) is the process in which the nucleus divides to form two identical nuclei. Each new nucleus is also identical to the original nucleus. Mitosis is described as a series of phases or steps. The steps are named prophase, metaphase, anaphase, and telophase.

VISUALIZING
Mitosis

Figure 4-5 The steps of mitosis for an animal cell are shown here. Each micrograph shown in this figure is magnified 600 times.

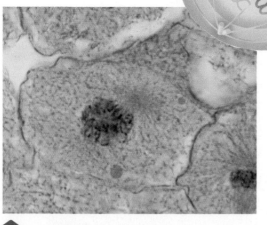

A **Prophase** During prophase, duplicated chromosomes become fully visible. The nucleolus and the nuclear membrane disintegrate. Two small structures called centrioles move to opposite ends of the cell. Between the centrioles, threadlike spindle fibers begin to stretch across the cell.

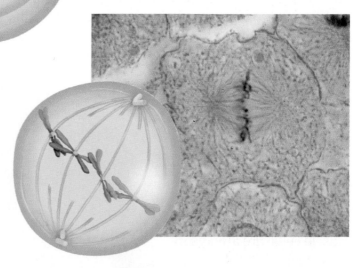

B **Metaphase** In metaphase, the duplicated chromosomes line up across the center of the cell. Each centromere becomes attached to two spindle fibers.

Animal Cell Mitosis

When a cell divides, the chromosomes in the nucleus play an important part. **Chromosomes** are structures in the nucleus that contain hereditary material. During *interphase,* you can't see chromosomes, but they are actively duplicating themselves. When the cell is ready to divide, each duplicated chromosome becomes visible because it coils tightly into two thick strands, as in **Figure 4-4.** Follow the steps of mitosis in the illustrations in **Figure 4-5** on these pages.

For most cells, after the nucleus has divided, the cytoplasm also separates, and two whole, new cells are formed. In animal cells, the cytoplasm pinches in to form the new cells. The new cells then begin the period of growth, or interphase, again. They will take in water and other nutrients that they need to carry out cell processes.

Plant Cell Mitosis

Plant cell mitosis is similar to animal cell mitosis, but there are differences. Plant cells form spindle fibers during mitosis but do not have centrioles.

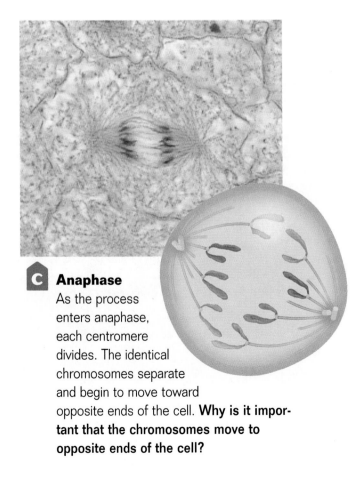

C **Anaphase**
As the process enters anaphase, each centromere divides. The identical chromosomes separate and begin to move toward opposite ends of the cell. **Why is it important that the chromosomes move to opposite ends of the cell?**

D **Telophase** In the final step, telophase, spindle fibers start to disappear. The chromosomes uncoil and are harder to see. A nuclear membrane forms around each mass of chromosomes, and a new nucleolus forms in each new nucleus.

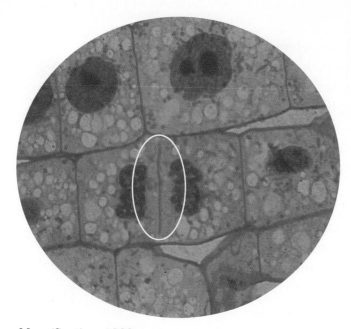

Magnification: 1230×

Figure 4-6 A cell plate (circled) forms during plant cell mitosis.

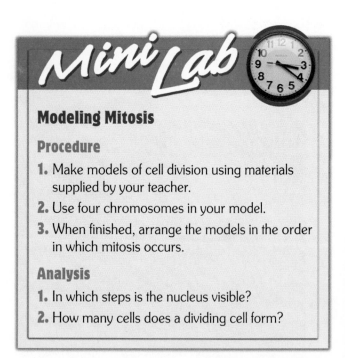

Mini Lab

Modeling Mitosis

Procedure

1. Make models of cell division using materials supplied by your teacher.
2. Use four chromosomes in your model.
3. When finished, arrange the models in the order in which mitosis occurs.

Analysis

1. In which steps is the nucleus visible?
2. How many cells does a dividing cell form?

Another difference is the rigid cell wall and how the cell membrane forms. In plants, a structure called a cell plate, shown in **Figure 4-6,** forms between the two new nuclei. New cell walls form along the cell plate. Then, new cell membranes develop inside the cell walls.

Results of Mitosis

There are two important things to remember about mitosis. First, it is the division of a nucleus. Second, mitosis produces two new nuclei that are identical to each other and the original nucleus. Each cell in your body, except sex cells, has a nucleus with 46 chromosomes, because you began as one cell with 46 chromosomes in its nucleus. **Figure 4-7** shows the 46 human chromosomes. Skin cells produced to replace or repair your skin have the same 46 chromosomes as the single cell you came from. Each cell in a fruit fly has eight chromosomes, so each new cell produced by mitosis has a copy of those eight chromosomes.

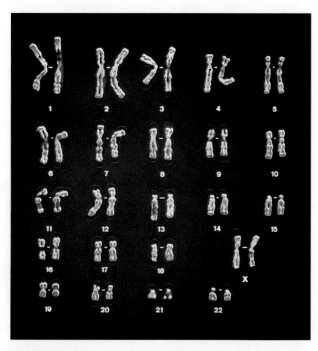

Figure 4-7 In the nucleus of most cells, there are pairs of chromosomes. Humans have 23 pairs of chromosomes including a pair of chromosomes that determine sex such as pair X above.

Asexual Reproduction

Reproduction is the process by which an organism produces others of the same kind. Among living organisms, there are two types of reproduction—asexual and sexual. Sexual reproduction is explained later in this chapter. In **asexual reproduction**, a new organism (sometimes more than one) is produced that has hereditary material identical to the hereditary material of the parent organism. Asexual reproduction of organisms with eukaryotic cells is done by mitosis. Bacteria reproduce asexually by fission. Fission is when a prokaryotic organism divides into two identical organisms.

If you've ever grown a sweet potato in a jar of water, you've seen asexual reproduction take place. All the stems, leaves, and roots that grow from the sweet potato have been produced by mitosis and have the same hereditary material. New strawberry plants can be asexually reproduced from horizontal stems called runners. In **Figure 4-8,** new cattail plants are reproduced asexually.

*inter*NET
CONNECTION

Visit the Glencoe Science Web Site at **www.glencoe. com/sec/science/ca** for more information about other ways plants reproduce asexually.

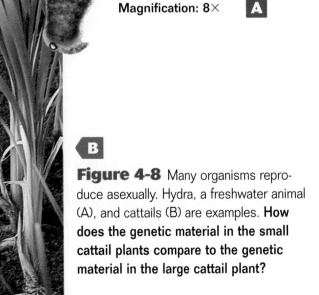

Magnification: 8× **A**

B

Figure 4-8 Many organisms reproduce asexually. Hydra, a freshwater animal (A), and cattails (B) are examples. **How does the genetic material in the small cattail plants compare to the genetic material in the large cattail plant?**

Budding and Regeneration

Budding is a type of asexual reproduction in which a new organism grows from the body of the parent organism. **Figure 4-8** illustrates an organism called a hydra reproducing by budding. When the bud on the adult becomes large enough, it breaks away to live on its own.

Another type of asexual reproduction possible for some organisms like sponges, planaria, and sea stars is regeneration. Regeneration is when a whole organism grows from a piece of an organism or regrows damaged or lost body parts. For some organisms, injury brings about the regeneration of two organisms, as in **Figure 4-9.** If a sponge is cut into small pieces, a new sponge may develop from each piece. How do you think sponge farmers increase their crop? ☑

Fission, budding, and regeneration are types of asexual reproduction. Through cell division, organisms grow, replace worn-out or damaged cells, or produce whole new organisms.

Reading Check ☑
What is regeneration?

Figure 4-9 Some animals produce new body parts by regeneration. A planarian is a worm that can regenerate a head or a tail when cut in two.

Magnification: 8✕

Section Assessment

1. What is mitosis and how does it differ in plants and animals?

2. Give two examples of asexual reproduction.

3. What happens to chromosomes before mitosis begins?

4. **Think Critically:** Why is it important for the nuclear membrane to disintegrate in mitosis?

5. **Skill Builder**
   Desigining an Experiment to Test a Hypothesis Do you know if a leaf can be used to grow a new plant? A piece of stem? A root section? Do the **Chapter 4 Skill Activity** on page 709 to design and experiment to test your hypothesis.

Using Math

Find out how much you weighed at birth. Subtract that weight from what you weigh now. Divide that number by your age to find the average weight you gained each year. Predict what you will weigh five years from now.

Activity
4 • 1

Mitosis in Plant and Animal Cells

Reproduction of cells in plants and animals is accomplished by mitosis. In this activity, you will study prepared slides of onion root-tip cells and whitefish embryo cells. These slides are used because they show cells in the various stages of mitosis.

Materials

- Prepared slide of an onion root tip
- Prepared slide of a white-fish embryo
- Microscope

What You'll Investigate

How mitosis in a plant cell is different from mitosis in an animal cell.

Goals

- **Compare** the sizes of the whitefish embryo cells and the onion root-tip cells.
- **Observe** the chromosomes of the whitefish embryo and onion root tip.

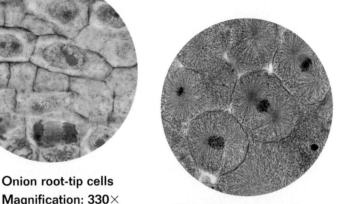

Onion root-tip cells
Magnification: 330×

Whitefish embryo cells
Magnification: 320×

Procedure

1. **Obtain** prepared slides of onion root-tip cells and whitefish embryo cells.

2. Set your microscope on low power and **examine** the onion root tip. Move the slide until you can see the area just behind the root tip. Turn the nosepiece to high power.

3. Use **Figure 4-5** to help you find a cell in prophase. **Draw** and **label** the parts of the cell you observe.

4. Repeat step 3 for metaphase, anaphase, and telophase.

5. Turn the microscope back to low power. Remove the onion root tip slide.

6. Place the whitefish embryo slide on the microscope stage under low power. Focus and find a region of dividing cells. Switch to high power.

7. Repeat steps 3 and 4 using the whitefish embryo slide.

8. Return the nosepiece to low power. Remove the whitefish embryo slide from the microscope stage.

Conclude and Apply

1. **Compare** the cells in the region behind the onion root tip to those in the root tip.

2. **Describe** the shapes of the cells in the onion root tip and the whitefish embryo.

3. **Infer** why embryo cells and root-tip cells are used to study mitosis.

4. Copy the following statements in your Science Journal then fill in each blank with the name of the correct phase of mitosis.

_____ Nuclear membrane re-forms.

_____ Chromosomes move to the center of the cell.

_____ Spindle fibers appear.

_____ Chromosomes move in opposite directions.

4•2 Sexual Reproduction and Meiosis

What You'll Learn

▶ The stages of meiosis and its end products
▶ The names of the cells involved in fertilization and how fertilization occurs in sexual reproduction

Vocabulary

sexual reproduction
fertilization
sperm
egg
meiosis
zygote

Why It's Important

▶ Because of meiosis, no one is exactly like you.

Sexual Reproduction

Sexual reproduction is another way that a new organism can be created. It happens when two sex cells, an egg and a sperm, come together. The joining of an egg and a sperm is called **fertilization.** Generally, the egg and the sperm come from two different organisms. Following fertilization, mitosis begins. A new organism develops that has its own unique identity.

Formation of Sex Cells

Your body forms two types of cells—body cells and sex cells. By far, your body has more body cells than sex cells. Your brain, skin, bones, and other tissues and organs are formed from body cells. Sex cells are formed from cells in reproductive organs. The **sperm** is formed in the reproductive organs of the male. A sperm has a whiplike tail and a head that is almost all nucleus. The **egg** is formed in the reproductive organs of the female and contains many food molecules along with the other cell parts. As seen in **Figure 4-10,** an egg is much larger than a sperm.

A human body cell has 46 chromosomes. Each chromosome has a similar mate, so human body cells have 23 pairs of chromosomes. Sex cells have half the number of chromosomes of a body cell. Human sex cells have only 23 chromosomes, one from each of the 23 pairs. Sex cells are produced by a process called **meiosis** (mi OH sus). Meiosis happens in the reproductive organs of plants and animals.

Figure 4-10 The large cell is a human egg cell, or ovum. The smaller cells on the egg are human sperm. **What is the chromosome number of each sex cell?**

Magnification: 400✕

The Importance of Sex Cells

When a cell has pairs of chromosomes, it is said to be *diploid* (DIHP loyd). Human body cells are diploid cells. Because sex cells do not have pairs of chromosomes, they are said to be *haploid* (HAP loyd). Haploid means "single form." The diploid number for humans is 46, and the haploid number is 23. For corn, the diploid number is 20, and the haploid number is 10. For most organisms, the haploid number is found only in sex cells.

Fertilization

Why are sex cells so important? Sexual reproduction starts with the formation of sex cells and ends with fertilization. The new cell that forms is called a **zygote.** If an egg with 23 chromosomes joins a sperm that has 23 chromosomes, a zygote forms that has 46 chromosomes, the diploid chromosome number for that organism. The zygote undergoes mitosis, and an organism develops. This process is illustrated in **Figure 4-11.**

CHEMISTRY
INTEGRATION

Fertilization
The human egg releases a chemical into the surrounding fluid that attracts sperm. Usually, only one sperm fertilizes the egg. After the sperm nucleus enters the egg, the cell membrane of the egg changes, preventing other sperm from entering. What adaptation in this process guarantees that the zygote will be diploid?

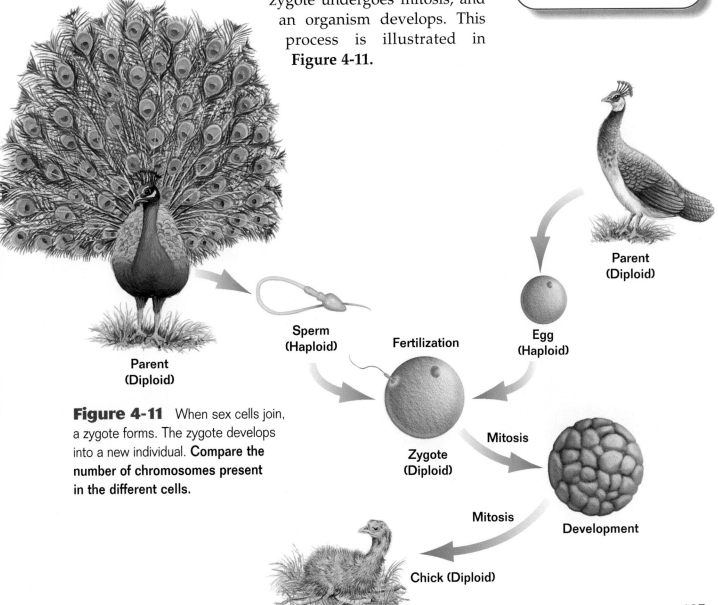

Figure 4-11 When sex cells join, a zygote forms. The zygote develops into a new individual. **Compare the number of chromosomes present in the different cells.**

Parent (Diploid)

Sperm (Haploid)

Fertilization

Egg (Haploid)

Parent (Diploid)

Zygote (Diploid)

Mitosis

Development

Mitosis

Chick (Diploid)

Meiosis

What would happen in sexual reproduction if the two cells that were formed through mitosis combined? The offspring would have twice as many chromosomes as its parent. Meiosis insures that this does not happen. During meiosis, two divisions of the nucleus occur, *meiosis I* and *meiosis II*. The different steps of each division have names like those in mitosis. Follow the steps of meiosis I and meiosis II in **Figure 4-12.**

Meiosis I

Before meiosis begins, each chromosome is duplicated, just as in mitosis. When the cell is ready for meiosis, each duplicated chromosome is visible because it coils tightly into two thick strands joined by a centromere. In *prophase I*, the spindle fibers form, and the nuclear membrane and the nucleolus disintegrate. Unlike mitosis, the duplicated chromosomes stay together as pairs. ☑

In *metaphase I*, the pairs of duplicated chromosomes line up in the center of the cell. Each centromere becomes attached to one spindle fiber. In *anaphase I,* the pair of duplicated

Problem Solving

Predicting Chromosome Numbers

A horse and a donkey can mate to produce a mule. The mule is almost always sterile. Horses have a diploid chromosome number of 66. Donkeys have a diploid number of 60.

Solve the Problem

1. How many chromosomes would the mule receive from each parent?

2. What is the diploid number of the mule?

3. What would happen when meiosis occurs in the mule's reproductive organs?

Think Critically: Why might a mule be sterile?

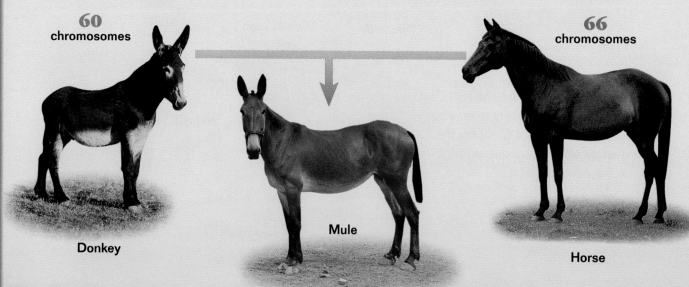

60 chromosomes

Donkey

Mule

66 chromosomes

Horse

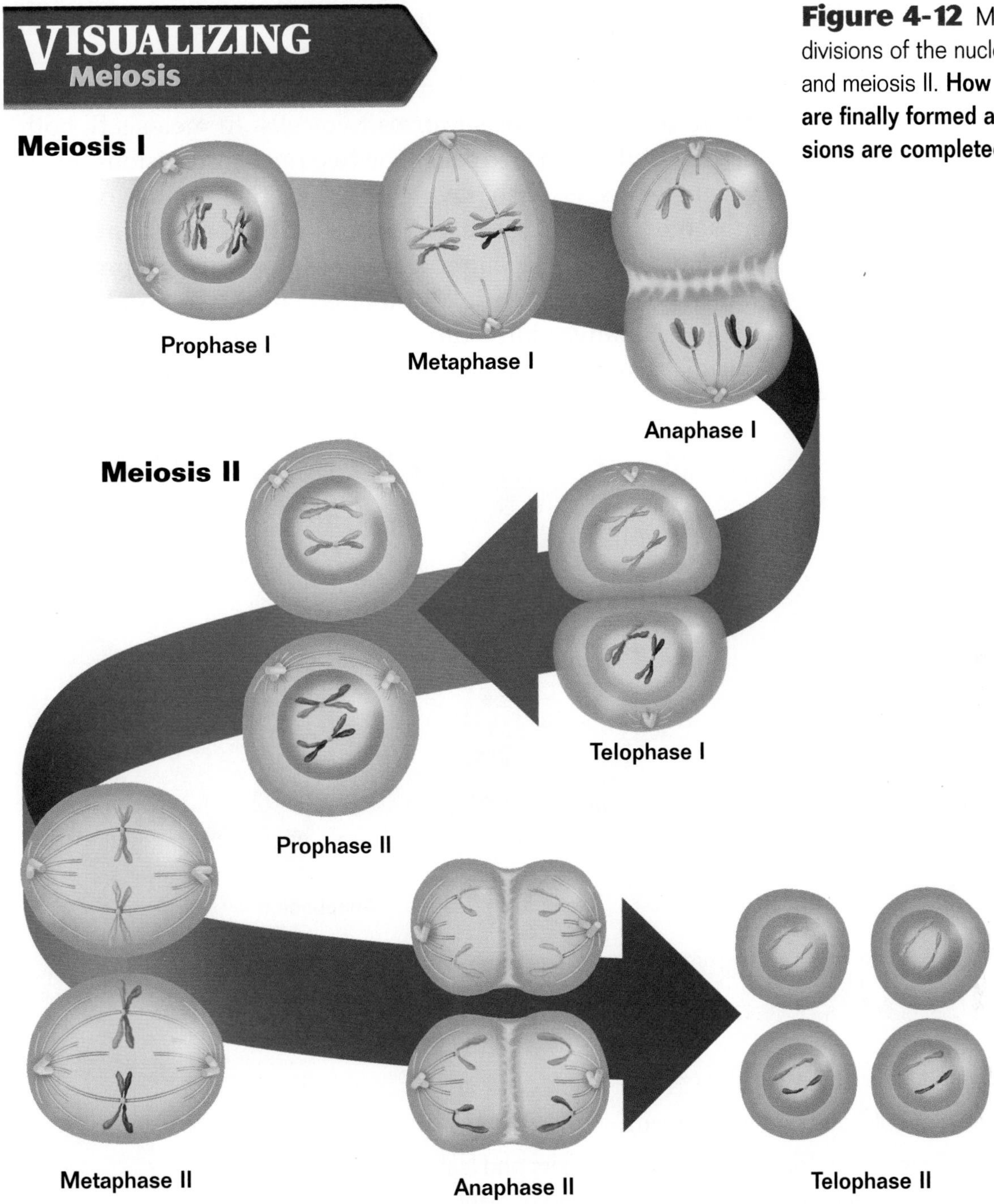

VISUALIZING Meiosis

Figure 4-12 Meiosis is two divisions of the nucleus, meiosis I and meiosis II. **How many sex cells are finally formed after both divisions are completed?**

Meiosis I

Prophase I

Metaphase I

Anaphase I

Meiosis II

Telophase I

Prophase II

Metaphase II

Anaphase II

Telophase II

chromosomes separate. The duplicated chromosomes of each pair are pulled to opposite ends of the cell. Then, in *telophase I*, the cytoplasm divides, and two cells form.

Meiosis II

Meiosis II, the second division of the nucleus, then begins. In *prophase II*, the duplicated chromosomes and spindle fibers reappear in each new cell. In *metaphase II*, the duplicated chromosomes move to the center of the cell. There, each centromere attaches to two spindle fibers. During *anaphase II*, the centromere divides, and the identical molecules of each duplicated chromosome separate and move to opposite ends of

Figure 4-13 Sometimes, a mistake is made. This diploid cell has four chromosomes. During Anaphase I, one pair of duplicated chromosomes did not separate. **How many chromosomes should each sex cell have?**

the cell. As *telophase II* begins, the spindle fibers disappear, and a nuclear membrane forms around the chromosomes at each end of the cell. When meiosis II is finished, the cytoplasm divides. Meiosis I forms two cells. In meiosis II, both of these cells form two cells. The two nuclear divisions result in four sex cells, each having only half the number of chromosomes in their nuclei that were in the original nucleus. From a cell with 46 paired chromosomes, meiosis produces four sex cells each with 23 unpaired chromosomes. Meiosis happens many, many times in reproductive organs. Rare mistakes, such as the one in **Figure 4-13,** do occur.

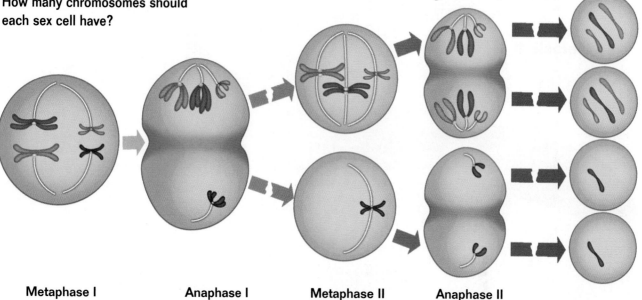

Metaphase I   Anaphase I   Metaphase II   Anaphase II

Section Assessment

1. Compare sexual and asexual reproduction.

2. What is a zygote, and how is it formed?

3. **Think Critically:** Plants grown from runners and leaf cuttings have exactly the same traits as the parent plant. Plants grown from seeds may vary from the parents in many ways. Suggest an explanation for this.

4. **Skill Builder**
   Making and Using Tables Make a table to compare mitosis and meiosis in humans. Vertical headings should include: *What type of cell* (Body or Sex), *Beginning cell* (Haploid or Diploid), *Number of cells produced, End-product cell* (Haploid or Diploid), and *Number of chromosomes in cells produced.* If you need help, refer to Making and Using Tables in the **Skill Handbook** on page 680.

Write a poem, song, or another memory device to help you remember the steps and outcome of meiosis.

Animal Cloning

What is an animal clone?

To scientists, a clone is an animal that is genetically identical to one of its parents. For many years, genetically identical organisms have been produced in the laboratory. Fertilized eggs are grown to two-, four-, or eight-cell embryos and then separated. These separated embryo cells behave like the original fertilized egg cell and grow into genetically identical siblings. However, these are not clones because their DNA is a combination of both parents' DNA.

Hello, Dolly!

In February 1997, researchers announced that they had cloned a sheep named Dolly. In the laboratory, they removed the nucleus of an egg cell taken from a female sheep. They replaced that nucleus with the nucleus from a cell of a second breed of sheep. The egg divided and formed an embryo. This embryo was implanted into the uterus of a female sheep of a third breed. Three breeds of sheep were used to show that Dolly received her genes from the transplanted nucleus of the second sheep—not the egg cell donor (the first sheep) or birth mother (the third sheep).

Beyond Dolly

Since Dolly was born, other scientists also have successfully cloned organisms. The next decades may bring enormous changes because of cloning. It may become possible to correct disorders and eliminate diseases by making genetic changes in embryos. Of particular interest are transgenic clones, organisms carrying genes from another species. Transgenic animals may be used for researching human diseases and their treatment, which would not be possible with human subjects. It may become common to clone transgenic animals, like the calves at left, that produce human antibiotics or other valuable protein products.

interNET CONNECTION

After reading this article, you may be wondering about the possibility of human cloning. Visit the Glencoe Science Web Site at **www.glencoe.com/sec/science/ca** to find the latest information about human cloning. Summarize this information in your Science Journal.

4•3 DNA

What is DNA?

Have you ever sent a message to someone using a code? To read your message, that person had to understand the meaning of the symbols you used in your code. The chromosomes in the nucleus of a cell contain a code. This code is in the form of a chemical called deoxyribonucleic (dee AHK sih ri boh noo klay ihk) acid, or DNA. **DNA** is an organism's information code. When a cell divides, the DNA code in the nucleus is copied and passed to the new cells. In this way, new cells receive the same coded information that was in the original cell. DNA controls all the activities of cells with this coded information. Every cell that has ever been formed in your body or in any other organism contains DNA.

History of DNA

Since the mid-1800s, scientists have known that the nuclei of cells contain chemicals called nucleic acids. What does DNA look like? Scientist Rosalind Franklin discovered that the DNA molecule was two strands of molecules in a spiral form.

What You'll Learn

- The parts of a DNA molecule and its structure
- How DNA copies itself
- How to describe the structure and function of each kind of RNA

Vocabulary

DNA
gene

RNA
mutation

Why It's Important

- DNA is in charge of everything your body is and does.

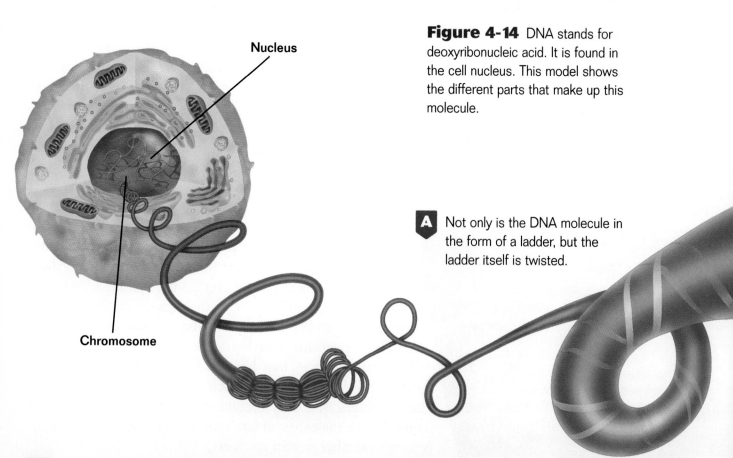

Nucleus

Chromosome

Figure 4-14 DNA stands for deoxyribonucleic acid. It is found in the cell nucleus. This model shows the different parts that make up this molecule.

A Not only is the DNA molecule in the form of a ladder, but the ladder itself is twisted.

By using an X-ray technique, Dr. Franklin showed that the spiral was so large that it was probably made up of two spirals. As it turned out, the structure of DNA is similar to a twisted ladder. In 1953, using the work of Franklin and others, scientists James Watson and Francis Crick made an accurate model of a DNA molecule.

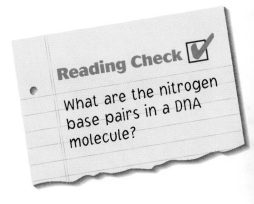

A DNA Model

According to the Watson and Crick DNA model, each side of the ladder is made up of sugar-phosphate molecules. Each molecule consists of the sugar called deoxyribose and a phosphate group. The rungs of the ladder are made up of other molecules called nitrogen bases. There are four kinds of nitrogen bases in DNA. These are adenine, guanine, cytosine, and thymine. In **Figure 4-14C,** the bases are represented by the letters *A, G, C,* and *T.* The amount of cytosine in cells always equals the amount of guanine, and the amount of adenine always equals the amount of thymine. This led to the hypothesis that these bases occur as pairs in the DNA molecule. The Watson and Crick model shows that adenine always pairs with thymine, and guanine always pairs with cytosine. Like interlocking pieces of a puzzle, each base bonds only with its correct partner. ☑

Reading Check ☑

What are the nitrogen base pairs in a DNA molecule?

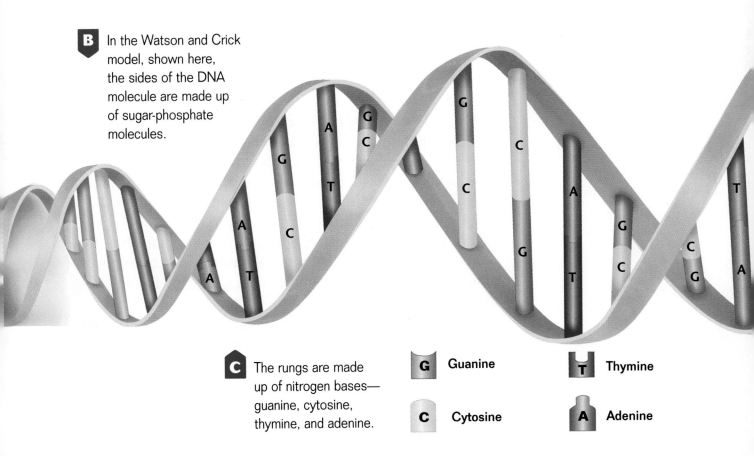

B In the Watson and Crick model, shown here, the sides of the DNA molecule are made up of sugar-phosphate molecules.

C The rungs are made up of nitrogen bases—guanine, cytosine, thymine, and adenine.

G Guanine

C Cytosine

T Thymine

A Adenine

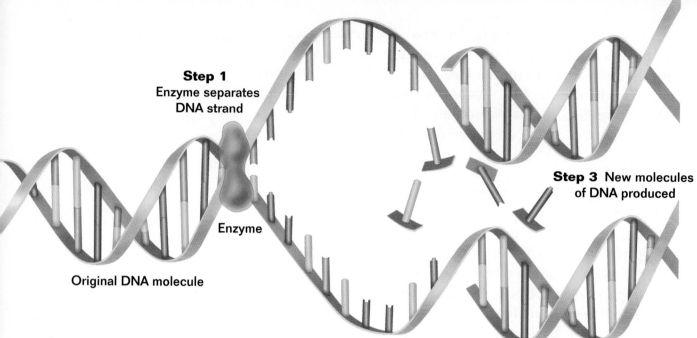

Step 1
Enzyme separates
DNA strand

Enzyme

Original DNA molecule

Step 3 New molecules
of DNA produced

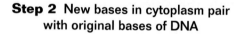

Step 2 New bases in cytoplasm pair
with original bases of DNA

Figure 4-15 DNA uses itself as a pattern when it is copied.

Copies of DNA

When chromosomes are duplicated before mitosis, the amount of DNA in the nucleus is doubled. How does DNA copy itself? The Watson and Crick model shows how this takes place. The two strands of the DNA molecule unwind and separate. Each strand then becomes a pattern on which a new molecule is formed. **Figure 4-15** follows a DNA molecule as it produces two new DNA molecules identical to the original DNA molecule.

Genes

Why is DNA important? All of your characteristics are in the DNA that you have in your cells. It controls the color of your eyes, the color of your hair, and whether or not you can digest milk. These characteristics are called traits. How traits appear depends on the kinds of proteins your cells make. DNA stores the blueprints for making proteins.

Proteins are made of units called amino acids that are linked together in a certain order. A protein may be made of hundreds or thousands of amino acids. Changing the order of the amino acids changes the protein that is made.

How does a cell know which proteins to make? The section of DNA on a chromosome that directs the making of a specific protein is called a **gene.** Genes control proteins that either build cells and tissues or work as enzymes. The gene gives the directions for the order in which amino acids will be arranged for a particular protein. Think about what might happen if an important protein couldn't be made in your cells.

RNA

Proteins are made on ribosomes in cytoplasm. How does the code in the nucleus reach the ribosomes in the cytoplasm? The codes for making proteins are carried from the nucleus to the ribosomes by another type of nucleic acid called ribonucleic acid, or **RNA.** RNA is different from DNA. It is made up of only one strand, the nitrogen base uracil (U). It replaces thymine and contains the sugar ribose. RNA is made in the nucleus on a DNA pattern.

The three main kinds of RNA made from DNA in the nucleus of a cell are messenger RNA (mRNA), ribosomal RNA (rRNA), and transfer RNA (tRNA). The production of a protein begins when mRNA moves through the nuclear membrane into the cytoplasm. There, ribosomes, made of rRNA, attach to it. Transfer RNA molecules, in the cytoplasm, bring amino acids to these ribosomes. Inside the ribosomes, three nitrogen bases on the tRNA temporarily match with three nitrogen bases on the mRNA. The same thing happens for another tRNA molecule and mRNA, as shown in **Figure 4-16.** The amino acids attached to the two tRNA molecules bond. This is the beginning of a protein.

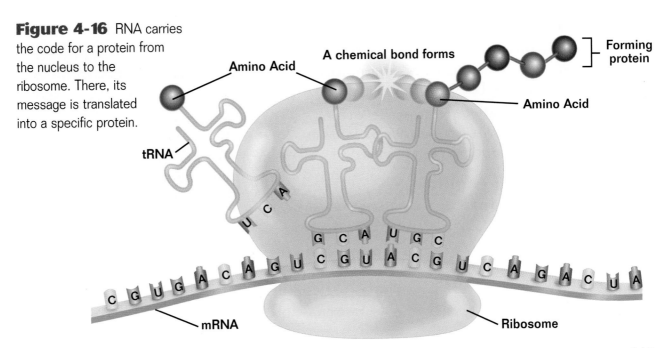

Figure 4-16 RNA carries the code for a protein from the nucleus to the ribosome. There, its message is translated into a specific protein.

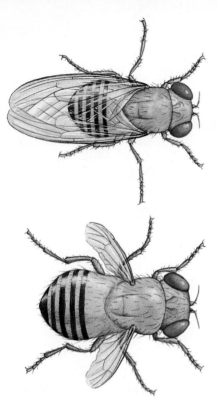

The code carried on mRNA directs the order of amino acid bonding. Once a tRNA molecule has lost its amino acid, it can move about the cytoplasm and pick up another one just like it. The ribosome moves along the mRNA. New tRNA molecules with amino acids match up and add amino acids to the protein molecule.

Mutations

Genes control the traits you inherit. Without correctly coded proteins, an organism can't grow, repair, or maintain itself. A change in a gene or chromosome, changes the traits of an organism, as illustrated in **Figure 4-17.** Sometimes an error is made during replication. Occasionally, a cell receives an entire extra chromosome. Outside factors such as X rays and chemicals have been known to cause changes in chromosomes. Any permanent change in a gene or chromosome of a cell is called a **mutation.** If the mutation occurs in a body cell, it may or may not be life threatening to the organism. If, however, a mutation occurs in a sex cell, then all the cells that are formed from that sex cell will have that mutation. Mutations add variety to a species when the organism reproduces. Many mutations are harmful to organisms, often causing their death. Some mutations do not appear to have any effect on the organism, and some may be beneficial.

Figure 4-17 Because of a defect on chromosome 2, the mutant fruit fly has short wings and cannot fly. **Could this defect be transferred to the mutant's offspring? Explain.**

Section Assessment

1. How does DNA make a copy of itself?
2. How are the codes for proteins carried from the nucleus to the ribosomes?
3. A single strand of DNA has the bases AGTAAC. Using letters, show what bases would match up to form a matching DNA strand from this pattern.
4. **Think Critically:** You begin as one cell. Compare the DNA in one of your brain cells to the DNA in one of your heart cells.
5. **Skill Builder**
   Concept Mapping Using a network tree concept map, show how DNA and RNA are alike and how they are different. If you need help, refer to Concept Mapping in the **Skill Handbook** on page 678.

Using Computers

Word Processing Make an outline of the events that led up to the discovery of DNA. Use library resources to find this information. If you need help, refer to page 696.

Modeling of DNA

Materials

- 6 colors of construction paper ($8\frac{1}{2} \times 11$) (2 of each color)
- Scissors
- 2 cardboard patterns, a circle and pentagon
- Tape

Bits of metal, pieces of wire, and cardboard cutouts are not usually considered scientific equipment. But, that's what Nobel prize winners James Watson and Francis Crick used to construct their model of DNA. In this lab, you will use colored construction paper to make a model of DNA.

What You'll Investigate

You will examine the structure of a DNA molecule.

Goals

- **Design and construct** a model of DNA that is four base pairs long.

Safety Precautions

Use scissors carefully.

Procedure

1. **Plan** your DNA molecule. Write down the four base pairs and enter them in your Science Journal.

2. **Assign** one color of paper to represent each of the following: phosphate groups, sugar molecules, guanines, adenines, thymines, and cytosines.

3. Using the circle pattern for each phosphate group and the pentagon pattern for each sugar molecule, **trace** and **cut out** enough figures to make the sugar-phosphate sides of your DNA molecule.

4. **Tape** a circle to each pentagon, as seen in illustration A.

5. Use the pentagon pattern to make the nitrogen bases. For each adenine and each guanine, **trace** and **cut out** two pentagons of the same color and tape them together, as seen in illustration B. Trace and cut out just one pentagon for each thymine and each cytosine.

6. **Tape** a nitrogen base to each sugar-phosphate unit.

7. **Construct** the DNA molecule that you planned in step 1 by taping the correct nitrogen bases together.

Conclude and Apply

1. **Compare** your models with those of other groups. Were the molecules your group created the same as those of other groups?

2. Compile a list of all the DNA sequences made and enter them in your Science Journal.

3. Based on your observations of the DNA molecule model, **infer** why a DNA molecule seldom copies itself incorrectly.

4. **Explain** why models are useful to scientists.

A.

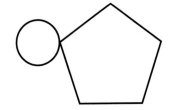

B.

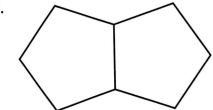

For a **preview** of this chapter, study this Reviewing Main Ideas before you read the chapter. After you have studied this chapter, you can use the Reviewing Main Ideas to **review** the chapter.

 The Glencoe MindJogger, Audiocassettes, and CD-ROM provide additional opportunities for review.

Section

4-1 CELL GROWTH AND DIVISION

The life cycle of a cell has two parts: growth and development, and cell division. Cell division includes mitosis and the division of the cytoplasm. In **mitosis,** the nucleus divides to form two identical nuclei. Mitosis happens in four continuous steps, or phases: prophase, metaphase, anaphase, and telophase. Cell division in animal cells and plant cells is similar, but plant cells do not have centrioles and animal cells do not form cell walls.

Asexual reproduction produces organisms with DNA identical to the parent's DNA. Fission, budding, and regeneration are types of asexual reproduction. *What are the two parts of cell division?*

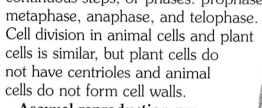

Section

4-2 SEXUAL REPRODUCTION AND MEIOSIS

Sexual reproduction results when a male sex cell, the **sperm,** enters the female sex cell, the **egg.** This event is called **fertilization,** and the cell that forms is the zygote. Before fertilization, **meiosis** happens in the reproductive organs, producing four haploid sex cells from one diploid cell. This insures that offspring produced by fertilization have the same number of chromosomes as their parents. *How do body cells differ from sex cells?*

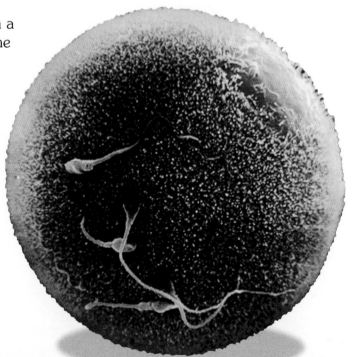

Reading Check ✔

• Write out in words what DNA and RNA stand for. Think about why these letters instead of others in the words were chosen for the abbreviations.

Section 4-3 DNA

DNA, the genetic material of all organisms, is a large molecule made up of two twisted strands of sugar-phosphate molecules and nitrogen bases. The sugar in DNA is deoxyribose, and the bases are adenine, thymine, cytosine, and guanine. They are always found as the pairs adenine-thymine and cytosine-guanine. DNA directs all of the activities of a cell. The section of DNA on a chromosome that directs the making of a specific protein is a **gene.** DNA can copy itself and is the pattern from which RNA is made. **RNA** is single stranded and contains the sugar ribose instead of deoxyribose and the nitrogen base uracil in place of thymine. Messenger RNA carries the codes for making proteins from the nucleus to the ribosomes. Transfer RNA and ribosomal RNA are also made from patterns on DNA. Sometimes, changes in DNA occur. Permanent changes in DNA are called **mutations.** *What are the similarities and differences between DNA and RNA?*

Career CONNECTION

Dr. Khristine Lindo, Surgeon
Khristine Lindo became interested in science in seventh grade when she read a book *The Making of a Woman Surgeon* by Elizabeth Morgan. The book inspired her to become a surgeon. In high school Dr. Lindo took every science class she could—biology, chemistry, and physics. She was especially interested in biochemistry, the chemistry of living cells. Now as a surgeon, Dr. Lindo uses science to save lives. *Why is an understanding of the nature of science important to being a surgeon?*

Chapter 4 Assessment

Using Vocabulary

a. asexual reproduction
b. chromosome
c. DNA
d. egg
e. fertilization
f. gene
g. meiosis
h. mitosis
i. mutation
j. RNA
k. sexual reproduction
l. sperm
m. zygote

In statements 1–5, replace each underlined word with the correct Vocabulary word.

1. Muscle and skin cells are sex cells.
2. Digestion produces two identical cells, and respiration produces four sex cells.
3. Two examples of nucleic acids are sugar and starch.
4. A cell is found on a tissue and is the code for a protein.
5. A diploid sperm is formed when mutation happens.

Checking Concepts

Choose the word or phrase that best answers the question.

6. Which of the following is a double spiral molecule with pairs of nitrogen bases?
   A) RNA
   B) An amino acid
   C) A protein
   D) DNA

7. What does RNA contain that DNA does **NOT**?
   A) thymine
   B) thyroid
   C) adenine
   D) uracil

8. If a diploid tomato cell has 24 chromosomes, how many chromosomes will the tomato's sex cells have?
   A) 6
   B) 12
   C) 24
   D) 48

9. During a cell's life cycle, when do chromosomes duplicate?
   A) anaphase
   B) metaphase
   C) interphase
   D) telophase

10. When during mitosis do duplicated chromosomes separate?
    A) anaphase
    B) prophase
    C) metaphase
    D) telophase

11. How many chromosomes are in the original cell compared to those in the new cells formed by mitosis?
    A) the same amount
    B) half as many
    C) twice as many
    D) four times as many

12. What are budding, fission, and regeneration forms of?
    A) mutations
    B) sexual reproduction
    C) cell cycles
    D) asexual reproduction

13. What is any permanent change in a gene or a chromosome?
    A) fission
    B) reproduction
    C) replication
    D) mutation

14. What does meiosis produce?
    A) cells with the diploid chromosome number
    B) cells with identical chromosomes
    C) sex cells
    D) a zygote

15. In what phase of the cell cycle is most of the life of any cell spent ?
    A) metaphase
    B) interphase
    C) anaphase
    D) telophase

Thinking Critically

16. If the sequence of bases on one strand of DNA is ATCCGTC, what is the sequence on its other strand?

17. A strand of RNA made from the DNA strand ATCCGTC would have what base sequence?

18. Will a mutation in a human skin cell be passed on to the person's offspring? Explain your answer.

19. What happens in mitosis that gives the new cells identical DNA?

20. How could a zygote end up with an extra chromosome?

Developing Skills

If you need help, refer to the **Skill Handbook.**

21. **Comparing and Contrasting:** Make a table about mitosis and meiosis. Include the number of divisions, cells produced, and chromosomes in parent cells and in sex cells.

22. **Hypothesizing:** Make a hypothesis about the effect of an incorrect mitotic division on the new cells produced.

23. **Concept Mapping:** Complete the events chain concept map of DNA synthesis.

24. **Making and Using Tables:** Copy and complete this table about DNA and RNA.

DNA and RNA		
Nucleic acid	DNA	RNA
Number of strands		
Type of sugar		
Letter names of bases		
Where found?		

25. **Sequencing:** Sequence the events that occur from interphase in the parent cell to the formation of the zygote. Tell whether the chromosome's number at each stage is haploid or diploid.

THE PRINCETON REVIEW

Test-Taking Tip

Don't Dwell On It Many test questions look more complicated than they really are. If you find yourself having to do a great deal of work to answer a question, look again and try to find a simpler way to find the answer.

Test Practice

Use these questions to test your Science Proficiency.

1. In sex cells, chromosomes duplicate, and the nucleus divides twice, producing four nuclei each with half the number of chromosomes of the original nucleus. What is this process called?
   A) differentiation   B) meiosis
   C) mitosis   D) respiration

2. What are all the activities of a cell directed by?
   A) proteins   B) lipids
   C) DNA   D) carbohydrates

3. How is RNA different from DNA?
   A) It is single stranded and has the base uracil.
   B) It is a double spiral of lipids.
   C) It is found only in the nucleus.
   D) It is copied from other RNA.

4. Which of the following sequences is correct for the formation of a protein?
   A) tRNA–ribosome–DNA–mRNA–protein
   B) mRNA–DNA–ribosome–tRNA–protein
   C) DNA–mRNA–ribosome–tRNA–protein
   D) ribosome–DNA–tRNA–mRNA–protein

Plant Reproduction

Chapter Preview

Skills Preview

Skill Builders

- Classify
- Hypothesize

Activities

- Compare and Contrast
- Design an Experiment to Test a Hypothesis

MiniLabs

- Observe
- Identify

Reading Check ✓

List ten questions that a young child might ask about plant reproduction. After you read the chapter, underline the questions that were answered in the chapter.

Explore Activity

I t's almost spring! The shelves in the garden center are over-flowing with seed packets. Many familiar plants, like some of the plants you see here, grow from seeds. Some seeds come from flowers and others from cones. Seeds are just one way plants reproduce. To find out more about seeds, try the activity below. Then, in the chapter that follows, learn about the different ways plants reproduce.

Observe the Inside of a Seed

1. Obtain a lima bean or other large seed.

2. If the seed is hard and dry, place it in water overnight.

3. Observe the seed and describe it in your Science Journal.

4. Remove the paperlike covering from the seed and carefully pull apart the seed halves.

5. Look for the parts of the immature plant on one side of the seed.

Science Journal

In your Science Journal, identify the different parts of the immature plant.

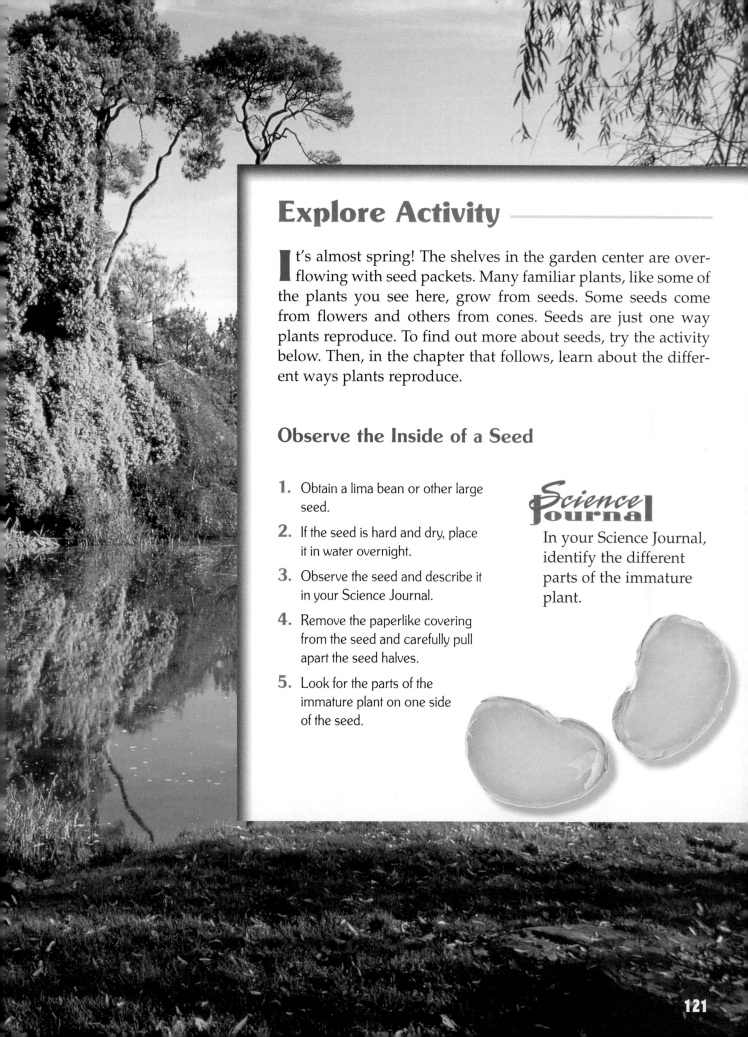

5•1 Introduction to Plant Reproduction

What You'll Learn

► The two types of plant reproduction

► The two stages in a plant's life cycle

► The life cycles of a moss and a fern

Vocabulary
gametophyte stage
sporophyte stage
alternation of generations
frond
rhizome
sori
prothallus

Why It's Important

► You'll be aware that you can grow new plants without using seeds.

Figure 5-1 Plants are living organisms that have all the characteristics of life.

Types of Reproduction

You and the garden plants shown in **Figure 5-1** are living organisms. But, you don't have leaves or roots, and a plant doesn't have a heart or a brain. Despite your differences, you are alike in many ways. You both can make similar copies of yourselves. This process is called reproduction. In this chapter, you'll learn how plants reproduce.

Sexual Reproduction

Plant sexual reproduction is similar to animal sexual reproduction. Both require fertilization, which is the combining of an egg and a sperm. Like animals, the plant's egg is produced in the female reproductive organs, and sperm are produced in male reproductive organs. The process of meiosis forms these sex cells. Meiosis is two divisions of a reproductive cell's nucleus. Meiosis results in four sex cells. Sex cells are haploid cells. That means that each sex cell has half the chromosomes of the original cell.

Male and female reproductive organs of plants may be on the same plant or on separate plants. For example, holly plants are referred to as male or female. A female holly, as shown in **Figure 5-2,** has flowers that have only female reproductive structures. Most plants have both sexes on one

Figure 5-2 Holly berries develop after the egg is fertilized.

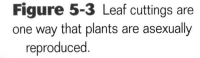

Visit the Glencoe Science Web Site at **www.glencoe.com/ sec/science/ca** for more information on plants that are male and female like holly.

plant and can reproduce by themselves. Plants, such as apples and pears, have flowers with both sexes, but it takes another plant for fertilization to happen.

Many plants depend on animals or environmental factors to help get the egg and sperm together. For most plants, a seed develops following fertilization. A spore develops in some plants, such as mosses and ferns.

Asexual Reproduction

Have you ever eaten seedless oranges and grapes? If these plants do not produce seeds, how do growers get new plants? Growers can produce new plants by asexual reproduction. Because some plant cells may undergo mitosis and eventually produce other cell types, a new plant may be produced from just part of a plant. For example, roots and leaves can grow from just a portion of the stem. The begonia shown in **Figure 5-3** is being asexually reproduced. A plant produced by asexual reproduction is genetically identical to the original plant. The plant part(s) used for asexual reproduction varies from species to species. People have used these methods of reproducing plants for centuries. You or someone you know may grow plants this way.

Figure 5-3 Leaf cuttings are one way that plants are asexually reproduced.

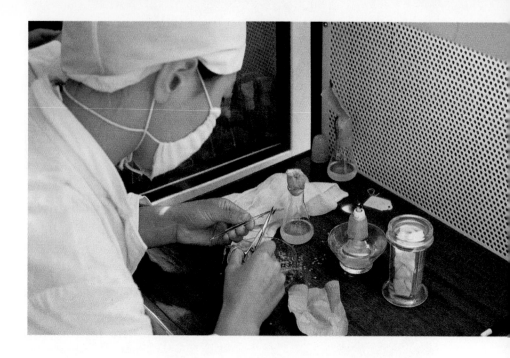

Figure 5-4 Many plants can be produced from just a few plant cells when grown using tissue culture techniques. Many orchids are reproduced by tissue culture.

Tissue culture is a form of asexual reproduction that uses a cluster of young cells to produce plants. This technology allows many identical plants to be produced from just a small portion of one plant. However, tissue culture requires special laboratory equipment and procedures, as in **Figure 5-4.**

Haploid and Diploid Stages

Every plant has a life cycle that contains two stages. The gametophyte (guh MEET uh fite) stage begins when cells in reproductive organs undergo meiosis. The cells formed are haploid (n). This means they contain half the number of chromosomes of a reproductive diploid cell. These haploid cells undergo mitosis to form plant structures. When all plant structures are made of haploid cells, it is called the **gametophyte stage.** Fertilization is the beginning of the sporophyte (SPOR uh fite) stage. Because cells in this stage are formed after fertilization, they have pairs of chromosomes, or are diploid. In the **sporophyte stage,** plant structures are made of cells with the diploid number ($2n$) of chromosomes. As you will learn in this chapter, these stages are different for different plant groups.

Seedless Plants

Have you ever walked in a cool, damp, shaded forest or woods and noticed that only leafy plants like ferns were growing near the ground? Sometimes, mosses cover the ground or grow on logs. Ferns and mosses are two types of seedless plants. They reproduce sexually by spores, not by seeds.

Using Math

A diploid apple has 34 chromosomes. How many chromosomes do cells in the gametophyte stage and cells in the sporophyte stage have?

The Moss Life Cycle

The life cycle of a moss is shown in **Figure 5-5.** You may know mosses as green, low-growing masses of plants. This is the gametophyte stage that produces the sex cells. Sometimes, a gametophyte moss plant has just male or female reproductive structures. Usually, both are on the same plant. For mosses, water is needed for fertilization. During a heavy dew or rain, water carries the sperm from the male reproductive structure to the female reproductive structure. Sperm swim to the eggs and fertilization occurs. A diploid cell, called a zygote, forms. This is the beginning of the sporophyte stage. The zygote undergoes mitosis and develops into an embryo. The embryo grows into the mature sporophyte. ✔

A moss sporophyte usually grows from the tip of the gametophyte. The sporophyte is not green and cannot carry on photosynthesis. It depends on the gametophyte for water and nutrients. The sporophyte consists of a stalk and a capsule. Inside the capsule, many cells undergo meiosis and form hundreds of haploid spores. When environmental conditions are just right, the capsule opens and releases the spores. If a spore lands on wet soil or rocks, it may grow into a green, threadlike structure. New moss gametophytes grow from this structure and the cycle begins again. When a plant's life cycle alternates between a sex-cell producing stage and a spore-producing stage, it is called **alternation of generations.** Liverworts have similar life cycles.

Reading Check

What event comes before the sporophyte stage of a moss's life cycle?

Figure 5-5 The life cycle of a moss alternates between gametophyte and sporophyte stages. **What is produced by the gametophyte stage?**

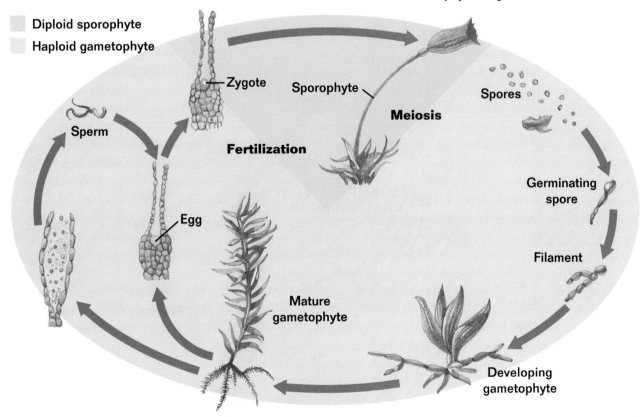

Diploid sporophyte
Haploid gametophyte

Zygote — Sporophyte — Spores

Sperm — Meiosis

Fertilization

Germinating spore

Egg

Filament

Mature gametophyte

Developing gametophyte

Mosses and liverworts may reproduce asexually. If a piece of a moss gametophyte plant breaks off, it may grow into a new plant. Liverworts reproduce asexually by forming small balls of cells on the surface of the gametophyte plant. These are carried away by water and may grow into new gametophyte plants.

The Fern Life Cycle

Like mosses, ferns have alternation of generations. The life cycle of a fern is illustrated in **Figure 5-6.** The fern plants that you see in nature or as houseplants are fern sporophyte plants. The leaves, called **fronds,** grow from an underground stem called a **rhizome.** Roots grow from the rhizome, anchor the plant, and absorb water and nutrients. Fern sporophytes make their own food.

Spores are produced in structures called **sori** (sing., *sorus*) on the underside of the fronds. Sori usually look like crusty rust-, brown-, or blackish-colored bumps. When a sorus opens, it exposes the spore cases. Inside each spore case, cells have undergone meiosis to form spores. Thousands of fern spores are ejected when spore cases open.

If fern spores land on damp soil or rocks, they can grow into small, green, heart-shaped gametophyte plants. The fern gametophyte is called a **prothallus** (proh THAL us). It can

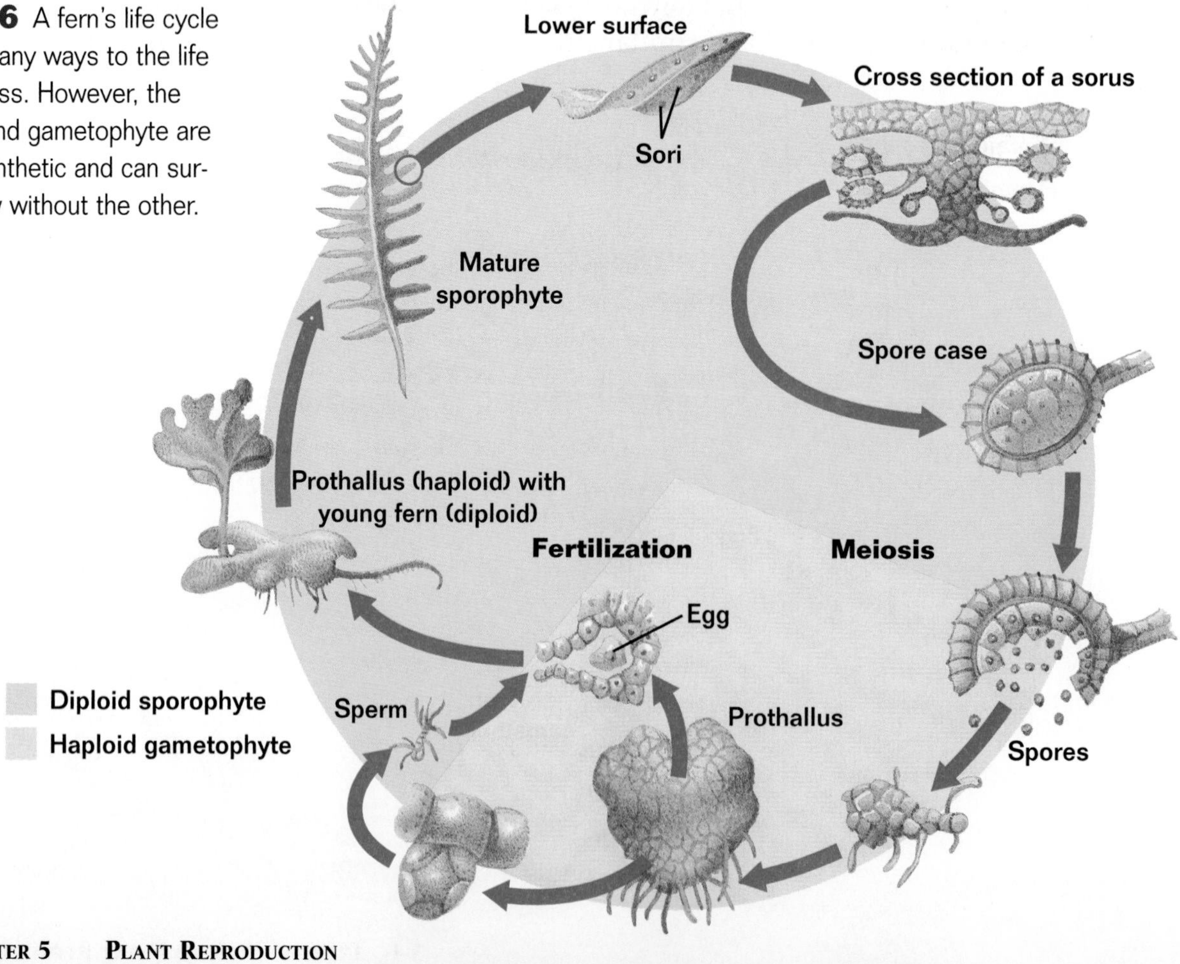

Figure 5-6 A fern's life cycle is similar in many ways to the life cycle of a moss. However, the sporophyte and gametophyte are both photosynthetic and can survive and grow without the other.

Lower surface

Sori

Cross section of a sorus

Mature sporophyte

Spore case

Prothallus (haploid) with young fern (diploid)

Fertilization

Meiosis

Egg

Prothallus

Sperm

Spores

Diploid sporophyte

Haploid gametophyte

make its own food and absorb water and nutrients from the soil. The prothallus has both male and female reproductive structures. Sex cells form, and water is needed to bring them together. The zygote forms by fertilization. It grows into the familiar fern plant.

Ferns may reproduce asexually, also. Fern rhizomes grow and form branches. New fronds develop from each branch as shown in **Figure 5-7.** The new rhizome branch and fronds can be separated from the main plant. It can grow on its own and form more fern plants.

Figure 5-7 New plants grow from the rhizome of a fern.

Section Assessment

1. Describe the life cycle of mosses.

2. Explain the stages in the life cycle of a fern.

3. **Think Critically:** You see a plant that you like and want to grow an identical one. What type of plant reproduction would you use? Why?

4. **Skill Builder**
   Sequencing The life cycle of a plant is a sequence of events. Do the **Chapter 5 Skill Activity** on page 710 to learn about the events in the life cycle of a fern and those in the life cycle of a pine.

Using Math

Spores of mosses are usually no more than 0.1 mm in diameter. Approximate the number of spores it would take to cover one side of a penny.

Materials

- Live mosses, liverworts, and ferns with gameto-phytes and sporophytes
- Hand lens
- Forceps
- Dropper
- Microscope slide and coverslip
- Microscope
- Dissecting needle
- Pencil with eraser

Comparing Mosses, Liverworts, and Ferns

Mosses and liverworts make up the division of plants called Bryophyta. Ferns make up the division Pterophyta and are called pteridophytes (tuh RIH duh fites). Try this activity to observe the similarities and differences in these groups of plants.

What You'll Investigate

How are the gametophyte and sporophyte stages of liver-worts, mosses, and ferns similar and different?

Goals

- **Describe** the sporophyte and gametophyte forms of liverworts, mosses, and ferns.
- **Identify** the spore-producing structures of liverworts, mosses, and ferns.

Procedure

1. Obtain a gametophyte of each plant. With a hand lens, **observe** the rhizoids, leafy parts, and stemlike parts, if any are present.

2. Obtain a sporophyte of each plant and use a hand lens to **observe** it.

3. Locate the spore structure on the moss plant. **Remove** it and place it in a drop of water on the slide. Place a coverslip over it. Use the eraser of a pencil to gently push on the cover-slip to release the spores. **CAUTION:** *Do not break the coverslip.* **Observe** the spores under low and high power.

4. Make labeled drawings of all observations in your Science Journal.

Conclude and Apply

1. For each plant, **compare** the gametophyte's appearance to the sporophyte's appearance.

2. List the structure(s) common to all three plants.

3. **Form a hypothesis** about why each plant produces a large number of spores.

Using Similar Triangles to Solve Problems

Trees, Trees, Trees

Prairie Creek, California, is home to the largest known coastal redwood in the United States. If you stood next to this towering tree on a sunny day, you could calculate its height. Remember that two similar triangles have the same shape but are different sizes. The sides of similar triangles are proportional. Using this relationship, you can follow these steps to find the tree's height.

Calculating Tree Height

At a certain time of day, the redwood's shadow measures 187.8 m. At the same time, a person 1.5 m tall stands near the tree and casts a shadow 3 m long. Both the tree and the person form 90° angles with the ground. The sun's angle is the same for both the tree and the person. Because the triangles formed by each shadow, each object, and the sun's angle are proportional, the height of the tree can be calculated.

1. Write a proportion comparing the heights of objects to lengths of shadows (all measurements are in meters):

$$\frac{\text{height of person}}{\text{height of tree}} = \frac{\text{length of person's shadow}}{\text{length of tree's shadow}}$$

$$\frac{1.5}{h} = \frac{3}{187.8}$$

2. Find the cross products of the proportion:
$$1.5 \times 187.8 = 3 \times h$$
$$281.7 = 3 \times h$$

3. To find the value of h, divide both sides of the equation by 3:

$$\frac{281.7}{3} = \frac{3\,h}{3} \qquad 93.9 = h$$

The height of the tree is about 93.9 m.

Practice
PROBLEMS

1. The largest American elm tree grows in Louisville, Kansas. When the elm casts a shadow of 17.4 m, a nearby, 0.9 m fence post has a 0.6 m shadow. Find the height of the American elm.

2. Cuba, New Mexico, is home to the largest piñon pine. When it casts a shadow of 27.6 m, a nearby, 0.45 m shrub casts a shadow of 0.6 m. Find the height of the piñon pine.

3. Try this method on a tall object in your neighborhood at two different times on the same day. Did the time of day affect your calculations?

5·2 Seed Plant Reproduction

What You'll Learn

▶ The life cycles of typical gymnosperms and angiosperms

▶ The structure and function of the flower

▶ Methods of seed dispersal in seed plants

Vocabulary

ovule	pistil
pollen grain	ovary
stamen	pollination

Why It's Important

▶ Learning about cones and flowers will help you understand where seeds come from.

Gymnosperm Reproduction

Have you ever collected pine cones or used them in a craft project? If you have, you probably noticed that there are many shapes and sizes of pine cones. Cones are the reproductive structures on plants called gymnosperms (JIHM nuh spurmz). Each gymnosperm species has a different cone.

Pines are typical gymnosperms. Each pine produces male cones and female cones on the sporophyte plant. A mature female cone consists of a spiral of woody scales on a short stem. At the base of each scale are two ovules. Each **ovule** contains an egg cell, food-storage tissue, and a sticky fluid. **Pollen grains** develop on the smaller male cone. Two sperm eventually form in each pollen grain. As seen in **Figure 5-8,** a cloud of pollen grains is released from each male cone.

Figure 5-8 Male cones of a Norway spruce release clouds of tiny pollen grains.

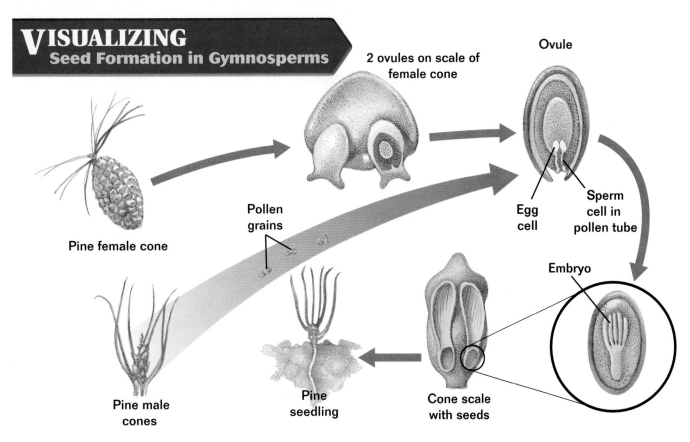

VISUALIZING
Seed Formation in Gymnosperms

Pine female cone

Pollen grains

2 ovules on scale of female cone

Ovule

Egg cell

Sperm cell in pollen tube

Embryo

Pine male cones

Pine seedling

Cone scale with seeds

Wind carries the pollen to female cones. However, most of the pollen falls on other plants, the ground, and bodies of water. If a pollen grain is blown between the scales of a female cone, it may be trapped in the sticky fluid secreted by the ovule. When the pollen grain and female cone are the same species, a pollen tube grows from the pollen grain toward the ovule. Fertilization may happen as much as 15 months later. The two sperm move down the pollen tube. One fertilizes the egg cell, and the other breaks down. As a result, a zygote forms that develops into an embryo. **Figure 5-9** illustrates this process.

Female cones of pines mature, open, and release their seeds, usually during the fall or winter months. It may take a long time for seeds to be released from a pine cone. From the moment a pollen grain falls on the female cone until the time the seeds are released may take two or three years. Released seeds are carried away, eaten, or buried by animals. Under favorable conditions, the buried seeds will grow into new pines.

Figure 5-9 It may take two or three years for the seed of a female cone to form. **Where would you find the seed?**

Mini Lab

Observing Gymnosperm Cones

Procedure

1. Using a hand lens, look at the parts of a gymnosperm cone.
2. On a large paper towel, open the cone and note where the seeds are located.

Analysis

1. Make a drawing of the cone and seeds in your Science Journal.
2. Where are the seeds located?
3. Predict how this location is an advantage for the tree species.

Angiosperm Reproduction

Angiosperms all produce flowers. Flowers are important because they contain the reproductive organs. When you think of a flower, you probably imagine something with a pleasant aroma and colorful petals. Although many such flowers do exist, some flowers are drab and have no aroma. Have you ever looked at the flowers of wheat, rice, or grass? Why do you think there is such variety among flowers?

The Flower

A flower's appearance may tell you something about the life of the plant it is part of. Large flowers with bright-colored petals often attract insects and other animals. These animals may eat the flower, its nectar, or pollen. As they move about the flower, the animals may get pollen on their wings, legs, or other body parts. As a result, these animals may spread the flower's pollen to other plants that they visit. Other flowers depend on wind, rain, or gravity to spread their pollen. Their petals may be small or absent. Flowers that open only at night, as seen in **Figure 5-10,** often have strong scents to attract animals.

Figure 5-10 Some flowers bloom only at night. They are usually light colored or white, and they produce large amounts of scent molecules, nectar, and pollen. **Aside from bats, what other animals might pollinate night-blooming plants?**

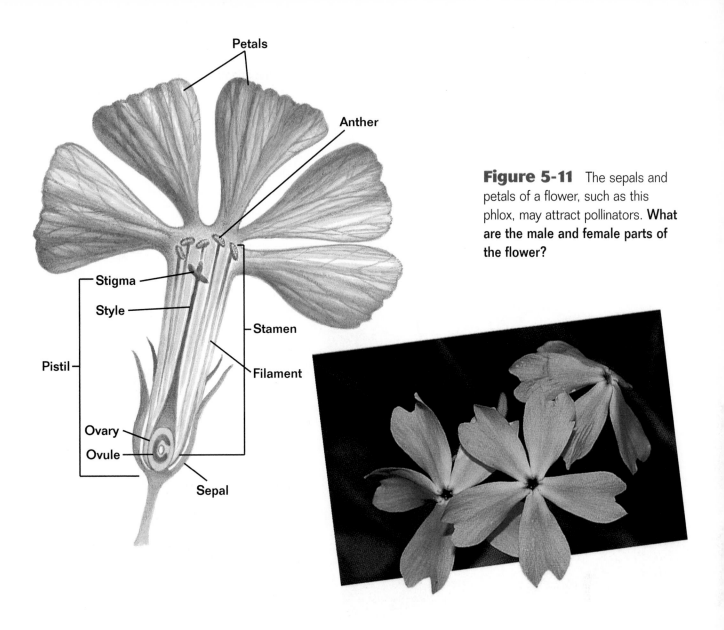

Petals

Anther

Stigma

Style

Stamen

Pistil

Filament

Ovary

Ovule

Sepal

Figure 5-11 The sepals and petals of a flower, such as this phlox, may attract pollinators. **What are the male and female parts of the flower?**

Generally, the colored parts of a flower are the petals. Outside the petals are usually leaflike parts called sepals. Sepals are easy to see when a flower is still a bud. Sepals form the outside of the bud and cover the petals. In some flowers, the sepals are as colorful as the petals.

Inside the flower are the reproductive organs of the plant. The **stamen** is the male reproductive organ. A stamen consists of a filament and an anther. Pollen grains form inside the anther. The sperm develop in each pollen grain.

The **pistil** is the female reproductive organ. A pistil consists of a sticky stigma where the pollen grains land, a long stalk-like style, and an ovary. The **ovary** is the swollen base of the pistil where ovules are formed. Eggs are produced inside the ovule as it develops. You can see the parts of a typical flower in **Figure 5-11.** ☑

Reading Check ☑

Where do pollen grains land in flowers?

Figure 5-12 The pollination process involves the transfer of pollen grains from the stamen to the stigma.

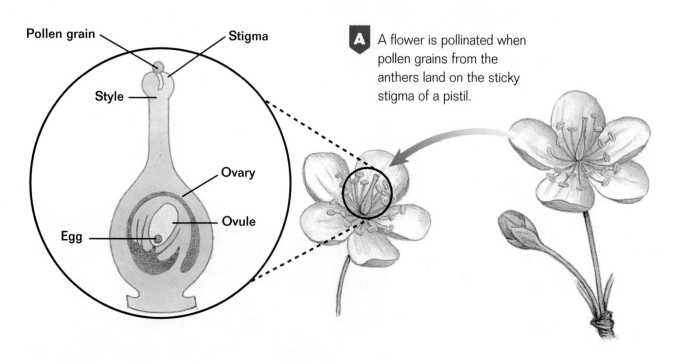

A A flower is pollinated when pollen grains from the anthers land on the sticky stigma of a pistil.

Pollen grain — Stigma

Style

Ovary

Ovule

Egg

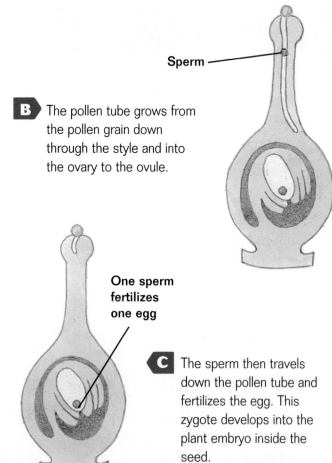

Sperm

B The pollen tube grows from the pollen grain down through the style and into the ovary to the ovule.

One sperm fertilizes one egg

C The sperm then travels down the pollen tube and fertilizes the egg. This zygote develops into the plant embryo inside the seed.

Development of a Seed

How does a seed develop? **Figure 5-12** illustrates this process. Pollen grains reach the stigma in a variety of ways. Pollen is carried by wind, rain, or animals such as insects, birds, and mammals. A flower is pollinated when pollen grains land on the sticky stigma. The transfer of pollen grains from the stamen to the stigma is the process of **pollination.** A pollen tube grows from the pollen grain down through the style. It enters the ovary and reaches an ovule. The sperm then travels down the pollen tube and fertilizes the egg. A zygote forms and grows into the plant embryo, which is inside the seed.

A seed is a mature ovule. It is surrounded by a protective seed coat. Inside the seed is the embryo. An embryo consists of an immature plant and stored food. The immature plant has structures that will eventually produce the plant's stem, leaves, and roots. In some plants, like beans and peanuts, the food is stored in structures called cotyledons. Other seeds like corn and wheat have food stored in a tissue called endosperm. This food provides the energy used by the seed as it sprouts. It also supplies energy for the immature plant's growth. You can see examples of these two seed types in **Figure 5-13.**

CONNECTION

What is a seed bank? Visit the Glencoe Science Web Site at **www.glencoe.com/ sec/science/ca** for more information about seed banks.

Figure 5-13 Seeds of land plants are capable of surviving unfavorable environmental conditions.

1. **Immature plant**
2. **Cotyledon(s)**
3. **Seed coat**
4. **Endosperm**

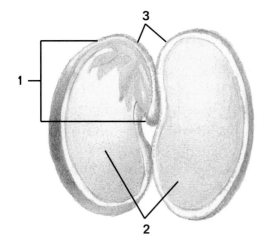
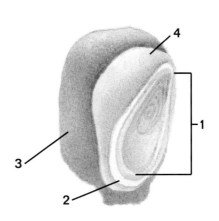

Problem Solving

Using Numbers to Test Seeds

While purchasing seeds to plant in his vegetable garden, Ling noticed that each seed packet had useful information on it. On each packet, he found a seed count, planting instructions, and germination rate for the seeds inside. The packet he chose stated that it contained about 200 carrot seeds. The planting instructions were to plant seeds about 5 cm apart and 6 mm deep. It also claimed that 95 percent of the seeds would germinate. Ling decided that he would test the seed company's claims.

Think Critically: What should Ling do to determine whether the claims are true? How could Ling use the weight of the seeds to determine the number of seeds in the packet?

Seed Dispersal

Most seeds grow only when placed on or in the ground. But, how do seeds naturally get from a plant to the ground? For many seeds, gravity is the answer.

Have you ever noticed how some plants just seem to appear in lawns, gardens, or the cracks of sidewalks? How did they get there? They probably grew from a seed, but where did the seed come from? In nature, seeds may travel great distances from the plants they grew on. Wind, water, and animals spread seeds. Some plants even have ways of ejecting their seeds. **Figure 5-14** shows ways that seeds are dispersed.

Wind dispersal happens usually because a seed has a structure attached to it that allows it to move with air currents. Dandelion, milkweed, and maple seeds are dispersed by the wind. Sometimes, seeds are so small that they become airborne when released by the plant.

Animals, including humans, disperse many seeds. Some seeds are eaten with fruits and dispersed as animals move from place to place. Often, for a seed to germinate, it must pass through an animal's digestive system. Hitchhiking on fur, feathers, and clothing is another way that animals disperse seeds. The fruit or seed may have a hooklike structure(s) or be coated with a sticky substance that allows it to stick to a passing animal. Humans often carry seeds without knowing it. Seeds wedge in the bottoms of shoes, drop into pockets or pant cuffs, and travel in our belongings.

Figure 5-14 Seeds can be dispersed by various methods.

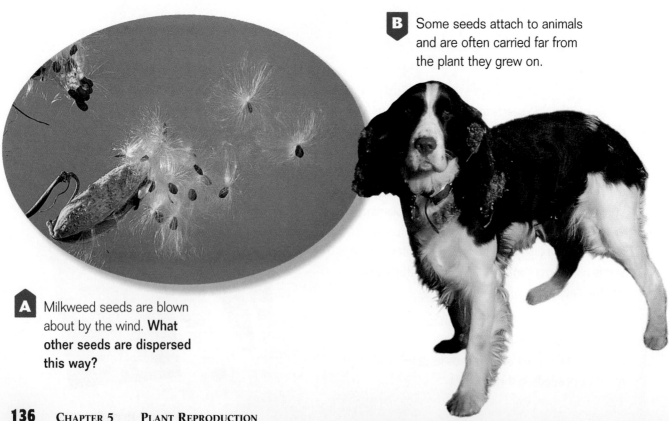

B Some seeds attach to animals and are often carried far from the plant they grew on.

A Milkweed seeds are blown about by the wind. **What other seeds are dispersed this way?**

Water also disperses seeds. Raindrops may knock seeds out of a dry fruit. Some fruits and seeds contain trapped air, which allows them to float on water. They also may have waxy coatings that delay water absorption. Floating seeds may travel great distances. The coconut palm's seed shown in **Figure 5-14C** has been dispersed hundreds of kilometers on ocean currents.

Have you ever touched the seedpod of an impatiens flower and watched as it exploded? The tiny seeds are ejected and spread some distance from the plant. This is another way that some plants disperse seeds.

Germination

Some seeds sprout or germinate in just a few days and other seeds take weeks or months to grow. Seeds will not sprout until environmental conditions are right. Some seeds can stay in a resting stage for hundreds of years. In 1982, seeds of the East Indian lotus sprouted after 466 years!

D The plant may disperse seeds by ejecting them.

C This coconut seed floats in the surf.

Figure 5-15 Germination is different in dicots and monocots.

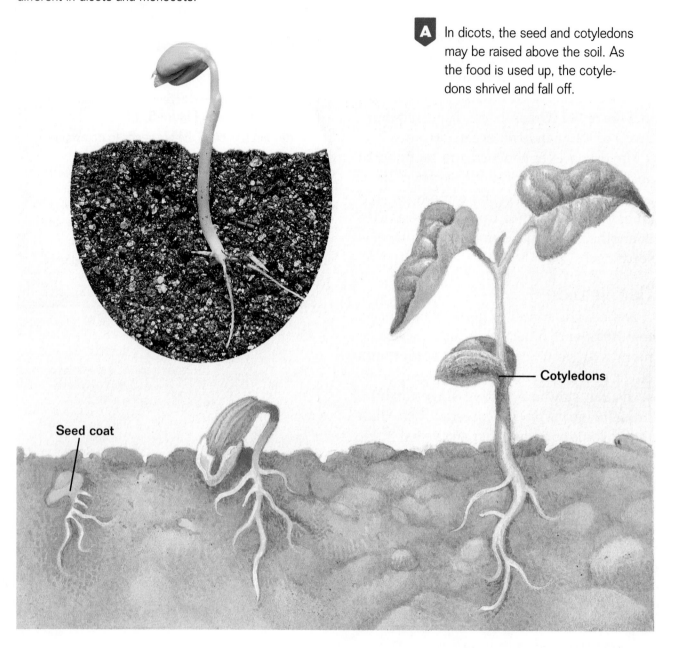

A In dicots, the seed and cotyledons may be raised above the soil. As the food is used up, the cotyledons shrivel and fall off.

Cotyledons

Seed coat

Germination, as shown in **Figure 5-15,** is a series of events that results in the growth of a plant from a seed. Temperature, the presence or absence of light, availability of water, and amount of oxygen present may affect germination. If the right combination of factors occurs, the seed will germinate. Germination begins when seed tissues absorb water. This causes the seed to swell. Then, a series of chemical reactions happens that releases energy from the stored food in the cotyledons or endosperm. Eventually, a root grows from the seed, followed by a stem and leaves. Once the plant is out of the soil, photosynthesis begins. Photosynthesis provides food and energy for the plant.

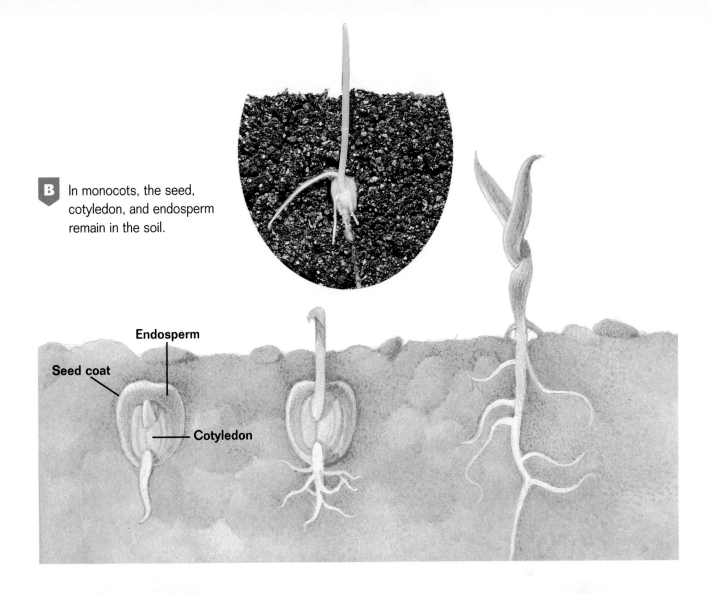

B In monocots, the seed, cotyledon, and endosperm remain in the soil.

Endosperm

Seed coat

Cotyledon

Section Assessment

1. **Compare** life cycles of angiosperms and gymnosperms.

2. Diagram a flower and label its parts.

3. List three methods of seed dispersal in plants.

4. **Think Critically:** Some conifers have female cones on the top half of the tree and male cones on the bottom half. Why do you think this arrangement of cones is important?

5.  **Skill Builder**
   Forming a Hypothesis A corn plant produces thousands of pollen grains on top of the plant in flowers that have no odor or color. The pistils grow from the cob lower down on the plant. Hypothesize how a corn plant is probably pollinated. If you need help, refer to Forming a Hypothesis in the **Skill Handbook** on page 686.

Science Journal Observe live specimens of several different types of flowers. In your Science Journal, describe their structures. Include numbers of petals, sepals, stamens, and pistil.

Design Your Own Experiment

Activity 5·2

Germination Rate of Seeds

Many environmental factors affect the germination rate of seeds. Among these are soil temperature, air temperature, moisture content of soil, and salt content of soil. What happens to the germination rate when one of these variables is changed? Can you determine a way to predict the best conditions for seed germination?

Possible Materials

- Seeds
- Water
- Salt
- Potting soil
- Plant trays or plastic cups
  * *seedling warming cables*
- Thermometer
- Graduated cylinder
- Beakers
  * *Alternate Materials*

Recognize the Problem

How does an environmental factor affect seed germination?

Form a Hypothesis

Based on your knowledge of seed germination, state a hypothesis about how environmental factors affect germination rates.

Goals

- **Design an experiment** to test the effect of an environmental factor on seed germination rate.
- **Compare** germination rates under different conditions.

Safety Precautions

Some kinds of seeds are poisonous. Do not place any seeds in your mouth. Be careful when using any electrical equipment to avoid shock hazards.

Test Your Hypothesis

Plan

1. As a group, agree upon and **write** out your hypothesis statement.

2. As a group, list the steps that you need to take to test your hypothesis. Be specific, and **describe** exactly what you will do at each step. List your materials.

3. **Identify** any constants, variables, and controls of the experiment.

4. What measurements will you take? What data will you collect?

Do

1. Make sure your teacher approves your plan before you proceed.

2. Carry out the experiment as planned.

3. While the experiment is going on, **record** any observations

How often will you collect data? If you need a data table, **design** one in your Science Journal so that it is ready to use as your group collects data. Will the data be summarized in a graph?

5. **Read** over your entire experiment to make sure that all steps are in logical order. How many tests will you run?

that you make and complete the data table in your Science Journal.

Analyze Your Data

1. **Compare** your results with those of other groups.

2. Did changing the variable affect germination rates? Explain.

3. **Graph** your results using a bar graph, placing germination rate on the *y*-axis and the environmental variables on the *x*-axis.

Draw Conclusions

1. **Interpret** your graph to estimate the conditions that give the best germination rate.

2. What things affect the germination rate?

FIELD GUIDE

to Cones

FIELD ACTIVITY

Find three different cones in your neighborhood, a park, around your school or as part of a craft item. Using this guide, identify the genus of each cone. In your Science Journal, make a sketch of each cone and write a description of the plant it came from.

When we hear the word *cone*, we may think of a holder for our favorite ice cream. Or, we may think of the orange cones that we see on highways and in public places to direct traffic. But, there's another type of cone in our environment that plays an important role for some plants. They are the reproductive organs of a large plant group called the *conifers,* or cone bearers. The seeds of pines, firs, spruces, and redwoods are formed on cones.

Types of Cones

All conifers have two types of cones, male and female. The male cones produce pollen grains. They are short lived, breaking apart shortly after they release pollen. Depending on the species of conifer, the familiar female cones may stay on plants for nearly one year, two years, or three years. Female cones may be woody or berrylike. Woody cones consist of scales growing from a central stalk. Berrylike cones are round and may be either hard or soft. Each genus of conifers has a different female cone. They are so different from one another that you can use them to identify a conifer's genus.

Cone Characteristics

- **cylindrical**—shaped like a cylinder; nearly uniform in size from the base to the tip of the cone

- **ovoid**—shaped like a cylinder but smaller at the ends than in the middle

- **globose**—rounded like a globe

- **conic**—shaped like a cone; decreasing in diameter from the base to the tip of the cone

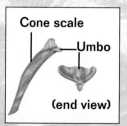

Cone scale
Umbo
(end view)

- **umbo**—a raised, triangular area at the tip of a cone scale; size and thickness of area varies

Cone Identification

This field guide contains some of the conifers. **Remember** that plant features may differ in appearance because of environmental conditions.

Juniper—*Juniperus*

- Hard, berrylike structures that stay on the tree or shrub for two to three years
- About 1.3 cm in diameter
- May be bluish, pale green, reddish, or brown and covered with a whitish, waxy coating called a bloom

Douglas Fir—*Psuedotsuga*

- Three-pointed, papery structure extends from below each cone scale
- Ovoid, on short stalks
- 5 cm to 10 cm in length

Spruce—*Picea*

- Cylindrical and brown, 6 cm to 15 cm in length
- Hang from branches on the upper third of the tree
- Thin cone scales, tips are usually pointed; brittle when mature
- Stay on the plant for two years

Redwood—*Sequoia*

- Ovoid, reddish brown, hang from the tips of neddled twigs
- Small in comparison to the size of the tree, only 1.2 cm to 3 cm
- Cone scales flattened on the end
- Mature in one year

Hemlock—*Tsuga*

- Small, ovoid to cylindrical, 2 cm to 7 cm long, hang from twigs
- Cone scales are few and have rounded tips
- Mature in one year but usually stay on tree for more than one year

Pine—*Pinus*

- Each thick, woody scale tipped with an umbo; the umbo may have a small spine or prickle
- Most cylindrical or conic and grow on a small stalk
- Vary in length from about 4 cm (scrub pine) to 45 cm (sugar pine)
- Remain on tree or shrub two to three years

Arborvitae—*Thuja*

- Egg-shaped cones, 1.2 cm to 1.5 cm long
- Paired cone scales, usually six to twelve, straplike and end in a sharp point
- Remain attached to shrub after opening and releasing seeds

Cypress—*Cupressus*

- Globose, usually 2 cm to 2.5 cm in diameter, only six to eight scales
- Cone scales have raised point in the center
- Mature in about 18 months and stay closed and attached to the tree

False Cypress—*Chamaecyparis*

- Small globose, only 0.5 cm to 4 cm in diameter with four to ten cone scales
- Open at maturity (unlike cones of *Cupressus* trees)

Swamp or Bald Cypress—*Taxodium*

- Globose, about 2.5 cm across
- Tips of cone scales are four sided, forming irregular pattern on the surface of cone
- Ripen in one year
- Trees in this genus recognizable by "knees" that form around the base of the tree trunk.

Fir—*Abies*

- Grow upright on branch
- Seldom used for identification because scales drop off at maturity leaving only the bare, central stalk
- 5 cm to 20 cm in length

Cedar—*Cedrus*

- Barrel-shaped cones with flattened tips grow upright on branches
- 5 cm to 10 cm in length and nearly half as wide
- Scales drop off at maturity (like firs) after two years
- Not produced until trees are 40 to 50 years old

For a **preview** of this chapter, study this Reviewing Main Ideas before you read the chapter. After you have studied this chapter, you can use the Reviewing Main Ideas to **review** the chapter.

The Glencoe MindJogger, Audiocassettes, and CD-ROM provide additional opportunities for review.

Section

5-1 INTRODUCTION TO PLANT REPRODUCTION

Plants reproduce sexually and asexually. Sexual reproduction involves the formation of sex cells and fertilization. Asexual reproduction does not involve sex cells and produces organisms genetically identical to the parent organism. Plant life cycles include a gametophyte and a sporophyte stage. The gametophyte stage begins with meiosis. The sporophyte stage begins when the egg is fertilized by a sperm. In some plant life cycles, these stages are separate and not dependent on each other. In other plant life cycles, they are part of the same organism. For liverworts and mosses, the **gametophyte stage** is the familiar plant form. The **sporophyte stage** produces spores. In ferns, the sporophyte stage, not the gametophyte stage, is the familiar plant form. Ferns, like mosses and liverworts, produce spores.

What does alternation of generations mean?

Reading Check ✓

Find five science words in this chapter that begin with the letter *a*. Identify the words in which *a* is the prefix that means "without."

Section 5-2 SEED PLANT REPRODUCTION

Seed plants include gymnosperms and angiosperms. The male reproductive organs produce **pollen grains** that eventually contain sperm. Eggs are produced in the **ovules** of the female reproductive organs. The reproductive organs of gymnosperms are called cones. Wind usually moves pollen from the male cone to the female cone for fertilization. The reproductive organs of angiosperms are in a flower. The male reproductive organ is the **stamen,** and the female reproductive organ is the **pistil.** Gravity, wind, rain, and animals may pollinate a flower. Seeds of gymnosperms and angiosperms are dispersed in many ways. *How are the reproductive organs of gymnosperms and angiosperms alike?*

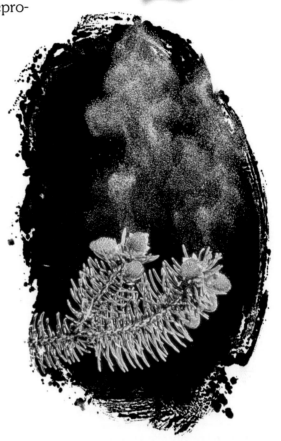

Career CONNECTION

Flora Ninomiya, Horticulturist

As a horticulturist, Flora Ninomiya is interested in the science of cultivating plants. She is responsible for 600 000 rose plants that occupy about 92 000 m² of greenhouse space. In addition to experimenting with new rose varieties, Flora schedules plant production, checks plants for diseases and insects, and oversees plant watering and fertilization. She uses the latest technologies, including computer-automated greenhouses and hydroponics.

Chapter 5 Assessment

Using Vocabulary

a. alternation of generations
b. frond
c. gametophyte stage
d. ovary
e. ovule
f. pistil
g. pollen grain
h. pollination
i. prothallus
j. rhizome
k. sori
l. sporophyte stage
m. stamen

Complete the following sentences with the best choices from the Vocabulary list.

1. A(n) _____ has an ovary and a(n) _____ has an anther.
2. In seed plants, the _____ contains the egg and the _____ contains the sperm.
3. Haploid cells make up the _____ _____ and diploid cells make up the _____ _____.
4. Moss capsules and moss plants are examples of _____ ___ _____.
5. Two parts of a sporophyte fern are _____ and _____.

Checking Concepts

Choose the word or phrase that best answers the question.

6. How are colorful flowers usually pollinated?
   A) insects   C) clothing
   B) wind   D) gravity

7. What is part of all plant life cycles?
   A) seeds   C) flowers
   B) fruits   D) alternation of generations

8. What part of the flower receives the pollen grain?
   A) sepal   C) stamen
   B) ovary   D) stigma

9. What do ferns form when they reproduce sexually?
   A) spores   C) seeds
   B) vascular tissue D) flowers

10. What contains food for the embryo?
    A) endosperm   C) stigma
    B) pollen grain D) root

11. What disperses most dandelion seeds?
    A) rain   C) wind
    B) animals   D) insects

12. What is the series of events that results in an organism from a seed?
    A) pollination   C) germination
    B) alternation of generations D) asexual reproduction

13. What is another name for seed leaves?
    A) root hairs   C) stigmas
    B) cotyledons   D) stomata

14. Ovules and pollen grains are involved in what process?
    A) germination   C) seed dispersal
    B) asexual reproduction D) sexual reproduction

15. Which of the following terms describes the cells in the gametophyte stage?
    A) haploid   C) diploid
    B) prokaryotic   D) missing a nucleus

Thinking Critically

16. Explain why male cones produce so many pollen grains.

17. Describe a flower that is pollinated by a hummingbird.

18. Discuss the importance of water in the reproduction of bryophytes and ferns.

19. In mosses, why is the sporophyte stage dependent on the gametophyte stage?

20. What features of flowers ensure pollination?

Developing Skills

If you need help, refer to the **Skill Handbook.**

21. Concept Mapping: Complete this concept map of a moss life cycle.

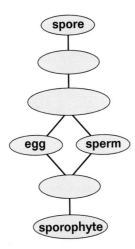

22. Comparing and Contrasting: Describe the differences and similarities between the fern sporophyte and gametophyte stages.

23. Observing and Inferring: Observe pictures of flowers or actual flowers and infer how each is pollinated. Explain your suggestion.

24. Sequencing: Number the following events in the correct order. *Pollen is trapped on the stigma; pollen tube reaches the ovule; fertilization; pollen released from the anther; pollen tube forms through the style; a seed forms.*

25. Making and Using Graphs: Make a bar graph for the following data table about onion seeds. Put the temperature on the horizontal axis and days on the vertical axis.

Onion Seed Data						
Temperature (°C)	10	15	20	25	30	35
Days to germinate	13	7	5	4	4	13

THE PRINCETON REVIEW

Test-Taking Tip

Use as Much Time as You Can You will not get extra points for finishing early. Work slowly and carefully on any test and make sure you don't make careless errors because you are hurrying to finish.

Test Practice

Use these questions to test your Science Proficiency.

1. What does the gametophyte stage of a moss or fern life cycle produce?
   A) sex cells   C) spores
   B) seeds   D) fruits
2. What is the usual pollinator for gymnosperms?
   A) wind   C) rain
   B) insects   D) gravity

3. If a flower has a pistil but no stamen, what type of flower is it?
   A) pollinator   C) infertile
   B) male   D) female

4. You see a dandelion growing near a rose. Which of the following **BEST** explains how the dandelion came to be there?
   A) It grew from an underground dandelion.
   B) The seed was carried there by the wind and grew.
   C) The plant was put there by an animal.
   D) Dandelions often grow from the roots of roses.

Chapter Preview

Skills Preview

Skill Builders
- Make and Use a Graph
- Map Concepts

Activities
- Predict
- Hypothesize

MiniLabs
- Collect and Analyze Data

Reading Check ✓

Choose an unfamiliar word from a section vocabulary list. Use its root, affixes, or section illustrations to predict its meaning. As you read, check the accuracy of your prediction.

Explore Activity

Pronghorn antelope like the ones in this photograph are the fastest mammals in the Western Hemisphere. They can run up to 86 km/hr and leap up to 6.1 m. Montana is home to many pronghorns. Like many other organisms, pronghorn antelope inherit traits from both of their parents. If you look closely, you will find small differences among individuals, though they have many traits in common. Most traits found in organisms have at least two different forms. In humans, there is a noticeable difference between a straight hairline and a hairline with a widow's peak. In the following activity, observe this genetic difference. In this chapter, you will learn how you and your classmates received the genetic traits you have.

Observe Differences in Human Hairlines

1. Notice the two different kinds of hairlines in the photo above. The girl on the right has a straight hairline. The girl on the left has a pointed hairline, also called a widow's peak.

2. Record the name of each of your classmates and the kind of hairline he or she has.

Do most of your classmates have the same kind of hairline as you? Record the percentage of each type of hairline in your Science Journal.

What is genetics?

What have you inherited?

People have always been interested in why one generation looks like another. A new baby may look much like one of its parents. It may have eyes the same color as its father or a nose like its mother. Eye color, nose shape, and many other physical features are types of traits that you inherited from your parents. Every organism is a collection of traits, all inherited from its parents. **Heredity** (huh RED ut ee) is the passing of traits from parent to offspring. What controls these traits? As you will learn, traits are controlled by genes.

How Traits Are Inherited

Genes are made up of DNA and are located on chromosomes. To a large degree, genes control the traits that show up in an organism. The different forms a gene may have for a trait are its **alleles** (uh LEELZ). When pairs of chromosomes separate into sex cells during meiosis, pairs of genes also separate from one another. As a result, each sex cell winds up with one allele for each trait that an organism shows, as demonstrated in **Figure 6-1.** The allele in one sex cell may

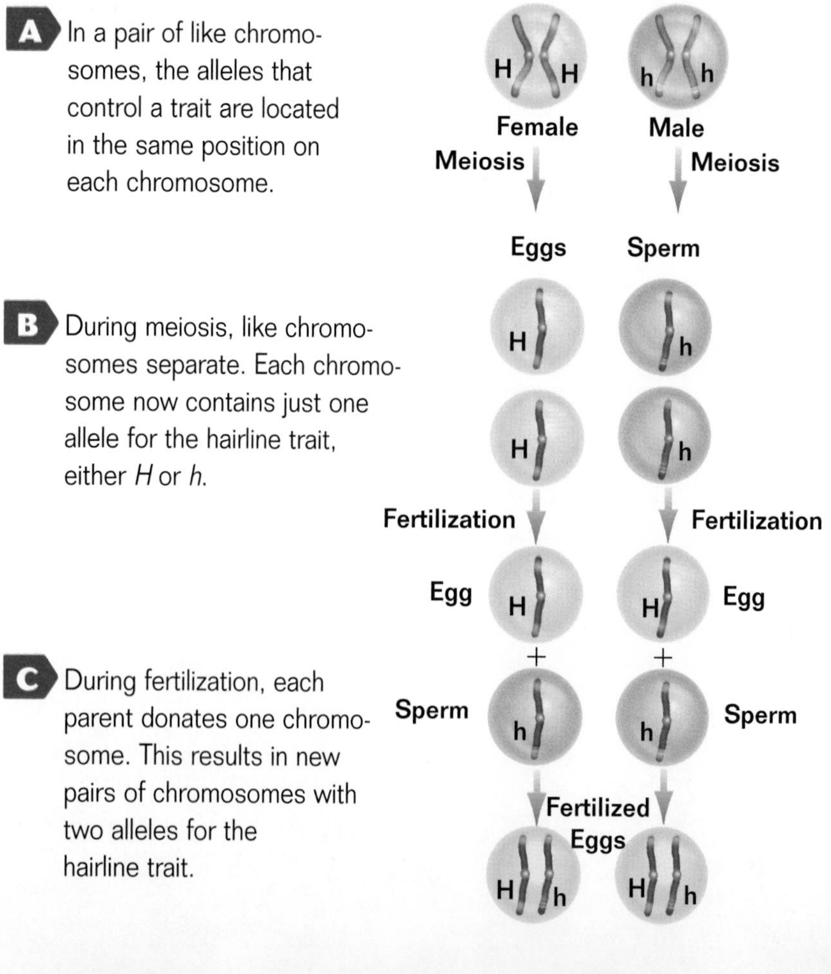

A In a pair of like chromosomes, the alleles that control a trait are located in the same position on each chromosome.

Figure 6-1 An allele is one form of a gene. Alleles separate during meiosis. In this example, the alleles that control the trait for hairlines include *H*, the widow's peak hairline allele, and *h*, the straight hairline allele.

B During meiosis, like chromosomes separate. Each chromosome now contains just one allele for the hairline trait, either *H* or *h*.

C During fertilization, each parent donates one chromosome. This results in new pairs of chromosomes with two alleles for the hairline trait.

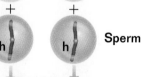
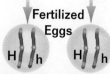

control one form of the trait, such as a widow's peak. The allele in the other sex cell may control an alternate form of the trait, such as a straight hairline. The study of how traits are inherited through the actions of alleles is the science of **genetics** (juh NET ihks).

The Father of Genetics

The first recorded scientific study of how traits pass from one generation to the next was done by Gregor Mendel, an Austrian monk born in 1822. He learned how to grow plants as a child working on his family's farm. Mendel studied science and math and eventually became a priest and teacher. While teaching, Mendel took over a garden plot at his monastery. In 1856, he began experimenting with garden peas like the ones shown in **Figure 6-2.** His observations of his father's orchard made him think that it was possible to predict the kinds of flowers and fruit a plant would produce. But, something had to be known about the parents of the plant before such a prediction could be made. Mendel made careful use of scientific methods in his research. After eight years of working with pea plants, Mendel presented a paper detailing the results of his research to the Natural History Society of Brünn, Austria. This paper was published by the Society in 1866 under the title "Experiments with Plant Hybrids."

In 1900, three other scientists working in botany rediscovered Mendel's work. These other scientists had come to the same conclusions that Mendel had reached. Since that time, Mendel has been known as the father of genetics.

Figure 6-2 Mendel's work with garden peas such as these led to the science of genetics. **Why is Mendel called the father of genetics?**

Mini Lab

Comparing Common Traits

Procedure

1. Always obtain the permission of any person included in an experiment on human traits.
2. Survey ten students in your class or school for the presence of freckles, dimples, cleft or smooth chins, and attached or detached earlobes.
3. Make a data table that lists each of the traits.
4. Fill in the table.

Analysis

1. Compare the number of people who have one form of a trait with those who have the other form. How do those two groups compare?
2. What can you conclude about the number of variations you noticed?

In Mendel's Garden

Reading Check ✓

What is a purebred?

Mendel chose ordinary garden peas, such as the ones you eat for dinner, for his experiments. Peas are easy to breed for pure traits. An organism that always produces the same traits generation to generation is called a purebred. Tall plants that always produce tall plants are purebred for the trait of tallness. Short plants that always have short offspring are purebred for the trait of shortness. In addition to height, Mendel studied six other traits of garden peas, shown in **Table 6-1.** ✓

Dominant and Recessive Factors

In nature, insects such as the bee shown in **Figure 6-3** pollinate randomly as they move from flower to flower. In his experiments, Mendel took pollen from the male reproductive structures of flowers from purebred tall plants. He then placed the pollen on the female reproductive structures of flowers from pure short plants. This process is called cross-pollination. The results of his cross are shown in **Figure 6-4.** Notice that tall plants crossed with short plants produced all tall plants. It seemed as if whatever had caused the plants to be short had disappeared.

Mendel called the tall-height form that appeared the **dominant** (DAHM uh nunt) factor because it dominated, or covered up, the short-height form. He called the form that seemed to disappear the **recessive** (rih SES ihv) factor. But, what had happened to the recessive form?

Mendel allowed the new tall plants to self-pollinate. Self-pollination occurs when pollen is transferred from the male to the female reproductive structure in the same plant. Then, he collected the seeds from these tall plants and planted

Figure 6-3 Bees and other animals often visit only one species of flower at a time. **Why is this important to plant species pollinated by animals?**

Table 6-1

Traits Compared by Mendel							
Traits	**Shape of seeds**	**Color of seeds**	**Color of pods**	**Shape of pods**	**Plant height**	**Position of flowers**	**Flower color**
Dominant Trait	Round	Yellow	Green	Full	Tall	At leaf junctions	Purple
Recessive Trait	Wrinkled	Green	Yellow	Flat or constricted	Short	At tips of branches	White

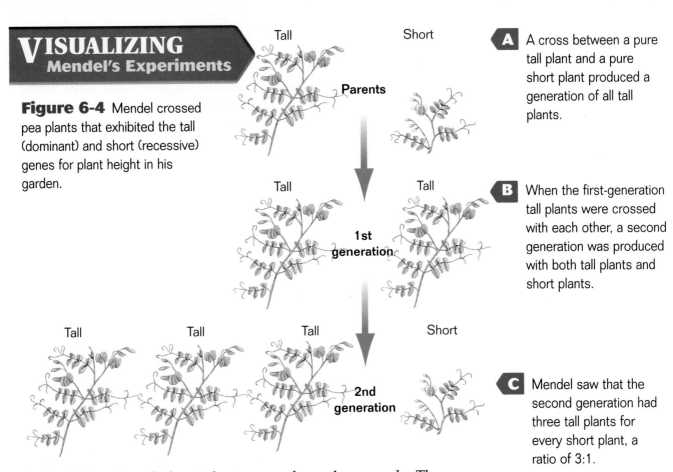

VISUALIZING Mendel's Experiments

Figure 6-4 Mendel crossed pea plants that exhibited the tall (dominant) and short (recessive) genes for plant height in his garden.

Tall   Short

Parents

Tall   Tall

1st generation

Tall   Tall   Tall   Short

2nd generation

A A cross between a pure tall plant and a pure short plant produced a generation of all tall plants.

B When the first-generation tall plants were crossed with each other, a second generation was produced with both tall plants and short plants.

C Mendel saw that the second generation had three tall plants for every short plant, a ratio of 3:1.

them. Both tall and short plants grew from these seeds. The recessive form had reappeared. Mendel saw that for every three tall plants, there was one short plant, or a 3:1 ratio. He saw this 3:1 ratio often enough that he knew he could predict his results when he started a test. He knew that the probability was great that he would get that same outcome each time.

Predictions Using Probability

Probability is a branch of mathematics that helps you predict the chance that something will happen. Suppose you and a friend want to go to different movies. You toss a coin to decide which movie you will see. Your friend chooses tails as the coin is in the air. What is the probability that the coin will land with the tail side of the coin facing up? Because there are two sides to a coin, you know there is one chance out of two possible outcomes that tails will land face up. The probability of one side of a coin showing is one out of two, or 50 percent. When you flip a coin, you are dealing with probabilities.

Mendel also dealt with probabilities. One of the things that made his predictions accurate was that he worked with large numbers. He counted every plant and thousands of seeds. In fact, Mendel raised and studied almost 30 000 pea plants over a period of eight years. By doing so, Mendel increased his chances of seeing a repeatable pattern. Valid scientific conclusions need to be based on repeatable results.

Using Math

Suppose Mendel had 100 second-generation pea plants. How many would he expect to be tall? How many would he expect to be short? Review **Figure 6-4** to help you determine the probability of each event.

Using a Punnett Square

Suppose you wanted to know what kinds of pea plants you would get if you used pollen from a pea plant with white flowers to pollinate a pea plant with purple flowers. How could you predict what the offspring would look like without actually making the cross? A handy tool used to predict results in Mendelian genetics is the **Punnett square** as seen in **Figure 6-6.** In a Punnett square, dominant and recessive alleles are represented by letters. A capital letter *(T)* stands for a dominant allele. A lowercase letter *(t)* stands for a recessive allele. The letters are a form of shorthand. They show the **genotype** (JEE nuh tipe), or genetic makeup, of an organism. Once you understand what the letters mean, you can tell a lot about the inheritance of a trait in an organism.

*inter*NET CONNECTION

Visit the Glencoe Science Web Site at **www.glencoe.com/sec/science/ca** for more information about early experiments in the field of genetics.

Alleles Determine Traits

Most cells in your body have two alleles for every trait. An organism with two alleles that are exactly the same is called **homozygous** (hoh muh ZI gus). This would be written as ***TT*** or ***tt.*** An organism that has two different alleles for a trait is called **heterozygous** (het uh roh ZI gus). This condition would be written ***Tt.*** The purebred pea plants that Mendel used were homozygous for tall, ***TT,*** and homozygous for short, ***tt.*** The hybrid plants he produced were all heterozygous, ***Tt.***

The physical expression of a particular genotype is its **phenotype** (FEE nuh tipe). Red is the phenotype for red flowering plants such as the one in **Figure 6-5.** Short is the phenotype for short plants. If you have brown hair, then the phenotype for your hair color is brown.

Figure 6-5 The color phenotype of this hibiscus flower is red. **Can you tell what the flower's genotype for color is? Why or why not?**

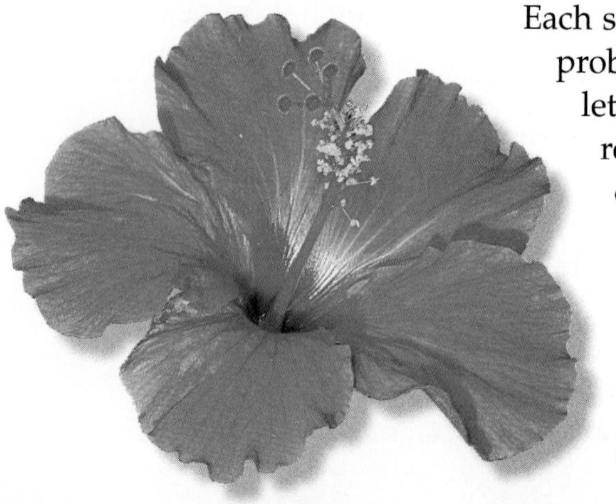

Determining Genotypes and Phenotypes

In a Punnett square, the letters representing the two alleles from one parent are written along the top of the square. Those of the second parent are placed along the side of the square. Each section of the square is filled in like a multiplication problem, with one allele donated by each parent. The letters that you use to fill in each of the squares represent the genotypes of offspring that the parents could produce.

The Punnett square in **Figure 6-6** represents the first type of experiment by Mendel. You can see that each homozygous parent plant has two alleles for height. One parent is homozygous for tall ***(TT).*** The other parent is homozygous for short ***(tt).*** The alleles inside the squares are the genotypes of the possible offspring. All of them have the genotype **Tt**. They all have tall as a phenotype because **T** represents tall, the dominant trait. Notice that you can't always figure out a genotype just by looking at the phenotype. The combinations of **TT** or **Tt** both produce tall plants when **T** is dominant to **t**. The examples below will help you understand further.

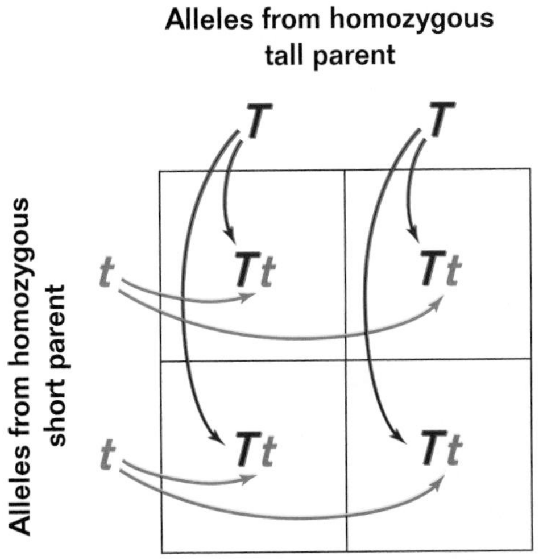

Alleles from homozygous tall parent

Figure 6-6 A Punnett square shows you all the ways in which alleles can combine. A Punnett square does not tell you how many offspring will be produced. By observing this Punnett square, you can see why all the plants in Mendel's first cross showed the dominant form of the trait in their phenotypes.

Using Punnett Squares

Example 1: Color in Peas

In peas, the color yellow is dominant to the color green. A homozygous yellow pea plant is crossed with a homozygous green pea plant. What will the genotypes and the phenotypes of all the possible offspring be?

Outcome

Genotypes of all possible offspring: All **Yy**

Phenotypes of offspring: All yellow

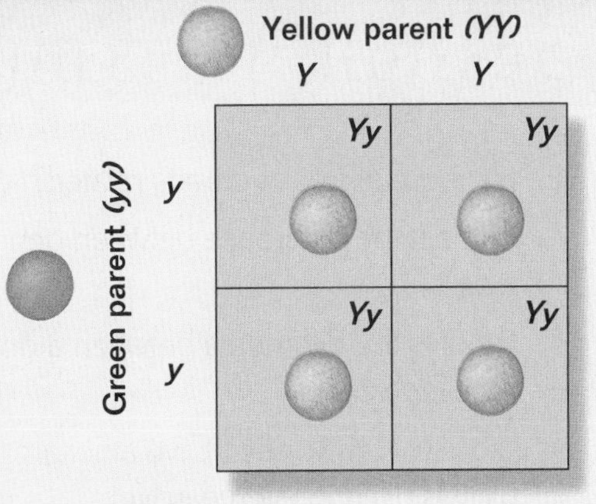

Yellow parent (YY)

Example 2: Wing Length in Fruit Flies

In fruit flies, long wings **(L)** are dominant to short wings **(l)**. Two heterozygous long-winged fruit flies (both **Ll**) are crossed. What are the possible genotypes of their offspring? What are the phenotypes?

Outcome

Genotypes of all possible offspring: **LL, Ll,** and **ll**

Phenotypes of all possible offspring:

    LL and **Ll** = long wings

    ll = short wings

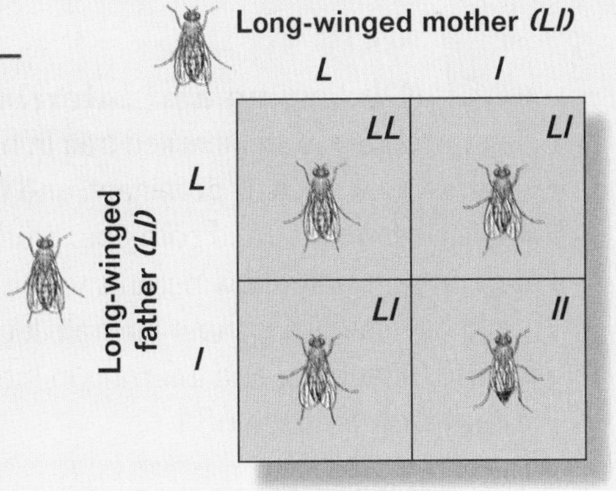

Long-winged mother (Ll)

Table 6-2

Mendel's Success

Gregor Mendel succeeded in describing how inherited traits are transmitted from parents to offspring. However, he didn't know anything about DNA, genes, or chromosomes. He did figure out that factors in the plants caused certain traits to appear. He also figured out that these factors separated when the plant reproduced. Mendel arrived at his conclusions by patient observation, careful analysis, and repeated experimentation. His work is summed up in **Table 6-2.**

Mendelian Inheritance

1. Traits are controlled by alleles on chromosomes.

2. An allele may be dominant or recessive in form.

3. When a pair of chromosomes separates during meiosis, the different alleles for a trait move into separate sex cells.

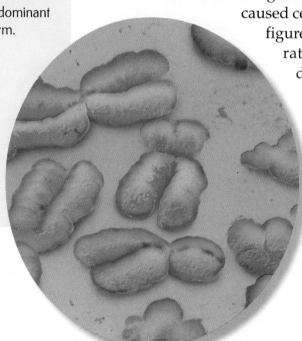

Chromosomes
Magnification: 12 000×

Section Assessment

1. How are alleles and traits related?
2. Explain the difference between genotype and phenotype.
3. What is the difference between a dominant and a recessive allele?
4. **Think Critically:** Give an example of how probability is used in everyday life.
5. **Skill Builder**
   Observing and Inferring
   Hairline shape is an inherited trait in humans. The widow's peak allele is dominant, and the straight hairline allele is recessive. From your study of Mendel's experiments, infer how parents with widow's peaks could have a child without the trait. If you need help, refer to Observing and Inferring in the **Skill Handbook** on page 684.

Using Math

Make a Punnett square showing a cross between two dogs. One dog is heterozygous with a black coat, and the other dog is homozygous with a white coat. Black is dominant to white. Use **B** for the dominant allele and **b** for the recessive allele. What percent of the offspring are expected to be white?

Expected and Observed Results

Materials
- Paper bags (2)
- Red beans (100)
- White beans (100)

Could you predict how many white flowers would result from crossing two heterozygous red flowers if you knew that white color was a recessive trait? Try this experiment to find out.

What You'll Investigate

How does chance affect combinations of genes?

Goals

- **Model** chance events in heredity.
- **Compare and contrast** predicted and actual results.

Safety Precautions

CAUTION: Do not taste, eat, or drink any materials used in lab.

Procedure

1. Place 50 red beans and 50 white beans into a paper bag. Place 50 red beans and 50 white beans into a second bag. Each bean represents an allele for flower color.

2. **Label** one of the bags "female" for the female parent. **Label** the other bag "male" for the male parent.

3. Without looking, remove one bean from each bag. The two beans represent the alleles that combine when sperm and egg join.

4. Use a Punnett square to **predict** how many red/red, red/white, and white/white combinations are possible.

5. **Use** a data table to **record** the combination of the beans each time you remove two beans. Your table will need to accommodate 100 picks. After recording, return the beans to their original bags.

6. **Count and record** the total numbers of combinations in your data table.

7. **Compile and record** the class totals.

Conclude and Apply

1. Which combination occurred most often?

2. **Calculate** the ratio of red/red to red/white to white/white.

3. **Compare** your predicted (expected) results with your observed (actual) results.

4. Does chance affect allele combination? Explain.

5. How do the results of a small sample compare with the results of a large sample?

6. **Hypothesize** how you could get predicted results to be closer to actual results.

Male   Female

Gene Combinations			
Beans	**Red/Red**	**Red/White**	**White/White**
Your total			
Class total			

6·2 Genetics Since Mendel

What You'll Learn

► How traits are inherited by incomplete dominance

► What multiple alleles and polygenic inheritance are, and examples of each

Vocabulary
incomplete dominance
multiple alleles
polygenic inheritance

Why It's Important

► Most genetic traits are inherited in a more complicated way than Mendel originally discovered. These patterns provide additional insights into heredity.

Incomplete Dominance

When Mendel's work was rediscovered, scientists repeated his experiments. For some plants, such as peas, Mendel's results proved true again and again. However, when different plants were crossed, the results sometimes varied from Mendel's predictions. One scientist crossed pure red four o'clock plants with pure white four o'clocks. He expected to get all red flowers. To his surprise, all the flowers were pink. Neither allele for flower color seemed dominant. Had the colors become blended like paint colors? He crossed the pink-flowered plants with each other and red, pink, and white flowers were produced. These results are shown in **Figure 6-7.** The red and white alleles had not become "blended." Instead, the allele for white flowers and the allele for red flowers had resulted in an intermediate phenotype, a pink flower. **Incomplete dominance** is the production of a phenotype that is intermediate to those of the two homozygous parents. Flower color in four o'clock plants is inherited by incomplete dominance.

Multiple Alleles

Mendel studied traits in peas that were controlled by just two alleles. However, many traits are controlled by more than two alleles. A trait that is controlled by more than two alleles is considered to be controlled by **multiple alleles.** One example of a trait controlled by multiple alleles is blood type in humans.

Figure 6-7 The diagrams show how color in four o'clock flowers is inherited by incomplete dominance.

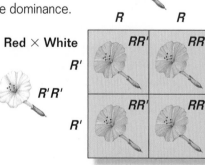

Red × White

Genotypes: All *RR'*
Phenotypes: All pink

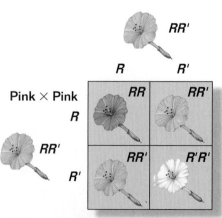

Pink × Pink

Genotypes: *RR, RR', R'R'*
Phenotypes: Red, pink, and white

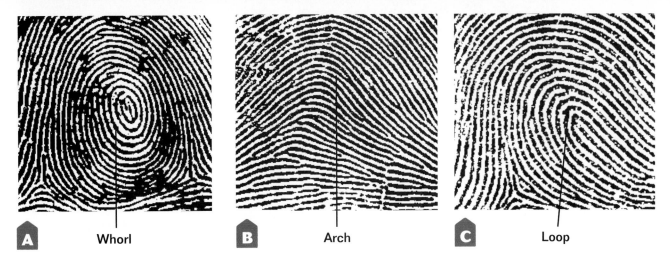

A **Whorl**

B **Arch**

C **Loop**

Figure 6-8 Fingerprints are an example of a trait inherited through the action of a group of gene pairs. The fingerprints in your class will probably show varieties of the whorl (A), arch (B), and loop (C) patterns. These patterns have many variations. **Why are everyone's fingerprints unique?**

In 1900, one scientist found three alleles for blood types in the human population. He called them A, B, and O. A and B alleles are both dominant. When a person inherits one A and one B allele for blood type, both are expressed. Thus, a person with AB blood type shows both alleles in his or her phenotype. Both A and B alleles are dominant to the O allele, which is recessive.

A person with phenotype A blood inherited either the genotype AA or AO. A person with phenotype B blood inherited either genotype BB or BO. For a person to have type AB blood, an A allele must be inherited from one parent and a B allele must be inherited from the other parent. Finally, a person with phenotype O blood has inherited an O allele from each parent and has the genotype OO.

Polygenic Inheritance

Eye color is an example of a single trait that is produced by a combination of many genes. **Polygenic** (pahl ih JEHN ihk) **inheritance** occurs when a group of gene pairs acts together to produce a single trait. The effect of each allele may be small, but the combination produces a wide variety. For this reason, it may be hard to classify all the different shades of blue or brown eyes in your class. Fingerprints, such as those shown in **Figure 6-8,** are inherited through a combination of gene pairs.

Try at Home

Mini Lab

Interpreting Fingerprints
Procedure

1. Look at **Figure 6-8** to see some of the differences shown by fingerprints.
2. With a pencil lead, rub a spot large enough for your finger onto a piece of paper.
3. Rub your finger in the pencil markings.
4. Stick clear tape to your finger.
5. Remove the tape and stick it on the paper.
   CAUTION: Wash hands after taking fingerprints.
6. Using a magnifying lens, observe your fingerprints to see if you can find a whorl, arch, or loop pattern.

Analysis
1. What patterns did you find?
2. Are fingerprints inherited as a simple Mendelian pattern or as a more complex pattern?

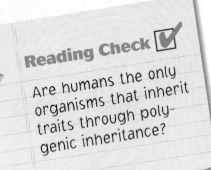

Reading Check ☑

Are humans the only organisms that inherit traits through polygenic inheritance?

Many human traits are controlled by polygenic inheritance, as shown in **Figure 6-9.** Height; weight; body build; and shape of eyes, lips, and ears are examples of some of these traits. It is estimated that skin color is controlled by three to six genes. Even more gene pairs may control the color of your hair and eyes. It is important to note that environment also plays an important role in the expression of traits controlled by polygenic inheritance.

Polygenic inheritance is, of course, not limited to human traits. Grain color in wheat, milk production in cows, and egg production in chickens are also polygenic traits. ☑

The study of genes is no longer a simple look at a single trait controlled by one pair of alleles. Do you think Mendel would be amazed if he could see the amount of progress in genetics that began with his work?

Figure 6-9 Hair color, skin color, and eye color in humans are the results of the expression of more than one pair of genes.

Section Assessment

1. Compare inheritance by multiple alleles and polygenic inheritance.

2. Explain why a trait inherited by incomplete dominance is not a blend of two alleles.

3. Give an example of a trait that is inherited by polygenic inheritance, one controlled by multiple alleles, and one that exhibits incomplete dominance.

4. **Think Critically:** A chicken that is purebred for black feathers is crossed with one that is purebred for white feathers. All the offspring produced have gray feathers. How is the trait inherited? Explain your answer.

5. **Skill Builder**
   Making and Using Graphs
   Many genetic traits are produced by a combination of genes. Do the **Chapter 6 Skill Activity** on page 711. Make and use a graph that shows the effect of polygenic inheritance.

Science Journal

In your Science Journal, write an essay that explains why the offspring of two parents may or may not show much resemblance to either parent.

How it Works

DNA Fingerprinting

DNA (deoxyribonucleic acid) is the molecule in each cell that contains information directing the cell's growth and development (see double helix, left background). DNA fingerprinting identifies you by distinguishing your DNA from the DNA of everyone else. DNA fingerprinting is based on the uniqueness of everyone's DNA, just as hand fingerprints are unique. Scientists extract cells from different areas of a person's body and process the DNA so that it appears as a pattern of dark bands. The bands show the composition of that person's DNA and form the DNA fingerprint.

HOW DNA FINGERPRINTS ARE MADE

1 Scientists use material from a person's cells to obtain DNA.

2 DNA is cut into pieces of varying sizes.

3 The pieces of DNA are placed in a gel. Then an electrical charge causes the DNA fragments to separate, with smaller pieces collecting toward the bottom of the gel.

4 The DNA sample is exposed to X-ray film or a stain so that a pattern of black bars can be seen.

5 Scientists "read" the pattern, which is unique to the person from whom the DNA was taken.

Forensic scientists (those who apply scientific knowledge to legal problems) use DNA fingerprints to identify a crime suspect or to prove someone innocent.

Medical scientists also use DNA fingerprinting to detect the presence of genetic diseases and to predict the chances of a successful transplant. Because a DNA fingerprint provides a genetic profile, scientists can predict the success of a transplant by comparing the profile of the donor with that of the recipient.

Think Critically

1. Cells from which parts of your body can be used to determine your DNA fingerprint?

2. In addition to the applications mentioned here, how else might DNA fingerprinting be used?

interNET CONNECTION

Visit the Glencoe Science Web Site at **www.glencoe.com/sec/ science/ca** to learn more about forensics and the process of DNA fingerprinting.

Determining Polygenic Inheritance

Materials
- Meter stick
- Graph paper
- Pencil

When several genes at different locations on chromosomes act together to produce a single trait, a wide range of phenotypes for the trait can result. By measuring the range of phenotypes and graphing them, you can determine if a trait is produced by polygenic inheritance. How would graphs differ if traits were inherited in a simple dominant or recessive pattern?

What You'll Investigate

How can the effect of polygenic inheritance be determined?

Goals

- **Measure** the heights of students to the nearest centimeter.
- **Create** a bar graph of phenotypes for a polygenic trait.

Safety Precautions

Always obtain the permission of any person included in an experiment on human traits.

Procedure

1. **Form a hypothesis** about what a bar graph that shows the heights of students in your class will look like.

2. **Measure** and record the height of every student to the nearest centimeter.

3. **Design** a table on your paper like the one shown. Count the number of students for each interval and complete the table.

4. **Plot** the results from the table on a bar graph. The height should be graphed on the horizontal axis and the number of students of each height along the vertical axis. If you need help, refer to Making and Using Graphs in the **Skill Handbook** on page 681.

5. The *range* of a set of data is the difference between the greatest measurement and the smallest measurement. The *median* is the middle number when the data are placed in order. The *mean* is the sum of all the data divided by the sample size. The *mode* is the number that appears most often in the measurements. Calculate each of these numbers and record them in your Science Journal.

Conclude and Apply

1. How does this bar graph differ from one produced for a trait controlled by a single gene?

2. How can you tell if a trait is controlled by more than one gene?

3. Can you **infer** from your data that height is controlled by more than two genes? Explain why or why not.

Student Height	
Height in cm	**Number of Students**
A 101–110	
B 111–120	
C 121–130	
D 131–140	
E 141–150	
F 151–160	
G 161–170	
H 171–180	

Human Genetics

Genes and Health

Sometimes, a gene undergoes a mutation that results in an unwanted trait. Not all mutations are harmful, but some have resulted in genetic disorders among humans. Sickle-cell anemia and cystic fibrosis are two disorders that result from changes in DNA.

Recessive Genetic Disorders

Sickle-cell anemia is a homozygous recessive disorder in which red blood cells are sickle shaped instead of disc shaped, as shown in **Figure 6-10.** Sickle-shaped cells can't deliver enough oxygen to the cells in the body. In addition, the misshapen cells don't move through blood vessels easily. As a result, body tissues may be damaged due to insufficient oxygen. Sickle-cell anemia is most commonly found in tropical areas and in a small percentage of African Americans. Many people with sickle-cell anemia die as children, but some live longer. Sickle-cell anemia patients can be treated with drugs to increase the amount of oxygen carried by red blood cells or by transfusions of blood containing normal cells. Because sickle-cell anemia is homozygous recessive, it is possible to carry the sickle-cell allele and not have the disease. In fact, those heterozygous for sickle-cell anemia have been shown to be more resistant to malaria than those not carrying the sickle-cell trait.

What You'll Learn

► Two human genetic disorders and how they are inherited
► How sex-linked traits are inherited
► The importance of genetic engineering

Vocabulary
sex-linked gene
pedigree
genetic engineering

Why It's Important

► Human genetics and heredity explain why you look the way you do.

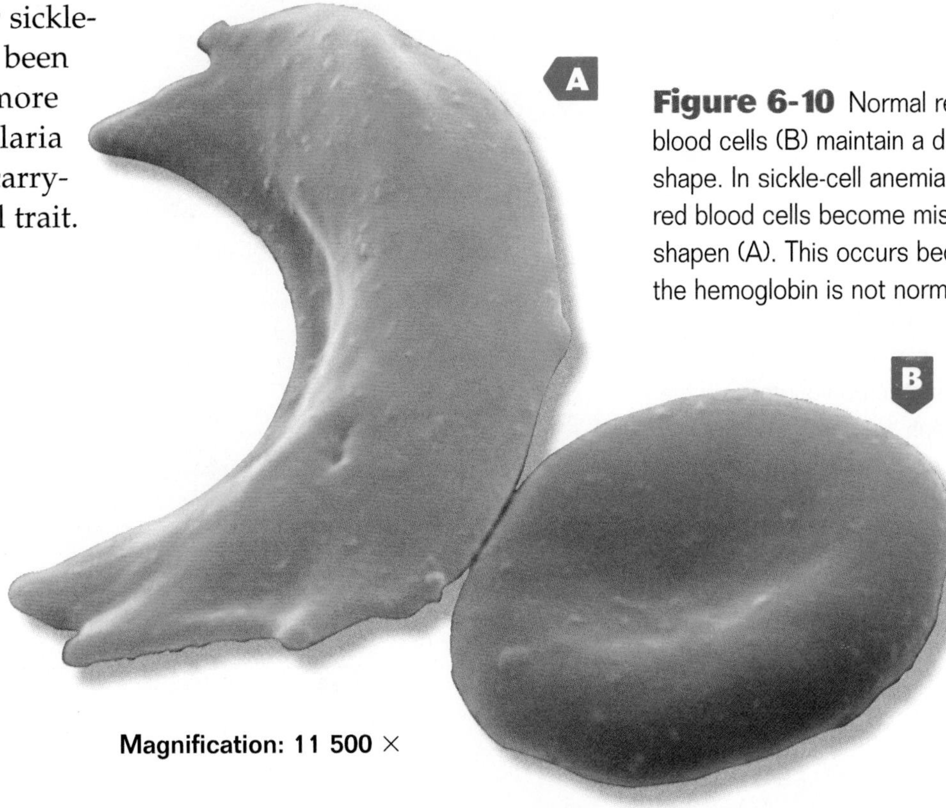

A

Figure 6-10 Normal red blood cells (B) maintain a disc shape. In sickle-cell anemia, red blood cells become misshapen (A). This occurs because the hemoglobin is not normal.

B

Magnification: 11 500 ×

Using Math

If 30 000 Caucasian Americans live in one town, how many are expected to carry the recessive allele for cystic fibrosis? To calculate the expected results, multiply the probability of two people being heterozygous for the trait. Multiply that result by the population.

Cystic fibrosis is another homozygous recessive disorder. In most people, a thin fluid is produced by the body to lubricate the lungs and intestinal tract. Instead of a thin fluid, people with cystic fibrosis have thick mucus in these areas which builds up in the lungs and digestive system. Mucus in the lungs makes it hard to breathe and is often the site of bacterial infection. Mucus in the digestive tract reduces or prevents the flow of digestive enzymes to food in the intestine. These enzymes are needed to break down food so that it can be absorbed by your body.

Cystic fibrosis is the most commonly inherited genetic disorder among Caucasians. Nearly one Caucasian in 25 carries a recessive allele for this disorder. In the United States, four Caucasian babies are born with this disorder every day. Patients with cystic fibrosis are often helped with antibiotics, special diets, and physical therapy to break up the thick mucus in their lungs and help them cough it out.

Sex Determination

What determines the sex of an individual? Information on sex inheritance in many organisms, including humans, came from a study of fruit flies. Fruit flies have eight chromosomes. Among these chromosomes are either two X chromosomes,

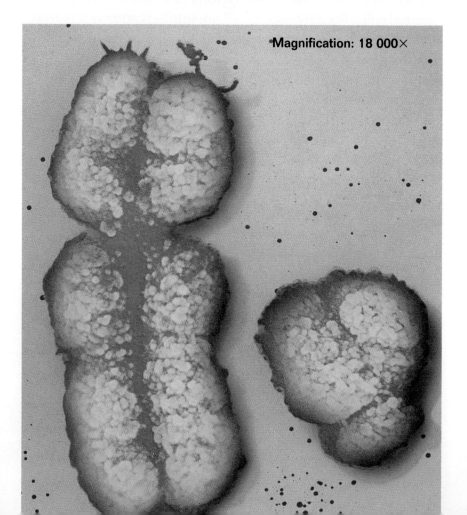

Figure 6-11 Sex in many organisms is determined by X (left) and Y (right) chromosomes. In the photograph, you can see how X and Y chromosomes differ from one another in shape and size.

or an X chromosome and a Y chromosome. Scientists have concluded that the X and Y chromosomes contain genes that determine the sex of an individual. Females have two X chromosomes in their cells. Males have an X chromosome and a Y chromosome. You can see an X and a Y chromosome in **Figure 6-11.** Is this individual male or female?

Females produce eggs that have only an X chromosome. Males produce both X-containing sperm and Y-containing sperm. When an egg from a female is fertilized by an X sperm, the offspring is XX, a female. When an egg from a female is fertilized by a Y sperm, the zygote produced is XY, and the offspring is a male. Sometimes chromosomes fail to separate properly during meiosis. When this occurs, an individual may inherit an abnormal number of sex chromosomes, as in **Figure 6-12.** What pair of sex chromosomes is in each of your cells?

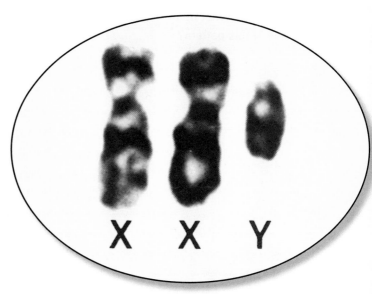

Figure 6-12 The chromosomes above are from an individual with Klinefelter syndrome. This syndrome, in which a male inherits an extra X chromosome, occurs once in every 2000 live births.

Problem Solving

Predicting a Baby's Gender

Probability refers to the chance that an event will occur. For example, if you flip a coin, it will land in only one of two ways—heads or tails. The probability of the coin landing heads or tails is one out of two, or 50 percent. If you were to toss two coins at the same time, each coin still has only a one-half probability of landing with heads or tails up.

What is the probability that any single pregnancy will result in the birth of a girl?

Rosalinda's mother is going to have a baby.

Rosalinda already has a brother, so she really hopes this baby is a girl. How would you determine the chance that this baby will be a girl?

Solve the Problem: How can the outcome of each pregnancy be predicted?

Think Critically: Does the fact that Rosalinda's mother already has one boy and one girl affect the probability of the next child being a girl? Why or why not?

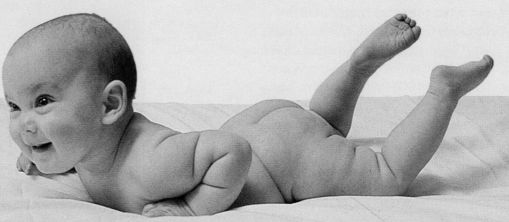

Figure 6-13 What number do you see in this pattern?

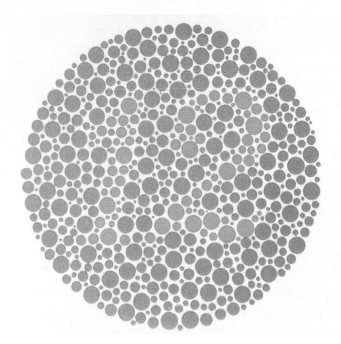

*inter*NET
CONNECTION

Visit the Glencoe Science Web Site at **www.glencoe.com/ sec/science/ca** for more information about recent developments in genetics.

Sex-Linked Disorders

Some inherited conditions are closely linked with the X and Y chromosomes that determine the sex of an individual. A story is told about a young boy who appeared to have normal intelligence but couldn't be taught to pick ripe cherries on the family farm. His parents took him to a doctor. After observing him, the doctor concluded that the boy couldn't tell the difference between the colors red and green. Individuals who are red-green color blind have inherited an allele on the X chromosome that prevents them from seeing these colors. Find out if you are color blind by looking at **Figure 6-13.**

An allele inherited on a sex chromosome is called a **sex-linked gene.** More males are color blind than females. Can you figure out why? If a male inherits an X chromosome with

Figure 6-14 Color blindness is a recessive sex-linked trait. Females who are heterozygous see colors normally, but their sons may be color blind. When a woman with normal vision who carries one allele for color blindness (XX^C) marries a man with normal vision (XY), their children may have normal vision (XX, XY), be carriers (XX^C), or be color blind (X^{C}Y). **Why aren't the daughters of this marriage color blind?**

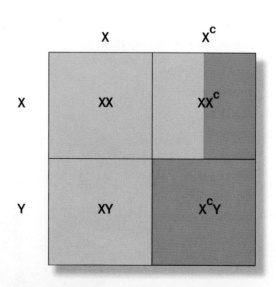

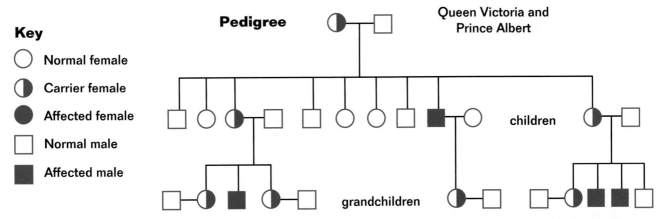

Key

○ Normal female

◐ Carrier female

● Affected female

□ Normal male

■ Affected male

Pedigree

Queen Victoria and Prince Albert

children

grandchildren

Figure 6-15 Pedigrees show the occurrence of a trait in a family. The icons in the key mean the same thing on all pedigree charts. Queen Victoria was a carrier of the recessive allele for hemophilia. **How many of her grandchildren on this chart are hemophiliacs? How many are carriers?**

the color-blind allele from his mother, he will be color blind. Color-blind females are rare. **Figure 6-14** shows how males and females inherit the genes that result in color blindness.

Another sex-linked disorder is hemophilia. For people with this disorder, even a scrape can be life threatening because blood does not clot properly. Like color blindness, males who inherit the X chromosome with the hemophilia allele will have the disorder. For a female to be a hemophiliac, she must inherit the defective allele on both X chromosomes. Hemophilia occurs in fewer than 1 in 7000 males. Females are usually carriers, having just one allele for hemophilia.

Pedigrees Trace Traits

How can you trace a trait through a family? A **pedigree** is a tool for tracing the occurrence of a trait in a family. Males are represented by squares and females by circles. A circle or square that is completely filled in shows that the person has the condition. Half-colored circles or squares indicate carriers. A carrier has an allele for a trait but does not express the trait. People represented by empty circles or squares are neither carriers nor affected by the trait. You can see how the trait for hemophilia was inherited in Queen Victoria of England's family in the pedigree in **Figure 6-15.** ☑

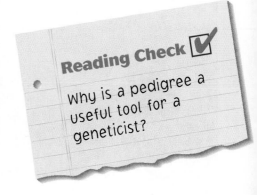

Reading Check ☑

Why is a pedigree a useful tool for a geneticist?

Why is genetics important?

If Mendel were to pick up a daily newspaper in any country today, he probably would be surprised. News articles about developments in genetic research appear almost daily. The term *gene* has become a household word. In this chapter, you have learned that nearly every trait you have inherited is the result of genes expressing themselves. The same laws that govern the inheritance of traits in humans govern the inheritance of traits in wheat and in mice.

In this section, you've seen that there are inherited disorders that affect the human population. You may even know someone with one of these disorders. Many genetic disorders are controlled by diet and preventive measures. Genetics is no longer something that you read about only in textbooks.

Knowing how genes are inherited causes some people to seek the advice of a genetic counselor before having children. Couples who discover genetic traits that could lead to disorders in their children sometimes elect to adopt healthy children instead.

Genetic Engineering

Through **genetic engineering,** scientists are experimenting with biological and chemical methods to change the DNA sequence that makes up a gene. Genetic engineering is already used to help produce large quantities of medicine, such as insulin, to meet the needs of people with a disease called diabetes. Genes also can be inserted into cells to change how those cells perform their normal functions, as shown in **Figure 6-16.** Genetic engineering research also is being used to find new ways to improve crop production and quality, including the development of plants that are resistant to disease.

Magnification: 4290×

Figure 6-16 Genetically engineered bacteria (A) have been developed to clean up environmental problems such as this oil spill in Wales (B). Such bacteria have alleles inserted into them that allow them to break down oil more efficiently than normal bacteria found in the environment.

New Plants from Old

One type of genetic engineering involves identifying genes that are responsible for desirable traits in one plant, then inserting these genes into other plants. In barley, for example, a single gene has been identified that controls several traits—including time of maturity, strength, height, and resistance to drought. Researchers plan to insert this gene into plants such as wheat, rice, and soybeans to create shorter, stronger, drought-resistant plants. Why are these traits of interest to scientists? Wheat, rice, and soybeans are subject to lodging, a condition in which plants fall over because of their own height and weight. If a new gene from the barley plant could result in shorter wheat or rice plants, fewer plants would be lost and crop yields would increase. This gene could even be used to develop lawn grass that stays a certain height and doesn't need to be watered as often. Already, corn and cotton have undergone genetic engineering to enable them to better withstand pests. Research on genetic engineering in plants is done at centers such as the one shown in **Figure 6-17.**

Figure 6-17 Researchers at the International Rice Research Institute in the Philippines are using genetic engineering techniques to develop new strains of rice.

Section Assessment

1. Describe two genetic disorders.
2. Explain why males are affected more often than females by sex-linked genetic disorders.
3. Describe the importance of genetic engineering.
4. **Think Critically:** Use a Punnett square to explain how a woman who is a carrier for color blindness can have a daughter who is color blind.
5.  **Skill Builder**
   Concept Mapping
   Use a network tree concept map to show how X and Y sex cells can combine to form fertilized eggs. Begin with female sex cells, each containing an X chromosome. Use two male sex cells. Indicate one with an X chromosome and one with a Y chromosome. If you need help, refer to Concept Mapping in the **Skill Handbook** on page 678.

Science Journal
Hugo de Vries, Walter Sutton, Barbara McClintock, and Thomas Hunt Morgan each made discoveries in the field of genetics. Research these scientists and summarize their work in your Science Journal, discussing the importance of their contributions.

For a **preview** of this chapter, study this Reviewing Main Ideas before you read the chapter. After you have studied this chapter, you can use the Reviewing Main Ideas to **review** the chapter.

The Glencoe MindJogger, Audiocassettes, and CD-ROM provide additional opportunities for review.

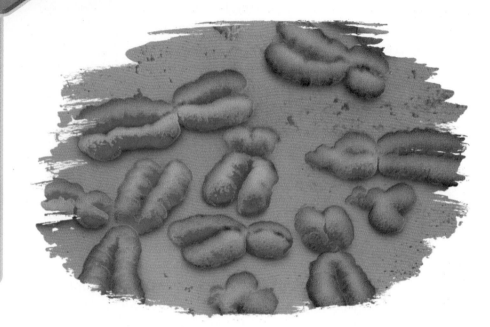

Section

6-1 GENETICS

Genetics is the study of how traits are inherited through the actions of **alleles.** Gregor Mendel determined the basic laws of genetics.

1. Traits are controlled by alleles on chromosomes.
2. An allele may be dominant or recessive in form.
3. When a pair of chromosomes separates during meiosis, the different alleles for a trait move into separate sex cells.

He found that traits followed the laws of probability and that he could predict the outcome of genetic crosses. *How can a Punnett square help to predict inheritance of traits?*

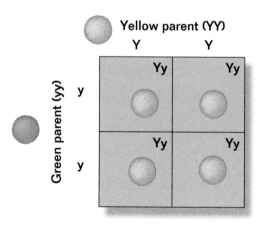

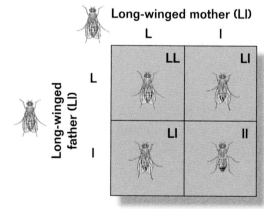

Reading Check ☑

List prefixes that help determine word meanings, such as *re-*, *in-*, and *poly-*. Look up the meanings of these prefixes.

Section 6-2 GENETICS SINCE MENDEL

Some inheritance patterns have been determined that Mendel did not see. Some patterns studied since Mendel include **incomplete dominance, multiple alleles,** and **polygenic inheritance**. These inheritance patterns allow a greater variety of phenotypes to be produced than would result from simple Mendelian inheritance. *Define incomplete dominance, multiple alleles, and polygenic inheritance, and give an example of each.*

Section 6-3 HUMAN GENETICS

Some disorders are the results of inheritance and can be harmful, even deadly, to those affected. **Pedigrees** may help to reveal patterns of inheritance of a trait in a family. Pedigrees show that males express **sex-linked** traits more often than females. Breakthroughs in the field of genetic engineering are allowing scientists to do many things, including producing plants that are resistant to disease. *How may genetic engineering result in solutions to problems caused by human genetic disorders?*

Chapter **6** Assessment

Using Vocabulary

a. alleles
b. dominant
c. genetic engineering
d. genetics
e. genotype
f. heredity
g. heterozygous
h. homozygous
i. incomplete dominance
j. multiple alleles
k. pedigree
l. phenotype
m. polygenic inheritance
n. Punnett square
o. recessive
p. sex-linked gene

Each phrase below describes a vocabulary term from the list. Write the term that matches the phrase describing it.

1. gene located on the X chromosome
2. different form of the same gene
3. a tool for predicting possible offspring
4. the study of heredity
5. shows the pattern of gene inheritance in a family

Checking Concepts

Choose the word or phrase that best answers the question.

6. Which of the following are located on chromosomes?
   A) genes
   B) pedigrees
   C) carbohydrates
   D) zygotes

7. Which of the following describes the allele that causes color blindness?
   A) dominant
   B) carried on the Y chromosome
   C) carried on the X chromosome
   D) present only in females

8. What is it called when two different alleles combine to form an intermediate phenotype?
   A) incomplete dominance
   B) polygenic inheritance
   C) multiple alleles
   D) sex-linked genes

9. What separates during meiosis?
   A) proteins
   B) phenotypes
   C) alleles
   D) pedigrees

10. What do genes control?
    A) chromosomes
    B) traits
    C) cell membranes
    D) mitosis

11. How is blood type inherited?
    A) polygenic inheritance
    B) multiple alleles
    C) incomplete dominance
    D) recessive genes

12. How is sickle-cell anemia inherited?
    A) polygenic inheritance
    B) multiple alleles
    C) incomplete dominance
    D) recessive genes

13. How is eye shape inherited?
    A) polygenic inheritance
    B) multiple alleles
    C) incomplete dominance
    D) recessive genes

14. For a normal female to be produced, what must the father contribute?
    A) an X chromosome
    B) XX chromosomes
    C) a Y chromosome
    D) XY chromosomes

15. Which of the following is a Punnett square used for?
    A) to dominate the outcome of a cross
    B) to predict the outcome of a cross
    C) to assure the outcome of a cross
    D) to number the outcome of a cross

Thinking Critically

16. Explain the relationship among DNA, genes, alleles, and chromosomes.

17. How can advances in genetic engineering help in places that are subject to food shortages caused by drought?

18. Explain how an organism with a genotype *Gg* and an organism with the genotype *GG* could have the same phenotype.

Developing Skills

If you need help, refer to the Skill Handbook.

19. **Designing an Experiment:** Design an experiment to determine if a trait is transmitted by a dominant or recessive gene.

20. **Concept Mapping:** On a separate sheet of paper, use the following terms to complete the network tree concept map below: *phenotypes, recessive, genes,* and *dominant.*

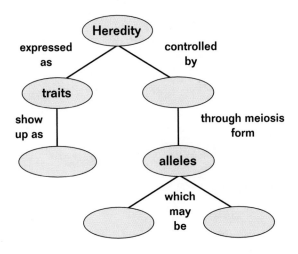

THE PRINCETON REVIEW

Test-Taking Tip

Don't Cram If you don't know the material by the week before the test, you're less likely to do well. Set up a time line for your practice and preparation so that you're not rushed. Then you will have time to deal with any problem areas.

Test Practice

Use these questions to test your Science Proficiency.

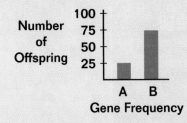

1. From the graph above, what is the inheritance pattern?
   A) dominant recessive
   B) incomplete dominance
   C) multiple alleles
   D) polygenic inheritance

2. Which of the following is true about inheritance of sex-linked traits?
   A) Sex-linked traits occur only in females.
   B) Sex-linked traits are inherited most frequently by males.
   C) Sex-linked traits require many genes to be inherited.
   D) Sex-linked traits occur equally often in males and females.

Change Through Time

Skills Preview

Skill Builders
- Make a Table
- Map Concepts

Activities
- Collect and Organize Data
- Formulate a Model

MiniLabs
- Make a Model
- Infer

Reading Check ✔

Before reading this chapter, list the kinds of images you expect to see. Compare this list with the images you find as you read.

Explore Activity

The Central Indian Tiger is a fierce hunter. It preys mostly on large mammals, including lions and other tigers. If injured or unable to get food, tigers have even been known to eat humans. Because tigers can run swiftly only for a short distance, they must conceal themselves so they can spring on their prey and kill it before it gets away. Tigers are camouflaged according to their natural environment. The tiger on the opposite page is colored perfectly for its surroundings. Its stripes blend in with the tall grass, making it almost invisible as it stalks its prey.

Model Camouflage

1. Spread a sheet of classified ads from a newspaper on the floor.

2. Using a hole punch, punch out 100 circles each from sheets of white paper, black paper, and classified ads.

3. Scatter the paper circles on the spread-out sheets of classified ads. Pick up as many paper circles as possible for 10 s. Have a partner time you.

4. Count each kind of paper circle that you picked up. Then, pour the circles back on the newspaper pages.

5. Repeat steps 3 and 4 three times. Graph your data.

Science Journal

In your Science Journal, describe which paper circles were most difficult to find. What can you infer from this activity?

7•1 Mechanisms of Evolution

Early Thoughts About Evolution

On Earth today, there are millions of different types of organisms. Among these organisms are different species of plants, animals, bacteria, fungi, and protists. A **species** is a group of organisms with members that reproduce among themselves in their natural environment. Have any of these species of organisms changed since they first appeared on Earth? Are they still changing today? Evidence from observation of fossils indicates that living things have changed through time and are still changing. Change in the hereditary features of a species over time is **evolution.** For example, **Figure 7-2** shows how the camel has changed over time.

In 1809, Jean Baptiste de Lamarck, a French scientist, proposed one of the first explanations as to how species evolve or change. Lamarck hypothesized that species evolve by keeping traits that their parents develop during their lives. Characteristics that are not used are lost from the species. According to Lamarck's theory of evolution, if the parents lift weights, their children will be born with muscles stronger or larger than children of people who do not lift weights. Lamarck's explanation of evolution is often called the theory of acquired characteristics.

Figure 7-1 Lamarck's explanation can be tested by experimentation. Weight lifters do not produce offspring with muscles that are larger or stronger than those of children produced by people who do not lift weights.

What You'll Learn

► Lamarck's explanation of evolution and Darwin's theory of evolution
► The importance of variations in organisms
► How gradualism and punctuated equilibrium describe the rate of evolution

Vocabulary

species
evolution
natural selection
variation
gradualism
punctuated equilibrium

Why It's Important

► The theory of evolution explains why living things are different and predicts changes that will occur.

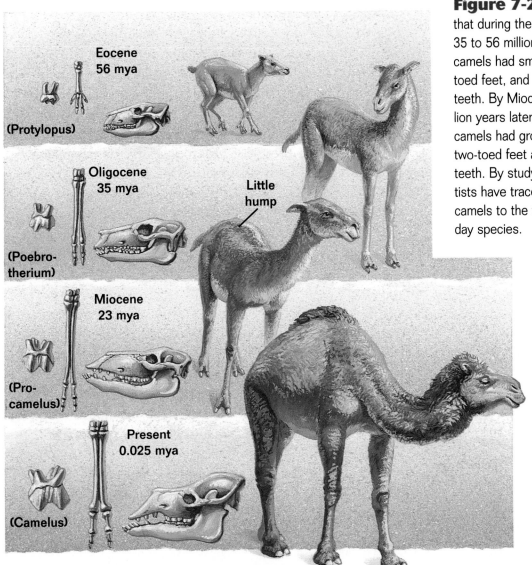

Figure 7-2 Fossils indicate that during the Eocene epoch, 35 to 56 million years ago, camels had small body size, four-toed feet, and low-crowned teeth. By Miocene times, 33 million years later, species of camels had grown larger and had two-toed feet and high-crowned teeth. By studying fossils, scientists have traced the evolution of camels to the forms of present-day species.

Genes on chromosomes control the inheritance of traits. The traits that develop during an organism's life, such as large muscles, as shown in **Figure 7-1,** are not inherited. After scientists collected large amounts of information on the inheritance of characteristics, Lamarck's explanation was rejected. The data showed that characteristics an organism develops or acquires during its lifetime aren't passed on to its offspring. ☑

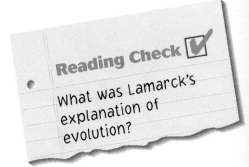

Reading Check ☑

What was Lamarck's explanation of evolution?

Evolution by Natural Selection

In the mid-1800s, Charles Darwin came up with the theory of evolution that is still accepted today. At the age of 22, Darwin became the ship's naturalist aboard HMS *Beagle.* The *Beagle* was on a trip to survey the east and west coasts of South America. The ship sailed from England in December 1831. Darwin's work was to record facts about all the plants and animals he observed during the journey.

Darwin's Observations

Darwin collected many plants, animals, and fossils from stops all along his route, which is shown in **Figure 7-3.** He was amazed by the variety of plants and animals he found in the Galápagos Islands. The Galápagos Islands are off the coast of Ecuador. The plants and animals Darwin saw in these islands must have come from Central and South America, yet on these 19 small islands, he found many species that he had not seen before. He observed giant cactus trees, 13 species of finches, and huge land tortoises, but he saw few other reptiles, only nine mammal species, and no amphibians at all. Darwin became particularly interested in the finches. He wondered how so many different, but closely related, species of finches could live on islands just a few miles apart.

For 20 years after the voyage, Darwin continued studying his collections. He thought about his observations and made further studies. He collected evidence of variations among species by breeding pigeons for racing. He also studied breeds of dogs and varieties of flowers. Darwin knew that people selected traits they wanted in plant and animal offspring by breeding parents that had those traits.

Figure 7-3 A map of Darwin's voyage is illustrated below. Some of the unique organisms he found in the Galápagos Islands included a cactus tree, a land iguana, a finch, and a giant tortoise.

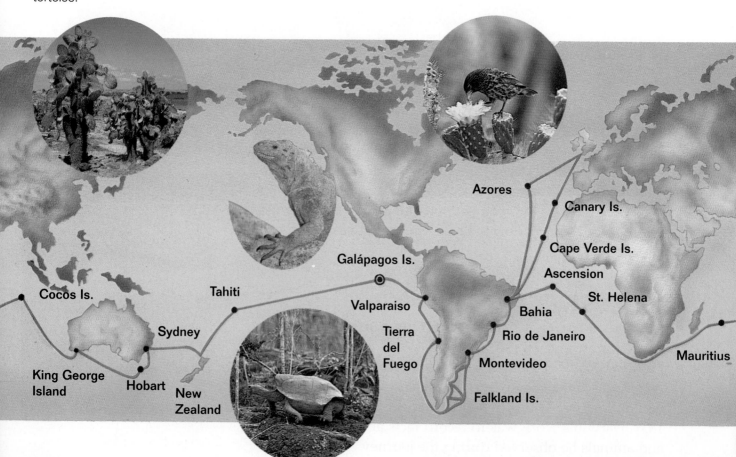

Azores

Canary Is.

Cape Verde Is.

Ascension

St. Helena

Cocos Is.

Tahiti

Galápagos Is.

Valparaiso

Bahia

Rio de Janeiro

Mauritius

Sydney

Tierra del Fuego

Montevideo

King George Island

Hobart

New Zealand

Falkland Is.

Principles of Natural Selection

Darwin's observations suggested that organisms with traits most favorable for their environment survived and passed these traits on to their offspring. After many experiments, Darwin's hypothesis became the theory of evolution by natural selection. **Natural selection** means that organisms with traits best suited to their environment are more likely to survive and reproduce. The factors identified in natural selection are as follows.

1. Organisms produce more offspring than can survive.
2. Variations are found among individuals of a species.
3. Variations are passed on to offspring.
4. Some variations allow members of a population to survive and reproduce better than others.
5. Over time, offspring of individuals with helpful variations make up more and more of a population.

Darwin wrote a book describing his theory of evolution by natural selection. His book, *On the Origin of Species by Means of Natural Selection*, was published in 1859. Some changes have been made to Darwin's theory as new information has been gathered. However, his theory remains one of the most important ideas in the study of life science.

*inter***NET**
CONNECTION

Visit the Glencoe Science Web Site at **www.glencoe.com/ sec/science/ca** for more information about the finches Darwin observed.

Problem Solving

When can some fish be sold?

Alejandro has decided to raise tropical fish as a hobby and to sell his extra fish to a local store to make some spending money. In his research, Alejandro learned that each tropical fish requires one gallon of water. Eventually, they will produce more young than can be kept in his 30-gallon aquarium. He knew that he wanted to keep his most beautiful fish and sell the others. Alejandro realized that selecting fish in this way would be similar to Charles Darwin's theory of evolution by natural selection.

Solve the Problem

1. Assume Alejandro buys one pair of adult fish that just produced young. The species of fish Alejandro bought produce equal numbers of males and females. Each adult pair of fish begins to breed when they are two months old and produce ten young every subsequent two months. Also

assume that all of the young survive to reproduce. How many fish will Alejandro have after two months?

2. If Alejandro continues to raise fish, how long will it be before he must sell some fish or get another aquarium?

Think Critically: How does Alejandro's problem relate to the first factor that governs natural selection as listed at the top of this page?

Adaptation and Variation

One of the points in Darwin's theory is that differences are found among individuals of a species. These differences are called variations. A **variation** is an inherited trait that makes an individual different from other members of the same species. Variations can be small, such as differences in the shape of human hairlines, or large, such as an albino squirrel in a population of gray squirrels, or fruit without seeds. Variations are important in populations of organisms. A population is a group of organisms of one species that live in an area. If enough variations occur in a population as it produces new offspring, a new species may evolve from the existing species. It may take hundreds, thousands, or even millions of generations for a new species to evolve.

The Sources of Variations

Some variations are more helpful than others. An adaptation is any variation that makes an organism better suited to its environment. The variations that result in adaptation can be in an organism's color, shape, behavior, or chemical makeup. Camouflage is an adaptation that lets an organism blend into its environment, as shown in **Figure 7-4A.** An organism that can camouflage itself is more likely to survive and reproduce. These types of variations result from mutations, which are changes in an organism's DNA.

What other factors bring about evolution? The movement of individuals of the same species into or out of an area brings in or removes new genes and variations. Have you ever had an exchange student come to your school? The student

Using Math

Use the data from the Explore Activity. The experimental probability of picking up a white circle is as follows.

Probability = white circles ÷ total circles

Find the probability of picking up white, black, and classified ad circles. Are these events equally likely? Is that what actually happened?

Figure 7-4 Variations may be beneficial, harmful, or neutral in a population.

A Camouflage causes some organisms to blend into their environment. **How does camouflage coloration give this spider an advantage in survival?**

B Variations that result in a disadvantage, such as albinism, tend to decrease in a population over time. **What would likely happen to an albino squirrel in its natural environment?**

probably brought new ideas, maybe a new style of dress, and even a new language. When new individuals come into an existing population, they can bring in new genes and variations in much the same way. Some organisms are separated from others by geography and changes in climate. This isolation can result in evolutionary change, as you can see in **Figure 7-5.** Each of these factors affects how fast evolution occurs.

How fast does evolution occur?

Scientists do not agree on the answer to this question. Many scientists hypothesize that evolution occurs slowly, perhaps taking tens or hundreds of millions of years. Other scientists hypothesize that evolution may occur quickly. As you study evolution, you will see that evidence supports both of these models.

Mini Lab

Relating Evolution to Species

Procedure

1. On a piece of paper, print the alphabet in lowercase letters.
2. Order the letters into three groups. Put all of the vowels in the first group. Place all of the consonants that do not drop below the line into the second group and all of the consonants that do drop below the line in the third group.

Analysis

1. How are the three groups of letters similar to each other?
2. If the letters were organisms, how would scientists know how closely related the letters were to each other?

Figure 7-5 The Tana river in Kenya separates two populations of giraffes. Over time, these two populations have become distinct. **Do these giraffes have different appearances? What does this tell you about their genetic makeup?**

A The common giraffe is known as Rothschild's giraffe, *Giraffa camelopardalis rothschildi.*

B This is the reticulated giraffe, *Giraffa camelopardalis reticulata.* The word *reticulated* means "having lines or veins."

Gradualism

Darwin hypothesized that the rate of evolution was steady, slow, and ongoing. The model that describes evolution as a slow change of one species to another, new species is known as **gradualism.** According to the gradualism model, continued mutations and variations will result in a new species over time. According to this model, there should be intermediate forms of all species. Evolution involves a change in the phenotype, or appearance, of a species as its hereditary features change. Look back at **Figure 7-2,** showing evolution of the camel. Fossil evidence shows gradual changes between the camel as it first appeared and how it looks today. Camels appear to have evolved gradually over millions of years. Fossil evidence shows the gradual evolution of many present-day species.

Punctuated Equilibrium

But gradualism doesn't explain the evolution of some species, especially those in which there is a gap in the fossil record because few intermediate forms have been discovered. The **punctuated equilibrium** model, as seen in **Figure 7-6,** shows that rapid evolution can come about by the mutation of just a few genes, resulting in the appearance of a new species. How fast is evolution by this model? New species could appear as quickly as every few million years and sometimes even more rapidly than that. For example, bacteria that cause illness in humans can sometimes be killed by antibiotics such as penicillin. Penicillin has been available only since 1940, yet some species of bacteria are now resistant to this drug. How did this happen so quickly? As in any population, some of the bacteria had variations that allowed them to keep from being

Figure 7-6 Evolution can occur slowly, as in gradualism, or rapidly, as in punctuated equilibrium. In the diagrams below, branches of different colors represent different species. Branches that do not continue to the top of the graph represent species that are extinct and, therefore, are no longer evolving. A change in the phenotype of a species is a change in its appearance.

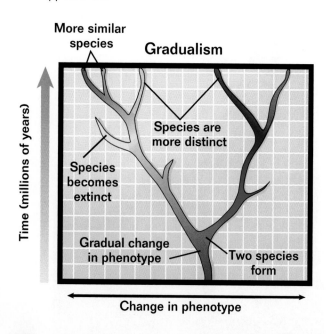

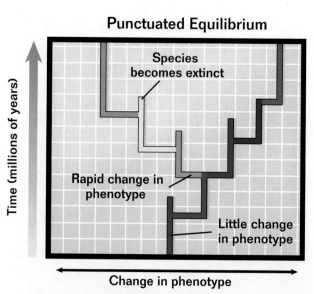

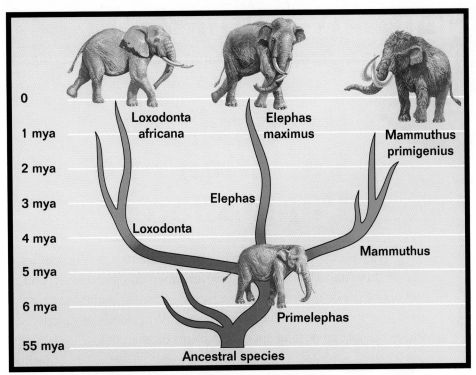

Figure 7-7 The evolution of the elephant illustrates how punctuated equilibrium usually occurs. Notice that three distinct species evolved over 1 million years—a relatively short amount of time. This same change would have taken several million years to occur in gradualism.

killed by penicillin. When the drug was used to kill bacteria, the few individuals with this variation lived to reproduce. Over a short period of time, the entire population of bacteria became resistant to penicillin. The bacteria had evolved quickly—an example of punctuated equilibrium. In this step-like pattern, large changes take place in a short period of time. The fossil record also gives examples of this type of evolution, as you can see in **Figure 7-7.** Punctuated equilibrium and gradualism are compared in **Figure 7-6.**

Section Assessment

1. Compare Lamarck's and Darwin's ideas of evolution.
2. How are variations important in a population?
3. Define what an adaptation is and give an example.
4. **Think Critically:** Explain how the gradualism model of evolution differs from the punctuated equilibrium model.
5. **Skill Builder**
   Making and Using Graphs Do the **Chapter 7 Skill Activity** on page 712 to learn how to make and use a graph.

Using Math

Figure **7-2** states that the evolution of the camel can be traced for at least 56 million years. Use the information in **Figure 7-2** to determine the approximate percent of this time that the modern camel has existed.

Possible Materials

- Leaves, flowers, and seeds from one species of plant
- Metric ruler
- Magnifying glass
- Graph paper

Recognizing Variation in a Population

When you first see a group of plants or animals of one species, they may all look alike. However, when you look closer, you will notice minor differences in each characteristic. Variations must exist in a population for evolution to occur. What kinds of variations have you noticed among species of plants or animals?

Recognize the Problem

How can you measure variation in a plant or animal population?

Form a Hypothesis

Make a hypothesis about the amount of variation in seeds, leaves, or flowers of one species of plant.

Goals

- **Design an experiment** that will allow you to collect data about variation in a population.
- **Observe, measure,** and **analyze** variations in a population.

Safety Precautions

Do not put any seeds, flowers, or plant parts in your mouth. Wash your hands after handling plant parts.

Test Your Hypothesis

Plan

1. As a group, agree upon and write out the hypothesis statement.

2. List the steps you need to take to **test your hypothesis.** Be specific. Describe exactly what you will do at each step. List your materials.

3. Decide what characteristic of seeds, leaves, or flowers you will study. For example, you could **measure** the length of seeds, the width of leaves, or the number of petals on the flowers of plants.

4. **Design a data table** in your Science Journal to collect data about one variation. Use the table to record the data your group collects as you complete the experiment.

5. **Identify** any constants, variables, and controls of the experiment.

6. How many seeds, leaves, or flowers will you examine? Will your data be more accurate if you examine larger numbers?

7. **Summarize** the data in a graph or chart.

Do

1. Make sure your teacher approves your plan before you proceed.

2. Carry out the experiment as planned.

3. While the experiment is going on, write down any observations that you make and complete the data table in your Science Journal.

Analyze Your Data

1. **Compare** your results with those of other groups.

2. How did you determine the amount of variation present?

Draw Conclusions

1. **Graph** your results, placing the *range* of variation on the *x*-axis and the number of organisms that had that measurement on the *y*-axis.

2. **Calculate** the *mean* and *range* of variation in your experiment.

The *range* of a set of data is the difference between the greatest measurement and the smallest measurement. The *mean* is the sum of all the data divided by the sample size.

Evidence for Evolution

Fossil Evidence

On a hot day in July 1975, in northern Texas, two people were walking along the shores of Lake Lavon. They came across some odd-looking rocks sticking up from the muddy shore. They noticed that the rocks seemed different from the surrounding limestone rocks. They took a few of the rocks to a scientist who studies reptiles and amphibians. The rocks were skull pieces of a fossil mosasaur, an extinct lizard that had lived in salt water.

A group of scientists returned to the site and carefully dug up the rest of the fossil mosasaur. This find indicates that about 120 million years ago, the northern Texas area—now more than 500 km from the Gulf of Mexico—was covered by a shallow sea. Fossils such as those found on the shores of Lake Lavon are studied by scientists called paleontologists (pay lee ahn TAHL uh justs), shown in **Figure 7-8**.

Figure 7-8 Digging for fossils requires careful work. Paleontologists, scientists who study the past by examining fossils, sift tons of earth and rock to find tiny bones. They may use dental equipment such as dental picks and toothbrushes to remove dirt as they work to uncover larger bones, such as these dinosaur bones found in Thailand.

VISUALIZING
Fossils

Figure 7-9 Three examples of fossils are shown. **Which of these would most likely be found in a layer of sedimentary rock?**

A This is an imprint fossil made by a leaf.

B An insect caught in amber that hardened over time is also a fossil.

C This is the cast fossil of an ammonite, an extinct marine organism.

Kinds of Fossils

The most evidence for evolution comes from fossils like those found on the shore of Lake Lavon in Texas. A fossil is any evidence of life from an earlier geological time, such as those illustrated in **Figure 7-9.** Examples of fossils include the following.

1. the imprint of a leaf, feather, or organism in rock

2. a cast made of minerals that filled in the hollows of an animal track, mollusk shell, or other parts of an organism

3. a piece of wood or bone replaced by minerals

4. an organism frozen in ice

5. an insect or other organism trapped in amber

Sedimentary rock contains the most fossils. **Sedimentary rock** is a rock type formed from particles of preexisting rocks. These particles can be deposited by water, wind, gravity, or ice. Limestone, sandstone, and shale are all examples of sedimentary rock. Fossils are found more often in limestone than in any other kind of sedimentary rock.

*inter*NET
CONNECTION

Visit the Glencoe Science Web Site at **www.glencoe.com/ sec/science/ca** for more information on fossils.

Table 7-1

Geologic Time Scale							
Era	Cenozoic		Mesozoic			Paleozoic	
Period	Quaternary	Tertiary	Cretaceous	Jurassic	Triassic	Permian	Pennsylvanian
Millions of years ago							

1.6   66   146   208   245   290

Using Math

The Cenozoic era represents approximately 66 million years of Earth's 4.6-billion-year history. Approximately what percent of Earth's total history does this era represent?

The Fossil Record

You learned that the mosasaur fossil found in Texas was 120 million years old. How did scientists come up with this date? Scientists have divided Earth's history into eras and periods. These divisions make up the geologic time scale as shown in **Table 7-1.** Unique rock layers and fossils give information about the geology, weather, and life-forms of each time period. There are two basic methods for reading the record of past life. When these methods are used together, estimates of the ages of certain rocks and fossils can be made.

Relative Dating

One way to find the approximate age of a rock layer, or fossils within the layer, is relative dating. Relative dating is based on the idea that in undisturbed areas, older rock layers lie below younger rock layers, as shown in **Figure 7-10.** Therefore, fossils found in lower layers of rock are older than those in upper layers. Relative dating cannot give the exact age of a fossil. It can give only an estimate of how old the fossil might be.

Radiometric Dating

Scientists can give a more accurate age to a rock layer using radioactive elements. A **radioactive element** gives off radiation due to an unstable nucleus. As radioactive elements give off radiation, they eventually change to more stable products. The radiation is given off at a steady rate

Paleozoic					Precambrian
Mississippian	Devonian	Silurian	Ordovician	Cambrian	
					4600

| 323 | 362 | 408 | 439 | 510 | 543 |

Reading Check ✓

Which is more accurate, relative dating or radiometric dating?

that is different for each element. Scientists can estimate the age of the rock by comparing the amount of radioactive element with the amount of nonradioactive element in the rock. However, this method of dating can produce inconsistent dates. For this reason, scientists analyze many samples of a rock using different methods to obtain more consistent results. ✓

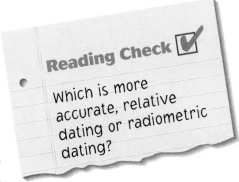

Figure 7-10 Fossils found in lower layers of sedimentary rock are usually older than the fossils found in upper layers.

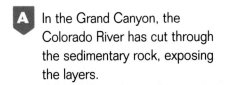

A In the Grand Canyon, the Colorado River has cut through the sedimentary rock, exposing the layers.

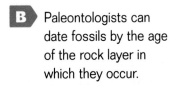

B Paleontologists can date fossils by the age of the rock layer in which they occur.

Figure 7-11 In the Pennsylvanian period, 300 million years ago, amphibians and land plants were the dominant life-forms on Earth. Many of the plants of this period eventually became peat and coal. **Why do we call these fossil fuels?**

Fossils Show Evolution Occurred

Fossils are a record of organisms that lived in the past. But, the fossil record has gaps, much like a book with pages missing. Because every living thing doesn't or can't become fossilized, the record will never be complete. By looking at fossils, scientists conclude that many simpler forms of life existed earlier in Earth's history, and more complex forms of life appeared later. The oldest fossil bacteria appeared about 3.5 billion years ago. Invertebrates with hard shells appeared in the Cambrian period, about 540 million years ago. The first land plants did not appear until the Silurian period, about 439 million years ago. Dinosaurs were common on Earth during the Jurassic and Cretaceous periods, from about 208 to 66 million years ago. The first mammals and birds did not appear until the Jurassic period, about 200 million years ago. **Figure 7-11** shows an artist's drawing of a scene of 300 million years ago. The fossil record gives scientists direct evidence that living things evolved. There are also other types of ideas that support the theory of evolution.

Other Evidence for Evolution

Besides fossils, what other evidence is there for evolution? Scientists have found more evidence by looking at similarities in chemical makeup such as DNA, development, and embryological structure among organisms. You know that the functions of a dolphin's flipper, a bat's wing, and a bird's wing are different. Yet, as you can see in **Figure 7-12,** each of these structures is made up of the same kind of bones. Each has about the same number of muscles and blood vessels. Each of these limbs developed from similar tissues. Body parts that are similar in origin and structure are called **homologous** (huh MAHL uh gus). Homologous structures indicate that two or more species might share common ancestors.

EARTH SCIENCE
INTEGRATION

Importance of Fossils
Many organisms have a history that has been preserved in sedimentary rock. Fossils of animals such as horses and whales have bones that have become reduced in size or number over geologic time as species have evolved. Explain what information can be understood from changes in structures over time.

Figure 7-12 A bird wing, a bat wing, and dolphin flipper are homologous. Each has about the same number of bones, muscles, and blood vessels.

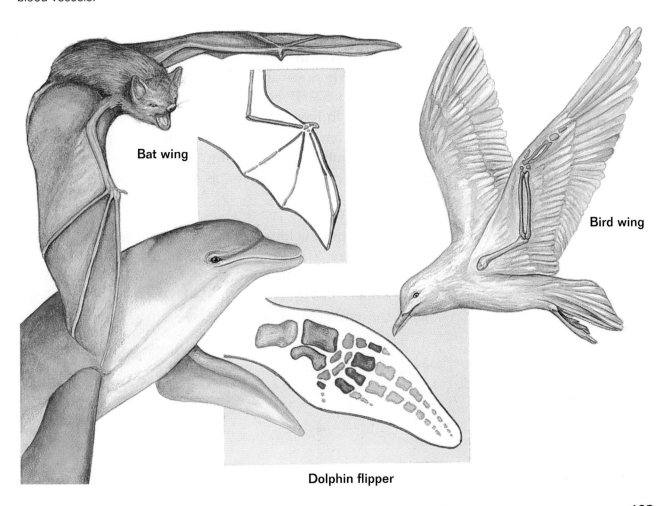

Bat wing

Bird wing

Dolphin flipper

Modern horse

Baleen whale

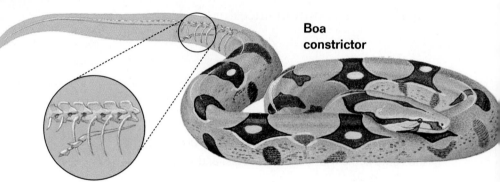

Boa constrictor

Figure 7-13 Do whales or snakes have back legs? You can see that they don't, yet both animals have vestigial hipbones and leg bones where legs may once have existed. Horses once had four functional toes. Now, they walk on just one toe. The others are no longer functional.

Vestigial Structures

Vestigial structures also give evidence for evolution. A **vestigial** (veh STIHJ ee ul) **structure** is a body part that doesn't seem to have a function. For example, manatees no longer have back legs, but they still have pelvic bones. Scientists hypothesize that vestigial structures are parts that once functioned in an ancestor, as seen in **Figure 7-13.**

Embryology

The study of development in organisms is called **embryology** (em bree AHL uh jee). An embryo is an organism in its earliest stages of development. Compare the embryos of the organisms in **Figure 7-14.** In the early stages of development, the embryos of fish, reptiles, birds, and mammals

Figure 7-14 Similarities in the embryos of fish, reptiles, birds, and mammals suggest evolution. Many of the same features are found in all of these organisms. **How can you tell which organism's embryo is which?**

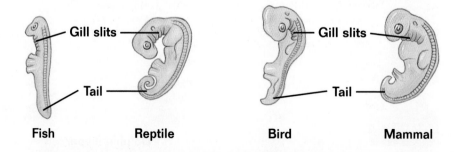

Gill slits

Tail

Fish

Gill slits

Tail

Reptile

Gill slits

Tail

Bird

Tail

Mammal

have a tail and gills or gill slits. The gill slits of fish continue to develop into gills, which are kept throughout life. The gill slits of other organisms are lost during development. Fish, birds, and reptiles keep their tails, but mammals may lose theirs. These similarities suggest an evolutionary relationship among all vertebrate species.

DNA

DNA is the molecule that controls heredity. It is contained on chromosomes and directs the development of every organism. Scientists can determine whether or not organisms are closely related by looking at their DNA. Organisms that are close relatives have similar DNA. By studying DNA, scientists have determined that dogs are the closest relatives of bears. You would not be surprised to learn that primates, such as gorillas, bonobos, and chimpanzees, like the one shown in **Figure 7-15,** also have DNA that is similar.

Genetic evidence also supports the view that primates all evolved from a common ancestor. Primates share many of the same proteins, including hemoglobin. Hemoglobin is a protein in red blood cells that carries oxygen. Many primates have hemoglobin that is nearly the same.

Figure 7-15 The DNA of humans and chimpanzees is similar in many ways.

Section Assessment

1. How are relative and radiometric dating used to interpret the fossil record?

2. How are fossils important evidence of evolution? List the different kinds of fossils.

3. How can DNA provide evidence of evolution?

4. **Think Critically:** Compare and contrast the five types of evidence for evolution.

5. **Skill Builder**
   Making and Using Tables
   Use **Table 7-1,** the geologic time scale, to answer the following questions. Which was the longest period of the Paleozoic era? Which was the shortest? What period began 1.6 million years ago? If you need help, refer to Making and Using Tables in the **Skill Handbook** on page 680.

Using Computers

Spreadsheet Prepare a spreadsheet that contains the name of each era and its corresponding length expressed in millions of years. Use the spreadsheet to make a chart that shows the information graphically. What information becomes more evident from a graphical presentation? If you need help, refer to page 702.

Footprints in Geologic Time

In 1978, a team led by renowned archaeologist Mary Leakey (shown in inset) made an astounding discovery in the Laetoli area of northern Tanzania in Africa. Amid the ancient tracks left by prehistoric giraffes, elephants, and rhinoceros were the fossilized footprints of three hominids—thought to be early ancestors of *Homo sapiens*. Preserved in volcanic ash, the Laetoli footprints (right) are estimated to be some 3.4 million years old.

Settling the Debate

In the minds of many, Leakey's discovery laid to rest the debate as to when our ancestors began to walk upright. The depth and spacing of the footprints indicated that these early hominids, nearly 3.4 million years ago, had erect posture and walked like modern humans. Leakey, who spent more than six decades conducting research in East Africa, considered the find her greatest achievement.

Preserving the Past

After studying the footprints, Leakey's team buried the fossils in sand for preservation. Unknown to them, the sand contained seeds of acacia trees, which soon sprouted. Scientists expressed concern that eventually the tree roots would damage the footprints. In 1994, scientists working with the Tanzanian government began a two-year project to uncover, repair, and then re-cover the footprints. They buried the site in sand, soil, and materials to prevent root growth. The scientists also photographed the footprints again to create more detailed diagrams of each imprint. The diagrams, accurate to within half a millimeter, may help answer lingering questions about the hominids who made the footprints, such as whether they were male or female.

In 1996, Mary Leakey attended an event held at Laetoli by the Masai, a local tribe. Knowing the significance of the site, the Masai have agreed to help protect it.

Science JOURNAL

Many fossils are dug up, then stored in museums for further study and safekeeping. Research why scientists decided not to dig up the Laetoli footprints. Write your findings in your Science Journal.

A Model of Natural Selection

Materials

- Red beans and white beans (10 each)
- Paper bag
- Pencil and paper

Natural selection has been observed in a variety of organisms in nature. Studying natural selection takes a long time because natural selection occurs in populations that may take years to produce a new generation. However, the process occurs in a way that can be explained by a simple model.

What You'll Investigate

What is the result of natural selection?

Safety Precautions

CAUTION: *Do not taste or eat any material used in the lab.*

Procedure

1. Take a paper bag and write "Rabbit Gene Pool" on it.

2. Place ten red beans and ten white beans in the bag.

3. **Make a table** that you can use to record the genetics in the population. **Assume** that the pairs of beans are rabbits. A pair of red beans make a brown rabbit. A red bean and a white bean make a gray rabbit, and a pair of white beans make a white rabbit.

4. Without looking into the bag, take out two beans to represent an offspring. Write the colors of beans in the table.

5. Continue taking beans out of the bag two at a time and writing the results.

6. To model selection, predators eat all of the white rabbits and half of the gray rabbits. For each brown rabbit, place six baby rabbits (two red beans for each rabbit) in the bag along with its parents. For each remaining gray rabbit, do the same thing (one red bean and one white bean for each rabbit).

7. Repeat steps 4 and 5 two more times.

Conclude and Apply

1. How did the rabbit gene pool change during the activity?

2. What eventually happens to the white rabbits?

3. Describe how this model is similar to the way natural selection occurs in nature.

4. How is this model unlike the way natural selection occurs in nature?

Rabbit Offspring	
Rabbit #	**Bean Colors**
1	
2	
3	
4	
5	
6	
7	
8	
9	
10	
11	
12	
13	
14	
15	

7•3 Primate Evolution

Primates

What You'll Learn

▶ The differences in living primates
▶ The adaptations of primates
▶ The evolutionary history of modern primates

Vocabulary
primates
hominids
Homo sapiens

Why It's Important

▶ Studying primate evolution will help you appreciate the differences between humans and other primates.

Monkeys, apes, and humans belong to the group of mammals called **primates.** The primates share several characteristics that lead scientists to think that all primates may have evolved from a common ancestor. All primates have opposable thumbs that allow them to reach out and grasp things, as shown in **Figure 7-16.** Having an opposable thumb allows you to cross your thumb over your palm and touch your fingers. Think of the problems you might have if you didn't have this type of thumb.

Primates also have binocular vision. Binocular vision permits a primate to judge depth or distance with its eyes. All primates have flexible shoulders and rotating forelimbs. These allow tree-dwelling primates to swing easily from branch to branch and allow you to swing on a jungle gym. Each of these characteristics suggests that all primates may share common ancestry.

Figure 7-16 An opposable thumb allows tree-dwelling primates to hold onto branches. It also allows you to use your hand in many ways.

Primate Classification

Primates are divided into two major groups. The first group includes organisms such as lemurs and tarsiers, the prosimians, as shown in **Figure 7-17.** These animals are active at night and have large eyes and excellent hearing. The second group of primates includes monkeys, apes, and humans.

Hominids

About 4 to 6 million years ago, our earliest ancestors branched off from the other primates. These ancestors, called **hominids,** were humanlike primates that ate both meat and vegetables and walked upright on two feet. Hominids shared some common characteristics with gorillas, orangutans, and chimpanzees, but a larger brain size separated them from these other great apes.

African Origins

In the early 1920s, Raymond Dart, a South African scientist, discovered a fossil skull in a quarry in South Africa. The skull had a small space for the brain, but humanlike jaw and teeth. Dart named his discovery *Australopithecus.* He chose the name *Australopithecus* for one of the earliest hominid groups discovered because it means "southern ape." In 1974,

EARTH SCIENCE
INTEGRATION

African Rift Valley
Many fossils from hominids and early humans have been found in the African Rift Valley. This area of Africa is where two tectonic plates of Earth's crust are moving past one another. Do research on this area and draw a map of it in your Science Journal. Write a paragraph that explains why you might expect to find many fossils there.

Figure 7-17 Tarsiers belong to a subgroup of primates called the prosimians, which means "before apes." They are commonly found in the rain forests of Southeast Asia.

Try at Home

Mini Lab

Living Without Thumbs

Procedure

1. Tape your thumb securely to your hand. Do this for both hands.

2. Leave your thumbs taped down for at least two hours. During this time, do the following activities: eat a meal, change clothes, and brush your teeth. Be careful not to try anything that could be dangerous.

3. Write about your experiences in your Science Journal.

Analysis

1. Did not having usable thumbs significantly affect the way you did things? Explain.

2. Infer how having opposable thumbs may have influenced primate evolution.

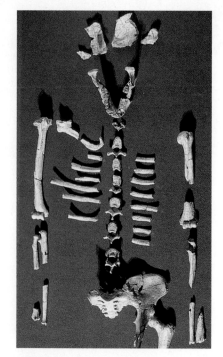

Figure 7-18 The fossil remains of Lucy, a hominid, are estimated to be 2.9 to 3.4 million years old.

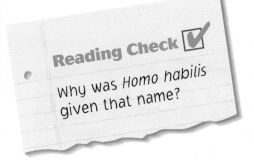

Reading Check ✓

Why was *Homo habilis* given that name?

Figure 7-19 In this photograph, the skull of a Neanderthal, right, can be compared with the skull of a Cro-Magnon, left. **What differences can you see between these two skulls?**

an almost-complete skeleton of *Australopithecus,* as shown in **Figure 7-18,** was discovered by American scientist Donald Johanson and his coworkers. They named the fossil Lucy. Lucy had a small brain but is thought to have walked upright. This fossil is important because it indicates how modern hominids may have evolved.

About 40 years after the discovery of *Australopithecus,* a discovery was made in East Africa by Louis, Mary, and Richard Leakey. The Leakeys discovered a fossil more like present-day humans than *Australopithecus.* They named this hominid *Homo habilis,* the "handy man," because they found simple stone tools near him. Scientists estimate *Homo habilis* to be 1.5 to 2 million years old. ✓

Based upon many fossil comparisons, anthropologists have suggested that *Homo habilis* gave rise to another species about 1.6 million years ago, *Homo erectus. Homo erectus* had a larger brain than *Homo habilis.* This hominid moved out of Africa about 1 million years ago. *Homo habilis* and *Homo erectus* both are thought to be ancestors of humans because they had larger brains and were more like humans than *Australopithecus.*

Modern Humans

Our species is named ***Homo sapiens,*** meaning "wise human." The fossil record indicates that the human species evolved about 400 000 years ago. By about 125 000 years ago, two early groups of *Homo sapiens,* Neanderthals and Cro-Magnon humans, probably lived at the same time in parts of Africa and Europe.

Neanderthals had short, heavy bodies with thick bones; small chins; and heavy browridges, as you can see in **Figure 7-19.** The Neanderthals lived in family groups in caves and, using well-made stone tools, hunted mammoths, deer, and

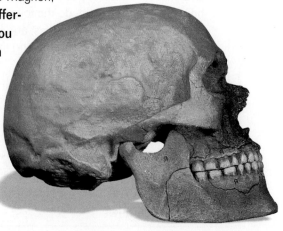

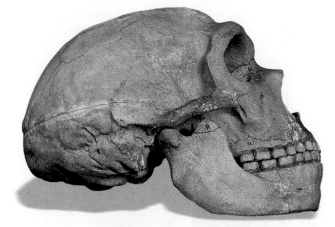

other large animals. For reasons that are not clear, Neanderthals disappeared from the fossil record about 35 000 years ago. Most scientists think Neanderthals were a side branch of human evolution but are not direct ancestors of modern humans.

Cro-Magnon fossils have been found in Europe, Asia, and Australia. These fossils are dated from 40 000 to about 10 000 years old. The oldest recorded art dates from the caves of France where Cro-Magnon humans first painted bison, horses, and spear-carrying people. Cro-Magnon humans lived in caves, made stone carvings, and buried their dead, as seen in **Figure 7-20.** Standing about 1.6 m to 1.7 m tall, the physical appearance of Cro-Magnon people was almost the same as that of modern humans. Cro-Magnon humans are thought to be direct ancestors of modern humans.

Figure 7-20 This grave contained objects thought to be placed there by Cro-Magnon humans. In addition to graves such as this, tools and paintings on cave walls have led scientists to hypothesize that Cro-Magnon humans had a well-developed culture.

Section Assessment

1. Describe at least three kinds of evidence that suggest all primates may have shared a common ancestor.

2. What is the importance of *Australopithecus?*

3. Describe the differences among Neanderthals, Cro-Magnon humans, and modern humans.

4. **Think Critically:** Propose a hypothesis about why teeth represent the most abundant available fossils of hominids.

5. **Skill Builder**
Concept Mapping Using information in this section, make a concept map to show the sequence of hominids. Use the following terms: Neanderthal, *Homo habilis, Australopithecus,* modern *Homo sapiens,* and Cro-Magnon human. If you need help, refer to Concept Mapping in the **Skill Handbook** on page 678.

Science Journal Write a story in your Science Journal about what life would be like for you if you did not have thumbs.

For a **preview** of this chapter, study this Reviewing Main Ideas before you read the chapter. After you have studied this chapter, you can use the Reviewing Main Ideas to **review** the chapter.

The Glencoe MindJogger, Audiocassettes, and CD-ROM provide additional opportunities for review.

Section
7-1 MECHANISMS OF EVOLUTION

Evolution is one of the central ideas of biology. It explains how living things changed in the past and provides predictions for how they may change in the future. Charles Darwin developed the theory of evolution by **natural selection** to explain how these changes account for the diversity of organisms. The factors that control natural selection are as follows.

1. Organisms produce more offspring than can survive.
2. **Variations** are found among individuals of a **species.**
3. Variations are passed on to offspring.
4. Some variations allow members of a population to survive and reproduce better than others.
5. Over time, offspring of individuals with helpful variations make up more and more of a population.

How did Darwin's theory differ from Lamarck's theory?

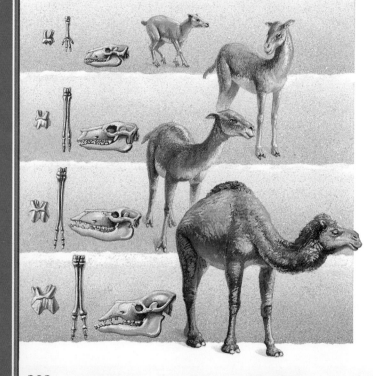

Reading Check ☑️

For a section of this chapter, rewrite the headings as questions. For instance, "What were early thoughts about evolution?" Answer each question.

Section 7-2 EVIDENCE FOR EVOLUTION

Fossils are one of the main sources of evidence for evolution. They are tested using relative dating and radiometric dating to estimate how old they are. Other evidence includes comparative **embryology, homologous** structures, **vestigial structures,** and chemical similarities. *How are chemical similarities evidence of evolution?*

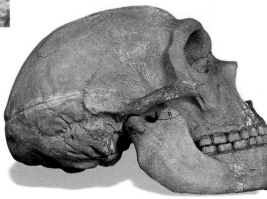

Section 7-3 PRIMATE EVOLUTION

Primates include monkeys, apes, and humans. **Hominids** are humanlike primates. The earliest known hominid is *Australopithecus.* Modern humans are thought to have evolved at least 400 000 years ago. *What are the common characteristics of primates?*

Using Vocabulary

a. embryology
b. evolution
c. gradualism
d. hominids
e. homologous
f. *Homo sapiens*
g. natural selection
h. primates
i. punctuated equilibrium
j. radioactive element
k. sedimentary rock
l. species
m. variation
n. vestigial structure

Each phrase below describes a science term from the list. Write the term that matches the phrase describing it.

1. model of evolution showing slow change
2. structure with no obvious use
3. similar organisms that successfully reproduce
4. body structures that are similar in origin
5. group containing monkeys, apes, and humans

Checking Concepts

Choose the word or phrase that best answers the question.

6. What is an example of adaptation?
   A) a fossil
   B) a homologous structure
   C) camouflage
   D) gradualism

7. How can the most accurate age of a fossil be estimated?
   A) natural selection
   B) radiometric dating
   C) relative dating
   D) camouflage

8. What do homologous structures, vestigial structures, and fossils all provide evidence of?
   A) gradualism
   B) food choice
   C) species populations
   D) evolution

9. What is a factor that controls natural selection?
   A) inheritance of acquired traits
   B) unused traits become smaller
   C) organisms produce more offspring than can survive
   D) the size of an organism

10. What may a series of helpful variations in a species result in?
    A) adaptation
    B) fossils
    C) embryology
    D) climate change

11. What describes organisms that are adapted to their environment?
    A) homologous
    B) not reproducing
    C) forming fossils
    D) surviving and reproducing

12. Which model of evolution shows rapid change?
    A) embryology
    B) punctuated equilibrium
    C) gradualism
    D) adaptation

13. What are opposable thumbs and binocular vision characteristics of?
    A) all primates
    B) hominids
    C) humans only
    D) monkeys and apes

14. What is the study of an organism's early development?
    A) adaptation
    B) relative dating
    C) natural selection
    D) embryology

15. A fossil has the same number of bones in its hand as a gorilla. What type of evidence for evolution does this represent?
    A) DNA
    B) homologous structures
    C) vestigial structures
    D) embryology

Thinking Critically

16. How would Lamarck and Darwin have explained the webbed feet of a duck?

17. Using an example, explain how a new species of organism could evolve.

18. How is the color-changing ability of chameleons an adaptation to their environment?

19. Describe the processes a scientist would use to figure out the age of a fossil.

20. Explain how a species could adapt to its environment. Give an example.

Developing skills

If you need help, refer to the Skill Handbook.

21. **Observing and Inferring:** Observe the birds' beaks pictured below. Describe each. Infer the types of food each would eat and explain why.

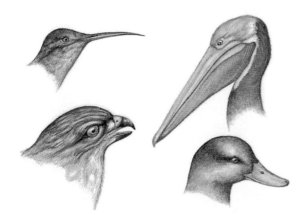

22. **Interpreting Data:** The chemicals present in certain bacteria were studied. Each letter below represents a different chemical found in the bacteria. Use this information to determine which of the bacteria are closely related.

Chemicals Present	
Bacteria 1	A, G, T, C, L, E, S, H
Bacteria 2	A, G, T, C, L, D, H
Bacteria 3	A, G, T, C, L, D, P, U, S, R, I, V
Bacteria 4	A, G, T, C, L, D, H

THE PRINCETON REVIEW

Test-Taking Tip

Make Yourself Comfortable When you take a test, try to make yourself as comfortable as possible. You will then be able to focus all your attention on the test.

Test Practice

Use these questions to test your Science Proficiency.

1. Which of the following statements **BEST** describes how evolution happens?
   A) An insect with an adaptation for surviving insecticide lives to reproduce after being sprayed. Its offspring inherit the trait.
   B) Two Great Danes have their ears cropped. They have a litter of puppies that also need to have their ears cropped.
   C) Two excellent musicians have a baby. After years of practice, the child learns to play instruments as well as the parents.
   D) After generations of stretching their necks to get leaves, all giraffes now have long necks.

2. Which of the following would **BEST** explain the punctuated equilibrium model of evolution?
   A) A mountain range is built up over millions of years due to tectonic plates colliding.
   B) During 54 million years of evolution, the camel evolved to its present form.
   C) Many species become extinct after a meteor strikes Earth, causing darkness for many months.
   D) Two populations become separated because of a flood, each evolving to look very different from the other.

2

Life's
Diversity

What's Happening Here?

In the shallow, sunlit waters between 30 degrees north and south of the equator are the rain forests of the ocean—coral reefs. Hundreds of species of organisms live in marine communities like this one (left) in the Bismarck Sea off New Britain Island, Papua New Guinea. Coral itself is an animal, although it stays put all its life. It belongs to the same phylum as jellyfish, which float freely in the current. Why is coral considered an animal and not a plant? How is it similar to jellyfish? These are some of the questions you will answer as you learn about life's diverse forms. You will also learn about forms of life that are difficult to pigeonhole. Some thrive in the world's most hostile places, such as this Morning Glory Pool (below) in Yellowstone's Upper Geyser Basin. Here, boiling springs bring to the surface minerals that nourish algae and bacteria and tint the formations in pastel colors.

interNET CONNECTION

Explore the Glencoe Science Web Site at **www.glencoe.com/sec/ science/ca** to find out more about topics found in this unit.

CHAPTER

8

Classifying Living Things

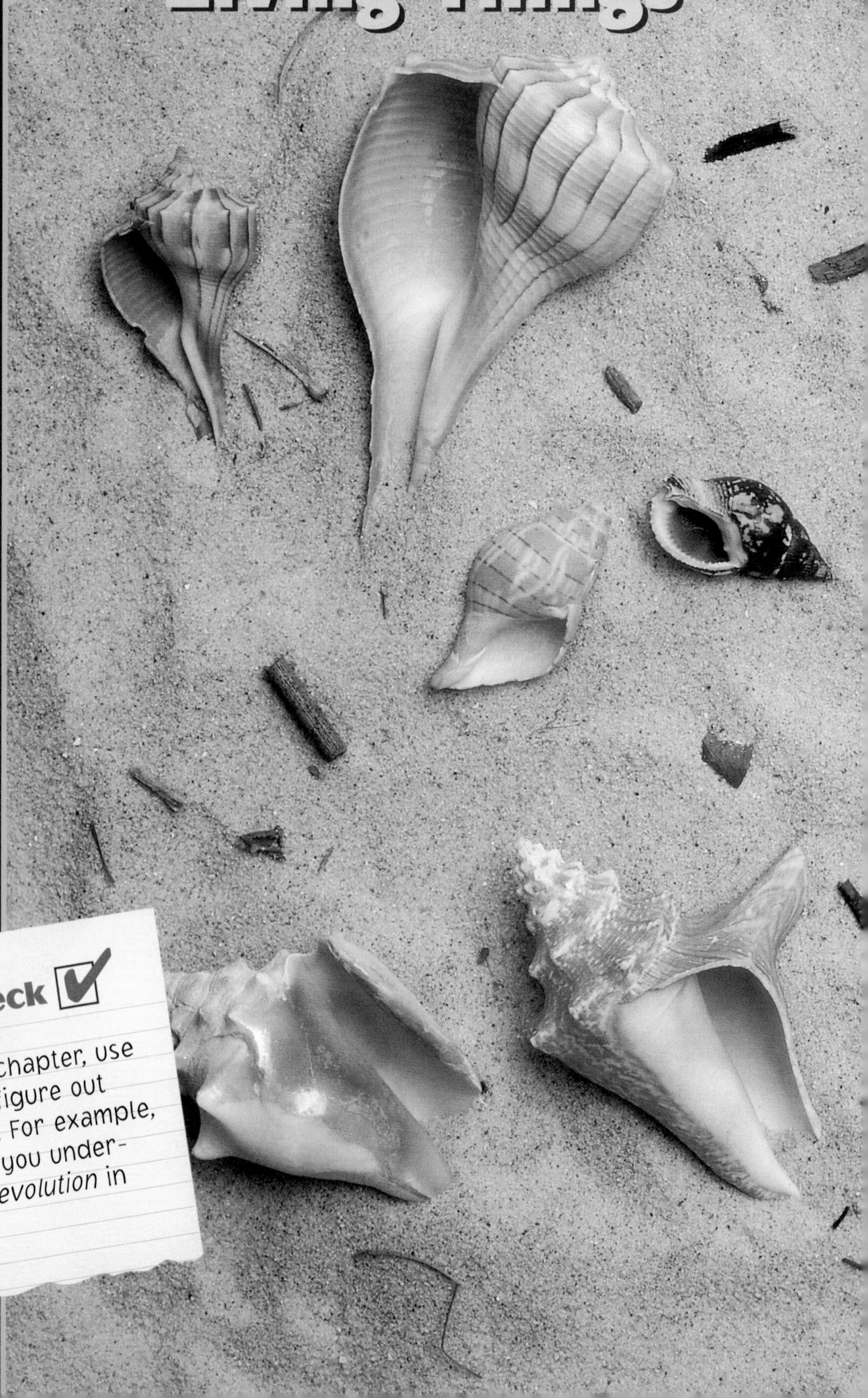

Chapter Preview

Section 8-1
- What is classification?

Section 8-2
- Modern Classification

Section 8-3
- Identifying Organisms

Skills Preview

Skill Builders
- Observe and Infer
- Map Concepts

MiniLabs
- Classify
- Communicate

Activities
- Form a Hypothesis
- Use a Key

Reading Check

As you read this chapter, use context clues to figure out unfamiliar terms. For example, what clues help you understand the term *evolution* in Section 8-2?

Explore Activity

How many plants and animals are discovered each year? You might think that the answer would be a small number, or perhaps none at all, but that would not be right. Life scientists discover, describe, and name hundreds of organisms every year. How do they decide if a certain plant belongs to the iris or orchid family of flowering plants? Or, if an insect is more like a grasshopper or a beetle? Think about how scientists might make these distinctions.

Classify Things

1. Observe the seashells pictured on these two pages. They were once parts of living organisms.

2. Notice the features that are the same and those that are different.

3. Make a list of their similarities and differences.

4. Separate the objects into two groups.

5. To which group does this snail belong?

Science Journal

In your Science Journal, predict how this activity models how biologists categorize living things.

What is classification?

Classifying

When you go into a grocery store, do you go to one aisle to get milk, to another to get margarine, and to a third to get yogurt? Most grocery stores group similar items together. You would find the dairy products mentioned above in one area. When you place similar items together, you classify them. To **classify** means to group ideas, information, or objects based on their similarities. The science of classifying is called **taxonomy** (tak SAHN uh mee).

Classification is an important part of your life. Grocery stores, bookstores, and department stores group similar items together. In what other places is classification important?

Early History of Classification

More than 2000 years ago, Aristotle, a Greek philosopher, developed a system to classify living things. Aristotle thought that all living things on Earth could be placed in either the plant kingdom or the animal kingdom.

Figure 8-1 Aristotle's system of classification did not work for some organisms. For example, frogs can live in water and on land. **What other organisms don't fit into Aristotle's classification system? Why don't they fit?**

In taxonomy, a **kingdom** is the first and largest category. Aristotle began his classification of animals by grouping them according to their physical traits. Then, he used such things as where they lived, the presence or absence of blood, how they reproduced, and wing types to sort them into smaller groups.

Eventually, scientists began to criticize Aristotle's system because it had too many exceptions. Animals were classified according to where they lived, but what about frogs? Frogs spend part of their lives in water and part on land, as shown in **Figure 8-1.** His method of classifying included philosophical ideas that added to the confusion.

Scientific Naming

By the mid-eighteenth century, the classifications of Aristotle had changed and new systems had been developed. However, a lot of confusion remained. Sometimes, an organism had a different name in each country it lived in. Sometimes, it was known by different names in the same country.

Another problem was the length of names for organisms. By this time, many plants, animals, and other organisms had been identified and named. To avoid confusion, scientists gave organisms names that described them in great detail. The name often consisted of several words. For example, the

CHEMISTRY
INTEGRATION

Acid or base?
Classification of matter may include categories like solids, liquids, or gases; elements or compounds; and organic or inorganic. Another way to group matter is as an acid or a base. Using resources, find definitions for acids and bases. In your Science Journal, write a short definition for each, including something about pH.

Problem Solving

Classifying an Organism

Laquitia and her family were on vacation in southern Arizona. One evening, they were driving through a national park just as the sun was setting. Suddenly, a tawny, heavily marked cat with a long tail ran across the road and disappeared into the dense brush. The cat's spots included rings, speckles, slashes, and bars. Laquitia and her family were startled to see such a beautiful animal. No one in the car knew what it was.

Solve the Problem:

1. What important characteristics might be needed to identify an animal?

2. Would Laquitia need other information to be able to determine the animal's species?

Think Critically: How would you begin to figure out what cat Laquitia saw?

interNET CONNECTION

Visit the Glencoe Science Web Site at **www.glencoe.com/sec/science/ca** for more information about the rules for naming or renaming organisms.

Figure 8-2 *Scabiosa caucasica* is also called the pincushion flower. During the fifteenth century, it was made into a medicine to treat scabies, a skin problem caused by mites. That's why the genus is named *Scabiosa.* The specific name means that the plant came from the Caucasus Mountains in Russia.

Reading Check ✓

What is the smallest, most precise classification category?

spearmint plant was named *Mentha floribus spicatis, foliis oblongis serratis.* This name means, more or less, "a member of the mint genus that has its flowers in a spike arrangement, and oblong, serrated leaves." These long names were difficult for scientists to work with. Can you imagine asking for "a member of the mint genus that has its flowers in a spike arrangement, and oblong, serrated leaves, chewing gum?" Carolus Linnaeus, a Swedish physician and naturalist, created a way to give each organism a simpler, unique name.

Binomial Nomenclature

Linnaeus's system, called **binomial nomenclature** (bi NOH mee ul•NOH mun klay chur), gives a two-word name to every organism. Binomial means "two names." The two-word name is commonly called the organism's scientific name. The first word of an organism's scientific name is the genus, and the second is the specific name. A **genus** (JEE nus) is a group of different organisms that have similar characteristics. Together, the genus name and the specific name make up the scientific name of a particular species, as shown in **Figure 8-2.** A **species** (SPEE sheez) is the smallest, most precise classification category. Organisms belonging to the same species can mate to produce fertile offspring. ✓

Mini Lab

Using Binomial Nomenclature

Procedure

1. Make a model of a fictitious organism.
2. Give your organism a scientific name.
3. Make sure that your name is Latinized and supplies information about the species.

Analysis

1. Present your organism to the class. Ask them to guess its name.
2. Why do scientists use Latin when they name organisms?

An example of a two-word name, or species, is *Canis famil-iaris*. This is a domesticated dog. Notice that the first word, the genus name, always begins with a capital letter. The second word, the specific name, begins with a lowercase letter. Both words in a scientific name are written in italics or underlined. Linnaeus's naming system uses Latin because when he developed it, Latin was the language used at European universities and understood by nearly all educated people. Today, it provides an international understanding of all scientific names. In Linnaeus's system, no two organisms have the same scientific name. Because of Linnaeus's system and the use of Latin, scientists around the world recognize the name *Canis familiaris* as a domesticated dog and not a gray wolf, *Canis lupus*. You can see the differences among a dog, a gray wolf, and a coyote in **Figure 8-3.**

Figure 8-3 The photo on the left shows a dog, *Canis familiaris*. Other members of the genus Canis are the coyote, *Canis latrans* (middle), and the gray wolf, *Canis lupus* (right). Notice that they are all different species. **Why are they placed in the same genus?**

Section Assessment

1. What is the purpose of classification?
2. What were the contributions of Aristotle and Linnaeus to taxonomy?
3. **Think Critically:** List two examples of things that are classified based on their similarities.
4. **Skill Builder**
   Observing and Inferring To learn how to classify organisms by observing them, do the **Chapter 8 Skill Activity** on page 713.

Using Math

You have eight different members of the same genus to classify. What is the least number of characteristics required to separate them into eight species?

Species Diversity

Human Footprints

Are there any places on Earth untouched by humans? The old-growth forests of the northwestern United States as well as the rain forests of South America and Asia—previously untouched areas—are increasingly under pressure from human demands. Loggers and lumber companies want to harvest old-growth timber. Farmers want to clear the rain forest to grow crops.

What is species diversity?

Rain forests, coral reefs, and other environments provide homes to hundreds of thousands of organisms. In a hectare (about 10 sq km) of rain forest, for example, there may be 200 species of plants and more than 1000 species of animals. This great variety of plants, animals, and other organisms makes up species diversity. An ecosystem that has a high diversity of species is more stable than one with fewer species.

How is species diversity changed?

In the past, because humans have entered into undisturbed areas, particular species, such as the Carolina parakeet and the passenger pigeon, have become extinct. Extinction reduces species diversity and the stability of ecosystems. Even though extinction is a natural process, humans are contributing to extinction today at a far greater rate than has ever occurred before.

Every minute, more than 20 hectares of rain forest are cut for timber or are cleared for farming or mining. Some areas of old-growth forests in the United States are protected from cutting because the northern spotted owl (right), an endangered species, lives there. Protecting an entire forest because of one endangered species is one way to prevent a decrease in species diversity, but it is a controversial method. International organizations, communities, and individuals concerned about species diversity are working to figure out how best to protect and develop these areas.

interNET
CONNECTION

The Smithsonian Institution created a biodiversity program in 1986 that focuses on problems associated with maintaining global forest diversity. Visit the Glencoe Science Web Site at **www.glencoe.com/sec/ science/ca** for more information on the Smithsonian Institution's program.

Modern Classification

Six-Kingdom System

How do the classification systems used today differ from those of the past? Aristotle and Linnaeus developed their systems of classification using only those characteristics of organisms that they could see. Today, scientists use those and other traits to classify organisms. For example, they may look at the chemical and genetic makeup of organisms. By studying fossils, they examine and compare ancestors to existing organisms. They may compare body structures or early stages of development. By studying all of these things and more, scientists can determine an organism's phylogeny. The **phylogeny** (fi LAH jon nee) of an organism is its evolutionary history or how it has changed over time. Phylogeny tells scientists who the ancestors of an organism were. Today, classification of organisms is based on phylogeny.

The classification system most commonly used today separates organisms into six kingdoms. These kingdoms are animal, plant, fungi, protists, eubacteria, and archaebacteria. Organisms are placed into a kingdom based on several characteristics. These characteristics include cell type, whether it is single celled or many celled, ability to make food, and others. The organisms in **Figure 8-4** all belong to the Kingdom Fungi.

Figure 8-4 Fungi have common characteristics. One characteristic is that they cannot make their own food.

B Some cap fungi are poisonous.

C Coral fungi resemble marine animals.

A To some people, morels are gourmet food.

Prokaryotes and Eukaryotes

Cell type separates two kingdoms from the other four kingdoms. The archaebacteria and eubacteria kingdoms contain organisms that are just one prokaryotic (proh kair ee AH tik) cell in size—a cell without a nucleus. Protists, fungi, plants, and animals have one or more eukaryotic (yew kair ee AH tik) cells—cells with a nucleus. **Table 8-1** lists information about each of the six kingdoms. Some scientists propose that before organisms are grouped into kingdoms, they should be placed in larger groups called domains. One proposed domain classification system is shown in **Figure 8-5.**

Groups Within Kingdoms

Suppose you go to a music store at the mall to buy a new CD. Will you look through all the CDs in the store until you find the one you're looking for? No, the CDs are separated into categories of similar types of music such as rock, soul, classical, country, and jazz. Within each category, the CDs are divided by artists, and then by specific titles. Because of this classification system, you can easily find the CD you want.

Scientists classify organisms into groups in the same way. Every organism is placed into a kingdom. Then, an organism is assigned to a **phylum** (FI lum), the next smallest group. In the plant kingdom, the word **division** is used in place of phylum. Each phylum or division is separated into **classes.** Classes are separated into **orders,** and orders are separated into **families.** A genus is a group within a family. A genus can have one or more species.

Scientists use these categories to classify and name an organism, in the same way that you use categories to find a CD. To understand how an organism is classified, look at the classification of the bottlenose dolphin in **Figure 8-6.**

DOMAIN
Bacteria

KINGDOM
Eubacteria

DOMAIN
Eukarya

KINGDOMS
Animalia

Plantae

Fungi

Protista

DOMAIN
Archaea

KINGDOMS
Euryarchaeota

Crenarchaeota

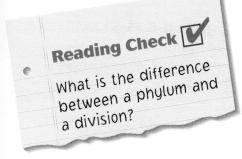

Reading Check

What is the difference between a phylum and a division?

Figure 8-6 The classification of the bottlenose dolphin shows that it is in the order Cetacea. This order includes whales and porpoises.

Kingdom ———— Animalia

Phylum ———— Chordata

Class ———— Mammalia

Order ———— Cetacea

Family ———— Delphinidae

Genus ———— *Tursiops*

Species ——— *Tursiops truncatus*

Table 8-1

Life's Six Kingdoms

Archaebacteria	Eubacteria	Protista	Fungi	Plantae	Animalia
Prokaryotic	Prokaryotic	Eukaryotic	Eukaryotic	Eukaryotic	Eukaryotic
One celled	One celled	One and many celled	One and many celled	Many celled	Many celled
Some members make their own food; others obtain it from other organisms. Some organisms live in extreme environments.	Some members make their own food; others obtain it from other organisms.	Some members make their own food; others obtain it from other organisms.	All members obtain food from other organisms.	Members make their own food.	Members eat plants, animals, or other organisms.

Section Assessment

1. Name and describe a member of each kingdom.

2. Why are there smaller groups within each kingdom?

3. **Think Critically:** Identify the kingdom a single-celled, eukaryotic organism that makes its own food belongs to.

4. **Skill Builder**
   Concept Mapping Use the following terms to make a network tree concept map: *cells, cell organelles, eukaryote, prokaryote, plants, animals, archaebacteria, eubacteria, no membrane-bound organelles, no nucleus, fungi, protists,* and *organized nucleus.* Provide linking words. If you need help, refer to Concept Mapping in the **Skill Handbook** on page 678.

Using Computers

Database Make a database that could be used to sort organisms based on any level of classification. Enter the classification information for humans, dogs, and cats. If you need help, refer to page 697.

Design Your Own Experiment

Classifying Seeds

Possible Materials

- Packets of seeds (10 different kinds)
- Hand lens
- Metric ruler
- Sheets of paper (2)

Scientists have developed classification systems to show how organisms are related. How do they determine what features they will use to classify organisms? Can you learn to use the same methods?

Recognize the Problem

You are given several kinds of seeds and are asked to classify them into groups of similar seeds. How would you begin?

Form a Hypothesis

Make a hypothesis about the traits or physical features that may be used to help classify various kinds of seeds.

Goals

- **Observe** the seeds provided and notice their distinctive features.
- **Classify** seeds using your model.

Safety Precautions

Do not eat any seeds or put them in your mouth. Some may have been treated with chemicals.

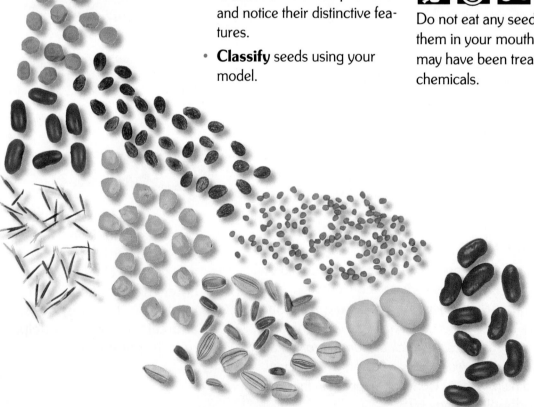

Test Your Hypothesis

Plan

1. As a group, list the steps that you need to take to classify seeds. Be specific, and describe exactly what you will do at each step. List your materials.

2. **Classify** your seeds by making a model.

3. Make a plan to identify your seeds.

4. Read over your entire experiment to make sure that all steps are in logical order.

Do

1. Make sure your teacher approves your model before you proceed.

2. Carry out the experiment as planned.

3. While you are working, write down any observations that you make that would cause you to change your model.

4. **Complete** the plan.

Analyze Your Data

1. **Compare** your key and model with those made by other groups.

2. Check your key by having another group use it.

Draw Conclusions

1. In what ways can groups of different types of seeds be classified?

2. Why is it an advantage for scientists to use a standardized system to classify organisms? What observations did you make to support your answer?

Identifying Organisms

Common Names and Scientific Names

Have you heard anyone call the bird in **Figure 8-7A** a *Turdus migratorius*? In much of the United States, this bird is commonly called a robin, or a robin redbreast. However, people who live in England call the bird in **Figure 8-7B** a robin. In much of Europe, the same bird is also called a redbreast. If you lived in Australia, you'd call the bird in **Figure 8-7C** a robin, or a yellow robin. Are these the same species of bird? No, these birds are obviously different from one another.

Figure 8-7 These three robins have the same common name but are three different species.

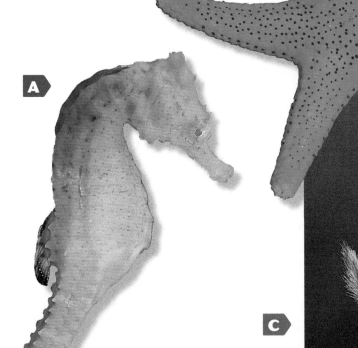

Figure 8-8 Common names can be misleading. Sea horses (A) are fish, but starfish (B) are not fish. Prairie dogs (C) are more closely related to squirrels than to dogs. **Do you know a misleading common name?**

Yet, they all have the same or a similar common name. **Figure 8-8** gives other examples of some common names that are confusing.

What would happen if life scientists used only common names when they communicated with others about organisms? There would be many misunderstandings. The system of binomial nomenclature developed by Linnaeus gives each bird a unique scientific name. The scientific names for the birds in **Figure 8-7** are: **A**, *Turdus migratorius*; **B**, *Erithacus rubecula*; and **C**, *Eopsaltria australis*.

Functions of Scientific Names

Scientific names serve four functions. First, they help scientists avoid errors in communication. A life scientist who studied the yellow robin, *Eopsaltria australis*, would not be confused by information he or she read about *Turdus migratorius*,

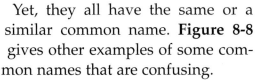

Try at Home

Mini Lab

Communicating Ideas

Procedure

1. Find a picture in a magazine of a piece of furniture that you could both sit or lie down on.

2. Show the picture to ten people and ask them to tell you what they call the piece of furniture.

3. Keep a record of the answers in your Science Journal.

Analysis

1. In your Science Journal, infer how using common names can be confusing when communicating with others.

2. How does using scientific names make communication between scientists easier?

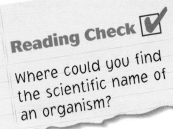

Using Math

1. Make a bar graph for the frequency of answers of your Try at Home MiniLab on the previous page.
2. Compile a list of all answers given to your classmates for the same MiniLab.
3. Make a bar graph for the frequency of responses of the compiled list.
4. Compare the two bar graphs.

Reading Check ✔

Where could you find the scientific name of an organism?

the American robin. Second, organisms with similar evolutionary histories are classified together. Because of this, you know that organisms with the same genus name are related. Third, scientific names give descriptive information about the species. What can you tell from the species name *Turdus migratorius?* It tells you that this bird migrates from place to place. Fourth, scientific names allow information about organisms to be organized and found easily and efficiently. Such information may be in a field guide, a book, or a pamphlet that lists related organisms and gives their scientific names.

Tools for Identifying Organisms

You've been asked to identify the organism in **Figure 8-9.** What do you do? The easiest thing would be to ask someone. You could contact a professor at a university, an exterminator, a county extension specialist, an expert at a natural history museum, or any knowledgeable person. However, no one knows or is expected to know all members of any taxonomic group. The person would probably tell you that the organism is a tick. He or she might look in a field guide to find its scientific name. If you were to use a field guide, you might be able to identify the organism. ✔

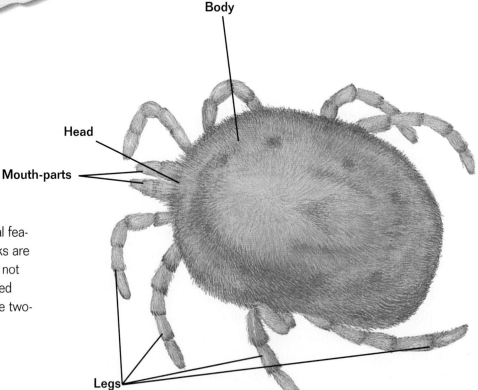

Figure 8-9 Two external features used for identifying ticks are eight legs and a body that is not in sections. Other eight-legged arthropods, like spiders, have two-section bodies.

Many kinds of field guides have been written like those in **Figure 8-10** and the field guide at the end of this chapter. Field guides about plants, fungi, fish, and nearly every other kind of organism are available. Most field guides have descriptions, illustrations of organisms, and information about habitats to help with identification. You can identify species from around the world by using the appropriate field guide.

Using Dichotomous Keys

A **dichotomous** (di KAH toh mus) **key** is a detailed list of characteristics used to identify organisms and includes scientific names. Dichotomous keys are arranged in steps with two descriptive statements at each step. Look at the dichotomous key for mites and ticks in **Table 8-2**. Notice that at each numbered step, the descriptions are labeled "a" and "b." To use the key, you must always begin with a choice from the first pair of descriptions. Notice that the end of each description is either the name of a species or directions to go to another step. If you use the dichotomous key properly, you will eventually end up with the correct name for your species.

Let's identify the soft tick in **Table 8-2**. Start at 1 of the key. Your tick is brown, so you go to 3. You measure your tick and find it is more than 5 mm in length, so you go on to 4. Your tick is brown with an oval, flattened body, so you choose "b."

Figure 8-10 Field guides are useful when trying to identify things.

Table 8-2

Key to Some Mites and Ticks of North America

Actual size: 5 mm

1. Animal color
   a. red, go to 2
   b. not red, go to 3

2. Body texture
   a. smooth; body globular and somewhat elongated; red freshwater mite, *Limnochares americana*
   b. dense velvety hair; body oval to rounded rectangle; velvet mite, *Trombidium* species

3. Body length
   a. 0.5 mm or less; two-spotted spider mite, *Tetranychus uriticae*
   b. more than 0.5 mm, go to 4

4. Body coloration
   a. dark brown with a small, whitish, patterned shield near the head; American dog tick, *Dermacentor* species
   b. brown; body is a flattened oval with a soft plate on the back; mammal soft tick, *Ornithodoros* species

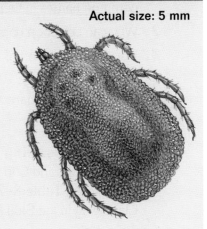

Figure 8-11 Each of these animals is a different species of mite or tick. **What things do they have in common?**

 Actual size: 3.2 mm

B Actual size: 3 mm

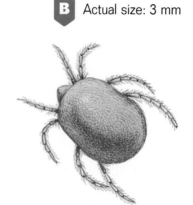

C Actual size: 0.5 mm

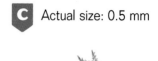

EARTH SCIENCE
INTEGRATION▶

The dichotomous key tells you that your tick is an example of an *Ornithodoros* species, which are mammal soft ticks.

Keys are useful in a variety of ways. It is important to know if a rock is igneous, metamorphic, or sedimentary when classifying fossils, for example. Minerals can be classified using a key that describes characteristics such as hardness, luster, color, streak, and cleavage. Why might you need to know several characteristics to classify a mineral or a living thing?

Section Assessment

1. List four reasons biologists use scientific names instead of common names in their communications.

2. Why can common names cause confusion?

3. What is the function of a dichotomous key?

4. **Think Critically:** Why would you infer that two species that look similar share a common evolutionary history?

5. **Skill Builder**
   Classifying Classify the ticks and mites marked A, B, and C in **Figure 8-11,** using the dichotomous key in **Table 8-2.** If you need help, refer to Classifying in the **Skill Handbook** on page 677.

Science Journal
Select a field guide for grasses, trees, insects, or mammals. Select two organisms in the field guide that closely resemble each other. Compare them and explain how they differ using labeled diagrams.

Using a Dichotomous Key

Materials
• Paper and pencil

Scientists who classify organisms have made many keys that allow you to identify unknown organisms. Try this activity to see how it is done.

What You'll Investigate

How a dichotomous key can be used to identify native cats in the United States.

Goals

• **Learn** to use a dichotomous key.
• **Identify** two native cats of North America.

Procedure

1. **Observe** the cats pictured below.

2. Begin with 1 of the key to the right. **Identify** the cat labeled A.

3. On your paper, write the common and scientific name for the cat and list all of its traits given in the key.

4. Use the same procedure to **identify** the species of the cat labeled B.

Conclude and Apply

1. According to the key, how many species of native cats reside in North America?

2. How do you know that this key doesn't contain all the species of native cats in the world?

3. **Infer** why you couldn't identify a lion using this key.

4. **Explain** why it wouldn't be a good idea to begin in the middle of a key instead of with the first step.

Key to Native Cats of North America

1. Tail length
   a. short, go to 2
   b. long, go to 3

2. Cheek ruff
   a. no cheek ruff; long ear tufts tipped with black; coat distinctly mottled; lynx, *Lynx canadensis*
   b. broad cheek ruffs; ear tufts short; coat with indistinct spots; bobcat, *Lynx rufus*

3. Coat
   a. plain colored, go to 4
   b. patterned, go to 5

4. Coat color
   a. yellowish to tan above with white to buff below; mountain lion, *Felis concolor*
   b. all brown or black; jaguarundi, *Felis yagouaroundi*

5. Coat pattern
   a. lines of black-bordered brown spots; ocelot, *Felis pardalis*
   b. irregular tan and black, go to 6

6. Animal size
   a. large cat; rows of black rosettes or rings unevenly distributed; jaguar, *Panthera onca*
   b. small cat; four dark-brown stripes on the back and one on the neck; some irregularly shaped spots; margay, *Felis wiedii*

A   B

FIELD GUIDE

to Insects

FIELD *ACTIVITY*

For a week, use this field guide to help you identify insect orders. Look in different places and at different times of day for insects. In your Science Journal, record the order of insect found, along with the date, time, and place. *Why do you think there are so many kinds of insects?*

It's brown and creepy, and has wings and six legs. If you call it a bug, you may be correct, but if you said it was an insect, you definitely would be correct. Insects belong to a large group of animals called the arthropods. They are related to shrimp, spiders, lobsters, and centipedes. There are more insect species than all other animal species on Earth. Insects are found from the tropics to the tundra. Some are aquatic all or part of their lives. There are even insects that live inside other animals. Insects play important roles in the environment. Many are helpful, but others are destructive.

How Insects Are Classified

An insect's body is divided into three parts: head, thorax, and abdomen. The head has a pair of antennae and eyes and paired mouthparts. Three pairs of jointed legs and, sometimes, wings are attached to the thorax. They have a hard covering over their entire body. Some insects shed this covering so that they can grow. Insects are classified into smaller groups called orders. By observing an insect and recognizing certain features, you can identify the order it belongs to. This field guide presents ten insect orders.

Insect Orders

Dermaptera Earwigs

- A pair of pincerlike structures extends from the end of the abdomen.
- They are usually active at night and hide under litter or in any dark, protected place during the day.
- Earwigs may damage plants.

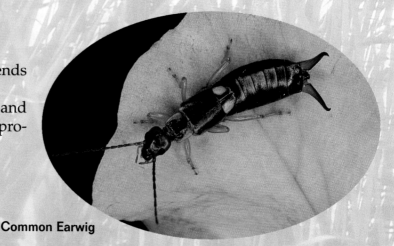

Common Earwig

Coleoptera **Beetles**

- A pair of thick, leathery, sometimes-knobby wings meets in a straight line and covers another pair of wings, the thorax, and all or most of the abdomen.
- Most beetles are considered serious pests, but some feed on other insects and others are scavengers.

This is the largest order of insects. There are many sizes, shapes, and colors of beetles. Not all beetles are called beetles. For example, ladybugs, fireflies, June bugs, and weevils are beetles.

Convergent Ladybug Beetle

Male Stag Beetle

Common Housefly

Diptera **Flies—Mosquitoes**

- They are small insects with large eyes.
- They have two pair of wings but only one pair is visible.
- Mouths are adapted for piercing and sucking, or scraping and lapping

Many of these insects are food for larger animals. Some spread diseases, others are pests, and some eat dead and decaying things. They are found in many different environments.

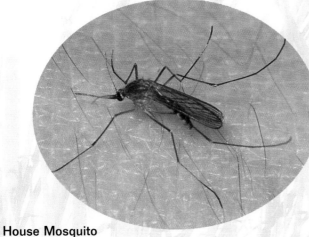

House Mosquito

Odonata **Dragonflies—Damselflies**

- They have two pairs of transparent, many-veined wings that are nearly equal in size and never folded against the insect's body.
- A pair of large eyes are on its head.
- They have a long, thin abdomen.

These insects are usually seen near bodies of water. All members of this group catch small insects, such as mosquitoes, while in flight.

Twelve Spotted Skimmer Dragonfly

Isoptera Termites

- Adults are small, dark brown or black, and may have wings.
- Immature forms are small, soft-bodied, pale yellow or white, and wingless.
- Termites live in colonies in the ground or in wood.

The adults are sometimes confused with ants. The thorax and abdomen of a termite look like one body part, but a thin waist separates the thorax and abdomen of an ant. Although most people consider termites to be destructive insects, they play an important role in recycling trees and other woody plants. Termites can digest wood because certain bacteria and protists live in their digestive tracts.

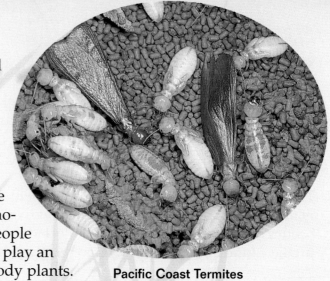

Pacific Coast Termites

Dictyoptera Cockroaches—Mantises

- They have long, thin antennae on the head.
- The front wings are smaller than back wings; back wings are thin and fanlike when opened.
- Front legs of a mantis are adapted for grasping; the other two pairs of legs are similar to those of a cockroach.

Praying mantises are called beneficial insects because they eat other, often harmful, insects. Cockroaches are pests wherever humans live.

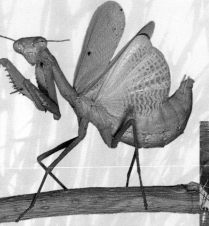

Carolina Praying Mantis

American Cockroach

Hymenoptera

Ants—Bees—Wasps

- They have two pairs of transparent wings, if present.
- They are found in many different environments, either in colonies or alone.

Members of this order may be so small that they can be seen only with a magnifier. Others may be nearly 35 mm long. They are important because they pollinate flowers, and some prey on harmful insects. Honeybees make honey and wax. Despite common beliefs, not all bees and wasps can sting.

American Bumble Bee

Black Carpenter Ant

Paper Wasp

Lepidoptera **Butterflies—Moths**

- They have two pairs of wings with colorful patterns created by thousands of tiny scales.
- A moth's antennae are feathery; a butterfly's antennae are thin and each has a small knob on the tip.
- An adult's mouth-parts are adapted as a long, coiled tube for drinking nectar.
- Moths are active at night; butterflies are active on warm, sunny days.

Caterpillars are immature butterflies and moths. They eat plants, fabrics made from animal hair, and stored grains and nuts.

Yellow Woolly Bear Moth

Buckeye Butterfly

Periodic Cicada

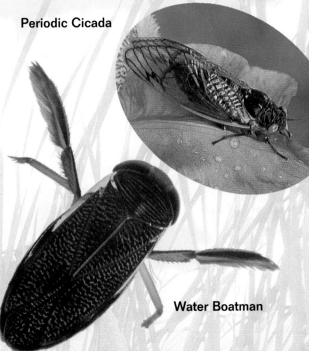

Water Boatman

Hemiptera **Bugs**

- Front wings are thick and leathery near the insect's head and thin at the tip.
- Wing tips usually overlap when folded over the insect's back and cover a smaller pair of thin wings.

The prefix of this order, *Hemi-*, means "half" and describes the front pair of wings. Some bugs live on land and others are aquatic. Some bugs are pests, while others are beneficial insects.

Field Cricket

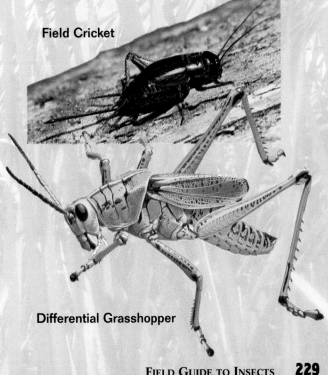

Orthoptera

Grasshoppers—Crickets—Katydids

- They have large, hind legs adapted for leaping.
- They usually have two pairs of wings; outer pair is hard and covers a transparent pair.

Many of these insects "sing" by rubbing one body part against another. Males generally do the singing. These insects are considered pests because swarms of them can destroy a farmer's crops in a few days.

Differential Grasshopper

For a **preview** of this chapter, study this Reviewing Main Ideas before you read the chapter. After you have studied this chapter, you can use the Reviewing Main Ideas to **review** the chapter.

The Glencoe MindJogger, Audiocassettes, and CD-ROM provide additional opportunities for review.

Section

8-1 WHAT IS CLASSIFICATION?

To **classify** means to group ideas, information, or objects based on their similarities. **Taxonomy** is the science of classification. Aristotle developed the first classification system, but it was confusing. Over time, other systems were created. Linnaeus gave taxonomy **binomial nomenclature,** which is the two-word naming system for organisms, still used today. The two-word species name is the organism's scientific name. The first word is the genus; the second word is the specific name. Methods of classification are important because they help us to see how groups of organisms are related, to identify organisms, and to find their scientific names. *Why was Aristotle's system confusing?*

Reading Check ✓

All organisms can be classified using only three features. Why can't these features be used to classify dogs? What features could you use to classify dogs?

Section

8-2 MODERN CLASSIFICATION

Organisms are classified into six **kingdoms** based on several characteristics. Cell type divides organisms into two groups, prokaryotes and eukaryotes. Adding other characteristics sorts organisms into smaller and smaller categories. The last level of classification is the **species.** *Which kingdoms contain prokaryotes and which contain eukaryotes?*

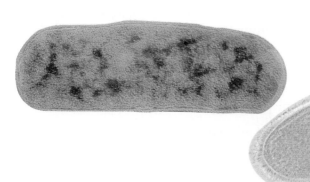

Section

8-3 IDENTIFYING ORGANISMS

Scientific names give descriptive information about species. Each species has its own unique name. Species names are used worldwide. Communication among scientists and others is easier and clearer with scientific names. Field guides and **dichotomous keys** are used to identify specific organisms. Identification of organisms is important in the study of living organisms. *Why do you always start with the number one entry of a dichotomous key?*

Chapter 8 Assessment

Using Vocabulary

a. binomial nomenclature
b. class
c. classify
d. dichotomous key
e. division
f. family
g. genus
h. kingdom
i. order
j. phylogeny
k. phylum
l. species
m. taxonomy

Distinguish between the terms in each of the following sets.

1. kingdom, species
2. division, phylum
3. dichotomous key, binomial nomenclature
4. classify, taxonomy
5. class, family

Checking Concepts

Choose the word or phrase that best answers the question.

6. Which group has the most members?
   A) family   C) genus
   B) kingdom   D) order

7. In what category do the most similar organisms belong?
   A) family   C) genus
   B) class   D) species

8. Which of the following are all many celled organisms?
   A) animals   C) fungi
   B) bacteria   D) protists

9. What is the closest relative of *Canis lupus*?
   A) *Quercus alba*   C) *Felis tigris*
   B) *Equus zebra*   D) *Canis familiaris*

10. What does the first word in a two-word scientific name of an organism identify?
    A) kingdom   C) phylum
    B) species   D) genus

11. To which kingdom do mushrooms belong?
    A) animal   C) fungi
    B) eubacteria   D) plant

12. What is the evolutionary history of an organism?
    A) taxonomy   C) phylogeny
    B) biology   D) chemistry

13. What are the simplest eukaryotes?
    A) animals   C) eubacteria
    B) fungi   D) protists

14. What are trees and flowers?
    A) animals   C) fungi
    B) plants   D) protists

15. What are cells without a nucleus?
    A) eukaryotes   C) species
    B) phylogeny   D) prokaryotes

Thinking Critically

16. Explain what binomial nomenclature is and why it is important.

17. Name each of the six kingdoms, and identify a member of each kingdom.

18. Write a short dichotomous key to identify five of your classmates. Use such things as sex, hair color, eye color, and age in your key. Each person's first and last name will be their scientific name.

19. Discuss the relationship between tigers and lions, members of the genus *Panthera*.

20. Scientific names often describe a characteristic of the organism. What does *Lathyrus odoratus* tell you about a sweet pea?

Developing Skills

If you need help, refer to the **Skill Handbook.**

21. **Concept Mapping:** Using information in Sections 8-1 and 8-2, make an events chain concept map to show events from Aristotle to modern classification.

22. **Comparing and Contrasting:** Compare the number and variety of organisms in a kingdom and in a genus.

23. **Classifying:** Use the Key to Native Cats of North America to identify these cats.

24. **Making and Using Graphs:** Make a circle graph using the data listed in the table below.

Number of Species of Organisms

Kingdom	Number of Species
Protists	51 000
Fungi	100 000
Plants	285 000
Animals	2 000 000

Test-Taking Tip

You Are Smarter Than You Think
Nothing on the science tests that you will take this year is so difficult that you can't understand it. You can learn to master any of it. Be self-confident and just keep practicing your test-taking skills.

Test Practice

Use these questions to test your Science Proficiency.

1. You are examining a cell under a microscope. Which of the following observations lets you know that the cell is **NOT** from the Kingdom Eubacteria?
   A) Its nucleus is surrounded by a membrane.
   B) The cell has a wall.
   C) The cell is small.
   D) Flagella are attached to the cell wall.

2. Two organisms look different from each other, but a taxonomist suspects they are members of the same species. Why would the taxonomist come to this conclusion?
   A) They fight with each other.
   B) They come from the same country.
   C) They seem to get along well.
   D) They mate and produce fertile offspring.

3. The blue jay, *Cyanocitta cristata*, is most closely related to which of the following birds?
   A) green jay, *Cyanocorax yncas*
   B) Stellar's jay, *Cyanocitta stelleri*
   C) eastern bluebird, *Sialia sialis*
   D) bluethroat, *Luscinia svecica*

Chapter Preview

Skills Preview

Skill Builders
- Hypothesize
- Map Concepts

Activities
- Design an Experiment
- Organize Data

MiniLabs
- Recognize Cause and Effect
- Infer

Reading Check ✔

As you read this chapter, find out the differences among the meanings of the prefixes *a-*, *anti-*, and *ana-*. List and define two words that begin with each prefix.

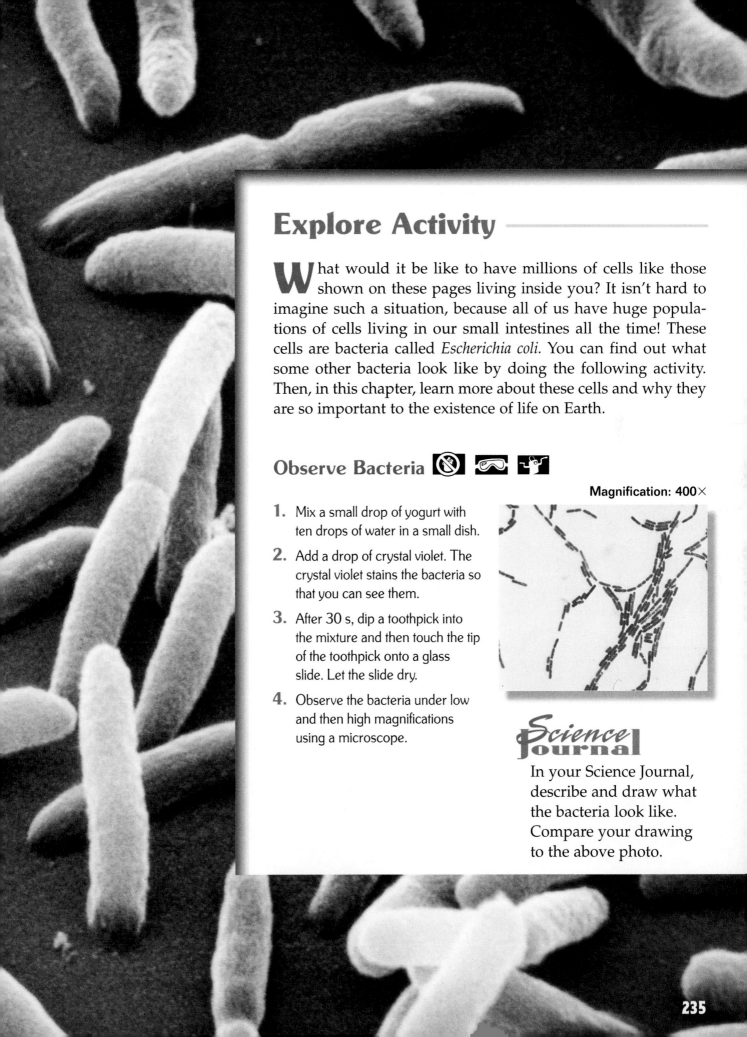

Explore Activity

What would it be like to have millions of cells like those shown on these pages living inside you? It isn't hard to imagine such a situation, because all of us have huge populations of cells living in our small intestines all the time! These cells are bacteria called *Escherichia coli.* You can find out what some other bacteria look like by doing the following activity. Then, in this chapter, learn more about these cells and why they are so important to the existence of life on Earth.

Observe Bacteria

Magnification: 400×

1. Mix a small drop of yogurt with ten drops of water in a small dish.

2. Add a drop of crystal violet. The crystal violet stains the bacteria so that you can see them.

3. After 30 s, dip a toothpick into the mixture and then touch the tip of the toothpick onto a glass slide. Let the slide dry.

4. Observe the bacteria under low and then high magnifications using a microscope.

Science Journal

In your Science Journal, describe and draw what the bacteria look like. Compare your drawing to the above photo.

Two Kingdoms of Bacteria

What are bacteria?

When most people hear the word *bacteria*, they probably associate it with sore throats or other illnesses. However, very few bacteria cause illness. Most are important for other reasons. Bacteria are almost everywhere—in the air you breathe, the food you eat, the water you drink, and even at great ocean depths. A shovelful of soil contains billions of them. Millions of bacteria live on and in your body. Many are beneficial to you.

There are two types of cells—prokaryotic and eukaryotic. Bacteria are prokaryotes because they have no true nucleus. The nuclear material of a bacterial cell is made up of one or more circular chromosomes. Bacteria have cell walls and cell membranes and also contain ribosomes. Structures inside bacterial cells are not surrounded by membranes.

Types of Bacteria

Bacteria are grouped into two kingdoms—eubacteria (yoo bak TIHR ee uh) and archaebacteria (ar kee bak TIHR ee uh). Some eubacteria, such as the cyanobacteria in **Figure 9-1,** contain chlorophyll, which enables them to make their own food. They obtain their energy from the sun by photosynthesis. Most eubacteria do not make their own food. Some break down dead organisms to obtain energy. Others live as parasites and absorb nutrients from living organisms. Archaebacteria live in habitats where few organisms can live and obtain energy in other ways.

Figure 9-1 These cyanobacteria make their own food. **What do cyanobacteria contain that enables them to make food?**

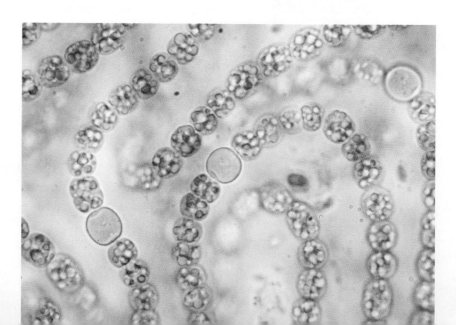

Magnification: 1250×

Figure 9-2 Bacterial characteristics and shapes make bacteria different from other cells. Spirilla-, cocci-, and bacilli-shaped bacteria can be found in almost any environment. **What common terms could be used to describe these cell shapes?**

B The flagella help the bacterium move in a liquid environment.

Gel-like capsule

Cell wall

Cell membrane

Flagella

Cytoplasm

Nuclear material

Cocci

A The capsule surrounding some bacteria protects them from attack by white blood cells.

C Bacterial cells are much smaller than eukaryotic cells. Most bacteria are about the size of a mitochondrion or chloroplast found in eukaryotic cells.

Bacilli

Bacterial cell

D Bacterial cells are prokaryotic. Their nuclear material is not surrounded by a membrane.

Spirilla

Bacterial Shapes

The bacteria that normally inhabit your home and body have three basic shapes—spheres, rods, and spirals. Sphere-shaped bacteria are called *cocci* (sing. *coccus),* rod-shaped bacteria are called *bacilli* (sing. *bacillus),* and spiral-shaped bacteria are called *spirilla* (sing. *spirillum).* The general characteristics of bacteria can be seen in the bacillus shown in **Figure 9-2.** It contains cytoplasm surrounded by a cell membrane and wall. Bacterial chromosomes are not located in a membrane-bound nucleus but are found in the cytoplasm. Some bacteria have a thick, gel-like capsule around the cell wall. The capsule helps the bacterium stick to surfaces. How does a capsule help a bacterium to survive?

Many bacteria float freely in the environment on air and water currents, your hands, your shoes, and even the family dog or cat. Many that live in moist conditions have whiplike tails called **flagella** to help them move. ✓

Reading Check ✓

What are flagella?

Observing Bacterial Growth

Procedure

1. Obtain two or three dried beans.
2. Break them into halves and place the halves into 10 mL of distilled water in a glass beaker.
3. Observe how many days it takes for the water to become cloudy and develop an unpleasant odor.
4. Use methylene blue to dye a drop of water from the beaker and observe it under the microscope.

Analysis

1. How long did it take for the water to become cloudy?
2. What did you observe on the slide that would make the water cloudy?
3. What do you think the bacteria were feeding on?

Eubacteria

Eubacteria is the larger of the two bacterial kingdoms. It contains so many organisms that it is hard to classify. All bacteria except archaebacteria, which you will learn about later in this chapter, are considered to be eubacteria, or "true bacteria." These organisms live in much less harsh environments than archaebacteria. As illustrated in **Figure 9-3,** eubacteria include many diverse groups, from species that live off other organisms to those that can make their own food.

Cyanobacteria

One type of eubacteria is known as cyanobacteria. Cyanobacteria are eubacteria that are producers. They make their own food using carbon dioxide, water, and energy from sunlight. Cyanobacteria contain chlorophyll and another pigment that is blue. This pigment combination gives cyanobacteria their common name, blue-green bacteria. However, some cyanobacteria are yellow, black, or red. The Red Sea gets its name from red cyanobacteria.

Figure 9-3 Bacteria are divided into two main groups—archaebacteria and eubacteria. **Which group contains the largest variety of organisms?**

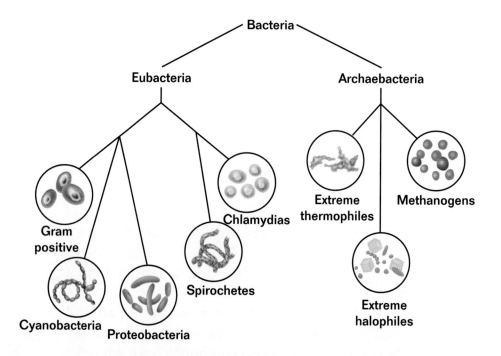

All species of cyanobacteria are one-celled organisms. However, some of these organisms live together in long chains or filaments. Look again at **Figure 9-1.** Many are covered with a gel-like substance. This adaptation enables cyanobacteria to live in globular groups called colonies. Cyanobacteria are important for food production in lakes and ponds. Since cyanobacteria make food from carbon dioxide, water, and the energy from sunlight, fish in a healthy pond can eat them and use the energy released from that food.

Have you ever seen a pond covered with smelly, green, bubbly slime? When large amounts of nutrients enter a pond, cyanobacteria and various algae increase in number and produce a matlike growth called a bloom. Available resources are quickly consumed and the cyanobacteria and various algae die. Bacteria feed on them and use up all the oxygen in the water. As a result, fish and other organisms die.

Using Math

Figure 9-4 shows a bacterium that is dividing into two cells. Measure the length of one of the new cells in millimeters. Determine the actual size of the cell by dividing the measured length by the magnification.

Problem Solving

Controlling Bacterial Growth

Bacteria may be controlled by slowing their growth, preventing their growth, or killing them. When trying to control bacteria that affect humans, it is often desirable to slow just their growth because substances that prevent bacteria from growing or that kill bacteria may harm humans. For example, bleach often is used to kill bacteria in bathrooms or on kitchen surfaces, but it is poisonous if swallowed. Antiseptic is the word used to describe substances that slow the growth of bacteria. Advertisers often claim that a substance kills bacteria, when in fact, the substance only slows the bacteria's growth. Many mouthwash advertisements, however, make this claim. How could you test several mouthwashes to see which one is the best antiseptic?

Solve the Problem

1. Choose three mouthwashes and describe an experiment that you could do to find the best antiseptic mouthwash of the three.

2. What controls would you use in your experiment?

Think Critically: Read the ingredients label on one of the bottles of mouthwash. List the ingredients in the mouthwash. What ingredient do you think is the antiseptic? Explain you answer.

Figure 9-4 In this color-enhanced electron micrograph, a bacterium is shown undergoing fission.

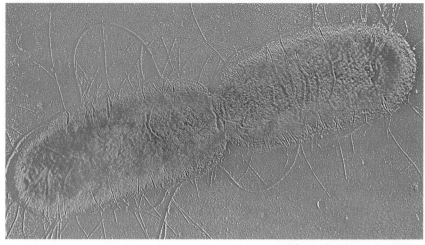

Magnification: 14 400×

Reproduction

Bacteria reproduce by fission, as shown in **Figure 9-4.** **Fission** produces two cells with genetic material identical to that of the parent cell. It is the simplest form of asexual cell reproduction. Some bacteria exchange genetic material through a process similar to sexual reproduction. Two bacteria line up beside each other and exchange DNA through a fine tube. This results in cells with different genetic material than their parents. As a result, the bacteria may have variations that give them an advantage for surviving in changing environments.

Most bacteria live in places where there is a supply of oxygen. An organism that uses oxygen for respiration is called an **aerobe** (AY rohb). You are an aerobic organism. In contrast, some organisms, called **anaerobes** (AN uh rohbz), have variations that allow them to live without oxygen.

Figure 9-5 Bacteria that live in mineral hot springs like Morning Glory Pool, shown below, are anaerobes. **What problems would bacteria have to overcome to live in conditions such as these?**

Archaebacteria

Kingdom Archaebacteria contains certain kinds of anaerobic bacteria, which, like eubacteria, are thought to have existed for billions of years. They are found in extreme conditions, such as the hot springs shown in **Figure 9-5,** salty lakes, muddy swamps, the intestines of cattle, and near deep ocean vents where life exists without sunlight. The conditions in which archaebacteria live today may resemble conditions found on early Earth.

Archaebacteria are divided into three groups, based on how they get energy. There are methanogens, halophiles, and thermophiles. The methanogens use carbon dioxide for energy and produce the methane gas that bubbles up out of swamps and marshes. The extreme halophiles live in salty environments such as the Great Salt Lake in Utah and the Dead Sea. Some of them require a habitat ten times saltier than seawater to grow. The last group of archaebacteria is the extreme thermophiles that survive in hot areas like the one shown in **Figure 9-6.**

EARTH SCIENCE
INTEGRATION

Figure 9-6 Thermophiles get energy by breaking down sulfur compounds such as those escaping from the deep-sea vent found near these tube worms.

Section Assessment

1. What are the characteristics of bacteria?
2. How do aerobic and anaerobic organisms differ?
3. How do bacteria reproduce?
4. **Think Critically:** A mat of cyanobacteria is found growing on a lake with dead fish floating along the edge. What has caused these events to occur?
5. **Skill Builder**
   Interpreting Data Do the **Chapter 9 Skill Activity** on page 714 to interpret the data to determine which substance best prevents bacterial growth.

Using Math

Some bacteria may reproduce every 20 minutes. Suppose that one bacterium is present at the beginning of a timed period. How long would it take for the number of bacteria to increase to more than 1 million?

Observing Cyanobacteria

Materials

- Micrograph photos (see below)
  * *prepared slides of Gloeocapsa and Anabaena*
  * *microscope*
  * *Alternate Materials*

You can obtain many species of cyanobacteria from ponds. When you look at these organisms under a microscope, you will find that they have many similarities but that they are also different from each other in important ways. In this activity, you will compare and contrast species of cyanobacteria.

What You'll Investigate

What do cyanobacteria look like?

Goals

- **Observe** several species of cyanobacteria.
- **Describe** the structure and function of cyanobacteria.

Safety Precautions

Procedure

1. **Make a data table** in your Science Journal. Indicate whether each cyanobacterium sample is in colony form or filament form. Write a *yes* or *no* for the presence or absence of each characteristic in each type of cyanobacterium.

2. **Observe** photos or prepared slides, if available, of *Gloeocapsa* and *Anabaena*. If using slides, observe under the low and high power of the microscope. Notice the difference in the arrangement of the cells. In your Science Journal, draw and label a few cells of each species of cyanobacterium.

3. **Observe** photos of *Nostoc* and *Oscillatoria*. In your Science Journal, draw and label a few cells of each.

Conclude and Apply

1. How does the color of cyanobacteria compare with the color of leaves on trees? What can you infer from this?

2. How can you tell by **observing** them that cyanobacteria belong to Kingdom Eubacteria?

3. **Describe** the general appearance of cyanobacteria.

Oscillatoria   **Anabaena**

Nostoc   **Gloeocapsa**

Cyanobacteria Observations				
Structure	**Ana-baena**	**Gloe-ocapsa**	**Nostoc**	**Oscill-atoria**
Filament or colony				
Nucleus				
Chlorophyll				
Gel-like layer				

Bacteria in Your Life

Beneficial Bacteria

Have you had any bacteria for lunch lately? Any time you eat cheese or yogurt, you eat some bacteria. Bacteria break down substances in milk to make many everyday products. Cheese-making is illustrated in **Figure 9-7.** If you have eaten sauerkraut, you ate a product made with cabbage and a bacterial culture. Vinegar is also produced by a bacterium.

Figure 9-7 Bacteria that break down proteins in milk are used in production of various kinds of cheese.

A Bacteria such as *Streptococcus lactis* added to milk cause the milk to curdle, or separate into curds (solids) and whey (liquids).

B Other bacteria are added to the curds. Curds are then allowed to ripen into cheese. Which type of cheese is made depends on the bacterial species added to the curds.

What You'll Learn

► Some ways bacteria are helpful
► The importance of nitrogen-fixing bacteria
► How some bacteria cause disease

Vocabulary
saprophyte
nitrogen–fixing bacteria
pathogen
antibiotic
vaccine
toxin
endospore

Why It's Important

► Discovering the ways bacteria affect your life can help you understand biological processes.

Uses of Bacteria

Bacteria called saprophytes (SAP ruh fitz) help maintain nature's balance. A **saprophyte** is any organism that uses dead material as a food and energy source. Saprophytes digest dead organisms and recycle nutrients so that they are available for use by other organisms. Without saprophytic bacteria, there would be layers of dead material deeper than you are tall spread over all of Earth. ✓

Reading Check ✓

What is a saprophyte?

VISUALIZING Nitrogen Fixation

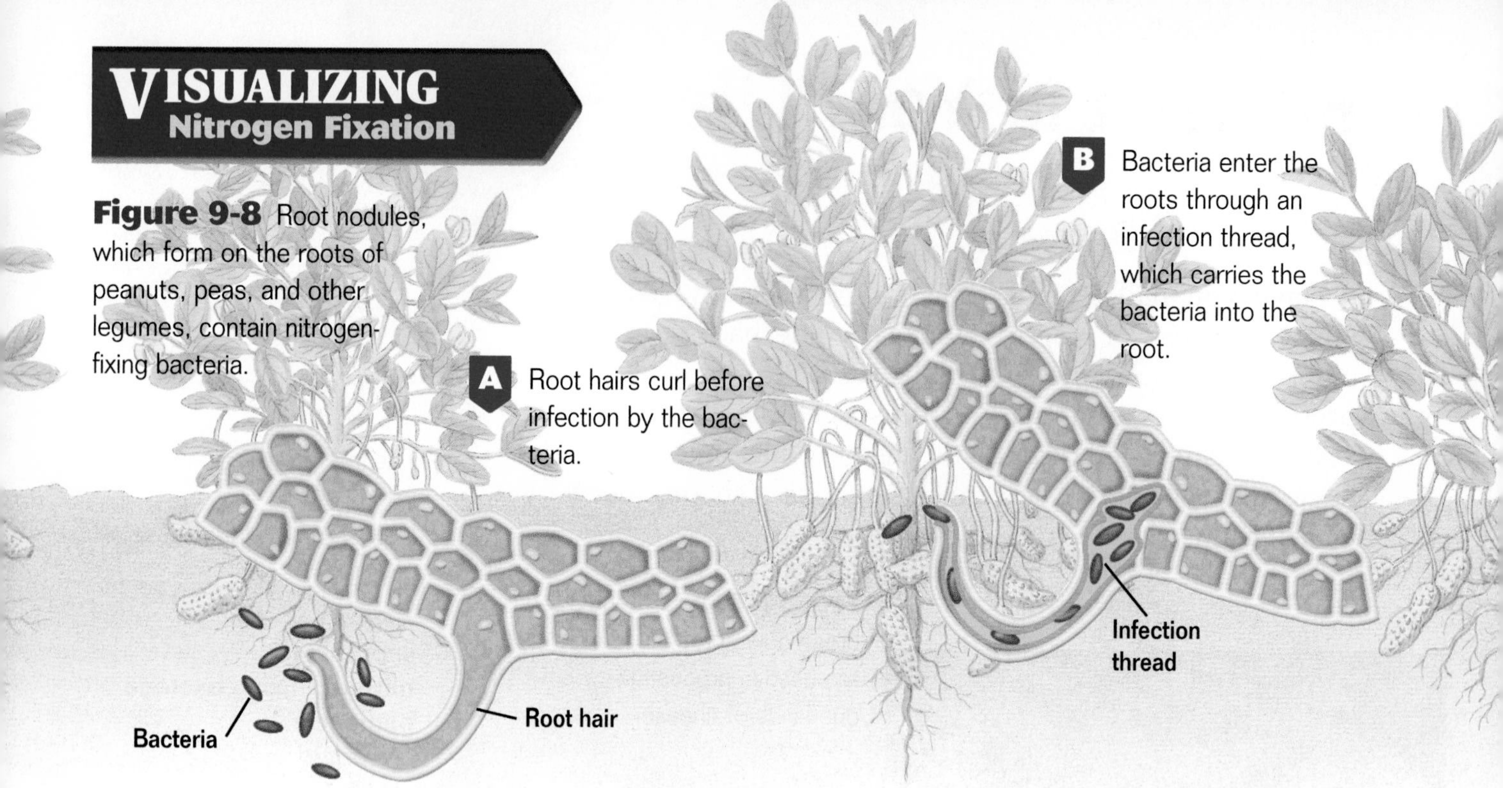

Figure 9-8 Root nodules, which form on the roots of peanuts, peas, and other legumes, contain nitrogen-fixing bacteria.

A Root hairs curl before infection by the bacteria.

B Bacteria enter the roots through an infection thread, which carries the bacteria into the root.

Infection thread

Bacteria

Root hair

The roots of some plants develop nodules when nitrogen-fixing bacteria enter them, as illustrated in **Figure 9-8.** This is especially true of legumes, a plant group that includes peas, peanuts, and clover. These **nitrogen-fixing bacteria** change nitrogen from the air into forms useful for plants and animals. Both plants and animals need nitrogen for making needed proteins and nucleic acids.

Many industries rely on bacteria. Biotechnology is putting bacteria to use in making medicines, enzymes, cleansers, adhesives, and other products. The ability of bacteria to digest oil has been extremely important in helping to clean up the extensive oil spills in Alaska, California, and Texas.

Harmful Bacteria

Some bacteria are pathogens. A **pathogen** is any organism that produces disease. If you have ever had strep throat, you have had firsthand experience with a bacterial pathogen. Other pathogenic bacteria cause anthrax in cattle, and diphtheria, tetanus, and whooping cough in humans. Bacterial diseases in humans and animals are usually treated effectively with antibiotics. An **antibiotic** is a substance produced by one organism that inhibits or kills another organism. Penicillin, a well-known antibiotic, works by preventing bacteria from making cell walls. Without cell walls, bacteria cannot survive.

Some bacterial diseases can be prevented by vaccines. A **vaccine** is made from damaged particles taken from bacterial

*inter*NET
CONNECTION

Visit the Glencoe Science Web Site at **www.glencoe. com/sec/science/ca** for more information about toxin-producing bacteria.

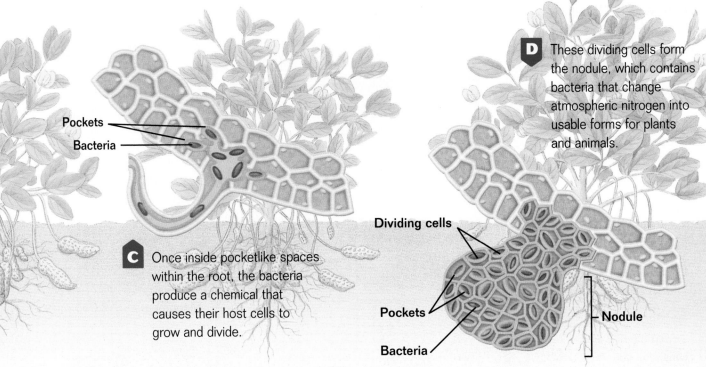

Pockets

Bacteria

C Once inside pocketlike spaces within the root, the bacteria produce a chemical that causes their host cells to grow and divide.

D These dividing cells form the nodule, which contains bacteria that change atmospheric nitrogen into usable forms for plants and animals.

Dividing cells

Pockets

Bacteria

Nodule

cell walls or from killed bacteria. Once injected, the white blood cells in the body learn to recognize the bacteria. If the particular bacteria then enter the body at a later time, the white blood cells immediately attack and overwhelm them. Vaccines have been produced that are effective against many bacterial diseases.

Some pathogens produce poisons. The poison produced by a bacterial pathogen is called a **toxin.** Botulism, a type of food poisoning, is caused by a toxin that can cause paralysis and death. The bacterium that causes botulism is *Clostridium botulinum.* Many bacteria that produce toxins are able to produce thick walls around themselves when conditions are unfavorable. This thick-walled structure is called an **endospore,** illustrated in **Figure 9-9.** Endospores can exist for hundreds of years before they begin to grow again. Botulism endospores must be exposed to heat for a long time to be destroyed. Once the endospores are in canned food, the bacteria can change back to regular cells and start producing toxins. Botulism bacteria are able to grow inside cans because they are anaerobes and do not need oxygen to live.

Try at Home

Mini Lab

Making Yogurt

Procedure

1. Bring a liter of milk almost to a boil in a saucepan. **CAUTION:** *Always be careful when using a stove or hot plate. Do not eat food used in a classroom activity.*

2. Remove the pan from the burner and allow it to cool until it is lukewarm.

3. Add one or two heaping tablespoons of yogurt starter with live cultures and stir.

4. Pour the mixture into a clean thermos and put on the lid.

5. Let stand for six hours and then refrigerate overnight.

Analysis

1. What do you think was in the yogurt starter?

2. Infer why you let the milk cool before adding the starter.

Figure 9-9 Bacteria sometimes form endospores when conditions become unfavorable. These structures can survive harsh winters, dry conditions, and heat. In this photo, the blue in the center of each structure is the endospore. The golden part is the cellular material. **How can botulism endospores be destroyed?**

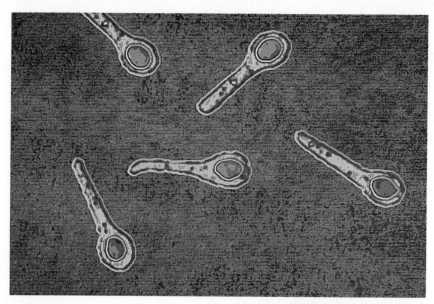

Magnification: 15 000×

PHYSICS
INTEGRATION

Vacuum Packing
A vacuum is a space from which all gas molecules have been removed. Vacuum-packed foods have most of the air removed from around the food. How would this prevent food from spoiling?

Pasteurization

Pasteurization, a process of heating food to a temperature that kills harmful bacteria, is used in the food industry. You are probably most familiar with pasteurized milk, but some fruit juices are also pasteurized. The process is named for Louis Pasteur, who first formulated the process for the wine industry during the nineteenth century in France.

Section Assessment

1. Why are saprophytes helpful and necessary?
2. Why are nitrogen-fixing bacteria important?
3. What makes penicillin an effective antibiotic?
4. **Think Critically:** Why is botulism associated with canned foods and not fresh foods?
5. **Skill Builder**
   Measuring in SI Air may have more than 3500 bacteria per cubic meter. How many bacteria might be in your classroom? If you need help, refer to Measuring in SI in the **Skill Handbook** on page 692.

Using Computers

Spreadsheet Create a spreadsheet that includes: Disease Name, Disease Organism, Method of Transmission, and Symptoms. Enter information for the following diseases: whooping cough, tuberculosis, tetanus, diphtheria, and scarlet fever. Sort your data using Method of Transmission. If you need help, refer to page 702.

Bioremediation

Each year, tons of pollutants are released into ecosystems because of human activities. Many of these pollutants are both poisonous and long lasting. Soil, surface, and groundwater contamination results from the buildup of these harmful compounds. Traditional methods of cleaning up damaged ecosystems, such as the use of landfills and toxic-waste dumps, can be costly and ineffective as long-term solutions.

An Unusual Solution

One approach to cleaning up polluted ecosystems is bioremediation—the use of living organisms, such as bacteria, fungi, and plants, to change pollutants into harmless compounds. Some microorganisms naturally have the ability to break down harmful compounds. Scientists find and isolate these organisms, often stimulating them to clean up polluted areas. Other times, it is necessary to genetically engineer a microorganism to break down specific pollutants. Archaebacteria and eubacteria are the main organisms used in bioremediation efforts. These micro-organisms break down polluting substances—even oil and gasoline—and change them into less damaging compounds, such as carbon dioxide and water. At left, technicians spray a fertilizer mix on an oil-soaked shore to promote the growth of oil-eating bacteria. Although bioremediation is not a complete cure, it is a new way to help repair damaged ecosystems.

Uses and Advantages of Bioremediation

About five to ten percent of all industrial, agricultural, and municipal wastes are being treated by bioremediation. To clean water, for example, bacteria are placed in lagoons or large containers. Then, wastewater is pumped through these sites, and the bacteria break down the pollutants in the water into harmless compounds. In another technique, pollutants are mixed into soil and broken down by microorganisms found there. An advantage of bioremediation is that it can eliminate hazardous waste where it occurs, rather than at a distant treatment site. Bioremediation has proven to be safe and effective, and it costs 60 to 90 percent less than many traditional methods.

interNET CONNECTION

Use the Glencoe Science Web Site at www.glencoe.com/sec/ science/ca to research local waste treatment companies. Do more companies use traditional methods or bioremediation? Try to find out why a company uses a particular method.

Are there bacteria in foods?

Materials

- 6 test tubes
- 6 stoppers
- test-tube rack
- felt-tip marker
- 3 droppers
- 3 craft sticks
- Milk, buttermilk, cottage cheese, yogurt, sour cream, water
- bromothymol blue solution (150 mL)

You've learned that bacteria are too small to be seen without a microscope, but is there some way that you can tell if they are present in foods? Because bacteria produce carbon dioxide like other living things, a chemical test that indicates the presence of carbon dioxide can be used to tell if bacteria are growing in foods you eat.

What You'll Investigate

Is there bacteria in the food you eat?

Goals

- **Observe** color changes in test tubes containing food.
- **Determine** which foods contain the most bacteria.

Procedure

1. Use the marker to label the test tubes 1 through 6 and place them in the test tube rack.

2. Add 25 mL of bromothymol blue-indicator solution to each test tube.

3. Using a different dropper each time, add four drops of water to tube 1, four drops of milk to tube 2, and four drops of buttermilk to tube 3. Be careful not to let the drops go down the sides of the tubes.

4. Using a different craft stick each time, add an amount of yogurt about the size of a green pea to tube 4, the same amount of cottage cheese to tube 5, and the same amount of sour cream to tube 6.

5. Loosely place a stopper in each tube and record the color of the contents of each tube in a data table.

6. Leave the tubes undisturbed until the end of the class period. Record the color of the contents of the tubes in the data table.

7. The next time you arrive in class, record the color of the contents of the tubes again.

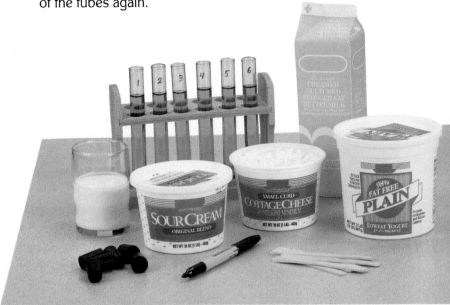

Conclude and Apply

1. Why was water added to tube 1?

2. What color does bromothymol turn if carbon dioxide is present?

3. Using strength of the color change as a guide, judge which tubes contain the most bacteria.

		Color at Start	Color at End of Class	Color One Day Later	Test + or −	Bacteria Present?
Data Table for Test of Bacteria in Food						
Tube	**Contents**	**Color at Start**	**Color at End of Class**	**Color One Day Later**	**Test + or −**	**Bacteria Present?**
1	Water					
2	Milk					
3	Buttermilk					
4	Yogurt					
5	Cottage Cheese					
6	Sour Cream					

For a **preview** of this chapter, study this Reviewing Main Ideas before you read the chapter. After you have studied this chapter, you can use the Reviewing Main Ideas to **review** the chapter.

The Glencoe MindJogger, Audiocassettes, and CD-ROM provide additional opportunities for review.

^{Section}
9-1   TWO KINGDOMS OF BACTERIA

Bacteria are prokaryotic cells that usually reproduce by **fission.** All bacteria contain DNA, ribosomes, and cytoplasm but lack membrane-bound organelles. Bacteria are placed into one of two kingdoms—eubacteria and archaebacteria. The eubacteria are considered to be true bacteria and contain a great variety of organisms. Archaebacteria are bacteria that exist in extreme conditions, such as deep-sea vents and hot springs. Most bacteria break down cells of other organisms to obtain food, but cyanobacteria make their own food. **Anaerobes** are bacteria that are able to live without oxygen, whereas **aerobes** need oxygen to survive. *How do prokaryotic cells differ from eukaryotic cells?*

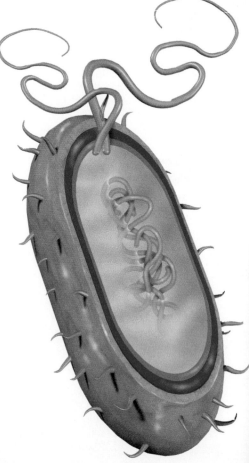

Reading Check ☑

Review **Figure 9-8.** Then, describe the nitrogen-fixing process in your own words, using numbered steps. You will probably have more than four steps.

Section

9-2 BACTERIA IN YOUR LIFE

Bacteria may be helpful or harmful. They may aid in recycling nutrients, fixing nitrogen, or helping in food production. They can even be used to break down harmful pollutants. Other bacteria are harmful because they can cause disease in the organisms they infect. Pasteurization is one process that can prevent harmful bacteria in food. *What are some diseases caused by harmful bacteria?*

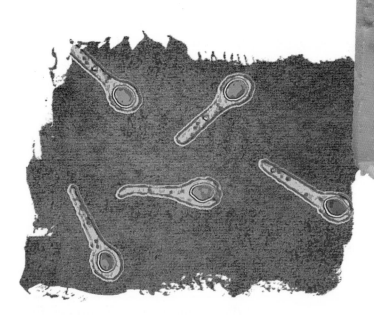

 **Career CONNECTION**

Alice Arellano, Wastewater Operator

Alice Arellano is a wastewater control-room operator responsible for cleaning wastewater in Austin, Texas. Wastewater from peoples' homes in Austin is discharged into the Colorado River, but it first has to be treated. Treatment is a complex process that involves screening, filtering, and chemical treatment. Part of treatment involves using microorganisms, like bacteria, to break down harmful bacteria that live in the wastewater. *How can understanding the way bacteria live help design water-treatment processes?*

Chapter 9 Assessment

Using Vocabulary

a. aerobe
b. anaerobe
c. antibiotic
d. endospore
e. fission
f. flagella
g. nitrogen-fixing bacteria
h. pathogen
i. saprophyte
j. toxin
k. vaccine

Each phrase below describes a science term from the list. Write the term that matches the phrase describing it.

1. organism that decomposes dead organisms
2. structure by which some organisms move
3. heat-resistant structure in bacteria
4. substance that can prevent, not cure, a disease
5. any organism that produces disease

Checking Concepts

Choose the word or phrase that best answers the question.

6. What is a way of cleaning up an eco-system using bacteria to break down harmful compounds?
   A) landfills
   B) toxic waste dumps
   C) waste storage
   D) bioremediation

7. What do bacterial cells contain?
   A) nuclei
   B) DNA
   C) mitochondria
   D) no chromosomes

8. What do bacteria that make their own food have?
   A) chlorophyll
   B) lysosomes
   C) Golgi bodies
   D) mitochondria

9. Which of the following describes most bacteria?
   A) anaerobic
   B) pathogens
   C) many-celled
   D) beneficial

10. What is the name for rod-shaped bacteria?
    A) bacilli
    B) cocci
    C) spirilla
    D) colonies

11. What structure(s) allow(s) bacteria to stick to surfaces?
    A) capsule
    B) flagella
    C) chromosome
    D) cell wall

12. What causes blooms in ponds?
    A) archaebacteria
    B) cyanobacteria
    C) cocci
    D) viruses

13. How are nutrients and carbon dioxide returned to the environment?
    A) producers
    B) flagella
    C) saprophytes
    D) pathogens

14. Which of the following is caused by a pathogenic bacterium?
    A) an antibiotic
    B) nitrogen fixation
    C) cheese
    D) strep throat

15. Which organisms do not need oxygen to survive?
    A) anaerobes
    B) aerobes
    C) humans
    D) fish

Thinking Critically

16. What would happen if nitrogen-fixing bacteria could no longer live on the roots of plants?

17. Why are bacteria capable of surviving in all environments of the world?

18. Farmers often rotate crops such as beans, peas, and peanuts with other crops such as corn, wheat, and cotton. Why might they make such changes?

19. One organism that causes bacterial pneumonia is called pneumococcus. What is its shape?

20. What precautions can be taken to prevent food poisoning?

Developing Skills

If you need help, refer to the **Skill Handbook.**

21. **Concept Mapping:** Use the events chain to sequence the events following a pond bloom.

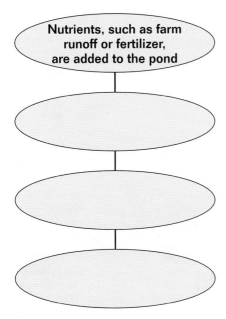

Nutrients, such as farm runoff or fertilizer, are added to the pond

22. **Making and Using Graphs:** Graph the data from the table below. Using the graph, determine where the doubling rate would be at 20°C.

Bacterial Reproduction Rates	
Temperature (°C)	**Doubling Rate per Hour**
20.5	2.0
30.5	3.0
36.0	2.5
39.2	1.2

23. **Interpreting Data:** What is the effect of temperature in question 22?

24. **Design an Experiment:** How could you decide if a kind of bacteria can grow anaerobically?

THE PRINCETON REVIEW

Test-Taking Tip

Investigate Ask what kinds of questions to expect on the test. Ask for practice tests so that you can become familiar with the test-taking materials.

Test Practice

Use these questions to test your Science Proficiency.

1. One group of bacteria are known as extremophiles, which literally means "lovers of the extreme." Which group of organisms would **BEST** fit this name?
   A) eubacteria
   B) archaebacteria
   C) cyanobacteria
   D) aerobes

2. Bioremediation has been shown to have several advantages over traditional methods of ecosystem cleanup. Which of the following is **NOT** an advantage of bioremediation?
   A) It is less time consuming.
   B) It is less costly.
   C) It is more effective.
   D) It can be done at the site of the pollution.

3. Many bacteria are considered beneficial organisms. Which of the following is **NOT** a reason they are considered beneficial?
   A) They change nitrogen in the air to a form useful for plants.
   B) They cause anthrax in cattle.
   C) They are used in food production.
   D) They are the source of some medicines.

Protists and Fungi

Chapter Preview

Section 10-1
Kingdom Protista

Section 10-2
Kingdom Fungi

Skills Preview

Skill Builders
- Compare and Contrast
- Use Variables, Constants, and Controls

Activities
- Observe
- Compare

MiniLabs
- Predict
- Estimate

Reading Check ✔

As you read this chapter, list three things you already knew about protists and fungi, and ten things you are learning about them.

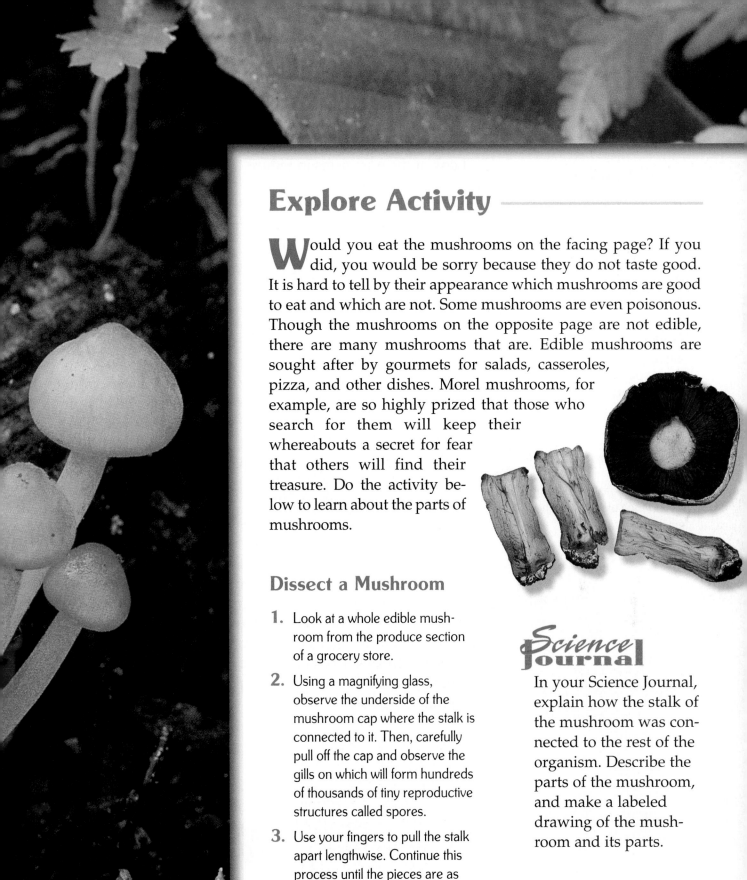

Explore Activity

Would you eat the mushrooms on the facing page? If you did, you would be sorry because they do not taste good. It is hard to tell by their appearance which mushrooms are good to eat and which are not. Some mushrooms are even poisonous. Though the mushrooms on the opposite page are not edible, there are many mushrooms that are. Edible mushrooms are sought after by gourmets for salads, casseroles, pizza, and other dishes. Morel mushrooms, for example, are so highly prized that those who search for them will keep their whereabouts a secret for fear that others will find their treasure. Do the activity below to learn about the parts of mushrooms.

Dissect a Mushroom

1. Look at a whole edible mushroom from the produce section of a grocery store.

2. Using a magnifying glass, observe the underside of the mushroom cap where the stalk is connected to it. Then, carefully pull off the cap and observe the gills on which will form hundreds of thousands of tiny reproductive structures called spores.

3. Use your fingers to pull the stalk apart lengthwise. Continue this process until the pieces are as small as you can get them.

Science Journal

In your Science Journal, explain how the stalk of the mushroom was connected to the rest of the organism. Describe the parts of the mushroom, and make a labeled drawing of the mushroom and its parts.

10·1 Kingdom Protista

What is a protist?

Look at the organisms in **Figure 10-1.** Do you see any similarities among them? As different as they appear, all of these organisms belong to the protist kingdom. A **protist** is a single- or many-celled organism that lives in moist or wet surroundings. All protists have a nucleus and are therefore eukaryotic. Despite these similarities, the organisms in Kingdom Protista (proh TIHS tuh) vary greatly. Some protists contain chlorophyll and make their own food, and others don't. Protists are plantlike, animal-like, and funguslike.

Evolution of Protists

Not much evidence of the evolution of protists can be found because many lack hard parts and, as a result, few fossils of these organisms have been found. However, by studying the genes of modern protists, scientists are able to trace their ancestors. Scientists hypothesize that the common ancestor of all protists was a one-celled organism with a nucleus, mitochondria, and other cellular structures. The cellular structures of this organism may have been different from those found in modern protists. Evidence suggests that protists that can't make their own food evolved differently from protists that do make their own food. Some scientists suggest that a cyanobacterium, a bacterium that contains chlorophyll, was taken up by a one-celled organism with mitochondria. As this organism changed over time, the cyanobacterium became the organism's chloroplast, the organelle where photosynthesis occurs. Plantlike protists probably developed from this kind of organism.

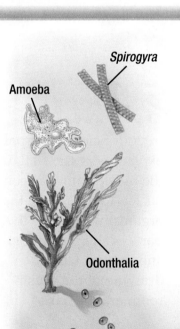

Spirogyra

Amoeba

Odonthalia

Sporozoan

Slime mold

Volvox

EXAMPLES OF
Protists

Figure 10-1 Kingdom Protista is made up of a variety of organisms. **Using what you see in the art, write a description of a protist.**

Plantlike Protists

Plantlike protists are known as **algae** (AL jee). Some species of algae are one celled and others are many celled. All algae can make their own food because they contain the pigment chlorophyll in their chloroplasts. Even though all algae have chlorophyll, not all of them look green. Many have other pigments that cover up their chlorophyll. Species of algae are grouped into six main phyla according to their structure, pigments, and the way in which they store food.

Euglenoids

Algae that belong to the phylum Euglenophyta (yoo GLEE nuh fi tuh) have characteristics of both plants and animals. A typical euglenoid, the Euglena, is shown in **Figure 10-2.** Like plants, these one-celled algae have chloroplasts and produce carbohydrates as food. When light is not present, euglenas feed on bacteria and protists. Although euglenas have no cell walls, they do have a strong, flexible layer inside the cell membrane that helps them move and change shape. Many move by using whiplike tails called flagella. Another animal-like characteristic of euglenas is that they have an adaptation called an eyespot that responds to light.

Diatoms

Diatoms, shown in **Figure 10-3,** belong to the phylum Bacillariophyta (buh sih law ree oh FI tuh) and are found in both freshwater and salt water. Diatoms are photosynthetic, which means they can make their own food. These one-celled algae store food in the form of oil. They have a golden-brown pigment that masks the green chlorophyll. For this reason, they are sometimes referred to as gold-brown algae.

Diatoms reproduce in extremely large numbers. When the organisms die, their small cell walls sink to the floor of the

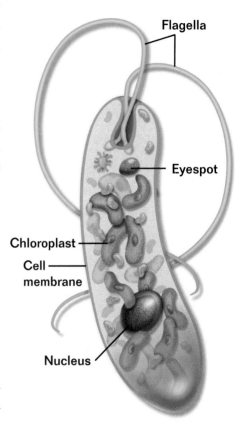

Figure 10-2 How are Euglenas similar to both plants and animals?

Flagella

Eyespot

Chloroplast

Cell membrane

Nucleus

Magnification: 130×

Figure 10-3 The cell wall of diatoms contain silica, the main element in glass. The body of a diatom is like a small box with a lid. Diatoms are covered with markings and pits that form patterns.

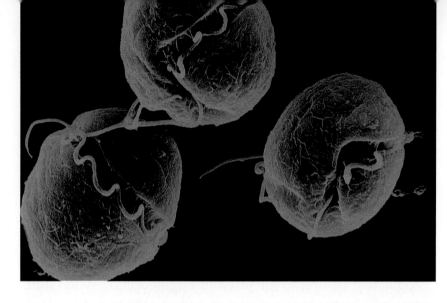

Figure 10-4 Dinoflagellates usually live in the sea. Notice the groove that houses one of the two flagella that mark all members of this group.

Magnification: 3000×

EARTH **SCIENCE**
INTEGRATION ➤

body of water and collect in deep layers. Ancient deposits of diatoms are mined with power shovels and used in insulation, filters, and road paint. The cell walls of diatoms produce the sparkle that makes some road lines visible at night and the crunch you feel when you use toothpaste to brush your teeth.

Dinoflagellates

Phylum Dinoflagellata contains species of one-celled algae called dinoflagellates that have red pigments. Because of their color, they are known as fire algae. The name *dino-flagellate* means "spinning flagellates." One of the flagella moves the cell, and the other circles the cell, causing it to spin with a motion similar to a top. Dinoflagellates, shown in **Figure 10-4,** store food in the form of starches and oils.

VISUALIZING
Green Algae

Figure 10-5 There are many different shapes among the species of green algae.

A *Chlamydomonas* is an example of a one-celled green alga. It is found in freshwater ponds and in moist soil.

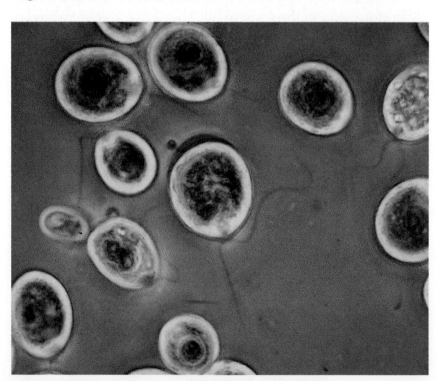

Magnification: 700×

Almost all dinoflagellates live in salt water. They are important food sources for many saltwater organisms. Some dinoflagellates, however, do live in freshwater and are suspected to have caused health problems for humans and other organisms on the East Coast.

Green Algae

Seven thousand species of green algae form the phylum Chlorophyta (klaw RAHF uh duh), giving it the most variety of any group of protists. The presence of chlorophyll in green algae tells you that they undergo photosynthesis and produce food. They are important because nearly half of the oxygen we consume is a result of the photosynthesis of green algae.

Although most green algae live in water, others can live in many other environments, including tree trunks and other organisms. Green algae can be one-celled or many-celled. **Figure 10-5** shows different forms of green algae.

EXAMPLES OF
Green Algae

- **River moss**
- *Chlamydomonas*
- *Volvox*
- *Spirogyra*
- *Ulva*

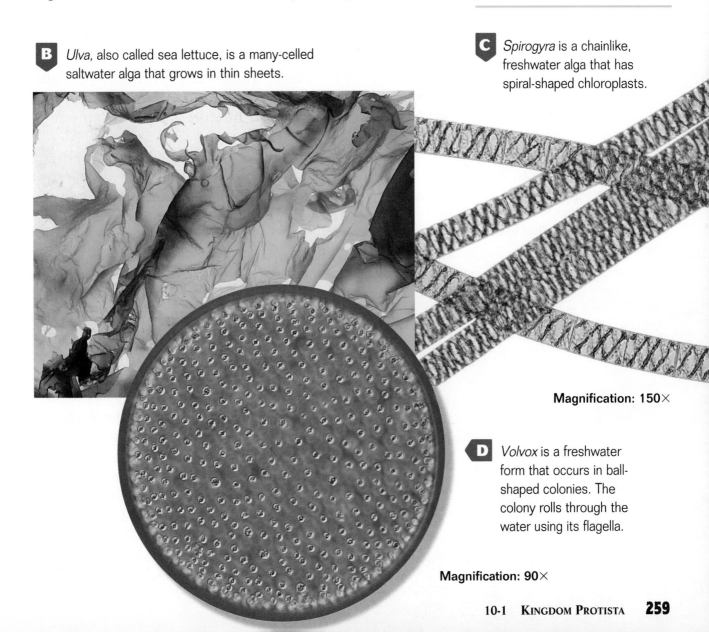

B *Ulva*, also called sea lettuce, is a many-celled saltwater alga that grows in thin sheets.

C *Spirogyra* is a chainlike, freshwater alga that has spiral-shaped chloroplasts.

Magnification: 150✕

D *Volvox* is a freshwater form that occurs in ball-shaped colonies. The colony rolls through the water using its flagella.

Magnification: 90✕

Figure 10-6 Carrageenan, a substance extracted from the red alga Irish moss, gives some puddings their smooth, creamy texture.

Reading Check ✓

What are some common household items that contain red algae?

Red Algae

Red algae belong to the phylum Rhodophyta (roh DAHF uh duh). *Rhodo-* means "red" and describes the color of members of this phylum. Pudding and toothpaste are made with red algae. Carrageenan is found in red algae, such as the Irish moss shown in **Figure 10-6.** It gives toothpaste and pudding their smooth, creamy textures. Most red algae are many-celled. Some species of red algae can live up to 175 m deep in the ocean. Their red pigment allows them to absorb the limited amount of light that penetrates to those depths and enables them to produce the starch on which they live. ✓

Brown Algae

Brown algae make up the phylum Phaeophyta (fee AHF uh duh). Members of this phylum are many-celled and vary greatly in size. They are mostly found growing in cool, saltwater environments. Kelp, shown in **Figure 10-7,** is an important food source for many fish and invertebrates. They form a dense mat of stalks and leaflike blades where small fish and other animals live. Giant kelp are the largest organisms in the protist kingdom.

People in many parts of the world eat brown algae. The thick texture of foods such as ice cream and marshmallows is produced by algin, which is found in these algae. Brown algae also are used to make fertilizer. **Table 10-1** summarizes the different phyla of plantlike protists.

Figure 10-7 Giant kelp may be as much as 100 m long and can form forests like this one located off the coast of California. **What are some practical uses for brown algae?**

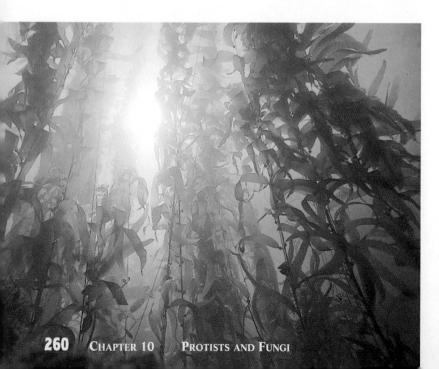

Table 10-1

The Plantlike Protists			
Phylum	**Example**	**Pigments**	**Other Characteristics**
Euglenophyta Euglenoids		Chlorophyll	One-celled alga that moves with flagella; has eyespot to detect light.
Bacillariophyta Diatoms		Golden Brown	One-celled alga with body made of two halves. Cell walls contain silica.
Dinoflagellata Dinoflagellates		Red	One-celled alga with two flagella. Flagella cause cell to spin. Some species cause red tide.
Chlorophyta Green Algae		Chlorophyll	One- and many-celled species. Most live in water; some live out of water, in or on other organisms.
Rhodophyta Red Algae		Red	Many-celled alga; carbohydrate in red algae is used to give some foods a creamy texture.
Phaeophyta Brown Algae		Brown	Many-celled alga; most live in salt water; important food source in aquatic environments.

Animal-Like Protists

One-celled, animal-like protists are known as **protozoans.** These complex organisms live in water, soil, and in both living and dead organisms. Many types of protozoans are parasites. A parasite is an organism that lives in or on another organism. Protozoans contain special vacuoles for digesting food and getting rid of excess water. Protozoans are separated into groups—rhizopods, flagellates, ciliates, and sporozoans—by how they move. **Figure 10-8** is an example of one type of protozoan.

TRAITS OF Animal-like Protists

- One-celled
- Many are parasites
- Grouped by how they move

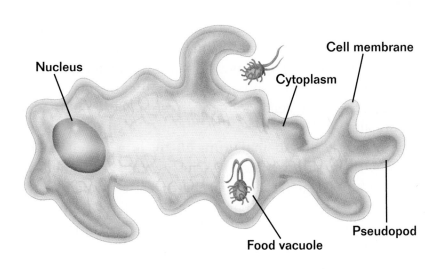

Nucleus

Cell membrane

Cytoplasm

Pseudopod

Food vacuole

Figure 10-8 An amoeba constantly changes shape as it extends its cytoplasm to capture food and move from place to place. Many areas of the world have a species of amoeba in the water that causes the condition dysentery. Dysentery leads to a severe form of diarrhea. **Why is an amoeba classified as a protozoan?**

Figure 10-9 Many saltwater rhizopods have skeletons made out of calcium carbonate, the material that makes up chalk.

 The White Cliffs of Dover in England are made almost entirely of the shells of billions of rhizopods.

 Rhizopod shells come in a variety of shapes.

Magnification: 100×

Figure 10-10 *Trypanosoma,* responsible for African sleeping sickness, is spread by the tsetse fly in Africa. This flagellate is the gray organism in the photo below. The red disks are blood cells. The disease causes fever, swollen glands, and extreme sleepiness.

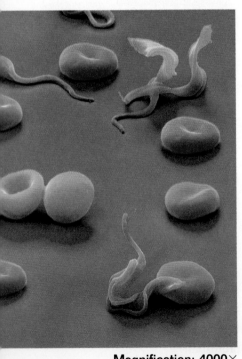

Magnification: 4000×

Rhizopods

The first protozoans were probably similar to members of the phylum Rhizopoda. The amoeba shown in **Figure 10-8** is a typical member of this phylum. Rhizopods move about and feed using temporary extensions of their cytoplasm called **pseudopods** (SEWD uh pahdz). The word *pseudopod* means "false foot." An amoeba extends the cytoplasm of a pseudopod on either side of a food particle such as a bacterium. Then, the pseudopod closes and the particle is trapped. A vacuole forms around the food and it is digested. Members of the phylum Rhizopoda, as shown in **Figure 10-9,** are found in freshwater and saltwater environments, and certain types are found in animals as parasites.

Flagellates

Protozoans that move using flagella are called flagellates and belong to the phylum Zoomastigina (zoe uh mas tuh JINE uh). All of the flagellates have long flagella that whip through a watery environment, moving the organism along. Many species of flagellates live in freshwater, though some are parasites.

Trypanosoma, shown in **Figure 10-10,** is a flagellate that causes African sleeping sickness in humans and other animals. Another flagellate lives in the digestive system of termites. The flagellates are beneficial to the termites because they produce enzymes that digest the wood the termites eat. Without the flagellates, the termites would not be able to digest the wood.

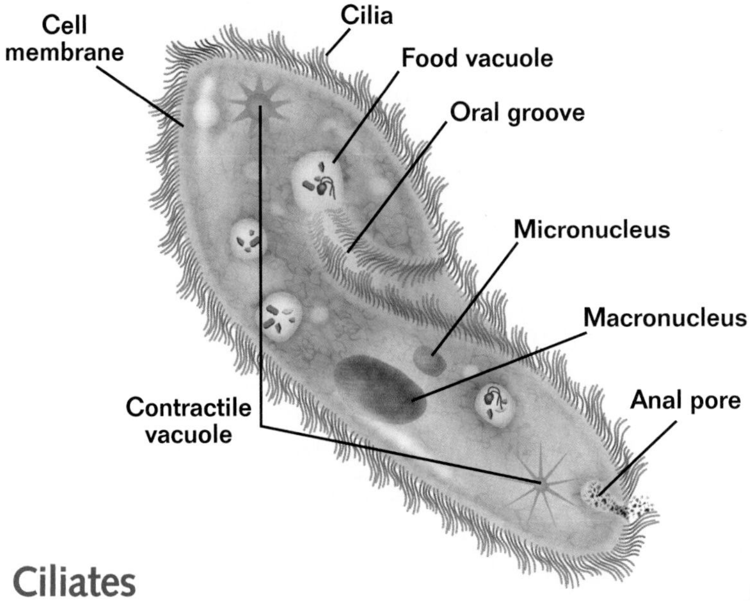

Cell membrane

Cilia

Food vacuole

Oral groove

Micronucleus

Macronucleus

Anal pore

Contractile vacuole

Figure 10-11 *Paramecium* is a typical ciliate found in many freshwater environments. These rapidly swimming protists consume bacteria. **Can you find the contractile vacuoles in the photo below? What is their function?**

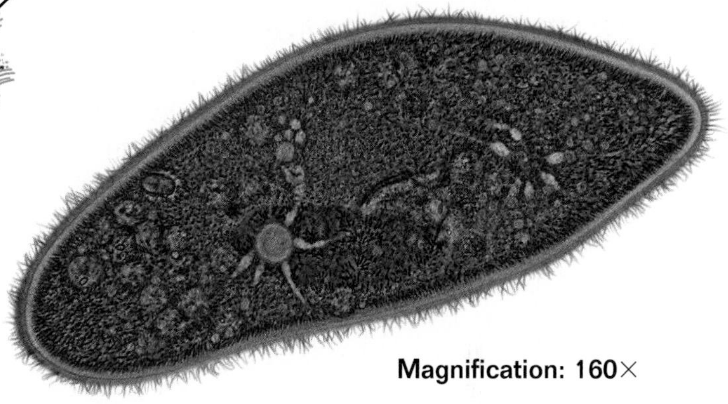

Magnification: 160×

Ciliates

The most complex protozoans belong to the phylum Ciliophora. Members of this phylum move by using cilia. **Cilia** (SIHL ee uh) are short, threadlike structures that extend from the cell membrane. Ciliates may be covered with cilia or have cilia grouped in specific areas of the cell. Cilia beat in an organized way that allows the organism to move swiftly in any direction.

A typical ciliate is *Paramecium,* shown in **Figure 10-11.** In *Paramecium,* you can see another characteristic of the ciliates: each has two nuclei—a macronucleus and a micronucleus. The macronucleus controls the everyday functions of the cell. The micronucleus is used in reproduction. Paramecia usually feed on bacteria swept into the oral groove by the cilia. Once the food is inside the cell, a food vacuole forms and the food is digested. Wastes are removed through the anal pore. As the name implies, a contractile vacuole contracts and excess water is ejected from the cell.

Sporozoans

The phylum Sporozoa contains only parasitic organisms. Sporozoans have no way of moving on their own. All are parasites that live in and feed on the blood of humans and other animals, as shown in **Figure 10-12.**

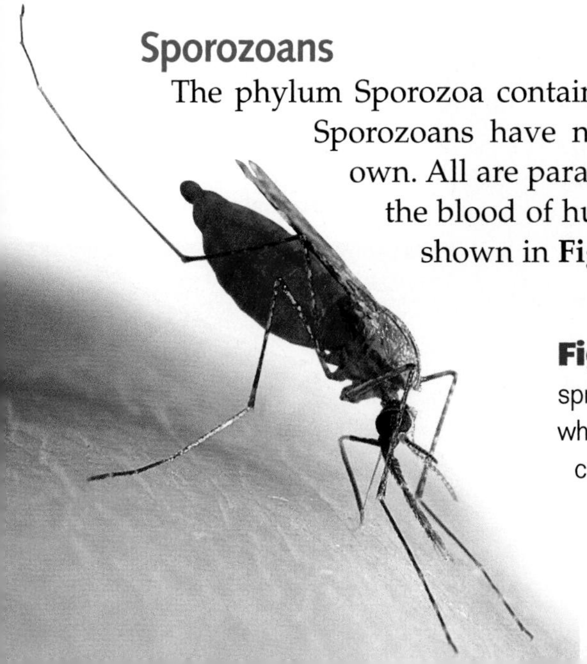

Using Math

A paramecium may be about 0.1 cm long. Giant kelp, a kind of brown algae, may be as much as 100 m long—about the same length as a football field. Using these measurements, how many times larger is a giant kelp than a paramecium?

Figure 10-12 Only female *Anopheles* mosquitoes spread the sporozoan that causes malaria. Malaria is spread when an infected mosquito bites a human. This disease still causes about 1 million deaths each year worldwide.

Mini Lab

Observing Slime Molds

Procedure

1. Obtain live specimens of the slime mold *Physarum polycephaalum* from your teacher.
2. Observe the mold for four days.

Analysis

1. Make daily drawings and observations of the mold as it grows. Use a magnifying glass.
2. Predict the conditions under which the slime mold will change from the amoeboid form to the spore-producing form.

Figure 10-13 Slime molds come in many different forms and colors ranging from brilliant yellow or orange to rich blue, violet, pink, and jet black. **How are slime molds similar to both protists and fungi?**

Blue slime mold

Pink slime mold

Pretzel slime mold

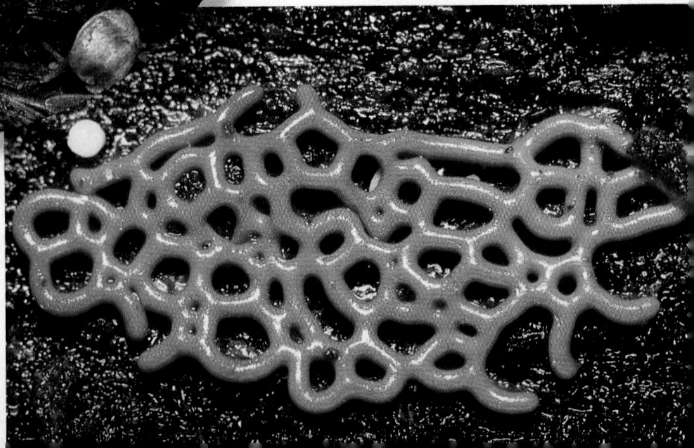

Funguslike Protists

Funguslike protists include several small phyla that have features of both protists and fungi. Slime molds and water molds are funguslike protists. They get energy by breaking down organic materials. Examples of slime molds are illustrated in **Figure 10-13.**

Slime Molds

Slime molds are much more attractive than their name sounds. Many are brightly colored. They form a delicate, weblike structure on the surface of their food supply. Slime molds have some protozoan characteristics. During part of their life cycle, the cells of slime molds move by means of pseudopods and behave like amoebas. Slime molds reproduce with spores the way fungi do. You will learn about reproduction in fungi in the next section.

Although most slime molds live on decaying logs or dead leaves in moist, cool, shady woods, one common slime mold is sometimes found crawling across lawns and mulch. It creeps along feeding on bacteria and decayed plants and animals. When conditions become less favorable, reproductive structures form on stalks and spores are produced.

Water Molds and Downy Mildews

Water molds, downy mildews, and white rusts make up another phylum of funguslike protists. Most members of this large and diverse group live in water or moist places. Most water molds appear as fuzzy, white growths on decaying matter. They are called funguslike protists because they grow as a mass of threads over a plant or animal, digest it, and then absorb the organism's nutrients. Water molds have cell walls as do fungi, but their relatively simple cells are more like protozoans. Unlike fungi, they produce reproductive cells with flagella at some point in their reproductive cycles. Some water molds are parasites of plants while others feed on dead organisms. **Figure 10-14B** shows a parasitic water mold that grows on decaying fish. If you have an aquarium, you may see water molds attack a fish and cause its death.

Another important member of this phylum is a downy or powdery mildew that causes a disease on the leaves of many plants when days have been warm and nights become cooler and moist. In fact, the most well-known member of this phylum is the downy mildew, pictured in **Figure 10-14A,** that caused the Irish potato famine in the 1840s. Potatoes were

*inter*NET
CONNECTION

Visit the Glencoe Science Web Site at **www.glencoe.com/ sec/science/ca** for more information about funguslike protists.

Problem Solving

Puzzled About Slime

At one time, slime molds were classified as fungi. This is because at times, when conditions are unfavorable, they dry up and look like tiny mushrooms. Now, they are classified as protists because they move like protists and have characteristics similar to protists.

Slime molds, such as the scrambled egg slime mold, can be found covering moist wood as in the photograph shown below. They may be white or bright red, yellow, or purple. If you looked at a piece of slime mold on a microscope slide, you would see that the cell nuclei move back and forth as the cytoplasm streams along. This is the method slime mold uses to creep over the wood.

Think Critically: What characteristics do slime molds share with protists? In what ways are slime molds similar to amoebas and fungi? In what ways are they different?

Scrambled egg slime mold

Figure 10-14 The potato plant (A) and the fish (B) show the effects of funguslike protists.

Ireland's main crop and the primary food source for its people. When the potato crop became infected with downy mildew, potatoes rotted in the fields, leaving many people with no food. Nearly 1 million people died in the resulting famine. Many others left Ireland and emigrated to the United States. This downy mildew continues to be a problem for potato growers, even in the United States.

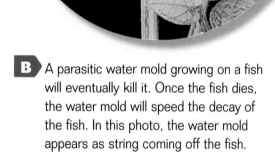

A The Irish potato famine in the 1840s was the result of a downy mildew.

B A parasitic water mold growing on a fish will eventually kill it. Once the fish dies, the water mold will speed the decay of the fish. In this photo, the water mold appears as string coming off the fish.

Section Assessment

1. What are the main characteristics of all protists?
2. Compare and contrast the three groups of protists.
3. How are plantlike protists classified into different phyla?
4. **Think Critically:** Why aren't there many fossils of the different groups of protists?
5. **Skill Builder**
   Making and Using Tables Do the **Chapter 10 Skill Activity** on page 715 and compare and contrast the protist groups.

Using Computers

Spreadsheet Use a spreadsheet to make a table that compares the characteristics of the four phyla of protozoans. Include phylum, example species, method of transportation, and other characteristics. If you need help, refer to page 702.

Comparing Algae and Protozoans

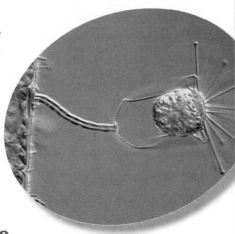

Algae and protozoan cells have characteristics that are similar enough to place them within the same kingdom. However, the variety of forms within Kingdom Protista is great. In this activity, you can observe many of the differences that make organisms in Kingdom Protista so diverse.

Materials

• Cultures of *Paramecium, Amoeba, Euglena,* and *Spirogyra*
  ＊prepared slides of above organisms
• Prepared slide of slime mold
• Coverslips (5)
• Microscope
  ＊stereomicroscope
• Dropper
• Microscope slides (5)
  ＊Alternate Materials

What You'll Investigate

What are the differences between algae and protozoans?

Goals

• **Draw and label** the organisms you examine.
• **Observe** the differences between algae and protozoans.

Safety Precautions

 Make sure to wash your hands after handling algae and protozoans.

Procedure

1. **Design** a data table in your Science Journal for your drawings and observations.

2. **Make** a wet mount of the *Paramecium* culture. If you need help doing this, refer to Appendix D.

3. **Observe** the wet mount first under low and then under high power. Draw and label the organism.

4. Repeat steps 2 and 3 with the other cultures. Return all preparations to your teacher and wash your hands.

5. **Observe** the slide of slime mold under low and high power. Record your observations.

Conclude and Apply

1. For each organism that could move, **label** the structure that enabled the movement.

2. Which protists make their own food? **Explain** how you know that they make their own food.

3. **Identify** those protists with animal characteristics.

Protist Observations				
	Paramecium	**Amoeba**	**Euglena**	**Spirogyra**
Drawing				

Kingdom Fungi

What are fungi?

Do you think you can find members of Kingdom Fungi in a quick trip around your house or apartment? You can find fungi in your kitchen if you have mushroom soup or fresh mushrooms. Yeasts are a type of fungi used to make bread and cheese. You also may find mold, a type of fungus, growing on an old loaf of bread, or mildew, another fungus, growing on your shower curtain.

As important as fungi seem in the production of different foods, they are most important in their role as organisms that decompose or break down organic materials. Food scraps, clothing, dead plants, and animals are all made of organic material. Fungi work to decompose, or break down, all these materials and return them to the soil. The materials returned to the soil are then reused by plants. Fungi, along with bacteria, are nature's recyclers. They keep Earth from becoming buried under mountains of waste materials.

Characteristics of Fungi

Fungi were once classified as plants because, like plants, they grow anchored in soil and have cell walls. But, unlike plants, fungi do not make their own food or have the specialized tissues and organs of plants, such as leaves and roots. Most species of fungi are many-celled. The body of a fungus is usually a mass of many-celled, threadlike tubes called **hyphae** (HI fee), as illustrated in **Figure 10-15.**

Fungi don't contain chlorophyll and therefore cannot make their own food. Most fungi feed on dead or decaying tissues. Organisms that obtain food in this way are called *saprophytes.* A fungus gives off enzymes that break down food outside of

What You'll Learn

▶ How to identify the characteristics shared by all fungi

▶ How to classify fungi into groups based on their methods of reproduction

▶ The difference between the imperfect fungi and all other fungi

Vocabulary
hyphae
spore
budding
lichen

Why It's Important

▶ Fungi are important sources of food and medicines, and they recycle Earth's wastes.

Hyphae

Figure 10-15 Most hyphae grow underground, though they also may form reproductive structures such as the mushrooms pictured here.

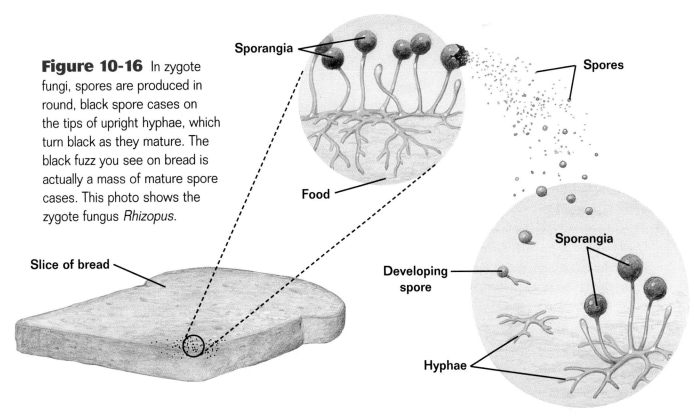

Figure 10-16 In zygote fungi, spores are produced in round, black spore cases on the tips of upright hyphae, which turn black as they mature. The black fuzz you see on bread is actually a mass of mature spore cases. This photo shows the zygote fungus *Rhizopus*.

Sporangia

Spores

Food

Developing spore

Sporangia

Hyphae

Slice of bread

itself. Then, the fungus cells absorb the digested food. Fungi that cause athlete's foot and ringworm are parasites. They obtain their food directly from living things.

Fungi grow best in warm, humid areas, such as tropical forests or the spaces between your toes.

A **spore** is a reproductive cell that forms new organisms without fertilization. The structures in which fungi produce spores are used to classify fungi into one of four phyla.

Zygote Fungi

The fuzzy black mold that you sometimes find growing on an old loaf of bread or perhaps a piece of fruit is a type of zygote fungus. Fungi that belong to this division, the phylum Zygomycota, produce spores in round spore cases called sporangia (spuh RAN jee uh) on the tips of upright hyphae, as illustrated in **Figure 10-16.** When each sporangium splits open, hundreds of spores are released into the air. Each spore will grow into more mold if it lands where there is enough moisture, a warm temperature, and a food supply.

Sac Fungi

Yeasts, molds, morels, and truffles are all examples of sac fungi. The spores of these fungi are produced in a little saclike structure called an ascus. The phylum Ascomycota (ahs coh my COH tuh) is named for these sacs. The ascospores are released when the tip of an ascus breaks open.

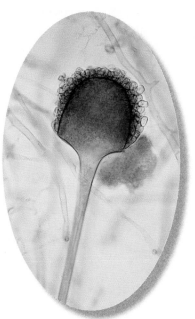

Magnification: 100×

Immature Rhizopus spore

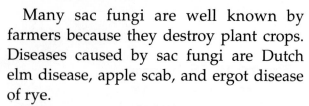

Try at Home

Interpreting Spore Prints

Procedure

1. Obtain several mushrooms from the grocery store and let them age until the undersides look brown.
2. Remove the stems and arrange the mushroom caps with the gills down on a piece of unlined white paper.
3. Let the mushroom caps sit undisturbed overnight and remove them from the paper the next day.

Analysis

1. Draw and label a sketch of the results in your Science Journal.
2. Describe the marks on the page and what made them.
3. How could you estimate the number of new mushrooms that could be produced from one mushroom cap?

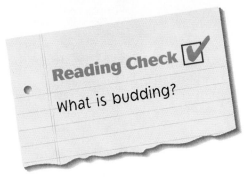

Reading Check ✓

What is budding?

Many sac fungi are well known by farmers because they destroy plant crops. Diseases caused by sac fungi are Dutch elm disease, apple scab, and ergot disease of rye.

Yeast is an economically important sac fungus. Yeasts don't always reproduce by forming spores. They also reproduce asexually by budding, as illustrated in **Figure 10-17. Budding** is a form of asexual reproduction in which a new organism grows off the side of the parent. Yeasts are used in the baking industry. As yeasts grow, they use sugar for energy and produce alcohol and carbon dioxide as waste products. The carbon dioxide causes bread to rise. ✓

Imperfect Fungi

The so-called imperfect fungi, phylum Deuteromycota, are species of fungi in which a sexual stage has never been observed. When a sexual stage of one of these fungi is observed, the species is immediately classified as one of the other three phyla. Instead, imperfect fungi reproduce asexually, most through the use of spores. *Penicillium* is one example from this group. Penicillin, an antibiotic, is an important product of this fungus. Other examples of imperfect fungi are species that cause ringworm and athlete's foot. Because changes in classification now allow asexual fungi to be included in other phyla, *Penicillium* is sometimes considered a sac fungus.

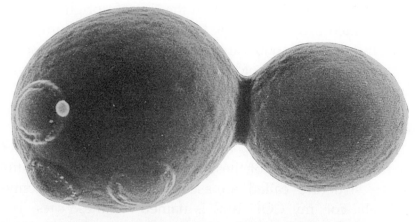

Figure 10-17 Yeasts can reproduce by forming buds off the side of the parents. The bud pinches off and forms an identical cell. **What are yeasts used for?**

Magnification: 6100×

Figure 10-18 A mushroom is the spore-producing structure of a club fungus. The gills are thin sheets of tissue found under the mushroom cap. Spores are contained in many club-shaped structures that line the gills. **What are these club-shaped structures called?**

Club Fungi

The mushrooms shown in **Figure 10-18** are members of the phylum Basidiomycota. These fungi are commonly known as club fungi. The spores of these fungi are produced in a club-shaped structure called a basidium. The spores you observed on the gills of the mushroom in the MiniLab on the previous page were produced in the basidia.

Many of the club fungi are economically important. Rusts and smuts cause billions of dollars worth of damage to food crops each year. Cultivated mushrooms are an important food crop, but you should never eat a wild mushroom because many are poisonous.

Lichens

The colorful organisms in **Figure 10-19** are lichens. A **lichen** (LI kun) is an organism that is made of a fungus and either a green alga or a cyanobacterium. When two organisms live together, they often have a relationship in which both organisms benefit. The cells of the alga live tangled up in the threadlike strands of the fungus. The alga gets a moist, protected place to live, and the fungus gets food made by the green alga or cyanobacterium. Lichens are an important food source for many animals, including caribou and musk oxen.

CHEMISTRY
INTEGRATION

pH
The measurement of how much acid or base a substance contains is its pH. Acids are measured on a pH scale that ranges from 1 to 14. Substances that have a pH lower than 7 are considered acidic. Acids become stronger as the pH decreases. The acids produced by lichens are weak, but given enough time, they can erode sedimentary rock. Look up the pH for some common acids, such as stomach acid, lemon juice, and battery acid. In your Science Journal, compare these to the pH of lichen.

Rocks crumble as they weather. Lichens are important in the weathering process because they are able to grow on bare rock. Lichens release acids as part of their metabolism. The acids break down the rock. As bits of rock accumulate and lichens die and decay, soil is formed. This soil supports the growth of other species. Organisms, such as the lichens seen in **Figure 10-19,** that grow on bare rock are called pioneer species because they are the first organisms to appear in a barren area.

Earth scientists also use lichens to monitor pollution levels because many species of lichens quickly die when they are exposed to pollution. When the lichen species return to grow on tree trunks and buildings, it is an indication that the pollution has been cleaned up.

EXAMPLES OF
Lichens

Figure 10-19 Lichens can grow upright, appear leafy, or look like a crust on bare rock. All three forms may grow near each other. **Can you think of one way that lichens might be classified?**

Crusty lichen

British soldier lichen

Leafy lichen

Section Assessment

1. How do fungi obtain food?
2. What common characteristics are shared by fungi?
3. What are some important functions of lichens?
4. **Think Critically:** If an imperfect fungus were found to produce basidia under some circumstances, how would the fungus be reclassified?
5. **Skill Builder**
   Comparing and Contrasting
   Organize information about fungi in a table. Use this information to compare and contrast the characteristics of the four divisions of fungi. Include information on lichens as a fifth division in your table. If you need help, refer to Comparing and Contrasting in the **Skill Handbook** on page 684.

Using Math

Of the 100 000 species of fungi, approximately 30 000 are sac fungi. From this information, estimate the percent of sac fungi as a part of the total fungi kingdom.

Monitoring Red Tides

What is a red tide?

Imagine a humpback whale dying and washing up on a beach. Then multiply this death by 14. Add to this grisly scene tons of dead fish littering beaches from Florida to Massachusetts. Such events actually happened in 1987. The cause was a single species of dinoflagellate, a type of microscopic algae (see inset). At times, certain kinds of dinoflagellates reproduce rapidly to form extremely dense populations, or "blooms," that turn the ocean surface red—a condition known as a red tide (see photo at left). Pigments in the dinoflagellates are responsible for the red color. It is not unusual for a red tide to stretch hundreds of kilometers along a coastline. Red tides often occur in warm, shallow parts of the ocean, or where runoff from the land adds nutrients to seawater.

Red tides can be deadly because some dinoflagellates produce poisonous substances called toxins. When a red tide occurs, the algae are so numerous that the amount of toxin in the water is concentrated enough to kill fish and marine mammals such as whales. Toxins also accumulate in the tissues of filter-feeding shellfish such as clams and mussels, making them poisonous. People who eat shellfish contaminated by a red tide can become ill and may die.

How are red tides monitored?

In the past, scientists monitored red tides by sampling seawater and shellfish for the presence of dinoflagellates. Wherever large numbers of dinoflagellates were detected, researchers would alert the public not to eat seafood from those areas. This method of monitoring red tides was not always effective, however, because only small stretches of ocean could be tested at any one time, and red tides often developed before scientists became aware of them.

More recently, satellites equipped with infrared cameras have been used to monitor red tides from space. Satellite images reveal sea-surface temperatures over huge areas of ocean and give scientists clues as to where red tides are most likely to occur. Predicting red tides before they develop can help save lives.

interNET CONNECTION

Visit the Glencoe Science Web Site at **www.glencoe.com/sec/ science/ca** for more information about red tides. Determine whether there is an area or time of year in which red tides occur with noticeable frequency.

Materials

- Cultures of fungi (bread mold, mushrooms, yeasts, lichens, or *Penicillium*)
- Cellophane tape
- Microscope
- Microscope slides
- Coverslips
- Magnifying lens

Comparing Types of Fungi

Fungi differ mainly in their reproductive structures. The diversity of these structures allows scientists to classify fungi as zygote fungi, club fungi, sac fungi, or imperfect fungi. In this activity, you will compare the reproductive structures in cultures of fungi.

What You'll Investigate

How do reproductive structures of fungi compare?

Goals

- **Observe** the appearance of fungi colonies.
- **Compare** the reproductive structures of fungi cultures.
- **Draw, label, and identify** different types of fungi.

Safety Precautions

Make sure to wash your hands after handling fungi.

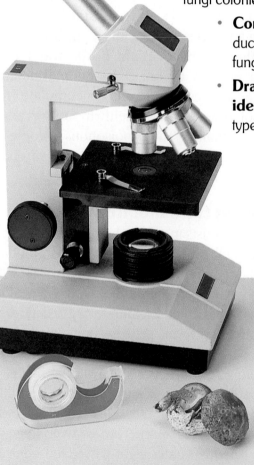

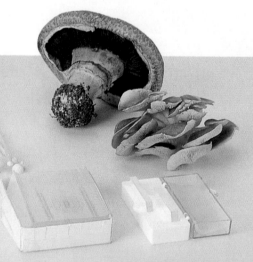

Procedure

1. **Design** a data table like the one below in your Science Journal with columns labeled *Fungus, Colony Appearance, Reproductive Structures,* and *Fungi Division.*

2. **Compare and contrast** the cultures of fungi in drawings that you label.

3. Your teacher will demonstrate how to collect the reproductive structures of fungi with cellophane tape by gently touching the tape to your samples.

4. Place the tape, adhesive side up, on a microscope slide and cover it with a coverslip. If you need help making a wet mount, see **Appendix D.**

5. Draw and label the reproductive structures.

6. Repeat this procedure for each culture of fungus.

7. Fill in the data table you designed. One column has been done for you below.

Conclude and Apply

1. Write a description of the reproductive structures you observed. Include relative numbers, shape of cells, and size.

2. From your descriptions, explain why fungi are classified based on their reproductive structures.

3. List the four divisions of fungi, and give an example of each division.

Fungi Observations			
Fungus	**Colony Appearance**	**Reproductive Structures**	**Fungi Division**
mushrooms	rounded stalks with clublike caps	basidia	club fungi

Chapter 10 Reviewing Main Ideas

For a **preview** of this chapter, study this Reviewing Main Ideas before you read the chapter. After you have studied this chapter, you can use the Reviewing Main Ideas to **review** the chapter.

The Glencoe MindJogger, Audiocassettes, and CD-ROM provide additional opportunities for review.

Section

10-1 KINGDOM PROTISTA

Protists are one- or many-celled eukaryotic organisms. They are thought to have evolved from a one-celled organism with a nucleus, mitochondria, and other cellular structures. The protist kingdom has members that are plantlike, animal-like, and funguslike. Plantlike protists are classified by their structure, their pigments, and the way in which they store food. Animal-like protists are separated into groups by how they move. Funguslike protists have characteristics of both protists and fungi.

What common names are given to each group of protists?

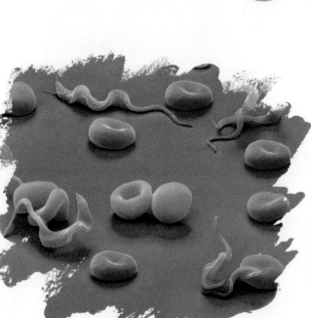

276   CHAPTER 10   PROTISTS AND FUNGI

Reading Check ☑

Review "Other Charac-teristics" in Table 10-1. How could you break the information under this heading into at least two columns?

Section
10-2 KINGDOM FUNGI

Fungi are organisms that reproduce using **spores.** They are saprophytes, or parasites, which means they feed off other things because they cannot make their own food. One of the most important roles of fungi is to decompose organic material and return the nutrients to the soil. There are four groups of fungi: zygote fungus, sac fungus, club fungus, and imperfect fungus. Fungi are placed into one of these groups according to the structures in which they produce spores. *Why are imperfect fungi given that name?*

Career

Dr. Regina Benjamin, Family Practice Physician

Dr. Benjamin runs a family practice in Bayou La Batre, Alabama. She's the only doctor in town, and about 80 percent of her patients live below the poverty level. Dr. Benjamin sees a lot of skin infections caused by fungi because the environment is humid, which promotes the growth of fungus. Fungal infections can be difficult to treat. *Why is classifying protists and fungi important for health care professionals?*

Chapter 10 Assessment

Using Vocabulary

a. algae
b. budding
c. cilia
d. hyphae
e. lichen
f. protist
g. protozoans
h. pseudopods
i. spore

Each phrase below describes a science term from the list. Write the term that matches the phrase describing it.

1. reproductive cell of a fungus
2. eukaryotic organism that is animal-like, plantlike, or funguslike
3. threadlike structures used for movement
4. plantlike protists
5. organism made up of a fungus and an alga or a cyanobacterium

Checking Concepts

Choose the word or phrase that best answers the question.

6. Which of the following is an example of one-celled algae?
   A) paramecia
   C) amoeba
   B) lichen
   D) diatom

7. What color are members of phylum Bacillariophyta?
   A) green
   C) golden-brown
   B) red
   D) brown

8. Which of the following organisms cause red tides when found in large numbers?
   A) *Euglena*
   C) *Ulva*
   B) diatoms
   D) dinoflagellates

9. What phylum do brown algae belong to?
   A) Rhodophyta
   C) Phaeophyta
   B) Dinoflagellata
   D) Euglenophyta

10. Which of the following moves using cilia?
    A) *Amoeba*
    C) *Trypanosoma*
    B) *Paramecium*
    D) *Euglena*

11. Where would you most likely find funguslike protists?
    A) on decaying logs
    B) in bright light
    C) on dry surfaces
    D) on metal surfaces

12. Decomposition is an important role of which organisms?
    A) protozoans
    C) plants
    B) algae
    D) fungi

13. Which of the following organisms are monitors of pollution levels?
    A) club fungus
    C) slime mold
    B) lichen
    D) imperfect fungus

14. What produce the spores in mushrooms?
    A) sporangia
    C) asci
    B) basidia
    D) hyphae

15. Which of the following is an example of an imperfect fungus?
    A) mushroom
    C) *Penicillium*
    B) yeast
    D) lichen

Thinking Critically

16. What kind of environment is needed to prevent fungal growth?

17. Look at **Figure 10-5C** again. Why is *Spirogyra* a good name for this green alga?

18. Compare and contrast one-celled, colonial, chain, and many-celled algae.

19. Why do scientists find it difficult to trace the origin of fungi? Explain your answer.

20. Explain the adaptations of fungi that enable them to get food.

Developing Skills

If you need help, refer to the **Skill Handbook.**

21. **Observing and Inferring:** Match the prefix of each alga, *Chloro-*, *Phaeo-*, and *Rhodo-*, with the correct color: brown, green, and red.

22. **Concept Mapping:** Complete the following concept map on a separate sheet of paper.

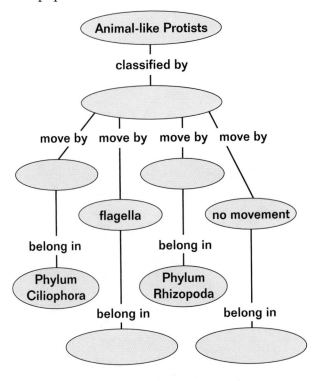

23. **Comparing and Contrasting:** Make a chart comparing and contrasting sac fungi, zygote fungi, club fungi, and imperfect fungi.

24. **Classifying:** Classify the following organisms based on their method of movement: *Euglena*, water molds, *Amoeba*, dinoflagellates, *Paramecium*, slime molds, *Trypanosoma*, and *Volvox*.

25. **Design an Experiment:** You find a new and unusual fungus growing in your refrigerator. Design an experiment to determine what phylum it belongs to.

Test-Taking Tip

Where's the Fire? Slow down! Double-check your math, and go back over reading passages. Remember that doing most of the questions and getting them right is always better than doing all the questions and getting lots of them wrong.

Test Practice

Use these questions to test your Science Proficiency.

1. Algae and plants have some characteristics in common. Which of the following **BEST** represents differences between algae and plants?
   A) Algae have cell walls, but plants do not.
   B) Plants have chlorophyll, but algae do not.
   C) Algae have cell membranes and nuclei, but plants do not.
   D) Plants have roots, stems, and leaves, but algae do not.

2. At one time, some protists were classified as animals because they moved and engulfed food. Which of the following protists are most like animals?
   A) protozoans
   B) algae
   C) slime molds and water molds
   D) zygote fungi

3. Fungi are classified according to how they produce sexual spores. Which of the following groups of fungi are **NOT** known to ever produce sexual spores?
   A) zygote fungi
   B) imperfect fungi
   C) club fungi
   D) sac fungi

Chapter Preview

Skills Preview

Skill Builders

- Hypothesize
- Map Concepts

Activities

- Predict
- Compare and Contrast

MiniLabs

- Measure in SI
- Observe and Infer

Reading Check ✓

As you read, list terms that describe parts of both plants and people, such as *vascular tissue, cuticle,* and *epidermis.* Define the terms as they relate to plants and to people.

Explore Activity

Plants are all around—in parks and gardens, by streams and on rocks, in houses, and even on dinner plates. Do you eat salads? Salads are made up of edible plants. What plants would you choose for a salad? Do you know what plant parts you would be eating? In the following activity, find out which plant parts are edible. Then, in the chapter, learn about plant life.

Infer Which Plant Parts Are Edible

1. Make a list of five foods that you might eat during a typical day.
2. Decide whether the foods contain any plant parts.
3. Infer what plant parts were used to make your five foods.

Science Journal

Plants provide many nutrients. List the nutrients from a package of dried fruit in your Science Journal. As a class, compare the nutrients in the dried fruits each student selected.

Characteristics of Plants

What You'll Learn

▶ The characteristics of plants
▶ What plant adaptations make it possible for plants to survive on land
▶ Similarities and differences between vascular and nonvascular plants

Vocabulary
cellulose
cuticle
vascular plant
nonvascular plant

Why It's Important

▶ Plants produce food and oxygen for most organisms on Earth. Without plants, there would be no life.

What is a plant?

Do you enjoy walking along nature trails in parks like the one shown in **Figure 11-1?** Maybe you've taken off your shoes and walked barefoot on soft, cool grass. Perhaps you've climbed a tree to see what your world looks like from high in its branches. In every instance, members of the plant kingdom surrounded you.

Now look at **Figure 11-2.** These organisms, mosses and liverworts, have characteristics that identify them as plants, too. What do they have in common with grasses, trees, and ferns? What makes a plant a plant?

Characteristics of Plants

All plants are made of eukaryotic cells that have cell walls. Cell walls provide structure and protection for plant cells. Many plant cells contain the green pigment chlorophyll. Plants range in size from microscopic water ferns to giant sequoia trees that are sometimes more than 100 m in height. They have roots or rootlike structures that hold them in the ground or onto something. Plants have successfully adapted to nearly every environment on Earth. Some grow in frigid, ice-bound polar regions and others grow in hot, dry deserts. Many plants must live in or near water.

About 285 000 plant species have been discovered and identified. Scientists think many more are still to be found, mainly in tropical rain forests. If you were to make a list of all

Figure 11-1 All plants are many celled and nearly all contain chlorophyll. Grasses, trees, and ferns all are members of Kingdom Plantae.

A

B

Figure 11-2 Plants include liverworts (A) and mosses (B).

the plants you could name, you probably would include vegetables, fruits, and field crops like wheat, rice, or corn. These plants are important food sources to humans and other consumers. Without plants, most life on Earth as we know it would not be possible.

Origin and Evolution of Plants

Where did the first plants come from? Like all life, early plants probably came from the sea, evolving from plantlike protists. What evidence is there that this is true? Both plants and green algae, a type of protist, have the same types of chlorophyll and carotenoids (KER uh tuh noydz) in their cells. Carotenoids are red, yellow, or orange pigments found in some plants and in all cyanobacteria.

Fossil Record

One way to understand the evolution of plants is to look at the fossil record. Unfortunately, plants usually decay before they form fossils. The oldest fossil plants are from the Silurian period and are about 420 million years old. Fossils of early plants are similar to the plantlike protists. Fossils of *Rhynia major*, illustrated in **Figure 11-3,** represent the earliest land plants. Scientists hypothesize that these kinds of plants evolved into some plants that exist today.

Cone-bearing plants, such as pines, probably evolved from a group of plants that grew about 350 million years ago. Fossils of these plants have been dated to the Paleozoic era, 300 million years ago. Flowering plants did not exist until the Cretaceous period, about 120 million years ago. The exact origin of flowering plants is not known.

Using Math

Fossil evidence shows that the first land plants lived about 420 million years ago. If Earth is 4.6 billion years old, what percent of Earth's age was Earth without land plants?

Figure 11-3 Fossils of *Rhynia major*, an extinct, small land plant, show that it had underground stems but no true roots or leaves.

Adaptations to Land

Imagine life for a one-celled green alga, a protist, floating in a shallow pool. The water in the pool surrounds and supports it. The alga can make its own food through the process of photosynthesis. Materials enter and leave the cell through the cell membrane and cell wall. The alga has everything it needs to survive.

Now, imagine a summer drought. The pool begins to dry up. Soon, the alga is on damp mud and is no longer supported by the pool's water, as shown in **Figure 11-4.** It won't starve because it still can make its own food. As long as the soil stays damp, the alga can move materials in and out through the cell membrane and cell wall. But, what will happen if the drought continues, and the soil becomes drier and drier? The alga will continue to lose water because water diffuses through the cell membrane and cell wall from where there is more water to where there is less water. Without water in its environment, the alga will dry up and die.

Protection and Support

What adaptations would make it possible for plants to survive on land? Losing water is a major problem for plants. What would help a plant conserve water? Plant cells have cell membranes, but they also have rigid cell walls outside the membrane. Cell walls contain **cellulose** (SEL yuh lohs), an organic compound made up of long chains of glucose molecules. Some woody plants, such as oaks and pines, are as much as 50 percent cellulose. Cell walls provide structure and support and help reduce water loss.

Figure 11-4 Algae must have water to survive.

A Each green alga produces its own food and moves materials in and out through the cell membrane. **By what process do algae make food?**

B If a pond completely dries up, the algae in it will die.

Figure 11-5 A waxy cuticle is an adaptation that enables plants to survive on land.

A Rain beads up on the leaves of some plants because of the cuticle. This reduces the amount of moisture on plant surfaces.

B A waxy cuticle prevents moisture loss from this prickly pear cactus. **Why is this important for a cactus?**

C Waxy cuticles are often found on flowers such as this orchid.

Covering the stems, leaves, and flowers of some land plants is a cuticle. The **cuticle** (KYEWT ih kul) is a waxy, protective layer secreted by the cell walls. It slows down the evaporation of water from a plant. After it rains, go outside and see how raindrops bead up on some plant surfaces, as illustrated in **Figure 11-5A.** Removing water from plant surfaces is important because too much moisture on a plant may affect cell functions. Too much surface moisture also may lead to fungal diseases. The cuticle is an adaptation that enabled plants to live on land. ☑

Life on land meant that plant cells could not depend on water to support them or to move substances from one cell to the next. Support came with the evolution of stems and substances that strengthen the cell walls. Eventually, plants developed tissues that distribute materials.

Reading Check ☑

What is the protective layer secreted by cell walls?

Reproduction

The move to land by plants not only meant changes to reduce water loss and increase support, but it also meant a change in plant reproduction. Plants evolved from organisms that reproduced in water. They completely depended on water for reproduction and survival. Some plants still require water to reproduce, but others do not. The development of cones and flowers that produce seeds allowed these plants to survive on land.

Life on Land

Life on land has some advantages for plants. There is more sunlight and carbon dioxide for plants on land than in water. Plants use sunlight and carbon dioxide for the food-making process, photosynthesis. During photosynthesis, plants give off oxygen. As more and more plants adapted to life on land, the amount of oxygen in Earth's atmosphere increased. This paved the way for the evolution of organisms that depend on oxygen. In some cases, it meant that some organisms evolved together. For example, some flowering plants provided animals with food, and the animals pollinated the plant's flowers.

Classification of Plants

Today, the plant kingdom is classified into major groups called divisions, as illustrated in **Figure 11-6.** A division is the same as a phylum in other kingdoms, as listed in Appendix E of this book. A less formal way to group plants is as vascular or nonvascular plants. **Vascular plants** have tissues that make up the organ system that carries water, nutrients, and other substances throughout the plant. **Nonvascular plants** have no vascular tissue and use other ways to move water and substances.

Problem Solving

Cause and Effect in Nature

People in all cultures have used and still use plants as medicine. Some Native American cultures used willow bark to cure headaches. Heart problems were treated with foxglove in England and sea onions in Egypt. In Peru, the bark of the cinchona tree was used to treat malaria. Scientists have found that many native cures are medically sound. Willow bark contains salicylates, the main ingredient in aspirin. Foxglove, as seen in the photo to the right, is still the main source of digitalis, a drug prescribed for heart problems. Cinchona bark contains quinine, an anti-malarial drug.

Think Critically: Predict how the destruction of the rain forests might affect research for new drugs from plants.

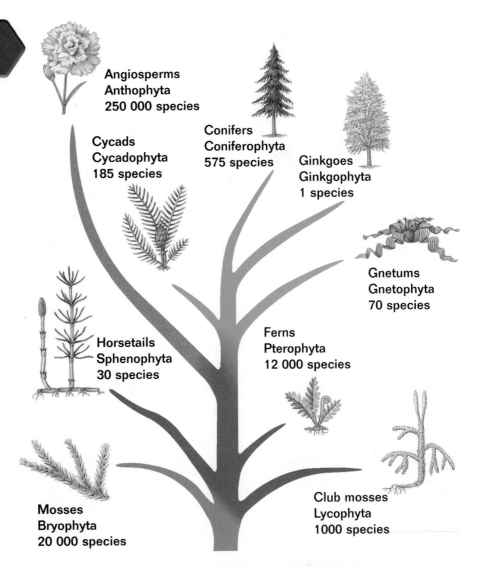

Figure 11-6 The diversity of Kingdom Plantae is represented by a branching tree, composed of different divisions. All of these plant groups are related but have differences that separate them. **What differences can you detect among the plant divisions in this illustration?**

Angiosperms
Anthophyta
250 000 species

Cycads
Cycadophyta
185 species

Conifers
Coniferophyta
575 species

Ginkgoes
Ginkgophyta
1 species

Gnetums
Gnetophyta
70 species

Horsetails
Sphenophyta
30 species

Ferns
Pterophyta
12 000 species

Mosses
Bryophyta
20 000 species

Club mosses
Lycophyta
1000 species

Section Assessment

1. List the characteristics of plants.

2. Compare vascular and nonvascular plants.

3. Name three adaptations that allow plants to survive on land.

4. **Think Critically:** If you left a board lying on the grass for a few days, what would happen to the grass underneath the board? Why?

5.  **Skill Builder**
   Forming a Hypothesis From what you have learned about adaptations necessary for life on land, make a hypothesis as to what types of adaptations land plants might have if they had to survive submerged in water. If you need help, refer to Forming a Hypothesis in the **Skill Handbook** on page 686.

Science Journal
The oldest surviving plant species is *Ginkgo biloba*. Research the history of this species, then write about it in your Science Journal.

11•2 Seedless Plants

Seedless Nonvascular Plants

If you were asked to name the parts of a plant, you probably would list roots, stems, leaves, and perhaps flowers. You also may know that many plants grow from seeds. But, did you know that some plants do not have all of these parts? **Figure 11-7** shows some common types of nonvascular plants.

Liverworts and Mosses (Bryophytes)

The bryophytes (BRI uh fites)—liverworts and mosses—are small, nonvascular plants that are usually just a few cells thick and only 2 cm to 5 cm in height. They have stalks that look like stems and leafy green growths. The threadlike roots of bryophytes are called **rhizoids.** Water is absorbed and distributed directly through their cell walls. Bryophytes grow in damp environments such as the forest floor, the edges of ponds and streams, and near the ocean. Bryophytes usually reproduce by spores because they do not have flowers to produce seeds.

Liverworts get their name because to some people, one type looks like a liver. It is a rootless plant that has a flattened, leaflike body. Liverworts usually have one-celled rhizoids. In the ninth century, liverworts were thought to be useful in treating diseases of the liver. The ending, *-wort,* means "herb," so the word *liverwort* means "herb for the liver." Of approximately 20 000 species of nonvascular plants, most are classified as mosses. Have you ever seen mosses growing on tree trunks, rocks, or the ground in damp or humid areas? Mosses have green, leaflike

What You'll Learn

► Characteristics of seedless nonvascular plants and seedless vascular plants
► The importance of some nonvascular and vascular plants

Vocabulary
rhizoid
pioneer species

Why It's Important

► Seedless plants are often the first to grow in damaged or disturbed environments.

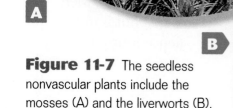

A

B

Figure 11-7 The seedless nonvascular plants include the mosses (A) and the liverworts (B).

Figure 11-8 Mosses are often among the first organisms to live in a new environment, such as this lava field. **Where do the mosses come from?**

EARTH SCIENCE
INTEGRATION

Soil Formation
Soil is a mixture of weathered rock and decaying organic matter (plant and animal). Infer what roles pioneer species such as lichens, mosses, and liverworts play in building soil.

growths in a spiral around a stalk. Their threadlike rhizoids are only a few cells in length.

The Importance of Bryophytes

Mosses and liverworts are important in the ecology of many areas. Although mosses require moist conditions to grow and reproduce, many of them can withstand long, dry periods. Often, they are among the first plants to grow in new environments, such as lava fields as shown in **Figure 11-8,** or disturbed environments, such as forests destroyed by fire.

When a volcano erupts, lava covers the land and destroys the plants living there. After the lava cools, spores of mosses and liverworts are carried by the wind to the new rocks. The spores will grow into plants if enough water is available and other growing conditions are right. Organisms that are the first to grow in new or disturbed areas like these are called **pioneer species.** As pioneer plants grow and die, decaying plant material builds up. This, along with the breakdown of rocks, begins the formation of soil. Pioneer plants change environmental conditions so that other plants can grow.

Mini Lab

Measuring Water Absorption by a Moss

Procedure

1. Place a few teaspoons of *Sphagnum* moss on a piece of cheesecloth. Twist the cheesecloth to form a ball and tie it securely.
2. Weigh the ball.
3. Put 200 mL of water in a container and add the ball.
4. Predict how much water the ball will absorb.
5. Wait 15 minutes. Remove the ball and drain the excess water back into the container.

Analysis

1. Weigh the ball and measure the amount of water left in the container.
2. In your Science Journal, calculate how much water the *Sphagnum* moss absorbed.

Seedless Vascular Plants

The plants in **Figure 11-9** are like mosses because they are seedless plants that reproduce by spores. They are different from mosses because they have vascular tissue. The vascular tissue in the seedless vascular plants is made up of long, tubelike cells. These cells carry water, minerals, and nutrients to cells throughout the plant. Why is having cells like these an advantage to a plant? Remember that bryophytes are only a few cells thick. Each cell absorbs water directly from its environment. As a result, these plants cannot grow large. Vascular plants, on the other hand, can grow bigger and thicker because the vascular tissue distributes water and nutrients. ☑

Types of Seedless Vascular Plants

Seedless vascular plants include the ground pines, spike mosses, horsetails, and ferns. Today, there are about 1000 species of ground pines, spike mosses, and horsetails. Ferns are more abundant, with at least 12 000 species known. Many species of seedless vascular plants are known only from fossils. They flourished during the warm, moist Paleozoic era. Fossil records show that some horsetails grew 15 m tall, unlike modern species that only grow 1 m to 2 m tall.

Figure 11-9 The seedless vascular plants include ground pines, spike mosses, horsetails, and ferns. **Why can these plants grow taller than mosses and liverworts?**

Ferns

Horsetails

Spike moss

Ground pine

Figure 11-10 Club mosses such as ground pines (A) and spike mosses (B) produce spores at the end of stems in tiny, conelike structures. Photographers once used the dry, flammable spores of club mosses as flash powder. It burned rapidly and produced the light to take photographs.

Ground Pines and Spike Mosses

The photographs in **Figure 11-10** show ground pines and spike mosses. Both groups of plants are often called club mosses. They are seedless vascular plants with needlelike leaves. Spores are produced at the end of the stems in structures that look like tiny pine cones. Ground pines are found from arctic regions to the tropics, but never in large numbers. In some areas, they are endangered because they have been overcollected to make wreaths and other decorations.

Spike mosses resemble ground pines. One species of spike moss, the resurrection plant, is adapted to desert conditions. When water is scarce, the plant curls up and seems dead. When water becomes available, the resurrection plant unfurls its green leaves and begins making food again. The plant can repeat this process whenever necessary.

Horsetails

Horsetails have a stem structure unique among the vascular plants. Their stems are jointed and have a hollow center surrounded by a ring of vascular tissue. At each joint, leaves grow around the stem. In **Figure 11-11,** you can see these joints easily. If you pull on a horsetail stem, it will pop apart in sections. Like the club mosses, spores from horsetails are produced in a conelike structure at the tips of some stems.

Figure 11-11 The spores of horsetails are found in conelike structures on the tips of some stems.

Figure 11-12 Most ferns produce spores in special structures on the leaves, but the spores of the cinnamon fern are on a separate stalk.

The stems of the horsetails contain silica, a gritty substance found in sand. For centuries, horsetails have been used for polishing objects, sharpening tools, and scouring cooking utensils. Another common name for horsetails is scouring rush.

Ferns

Ferns belong to the largest group of seedless vascular plants. Ferns, like those in **Figure 11-12,** have stems, leaves, and roots. They also have characteristics of both nonvascular and vascular plants.

Like the bryophytes, ferns produce spores, and they have vascular tissue like vascular plants. Today, thousands of species of ferns grow on Earth, but once there were many more. From clues left in rock layers, scientists know that during the Carboniferous period of the Paleozoic era, much of Earth was tropical. Steamy swamps covered large areas, as illustrated in **Figure 11-13.** The tallest plants were species of ferns. The ancient ferns grew as tall as 25 m—much taller than any fern species alive today. The tallest, modern tree ferns are about 3 m to 5 m in height.

Formation of Fuel

When ferns and other plants of the Carboniferous period died, many of them became submerged in water and mud before they could decompose. This plant material built up, became compacted and compressed, and eventually turned into coal. This process took millions of years.

Today, a similar process is taking place in bogs. A bog is a poorly drained area of land that contains decaying plants. The decay process is slow because waterlogged soils do not

contain oxygen. The plants in bogs are mostly seedless plants like mosses and ferns. Peat, the remains of peat mosses, is mined from bogs in some countries for a low-cost fuel. Scientists hypothesize that over time, if additional layers of soil bury, compact, and compress the peat, it will become coal.

Figure 11-13 Many more species of club mosses, horsetails, and ferns grew in carboniferous swamp forests than are alive today.

Section Assessment

1. Compare and contrast the mosses and ferns.

2. What do fossil records tell us about seedless plants?

3. Under what conditions would you expect to find pioneer plants?

4. **Think Critically:** List ways seedless plants affect your life each day. (HINT: Where do electricity and heat for homes come from?)

5. **Skill Builder**
   Concept Mapping Make a concept map showing how seedless nonvascular and seedless vascular plants are related. Include these terms in the concept map: *plant kingdom, bryophytes, seedless nonvascular plants, seedless vascular plants, ferns, ground pines, horsetails, liverworts, mosses,* and *spike mosses.* If you need help, refer to Concept Mapping in the **Skill Handbook** on page 678.

Using Math

There are approximately 8000 species of liverworts and 9000 species of mosses. Estimate what fraction of bryophytes are mosses.

Comparing Seedless Plants

Materials

One living example of each of these plants:
- Moss
- Liverwort
- Club moss
- Horsetail
- Fern
  - *detailed photographs of the above plant types*
  - *Alternate Material*

Liverworts, mosses, ferns, horsetails, and club mosses have at least one common characteristic—they reproduce by spores. But, do they have other things in common? In this activity, discover their similarities and differences.

What You'll Investigate

How are seedless plants alike and how are they different?

Goals

- **Observe** types of seedless plants.
- **Compare and contrast** seedless plants.

Procedure

1. Copy the Plant Observations table into your Science Journal.

2. Examine each plant and fill in the table using the following guidelines:
   Color—green or not green
   Growth—mostly flat and low or mostly upright
   Root Type—small and fiberlike or rootlike
   Leaf Form—needlelike, scalelike, or leaflike

Conclude and Apply

1. **Observe and infer** what characteristics seedless plants have in common.

2. **Hypothesize** about the differences in growth.

3. **Compare and contrast** the seedless plants.

Plant Observations				
Plant	**Color**	**Growth**	**Root Type**	**Leaf Form**
Moss				
Liverwort				
Club moss				
Horsetail				
Fern				

Preservation in Peat Bogs

A bog is a wetland, characterized by wet, spongy, poorly drained ground. It typically contains a thin layer of living plants overlying a thick layer of partially decomposed plant material called peat. One of the major types of peat is moss peat. It is formed mostly from *Sphagnum* moss. Peat bogs are acidic, low in minerals, and lack oxygen. These conditions provide a unique environment. When some types of organisms become trapped and buried in a peat bog, they do not decay. In Europe and North America, the well-preserved bodies of humans and other animals have been found in peat bogs.

STEP BY STEP

1 Mosses and other wetland plants grow on the surface of a bog.

2 Over time, a layer of partially decayed plant matter accumulates. Eventually, this becomes a thick layer of peat.

3 A substance in the cell walls of *Sphagnum* moss reacts with, and ties up, certain nutrients. These nutrients are essential for the survival of decay-causing bacteria. Without these nutrients, the bacteria cannot live in a bog.

4 When an animal is buried in a bog, its soft tissues, such as skin and internal organs, are not destroyed by decay. But, the animal's bones are dissolved away because of the acidic environment.

5 The skin of animals buried in a peat bog undergoes a sort of tanning process. Human skin becomes leatherlike and coffee colored, as seen in the photograph below.

Think Critically

1. What kinds of information might scientists gain by studying bog-preserved ancient humans?
2. Another type of peat is fuel peat. What property of peat do you think makes it usable as a fuel?

Career CONNECTION

Archaeologists have found hundreds of preserved animals in peat bogs. An archaeologist studies ancient peoples, their remains, and their culture. Pretend you are an archaeologist. Imagine what it must be like for archaeologists to discover human remains.

11•3 Seed Plants

What is a seed plant?

Have you ever eaten vegetables like the ones shown in **Figure 11-14?** All of these foods come from seed plants. What fruits and vegetables have you eaten today? If you had an apple, a peanut butter and jelly sandwich, or a glass of orange juice for lunch, you ate foods that came from seed plants.

Nearly all the plants you are familiar with are seed plants. Seed plants have roots, stems, leaves, and vascular tissue and produce seeds. A seed usually contains an embryo and stored food. The stored food is the source of energy for growth of the embryo into a plant. More than 250 000 species of seed plants are known in the world today. Seed plants are generally classified into two major groups: the gymnosperms and the angiosperms.

What You'll Learn

► The characteristics of seed plants
► The structures and functions of roots, stems, and leaves
► The main characteristics of gymnosperms and angiosperms and their importance
► Similarities and differences of monocots and dicots

Vocabulary

xylem   gymnosperm
phloem   angiosperm
cambium   monocot
stomata   dicot
guard cell

Why It's Important

► Understanding seed plants will help you appreciate how much you depend on them.

Figure 11-14 The products of plants, like these being sold at a market in Ecuador, provide food for humans. **How are plants an important part of the world's food supply?**

Figure 11-15 The vascular tissue of some seed plants includes xylem, phloem, and cambium. **Which of these tissues transports food throughout the plant?**

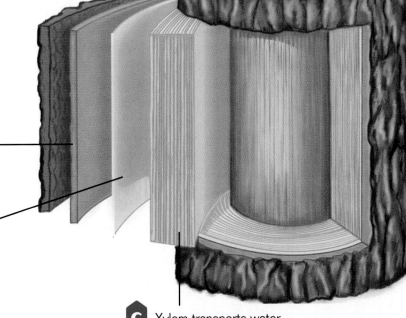

 **A** Phloem transports dissolved sugar throughout the plant.

B Cambium produces xylem and phloem as the plant grows.

C Xylem transports water and dissolved substances throughout the plant.

Vascular Tissue

Three tissues usually make up the vascular system in a seed plant. **Xylem** (ZI lum) tissue transports water and dissolved substances from the roots throughout the plant. **Phloem** (FLOH em) tissue moves food up from where it is made to other parts of the plant where it is used or stored. In some plants, a cambium is between xylem and phloem, as shown in **Figure 11-15**. **Cambium** (KAM bee um) is a tissue that produces new xylem and phloem cells. These three tissues completely circle some stems and roots. Groups of vascular tissue called vascular bundles are found in other plants.

Stems

Did you know that the trunk of a tree is really its stem? Stems are usually above ground and support the branches, leaves, and flowers. Some stems, such as potatoes and onions, are underground. The stem allows movement of materials between leaves and roots. Some stems store food. Sugarcane has an aboveground stem that stores large quantities of food. Stems of cacti are adapted to carry on photosynthesis and make food for the rest of the plant.

Mini Lab

Observing Water Moving in a Plant

Procedure

1. Into a clear container, about 10 cm tall and 4 cm in diameter, pour water to a depth of 1.5 cm. Add 15 drops of red food coloring to the water.
2. Put the root end of a whole green onion in the colored water in the container. Do not cut the onion in any way.
3. Let the onion stand overnight.
4. The next day, examine the outside of the onion. Peel off the layers of leaves and examine them.

Analysis

1. In your Science Journal, compare the appearance of the onion before and after it was in the colored water.
2. Describe the location of red color inside the onion.
3. Infer how the red color inside the onion might be related to vascular tissue.

Figure 11-16 The root system of a dandelion is longer than the plant is tall. When you pull up a dandelion, you often pull off the top portion of the plant. The root quickly produces new leaves, and another dandelion grows.

Plant stems are either herbaceous (hur BAY shus) or woody. Herbaceous stems usually are soft and green, like the stems of peppers, corn, and tulips. Oak, birch, and other trees and shrubs have hard, rigid, woody stems.

Roots

Imagine a large tree growing alone on top of a hill. What is the largest part? Maybe you said the trunk or the branches. Did you consider the roots? The root systems of most plants are as large or larger than the aboveground stems and leaves, like the dandelion in **Figure 11-16.**

Roots are important to plants. Water and other substances enter a plant through its roots. Roots have vascular tissue to move water and dissolved substances from the ground up through the stems to the leaves. Roots also anchor plants. If they didn't, plants could be blown away by wind or washed away by water. Each root system must support the plant parts that are above the ground—the stem, branches, and leaves of a tree, for example. Sometimes, part or all of roots are above ground, too.

Roots may store food. When you eat carrots or beets, you eat roots that contain stored food. Root tissues also may perform special functions such as absorbing oxygen that is used in the process of respiration.

Leaves

Have you ever rested in the shade of a tree's leaves on a hot, summer day? Leaves are the organs of the plant that usually trap light and make food through the process of photosynthesis. Leaves come in many shapes, sizes, and colors.

Leaf Structure

Look at the structure of a typical leaf shown in **Figure 11-17.** The epidermis is a thin layer of cells that covers and protects both the upper and lower surfaces of a leaf. A waxy cuticle that protects and reduces water loss covers the epidermis of many leaves. A feature of most leaves is stomata. **Stomata** are small pores in the leaf surfaces that allow carbon dioxide, water, and oxygen to enter and leave a leaf. The stomata are surrounded by **guard cells** that open and close the pores. The cuticle, stomata, and guard cells all are adaptations that help plants survive on land. ☑

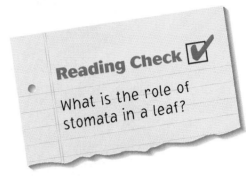
Leaf Cells

A typical leaf is made of different layers of cells. Covering the upper and lower surfaces of a leaf is the epidermis. Just below the upper epidermis is the palisade layer. It consists of closely packed, long, narrow cells that usually contain many chloroplasts. Most of the food produced by plants is made in the palisade cells. Between the palisade layer and the lower epidermis is the spongy layer. It is a layer of loosely arranged cells separated by air spaces. In a leaf, xylem and phloem are in the spongy layer.

Figure 11-17 The structure of a typical leaf is adapted for photosynthesis. **Why do cells in the palisade layer have more chloroplasts than cells in the spongy layer?**

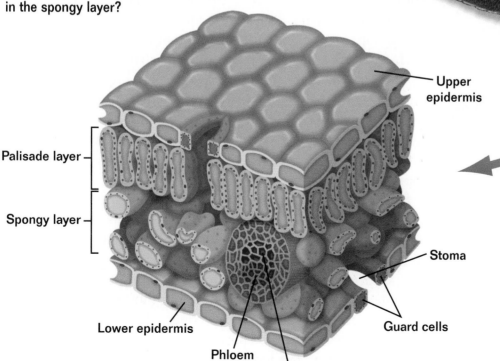

Upper epidermis

Palisade layer

Spongy layer

Stoma

Lower epidermis

Guard cells

Phloem

Xylem

A Conifers are the largest, most diverse division of the gymnosperms. Most conifers are evergreen plants, such as this blue spruce.

B About 100 species of cycads exist today. Only one genus grows naturally in the United States. This sago palm comes from Java, an island in Indonesia.

Figure 11-18 The gymnosperms include conifers (A), cycads (B), ginkgoes (C), and gnetophytes (D).

EXAMPLES OF
Gymnosperms

- Pine
- Hemlock
- Spruce
- Sago Palm
- Ginkgo
- Joint Fir

Gymnosperms

The oldest trees alive today are gymnosperms (JIHM nuh spurmz). A bristlecone pine tree in the White Mountains of eastern California is estimated to be 4900 years old. **Gymnosperms** are vascular plants that produce seeds on the surface of the female reproductive structure. The word *gymnosperm* comes from the Greek language and means "naked seed." Seeds of gymnosperms are not protected by a fruit. Gymnosperms do not produce flowers. Leaves of most gymnosperms are needlelike or scalelike. Gymnosperms are often called evergreens because most keep their leaves for more than one year.

Four divisions of plants—conifers, cycads, ginkgoes, and gnetophytes—are classified as gymnosperms. **Figure 11-18** shows examples of the four divisions. You are probably most familiar with the division Coniferophyta, the conifers. Pines, firs, spruces, redwoods, and junipers belong to this division. It contains the greatest number of gymnosperm species. All conifers produce two types of cones, the male and female reproductive structures. These are usually on the same plant. Seeds develop on the female cone.

D The 70 species of gnetophytes are classified into three genera. More than half of the species, such as this joint fir, are in one genus. Another genus has just one species, and the rest of the species are in the third genus.

C Today, the ginkgoes are represented by only one living species. Ginkgoes lose their leaves in the fall. **How is this different from most gymnosperms?**

Angiosperms

When people are asked to name a plant, most people name an angiosperm (AN jee uh spurm). Angiosperms are familiar plants no matter where you live. They grow in parks, fields, forests, jungles, deserts, freshwater, salt water, cracks of sidewalks, or dangling from wires or other plants. One species of orchid even grows underground. Angiosperms make up the plant division Anthophyta. More than eighty-five percent of plant species known today belong to this division.

An **angiosperm** is a vascular plant that flowers and has a fruit that contains seeds. The fruit develops from a part or parts of one or more flowers. The flowers of angiosperms vary in size, shape, and color. Duckweed, an aquatic plant, has a flower that is only 0.1 mm long. A plant in Indonesia has a flower that is nearly 1 m in diameter and can weigh 9 kg. Nearly every color can be found in some flower, although some people would not include black. Multicolored flowers are common. Some plants have flowers that are not easily recognized as flowers, such as those found on oak and birch trees.

> **EXAMPLES OF**
> **Angiosperms**
>
> • Grasses and grains
>
> • Cacti
>
> • Palms
>
> • Garden flowers
>
> • Vegetables
>
> • Fruits
>
> • Nuts
>   (except pine nuts)
>
> • Leafy trees
>   (except ginkgoes)

Figure 11-19 By observing a monocot and a dicot, their plant characteristics can be determined.

Monocots

A Monocots, such as these lilies, have flower parts in multiples of three. If you had cereal for breakfast, you ate part of a monocot. Corn, rice, oats, and wheat are monocots.

Seed   **Seedling**

B In monocots, vascular tissues are arranged as bundles scattered throughout the stem. Monocot leaves are usually more narrow than long. The vascular bundles show up as parallel veins in leaves.

Monocots and Dicots

The two classes of angiosperms are the monocots and the dicots. The terms *monocot* and *dicot* are shortened forms of the words *monocotyledon* and *dicotyledon*. The prefix *mono* means "one," and *di* means "two." A cotyledon is a seed leaf inside a seed. Therefore, **monocots** have one seed leaf inside their seeds and **dicots** have two. **Figure 11-19** compares the characteristics of monocots and dicots.

Importance of Seed Plants

Imagine that your class is having a picnic in the park. You cover the wooden picnic table with a red-checked, cotton tablecloth and pass out paper cups and plates. Your lunch includes hot dogs, potato chips, and apple cider. Perhaps you collect leaves or flowers for a science project. Later, you clean up and put leftovers in paper bags.

Now, let's imagine this scene if there were no seed plants on Earth. There would be no wooden picnic table and no

Dicots

C Dicots, such as the hibiscus, have flower parts in multiples of four or five. Oaks, maples, and many other trees are dicots. Most vegetables and fruits are dicots, as are many garden flowers.

Seed   Seedling

D In dicot stems, vascular bundles occur in rings. These bundles of rings are the annual rings in woody stems. The vascular bundles are the network of veins in dicot leaves.

pulp to make paper products such as cups, plates, and bags. The hot dog came from the meat of animals that eat only plants. Bread for buns, apples for cider, and potatoes for chips all come from plants. The tablecloth is made from cotton, a plant. Without seed plants, there would be no picnic.

Uses of Gymnosperms and Angiosperms

Conifers are the most economically important gymnosperms. Most of the wood used for construction, as in **Figure 11-20,** and for paper production, comes from conifers such as pines and spruces. Resin, a waxy substance secreted by conifers, is used to make chemicals found in soap, paint, varnish, and some medicines.

Figure 11-20 The wood from conifers, such as pines, is commonly used in construction. Resin is used to make household products.

Figure 11-21 Cotton is a flowering plant that yields long fibers that can be woven into a wide variety of fabrics. **What chemical compound makes up these fibers?**

The most common plants on Earth are the angiosperms. They are important to all life because they form the basis for the diets of most animals. Grains such as barley and wheat and legumes such as peas and lentils were among the first plants ever grown by humans. Angiosperms also are the source of many of the fibers used in clothing. Cotton fibers, as seen in **Figure 11-21,** grow from the outer surface of cotton-seeds. The fibers of the flax plant are processed and woven into linen fabrics. The production of medicines, rubber, oils, perfumes, pesticides, and some industrial chemicals uses substances found in angiosperms.

Section Assessment

1. What are the characteristics of a seed plant?
2. Compare and contrast the characteristics of gymnosperms and angiosperms.
3. You are looking at a flower with five petals, five sepals, one pistil, and ten stamens. Is it from a monocot or dicot plant?
4. **Think Critically:** The cuticle and epidermis of leaves are transparent. If they were not transparent, what might be the result?
5. **Skill Builder**
   Classifying Conifers have needlelike or scalelike leaves. Do the **Chapter 11 Skill Activity** on page 716 to learn how to use this characteristic to classify conifers.

Using Computers

Word Processing Use a word-processing program to outline the structures and functions that are associated with roots, stems, and leaves. If you need help, refer to page 696.

Activity 11•2

Comparing Monocots and Dicots

Materials
- Monocot and dicot flowers
- Monocot and dicot seeds
- Scalpel
- Forceps
- Iodine solution

Y ou have read that monocots and dicots are similar because they are both groups of flowering plants. However, you also have learned that these two groups are different. Try this activity to compare and contrast monocots and dicots.

What You'll Investigate
How do the characteristics of monocots and dicots compare?

Goals
- **Observe** similarities and differences between monocots and dicots.
- **Classify** plants as monocots or dicots based on flower characteristics.
- **Infer** what type of food is stored in seeds.

Procedure
1. Copy the Plant Data table in your Science Journal.
2. **Observe** the leaves on the stem of each flower. In your Science Journal, describe the monocot and the dicot leaves.

3. **Examine** the monocot and the dicot flower. For each flower, remove and count the sepals and petals. Enter these numbers on the table.
4. Inside each flower, you should see a pistil(s) and several stamens. **Count** each type and enter these numbers as "Other Observations."
5. **Examine** the two seeds. **Cut** the seeds lengthwise, **observe** each half, and **identify** the embryo and cotyledon(s).
6. Place a drop of iodine on different parts of the seed. A blue-black color indicates the presence of starch. **CAUTION:** *Iodine is poisonous. It will stain and can burn your skin.*

Conclude and Apply
1. **Compare** the numbers of sepals and petals of monocot and dicot flowers.
2. What characteristics are the same for monocot and dicot flowers?
3. Distinguish between a monocot and a dicot seed.
4. What type of food is stored in monocot and in

Plant Data				
	Number of Sepals	Number of Petals	Number of Cotyledons	Other Observations
Monocot				
Dicot				

For a **preview** of this chapter, study this Reviewing Main Ideas before you read the chapter. After you have studied this chapter, you can use the Reviewing Main Ideas to **review** the chapter.

The Glencoe MindJogger, Audiocassettes, and CD-ROM provide additional opportunities for review.

Section
11-1 CHARACTERISTICS OF PLANTS

Plants are made up of eukaryotic cells. They usually have some form of leaves, stems, and roots. Plants vary greatly in size and shape. Most plants are adapted to live on land. As plants evolved from aquatic to land forms, changes in structure and function occurred. The changes included how they reproduced, supported themselves, and moved substances from one part of the plant to another. The plant kingdom is classified into groups called divisions. *What are some plant adaptations for living on land?*

Section
11-2 SEEDLESS PLANTS

Seedless plants include **nonvascular** and **vascular** types. Bryophytes—mosses and liverworts—are seedless **nonvascular plants.** They have no true leaves, stems, roots, or vascular tissues and live in moist environments. For bryophytes, reproduction usually is by spores. Bryophytes may be considered **pioneer species** because they are some of the first plants to grow in new or disturbed environments. They change the environment so that other plant species may grow there. Club mosses, horsetails, and ferns are seedless **vascular plants.** They have vascular tissues, a pipeline that moves substances throughout the plant. Like bryophytes, these plants may reproduce by spores. When ancient forms of these plants died, they underwent a process that, over time, resulted in the formation of coal. *How are bryophytes and ferns alike?*

Reading Check ✔

Choose a topic in this chapter that interests you. Look it up in a reference book, an encyclopedia or on a CD. Think of a way to share what you learn.

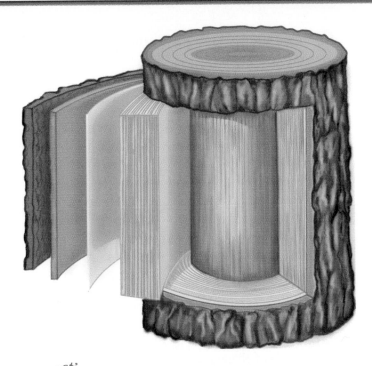

Section 11-3 SEED PLANTS

Seed plants are what most people think of when they hear the word *plants.* These plants have adapted to survive in nearly every environment on Earth. Seed plants produce seeds and have vascular tissue, stems, roots, and leaves. Vascular tissues transport food, water, and dissolved substances in the roots, stems, and leaves. The two major groups of seed plants are gymnosperms and angiosperms. **Gymnosperms** generally have needlelike leaves and some type of cone. **Angiosperms** are plants that flower and are classified as **monocots** or **dicots.** Seed plants provide food, shelter, clothing, and many other products. *What structures are common to all seed plants?*

Chapter 11 Assessment

Using Vocabulary

a. angiosperm
b. cambium
c. cellulose
d. cuticle
e. dicot
f. guard cell
g. gymnosperm
h. monocot
i. nonvascular plant
j. phloem
k. pioneer species
l. rhizoid
m. stomata
n. vascular plant
o. xylem

Explain the differences between the terms in each of the following sets.

1. xylem, phloem, cambium
2. angiosperm, dicot, monocot
3. guard cell, stomata
4. cuticle, cellulose
5. vascular plant, gymnosperm

Checking Concepts

Choose the word or phrase that best answers the question.

6. Which of the following is a seedless, vascular plant?
   A) moss   C) horsetail
   B) liverwort   D) pine

7. What are the small openings in the surface of a leaf surrounded by guard cells?
   A) stomata   C) rhizoids
   B) cuticles   D) angiosperms

8. What is the plant structure that anchors the plant?
   A) stem   C) roots
   B) leaves   D) guard cell

9. What kind of plants have structures that move water and other substances?
   A) vascular   C) nonvascular
   B) protist   D) moneran

10. What division has plants that are only a few cells thick?
    A) Anthophyta   C) Pterophyta
    B) Cycadophyta D) Bryophyta

11. Where is new xylem and phloem produced?
    A) guard cells C) stomata
    B) cambium   D) cuticle

12. Which of the following is **NOT** part of an angiosperm?
    A) flowers   C) cones
    B) seeds   D) fruit

13. In what part of a leaf does most photosynthesis happen?
    A) epidermis   C) stomata
    B) cuticle   D) palisade layer

14. Which of these is an advantage to life on land for plants?
    A) more direct sunlight
    B) less carbon dioxide
    C) greater space to grow
    D) less competition for food

15. What do ferns **NOT** have?
    A) fronds   C) spores
    B) rhizoids   D) vascular tissue

Thinking Critically

16. What might happen if a land plant's waxy cuticle were destroyed?

17. Well-preserved human remains have been found in peat bogs. Explain why this occurs.

18. Plants called succulents store large amounts of water in their leaves, stems, and roots. In what environments would you expect to find succulents growing naturally?

19. Explain why mosses are usually found on moist areas.

20. How do pioneer species change environments so that other plants may grow there?

Developing Skills

If you need help, refer to the **Skill Handbook.**

21. **Concept Mapping:** Complete this map for the seedless plants of the plant kingdom.

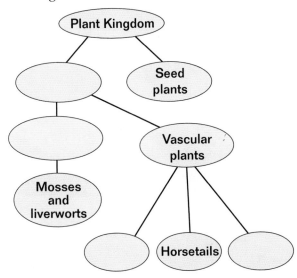

22. **Interpreting Data:** What do the data in this table tell you about where gas exchange occurs in each plant leaf?

Stomata (per mm^2)		
	Upper Surface	Lower Surface
Pine	50	71
Bean	40	281
Fir	0	228
Tomato	12	13

23. **Making and Using Graphs:** Make two circle graphs using the table in question 22.

24. **Interpreting Scientific Illustrations:** Using **Figure 11-19,** compare and contrast the *number of seed leaves, bundle arrangement in the stem, veins in leaves,* and *number of flower parts* for monocots and dicots.

THE PRINCETON REVIEW

Test-Taking Tip

You Are Smarter Than You Think
Nothing on the science tests that you will take this year is so difficult that you can't understand it. You can learn to master any of it. Be confident and just keep practicing your test-taking skills.

Test Practice

Use these questions to test your Science Proficiency.

1. What does the cuticle found on the surface of many plant cells help to do?
   A) increase the carbon dioxide released
   B) change the method of reproduction
   C) reduce water loss for the plant
   D) keep the surface area as small as possible

2. What is one explanation for why bryophytes grow just a few centimeters tall?
   A) They lack reproductive structures.
   B) Their rhizoids are not real roots.
   C) Many creatures trample them on the forest floor.
   D) They do not have vascular tissues.

3. What is one feature that gymnosperms and flowering plants have in common?
   A) reproduce naturally from seeds
   B) have leaves that stay on the plant for more than one year
   C) produce the same types of fruit
   D) are nonvascular plants

Invertebrate Animals

Chapter Preview

Skills Preview

Skill Builders
- Map Concepts

Activities
- Design an Experiment

MiniLabs
- Model

Reading Check ✔

As you read, create an outline of the chapter that includes the headings and subheadings. List important points under each one.

Explore Activity

What is an animal? Is the insect in the photo an animal? What characteristics does the praying mantis have that makes it an animal? More than 1.8 million different kinds of animals have been identified by scientists. How are these animals organized? In the following activity, your class will learn about organizing animals by building a bulletin board display.

Organize Animal Groups

1. Your class is going to make a bulletin board display of different groups of animals. It will look similar to the concept map in **Figure 12-2.**

2. Label large envelopes with the names of different groups.

3. Pick one animal group to study. Make information cards of animals that belong in your group. These cards should have pictures on one side and information on the other.

4. Place your finished cards inside the appropriate envelope on the bulletin board.

Science Journal

In your Science Journal, write down the group of animals you want to study. Collect information on animals that belong to your group. List similarities and differences between your animals and animals of different groups.

12•1 What is an animal?

Animal Characteristics

What You'll Learn

► The characteristics of animals
► The difference between vertebrates and invertebrates
► How the symmetry of animals differs

Vocabulary
vertebrate
invertebrate
symmetry

Why It's Important

► All animals share common characteristics.

Think about the animals shown in **Figure 12-1.** These animals would be described differently. They have a wide variety of body parts, as well as ways to move, get food, and protect themselves. So, what do all animals have in common? What makes an animal an animal?

1. Animals cannot make their own food. Some animals eat plants to supply their energy needs. Some animals eat other animals, and some eat both plants and animals.
2. Animals digest their food. Large food substances are broken down into smaller substances that their cells can use.
3. Most animals can move from place to place. They move to find food, shelter, and mates and to escape from predators.
4. Animals are many-celled organisms that are made of many different kinds of cells. These cells digest food, get rid of wastes, and reproduce.
5. Most animal cells have a nucleus and organelles surrounded by a membrane. This type of cell is called a eukaryotic cell.

Figure 12-1 Animals come in a variety of shapes and sizes.

A The thorny devil lizard lives in the Australian desert. It feeds on ants and survives with little water to drink.

B The largest lion's mane jellyfish was found dead on shore. It had a bell over 2 m across with tentacles that dangled over 36 m long.

C The East African crowned crane is the only crane that will roost in trees. The adults perform spectacular dances when excited.

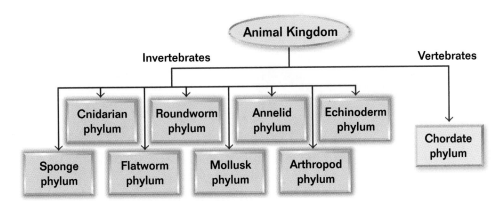

Figure 12-2 This diagram shows the relationships among different groups in the animal kingdom. Different forms of this diagram will appear at the beginning of each section in this and the following chapter. The groups that are highlighted with an orange outline are the groups that will be discussed in that particular section. For example, this section will deal with the invertebrates, which includes the sponge, cnidarian, flatworm, roundworm, mollusk, annelid, arthropod, and echinoderm phylums.

Animal Classification

Deciding whether an organism is an animal is only the first step in classifying it. Scientists place all animals into smaller, related groups. They begin by separating animals into two distinct groups—vertebrates and invertebrates. **Vertebrates** (VURT uh brayts) are animals that have a backbone. **Invertebrates** (ihn VURT uh brayts) are animals that do not have a backbone. There are far more invertebrates than vertebrates. About 97 percent of all animals are invertebrates.

Scientists classify or group the invertebrates into several different phyla (FI lah), as shown in **Figure 12-2.** The animals within each phylum share similar characteristics. These characteristics indicate that the animals within the group descended from a common ancestor. The characteristics also show a change from less complex to more complex animals as you move from phylum to phylum.

Symmetry

As you study the different groups of invertebrates, one feature becomes apparent—symmetry. **Symmetry** (SIH muh tree) refers to the arrangement of the individual parts of an object. Scientists also use body symmetry to classify animals.

Most animals have either radial or bilateral symmetry. Animals with body parts arranged in a circle around a central point have radial symmetry. These animals can locate food and gather other information from all directions. Animals with radial symmetry, such as jellyfish and sea urchins, live in water.

Reading Check
What is symmetry?

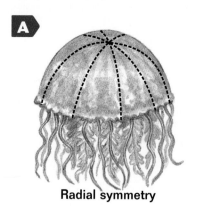

Radial symmetry

Bilateral symmetry

Asymmetry

Figure 12-3 Jellyfish (A) have radial symmetry, butterflies (B) have bilateral symmetry, and sponges (C) are asymmetrical. **What type of symmetry do humans exhibit?**

On the other hand, animals with bilateral symmetry have parts that are mirror images of each other. A line can be drawn down the center of their bodies to divide them into two matching parts. Grasshoppers and lobsters are bilaterally symmetrical.

Some animals have no definite shape. They are called asymmetrical. Their bodies cannot be divided into matching halves. Many sponges are asymmetrical (AY suh meh trih kul). As you learn more about invertebrates, see how their body symmetry is related to how they gather food. **Figure 12-3** shows the three ways an animal's body parts can be arranged.

Section Assessment

1. What are the characteristics of animals?

2. How are invertebrates different from vertebrates?

3. What are the types of symmetry? Name an animal that has bilateral symmetry.

4. **Think Critically** Radial symmetry is found among species that live in water. Why might radial symmetry be an adaptation uncommon among animals that live on land?

5. **Skill Builder**
   Concept Mapping Using the information in this section, make a concept map showing the steps a scientist might use to classify a new animal. If you need help, refer to Concept Mapping in the **Skill Handbook** on page 678.

Using Computers

Word Processing
Create a table that you will use as you complete this chapter. Label the following columns: *animal, group,* and *body symmetry*. Create ten rows to enter animal names. If you need help, refer to page 696.

Sponges, Cnidarians, Flatworms, and Roundworms

Sponges

Sponges are the simplest of animals. They bridge the gap between single-celled organisms and more complex animals. Their body structure is made of two layers of cells. Adult sponges live attached to one place. Organisms that remain attached to one place during their lifetimes are called sessile (SES ul). Because they do not move about in search of food, scientists used to classify sponges, shown in **Figure 12-4,** as plants. Once scientists found out that sponges can't make their own food, they reclassified them as animals.

What You'll Learn

► The structures that make up sponges and cnidarians
► How sponges and cnidarians get food and reproduce
► The body plans of flatworms and roundworms

Vocabulary

cnidarian   free-living
polyp   parasite
medusa

Why It's Important

► Sponges, cnidarians, flat-worms, and roundworms exhibit simple cell and tissue organization.

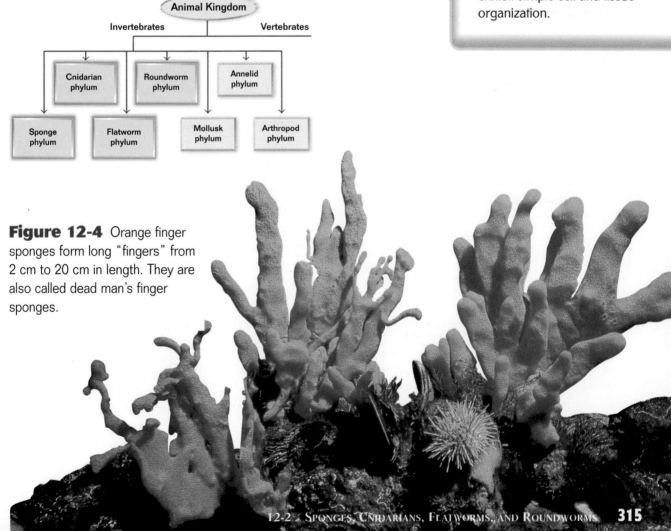

```
                    Animal Kingdom
        Invertebrates    │    Vertebrates
              ┌──────────┼──────────┐
              ↓          ↓          ↓
         ┌─────────┐ ┌─────────┐ ┌─────────┐
         │Cnidarian│ │Roundworm│ │ Annelid │
         │ phylum  │ │ phylum  │ │ phylum  │
         └─────────┘ └─────────┘ └─────────┘
    ↓            ↓          ↓          ↓
┌─────────┐ ┌─────────┐ ┌─────────┐ ┌─────────┐
│ Sponge  │ │Flatworm │ │ Mollusk │ │Arthropod│
│ phylum  │ │ phylum  │ │ phylum  │ │ phylum  │
└─────────┘ └─────────┘ └─────────┘ └─────────┘
```

Figure 12-4 Orange finger sponges form long "fingers" from 2 cm to 20 cm in length. They are also called dead man's finger sponges.

Filter Feeders

Sponges live in water. They are called filter feeders because they filter food out of the water that flows through their bodies. Microscopic organisms and oxygen are carried with the water through pores into the central cavity of the sponge. The phylum that sponges belong to, Porifera, gets its name from these pores. The inner surface of the central cavity is lined with specialized cells called collar cells. Thin, whiplike structures, called flagella, extend from the collar cells and keep the water moving through the sponge. Other specialized cells digest the food, carry nutrients to all parts of the sponge, and remove wastes.

Body Support and Defense

At first glance, you might think that sponges have few defenses against predators. Actually, not many animals eat sponges. The soft bodies of many sponges are supported by sharp, glasslike structures called spicules. Many other sponges have a material called spongin. Spongin can be compared to foam rubber because it makes sponges both soft and elastic. Some sponges have both spicules and spongin, which protects their soft bodies.

Sponge Reproduction

Sponges are able to reproduce both sexually and asexually. Asexual reproduction occurs when a bud located on the side of the parent sponge develops into a small sponge. The small sponge breaks off, floats away, and attaches itself to a new surface. New sponges also grow when a sponge is cut or broken into pieces. The broken pieces regenerate or grow into a complete new sponge.

Most sponges that reproduce sexually produce both eggs and sperm. The sponge releases sperm into the water. Currents carry the sperm to eggs of another sponge, where fertilization occurs. The fertilized eggs grow into larvae that look different from the adult sponge. The larvae are able to swim to a different area before attaching themselves to a rock or other surface.

Mini Lab

Observing Sponge Spicules

Procedure

1. Add a few drops of bleach to a microscope slide. **CAUTION:** *Do not inhale the bleach. Do not spill it on your hands, clothing, or the microscope.*

2. Put a small piece of the sponge into the bleach on the slide. Add a coverslip. Observe the cells of the sponge.

Analysis

1. Are spicules made of the same materials as the rest of the sponge? Explain.

2. What is the function of spicules?

Cnidarians

Have you ever cast a fishing line into the water to catch your dinner? In a somewhat similar way, animals in the phylum Cnidaria have tentacles that are used to capture prey. Jellyfish, sea anemones, hydra, and corals belong to this phylum.

Cnidarians (NIH dar ee uns) are a phylum of hollow-bodied animals that have stinging cells. They have radial symmetry that allows them to locate food that floats by from any direction. Their bodies have two cell layers that are organized into tissues. The inner layer forms a digestive cavity where food is broken down. Their tentacles surround the mouth. Stinging cells shoot out to stun or grasp prey. The word *cnidaria* is Latin for "stinging cells." Oxygen moves into the cells from the surrounding water, and carbon dioxide waste moves out of the cells. Nerve cells work together as a nerve net throughout the whole body.

Two Body Plans

Study the two cnidarians in **Figure 12-5.** They represent the two different body plans found in this animal's phylum. The vase-shaped body of the hydra is called a **polyp** (PAHL up). Although hydras are usually sessile, they can twist to capture prey. They also can somersault to a new location. Jellyfish have a free-swimming, bell-shaped body that is called a **medusa.** Jellyfish are not strong swimmers. Instead, they drift along with the ocean currents. Some cnidarians go through both the polyp and medusa stages during their life cycles. ☑

EXAMPLES OF Cnidarians

- Jellyfish
- Sea anemones
- Hydra
- Corals
- Portuguese man-of-war

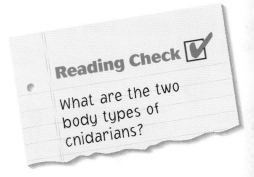

Reading Check

What are the two body types of cnidarians?

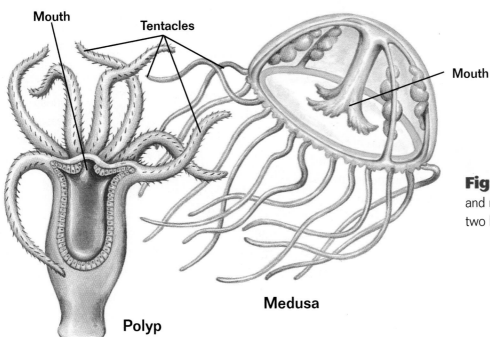

Mouth

Tentacles

Mouth

Figure 12-5 The polyp and medusa forms are the two body plans of cnidarians.

Medusa

Polyp

Figure 12-6 Polyps, like these hydra, reproduce by budding.

Cnidarian Reproduction

Cnidarians produce both asexually and sexually. Polyp forms of cnidarians, such as hydras, reproduce asexually by budding, as illustrated in **Figure 12-6.** The bud eventually falls off of the parent organism and develops into a new polyp. Some polyps also can reproduce sexually by releasing eggs or sperm into the water. The eggs are fertilized by sperm and develop into a new polyp. Medusa forms of cnidarians, such as jellyfish, have both an asexual and a sexual stage, which are illustrated in **Figure 12-7.** These stages alternate between generations. Medusa reproduce sexually to produce polyps, which in turn, reproduce asexually to form new medusa.

VISUALIZING
Cnidarian Reproduction

Figure 12-7 Medusa forms of cnidarians have both a sexual and an asexual stage.

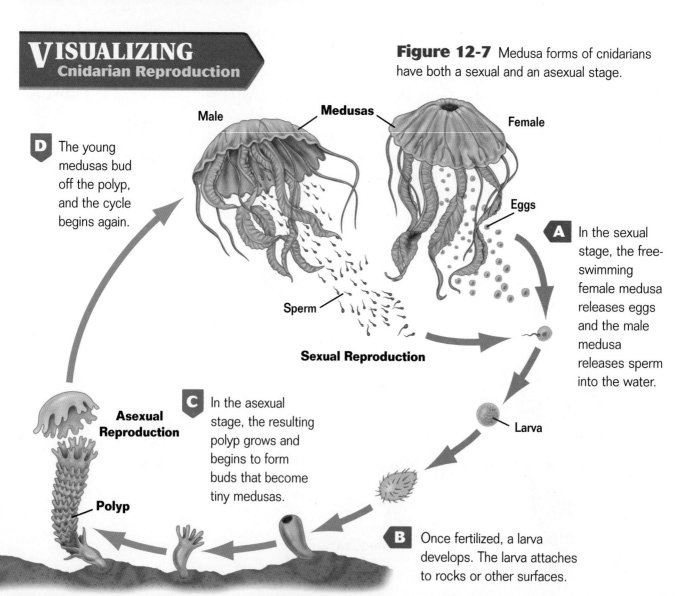

D The young medusas bud off the polyp, and the cycle begins again.

Male

Medusas

Female

A In the sexual stage, the free-swimming female medusa releases eggs and the male medusa releases sperm into the water.

Eggs

Sperm

Sexual Reproduction

Larva

C In the asexual stage, the resulting polyp grows and begins to form buds that become tiny medusas.

Asexual Reproduction

Polyp

B Once fertilized, a larva develops. The larva attaches to rocks or other surfaces.

Flatworms

Unlike sponges and cnidarians that wait for food to pass their way, flatworms actively search for their food. Worms are invertebrates with soft bodies and bilateral symmetry. Flatworms are members of the phylum Platyhelminthes (plat ih hel MIHN theez). They have long, flattened bodies. They also have three distinct layers of tissue organized into organs and organ systems.

Some flatworms are free-living, such as the planarian in **Figure 12-8B**. Free-living organisms don't depend on one particular organism for food or a place to live. But, most flatworms are parasites that live in or on their hosts. A **parasite** depends on its host for food and a place to live.

Tapeworms

One parasitic flatworm that lives in humans is called the tapeworm. It lacks a digestive system. To survive, it lives in the intestines of its hosts. The tapeworm absorbs nutrients directly into its body from digested material in the host's intestines. Find the hooks and suckers on the tapeworm's head in **Figure 12-8A**. The hooks and suckers attach the tapeworm to the host's intestines.

Figure 12-8 Flatworms have members that are free-living and other members that are parasites.

Eyespot

Head

Cilia

Mouth/Anus

Digestive tract

Excretory system

B Planarians have eyespots that have been known to respond to light. They also have the power to regenerate. A planarian can be cut in two, and each piece will grow into a new worm.

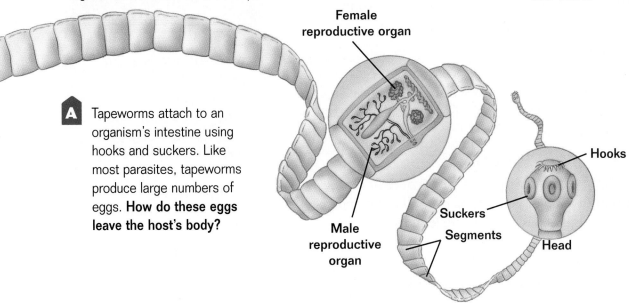

Female reproductive organ

A Tapeworms attach to an organism's intestine using hooks and suckers. Like most parasites, tapeworms produce large numbers of eggs. **How do these eggs leave the host's body?**

Male reproductive organ

Hooks

Suckers

Segments

Head

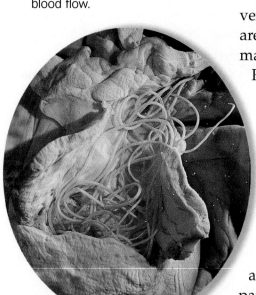

Figure 12-9 Mosquitoes are the carriers of dog heartworm. Mosquitoes bite infected dogs and, in turn, infect still other dogs by biting them. The worm larva travels through the circulatory system and lodges in the heart where it interrupts normal blood flow.

A tapeworm grows by adding sections directly behind its head. Each body segment produces both eggs and sperm from separate male and female reproductive organs. The eggs and sperm are released into the segment. Once filled with fertilized eggs, the segment breaks off and passes out of the host's body. If another host eats a fertilized egg, the egg hatches and develops into a new worm.

Roundworms

Dog owners regularly give their pets a medicine that prevents heartworm disease. Heartworms can kill a dog. They are just one kind of the many thousands of roundworms that make up the phylum Nematoda (nem uh TOH duh). Roundworms are the most widespread animal on Earth. Billions can live in a single acre of soil.

A roundworm's body is described as a tube within a tube, with fluid in between. The cavity separates the digestive tract from the body wall. Roundworms are also more complex than flatworms because their digestive tract is complete with two openings. Food enters through the mouth and wastes exit through an anus.

Roundworms are a diverse group. Some are decomposers. Some are predators. Some are parasites of animals and some are parasites of plants. **Figure 12-9** shows a parasitic heartworm that can infect dogs. What type of body symmetry does a roundworm have?

Section Assessment

1. How do sponges and cnidarians get food?
2. What are three common characteristics of worms?
3. Compare the body plans of flatworms and roundworms.
4. **Think Critically:** Sponges are sessile organisms. They remain attached to one place during their lifetimes. Explain why a sponge is still considered to be an animal.
5. **Skill Builder**
   Comparing and Contrasting Do the **Chapter 12 Skill Activity** on page 717 to compare and contrast types of symmetry found in different animals.

Using Math

A sponge is 1 cm in diameter and 10 cm tall. It can move 22.5 L of water through its body in a day. Calculate the volume of water it pumps through its body in one minute.

Mollusks and Segmented Worms

Mollusks

Imagine yourself walking along the beach at low tide. On the rocks by a small tide pool, you see small conelike shells. The blue-black shelled mussels are exposed along the shore, and one arm of a shy octopus can be seen inside the opening of its den. How could all of these different animals belong to the same phylum? What do they have in common?

Common Characteristics

The snail, slug, mussel, and octopus belong to the phylum Mollusca. **Mollusks** are soft-bodied invertebrates that usually have a shell. Characteristics shared by mollusks include a mantle and a large, muscular foot. The **mantle** is a thin layer of tissue covering the mollusk's soft body. It secretes the protective shell of those mollusks that have a shell. The foot is used for moving the animal or for attaching it to an object.

Between the soft body and the mantel is a space called the mantle cavity. Water-dwelling mollusks have gills in the mantle cavity. **Gills** are organs that exchange oxygen and carbon dioxide with the water. Land-dwelling mollusks have lungs to exchange gases with air. Mollusks have a complete digestive system with two openings. Many also have a scratchy, tonguelike organ called the radula. The **radula** (RAJ uh luh) acts like a file with rows of teeth to break up food into smaller pieces.

Figure 12-10

What You'll Learn

▶ The characteristics of mollusks

▶ The similarities and differences between an open and a closed circulatory system

▶ The characteristics of segmented worms

▶ The structures and digestive process of an earthworm

Vocabulary

mollusk
mantle
gills
radula
open circulatory system
closed circulatory system

Why It's Important

▶ Mollusks and segmented worms have specialized structures that allow them to live in their environments.

Fire Bristleworm

Octopus

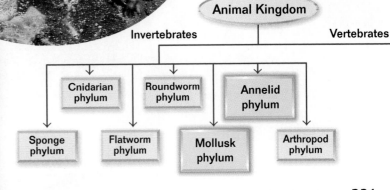

Animal Kingdom

Invertebrates — Vertebrates

Cnidarian phylum
Roundworm phylum
Annelid phylum

Sponge phylum
Flatworm phylum
Mollusk phylum
Arthropod phylum

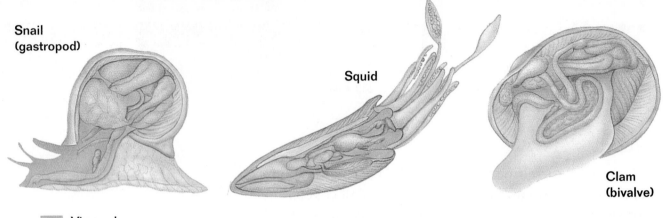

Snail
(gastropod)

Squid

Clam
(bivalve)

■ Visceral mass
■ Mantle
■ Shell
■ Foot

Figure 12-11 All mollusks have the same basic body plan: with a mantle, a shell, a foot, and an area called visceral mass where the body organs are located.

EXAMPLES OF
Bivalves Gastropods

Figure 12-12 Although these animals look different from one another, they are all mollusks.

A Tree snails are cone-shaped gastropods ranging in size from 1 cm to 6 cm long. They feed on tiny lichens, fungi, and algae that grow on the bark, leaves, and fruit of trees.

Some mollusks have an open circulatory system. Animals with an **open circulatory system** do not have their blood contained in vessels. Instead, the blood surrounds the organs. These organs are grouped together in a fluid-filled body cavity. **Figure 12-11** shows the basic structure of all mollusks.

Types of Mollusks

To classify mollusks, scientists first find out whether the mollusk has a shell. Then, they look at the kind of shell. They also look at the kind of foot. In this section, you will learn about three kinds of mollusks. **Figure 12-12** shows examples of two groups of mollusks—the gastropods and bivalves.

Gastropods and Bivalves

Gastropods are the largest class of mollusks. Most gastropods, such as the snails and conches, have a single shell. Slugs are also gastropods, but they don't have a shell. All move about on the large, muscular foot. A secretion of mucus allows them to glide across objects. Gastropods live in water or on land.

Bivalves are another class of mollusks. How many shells do you think bivalves have? Think of other words that start

B Scallops are marine bivalves. They swim by flapping their shells with a powerful muscle, the only part that humans eat.

Figure 12-13 Although the chambered nautilus's shell resembles a snail's shell, the nautilus is a cephalopod. Like the octopus and the squid, it swims using jet propulsion, as shown in **Figure 12-14.**

with *bi-*. A clam is a bivalve, or an organism with two shell halves joined by a hinge. Powerful, large muscles open and close the shells. Bivalves are water animals that are also filter feeders. Food is removed from water that is brought into and filtered through the gills.

Cephalopods

Cephalopods (SEF ah loh pawdz) are the most complex type of mollusk. Squid, octopuses, and the chambered nautilus, pictured in **Figure 12-13,** are all cephalopods. Most cephalopods have no shell but they do have a well-developed head. The "foot" is divided into tentacles with strong suckers. These animals also have a **closed circulatory system** in which blood is carried through blood vessels.

Both the squid and octopus are adapted for quick movement in the ocean. The squid's mantle is a muscular envelope that surrounds its internal organs. Water enters the space between the mantle and the other body organs. When the mantle closes around the collar of the squid, the water is squeezed rapidly through a siphon, which is a funnel-like structure. The rapid expulsion of water from the siphon causes the squid to move in the opposite direction of the stream of water. **Figure 12-14** shows how this propulsion system works.

EXAMPLES OF
Cephalopods

- **Octopus**
- **Squid**
- **Chambered nautilus**

PHYSICS
◄**INTEGRATION**

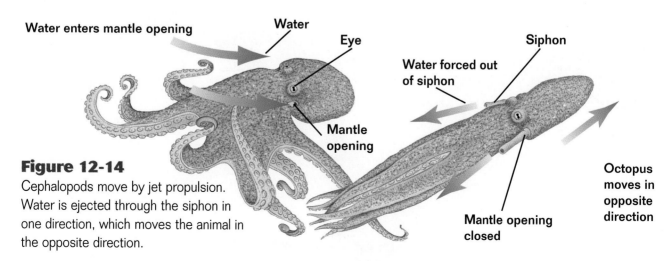

Water enters mantle opening

Water

Eye

Siphon

Water forced out of siphon

Mantle opening

Figure 12-14
Cephalopods move by jet propulsion. Water is ejected through the siphon in one direction, which moves the animal in the opposite direction.

Mantle opening closed

Octopus moves in opposite direction

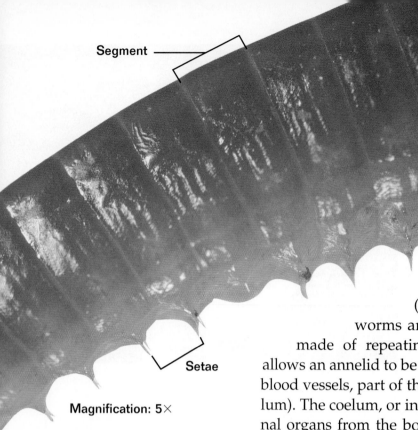

Segment
Setae
Magnification: 5×

Figure 12-15 Earthworms move using bristlelike hairs called setae. **How would the setae help the earthworms move?**

Segmented Worms

What kind of animal do you think of when you hear the word *worm?* Most likely, you think of an earthworm. Earthworms belong to a group of segmented worms in the phylum Annelida (an NEL ud uh). Leeches and marine worms are also annelids. An annelid's body is made of repeating segments or rings. Segmentation allows an annelid to be flexible. Each segment has nerve cells, blood vessels, part of the digestive tract, and the coelum (SEE lum). The coelum, or internal body cavity, separates the internal organs from the body wall. Annelids also have a closed circulatory system and a complete digestive system with two body openings.

EXAMPLES OF Segmented Worms

- Earthworms
- Leeches
- Marine worms

Earthworms

Earthworms have more than 100 body segments. Setae (SEE tee), or bristlelike structures pictured in **Figure 12-15,** are found on the outside of these segments. Earthworms use the setae and two sets of muscles to move through or hold onto

Figure 12-16 Segmented worms have circulatory, respiratory, excretory, digestive, muscular, and reproductive systems.

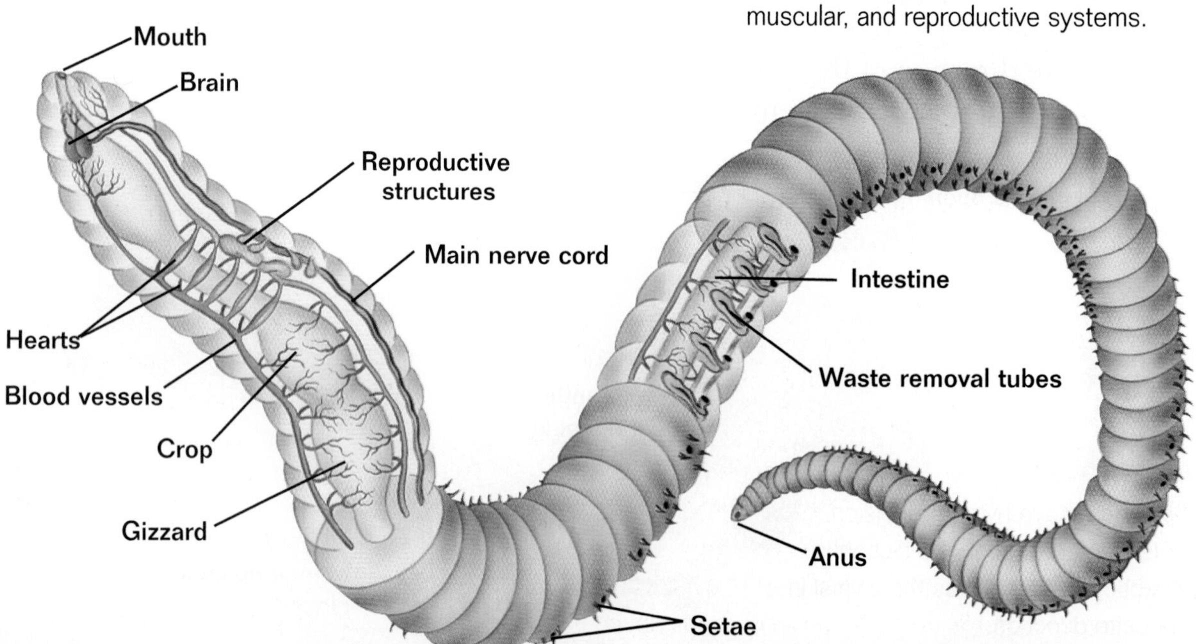

Mouth
Brain
Reproductive structures
Main nerve cord
Hearts
Blood vessels
Crop
Gizzard
Intestine
Waste removal tubes
Anus
Setae

soil. Moving through soil is important for earthworms because they eat it. Earthworms get the energy they need to live from the bits of leaves and other living matter found in the soil. You can trace the path through an earthworm's digestive system in **Figure 12-16.** First, the soil moves to the crop, where it is stored. Behind the crop is a muscular structure called the gizzard. Here, the soil is ground. As the food passes to the intestine, it is broken down and absorbed by the blood. Undigested soil and wastes leave the worm through the anus. ☑

What body structures are not present in the earthworm shown in **Figure 12-16?** Notice that you don't find gills or lungs. An earthworm lives in a thin film of water. It exchanges carbon dioxide and oxygen by diffusion through its skin.

Reading Check ☑

What are setae?

Leeches

Leeches are parasites that have a lifestyle that is different from earthworms'. These worms have flat bodies from 5 mm to 46 cm long and have sucking disks on both ends of their bodies. Leeches attach themselves to and remove blood from the body of a host. Some leeches can store as much as ten times their own weight in blood. The blood can be stored for months and released a little at a time into the digestive system. Leeches are found in freshwater, marine waters, and on land in mild and tropical regions.

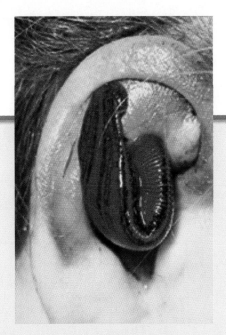

Problem Solving

Leeches to the Rescue

Since ancient times, doctors have used leeches to treat a variety of diseases. Early doctors thought leeches removed the bad blood that resulted in disease. Unfortunately, so many leeches were used sometimes that patients died from blood loss. With the rise of modern medical treatments, the use of leeches was abandoned. People thought it was useless.

Now, the leech is back! Surgeons are able to reattach severed ears or fingers, but it is difficult to keep blood flowing to the reattached body part. If blood clots appear, they stop blood circulation and the cells in the ear or finger die. Medicinal leeches are the key to success. Surgeons place a leech on the reattached ear or finger. It inflicts a painless bite from a sucking disk at each end of its body. As the leech feeds on the blood, chemicals in the saliva break up clots that have already formed and prevent new clots from forming. Eventually, normal circulation is established. The leech is removed and the reattached part survives.

Think Critically: Blood clots are major factors in strokes and some heart and blood vessel diseases. How might research about leeches play an important role in developing treatments for these conditions?

Figure 12-17 Polychaetes come in a variety of forms and colors. The Christmas tree (A) and feather duster (B) use their appendages to filter out food from their watery environments. **How are these organisms similar to cnidarians and sponges?**

Marine Worms

Look at the animals in **Figure 12-17.** You may wonder how these feathery animals can possibly be related to the earthworm and leech. These animals belong to a third group of annelids called polychaetes (PAHL ee kitz). The word *polychaete* means "many spines." There are more species of polychaetes than of any other kind of annelid. More than 6000 known species of polychaetes have been discovered.

The setae of these annelids occur in bundles along their segments. Marine worms are polychaetes that float, burrow, build structures, or walk on the ocean floor. While earthworms find nutrients in the soil and leeches are parasites, polychaetes are predators. Some use powerful jaws or tentacles to catch prey. Some of these strange-looking annelids can even produce their own light.

While annelids may not look complex, they are much more complex than sponges and cnidarians. In the next section, you will learn how they compare to the most complex invertebrates.

Section Assessment

1. Name the three classes of mollusks and identify a member from each class.

2. What are the characteristics of segmented worms?

3. Describe how an earthworm feeds and digests its food.

4. **Think Critically:** How does an annelid's segmentation help it move?

5. **Skill Builder**
   Comparing and Contrasting Compare and contrast an open circulatory system with a closed circulatory system. If you need help, refer to Comparing and Contrasting in the **Skill Handbook** on page 684.

Choose a mollusk and write about it in your Science Journal. Describe its appearance, how it gets food, where it lives, and other interesting facts.

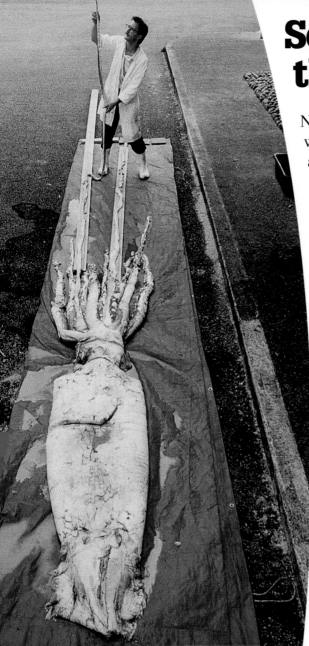

Searching for the Giant Squid

No one has ever seen a giant squid in its natural habitat, which is 300 m to 1500 m below the ocean's surface. Nor has any live, healthy giant squid been kept in an aquarium or research facility to be studied by scientists. The only live specimens of giant squid available for study have been those that washed up on beaches or were brought up in deep-sea commercial fishing nets. These squids have been sick and unsuitable for study.

Rare Find

In the late 1500s, accounts were written about several large sea creatures stranded on Norwegian shores. It was not until 1854 that scientists concluded that these creatures were giant squid. In the late 1800s, a dead giant squid caught by commercial fishers in Newfoundland became the first specimen available for study. The one-metric-ton giant squid at left was netted at a depth of 425 m in the waters off New Zealand. The creature was nearly dead when pulled on board the research vessel. The three-year-old squid measured 8 m from top to tip of tentacle and might have reached a much greater length at maturity.

The Search Goes On

The Smithsonian's Clyde Roper, one of the world's leading experts on the giant squid, has spent more than 30 years studying these remarkable animals. In 1997, Roper and his crew used the *Odyssey*, a robotic underwater vehicle, and a camera to explore the cold, black depths of Kaikoura Canyon, a deep-sea ecosystem located off New Zealand's South Island. Dr. Roper and his colleagues collected valuable information on the temperature, salt content, and depth of the ocean. On a ship at the surface, they viewed many hours of videotapes of this deep-water ecosystem—but alas, no giant squids. One day, perhaps crewed submersibles in the area will be the first to catch a glimpse of the giant squid at home.

Science JOURNAL

How big is a giant squid? Find out the length of the wall in your classroom, a school bus, and an airplane. Record the lengths in your Science Journal. Compare the lengths of these objects to an 18 m giant squid. Which is longest?

Garbage-eating Worms

Possible Materials

- Worms (red wigglers)
- Plastic containers with drainage holes (4 L) (2)
- Soil (7 L)
- Chopped food scraps including fruit and vegetable peels, pulverized eggshells, tea bags, and coffee grounds
- Shredded newspaper
- Spray bottle

You know that soil conditions can influence the growth of plants. You are trying to decide what factors might improve the soil in your backyard garden. A friend suggests that earthworms improve the quality of the soil. Does the presence of earthworms have any value in improving soil conditions?

Recognize the Problem

How does the presence of earthworms change the condition of the soil?

Form a Hypothesis

Based on your reading and observations, state a hypothesis about how earthworms might improve the conditions of soil.

Goals

- **Design an experiment** that compares the condition of soil in two environments, one with earthworms and one without.
- **Observe** the change in soil conditions for two weeks.

Safety Precautions

Be careful when working with live animals. Always keep your hands wet when handling earthworms. Dry hands will remove the mucus from the earthworms.

Test Your Hypothesis

Plan

1. As a group, agree upon the hypothesis and **decide** how you will test it. **Identify** what results will confirm the hypothesis.

2. **List** the steps you will need to take to test your hypothesis. Be specific. **Describe** exactly what you will do in each step. **List** your materials.

3. Prepare a data table in your Science Journal to **record** your observations.

4. **Read** over the entire experiment to make sure all steps are in logical order.

5. **Identify** all constants, variables, and controls of the experiment.

Do

1. Make sure your teacher approves your plan and your data table before you proceed.

2. Carry out the experiment as planned.

3. While doing the experiment, **record** your observations and complete the data table in your Science Journal.

Analyze Your Data

1. **Compare** the changes in the two sets of soil samples.

2. **Compare** your results with those of other groups.

3. What was your control in this experiment?

4. What were your variables?

Draw Conclusions

1. Did the results support your hypothesis? **Explain.**

2. **Describe** what effect you think rain would have on the soil and worms.

Arthropods

By far, the largest group of animals belongs in the phylum Arthropoda. More than 900 000 species of arthropods have been discovered. The term **arthropod** comes from *arthros*, meaning "jointed," and *poda*, meaning "foot." Arthropods are animals that have jointed appendages. They are similar to annelids because they have segmented bodies. Yet, in most cases, they have fewer, more specialized segments. Instead of setae, they have different kinds of appendages. **Appendages** are the structures such as claws, legs, and even antennae that grow from the body.

Every arthropod has an **exoskeleton** that protects and supports its body. The exoskeleton also protects the arthropod from drying out. This lightweight body covering is made of a carbohydrate and a protein. As the animal grows, the exoskeleton is shed in a process called molting. The weight of the outer covering increases as the size of the animal increases. Weight and hardness of the exoskeleton produce a problem for the animal. They make it more difficult to move. The jointed appendages solve part of this problem.

Figure 12-18 shows an example of the five different types of arthropods: insects, spiders, centipedes, millipedes, and crustaceans. Find the body segments on these animals. Which arthropods appear most like the annelids?

Figure 12-18 Arthropods include insects (A), spiders (B), centipedes (C), millipedes (D), and crustaceans (E).

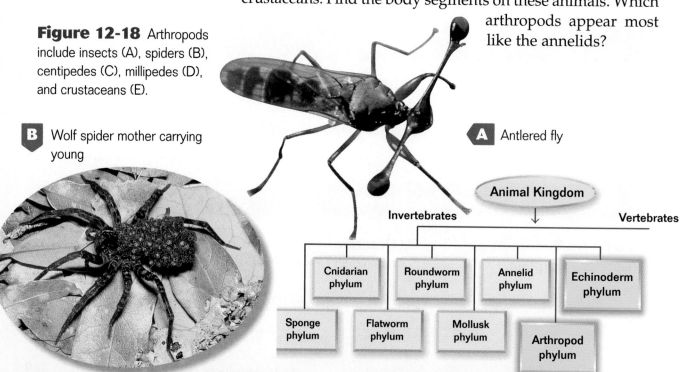

B Wolf spider mother carrying young

A Antlered fly

Animal Kingdom

Invertebrates — Vertebrates

Cnidarian phylum
Roundworm phylum
Annelid phylum
Echinoderm phylum
Sponge phylum
Flatworm phylum
Mollusk phylum
Arthropod phylum

Insects

When asked to name an insect, your answer might be some kind of flying insect, such as bee, fly, beetle, or butterfly. In fact, insects are the only invertebrates that can fly. Insects make up the largest group of invertebrates. There are more than 700 000 classified species of insects, and scientists describe more each year.

Insects have three distinct body regions, as shown in **Figure 12-18A:** the head, thorax, and abdomen. The head has well-developed sensory organs, including the eyes and antennae. The thorax has three pairs of jointed legs and, in many species, one or two pairs of wings. The wings and legs of insects are highly specialized.

The abdomen is divided into segments and has neither wings nor legs attached to it. Reproductive organs are located in this region. Insects produce many more young than can survive. For example, a single female fly can produce thousands of eggs.

Insects have an open circulatory system. Oxygen is not transported by blood in the system, but food and waste materials are. Oxygen is brought directly to tissues inside of the insect through small holes called spiracles (SPIHR ih kulz) located along the thorax and abdomen.

*inter***NET**
CONNECTION

Visit the Glencoe Science Web Site at **www.glencoe.com/ sec/science/ca** for more information about butterflies.

E Sally lightfoot crab

C Centipede

D Forest floor millipede

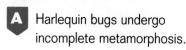

VISUALIZING Metamorphosis

Figure 12-19

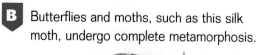

B Butterflies and moths, such as this silk moth, undergo complete metamorphosis.

A Harlequin bugs undergo incomplete metamorphosis.

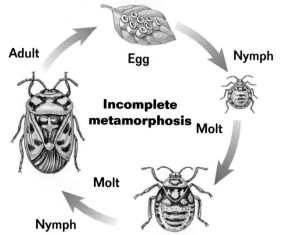

Adult

Egg

Nymph

Incomplete metamorphosis

Molt

Molt

Nymph

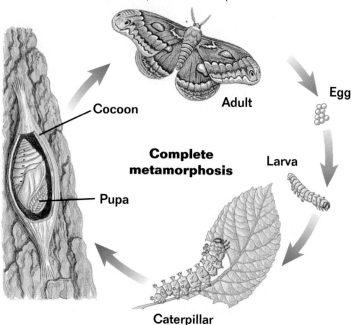

Cocoon

Adult

Egg

Complete metamorphosis

Larva

Pupa

Caterpillar

Figure 12-20 A spider's web is made from a liquid silk that the arachnid produces in its abdomen. Each kind of spider weaves its own unique style of web.

EXAMPLES OF Arachnids

- Spiders
- Mites
- Ticks
- Scorpions
- Lice

Metamorphosis

Identifying the young of some insects can be difficult. They don't look anything like the adult forms. This happens because many insects completely change their body form as they mature. This change in body form is called **metamorphosis** (met uh MOR fuh sus). There are two kinds of metamorphosis. Butterflies, ants, bees, and moths undergo complete metamorphosis. Complete metamorphosis has four stages: egg, larva, pupa (PYEW puh), and adult. You can trace the stages of this process in **Figure 12-19.** Notice how different the larva and pupa stages are from the adults.

Other insects go through incomplete metamorphosis, which is made up of only three stages: egg, nymph, and adult. Grasshopper nymphs look like a tiny version of the parents except they don't have wings. A nymph molts several times before reaching the adult stage. They replace their old exoskeletons as they grow larger. Grasshoppers get their wings and become adults after their final molt.

Arachnids

Spiders, ticks, mites, and scorpions are often confused with insects. They actually belong to a separate group of arthropods known as arachnids. Arachnids have two body regions. The first, called the cephalothorax (sef uh luh THOR aks), is made of the fused head and thorax regions. The abdomen is the second region. All arachnids have four pairs of legs attached to the cephalothorax.

Figure 12-21 Millipedes (A) may have more than 100 segments in their long abdomens. Centipedes (B) may have from 15 segments to 181 segments—always an odd number.

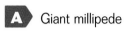

Spiders are predators, but they can't chew and eat prey the way insects do. Instead, a spider uses a pair of fanglike appendages in its mouth to inject venom into the prey and paralyze it. The spider releases enzymes that turn its victim into a liquid. The spider then drinks its food. In **Figure 12-20,** a spider is weaving a web that will trap prey.

Centipedes and Millipedes

Centipedes and millipedes are long, thin, segmented arthropods that look like worms. Instead of setae, these arthropods have pairs of jointed legs. Centipedes have one pair of joined legs attached to each body segment. Millipedes have two pairs. Centipedes are predators that use poisonous venom to capture their prey. Millipedes eat plants. Besides the number of legs, how else is the centipede different from the millipede in **Figure 12-21?**

Crustaceans

The exoskeleton gets larger and heavier each time an arthropod molts. The weight of the exoskeleton can limit the size of the animal. Now, think about where you can lift the most weight—on land or in water? Water is more buoyant than air, and it provides a greater upward force on an object. Because of this buoyant property, a large, heavy exoskeleton is less limiting for arthropods that live in water. These arthropods belong to a class known as crustaceans.

Most crustaceans live in water. Examples include crabs, crayfish, lobsters, shrimp, barnacles, and water fleas. They have five pairs of jointed legs. The first pair is usually larger and thicker and is used as claws to hold food, as illustrated in **Figure 12-22.** The other four pairs are walking legs. The five pairs of appendages on the abdomen are swimmerets. These are used to help move the animals through water and for reproduction. The swimmerets also force water over the feathery gills. If a crustacean loses an appendage, it can regenerate the lost part.

EXAMPLES OF
Crustaceans

- Crabs
- Crayfish
- Lobsters
- Shrimp
- Barnacles

Figure 12-22 This rock crab, found in the Atlantic Ocean, is using its claws to hold the scallop it eats.

B Sand dollar

Figure 12-23 Echinoderms include sea stars (A), sand dollars (B), and basket stars (C). **What do these organisms have in common?**

A Fireback sea star

C Basket star

Reading Check ✓

What does the word *echinoderm* mean?

EXAMPLES OF
Echinoderms

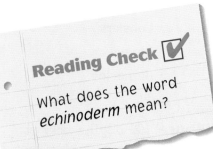

- **Sea stars**
- **Sea urchins**
- **Sand dollars**
- **Basket star**
- **Sea cucumber**

Echinoderms

Unless you live near the ocean, you may not have seen an echinoderm (ih KI nuh durm), but most people know what a sea star is. Echinoderms have radial symmetry and are represented by sea stars, brittle stars, sea urchins, sand dollars, and sea cucumbers. They also don't have heads, brains, or advanced nervous systems.

The name *echinoderm* means "spiny skin." You can see from those shown in **Figure 12-23** that echinoderms have spines of various lengths that cover the outside of their bodies. Most echinoderms, such as sea stars, are supported and protected by an internal skeleton made up of calcium carbonate plates. These plates are covered by thin, spiny skin. ✓

Water-Vascular System

Sea stars have a unique characteristic shared by all echinoderms—a water-vascular system. The water-vascular system is a network of water-filled canals. Thousands of tube feet are connected to this system. As water moves into and out of the water-vascular system, the tube feet act as suction cups and help the sea star move and eat. **Figure 12-24** shows these tube feet and how they are used to pry open a dead rock crab.

Sea stars also have a unique way of eating. Think about how you eat. You bring food to your mouth and swallow. The food then travels down to your stomach. The sea star actually pushes its stomach out of its mouth and into the opened shell of the oyster. It then digests the oyster's body while it is still inside the shell.

Like some other invertebrates, sea stars can regenerate damaged parts. Early settlers of the Chesapeake Bay area found the bay teeming with oysters. Eventually, more people moved into the area and deposited their wastes into the bay. Because some sea stars do well in polluted water, their population grew. People who harvested oysters found that the oyster population was decreasing. They decided to kill the sea stars by cutting them into pieces and

Figure 12-24 Sea bat sea stars use their tube feet to feed on a dead rock crab.

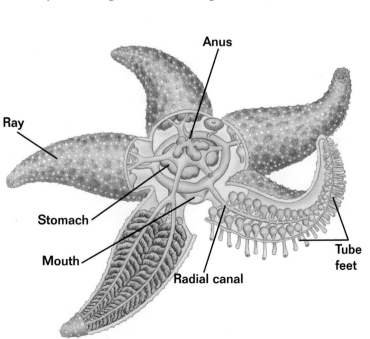

Anus

Ray

Stomach

Mouth

Radial canal

Tube feet

throwing them back into the bay. Within a short time, the sea star population was five times larger than before due to regeneration. The entire oyster bed was destroyed!

Sea Cucumbers

The sea cucumber in **Figure 12-25** looks nothing like the other members of the echinoderm class. They have soft bodies with a leathery covering. They have few calcium carbonate plates. Sea cucumbers have tentacles around their mouths that are used to capture food. Although they have five rows of tube feet on the sides of their bodies, they appear to be more bilaterally symmetrical than the other echinoderms. When threatened, sea cucumbers may expel their internal organs. These organs regenerate in a few weeks.

Scientists continue to study echinoderms to learn more about the process of regeneration. These animals are also important in keeping saltwater environments free of pollution. They feed on dead organisms and help recycle materials within the environment.

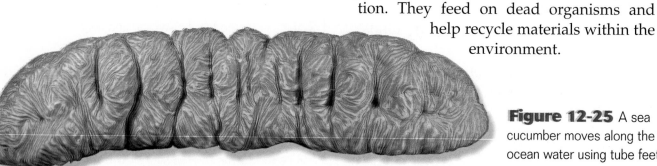

Figure 12-25 A sea cucumber moves along the ocean water using tube feet.

Section Assessment

1. What are three characteristics of all arthropods?
2. What are the advantages and disadvantages of an exoskeleton?
3. What characteristics set echinoderms apart from other invertebrates?
4. **Think Critically:** What might happen to the sea star population after the oyster beds are destroyed? Explain your answer.
5. **Skill Builder**
   Observing and Inferring Observe the echinoderms pictured in **Figure 12-23.** Infer why they are slow moving. If you need help, refer to Observing and Inferring in the **Skill Handbook** on page 684.

Observing Complete Metamorphosis

Many insects go through the four stages of complete metamorphosis during their life cycles. Chemicals that are secreted by the body of the animal control the changes. How different do the body forms look between the stages of metamorphosis?

Materials

- Large-mouth jar or old fish bowl
- Bran or oatmeal
- Dried bread or cookie crumbs mixed with flour
- Slice of apple or carrot
- Paper towel
- Cheesecloth
- Mealworms
- Rubber band

What You'll Investigate

What do the stages of metamorphosis look like for a mealworm?

Goals

- **Observe** the stages of metamorphosis of mealworms to adult darkling beetles.
- **Compare** the physical appearance of mealworms as they go through two stages of metamorphosis.

Procedure

1. **Set up** a habitat for the mealworms by placing a 1-cm layer of bran or oatmeal on the bottom of the jar. Add a 1-cm layer of dried bread or cookie crumbs mixed with flour. Then, add another layer of bran or oatmeal.

2. **Add** a slice of apple or carrot as a source of moisture. Replace the apple or carrot daily.

3. **Place** 20 to 30 mealworms in the jar. Add a piece of crumpled paper towel.

4. **Cover** the jar with a piece of cheesecloth. Use the rubber band to secure the cloth to the jar.

5. **Observe** the mealworms daily for two to three weeks. **Record** daily observations in your Science Journal.

Conclude and Apply

1. In your Science Journal, **draw** and **describe** the mealworms' metamorphosis to adults.

2. **Identify** the stages of metamorphosis that mealworms go through to become adult darkling beetles.

3. Which of these stages did you not see during this investigation?

4. What are some of the advantages of an insect's young being different from the adult form?

5. Based on the food you placed in the habitat, **infer** where you might find mealworms or the adult darkling beetles in your house.

6. Why do you think pet stores would stock and sell mealworms?

For a **preview** of this chapter, study this Reviewing Main Ideas before you read the chapter. After you have studied this chapter, you can use the Reviewing Main Ideas to **review** the chapter.

The Glencoe MindJogger, Audiocassettes, and CD-ROM provide additional opportunities for review.

Section

12-1 WHAT IS AN ANIMAL?

Animals are many-celled organisms that must find and digest their own food. **Invertebrates** are animals without backbones. **Vertebrates** have backbones. Animals that have body parts arranged the same way on both sides of their bodies have bilateral **symmetry.** Animals with body parts arranged in a circle around a central point have radial symmetry. Asymetrical animals have no definite shape. *What are five characteristics of animals?*

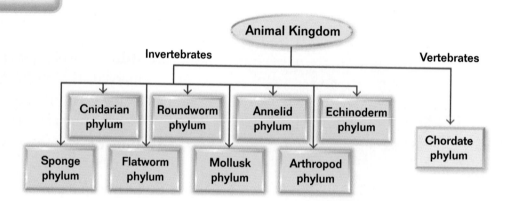

Section

12-2 SPONGES, CNIDARIANS, FLATWORMS, AND ROUNDWORMS

Sponges and cnidarians are only two layers thick. Sponge cells do not form tissues, organs, or organ systems. Sponges are sessile and obtain food and oxygen by filtering water through pores. **Cnidarian** bodies have tissues and are radially symmetrical. Most have tentacles with stinging cells that get food. Regeneration allows an organism to replace lost or damaged parts or to reproduce sexually. Flatworms and roundworms have bilateral symmetry. They have both parasitic and **free-living** members. *Why are sponges considered the least complex of all animals?*

Reading Check ☑

Choose a group of unlike objects, such as the items in your book bag or your locker. Classify these objects into groups and subgroups.

Section
12-3 MOLLUSKS AND SEGMENTED WORMS

Mollusks with one shell are gastropods. Bivalve mollusks have two shells. Cephalopods have a foot divided into tentacles and no outside shell. Except for cephalopods, mollusks have an **open circulatory system** in which the blood surrounds the organs directly. Cephalopods have a **closed circulatory system** with the blood contained in vessels. Annelids have a body cavity that separates the internal organs from the body wall. Setae help annelids move. *How are cephalopods adapted for swimming?*

Section
12-4 ARTHROPODS AND ECHINODERMS

Arthropods are classified by the number of body segments and **appendages.** Their **exoskeletons** cover, protect, and support their bodies. Arthropods develop either by complete or incomplete **metamorphosis.** Echinoderms are spiny-skinned invertebrates most closely related to vertebrates. They move by means of a water-vascular system. *What are some common characteristics for all arthropods?*

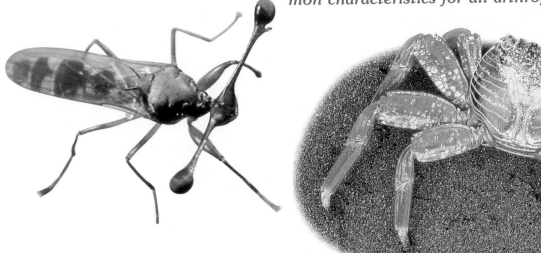

Chapter 12 Assessment

Using Vocabulary

a. appendage
b. arthropod
c. closed circulatory system
d. cnidarian
e. exoskeleton
f. free-living
g. gills
h. invertebrate
i. mantle
j. medusa
k. metamorphosis
l. mollusk
m. open circulatory system
n. parasite
o. polyp
p. radula
q. symmetry
r. vertebrate

Explain the differences between the terms in each of the following sets.

1. medusa, polyp
2. closed circulatory system, open circulatory system
3. vertebrate, invertebrate
4. arthropod, mollusk
5. exoskeleton, mantle

Checking Concepts

Choose the word or phrase that best answers the question.

6. Which of the following refers to animals that can be divided in half along a single line?
   A) asymmetrical
   B) bilaterally symmetrical
   C) radially symmetrical
   D) anterior

7. Which of the following do **NOT** belong to the same group?
   A) fish   C) jellyfish
   B) hydras   D) sea anemones

8. Which of the following phylums do sponges belong to?
   A) Cnidaria   C) Porifera
   B) Nematoda   D) Platyhelminthes

9. The body plans of cnidarians are polyp and which of the following?
   A) larva   C) ventral
   B) medusa   D) bud

10. Which of the following is an example of a parasite?
    A) sponge   C) tapeworm
    B) planarian   D) jellyfish

11. Which of the following covers the organs of mollusks?
    A) radula   C) gill
    B) mantle   D) foot

12. Which organism has a closed circulatory system?
    A) octopus   C) oyster
    B) snail   D) sponge

13. Which organism has two body regions?
    A) insect   C) arachnid
    B) mollusk   D) annelid

14. Which phylum has many organisms with radial symmetry?
    A) annelids   C) echinoderms
    B) mollusks   D) arthropods

15. Which of the following are sharp and cause predators to avoid eating sponges?
    A) thorax   C) collar cells
    B) spicules   D) tentacles

Thinking Critically

16. What aspect of sponge reproduction would be evidence that they are more like animals than plants?

17. What is the advantage for simple organisms to have more than one means of reproduction?

18. What are the differences between the tentacles of cnidarians and cephalopods?

19. What is the difference between budding and regeneration?

20. Centipedes and millipedes have segments. Why are they **NOT** classified as worms?

Developing Skills

If you need help, refer to the Skill Handbook.

21. **Comparing and Contrasting:** Compare and contrast the feeding habits of sponges and cnidarians.

22. **Using Variables, Constants, and Controls:** Design an experiment to test the sense of touch in planarians.

23. **Observing and Inferring:** Why are gastropods sometimes called univalves? Use examples in your answer.

24. **Classifying:** Classify the following animals into arthropod classes: *spider, grasshopper, ladybug, beetle, crab, scorpion, lobster, butterfly, tick,* and *shrimp*.

25. **Concept Mapping:** Complete the concept map of classification in the cnidarian phylum.

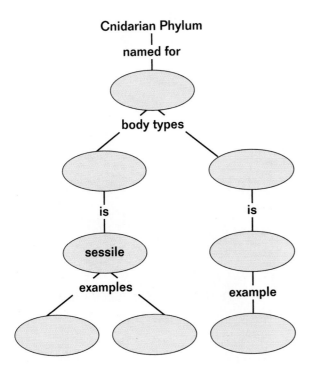

Test-Taking Tip

Words Are Easy to Learn Make a huge stack of vocabulary flash cards and study them. Use your new words in daily conversation. The great thing about learning new words is the ability to express yourself more specifically.

Test Practice

Use these questions to test your Science Proficiency.

1. Symmetry refers to the arrangement of the individual parts of an object. Which of the following organisms have radial symmetry?
   A) cnidarians
   B) sponges
   C) tapeworms
   D) mollusks

2. Echinoderms have a unique way of eating. Which of the following structures are used by echinoderms to move about and open a mollusk's shell?
   A) spicules
   B) arms
   C) spines
   D) tube feet

3. A water-vascular system is a network of water-filled canals. Which of the following phylums of invertebrates possess a water-vascular system?
   A) echinoderms
   B) arthropods
   C) mollusks
   D) cnidarians

CHAPTER

13 Vertebrate Animals

Chapter Preview

Skills Preview

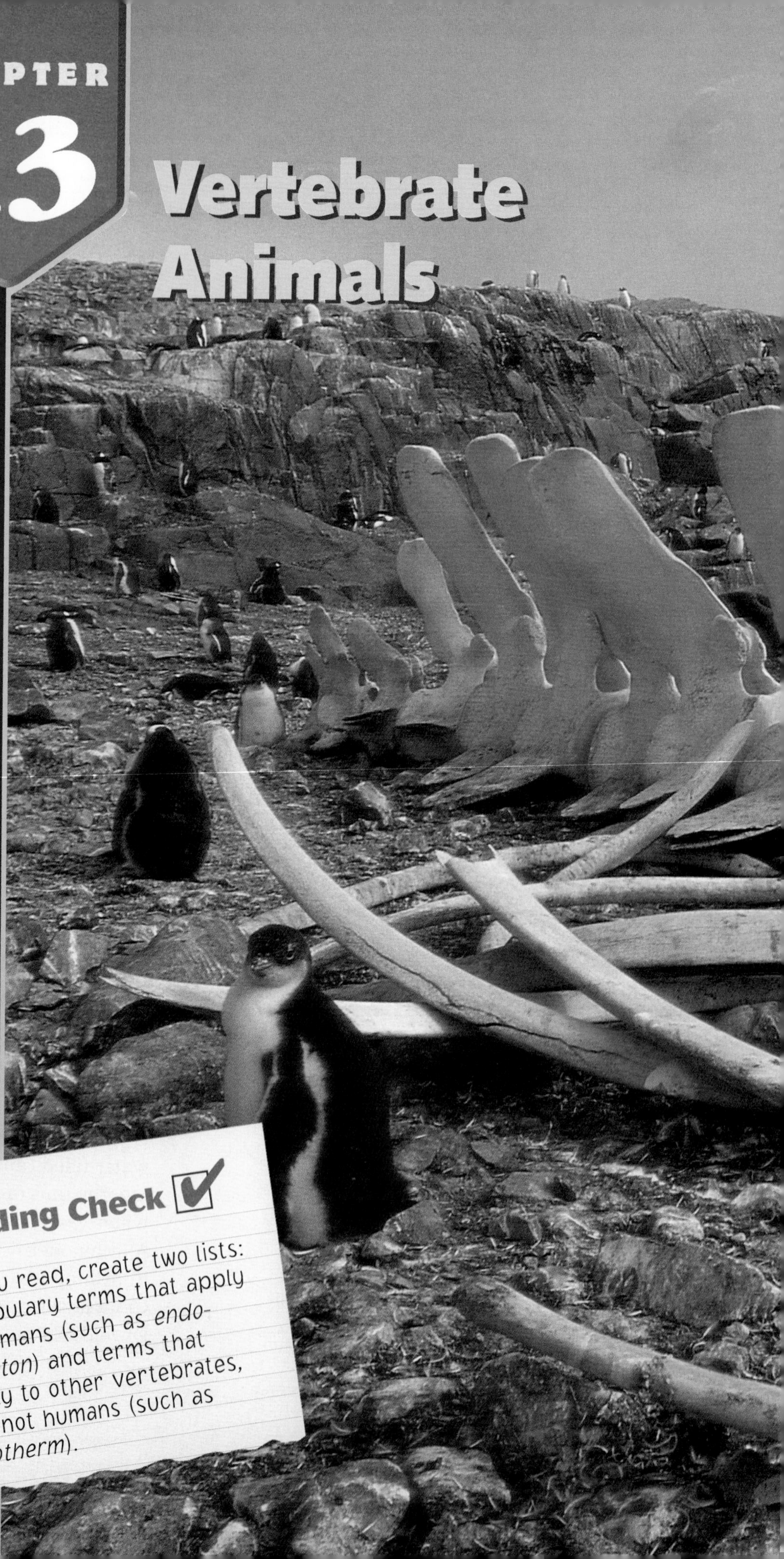

Skill Builders

- Map Concepts
- Classify

Activities

- Design an Experiment
- Observe and Infer

MiniLabs

- Make a Model
- Compare and Contrast

Reading Check

As you read, create two lists: vocabulary terms that apply to humans (such as *endoskeleton*) and terms that apply to other vertebrates, but not humans (such as *ectotherm*).

Explore Activity

You have something in common with the whale remains on the opposite page. This common feature protects some of the organs inside your body. It supports and gives your body shape. It also works with your muscles to help move your body. This common feature is your skeleton. Most internal skeletons are made of bone. Bones are many shapes and sizes. They must be strong enough to carry your weight yet light enough for you to move. To learn more about the structure of bones, complete the following Explore Activity.

Model Bones

1. Think about the different shapes of your bones. What shape is your shoulder blade? Your hip bone? Your neck? Your ribs?

2. Use five index cards to make bone models. Fold and bend the cards into different shapes. Use tape to hold the shapes if necessary.

3. Stack books on top of each card to find out which shape supports the most weight.

In your Science Journal, draw a picture of each bone model. Infer which shape would make the strongest bone. Write a paragraph comparing the strengths of each bone model.

What is a vertebrate?

Suppose you took a survey in which you asked your classmates to list their pets. Probably dogs, cats, birds, snakes, and fish appear on the list. A large percentage of the animals listed, along with yourself, would belong to a group called vertebrates. Vertebrates are animals with backbones. They are the most complex of three animal groups that belong to the Chordate phylum, as illustrated in **Figure 13-1.** All **chordates** have a notochord, which is a rod of stiffened tissue. Chordates also have a hollow nerve cord in their backs and gill slits. In most vertebrates, a backbone made of vertebra replaces the notochord as the animal develops.

Whereas most invertebrates have exoskeletons, vertebrates have an internal system of bones called an **endoskeleton.** *Endo-* means "within." The vertebrae, skull, and other bones of the endoskeleton support and protect the animal's internal organs. The skeleton also provides a place where muscles are attached.

Vertebrates have two different ways of dealing with internal body temperature. Most vertebrates are ectotherms. **Ectotherms** are vertebrates whose body temperature changes with the temperature of their surroundings. **Endotherms** are animals with a constant body temperature. The body temperature of an endotherm usually remains the same no matter what the temperature of its surrounding environment.

Figure 13-1 This concept map showing the different groups of animals will appear at the beginning of each section. The groups that are highlighted with a red outline are the groups to be discussed. This diagram shows that the Chordate phylum is made up of three groups: the tunicates, the lancelets, and the vertebrates.

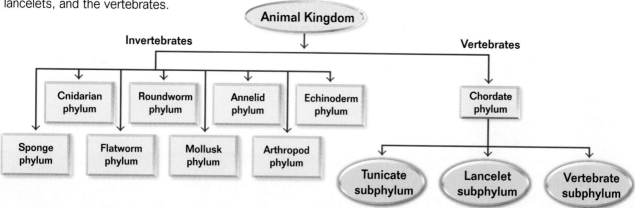

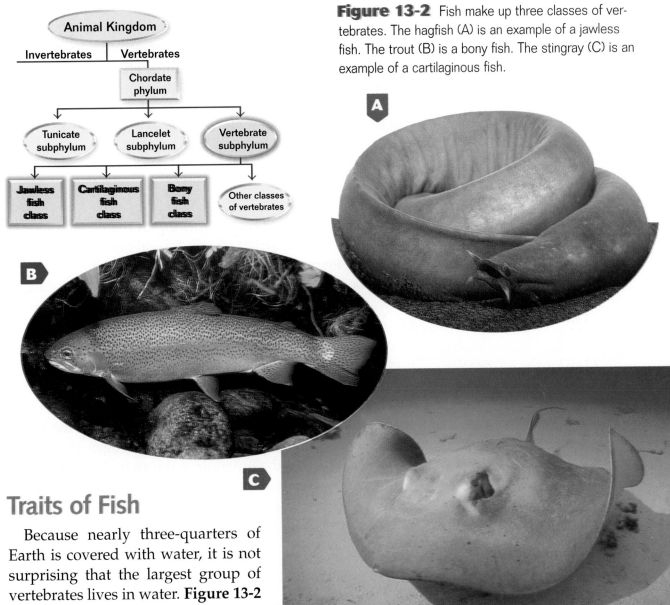

Figure 13-2 Fish make up three classes of vertebrates. The hagfish (A) is an example of a jawless fish. The trout (B) is a bony fish. The stingray (C) is an example of a cartilaginous fish.

Animal Kingdom

Invertebrates | Vertebrates

Chordate phylum

Tunicate subphylum | Lancelet subphylum | Vertebrate subphylum

Jawless fish class | Cartilaginous fish class | Bony fish class | Other classes of vertebrates

Traits of Fish

Because nearly three-quarters of Earth is covered with water, it is not surprising that the largest group of vertebrates lives in water. **Figure 13-2** illustrates how fish relate to other vertebrates. Fish can be found in warm desert pools and the subfreezing Arctic ocean. They swim in shallow streams and far down in the ocean depths.

Fish are ectotherms that live in water and use gills to get oxygen. Gills are fleshy filaments that are filled with tiny blood vessels. The heart of the fish pumps blood to the gills. As blood passes through the gills, it picks up oxygen from water that is passing over the gills. Carbon dioxide is released from the blood into the water.

Most fish have fins. **Fins** are fanlike structures used for steering, balancing, and moving. Usually, they are paired. Those on the top and bottom stabilize the fish. Those on the side steer and move the fish. Scales are another common characteristic of fish although not all fish have scales. Scales are hard, thin, overlapping plates that cover the skin. These protective plates are made of a bony material.

Using Math

Make a circle graph of the number of fish species currently classified. There are 70 species of jawless fish, 820 species of cartilaginous fish, and 23 500 species of bony fish. What percent of this graph is accounted for by cartilaginous fish?

Types of Fish

Scientists group fish into three distinct classes. They are bony fish, jawless fish, and cartilaginous fish. Bony fish have skeletons made of bone, while cartilaginous fish and jawless fish both have endoskeletons made of cartilage. **Cartilage** (KART uh lihj) is a tough, flexible tissue that is similar to bone but is not as hard. Your ears and the tip of your nose are made of cartilage.

Bony Fish

About 95 percent of all fish belong to the class known as bony fish. The body structure of a typical bony fish, a tuna, is shown in **Figure 13-3.** These fish have skeletons made of bone. Their scales are covered with slimy mucus that allows the water to easily flow over the fishes' bodies as they swim in water. The majority of bony fish use external fertilization to reproduce. Females release large numbers of eggs into the water. Males release sperm as they swim over the eggs.

An important adaptation in most bony fish is the swim bladder. This air sac helps control the depth at which the fish swim. Transfer of gases between the swim bladder and the blood, mostly oxygen in deep-water fish and nitrogen in shallow-water fish, changes the inflation of the swim bladder. As the swim bladder fills with gases, the fish becomes more buoyant and rises in the water. When the bladder deflates, the fish becomes less buoyant and sinks lower in the water.

EXAMPLES OF
Bony Fish

- Trout
- Cod
- Salmon
- Catfish
- Tuna
- Sea horse

PHYSICS
INTEGRATION

Regulating Buoyancy
Unlike fish that regulate the gas content of their fish bladders, submarines pump water into and out of special chambers to regulate the vertical forces that cause the submarine to sink or rise.

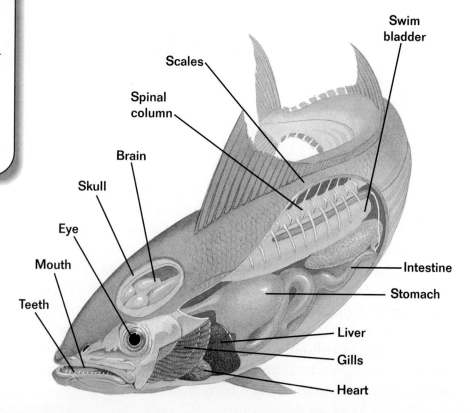

Figure 13-3 Although there are many different kinds of bony fish, they all share basic structures. **What are two unique fish structures?**

Figure 13-4 This sea lamprey (A) with its sucker disk mouth belongs to the class of jawless fish. Sharks (B) belong to the cartilaginous class and are efficient at finding and killing food.

Jawless and Cartilaginous Fish

Few fish belong to the class known as jawless fish. Jawless fish have long, scaleless, tubelike bodies and an endoskeleton made of cartilage. They have round mouths but no jaws, as seen in **Figure 13-4A.** Their mouths act like suckers with sharp toothlike parts. Once a lamprey attaches itself to another larger fish, it uses the toothlike parts to scrape through the host's skin. It then feeds on the blood of the larger fish.

Sharks, skates, and rays are cartilaginous fish. Cartilaginous fish have skeletons made of cartilage just like the jawless fish. However, cartilaginous fish, such as the shark in **Figure 13-4B,** have movable jaws and scales. Their scales feel rough like sandpaper. Most cartilaginous fish are predators.

Section Assessment

1. What are three characteristics of chordates?

2. Name the three classes of fish. What materials make up their skeletons?

3. Compare and contrast ectotherms and endotherms.

4. **Think Critically:** Female fish lay thousands of eggs. Why aren't lakes overcrowded with fish?

5. **Skill Builder**
   Observing and Inferring Fish without swim bladders, such as sharks, must move constantly, or they sink. They need more energy to maintain this constant movement. What can you infer about the amount of food sharks must eat when compared to another fish of similar size that have swim bladders? If you need help, refer to Observing and Inferring in the **Skill Handbook** on page 684.

Using Math

There are 353 known species of sharks. Of that number, only about 30 species have been known to attack humans. What percentage of shark species is known to attack humans?

13·2 Amphibians and Reptiles

What You'll Learn

▶ How amphibians have adapted to live in water and on land

▶ What happens during frog metamorphosis

▶ The adaptations that allow reptiles to live on land

Vocabulary

amphibian   estivation
hibernation   reptile

Why It's Important

▶ Amphibians are adapted to living in both water and on land while reptiles live only on land.

Amphibians

Have you ever heard of a person leading a double life? Amphibians are animals that lead double lives. In fact, the term *amphibian* comes from the Greek word *amphibios*, which means "double life." **Amphibians** are vertebrates that spend part of their lives in water and part on land. They are also ectotherms, which means that their internal body temperatures changes with their environment. Frogs, toads, and salamanders such as the barred tiger salamander pictured in **Figure 13-5** are the most common kinds of amphibians.

Amphibian Adaptations

Living on land is different from living in water. Air temperature changes more quickly and more often than water temperature. Also, air doesn't support body weight as well as water. Certain adaptations help amphibians survive both in water and on land.

Amphibians have behavioral adaptations that allow them to cope with swings in the air temperature of their particular environment. During cold winter months, they are inactive. They bury themselves in mud or leaves until the temperature warms up. In winter, this period of inactivity and lower metabolic needs

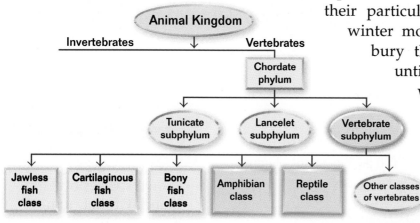

Figure 13-5 This barred tiger salamander has legs that extend straight out from the body.

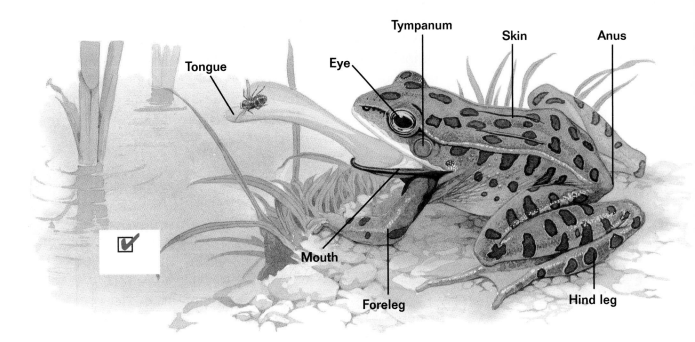

Figure 13-6 A frog's body is adapted for life in the water and on land. **What adaptations can you see in this illustration?**

is called **hibernation.** Metabolic needs refer to the chemical activities in an organism that enable it to live, grow, and reproduce. Amphibians that live in hot, drier environments are inactive and hide in the ground where it is likely to be cooler and more humid. This kind of inactivity during hot, dry summer months is called **estivation.** ☑

Amphibians have a strong endoskeleton made of bones. The skeleton helps to support the bodies of amphibians while on land. Adult frogs and toads have short, broad bodies, with four legs and no neck or tail. The strong hind legs are used for swimming and jumping.

Another adaptation increases amphibians' chances of survival on land. Instead of using gills to obtain oxygen from water, lungs become the primary method of obtaining oxygen from air. To increase the oxygen supply, amphibians exchange oxygen and carbon dioxide through their moist, scaleless skin or the lining of their mouths.

Moving to land provides an increased food supply for adult amphibians. Land habitats offer a variety of insects as food for these organisms. **Figure 13-6** shows some adaptations used to catch prey. The tympanic membranes, or eardrums, vibrate in response to sound and are used for hearing. Large eyes provide excellent vision. The long sticky tongue extends quickly to capture the insect and bring it into the waiting mouth.

Reading Check ☑

What is the difference between hibernation and estivation?

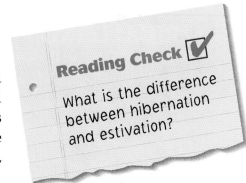

Visit the Glencoe Science Web Site at **www.glencoe.com/ sec/science/ca** for more information about amphibians.

Amphibian Metamorphosis

Although young animals such as kittens and calves are almost miniature duplicates of their parents, young amphibians look nothing like their parents. Metamorphosis is a series of body changes that occur during the life cycle of an amphibian. Most amphibians go through a two-stage metamorphosis as illustrated in **Figure 13-7.** The larval stage lives in water, and the adult lives on land.

Most amphibians mate in water. Here, the eggs hatch, and the young larval forms live. The larvae have no legs and breathe through gills. You can see that as the larval form of frogs, called tadpoles, go through metamorphosis, they change form. The young tadpoles develop body structures needed for life on land, including legs and lungs. The rate at which metamorphosis occurs depends on the species, the water temperature, and the amount of available food. The less available food is and the cooler the water temperatures are, the longer it takes for metamorphosis to occur.

VISUALIZING
Frog Metamorphosis

Figure 13-7 Frogs undergo a two-stage metamorphosis from the larval stage that lives in water to the adult stage that lives on land.

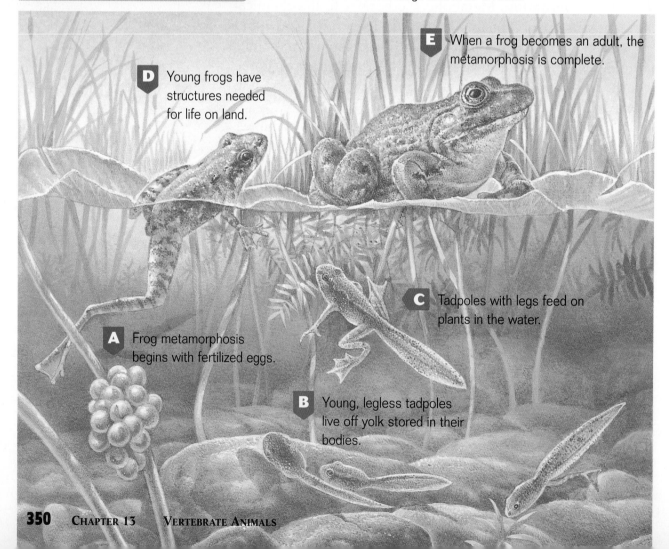

E When a frog becomes an adult, the metamorphosis is complete.

D Young frogs have structures needed for life on land.

C Tadpoles with legs feed on plants in the water.

A Frog metamorphosis begins with fertilized eggs.

B Young, legless tadpoles live off yolk stored in their bodies.

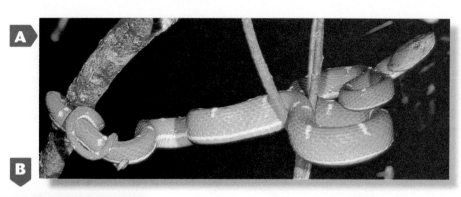

Figure 13-8 The green tree viper snake (A), the collared lizard (B), the spotted turtle (C), and the American alligator (D) are all reptiles.

Reptiles

The snake, lizard, turtle, and crocodile in **Figure 13-8** are all reptiles. A **reptile** is an ectothermic vertebrate with dry, scaly skin. Reptiles are vertebrates that do not depend on water for reproduction. Several adaptations allow reptiles to live on land.

Types of Reptiles

Reptiles vary greatly in size, shape, and color. Turtles are covered with a hard shell. They withdraw into the shell for protection. They eat insects, worms, fish, and plants. Alligators and crocodiles are feared predators that live in and near water. These large reptiles live in tropical climates.

Lizards and snakes are the largest group of reptiles. Lizards have movable eyelids, external ears, and legs with clawed toes. Snakes don't have eyelids, ears, or legs. Instead of hearing sounds, they feel vibrations in the ground. Snakes are also sensitive to chemicals in the air. They use their tongue to "smell" these chemicals.

Reptile Adaptations

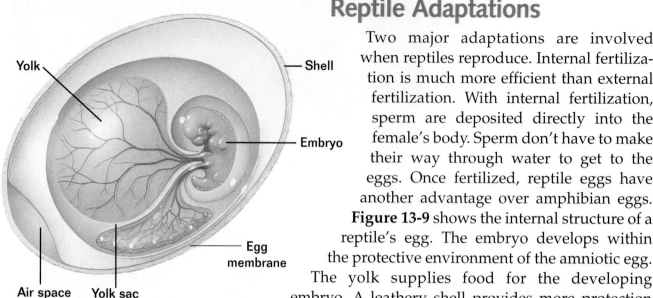

Yolk

Shell

Embryo

Egg membrane

Air space   Yolk sac

Figure 13-9 The amniotic egg is one of the adaptations reptiles have for living on land. Young reptiles hatch from their eggs fully developed.

Two major adaptations are involved when reptiles reproduce. Internal fertilization is much more efficient than external fertilization. With internal fertilization, sperm are deposited directly into the female's body. Sperm don't have to make their way through water to get to the eggs. Once fertilized, reptile eggs have another advantage over amphibian eggs.

Figure 13-9 shows the internal structure of a reptile's egg. The embryo develops within the protective environment of the amniotic egg. The yolk supplies food for the developing embryo. A leathery shell provides more protection than the jelly-covered frog's egg. When hatched, the young reptiles are fully developed. With some snakes, the young even develop and mature within the female's body. Then, the young snakes are born alive.

Another adaptation for life on land includes a thick, dry, waterproof skin. This skin is covered with scales and prevents dehydration and injury. All reptiles breathe with lungs. Even sea snakes and sea turtles must come to the surface to breathe.

Section Assessment

1. List the adaptations amphibians have for living in water and on land.

2. Sequence the steps of frog metamorphosis.

3. List the adaptations reptiles have for living on land.

4. **Think Critically:** Some harmless snakes have the same red, yellow, and black colors as the poisonous coral snake. How is this coloring an advantage for a nonpoisonous snake?

5. **Skill Builder**
   Comparing and Contrasting Compare and contrast the types of eggs amphibians and reptiles have. If you need help, refer to Comparing and Contrasting in the **Skill Handbook** on page 684.

Science Journal In your Science Journal, explain why it is important for amphibians to live in moist or wet environments.

Frog Metamorphosis

Materials

- Aquarium or jar (4 L)
- Frog egg mass
- Lake or pond water
- Stereoscopic microscope
- Watch glass
- Small fishnet
- Aquatic plants
- Washed gravel
- Lettuce (previously boiled)
- Large rock

Frogs and other amphibians use external fertilization to reproduce. Female frogs lay hundreds of jellylike eggs in water. Male frogs then fertilize these eggs. Once larvae hatch, the process of metamorphosis begins. Over a period of time, young tadpoles develop into adult frogs.

What You'll Investigate

What changes occur as a tadpole goes through metamorphosis?

Goals

- **Observe** how body structures change as a tadpole develops into an adult frog.
- **Determine** how long metamorphosis takes to be completed.

Procedure 🐭 💪 🥽

1. **Copy** the data table in your Science Journal.
2. As a class, use the aquarium, pond water, gravel, rock, and plants to prepare a water habitat for the frog eggs.
3. **Place** the egg mass in the water of the aquarium. Use the fishnet to separate a few eggs from the mass. **Place** these eggs in the watch glass. The eggs should have the dark side up. **CAUTION:** *Handle the eggs with care.*
4. **Observe** the eggs. **Record** your observations in the data table.
5. **Observe** the eggs twice a week. **Record** any changes that occur.
6. Continue observing the tadpoles twice a week after they hatch. **Identify** the mouth, eyes, gill cover, gills, nostrils, fin on the back, hind legs, and front legs. **Observe** how tadpoles eat boiled lettuce that has been cooled.

Conclude and Apply

1. How long does it take for the eggs to hatch and the tadpoles to develop legs?
2. Which pair of legs appears first?
3. **Explain** why the jellylike coating around the eggs is important.
4. **Compare** the eyes of young tadpoles with the eyes of older tadpoles.
5. **Calculate** how long it takes for a tadpole to change into a frog.

Frog Metamorphosis	
Date	**Observations**

13•3 Birds

What You'll Learn

► The characteristics of birds
► How birds have adapted in order to fly

Vocabulary
bird
contour feather
down feather

Why It's Important

► Many birds demonstrate structural and behavioral adaptations for flight.

Characteristics of Birds

Have you ever heard the term *pecking order?* Originally, it meant the ranking order of all the birds within a flock. High-ranking birds peck at lower-ranking birds to keep them away from food. This action is an example of a behavioral characteristic. Now, let's look at some physical characteristics of birds.

Despite the wide variety of birds, they all share some common characteristics. **Birds** are vertebrates with two legs, two wings, and bills, or beaks. They lay hard-shelled eggs, have feathers, and are endotherms. Recall that endothermic vertebrates keep a constant body temperature no matter what the temperature of the environment. Birds are the only animals that have feathers. The hard-shelled eggs protect the developing birds. Birds often sit on these eggs to keep them warm until they hatch. You learned that endotherms maintain a constant body temperature. A bird's body temperature is about 40°C. Your body temperature is about 37°C. Bird watchers can tell where a bird lives and what it eats by looking at the type of wing, beak, and feet it has. **Figure 13-10** illustrates some of the more than 8600 species of birds.

Figure 13-10 Birds are classified into orders based on the characteristic beaks, feet, feathers, and other physical features.

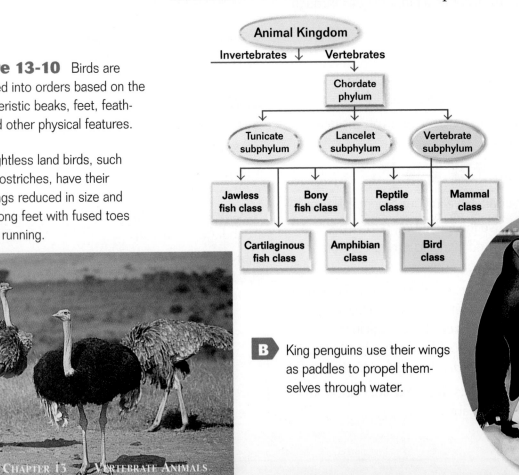

A Flightless land birds, such as ostriches, have their wings reduced in size and strong feet with fused toes for running.

B King penguins use their wings as paddles to propel themselves through water.

C The more than 200 species of ducks, such as this Mandarin duck, have webbed feet and short tails, as do geese and swans.

D Eagles and other birds of prey have sharp, hooked beaks for tearing flesh and large talons for grasping prey.

E Chickens, grouse, quail, turkeys, and this ringneck pheasant are ground-dwelling birds capable of short bursts of flight.

F Long-legged herons, storks, and these flamingos feed on fish and other aquatic organisms. Many of these species form nesting colonies in trees.

G Hummingbirds have specialized beaks for feeding on the nectar of flowers.

H Hairy woodpeckers have long, thin beaks adapted for digging insects out of wood and four toes—two toes in front and two toes in back. Such feet enable them to climb trees effectively.

I Mockingbirds and other perching birds, including crows and jays, have three toes facing forward and one backward. Their feet are adapted for perching on twigs.

J With two toes facing forward and two facing backward, roadrunners are adapted for running.

Using Math

Count the number of different birds you observe outside during a certain time each day for three days. Graph your data.

PHYSICS
INTEGRATION➤

Adaptations for Flight

Most body adaptations for birds are designed to enable them to fly. Their bodies are streamlined. Their skeletons are light, yet strong. If you could look inside the bone of a bird, you would see that it is hollow. Flying requires that they have a rigid body. Fused vertebrae provide the needed rigidity, strength, and stability. Birds need a good supply of oxygen to fly. Efficient hearts and lungs aid in respiration. The lungs are connected to air sacs that can be found throughout the body. Air sacs make a bird lighter for flight and help bring more oxygen to the blood. Large, powerful flight muscles in the wings are attached to the breastbone or sternum. Birds beat their wings to attain both thrust and lift. Slow motion pictures show that birds beat their wings both up and down as well as forward and back.

A bird's wing provides lift without constant beating. Like the airplane wing in **Figure 13-11,** a bird's wing is curved on top. It is flat or slightly curved on the bottom. A wing with this shape is important. As air moves across the wings, it has a greater distance to move across the top of the wing than along the bottom. The longer path taken by the air moving over the upper surface reduces the air pressure there. As a result, greater pressure is felt on the lower surface of the wing. The difference in air pressure results in lift.

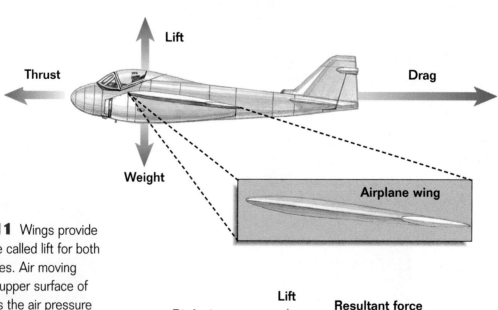

Figure 13-11 Wings provide the upward force called lift for both birds and airplanes. Air moving over the curved upper surface of the wing reduces the air pressure there, resulting in an upward force. The amount of lift depends on wing area, the speed of air across the wing, and the shape and angle of the wing.

Figure 13-12 Adult birds such as this great gray owl have an insulating layer of down feathers under their contour feathers. The owlets, like other young birds, are completely covered with down.

The Function of Feathers

Every body part of a bird is designed with flight in mind. Each feather is designed for flight. A bird's body is covered with two types of feathers, contour feathers and down feathers. Strong, lightweight **contour feathers** give birds their coloring and streamlined shape. Surface contour feathers overlap each other. This means that the bird can move more easily through the air or water. Feather colors and pattern are important because they identify a bird's species and sex. They also serve as protection that helps blend some birds into their surroundings. Contour feathers are also used to fly. It is these long feathers on the wings and tail that help the bird to steer and keep from spinning out of control.

Have you ever noticed that the hair on your arm stands up on a cold day? This response is your body's way to trap and keep warm air next to your skin. Birds have a similar response. This response helps birds maintain a constant body temperature. The birds in **Figure 13-12** have down feathers that trap and keep warm air next to their bodies. Soft, fluffy **down feathers** provide an insulating layer next to the skin of adult birds and cover the bodies of young birds. ☑

Mini Lab

Observing Bird Feathers

Procedure

1. Use a hand lens to examine a contour feather.
2. Hold the shaft end while carefully bending the opposite end. Observe what happens when you release the bent end.
3. Examine a down feather with a hand lens.
4. Hold each feather separately. Blow on them. Note any differences in the way each reacts to the stream of air.

Analysis

1. What happens when you release the bent end of the contour feather?
2. Which of the two feathers would you find on a bird's wing?
3. Which type of feather would you find in a pillow? Why?

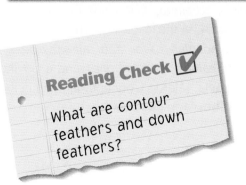

Reading Check ☑

What are contour feathers and down feathers?

Figure 13-13 Each barb in a contour feather has many smaller barbules that act like the teeth of a zipper. As a bird smoothes out the feather, the teeth of the barbules catch and zip together.

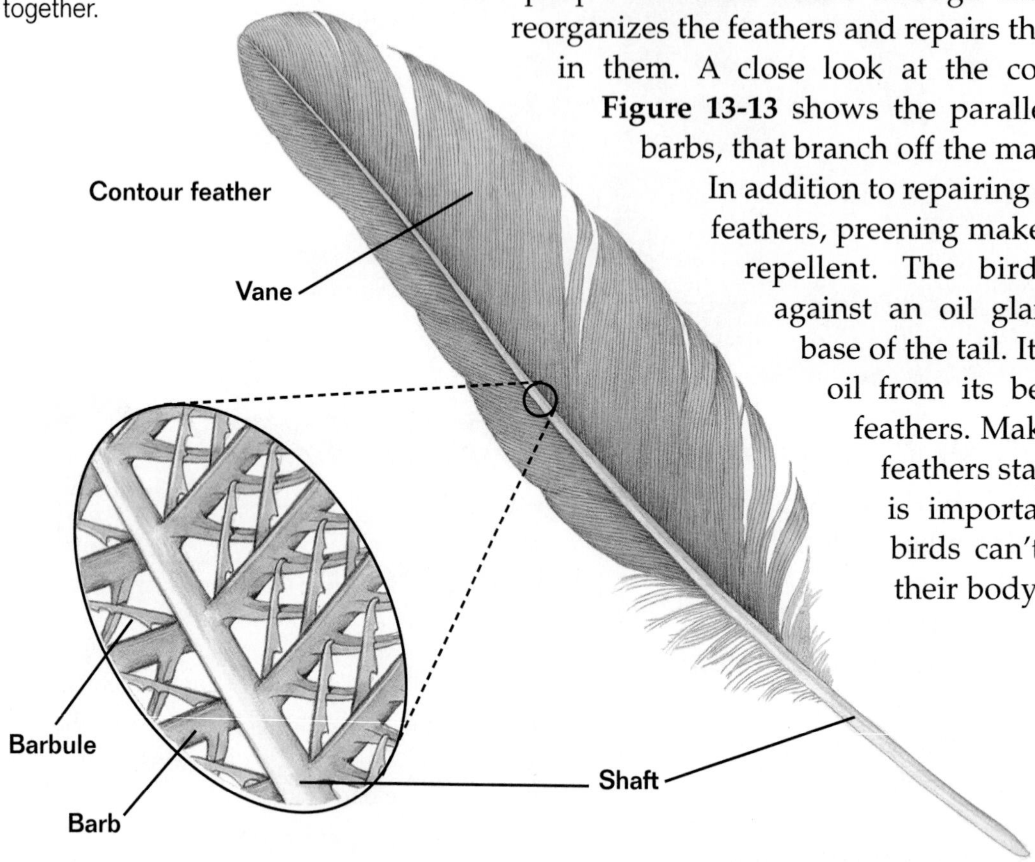

Contour feather

Vane

Barbule

Barb

Shaft

Care of Feathers

Feathers may be strong but they need to be kept in good condition. Only then can they keep birds warm, dry, and able to fly. Birds preen their feathers to take care of them. When they preen, they run their beaks through the feathers, much like people run their hands through their hair. Preening reorganizes the feathers and repairs the breaks, or gaps, in them. A close look at the contour feather in **Figure 13-13** shows the parallel strands, called barbs, that branch off the main shaft.

In addition to repairing and reorganizing feathers, preening makes feathers water-repellent. The bird rubs its beak against an oil gland found at the base of the tail. It then rubs off the oil from its beak and onto its feathers. Making sure that the feathers stay water-repellent is important. Watersoaked birds can't fly or maintain their body temperature.

Section Assessment

1. List four characteristics shared by all birds.
2. Explain how a bird's skeleton is adapted for flight.
3. **Think Critically:** Explain why birds can reproduce in the arctic but reptiles cannot.
4. **Skill Builder**
   Concept Mapping Make a network tree concept map that details the characteristics of birds. Use the following terms in your map: *birds, adaptations for flight, air sacs, beaks, eggs, feathers, hollow bones,* and *wing.* If you need help, refer to Concept Mapping in the **Skill Handbook** on page 678.

Using Computers

Spreadsheet Every 10 s a crow beats its wings 20 times, a robin 23 times, a chickadee 270 times, and a hummingbird 700 times. Using a spreadsheet, find out how many times the wings of each bird beat during a five-minute flight? If you need help, see page 702.

Flight Through the Ages

For thousands of years, people watched birds soar through the sky and yearned to experience the freedom of flight. The Maori people of what is now New Zealand made kites shaped like birds. The ancient Chinese loved kites, too (inset), and made them in all shapes and sizes.

In the early sixteenth century, artist and inventor Leonardo da Vinci made notes and diagrams about birds and flying machines. He reasoned that a bird's wings must work according to certain laws of physics and math and that therefore people should be able to build a device that could imitate the action of a bird in flight.

Da Vinci's drawings of flying machines inspired the invention of the ornithopter, or flapping-wing machine. People continued to experiment with these odd-looking devices—made out of willow, silk, and feathers—but never managed to get more than a few feet off the ground.

In the early 1800s, English scientist Sir George Cayley carried out his own studies of birds and bird flight. He concluded that it was impossible for people to fly using artificial flapping wings. Eventually, Cayley designed the first successful fixed-wing glider that could carry a person—a milestone that inspired Wilbur and Orville Wright.

Only after the Wright brothers solved a number of problems with gliding aircraft and built several gliders themselves did they focus on building an engine-powered aircraft. The Wright brothers identified the successful features of other aircraft and then added their own ideas about lift, the action of air currents, and the shape of wings. On December 17, 1903, Orville and Wilbur Wright made the world's first powered, sustained, and controlled flights in an airplane, the longest of which was 260 m. That momentous day set the stage for the evolution of many different kinds of engine-powered craft, from biplanes to supersonic jets and space shuttles.

Science JOURNAL

Think of how a bird flies. In your Science Journal, record the similarities and differences between airplane flight and the flight of birds.

13•4 Mammals

Characteristics of Mammals

How many different kinds of mammals can you name? Cats, dogs, bats, dolphins, horses, and people are all mammals. They live on land and in water, in cold and in hot climates. They burrow through the ground or fly through the air. Mammals have many characteristics that they share with other vertebrates. For example, they all have an internal skeleton with a backbone. But what characteristics make mammals unique?

Mammals are endotherms that have hair and produce milk to nourish their young. Being endothermic is not unique. Birds also are endotherms. However, mammals are unique because their skin is covered with hair or fur. Hair is mostly made of a protein called keratin. Some mammals, such as bears, are covered with thick fur. Others, like humans, have patches of hair. Still others, like the whale pictured in **Figure 13-14,** are almost hairless. Hair insulates the mammal's body from both cold and heat. It also protects the animal from wind and rain. Wool, spines, quills, and certain horns are made of keratin. What function do you think quills and spines serve?

Mammary Glands

Mammals put a great deal of time and energy into the care of their young. This begins at birth. Female mammals have mammary glands that form in the skin. During pregnancy, they increase in size. After birth, milk is produced and released in these glands. For the first weeks or months, the milk provides all of the nutrition that the young mammal needs.

What You'll Learn

▶ The characteristics of mammals
▶ How mammals adapt to different environments
▶ The difference among monotremes, marsupials, and placental mammals

Vocabulary

mammal   herbivore
monotreme   carnivore
marsupial   omnivore
placental
   mammal

Why It's Important

▶ Mammals—which include humans—all share many structural characteristics.

Figure 13-14 Unlike other mammals, whales, such as this humpback whale, are practically hairless with the exception of a few sensory whiskers on their snouts.

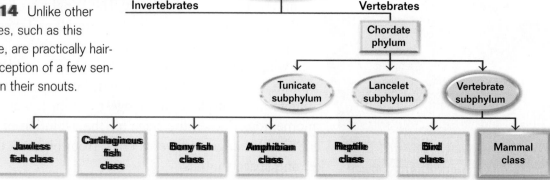

Body Systems

Think of all the different activities that mammals do. They run, swim, climb, hop, fly, and so on. They live active lives. Their body systems must be able to support all of these activities. Well-developed lungs made of millions of microscopic sacs called alveoli allow the exchanges of carbon dioxide and oxygen.

Mammals also have a more complex nervous system than other animals. The brain, spinal cord, and nerves allow these animals to utilize their senses and to gather information from their surrounding environment. They quickly sense and react to changes in their environment. Mammals are able to learn and remember more than other animals. The large brain plays an important part in this ability. In fact, the brain of a mammal is usually larger than the brain of other animals of the same size. Another factor in a mammal's ability to learn is the time spent by its parents to care for and teach it as it matures.

All mammals reproduce sexually and have internal fertilization. Most mammals give birth to live young after a period of development inside an organ called a uterus. While some mammals are nearly helpless when born, others must be able to stand and move quickly after birth. Why do you think a young deer must be able to run soon after it is born?

Mammal Classification

Once an egg is fertilized, the developing mammal is called an embryo. Mammals can be divided into three groups based on how their embryos develop.

Monotremes

Look at the animal in **Figure 13-15.** The duck-billed platypus looks like someone took parts from several different animals and put them together as a practical joke.

Observing Hair

Procedure

1. Brush or comb your hair to remove a few loose hairs.
2. Take two hairs from your brush that look like they still have the root attached.
3. Make a wet mount slide of the two hairs, being sure to include the root.
4. Focus on the hairs with the low-power objective. Draw what you see.
5. Switch to the high-power objective and focus on the hairs. Draw what you see.

Analysis

1. Describe the characteristics of hair and root.
2. Infer how hair keeps an organism warm.

Figure 13-15 A duck-billed platypus is a mammal, yet it lays eggs. **Why is it classified as a mammal?**

But, in fact, the duck-billed platypus belongs to the smallest group of mammals called monotremes. **Monotremes** lay eggs with tough leathery shells. The female incubates the eggs for about ten days. Mammary glands that produce the milk of monotremes lack nipples. When the young hatch, they nurse by licking up the milk that seeps through the skin surrounding the glands. The duck-billed platypus and two species of spiny anteaters are the only surviving members of this group.

Marsupials

Can you think of an animal that carries its young in a pouch? Mammals that do this are called marsupials. **Marsupials** are pouched mammals that give birth to immature offspring. Their embryos develop for only a few weeks within the uterus. When the young are born, they are naked, blind, and not fully formed. Using their sense of smell, the young crawl into the pouch and attach themselves to a nipple. Here they complete their development. Most marsupials live in Australia, Tasmania, and New Guinea. Kangaroos, koalas, Tasmanian devils, and wallabies are marsupials. The opossum in **Figure 13-16** is a marsupial that lives in North America.

Figure 13-16 Marsupials carry their developing young in a pouch on the outside of their bodies. Opossums are the only marsupials found in North America.

Problem Solving

Predicting Bat Behavior

Bats are acrobats of the night. They can fly around obstacles and can find insects to eat in complete darkness. Have you ever wondered how they do this? Some bats emit, or send out, extremely high-pitched sounds through the mouth and nose when hunting for food. These sounds are usually too high pitched for humans to hear. Bats also make noises that people hear, from whining sounds to loud twitters and squeaks. Bats can catch fast-flying insects or darting fish and at the same time avoid branches, wires, and other obstacles in a process called echolocation. The sound waves they send out travel in front of them, and this helps them locate objects.

The diagram illustrates what happens when a sound wave emitted by a bat comes in contact with an object.

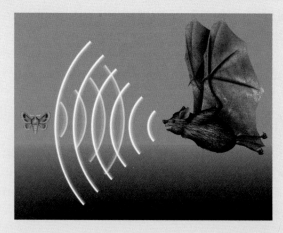

Think Critically: How does a bat locate an object in the dark? Explain what might happen to bats if they were allowed to search for food in a sound-proof room, where walls absorb most of the sound. Infer what would happen if a bat's mouth and nose are covered.

Placental Mammals

By far, the largest number of mammals belongs to the third group known as placental mammals. The most important characteristic of **placental mammals** is that their embryos develop in the uterus of the female. This time of development, from fertilization to birth, is the gestation period. Gestation periods vary greatly among placental mammals. Imagine waiting almost two years for the young elephant in **Figure 13-17** to be born! Placental mammals are named for the placenta, a saclike organ developed by the growing embryo that is attached to the uterus. The placenta absorbs oxygen and food from the mother's blood. An umbilical cord, **Figure 13-18,** attaches the embryo to the placenta. Several blood vessels in the umbilical cord act as a transportation system. Food and oxygen are transported from the placenta to the embryo. Waste products are taken away.

Figure 13-17 Gestation periods vary among mammals. While an elephant carries its young for 624 days, a golden hamster's gestation period is about 16 days.

*inter***NET**
CONNECTION

Visit the Glencoe Science Web Site at **www.glencoe.com/ sec/science/ca** for more information about small mammals.

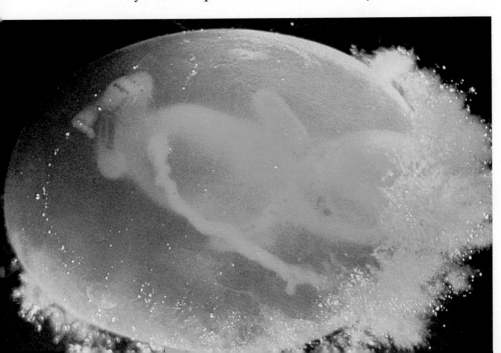

Figure 13-18 A placental mammal's embryo, such as this human embryo, develops in the uterus of a female. The umbilical cord allows the embryo to receive food and oxygen from the mother.

Figure 13-19 In addition to monotremes (A) and marsupials (B), many of the major orders of placental mammals are shown here.

You have learned the basic characteristics that distinguish mammals—vertebrae, hair or fur, mammary glands that produce milk, type of teeth, and the ability of young to learn. In addition, each kind of animal has certain adaptations that enable it to live successfully within its environment. Some of the 4000 species of mammals are shown in **Figure 13-19**.

A **Monotremata** (mahn uh tru MAH tah): Monotremes, such as this duck-billed platypus, are the only egg-laying mammals.

B **Marsupiala** (mar sew pee AH luh): Pouched mammals include kangaroos, shown here, and opossums.

C **Insectivora** (ihn sek tih VOR ah): Burrowing woodland moles have poor eyesight but an excellent sense of touch to catch insects.

D **Edentata** (ee duhn TAH tuh): Armadillos, shown here, anteaters, and tree sloths are toothless or have few teeth with which to eat insects.

E **Chiroptera** (cher OP ter uh): Bats are the only true flying mammals. Their front limbs are designed for flight. They use echolocation, a process that uses sound and echoes, to navigate while flying.

F **Carnivora** (kar NIH vor uh): The household cat and dog are meat-eaters that have canine teeth used to capture prey. This red fox is also a carnivore.

G **Cetacea** (sih TAY shuh): Marine mammals, including dolphins, spend their entire lives in the ocean.

H **Proboscidea** (proh boh SIH dee uh): Elephants are the largest land mammals. They have an elongated nose that forms a trunk.

I **Perissodactyla** (per ih soh DAHK tih luh): Herbivorous hoofed mammals with an odd number of toes. Horses, zebras, tapirs (shown here), and rhinoceroses belong to this group.

J **Artiodactyla** (ar tee oh DAHK tih luh): Herbivorous, hoofed mammals have an even number of toes. They also have large, flat molars and complex stomachs. Cows, camels, deer, giraffes, and the moose (shown here) belong to this group.

K **Rodentia** (roh DEN cha): The largest order, these gnawing mammals have two pairs of chisel-shaped teeth that never stop growing. These teeth wear down through use. This golden mouse, along with squirrels, beavers, porcupines, and gophers are in this group.

L **Lagomorpha** (lah gah MOR fuh): Lagomorphs include herbivorous rabbits, hares, and pikas. This Eastern cottontail rabbit has long hind legs that are adapted for jumping and running. It also has two pairs of upper incisors.

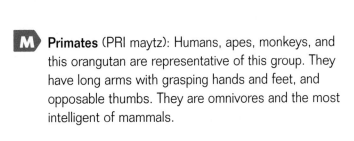

M **Primates** (PRI maytz): Humans, apes, monkeys, and this orangutan are representative of this group. They have long arms with grasping hands and feet, and opposable thumbs. They are omnivores and the most intelligent of mammals.

Figure 13-20 Mammals have teeth specialized for the food they eat. **How would you classify a horse (A), a hyena (B), and a human (C)? Herbivore? Carnivore? Omnivore?**

Different Teeth

Mammals have teeth that are specialized for the type of food they eat. There are four types of teeth: incisors, canines, premolars, and molars. Incisors are the sharp, chisel-shaped front teeth used to bite and cut off food. Grazing mammals, which eat plants, are called **herbivores.** They have sharp incisors to grab and cut grass. Horses, buffalo, and rabbits are some mammals that eat plants. Some mammals, such as lions and tigers, are predators and eat flesh. Flesh-eating mammals are called **carnivores.** They use long and pointed canine teeth to stab, grip, and tear flesh. They also have sharp-edged premolars that cut and shred food. Large premolars and molars shred, crush, and grind food. Horses have large, flat molars that grind both grains and grasses.

Some mammals eat both plants and animals. These mammals are called **omnivores.** Humans are capable of being omnivores. They have all four types of teeth. You usually can tell whether a mammal eats plants, other animals, or both from the kind of teeth it has. Look at **Figure 13-20.** ☑

Reading Check ☑

What are herbivores, carnivores, and omnivores?

Mammals Today

Mammals are important in maintaining a balance in the environment. Large carnivores, such as lions, help control populations of grazing animals. Bats help pollinate flowers, and some pick up plant seeds in their fur and distribute them. But mammals are in trouble today. As millions of acres of wildlife habitat are developed for housing and recreational areas, many mammals are left without food, shelter, and space to survive. The Bengal tiger pictured in **Figure 13-21** lives in India and is considered an endangered species.

Figure 13-21 Illegal poaching and decreasing habitat help account for the extreme decline in the Bengal tiger population in nature. In the early 1900s, there were around 100 000 tigers, but that has declined by roughly 95 percent this century.

Section Assessment

1. Describe five characteristics of all mammals and explain how these characteristics allow mammals to survive in different environments.

2. Compare and contrast herbivores with omnivores.

3. **Think Critically:** Compare reproduction in placental mammals with that of monotremes and marsupials.

4. **Skill Builder**
   Observing and Inferring Mammals have many adaptations to their environments. Do the **Chapter 13 Skill Activity** on page 718 to observe tracks to infer how mammals' feet are adapted.

Using Math

The tallest mammal is the giraffe, which stands at 5.6 m tall. Calculate your height in meters and determine how many of you it would take to be as tall as a giraffe.

Bird Counts

Birds can be found almost everywhere. No single place is best. You can see them in many different habitats—in a city park or an open field, along the riverbank, or at the shore. Many bird-watchers make their observations in the early morning when birds are most active. While bird-watching, care must be taken not to scare the birds with movement or noise.

It's simple to get started bird-watching. You can attract birds to your yard at home or at school by filling a bird feeder with seeds that birds like most. Then, sit back and observe the birds while they enjoy your hospitality.

Recognize the Problem

What type of bird is present in your neighborhood in the largest number?

Form a Hypothesis

Think about the types of birds that you observe around your neighborhood. What types of food do they eat? Do all birds come to a bird feeder? Make a hypothesis about the type of bird that you think you will see most often at your bird feeder.

Goals

- **Observe** the types of birds in your neighborhood.
- **Research** how to attract birds to a bird feeder.
- **Build** a bird feeder.
- **Identify** the types of birds observed.
- **Graph** your results in order to communicate them with other students.

Data Source

Go to the Glencoe Science Web Site at **www.glencoe.com/ sec/science/ca** for more information about how to build a bird feeder, hints on bird watching, and data from other students.

Test Your Hypothesis

Plan

1. **Research** general information about how to attract and identify birds. Determine where you will make your observations.

2. **Search** reference materials to find out how to build a bird feeder. Do all birds eat the same types of seeds?

3. What variables can you control in this activity? How long will you make your observations? Does the season or the weather conditions affect your observations?

4. What will you do to **identify** the birds that you do not recognize?

Do

1. Make sure your teacher approves your plan before you start.

2. **Record** your data in your Science Journal each time you **observe** your bird feeder.

Analyze Your Data

1. **Describe** the location where you made your observations and the time of year.

2. **Calculate** the total number of each type of bird by adding the numbers you recorded each day.

3. **Graph** your data. Will your results be best displayed in a line, circle, or bar graph?

4. **Post** your data on the Glencoe Science Web Site.

Draw Conclusions

1. What type of bird was present in your neighborhood in the largest number?

2. Did all of your classmates' data agree with yours? Why or why not?

3. **Compare and contrast** your observations with the observations posted by other students on the Glencoe Science Web Site. **Map** the data you collect from the Web site to **recognize** patterns in bird populations.

4. Many birds include an enormous number of insects in their diet. **Infer** the need for humans to maintain a healthy environment for birds.

Chapter 13 Reviewing Main Ideas

For a **preview** of this chapter, study this Reviewing Main Ideas before you read the chapter. After you have studied this chapter, you can use the Reviewing Main Ideas to **review** the chapter.

The Glencoe MindJogger, Audiocassettes, and CD-ROM provide additional opportunities for review.

Section

13-1 FISH

All animals in the Chordate Phylum have a notochord, dorsal hollow nerve cord, and gill slits. The body temperature of an **ectotherm** changes with its environment. **Endothermic** animals maintain body temperature. **Fish** are ectotherms that have scales and **fins.** Classes of fish include jawless fish, cartilaginous fish, and bony fish. *Why can't jawless fish be predators?*

White shark

Section

13-2 AMPHIBIANS AND REPTILES

Amphibians are vertebrates that spend part of their lives in water and part on land. Most frogs, toads, and salamanders are amphibians that go through metamorphosis from a water-living larva to a land-living adult. **Reptiles** are ectothermic land animals that have dry, scaly skin. Turtles, crocodiles, alligators, snakes, and lizards are reptiles. Reptiles lay eggs with a leathery skin. *Why does the reptile's egg provide better protection for the embryo than a frog's egg?*

Collared lizard

Barred tiger salamander

Reading Check ✓

Explain the major differences among the five groups of vertebrates described in this chapter in a way that a child could understand. (You might create a chart).

Hummingbird

Section
13-3 BIRDS

Birds are endotherms that are covered with feathers and lay eggs. Their front legs are modified into wings. Adaptations birds have for flight include wings, feathers, and a light, strong skeleton. Birds lay eggs enclosed in hard shells. Most birds keep their eggs warm until they hatch. *How do down feathers keep a bird warm?*

Mandarin duck

Flamingo

Bat

Section
13-4 MAMMALS

Mammals are endotherms with hair. Female mammals have mammary glands that produce milk. There are three groups of mammals. **Monotremes** are mammals that lay eggs. **Marsupials** are mammals that have pouches for the development of their embryos. **Placental mammals** have offspring that develop within the female's uterus. *What are some adaptations of mammals that allow them to be endothermic?*

Red fox

Chapter 13 Assessment

Using Vocabulary

a. amphibian
b. bird
c. carnivore
d. cartilage
e. chordate
f. contour feather
g. down feather
h. ectotherm
i. endoskeleton
j. endotherm
k. estivation

l. fin
m. fish
n. herbivore
o. hibernation
p. mammal
q. marsupial
r. monotreme
s. omnivore
t. placental mammal
u. reptile

Define the following Vocabulary terms and give two examples of each.

1. fish
2. amphibian
3. reptile
4. bird
5. mammal

Checking Concepts

Choose the word or phrase that best answers the question.

6. Which of the following animals have fins, scales, and gills?
   A) amphibians   C) reptiles
   B) crocodiles   D) fish

7. Which of the following stuctures is used for steering and balancing?
   A) cartilage   C) bone
   B) endoskeleton   D) fin

8. Which of the following is **NOT** an example of a bony fish?
   A) trout   C) shark
   B) bass   D) goldfish

9. Which of the following has a swim bladder?
   A) shark   C) trout
   B) lamprey   D) skate

10. Which of the following is **NOT** an adaptation that helps a bird fly?
    A) hollow bones   C) hard-shelled eggs
    B) fused vertebrae D) feathers

11. Which of the following does **NOT** have scales?
    A) birds   C) frogs
    B) snakes   D) fish

12. Which of the following are vertebrates with lungs and moist skin?
    A) amphibians   C) reptiles
    B) fish   D) lizards

13. Which of the following are mammals that lay eggs?
    A) carnivores   C) monotremes
    B) marsupials   D) placental mammals

14. Which of the following have mammary glands but no nipples?
    A) marsupials   C) monotremes
    B) placental mammals D) omnivores

15. Which of the following animals eat only plant materials?
    A) carnivores   C) omnivores
    B) herbivores   D) endotherms

Thinking Critically

16. Why do you think there are fewer species of amphibians on Earth than any other type of vertebrate?

17. What important adaptation allows a reptile to live on land while an amphibian must return to water to live out part of its life cycle?

18. Give two reasons why whales have little hair.

19. You observe a mammal catching and eating a rabbit. What kind of teeth does this animal probably have? Tell how it uses its teeth.

20. Explain how the development of the amniotic egg led to the early success of reptiles.

Developing Skills

If you need help, refer to the **Skill Handbook.**

21. Comparing and Contrasting: Compare and contrast the eggs of fish, reptiles, birds, and mammals. How well does each egg type protect the developing embryo?

22. Concept Mapping: Complete the concept map describing groups of mammals.

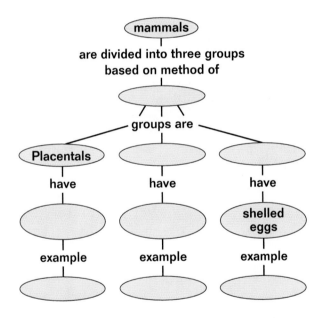

23. Designing an Experiment: Design an experiment to find out the effect of water temperature on frog egg development.

24. Observing and Inferring: How could you use the feet of a bird to identify it?

25. Comparing and Contrasting: Compare and contrast the teeth of herbivores, carnivores, and omnivores. How is each tooth type adapted to the animal's diet?

THE PRINCETON REVIEW

Test-Taking Tip

Let Bygones Be Bygones Once you have read a question, consider the answers and choose one. Then, put that question behind you. Don't try to keep the question in the back of your mind, thinking that maybe a better answer will come to you as the test continues.

Test Practice

Use these questions to test your Science Proficiency.

1. Vertebrates make up a large percentage of animals. Which of the following statements is true of all vertebrates?
A) Vertebrates are animals without backbones.
B) All vertebrates have a notochord.
C) Only fish have gill slits.
D) Dorsal hollow nerve cords always develop into a spinal cord with a brain at the front end.

2. Placental mammals, along with monotremes and marsupials, are the orders that make up mammals. Which of the following animals is an example of a placental mammal?
A) elephant
B) koala
C) duck-billed platypus
D) turtle

3. Which of the following terms describes inactivity during the summer?
A) estivation
B) hibernation
C) metamorphosis
D) preening

Ecology

What's Happening Here?

A small plane flies over one of the soda lakes of eastern Africa (left). Dotted with islands of foam, where liquid and gas bubble through its salt crust, Tanzania's Lake Natron appears to be a wasteland. Yet, notice the color. Pink algae bloom everywhere. After a rain, fresh water collects on the salt flats, and there the algae survive. The algae feed the flamingos (below) that flock to the lake by the millions to breed, and the birds' droppings feed the algae. The algae also give the birds' feathers their pink hue. Moreover, the harsh salt crust keeps many predators from crossing the treacherous flats—thereby providing a safe place for the flamingos to nest. Thus, living and non-living parts of the environment—the algae and the salt crust—work together to support life. In this unit, you will learn that complex webs connect living things and are key to supporting life, even in hostile environments.

interNET CONNECTION

Explore the Glencoe Science Web Site at **www.glencoe.com/sec/ science/ca** to find out more about topics found in this unit.

CHAPTER

14 Life and the Environment

Chapter Preview

Skills Preview

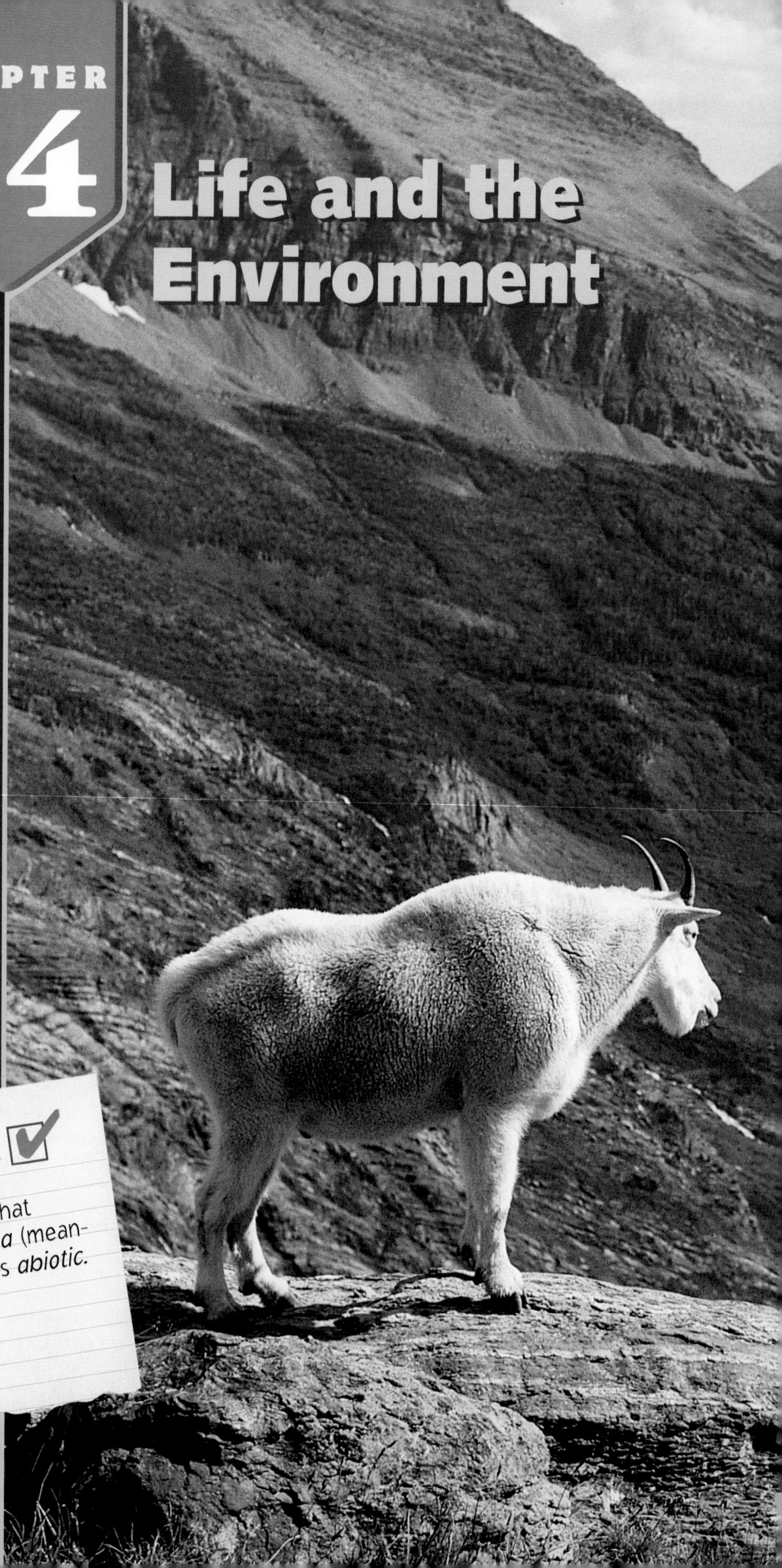

Skill Builders
- Classify

Activities
- Graph

MiniLabs
- Infer

Reading Check ✓

Define several terms that begin with the prefix *a* (meaning "without"), such as *abiotic.*

Explore Activity

Mountain goats rely on winter winds to uncover food plants buried beneath the snow. Surefooted and strong, they scale high cliffs to get their next meal. A mountain goat's range consists of high terrain where few other animals dare to tread. This reduces competition from different organisms for food. How does the number of related organisms in an area affect each individual? You share your science classroom with other students. How much space is available to each student?

Measure Space

1. Use a meterstick to measure the length and width of the classroom.

2. Multiply the length times the width to find the area of the room in square meters.

3. Count the number of individuals in your class. Divide the number of square meters in the classroom by the number of individuals.

In your Science Journal, record how much space each person has. Determine the amount of space each person would have if the number of individuals in your class doubled. Predict how having that amount of space would affect you and your classmates.

The Living and Nonliving Environment

What You'll Learn

▶ How to identify biotic and abiotic factors in an ecosystem
▶ The levels of biological organization

Vocabulary
biosphere
ecology
abiotic factor
biotic factor
population
community
ecosystem

Why It's Important

▶ Abiotic and biotic factors work together to form your ecosystem.

The Biosphere

Think of all the organisms on Earth. Millions of species exist. Where do all these organisms live? Living things can be found 11 000 m below the surface of the ocean and on tops of mountains 9000 m high. The part of Earth that supports organisms is known as the **biosphere** (BI uh sfihr). The biosphere seems huge, but it is actually only a small portion of Earth. The biosphere includes the topmost portion of Earth's crust, all the waters that cover Earth's surface, and the surrounding atmosphere. Overall though, the thickness could be compared to the thickness of the skin of an apple.

Within the biosphere, many different environments can be found. For example, red-tailed hawks are found in environments where tall trees live near open grassland. The hawks nest high in the trees and soar over the land in search of rodents and rabbits to eat. In environments with plenty of moisture, such as the banks of streams, willow trees provide food and shelter for birds, mammals, and insects. All organisms interact

Figure 14-1 The biosphere is the region of Earth that contains all living organisms. An ecologist is a scientist who studies relationships among organisms and between organisms and the physical features of the biosphere.

with the environment. The science of **ecology** is the study of the interactions that take place among organisms and between organisms and the physical features of the environment. Ecologists, such as the one in **Figure 14-1,** are the scientists who study interactions between organisms and the environment.

Abiotic Factors

A forest environment is made up of trees, birds, insects, and other living things that depend on one another for food and shelter. But, these organisms also depend on factors that surround them such as soil, sunlight, water, temperature, and air. These factors—the nonliving, physical features of the environment—are called **abiotic factors.** Abiotic—*a* meaning "not" and *biotic* meaning "living"—factors have effects on living things and often determine the organisms that are able to live in a certain environment. Some abiotic factors are shown in **Figure 14-2.**

Figure 14-2 Abiotic factors help determine which species can survive in an area.

 A **Soil**
Soil consists of minerals mixed with decaying, dead organisms. It contains both living and nonliving components.

B **Light**
Seasonal events, such as flowering in plants or migration of birds, are often triggered by a change in the number of hours of daylight.

C **Water**
Many organisms live in water, such as this lake in Pennsylvania, rather than air.

D **Temperature**
Temperatures change with daily and seasonal cycles. Desert-dwelling rattlesnakes, like this sidewinder in the Colorado desert, are active only in the cool, early morning hours. During the hottest part of the day, they rest in the shade.

Water

Water is an important abiotic factor. The bodies of most organisms are 50 to 95 percent water. Water is an important part of cytoplasm and the fluid that surrounds cells. Respiration, photosynthesis, digestion, and other important life processes can take place only in the presence of water.

Soil

The type of soil in a particular location helps determine which plants and other organisms live in that location. Most soil is a combination of sand, clay, and humus. Soil type is determined by the relative amounts of sand, clay, and humus in the soil. Humus is the decayed remains of dead organisms. The greater the humus content, the more fertile the soil.

Light and Temperature

The abiotic factors of light and temperature also impact the environment. Through the process of photosynthesis, the radiant energy of sunlight is transformed into chemical energy that drives virtually all of life's processes. The availability of sunlight is a major factor in determining where green plants and other photosynthetic organisms live, as shown in **Figure 14-3.** Sunlight does not penetrate far into deep water. Most green algae benefit from living near the surface. In a similar situation, because little sunlight reaches the shady darkness of the forest floor, plant growth there is limited.

Figure 14-3 Many wildflowers that live on the forest floor, such as these padres shooting stars and Johnny jump-ups, produce seeds early in the spring. At this time, they receive the maximum amount of sunlight. When the leaves are fully out on the trees, they receive little direct sun.

Biotic Factors

Abiotic factors do not provide everything an organism needs for survival. Mushrooms would not be able to grow without the decaying bodies of other organisms to feed on. Honeybees could not survive without pollen from flowers. Some species of owls and woodpeckers prefer to nest in the hollow trunks of dead trees. Organisms depend on other organisms for food, shelter, protection, or reproduction. Living or once-living organisms in the environment are called **biotic factors.** ☑

Reading Check ☑

What are the living organisms in the environment called?

Levels of Biological Organization

The living world is highly organized. Atoms are arranged into molecules, which are in turn organized into cells. Cells form tissues, tissues form organs, and organs form systems. Similarly, the biotic and abiotic factors studied by ecologists can be arranged into layers of organization, as shown in **Figure 14-4.**

Figure 14-4 The living world is organized into several levels.

Organism
An organism is a single individual from a population.

Population
A population is all of the individuals of one species that live and reproduce in the same area at the same time.

Community
A community is made up of populations of different species that interact in some way.

Ecosystem
An ecosystem consists of communities and the abiotic factors that affect them.

Biosphere
The biosphere is the highest level of biological organization. It is made up of all the ecosystems on Earth.

Figure 14-5 This coral reef is an example of an ecosystem. It is made up of hundreds of populations of organisms, as well as ocean water, sunlight, and other abiotic factors.

Populations

Individual organisms of the same species that live in the same place and can produce young form a **population.** Members of several populations on a coral reef are seen in **Figure 14-5.** Members of populations of organisms compete with each other for food, water, mates, and space. The resources of the environment and how the organisms use these resources determine how large a population can be.

Communities

Most populations of organisms do not live alone. They live and interact with populations of other organisms. Groups of populations that interact with each other in a given area form a **community.** Populations of organisms in a community depend on each other for food and shelter and for other needs.

Ecosystem

An **ecosystem** is made up of a biotic community and the abiotic factors that affect it. The rest of this chapter will discuss in more detail the kinds of interactions that take place between abiotic and biotic factors in an ecosystem.

Section Assessment

1. What is the difference between an abiotic factor and a biotic factor? Give at least five examples of each.

2. What is the difference between a population and a community? A community and an ecosystem?

3. **Think Critically:** Could oxygen in the atmosphere be considered an abiotic factor? Why or why not? What about carbon dioxide?

4. **Skill Builder**
   Observing and Inferring Each person lives in a population as part of a community. Describe your population and community. If you need help, refer to Observing and Inferring in the **Skill Handbook** on page 684.

Using Computers

Spreadsheet Obtain two months of temperature and rainfall data from your local newspaper or the Internet. Enter the data in a spreadsheet and then average the totals for temperature and the totals for rainfall. What kind of climate do you think you have based on your calculations? If you need help, refer to page 702.

Activity 14•1

Soil Composition

Soil is more than minerals mixed with the decaying bodies of dead organisms. It contains other biotic and abiotic factors.

What You'll Investigate

What are the components of soil?

Goals

- **Determine** what factors are present in soil.

Materials

- Small paper cups containing freshly dug soil (3)
- Newspaper
- Beaker of water
- Hand lens
- Jar with lid
- Scale

Procedure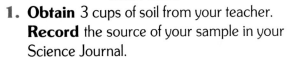

1. **Obtain** 3 cups of soil from your teacher. **Record** the source of your sample in your Science Journal.

2. **Pour** one of your samples onto the newspaper. **Sort** through the objects in the soil. Try to separate abiotic and biotic items. Use a hand lens to help identify the items. **Describe** your observations in your Science Journal.

3. Carefully place the second sample in the jar, disturbing it as little as possible. Quickly fill the jar with water and screw the lid on tightly. Without moving the jar, **observe** its contents for several minutes. **Record** your observations in your Science Journal.

4. **Weigh** the third sample. **Record** the weight in your Science Journal. Leave the sample undisturbed for several days, then weigh it again. **Record** the second weight in your Science Journal.

Conclude and Apply

1. Can you **infer** the presence of any organisms? Explain.

2. **Describe** the abiotic factors in your sample. What biotic factors did you **observe?**

3. Did you **record** any change in the soil weight over time? If so, why?

14·2 Interactions Among Living Organisms

What You'll Learn

▶ The characteristics of populations
▶ The types of relationships that occur among populations in a community
▶ The habitat and niche of a species in a community

Vocabulary
population density
limiting factor
carrying capacity
symbiosis
habitat
niche

Why It's Important

▶ You must directly or indirectly interact with other organisms to survive.

Characteristics of Populations

As shown in **Figure 14-6,** populations can be described by their characteristics. These include the size of the population, spacing (how the organisms are arranged in a given area), and density (how many individuals there are in a specific area). Suppose you spent several months observing a population of field mice living in a pasture. You would probably observe changes in the size of the population. Older mice die, baby mice are born, some are eaten by prey, and some mice wander away to new homes. The size of a population—the number of individual organisms it contains—is always changing, although some populations change more rapidly than others. In contrast to a mouse population, the number of pine trees in a forest changes fairly slowly, but a forest fire could quickly reduce the population of pine trees in the forest.

Figure 14-6 Populations have several characteristics that define them.

Each dot represents 1000 people

A Spacing
A characteristic of populations is spacing. In some populations, such as the oak trees of an oak-hickory forest, individuals are spaced fairly evenly throughout the area.

B Density
Human population density is higher in and around cities than in rural areas. **Which part of the United States has the highest population density?**

Population Density

At the beginning of this chapter, when you figured out how much space is available to each student in your classroom, you were measuring another population characteristic. The size of a population that occupies an area of limited size is called **population density.** The more individuals there are in a given amount of space, as seen in **Figure 14-7,** the more dense the population. For example, if 100 mice live in an area of a square kilometer, the population density is 100 mice per km².

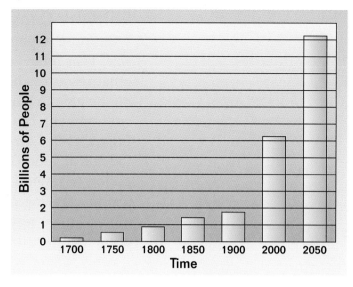

Figure 14-7 The size of the human population is increasing at a rate of about 1.6 percent per year. At the present time, it is about 6 billion. In 2050, the population will be about 12 billion.

Limiting Factors

Populations cannot continue to grow larger and larger forever. In any ecosystem, there are limits to the amount of food, water, living space, mates, nesting sites, and other resources available. A **limiting factor** is any biotic or abiotic factor that restricts the number of individuals in a population. A limiting factor can also indirectly affect other populations in the community. For example, a drought might restrict the growth of seed-producing plants in a forest clearing. Fewer plants means that food may become a limiting factor for a mouse population that feeds on the seeds. Food also may become a limiting factor for hawks and owls that feed on the mice, as well as for the deer in **Figure 14-8.**

Competition is the struggle among organisms to obtain the resources they need to survive and reproduce. As population density increases, so does competition among individuals.

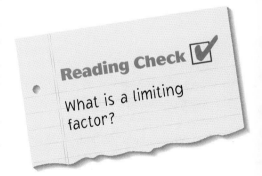

Reading Check

What is a limiting factor?

Figure 14-8 In many parts of the United States, deer populations, such as this one in northern Wisconsin, have become large enough to exceed the environment's ability to produce adequate food. Individuals starve or, weakened from lack of food, fall victim to disease.

Carrying Capacity

Suppose a population of robins continues to increase in size, year after year. At some point, food, nesting space, or other resources become so scarce that some individuals may not be able to survive or reproduce. When this happens, the environment has reached its carrying capacity, as seen in **Figure 14-9. Carrying capacity** is the largest number of individuals an environment can support and maintain for a long period of time. If a population begins to exceed the environment's carrying capacity, some individuals will be left without adequate resources. They may die or be forced to move elsewhere.

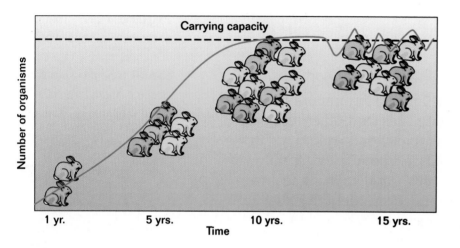

Figure 14-9 This graph shows how the size of a population increases until it reaches the carrying capacity of its environment. At first, growth is fairly slow. It speeds up as the number of adults capable of reproduction increases. Once the population reaches carrying capacity, its size remains fairly stable. **Why don't most populations achieve their biotic potential?**

Biotic Potential

What would happen if there were no limiting factors? A population living in an environment that supplies more than enough resources for survival will continue to grow. The maximum rate at which a population increases when there is plenty of food, water, ideal weather, and no disease or enemies is its biotic potential. However, most populations never reach their biotic potential, or do so for only a short period of time. Eventually, the carrying capacity of the environment is reached and the population stops increasing.

Interactions in Communities

Populations are regulated not only by the supply of food, water, and sunlight, but also by the actions of other populations. The most obvious way one population can limit another is by predation (prih DAY shun). One organism feeds on another. Owls and hawks are predators that feed on mice. Mice are their prey. Predators are biotic factors that limit the size of prey populations. Predation also helps to maintain the health of a prey population. Old, ill, or young individuals are more often captured than strong healthy animals. Thus, the overall health of the prey population improves. **Figure 14-10** shows how some predators work together to hunt their food.

Figure 14-10 Hyenas work together to hunt their food. This is called cooperation and helps all members of their population survive.

Symbiosis

Many types of relationships exist between organisms in ecosystems. Many species of organisms in nature have close, complex relationships in order to survive. When two or more species live close together, their relationship is called a symbiotic relationship. **Symbiosis** (sihm bee OH sus) is any close relationship between two or more different species.

Using Math

Calculating Population Growth

Example Problem: Estimates show the total human population will be about 6 billion in the year 2000. This number is thought to increase by 1.6 percent each year. What will the population be in the year 2005?

Problem-Solving Steps

1. What is known? Current population is 6 000 000 000. Yearly increase is 1.6%.
2. What is unknown? The population in 2001, 2002, 2003, 2004, and 2005.
3. **Solution:** Calculate the population increase for one year. Then, repeat the process four more times using the answer you came up with as a starting point.

```
  6 000 000 000              6 000 000 000
          × 0.016           +   96 000 000
 36 000 000 000              6 096 000 000 people in 2001
 60 000 000 000
     96 000 000 more people
```

The estimated population in the year 2005 is 6 495 607 732 people.

Practice Problem

An endangered species of fish currently has a population of 136 individuals. If the population increases by two percent every year, how many individuals will there be in three years?

Strategy Hint: When calculating percentages, remember to move your decimal two spaces to the left (0.02).

Mini Lab

Observing Symbiosis

Procedure

1. Carefully wash then examine the roots of a legume plant and a nonlegume plant.
2. Examine a prepared microscope slide of the bacteria that live in the roots of legumes.

Analysis

1. What differences do you observe in the roots of the two plants?
2. The bacteria help legumes thrive in poor soil. What type of symbiotic relationship is this? Explain.

Not all relationships benefit one organism at the expense of another as in predation. Symbiotic relationships can be identified by the type of interaction between organisms, as shown in **Figure 14-11.** Many types of symbiotic relationships occur between organisms. These are usually described by how each organism in the relationship is affected by the relationship.

A symbiotic relationship that benefits both species is called mutualism. An example of mutualism is the lichen. Each lichen species is made up of a fungus and an alga or cyanobacterium. The fungus provides a protected living space, and the alga or bacterium provides the fungus with food.

B Tropical orchids grow on the trunks of trees. The tree provides the orchid with a sunlit living space high in the forest canopy. This relationship is an example of commensalism because the orchid benefits from the relationship without harming or helping the tree.

Figure 14-11 Many examples of symbiotic relationships occur in nature.

A The partnership between the desert yucca plant and the yucca moth is an example of mutualism. Both species benefit from the relationship. The yucca depends on the moth to pollinate its flowers. The moth depends on the yucca for a protected place to lay its eggs and a source of food for its larvae.

C Tapeworms are parasites that feed inside the intestines of some mammals. This one was found inside a cat.

In shallow tropical seas, brightly colored anemone fish find protection from predators by swimming among the stinging tentacles of sea anemones. The presence of the fish does not affect the anemone in a harmful or beneficial way. Commensalism is a symbiotic relationship that benefits one partner but does not harm or help the other.

Parasitism is a symbiotic relationship that benefits the parasite and does definite harm to the parasite's host. Many parasites live on or in the body of the host, absorbing nutrients from the host's body fluids. Tapeworms live as parasites in the intestines of mammals. Mistletoe is a parasitic plant that penetrates tree branches with its roots.

Figure 14-12 Each organism in an ecosystem uses and affects its environment in particular ways. **What role does the earthworm play in the environment?**

Habitats and Niches

In a community, every species plays a particular role. Each also has a particular place to live. The physical location where an organism lives is called its **habitat.** The habitat of an earthworm is soil. The role of an organism in the ecosystem is called its **niche.** The niche of an earthworm is shown in **Figure 14-12.** What a species eats, how it gets its food, and how it interacts with other organisms are all parts of its niche. An earthworm takes soil into its body to obtain nutrients. The soil that leaves the worm enriches the soil. The movement of the worm through soil also loosens it and aerates it, creating a better environment for plant growth.

EARTH SCIENCE
◄ **INTEGRATION**

Section Assessment

1. Describe how limiting factors can affect the organisms in a population.

2. Describe the difference between a habitat and a niche.

3. **Think Critically:** A parasite can obtain food only from its host. Most parasites weaken but do not kill their hosts. Why?

4. **Skill Builder**
   Predicting There are methods used to determine the size of a population without counting each organism. Do the **Chapter 14 Skill Activity** on page 719 to learn how to infer population size.

Using Math

In a 12 m² area of weeds, 46 dandelion plants, 212 grass plants, and 14 bindweed plants are growing. What is the population density per square meter of each species?

Design Your Own Experiment

Identifying a Limiting Factor

Possible Materials

- Bean seeds
- Small planting containers
- Soil
- Water
- Labels
- Trowel or spoon
- Aluminum foil
- Sunny window or other light source
- Refrigerator or oven

Organisms depend on many biotic and abiotic factors in their environment to survive. When these factors are limited or are not available, it can affect an organism's survival. By experimenting with some of these limiting factors, you will see how organisms depend on all parts of their environment.

Recognize the Problem

How do abiotic factors such as light, water, and temperature affect the germination of seeds?

Form a Hypothesis

Based on what you have learned about limiting factors, make a hypothesis about how one specific abiotic factor may affect the germination of a bean seed. Be sure to consider factors that you can change easily.

Goals

- **Observe** the effects of an abiotic factor on the germination and growth of bean seedlings.

- **Design** an experiment that demonstrates whether or not a specific abiotic factor limits the germination of bean seeds.

Safety Precautions

Wash hands after handling soil and seeds.

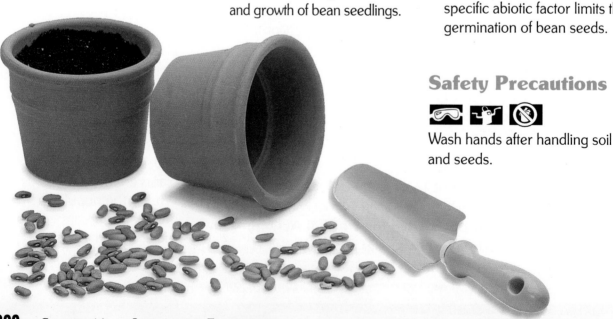

Test Your Hypothesis

Plan

1. As a group, agree upon and write out a hypothesis statement.

2. Decide on a way to test your group's hypothesis. Keep available materials in mind as you plan your procedure. **List** your materials.

3. **Prepare** a data table in your Science Journal.

4. Remember to **test** only one variable at a time and use suitable controls.

5. **Read** over your entire experiment to make sure that all steps are in logical order.

6. **Identify** any constants, variables, and controls in your experiment.

7. Be sure the factor you test is measurable.

Do

1. Make sure your teacher has approved your plan before you proceed.

2. Carry out the experiment as planned.

3. While the experiment is going on, write down any observations that you make and complete the data table in your Science Journal.

Analyze Your Data

1. **Compare** your results with those of other groups.

2. **Infer** how the abiotic factor you tested affected the germination of bean seeds.

3. **Graph** your results in a bar graph that compares the number of bean seeds that germinated in the experimental container with the number of seeds that germinated in the control container.

Draw Conclusions

1. **Identify** which factor had the greatest effect on the seeds.

2. **Determine** whether you could substitute one factor for another and still grow the seeds.

14·3 Matter and Energy

Energy Flow Through Ecosystems

As you can see, life on Earth is not simply a collection of living organisms. Even organisms that seem to spend most of their time alone interact with other members of their species. They also interact with other organisms. Most of the interactions between members of different species are feeding relationships. They involve the transfer of energy from one organism to another. Energy moves through an ecosystem in the form of food. Producers are organisms that capture energy from the sun. They use the sun's energy for photosynthesis to produce chemical bonds in carbohydrates. Consumers are organisms that

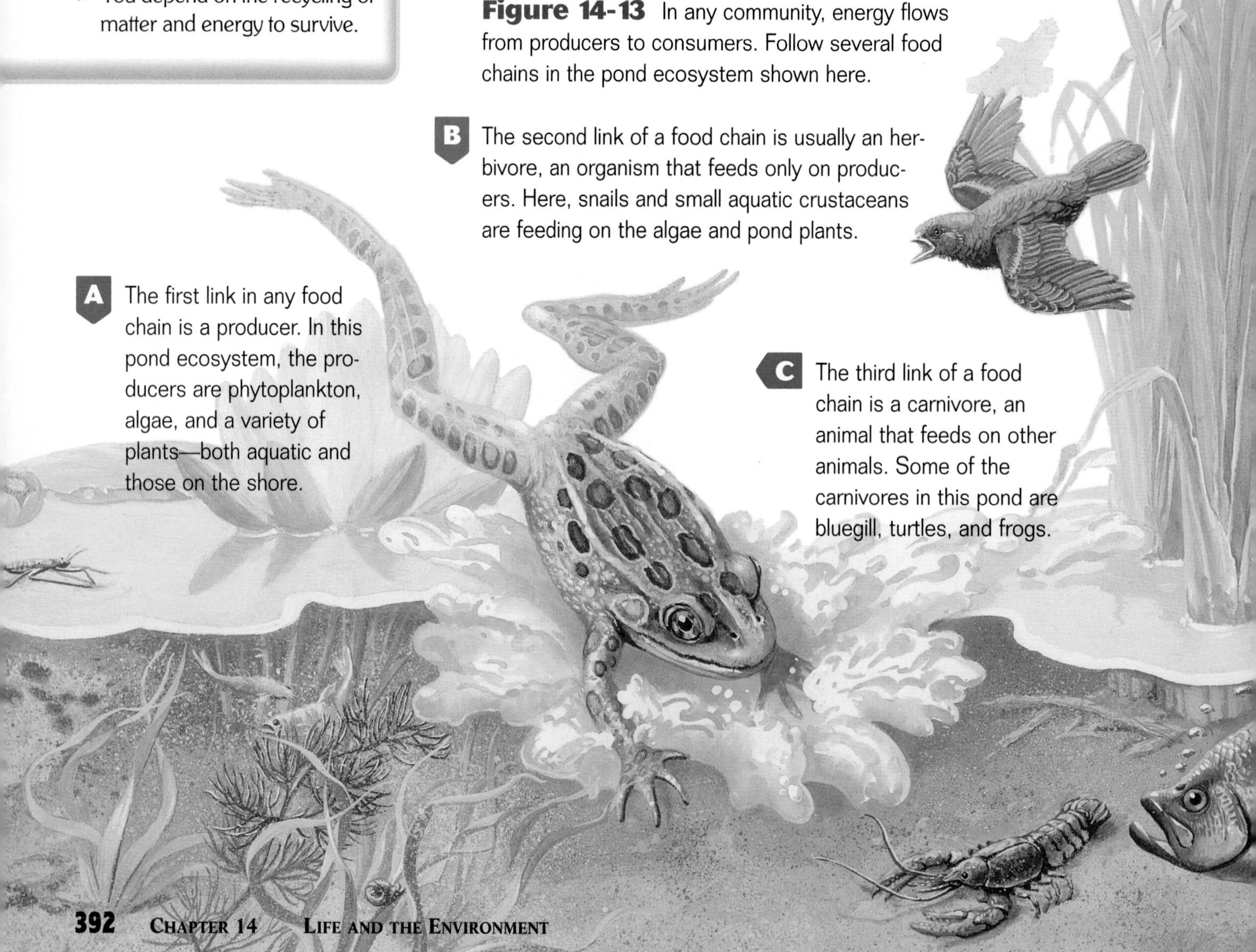

What You'll Learn

▶ How energy flows through ecosystems
▶ The cycling of matter in the biosphere

Vocabulary
food chain
food web
ecological pyramid
water cycle
nitrogen cycle

Why It's Important

▶ You depend on the recycling of matter and energy to survive.

Figure 14-13 In any community, energy flows from producers to consumers. Follow several food chains in the pond ecosystem shown here.

B The second link of a food chain is usually an herbivore, an organism that feeds only on producers. Here, snails and small aquatic crustaceans are feeding on the algae and pond plants.

A The first link in any food chain is a producer. In this pond ecosystem, the producers are phytoplankton, algae, and a variety of plants—both aquatic and those on the shore.

C The third link of a food chain is a carnivore, an animal that feeds on other animals. Some of the carnivores in this pond are bluegill, turtles, and frogs.

obtain energy when they feed on producers or other consumers. The transfer of energy does not end there. When organisms die, other organisms called decomposers obtain energy when they break down the bodies of the dead organisms. This movement of energy through a community can be drawn as food chains, and food webs.

Food Chains and Food Webs

A **food chain** is a simple way of showing how energy in the form of food passes from one organism to another. The pond community pictured in **Figure 14-13** shows examples of several aquatic food chains. When drawing a food chain, arrows between organisms indicate the direction of energy transfer. An example of a pond food chain would be as follows.

phytoplankton → insects → bluegill → bass

Food chains usually have three or four links. Most have no more than five links. This is due to the decrease in energy available at each link. The amount of energy left by the fifth link is only a small portion of the total amount of energy available at the first link. This is because at each transfer of energy, a portion of the energy is lost as heat due to the activities of the organisms as they search for food and mates.

D The fourth link of a food chain is a top carnivore, which feeds on other carnivores. Examples of these consumers in this pond are large fish such as crappies and bass.

E When an organism dies in any ecosystem, bacteria and fungi, which are decomposers, feed on the dead organism, breaking down the remains of the organism.

CHEMISTRY
INTEGRATION

Making Food
Certain bacteria obtain their energy through a process called chemosynthesis. In chemosynthesis, the bacteria produce food and oxygen using chemical compounds. Where do you think these bacteria are found?

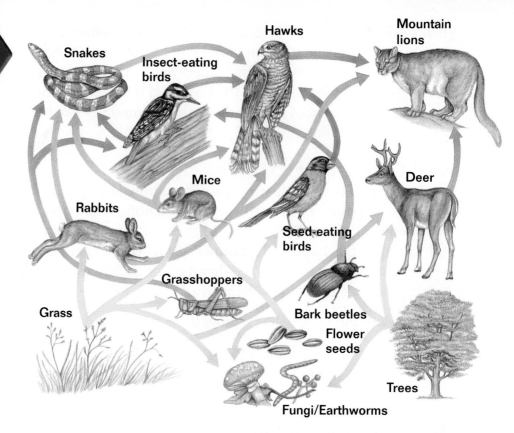

VISUALIZING
Food Webs

Figure 14-14 A food web includes many food chains. It provides a more accurate model of the complex feeding relationships in a community than a single food chain does.

Snakes

Insect-eating birds

Hawks

Mountain lions

Mice

Deer

Rabbits

Seed-eating birds

Grasshoppers

Bark beetles

Flower seeds

Grass

Trees

Fungi/Earthworms

Single food chains are too simple to describe the many interactions among organisms in an ecosystem. Many food chains exist in any ecosystem. A **food web** is a series of overlapping food chains, as seen in **Figure 14-14.** This concept provides a more complete model of the way energy moves through a community. Food webs are also more accurate models because they show the many organisms that feed on more than one level in an ecosystem.

Ecological Pyramids

Almost all the energy used in the biosphere comes from the sun. Producers capture and transform only a small part of the energy that reaches Earth's surface. When an herbivore eats a plant, some of the energy in the plant is passed on to the herbivore. However, most of it is given off into the atmosphere as heat. The same thing happens when a carnivore eats an herbivore. This transfer of energy can be modeled by an **ecological pyramid.** The bottom of an ecological pyramid represents the producers of an ecosystem. The rest of the levels represent successive organisms in the food chain. ☑

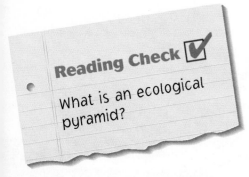

Reading Check ☑

What is an ecological pyramid?

Energy Pyramid

The flow of energy from grass to the hawk in **Figure 14-15** can be illustrated by an energy pyramid. An energy pyramid compares the energy available at each level of the food chain in an ecosystem. Just as most food chains have three or four links, a pyramid of energy usually has three or four levels. Only about ten percent of the energy available at each level of the pyramid is available to the next level. By the time the top level is reached, the amount of energy is greatly reduced.

The Cycles of Matter

The energy available at each link in the food chain is constantly renewed by sunlight. But, what about the physical matter that makes up the bodies of living organisms? The laws of conservation of mass and energy state that matter on Earth is never lost or gained. It is used over and over again. In other words, it is recycled. The carbon atoms present in your body right now have been on Earth since the planet formed billions of years ago.

Figure 14-15

An energy pyramid illustrates that energy decreases at each successive feeding step. **Why aren't there more levels in an energy pyramid?**

Problem Solving

Changes in Antarctic Food Webs

The food chain in the ice-cold Antarctic Ocean is based on phytoplankton—microscopic algae that float near the water's surface. The algae are eaten by tiny shrimp-like krill, which are consumed by baleen whales, squid, and fish. The fish and squid are eaten by toothed

whales, seals, and penguins. In the past, humans have hunted baleen whales. Now with laws against it, there is hope that the population of baleen whales will increase. How will an increase in the whale population affect this food web? Which organisms compete for the same source of food?

Think Critically

1. Populations of seals, penguins, and krill-eating fish increased in size as populations of baleen whales declined. Why?

2. What might happen if the number of baleen whales increases, but the amount of krill does not?

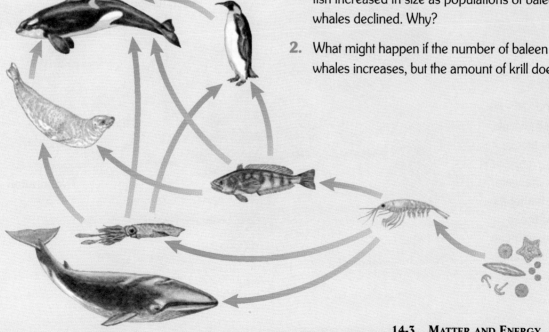

Try at Home

Mini Lab

Modeling the Water Cycle

Procedure

1. With a marker, make a line halfway up on a plastic cup. Fill the cup to the mark with water.
2. Cover the top with plastic wrap and secure it with a rubber band or tape.
3. Put the cup in direct sunlight. Observe the cup for three days. Record your observations.
4. Remove the plastic wrap and observe it for a week.

Analysis

1. What parts of the water cycle did you observe in this activity?
2. What happened to the water level in the cup when the plastic wrap was removed?

They have been recycled untold billions of times. Many important materials that make up your body cycle through ecosystems. Some of these materials are water, carbon, and nitrogen.

The Water Cycle

Water molecules on Earth are on a constant journey, rising into the atmosphere, falling to land or the ocean as rain or snow, and flowing into rivers and oceans. The **water cycle** involves the processes of evaporation, condensation, and precipitation.

When energy, such as heat, is added to a liquid, its molecules begin to move faster. The more energy the molecules absorb, the faster they move, until they are moving so fast they break free and rise into the atmosphere. The liquid evaporates, or changes from a liquid to a gas. The heat of the sun causes water on the surface of Earth to evaporate and rise into the atmosphere as water vapor.

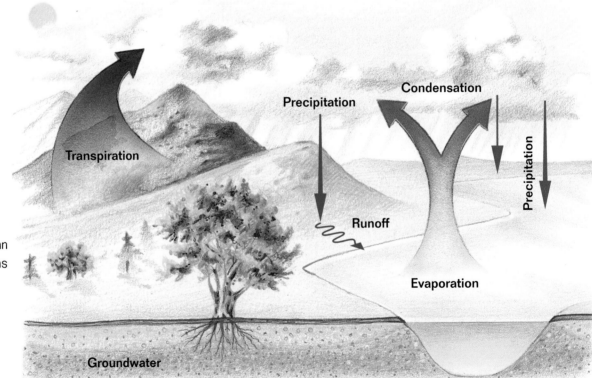

Figure 14-16
A water molecule that falls as rain can follow several paths through the water cycle. **Identify as many of these paths as you can in this diagram.**

VISUALIZING
The Carbon Cycle

Figure 14-17 Carbon is cycled between the atmosphere and living organisms. **Why is the carbon cycle important?**

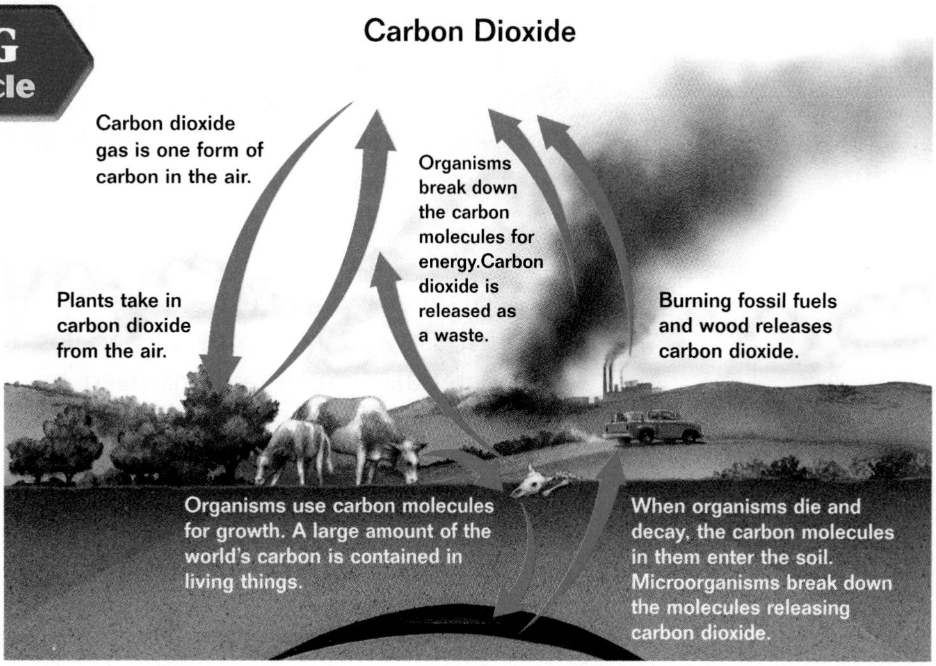

Carbon dioxide gas is one form of carbon in the air.

Plants take in carbon dioxide from the air.

Organisms break down the carbon molecules for energy. Carbon dioxide is released as a waste.

Burning fossil fuels and wood releases carbon dioxide.

Organisms use carbon molecules for growth. A large amount of the world's carbon is contained in living things.

When organisms die and decay, the carbon molecules in them enter the soil. Microorganisms break down the molecules releasing carbon dioxide.

As the water vapor rises, it encounters colder and colder air temperatures. As the molecules of water vapor become colder, they slow down. Eventually, the water vapor changes back into tiny droplets of water. It condenses, or changes from a gas to a liquid. These water droplets clump together to form clouds. When the droplets become large and heavy enough, they fall back to Earth as rain, or precipitation. This process is illustrated in **Figure 14-16.**

The Carbon Cycle

What do you have in common with all organisms? You all contain carbon. Earth's atmosphere contains about 0.03 percent carbon in the form of a gas called carbon dioxide. The movement of the element carbon through Earth's ecosystem is called the carbon cycle.

The carbon cycle begins with plants. During photosynthesis, plants remove carbon from the air and use it along with sunlight and water to make carbohydrates. These carbohydrates are used by other organisms and then returned to the atmosphere through cellular respiration, combustion, and erosion. See **Figure 14-17.** Once the carbon is returned to the atmosphere, the cycle begins again.

The Nitrogen Cycle

Nitrogen is an important element that is used by organisms to make proteins. Even though nitrogen gas makes up 78 percent of the atmosphere, most living organisms cannot use nitrogen in this form. It has to be combined with other elements through a process that is called nitrogen fixation.

*inter*NET
CONNECTION

Visit the Glencoe Science Web Site at **www.glencoe.com/ sec/science/ca** for more information about food chains and food webs.

You can see in **Figure 14-18** how nitrogen is changed into usable compounds by bacteria associated with certain plants. A small amount is changed into nitrogen compounds by lightning. The transfer of nitrogen from the atmosphere to plants and back to the atmosphere or directly into plants again is the **nitrogen cycle.**

Phosphorus, sulfur, and other elements needed by living organisms also are used and returned to the environment. Just as we recycle aluminum, glass, and paper products, the materials that organisms need to live are recycled continuously in the biosphere.

Figure 14-18 Nitrogen can be cycled from bacteria on plant roots to plants, then to animals, and directly back to plants again as a result of decomposition.

Atmospheric nitrogen is converted by lightning.

Plants use nitrogen.

Animals eat plants.

Animals and plants die and decompose.

Bacteria on special plants fix nitrogen and change it to a usable form.

Section Assessment

1. What is the difference between a food chain and a food web?
2. How does the cycling of matter affect a food chain?
3. **Think Critically:** Use your knowledge of food chains and the energy pyramid to explain why fewer lions than gazelles live on the African plains.
4. **Skill Builder**
   Classifying Look at the food web pictured in **Figure 14-14.** Classify each organism pictured as a producer, an herbivore, a carnivore, or a decomposer. If you need help, refer to Classifying in the **Skill Handbook** on page 677.

Science Journal
In your Science Journal, compare the water cycle, carbon cycle, and nitrogen cycle. Use this information to discuss the processes that are involved in each cycle and how each cycle is important to living organisms.

Never Cry Wolf
by Farley Mowat

In the book *Never Cry Wolf*, Canadian biologist Farley Mowat details his yearlong expedition learning about wolves and surviving on the frozen tundra of northern Canada. When Mowat set up camp in a remote wilderness area, he didn't know he would end up eating mice to prove a point. Mowat was hired by the Canadian Wildlife Service to investigate and live among the wolves to help solve the country's growing "*Canis lupus* problem." Hunters were reporting that packs of bloodthirsty wolves were slaughtering caribou by the thousands and contributing to their extinction.

Mowat's Discovery

This action-packed book is more than just an adventure story. It's also the report of a stunning scientific discovery. Instead of fierce killers, Mowat found wolves to be gentle, skillful providers and devoted protectors of their young. Mowat challenged the idea that wolves were causing the decline in the caribou population. He showed that his wolf population fed almost exclusively on mice during the warmer summer months when the mouse population skyrocketed. To prove that a large mammal could survive on mice, he ate them himself. Following the publication of *Never Cry Wolf,* Mowat's conclusions about the habits and behaviors of wolves were criticized by people clinging to the old image of wolves as vicious killers.

Filled with beautiful images of animals in their natural setting, *Never Cry Wolf* describes one person's struggle to preserve a vanishing species. Mowat's heroic efforts to document never-before-seen behaviors in wild wolves focused international attention on wolves, which are threatened with extinction in North America and elsewhere. In 1983, Mowat's groundbreaking book was made into an entertaining movie.

Science
JOURNAL ▶

Never Cry Wolf was made into a movie based on the book. In your Science Journal, explain how books and movies like *Never Cry Wolf* can be used to persuade or to change a person's attitude toward a subject.

For a **preview** of this chapter, study this Reviewing Main Ideas before you read the chapter. After you have studied this chapter, you can use the Reviewing Main Ideas to **review** the chapter.

The Glencoe MindJogger, Audiocassettes, and CD-ROM provide additional opportunities for review.

Section 14-1 THE LIVING AND NONLIVING ENVIRONMENT

The region of Earth in which all organisms live is the **biosphere.** The nonliving features of the environment are **abiotic factors,** and the organisms in the environment are **biotic factors. Populations** and **communities** make up an **ecosystem. Ecology** is the study of interactions among organisms and their environment. *How does the relationship between an organism, a population, and a community affect an ecosystem?*

Section 14-2 INTERACTIONS AMONG LIVING ORGANISMS

A **population** can be described by characteristics that include size, spacing, and density. Any biotic or abiotic factor that limits the number of individuals in a population is a **limiting factor.** A close relationship between two or more species is a symbiotic relationship. The place where an organism lives is its **habitat,** and its role in the environment is its **niche.** *How could two similar species of birds live in the same area and nest in the same tree without occupying the same niche?*

Reading Check

Translate the information in **Figure 14-14** into a diagram. Clearly show the relationships among the links in a food chain.

Section 14-3 MATTER AND ENERGY

Food chains and **food webs** are models that describe the feeding relationships in a community. An **energy pyramid** describes the flow of energy through a community. Energy is distributed at each level of the food chain but is replenished by the sun. Matter is never lost or gained but is recycled. ***If the rabbits, birds, mice, beetles, and deer were removed from the food web shown in this figure, which organisms would be affected and how?***

Career CONNECTION

Isidro Bosh, Aquatic Biologist

As an aquatic biologist, Isidro Bosh studies ocean invertebrates such as sea urchins, sea slugs, and sponges. He is interested in how these animals live in tough environmental conditions, such as cold polar oceans and the dark deep sea with its high pressure. He has explored the oceans in everything from huge research vessels to small, inflatable rafts. He also has explored tropical coral reefs and giant kelp forests. ***Why is it important to study how animals adapt to tough environments?***

Chapter 14 Assessment

Using Vocabulary

a. abiotic factor	**j.** food web
b. biosphere	**k.** habitat
c. biotic factor	**l.** limiting factor
d. carrying capacity	**m.** niche
e. community	**n.** nitrogen cycle
f. ecological pyramid	**o.** population
	p. population density
g. ecology	
h. ecosystem	**q.** symbiosis
i. food chain	**r.** water cycle

Match each phrase with the correct term from the list of Vocabulary words.

1. any living thing in the environment
2. number of individuals of a species living in the same place at the same time
3. all the populations in an ecosystem
4. series of overlapping food chains
5. where an organism lives in an ecosystem

Checking Concepts

Choose the word or phrase that best answers the question.

6. Which of the following is a biotic factor?
   A) animals　　　 C) sunlight
   B) air　　　　　 D) soil

7. What are coral reefs and oak-hickory forests examples of?
   A) niches　　　　 C) populations
   B) habitats　　　 D) ecosystems

8. What is made up of all populations in an area?
   A) niche　　　　 C) community
   B) habitat　　　 D) ecosystem

9. What does the number of individuals in a population occupying an area of a specific size describe?
   A) clumping　　　 C) spacing
   B) size　　　　　 D) density

10. Which of the following is an example of an herbivore?
    A) wolf　　　　 C) tree
    B) moss　　　　 D) rabbit

11. Which level of the food chain has the most energy?
    A) omnivores　　 C) decomposers
    B) herbivores　　 D) producers

12. What is a relationship in which one organism is helped and the other is harmed?
    A) mutualism　　 C) commensalism
    B) parasitism　　 D) symbiosis

13. Which of the following is **NOT** cycled in the biosphere?
    A) nitrogen　　　 C) water
    B) soil　　　　　 D) carbon

14. Which of the following is a model that shows how energy is lost as it flows through an ecosystem?
    A) pyramid of biomass
    B) pyramid of numbers
    C) pyramid of energy
    D) niche

15. What does returning wolves to Yellowstone National Park add to the food web?
    A) producer　　　 C) top carnivore
    B) herbivore　　　 D) decomposer

Thinking Critically

16. What would be the advantage to a human or other omnivore of eating a diet of organisms that are lower rather than higher on the food chain?

17. Why are viruses considered parasites?

18. What does carrying capacity have to do with whether or not a population reaches its biotic potential?

19. Why are decomposers vital to the cycling of matter in an ecosystem?

20. Describe your own habitat and niche.

Developing Skills

If you need help, refer to the **Skill Handbook.**

21. **Classifying:** Classify each event in the water cycle as the result of either evaporation or condensation.

    A) A puddle disappears after a rainstorm.

    B) Rain falls.

    C) A lake becomes shallower.

    D) Clouds form.

22. **Making and Using Graphs:** Use the following data to graph the population density of a deer population over the years. Plot the number of deer on the *y*-axis and years on the *x*-axis. Propose a hypothesis to explain what might have happened to cause the changes in the size of the population.

Arizona Deer Population	
Year	Deer per 400 hectares
1905	5.7
1915	35.7
1920	142.9
1925	85.7
1935	25.7

23. **Observing and Inferring:** A home aquarium contains water, an air pump, a light, algae, a goldfish, and algae-eating snails. What are the abiotic factors in this environment? Which of these items would be considered a population? A community?

24. **Concept Mapping:** Use the following information to draw a food web of organisms living in a goldenrod field. *Goldenrod sap is eaten by aphids, goldenrod nectar is eaten by bees, goldenrod pollen is eaten by beetles, goldenrod leaves are eaten by beetles, stinkbugs eat beetles, spiders eat aphids, assassin bugs eat bees.*

THE PRINCETON REVIEW

Test-Taking Tip

Skip Around, If You Can Just because the questions are in order doesn't mean you have to answer them that way. You may want to skip over hard questions and come back to them later. Answer all the easier questions first to guarantee you more points toward your score.

Test Practice

Use these questions to test your Science Proficiency.

1. According to the table, at which point are there more deer than available food?
   A) 1
   B) 2
   C) 3
   D) 4

2. In the water cycle, how is water returned to the atmosphere?
   A) evaporation
   B) condensation
   C) precipitation
   D) fixation

3. What are the food relationships among all organisms in the same environment called?
   A) food chain
   B) ecological pyramid
   C) food web
   D) energy pyramid

4. In an energy pyramid, which level has the most available energy?
   A) first
   B) second
   C) third
   D) fourth

Chapter Preview

Skills Preview

Skill Builders
- Map Concepts
- Compare and Contrast

Activities
- Observe

MiniLabs
- Observe
- Infer

Reading Check ✔

As you read about succession, record words and phrases that indicate a time sequence, such as *long ago*, *gradually*, and *as time passed*.

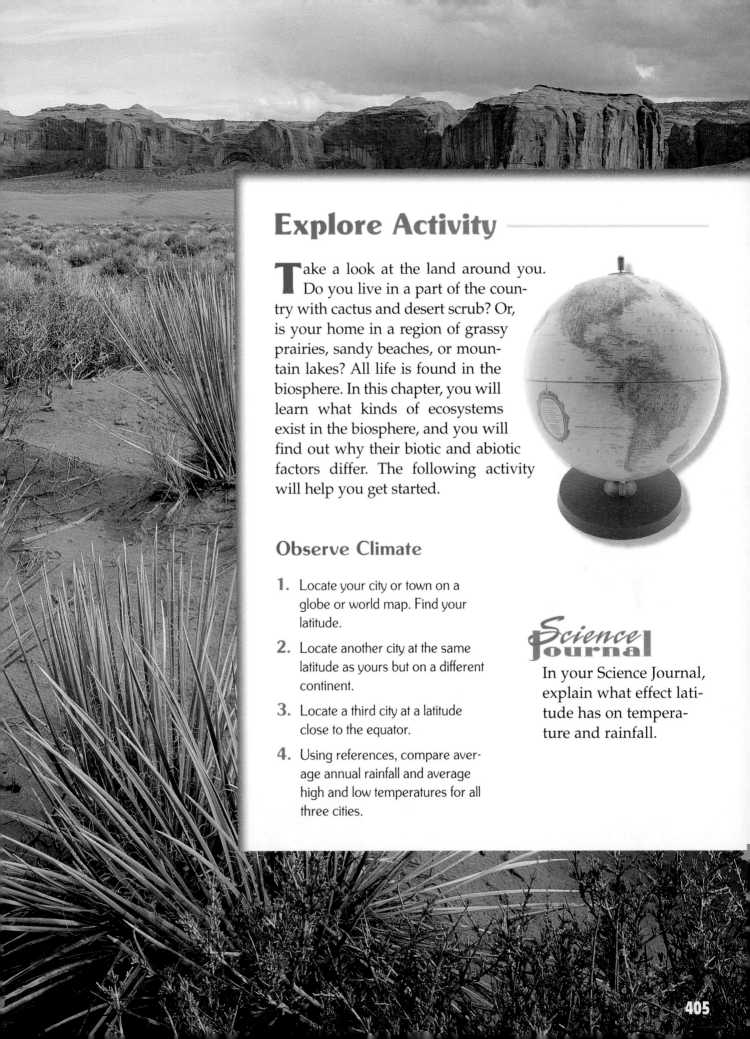

Explore Activity

Take a look at the land around you. Do you live in a part of the country with cactus and desert scrub? Or, is your home in a region of grassy prairies, sandy beaches, or mountain lakes? All life is found in the biosphere. In this chapter, you will learn what kinds of ecosystems exist in the biosphere, and you will find out why their biotic and abiotic factors differ. The following activity will help you get started.

Observe Climate

1. Locate your city or town on a globe or world map. Find your latitude.

2. Locate another city at the same latitude as yours but on a different continent.

3. Locate a third city at a latitude close to the equator.

4. Using references, compare average annual rainfall and average high and low temperatures for all three cities.

Science Journal

In your Science Journal, explain what effect latitude has on temperature and rainfall.

How Ecosystems Change

What You'll Learn

► How ecosystems change over time
► How new communities arise in areas that were bare of life
► How to compare and contrast pioneer communities and climax communities

Vocabulary
ecological succession
primary succession
pioneer community
secondary succession
climax community

Why It's Important

► Your ecosystem is changing right now.

Ecological Succession

Imagine hiking through a forest. Huge trees tower over the trail. You know it can take many years for trees to grow this large, so it's easy to think of the forest as something that has always been here. But, this area has not always been covered with trees. Long ago, it may have been a pond full of fish and frogs surrounded by water-loving plants. As time passed, the decomposed bodies of plants and animals slowly filled in the pond until it eventually became a lush, green meadow full of grass and wildflowers. Gradually, over many more years, seeds blew in, trees began to grow, and a forest developed. The process of gradual change from one community of organisms to another is called **ecological succession.** The changes associated with succession usually take place in a fairly predictable order and involve animals, plants, and other organisms.

VISUALIZING Succession

Figure 15-1 The following are the stages in primary succession.

A Life on this bare rock begins with a pioneer community of lichens. These hardy organisms produce acids that help to break down the rock. The acids release chemicals and nutrients from the rock that can then be absorbed by the lichens. The decaying bodies of dead lichens contribute to soil formation.

B Mosses and ferns gradually replace the lichens. These plants can grow even in extremely poor, thin soil. As they die, their decomposed bodies add humus to the soil. Insects and other small animals appear.

Primary Succession

Think about conditions around an erupting volcano. Incredibly hot, molten lava flows along the ground, destroying everything in its path. As the lava cools, it forms new land. Soil is formed from bare rock. Similar events happen to this newly formed land. Particles of dust and ash fall to the ground. The forces of weather and erosion break up the lava rock. A thin layer of soil begins to form. Birds, wind, and rain deposit more dust, along with bacteria, seeds, and fungal spores. Plants start to grow and decay. A living community has begun to develop.

Ecological succession that begins in a place that does not have soil is called **primary succession.** The first community of organisms to move into a new environment is called the **pioneer community,** as shown in **Figure 15-1.** Members of pioneer communities are usually hardy organisms that can survive drought, extreme heat and cold, and other harsh conditions. Pioneer communities change the conditions in their environments. These new conditions support the growth of other types of organisms that gradually take over.

C As the soil layer thickens, its ability to absorb and hold water improves. Grasses, wildflowers, and other plants that require richer, more moist soil begin to take over. Butterflies, bees, and caterpillars come to feed on the leaves and flowers. When these plants die, they also enrich the soil, which will become home to earthworms and other large soil organisms.

D Thicker, richer soil supports the growth of shrubs and trees. More insects, birds, mammals, and reptiles move into the area. After hundreds or thousands of years of gradual change, what was once bare rock has become a forest.

Figure 15-2 The tangled growth of weeds and grasses in untended yards and vacant lots, on abandoned farms, and along country roadsides is the beginning stage of secondary succession.

Reading Check ✔

What is secondary succession?

*inter***NET**
C O N N E C T I O N

Visit the Glencoe Science Web Site at **www. glencoe.com/sec/ science/ca** for more information about the Yellowstone fires and how they contributed to succession.

Secondary Succession

What happens when a forest is destroyed by a fire or a city building is torn down? After a forest fire, nothing is left except dead trees and ash-covered soil. Once the rubble of a demolished building has been taken away, all that remains is bare soil. But, these places do not remain lifeless for long. The soil may already contain the seeds of weeds, grasses, and trees. More seeds are carried to the area by wind and birds. As the seeds germinate and plants begin to grow, insects, birds, and other wildlife move in. Ecological succession has begun again. Succession that begins in a place that already has soil and was once the home of living organisms is called **secondary succession,** shown in **Figure 15-2.** ✔

Climax Communities

Succession involves changes in abiotic factors as well as biotic factors. You have already seen how lichens, mosses, and ferns change the environment by helping to form the rich, thick soil needed for the growth of shrubs and trees. Shrubs and trees also cause changes in abiotic factors. Their branches shade the ground beneath them, reducing the temperature. Shade also reduces the rate of evaporation, increasing the moisture content of the soil. Amount of sunlight, temperature, and moisture level determine which species will grow in soil.

The redwood forest shown in **Figure 15-3** is an example of a community that has reached the end of succession. As long as the trees are not cut down or destroyed by fire or widespread disease, the species that make up the redwood community tend to remain the same. When a community has reached the final stage of ecological succession, it is called a **climax community.** Because primary succession begins in areas with no life at all, it can take hundreds or even thousands of years for a pioneer community to develop into a climax community. Secondary succession is a shorter process, but it still may take a century or more.

Comparing Communities

As you have seen, pioneer communities are simple. They contain only a few species, and feeding relationships usually can be described with simple food chains. Climax communities are much more complex. They may contain hundreds of thousands of species, and feeding relationships usually involve complex food webs. Interactions among the many biotic and abiotic factors in a climax community create a more stable environment that does not change much over time. Climax communities are the end product of ecological succession. A climax community that has been disturbed in some way will eventually return to the same type of community, as long as all other factors remain the same. However, it may take a century or more for the community to return to its former state.

Figure 15-3 This forest of redwood trees in California is an example of a climax community. Redwoods live for hundreds of years. They create shade on the ground beneath them. Needles constantly fall from their branches. Eventually, they form an acidic soil that allows the growth of young redwoods but prevents the growth of many other types of plants.

Section Assessment

1. What is ecological succession?
2. What is the difference between primary and secondary succession?
3. What is the difference between pioneer and climax communities?
4. **Think Critically:** What kind of succession will take place on an abandoned, unpaved country road? Why?
5. **Skill Builder**
   Sequencing Describe the sequence of events in primary succession. Include the term *climax community.* If you need help, refer to Sequencing on page 678.

In your Science Journal, draw a food chain for a pioneer community of lichens and a food web for the climax community of an oak-maple forest. Write a short paragraph comparing the two communities.

On The Internet

Endangered and Threatened Species

Aspecies becomes endangered when its numbers are so low that it is in danger of extinction in the near future. The list of threatened and endangered species in the United States and around the world is constantly growing due to a variety of reasons. In 1998, about 965 species in the United States were listed as endangered or threatened.

Recognize the Problem

What endangered or threatened species have been identified for your region of the country?

Form a Hypothesis

Form a hypothesis to explain some of the reasons why the organisms identified as threatened or endangered in your region are on the list.

Goals

- **Obtain** and **organize** data.
- **Infer** relationships between the plant or animal and its environment.
- **Use the Internet** to collect and compare data from other students.

Data Sources

Go to the Glencoe Science Web Site at **www.glencoe. com/sec/science/ca** to find links to information about endangered plants and animals around the country. You also will find information posted by other students from around the country.

Species Data

Organism Genus species	Threatened or Endangered	Length of Time on List	Recovery Plan	General Information

Test Your Hypothesis

Plan

1. Find links to information on the Glencoe Science Web Site. You can also find information on endangered species at the local library or a local zoo.

2. Prepare a data table similar to the one below to record your findings.

3. If possible, observe one of the endangered or threatened species you've identified either in a zoo or in the wild.

Do

1. **Describe** the habitat and range of the organism you chose to study.

2. **Identify** any steps being taken to protect the organism. Outline the recovery plan written for one of the organisms in your region.

3. **Post** the information you collected in the table provided for this activity on the Glencoe Science Web Site.

4. **Check** the postings by other students for more information on your organism and on other organisms.

Analyze Your Data

1. Brainstorm possible reasons why your organism is threatened or endangered.

2. What factors were you able to identify as reasons for the organism becoming endangered?

3. Was your hypothesis supported by the information you collected? **Explain** your answer.

Draw Conclusions

1. What might help the organism you are studying survive the changes in conditions or other changes that have occurred in its range that caused its numbers to decrease.

2. How successful have any techniques established to protect the organism been?

3. Did you find more threatened or endangered species of plants or animals in your region? What explanation might there be for your findings?

4. What steps do you think should be taken, if any, to protect endangered or threatened species in your region? What objections might be raised for the steps taken to protect a species?

Factors That Determine Climate

What does a desert in Arizona have in common with a desert in Africa? They both have water-conserving plants with thorns, lizards, heat, little rain, and poor soil. How are the plains of the American West like the veldt of central Africa? Both regions have dry summers, wet winters, and huge expanses of grassland that support grazing animals such as elk and antelope. Many widely separated regions of the world have similar ecosystems. Why? Because they have similar climates. Climate is the general weather pattern in an area. The factors that determine a region's climate include temperature and precipitation.

Temperature

The sun supplies life on Earth not only with light energy for photosynthesis, but also with heat energy for warmth. The temperature of a region is regulated primarily by the amount of sunlight that reaches it. In turn, the amount of sunlight is determined by an area's latitude and elevation.

Latitude

As **Figure 15-4** shows, not all parts of Earth receive the same amount of energy from the sun. When you conducted the Explore Activity at the beginning of this chapter, you probably concluded that temperature is affected by latitude.

What You'll Learn

▶ How climate influences land environments
▶ The six biomes that make up land environments on Earth
▶ The adaptations of plants and animals found in each biome

Vocabulary

biome
tundra
taiga
temperate deciduous forest
tropical rain forest
grassland
desert

Why It's Important

▶ Resources that you need to survive are found in a variety of biomes.

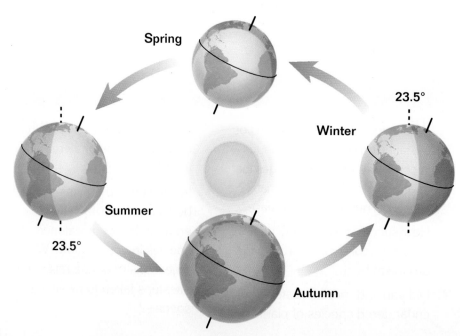

Figure 15-4 Because Earth is tilted on its axis, the angle of the sun's rays changes during the year. These changes create the seasons. The tilt of Earth's axis does not have as much of an effect on regions near the equator.

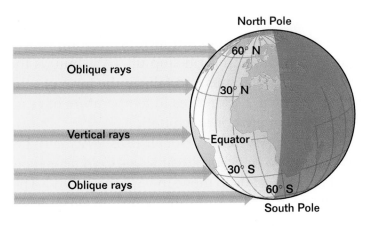

North Pole

60° N

Oblique rays

30° N

Vertical rays

Equator

30° S

Oblique rays

60° S

South Pole

Figure 15-5 Because Earth is curved, oblique rays of sunlight reaching higher latitudes near the poles are more spread out. These rays are therefore weaker than the sunlight reaching lower latitudes near the equator. Climates near the equator are warmer, and those near the poles are colder.

The nearer a region is to the north or south pole, the higher its latitude, the smaller the amount of energy it receives from the sun, as seen in **Figure 15-5,** and the colder its climate.

Seasonal changes in sunlight also have an effect on the temperature of a climate. Because Earth is tilted on its axis, the angle of the sun's rays changes as Earth moves through its yearly orbit. During winter in the northern hemisphere, regions north of the equator are tilted away from the sun. Rays of sunlight are spread over a larger area, reducing their warming effect. As a result, winter temperatures are colder than summer temperatures.

Elevation

A region's elevation, or distance above sea level, also has an influence on temperature. Earth's atmosphere acts as insulation that traps some of the heat that reaches Earth's surface. At higher elevations, the atmosphere is thinner, so more heat escapes back into space. As a result, the higher the elevation, the colder the climate. The climate on a mountain will be cooler than the climate at sea level at the same latitude. Higher elevations affect plant growth, as seen in **Figure 15-6.**

EARTH SCIENCE
◀ INTEGRATION

Using Math

Earth is tilted at an angle of 23.5°. Without using a protractor, sketch an angle that measures about 23.5°. Then, check your angle by measuring it with a protractor.

Figure 15-6 These Rocky Mountain bristlecone pines show the effects of higher elevations on plants. These trees are shaped by the wind and stunted by the cold, harsh conditions.

Precipitation

Water is one of the most important factors affecting the climate of an area. Precipitation (prih sihp uh TAY shun) is the amount of water that condenses and falls in the form of rain, snow, sleet, hail, and fog. Differences in temperature have an important effect on patterns of precipitation.

Have you heard the expression "Hot air rises"? Actually, hot air is pushed upward whenever cold air sinks. Cold air is more dense than hot air, so it tends to move toward the ground. This pushes warm air near Earth's surface upward. In warm tropical regions near the equator, the air, land, and oceans are constantly being heated by the direct rays of the sun. As the cooler air sinks, the warm air is pushed upward into the atmosphere. This warm air carries large amounts of water vapor from the oceans. When the air reaches a high enough altitude in the atmosphere, the water vapor it contains cools and condenses as rain. While the air rises, it also moves slowly toward either the north or south pole. The air loses virtually all of its moisture by the time it reaches a latitude of about 30°. Because of this pattern, deserts are common at latitudes near 30° in both the northern and southern hemispheres. Latitudes between 0° and 22° receive much larger amounts of rain.

The Rain Shadow Effect

The presence of mountain ranges also has an effect on rainfall patterns. As **Figure 15-7** shows, air that is moving toward a mountain range is forced upward by the shape of the land. As warm air is forced upward, it cools, condensing the water vapor it contains and creating rain or snow. By the time the air has passed over the mountains, it has lost its moisture. The region on the opposite side of the mountain range receives very little rain because it is in a "rain shadow" created by the mountains.

interNET
C O N N E C T I O N

Little precipitation falls in the desert. Visit the Glencoe Science Web Site at **www.glencoe. com/sec/science/ca** for more information about how cacti thrive.

Figure 15-7 Moist air moving into California from the Pacific Ocean is forced upward when it reaches the Sierra Nevada Mountains. As air rises, it cools and loses its moisture in the form of rain or snow. By the time the air reaches Nevada and Utah, on the other side of the mountains, it is dry. This area is in the mountains' "rain shadow." It receives so little rain that it has become a desert.

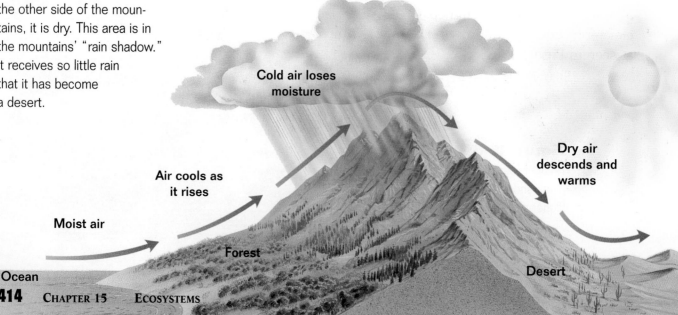

Cold air loses moisture

Dry air descends and warms

Air cools as it rises

Moist air

Forest

Ocean

Desert

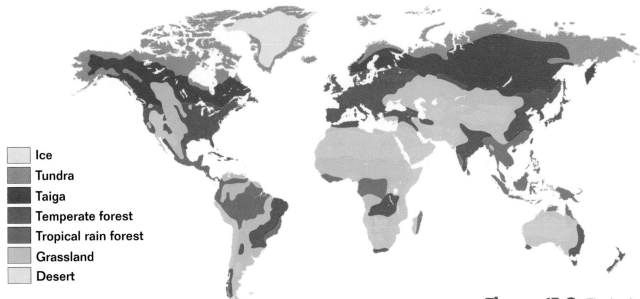

Ice
Tundra
Taiga
Temperate forest
Tropical rain forest
Grassland
Desert

Figure 15-8 The land portion of the biosphere can be divided into several biomes. Tundra, taiga, temperate forest, tropical rain forest, grassland, and desert are the most commonly known. **Which biome is most common in the United States?**

Land Biomes

As you will see in the **Field Guide to Biomes** at the end of this chapter, regions with similar climates tend to have ecosystems with climax communities of similar structure. Tropical rain forests are climax communities found near the equator, where temperatures are warm and rainfall is plentiful. Coniferous forests grow where winter temperatures are cold and rainfall is moderate. Large geographic areas that have similar climates and ecosystems are called **biomes** (BI ohmz). The six most common biomes are mapped in **Figure 15-8.**

Tundra

At latitudes surrounding the north pole lies a biome that receives little precipitation but is covered with ice most of the year. The **tundra** (TUN dra) is a cold, dry, treeless region, sometimes called a cold desert, where winters are six to nine months long. For some of those months, the land remains dark because the sun never rises above the horizon. For a few days during the short, cold summer, the sun never sets. Precipitation averages less than 25 cm per year, and winter temperatures drop to −40°C, so water in the tundra soil remains frozen solid during the winter. During the summer, only the top few inches thaw.

Try at Home

Mini Lab

Comparing Tundra and Taiga

Procedure

1. Compare the latitudes where tundra is found in the northern hemisphere with the same latitudes in South America.

2. Compare the latitudes where taiga is found in the northern hemisphere with the same latitudes in South America.

Analysis

Are either of these biomes found in South America? Explain why or why not.

Below the thawed surface is a layer of permanently frozen soil called permafrost. The cold temperatures slow down the process of decomposition, so the soil is also poor in nutrients.

Tundra plants are resistant to drought and cold. They include species of lichens known as reindeer moss, true mosses, grasses, and small shrubs, as seen in **Figure 15-9.** During the summer, mosquitoes, blackflies, and other biting insects are abundant. Many birds, including ducks, geese, various shorebirds, and songbirds, migrate to the tundra to nest during the summer. Hawks, snowy owls, mice, voles, lemmings, arctic hares, caribou, and musk oxen are also found there.

Taiga

Just below the tundra, at latitudes between about 50°N and 60°N, and stretching across Canada, northern Europe, and Asia, lies the world's largest biome. The **taiga** (TI guh), as shown in **Figure 15-10,** is a cold region of cone-bearing evergreen trees. This biome is also called the northern coniferous forest. Although the winter is long and cold, the taiga is warmer and wetter than the tundra. Precipitation is mostly snow and averages 35 cm to 100 cm each year.

Figure 15-9 Land is so flat in the tundra that water does not drain away. Because the frozen soil also prevents water from soaking into the soil, part of the tundra becomes wet and marshy during the summer. Frozen soil also prevents trees and other deep-rooted plants from growing in the tundra biome.

Figure 15-10 The climax community of the taiga is dominated by fir and spruce trees. Mammal populations include moose, black bears, lynx, and wolves.

Permafrost is found in northern areas of the taiga. The ground thaws completely during the summer, making it possible for trees to grow. There are few shrubs and grasses, primarily because the forests of the taiga are so dense that little sunlight penetrates through the trees. Lichens and mosses grow on the forest floor.

Temperate Deciduous Forest

Temperate forests are found in both the northern and southern hemispheres, at latitudes below about 50°. Temperate regions usually have four distinct seasons each year. Precipitation ranges from about 75 cm to 150 cm and is distributed evenly throughout the year. Temperatures range from below freezing during the winter to 30°C or more during the warmest days of summer.

Many coniferous forests exist in the temperate regions of the world, particularly in mountainous areas. However, most of the temperate forests in Europe and North America are dominated by climax communities of deciduous trees, which lose their leaves every autumn. These forests, like the one in **Figure 15-11,** are called **temperate deciduous forests.** In the United States, they are found primarily east of the Mississippi River. ☑

The loss of leaves in the fall signals a dramatic change in the life of the deciduous forest. Food becomes less abundant, and the leafless trees no longer provide adequate shelter for many organisms. Some animals, particularly birds, migrate to warmer regions during the winter. Other organisms reduce their activities and their need for food by going into hibernation until spring.

Reading Check ☑

Where are temperate deciduous forests found?

Figure 15-11 The mild climate and rich soil of the temperate deciduous forest support a wide variety of organisms. Animal life includes deer, foxes, squirrels, mice, snakes, and a huge number of bird and insect species. **Why do you think the temperate forests support a wide variety of organisms?**

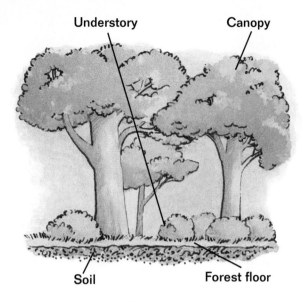

Understory   Canopy

Soil   Forest floor

Figure 15-12 All forests are made up of layers with distinctly different biotic and abiotic factors.

Layers of Vegetation

Forests form layers of vegetation, as illustrated in **Figure 15-12.** At the top of the forest is the canopy, which consists of the leafy branches of trees. The *canopy* shades the ground below and provides homes for birds, insects, mammals, and many other organisms.

Beneath the canopy and above the forest floor is the shrub layer, or *understory*. The understory is made up of shorter plants that tolerate shade, along with organisms that depend on these plants for food and shelter.

The forest floor is dark and moist. It is home to many insects, worms, and fungi, as well as plants that can survive in dim light. Leaves, twigs, seeds, and the bodies of dead animals that fall to the forest floor either decompose or are eaten.

Problem Solving

Saving the Rain Forests

Many of the world's rain forests are being destroyed for economic reasons. Logging and farming provide income for people living in these areas. When a section of rain forest is cleared, trees that can be used as lumber are removed and sold. The remaining plants are cut down and burned, the ash is used to fertilize the soil, and food crops are planted. After a couple of years, the soil becomes too poor to produce a harvest, so the land is abandoned and another patch of forest is cleared.

People can make a living from the rain forest in other ways. Latex, a material used in surgical gloves, rubber bands, tires, and shoes, is the sap of rubber trees. Carefully tapping the trees provides a continual harvest without harming the forest. Many rain forest plants produce edible fruits, nuts, and oils that can be harvested year after year, without the need for clearing land. Harvesting these plants, rather than clearing land on which other crops can be grown for only a short time, could provide people with a sustainable income.

Think Critically: Suppose a family could earn the same amount of money in two different ways. One is to clear several hectares of rain forest, sell the timber, and grow food crops for two years. The other is to harvest latex and edible fruits and nuts from a larger area of rain forest for four years. Which course of action would you recommend? Why? Give reasons why the family might choose the other method.

Tropical Rain Forest

The most important climax community in the equatorial regions of the world is the lush, green plant growth of the **tropical rain forest.** Rainfall averages 200 cm to 225 cm each year, and some areas receive as much as 400 cm of rain annually. Temperatures are warm and stable, never varying much above or below about 25°C. The abundant rainfall and high temperatures combine to create a hot, humid environment that can be compared to the atmosphere inside a greenhouse.

Plants

The highest part of the rain forest canopy is formed by the leaves and branches of trees that may reach 30 m to 40 m in height. A rain forest may contain more than 700 species of trees and more than 1000 species of flowering plants. The canopy is so dense that it prevents much sunlight from filtering through to the regions below. Vines that are rooted in the soil grow up along tree trunks to reach the sun. Some types of plants such as orchids reach the light by anchoring themselves on tree trunks instead of in the soil. The understory is only dimly lit. Many of the plants growing here have huge leaves that catch what little sunlight is available. The forest floor is almost completely dark, with few plants other than ferns and mosses. Many of the tallest trees have support roots that rise above the ground. Most plants have shallow roots that form a tangled mat at the soil surface.

Animals

The rain forest is home to a huge number of animals. It is estimated that 1000 hectares (about 2500 acres) of rain forest in South America contain thousands of insect species, including 150 different kinds of butterflies. The same patch of forest also contains dozens of species of snakes, lizards, frogs, and salamanders, and hundreds of varieties of brightly colored birds, including parrots, toucans, cockatoos, and hummingbirds. Tree-dwelling mammals include monkeys, sloths, and bats. Ocelots and jaguars are tropical cats that prowl the forest floor in search of small mammals such as pacas and agoutis, or piglike peccaries, shown in **Figure 15-13.**

Using Math

Make a bar graph that shows the average yearly precipitation in each of the land biomes.

Grassland

Temperate and tropical regions that receive between 25 cm and 75 cm of precipitation each year and are dominated by climax communities of grasses are known as **grasslands.** Most grasslands have a dry season, when little or no rain falls, which prevents the development of forests. Virtually every continent has grasslands, like the one in **Figure 15-14,** and they are known by a variety of names. The prairie and plains of North America, the steppes of Asia, the veldts of Africa, and the pampas of South America are all grasslands.

Grass plants have extensive root systems, called sod, that absorb water when it rains and can withstand drought during long dry spells. The roots remain dormant during winter and sprout new stems and leaves when the weather warms in the spring. The soil is rich and fertile, and many grassland regions of the world are now important farming areas. Cereal grains such as wheat, rye, oats, barley, and corn, which serve as staple foods for humans, are types of grasses.

The most noticeable animals in grassland ecosystems are usually mammals that graze on the stems, leaves, and seeds of grass plants. Kangaroos graze in the grasslands of Australia. In Africa, common grassland inhabitants include wildebeests and zebras.

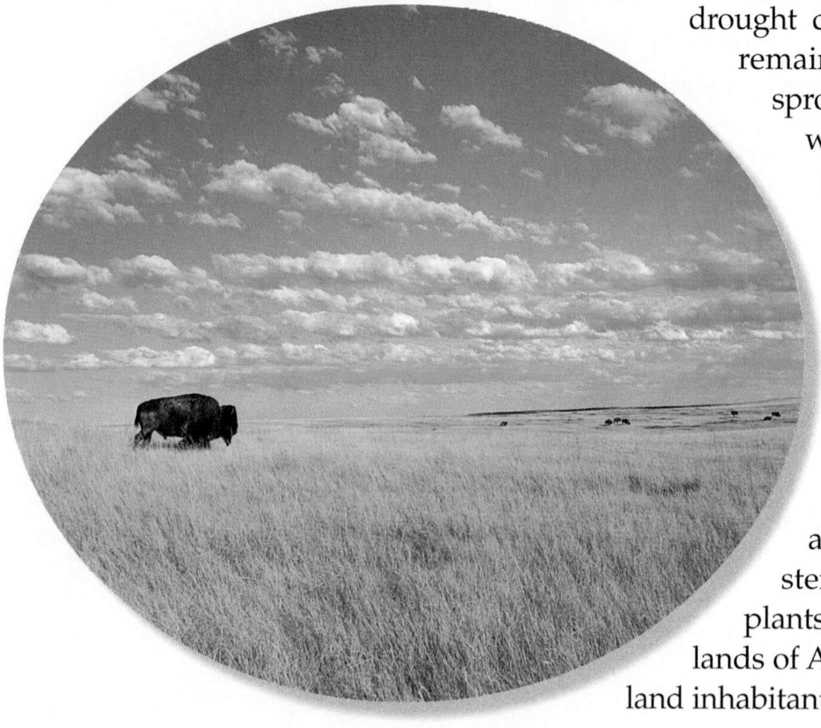

Figure 15-14 Grasslands, like this one in South Dakota, are hot and dry during the summer and cold and wet during the winter. They once supported huge herds of bison. Today, they are inhabited by pronghorn, gophers, ground squirrels, prairie chickens, and meadowlarks.

Desert

The **desert,** the driest biome on Earth, receives less than 25 cm of rain each year and supports little plant life. Some desert areas may receive no rain for years. When rain does come, it quickly drains away due to the sandy soil. Any water that remains on the ground evaporates rapidly, so the soil retains almost no moisture.

Because of the lack of water, desert plants are spaced widely apart, and much of the ground is bare. Some areas receive enough rainfall to support the growth of a few shrubs and small trees. Barren, windblown sand dunes are characteristic of the driest deserts, where rain rarely falls. Most deserts are covered with a thin, sandy or gravelly soil that contains little humus.

Adaptations of Desert Plants and Animals

Desert plants have developed a variety of adaptations for survival in the extreme dryness and hot and cold temperatures of this biome. Cactus plants, like the one in **Figure 15-15A,** with their reduced, spiny leaves, are probably the most familiar desert plants. Cacti have large, shallow roots that quickly absorb any water that becomes available.

Water conservation is important to all desert animals. Some, like the kangaroo rat, never need to drink water. They get all the moisture they need from the breakdown of food during digestion. Other adaptations involve behavior. Most animals are active only during the early morning or late afternoon, when temperatures are less extreme. Few large animals are found in the desert because there is not enough water or food to support them.

Figure 15-15 Desert organisms are adapted to hot, dry conditions.

 Giant saguaro cacti expand to store water after it rains.

 Desert iguanas, common in deserts of the southwestern United States and Mexico, prefer temperatures above 100°F.

Section Assessment

1. Name two biomes that receive less than 25 cm of rain each year.

2. Compare the adaptations of tundra organisms to their environment with those of a desert organism to its environment.

3. **Think Critically:** Compare and contrast the canopies of temperate deciduous forests and tropical rain forests.

4. **Skill Builder**
   Observing and Inferring Animals adapt to their environments in order to survive. Do the **Chapter 15 Skill Activity** on page 720 to infer how some organisms adapt.

Using Computers

Database Create a database of information on Earth's land biomes. Include data on temperature range, precipitation, limiting factors, and descriptions of climax communities. If you need help, refer to page 663.

Studying a Land Environment

An ecological study includes observation and analysis of living organisms and the physical features of the environment.

What You'll Investigate

How do you study an ecosystem?

Goals

- **Observe** biotic and abiotic factors of an ecosystem.
- **Analyze** the relationships among organisms and their environment.

Materials

- Graph paper
- Thermometer
- Tape measure
- Hand lens
- Notebook
- Binoculars
- Pencil
- Field guides

Procedure

1. **Choose** a portion of an ecosystem near your school or home as your area of study. You might choose to study a pond, a forest area in a park, a garden, or another area.

2. **Decide** the boundaries of your study area.

3. Using a tape measure and graph paper, **make a map** of your study area.

4. Using a thermometer, **measure and record** the air temperature in your study area.

5. **Observe** the organisms in your study area. Use field guides to identify them. Use a hand lens to study small organisms. Use binoculars to study animals you cannot get near. Also, look for evidence (such as tracks or feathers) of organisms you do not see.

6. Record your observations in a table like the one shown. Make drawings to help you remember what you see.

7. Visit your study area as many times as you can and at different times of the day for four weeks. At each visit, be sure to make the same measurements and record all observations. Note how biotic and abiotic factors interact.

Conclude and Apply

1. **Identify** relationships among the organisms in your study area, such as predator-prey or symbiosis.

2. **Diagram** a food chain or food web for your ecosystem.

3. **Predict** what might happen if one or more abiotic factors were changed suddenly.

4. **Predict** what might happen if one or more populations were removed from the area.

Environmental Data				
Date	Time of Day	Temperature	Organisms Observed	Observations and Comments

Protecting Antarctica

The Coldest Place on Earth

Antarctica is a vast continent of rock covered with ice and surrounded by ocean. It is the least changed landmass in the world, in part because it is an environment hostile to humans. Winters are dark and long, with temperatures dipping to –90°C. During winter, shelves of ice extend from the land out over the ocean, essentially doubling the size of the continent. The yearly freezing and thawing of this ice has important effects on worldwide weather patterns and is a force that drives ocean currents.

Antarctica's Resources

Although the land is barren, seals and penguins, like the ones at left, use the shores as breeding grounds, and the waters of the Antarctic Ocean teem with life. Under the surface of Antarctica lie untouched mineral resources. Coal and oil probably exist in enormous quantities, as do other minerals that have already been discovered.

Antarctica and its remarkable natural resources are fully protected by a treaty that was drawn up in 1959 and signed by 12 nations—the United States, Great Britain, Argentina, Chile, France, Belgium, Norway, Australia, New Zealand, Japan, South Africa, and what was then the USSR. The Antarctic Treaty made the entire continent "a natural reserve, devoted to peace and science." Military activities, hunting, mining, and other actions that might harm the environment and its wild inhabitants are banned.

Since 1959, the Antarctic Treaty has been expanded to promote even greater environmental protection, international cooperation, and freedom for scientific research. Thanks to this agreement, Antarctica will remain an essentially undisturbed wilderness far into the future.

interNET CONNECTION

Visit the Glencoe Science Web Site at **www.glencoe.com/sec/science/ca** to find out more about research in Antarctica.

Water Environments

What You'll Learn

► The difference between flowing freshwater and standing freshwater ecosystems
► Important seashore and deep-ocean ecosystems

Vocabulary
plankton
estuary
intertidal zone

Why It's Important

► You depend on water for your life processes.

Freshwater Biomes

You've learned that temperature and precipitation are the most important factors determining which species can survive in a land environment. The limiting factors in water environments are the amount of salt in the water, dissolved oxygen, water temperature, and sunlight. The amount of salts dissolved in the water is called salinity. Freshwater contains little or no dissolved salts, so it has a low salinity. Earth's freshwater biomes include flowing water like these rivers and streams, as well as still or standing water, such as lakes and ponds.

Rivers and Streams

Flowing freshwater environments range from small, swiftly flowing streams, like the one in **Figure 15-16A,** to large, slow rivers. The faster a stream flows, the clearer its water tends to be and the higher its oxygen content. Swift currents quickly wash loose particles downstream, leaving a rocky or gravelly bottom. The tumbling and splashing of swiftly flowing water mixes in air from the atmosphere, increasing the oxygen content of the water.

Most of the nutrients that support life in flowing-water ecosystems are washed into the water from land. In areas where the water movement slows down, such as wide pools in streams or large rivers, debris settles to the bot-

Figure 15-16

 A Freshwater streams are important in the ecosystem.

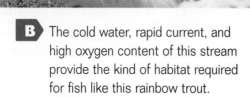 **B** The cold water, rapid current, and high oxygen content of this stream provide the kind of habitat required for fish like this rainbow trout.

Figure 15-17 Ponds and lakes differ in the types of communities inhabiting them. **What are some other differences between ponds and lakes?**

A The warm, sunlit waters of this pond are home to a large variety of organisms. Plants and algae form the basis of a food web that includes snails, insects, frogs, snakes, turtles, and fish.

tom. These environments tend to have higher nutrient levels and lower dissolved oxygen levels. They contain organisms such as freshwater mussels, minnows, and leeches that are not so well adapted for swiftly flowing water. They also tend to have more plant growth.

Lakes and Ponds

A lake or pond forms when a low place in the land fills with rainwater, snowmelt, or water from a stream. The waters of lakes and ponds hardly move at all. They contain more plant growth than flowing-water environments contain.

Ponds, like the one in **Figure 15-17A,** are smaller, shallow bodies of water. Because they are shallow, sunlight can usually penetrate all the way to the bottom, making the water warmer and promoting the growth of plants and algae. In fact, many ponds are almost completely filled with plant material, so the only clear, open water is at the center. Because of the lush growth in pond environments, they tend to be high in nutrients.

Lakes are larger and deeper than ponds. They tend to have more open water because most plant growth is limited to shallow areas along the shoreline. In fact, organisms found in the warm, sunlit waters of the lakeshore are often similar to those found in ponds.

Floating in the warm, sunlit water near the surface of freshwater lakes and ponds are algae and other microscopic organisms known all together as plankton. **Plankton** includes algae, plants, and other organisms. If you were to dive all the way to the bottom, you would discover few, if any, plants or algae growing. Colder temperatures and lower light levels limit the types of organisms that can live in deep lake waters. Most lake organisms are found along the shoreline and in the warm water near the surface. ☑

B The population density of the warm, shallow water of the lakeshore is high. Fewer types of organisms live in the deeper water.

Reading Check ☑

What is plankton?

Saltwater Biomes

Figure 15-18 These Canada geese are swimming in an estuary of the Chesapeake Bay.

About 95 percent of the water on the surface on Earth contains high concentrations of salts. The saltwater biomes include the oceans, seas, and a few inland lakes, such as the Great Salt Lake in Utah.

Estuaries

Virtually every river on Earth eventually flows into the ocean. The area where a river meets the ocean and contains a mixture of freshwater and salt water is called an **estuary.** Estuaries are located near coastlines and border the land. Salinity changes with the amount of freshwater brought in by rivers and streams, and with the amount of salt water pushed inland by the tides.

Estuaries like the one in **Figure 15-18** are extremely fertile, productive environments because freshwater streams bring in tons of nutrients from inland soils. Nutrient levels in estuaries are higher than those in freshwater or other saltwater ecosystems. Estuarine organisms include many species of algae, a few salt-tolerant grasses, shrimp, crabs, clams, oysters, snails, worms, and fish. Estuaries serve as important nursery grounds for many species of ocean fish.

Seashores

All of Earth's landmasses are bordered by ocean water. The fairly shallow waters along the world's coastlines contain a variety of saltwater ecosystems, all of which are influenced by the tides and by the action of waves. The gravitational pull of the sun and moon causes the tides to rise and fall twice each day in most parts of the world. The **intertidal zone** is the portion of the shoreline that is covered with water at high tide and exposed to the air during low tide. Organisms living in the intertidal zone must not only be adapted to dramatic changes in temperature, moisture, and salinity, but also be able to withstand the force of wave action. Two kinds of intertidal zones are shown in **Figure 15-19.**

Mini Lab

Modeling Freshwater Environments

Procedure

1. Cover the bottom of a 2-L bottle with about 2 cm of gravel, muck, and other debris from the bottom of a pond. If plants are present, add one or two to the bottle. Use a dip net to capture small fish, insects, or tadpoles.
2. Carefully pour pond water into the bottle until it is about two-thirds full. Seal the bottle.
3. Keep the bottle indoors at room temperature and out of direct sunlight.

Analysis

1. Using a hand lens, observe as many organisms as possible. Record your observations. After two or three days, return your sample to the original habitat.
2. Write a short paper describing the organisms in your sample ecosystem and explaining their interactions.

Figure 15-19 Organisms living in intertidal zones have adaptations to survive in these changing environments.

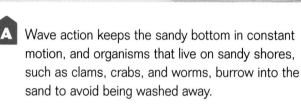

A Wave action keeps the sandy bottom in constant motion, and organisms that live on sandy shores, such as clams, crabs, and worms, burrow into the sand to avoid being washed away.

B Algae, mussels, barnacles, snails, and other organisms adapted for clinging to the rocks are typically found on rocky shores. These organisms must be able to tolerate the heavy force of breaking waves.

Open Ocean

Life abounds in the open ocean, where there is no land. The ocean can be divided into life zones based on the depth to which sunlight can penetrate the water. The lighted zone of the ocean is the upper 200 m or so. It is the home of the plankton that make up the foundation of the food chain in the open ocean. Below about 200 m, where sunlight cannot reach, is the dark zone of the ocean. Animals living in this region feed on material that floats down from the lighted zone, or they feed on each other.

Section Assessment

1. What are the similarities and differences between a lake and a stream?

2. What biotic or abiotic factor limits life on the floor of a tropical rain forest and the bottom of the deep ocean? Why?

3. **Think Critically:** Why do few plants grow in the waters of a swift-flowing mountain stream?

4. 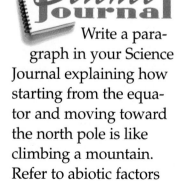 **Skill Builder**
   Comparing and Contrasting Compare and contrast the effects of (1) temperature in the tundra and desert and (2) sunlight in deep-lake and deep-ocean waters. If you need help, refer to Comparing and Contrasting in the **Skill Handbook** on page 684.

Science Journal Write a paragraph in your Science Journal explaining how starting from the equator and moving toward the north pole is like climbing a mountain. Refer to abiotic factors in your explanation.

FIELD GUIDE to BIOMES

FIELD ACTIVITY

Research the average monthly rainfall, high temperature, and low temperature for each month of the past year for the area where you live. Prepare a graph of data using the example below. Based on your findings, which biome graph most closely matches your data? What biome do you live in? What type of plant and animal life do you expect to find in your biome?

Have you ever wondered why you do not find polar bears in Florida or palm trees in Alaska? Organisms are limited to where they can live and survive due to temperature, amount of rainfall, and type of soil found in a region. A biome's boundaries are determined by climate more than anything else. Climate is a way of categorizing temperature extremes and yearly precipitation patterns. Use this field guide to identify some of the world's biomes and to determine which biome you live in.

Interpreting Land Biome Climates

The following graphs represent the climates of six different biomes. To read each biome graph, use the following information. Axis *A* shows the months of the year. Axis *B* shows the average amount of precipitation for each month. Axis *C* shows the average high and low temperature for each month.

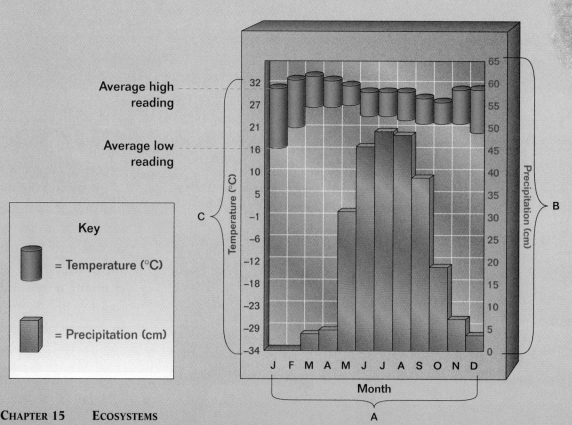

Average high reading

Average low reading

Key

= Temperature (°C)

= Precipitation (cm)

Temperature (°C)

Precipitation (cm)

C

B

Month

A

J F M A M J J A S O N D

Biome: Tundra

- Seasons: long, harsh winters; short summers; very little precipitation
- Plants: mosses, lichens, grasses, and sedges
- Animals: weasels, arctic foxes, snowshoe hares, snowy owls, and hawks

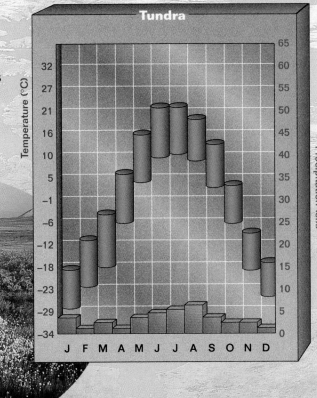

Biome: Taiga

- Seasons: cold, severe winters with much snow; short growing seasons
- Plants: conifers such as spruces, firs, and larches
- Animals: caribou, wolves, moose, bear, and summer birds

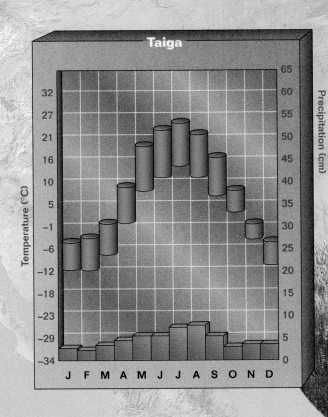

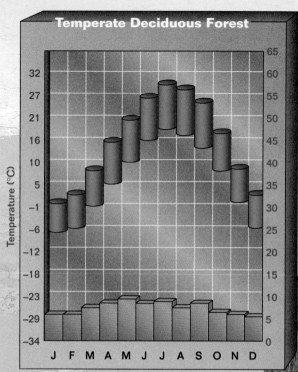

Temperate Deciduous Forest

Biome: Temperate Deciduous Forest

- Seasons: cold winters, hot summers, and moderate precipitation
- Plants: deciduous trees such as oak, hickory, and beech, which lose their leaves every autumn
- Animals: wolves, deer, bears, small mammals, and birds

Biome: Grassland

- Seasons: cold winters, hot summers with little precipitation
- Plants: grasses and a few trees
- Animals: grazing animals, wolves, prairie dogs, foxes, ferrets, snakes, lizards, and insects

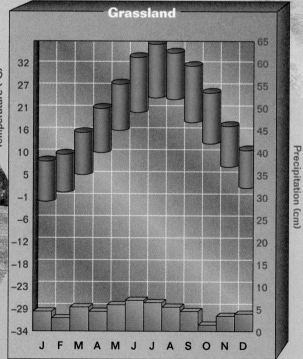

Grassland

Biome: Desert

- Seasons: warm to hot in daytime, cool in the evening, little precipitation
- Plants: cacti, yuccas, Joshua trees, and bunchgrasses
- Animals: small rodents, jackrabbits, birds of prey, and snakes

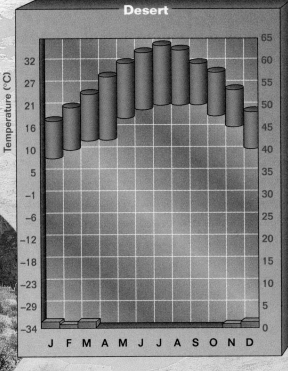

Desert

Biome: Tropical Rain Forest

- Seasons: hot all year with precipitation almost every day
- Plants: trees and orchids
- Animals: birds, reptiles, insects, monkeys, and sloths

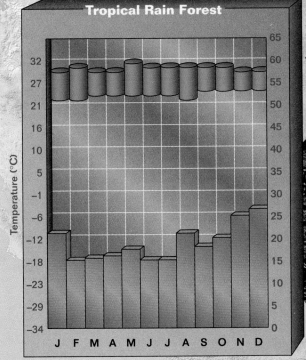

Tropical Rain Forest

For a **preview** of this chapter, study this Reviewing Main Ideas before you read the chapter. After you have studied this chapter, you can use the Reviewing Main Ideas to **review** the chapter.

The Glencoe MindJogger, Audiocassettes, and CD-ROM provide additional opportunities for review.

15-1 HOW ECOSYSTEMS CHANGE

The process of gradual change from one community of organisms to another is **ecological succession.** It involves changes in both abiotic and biotic factors. Succession can be divided into **primary** and **secondary succession. Pioneer communities** are the first to move into an environment, and **climax communities** are the final organisms to move in. *How can you explain that lawns usually do not go through succession?*

Section

15-2 LAND ENVIRONMENTS

Climate is the general weather pattern in an area. The factors that determine a region's climate are temperature and precipitation. Large geographic areas with similar climates and climax communities are biomes. The six major biomes are the **tundra, taiga, temperate deciduous forests, tropical rain forests, grasslands,** and **deserts.** *How does climate influence the type of biomes?*

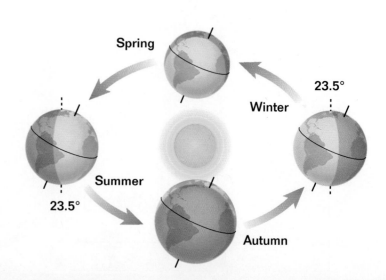

Spring

Summer

23.5°

Autumn

Winter

23.5°

Reading Check ☑

Diagram changes in an ecosystem as a series of causes and effects. You might start with this cause: an ecosystem's soil is thin and poor. What is a possible effect?

Section

15-3 WATER ENVIRONMENTS

The limiting factors in water environments include the amount of salt in the water, dissolved oxygen, water temperature, and sunlight. Freshwater ecosystems include rivers, streams, lakes, and ponds. Saltwater ecosystems include the oceans, seas, and a few inland lakes. An area where a river meets the ocean is called an **estuary.** All land on Earth is surrounded by ocean water. The **intertidal zone** is the portion of the shoreline that is covered with water at high tide and exposed to the air during low tide. The open ocean is divided into life zones based on the depth to which sunlight can penetrate the water. *Describe where estuaries form. How are they important?*

Using Vocabulary

a. biome
b. climax community
c. desert
d. ecological succession
e. estuary
f. grassland
g. intertidal zone
h. pioneer community
i. plankton
j. primary succession
k. secondary succession
l. taiga
m. temperate deciduous forest
n. tropical rain forest
o. tundra

Each of the following sentences is false. Make the sentence true by replacing the italicized word with a word from the list above.

1. *Primary succession* has occurred when one community of organisms replaces another.
2. *Plankton* are the first organisms to inhabit an area.
3. An *estuary* is a region with similar climate and climax communities.
4. A *biome* is an equatorial region that receives large amounts of rainfall.
5. A *tropical rain forest* is where freshwater mixes with salt water.

Checking Concepts

Choose the word or phrase that best answers the question.

6. What determines the climate of an area?
   A) plankton   C) limiting factors
   B) succession   D) abiotic factors

7. What are tundra and desert examples of?
   A) ecosystems   C) habitats
   B) biomes   D) communities

8. What is a treeless, cold, and dry biome called?
   A) taiga   C) desert
   B) tundra   D) grassland

9. Which is **NOT** a grassland?
   A) pampas   C) steppes
   B) veldts   D) estuaries

10. Mussels and barnacles have adapted to the wave action of what?
    A) sandy beach   C) open ocean
    B) rocky shore   D) estuary

11. Which biome contains the largest number of species?
    A) taiga
    B) temperate deciduous forest
    C) tropical rain forest
    D) grassland

12. What is the end result of succession?
    A) pioneer community
    B) limiting factor
    C) climax community
    D) permafrost

13. Which biome does **NOT** have trees as a climax community?
    A) tundra   C) tropical rain forest
    B) taiga   D) grassland

14. Which does **NOT** contain freshwater?
    A) lakes   C) rivers
    B) ponds   D) oceans

15. Which does **NOT** have flowing water?
    A) ponds   C) seashores
    B) rivers   D) streams

Thinking Critically

16. Would a soil sample from a temperate deciduous forest contain more or less humus than soil from a tropical rain forest? Explain.

17. A grassy meadow borders an oak-maple forest. Is one of these ecosystems undergoing succession? Why?

18. Describe how ecological succession eventually results in the layers of vegetation found in forests.

19. Why do many tropical rain forest plants make good houseplants?

Developing Skills

If you need help, refer to the **Skill Handbook.**

20. **Concept Mapping:** Make a concept map for water environments. Include these terms: *saltwater ecosystems, freshwater ecosystems, intertidal zone, lighted zone, dark zone, lake, pond, river, stream, flowing water,* and *standing water.*

21. **Making and Using Graphs:** Make a bar graph of the amount of rainfall per year in each biome.

Rainfall Amounts

Biome	Rainfall/Year
Deciduous forests	100 cm
Tropical rain forests	225 cm
Grasslands	50 cm
Deserts	20 cm

22. **Hypothesizing:** Make a hypothesis as to what would happen to succession in a pond if the pond owner removed all the cattails and reeds from around the pond edges every summer.

23. **Comparing and Contrasting:** Compare and contrast the adaptations of organisms living in swiftly flowing streams and organisms living in the rocky intertidal zones.

24. **Recognizing Cause and Effect:** Devastating fires, like the one in Yellowstone National Park in 1988, cause many changes to the land. Determine the effect of a fire to an area that has reached its climax community.

THE PRINCETON REVIEW

Test-Taking Tip

Where's the fire? Slow down! Go back over reading passages and double check your math. Remember that doing most of the questions and getting them right is always better than doing all the questions and getting lots of them wrong.

Test Practice

Use these questions to test your Science Proficiency.

1. What determines whether a land supports a deciduous forest or a grassland?
   A) temperature
   B) latitude
   C) precipitation
   D) length of growing season

2. What causes the vertical distribution of plants in a deep lake?
   A) color of the water
   B) depth that light can penetrate
   C) kind of plants in the lake
   D) kind of animals in the lake

3. How are primary succession and secondary succession similar?
   A) both begin where no soil is present
   B) both end in climax communities
   C) both begin with a pioneer community
   D) both develop where lava has cooled

4. What is the layer of vegetation that shades the ground below and provides homes for birds, insects, and mammals called?
   A) soil
   B) understory
   C) canopy
   D) forest floor

The Human Body

What's Happening Here?

A stream of bubbles (left) is the only sign of this swimmer's exertion. Yet, a sequence of millions of events must occur for her merely to stretch her arms over her head. Electric signals travel along nerve fibers (shown below, resembling a squiggle of toothpaste) at speeds up to 140 meters per second to instruct the adjacent skeletal muscle. Food is transformed into energy within her cells. Poised to begin her stroke, she uses the shoulder joint, which has the widest range of motion of the body's 68 joints. Her eyes and other sensory organs help her sense her position on her back in the water. In this unit, you will learn about the human body and how its many systems work together to accomplish even the simplest of feats.

interNET
CONNECTION

Explore the Glencoe Science Web Site at **www.glencoe.com/ sec/science/ca** to find out more about topics found in this unit.

Bones, Muscles, and Skin

Skills Preview

Skill Builders
- Outline
- Map Concepts

Activities
- Observe and Collect Data

MiniLabs
- Observe and Experiment

Reading Check ✔

Before reading this chapter, find out what these prefixes mean: *osteo-, peri-, im-,* and *epi-*. Identify and define several words that begin with each of these prefixes.

Explore Activity

Like this athlete on the left, you might have experienced tired muscles after completing some strenuous physical activity. You round the bend one last time at the school track, proud to have finished an unusually long run in good time. Your muscles feel as though they couldn't carry you another meter. You have improved your time, and you know your muscles are clenched. Try the following activity to measure muscles in different states.

Observe Muscle Size

1. Hang your straightened arm to your side in a relaxed position. Use a measuring tape to determine the size (circumference) of your upper arm when it is relaxed.

2. Flex your arm by bending it and making a fist. Measure your upper arm again.

3. How did the size of your upper arm change when you flexed your arm?

4. What happened to the muscle to cause this change? Did the muscle become larger? Or, did it shorten and bunch up?

Science **Journal**

Write a paragraph about what you think is happening to the muscles as you straighten and flex your arm.

16•1 The Skeletal System

A Living Framework

The skull and crossbones flag flying on a pirate ship has long been a symbol of death. You might think that bones are dead structures made of rocklike material. It's true that a skeleton's bones are no longer living, but the bones in your body are very much alive. Each bone is a living organ made of several different tissues. Cells in these bones take in nutrients and expend energy. They have the same requirements as your other cells.

Major Functions of Your Skeletal System

All the bones in your body make up your **skeletal system,** which is the framework of your body. The human skeletal system has five major functions. First, it gives shape and support to your body, like the framework of the building in **Figure 16-1.** Second, bones protect your internal organs: ribs surround the heart and lungs, and a skull encloses the brain. Third, major muscles are attached to bone. Muscles move bones. Fourth, blood cells are formed in the red marrow of some bones. Bone **marrow** is a soft tissue in the center of many bones. Finally, the skeleton is where major quantities of calcium and phosphorous compounds are stored for later use. Calcium and phosphorus make bone hard.

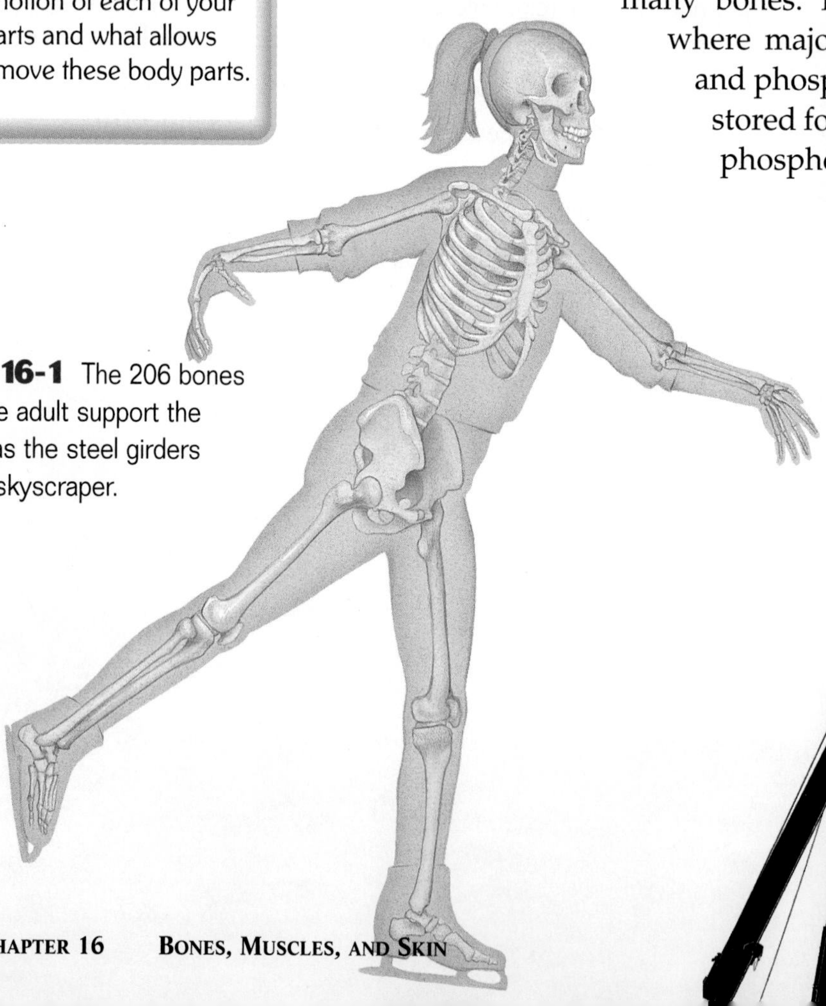

What You'll Learn

▶ The five major functions of the skeletal system
▶ How to compare and contrast movable and immovable joints

Vocabulary
skeletal system
marrow
periosteum
cartilage
joint
ligament
immovable joint
movable joint

Why It's Important

▶ You'll gain an understanding of the motion of each of your body parts and what allows you to move these body parts.

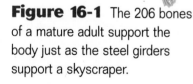

Figure 16-1 The 206 bones of a mature adult support the body just as the steel girders support a skyscraper.

Looking at Bone

As you study bones, you'll notice several characteristics. The differences in sizes and shapes are probably most obvious. Bones are frequently classified according to shape. Bone shapes, shown in **Figure 16-2,** are genetically controlled and also are modified by the work of muscles that are attached to them.

Bone Structure

Upon close examination, you'll find that a bone isn't all smooth. Bones have bumps, edges, round ends, rough spots, and many pits and holes. Muscles and ligaments attach to some of the bumps and pits. Blood vessels and nerves enter and leave through the holes. Many internal and external characteristics of bone are seen in the picture of the humerus shown in **Figure 16-3.**

As you can see in **Figure 16-3,** the surface of the bone is covered with a tough, tight-fitting membrane called the **periosteum** (per ee AHS tee um). Small blood vessels in the periosteum carry nutrients into the bone. Cells involved in the growth and repair of bone also are found here. Under the periosteum is compact bone, which is a hard, strong layer of bone. Compact bone contains bone cells, blood vessels, and a

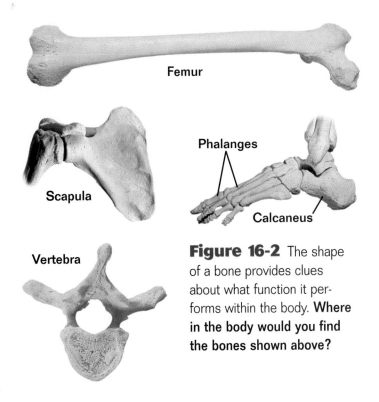

Figure 16-2 The shape of a bone provides clues about what function it performs within the body. **Where in the body would you find the bones shown above?**

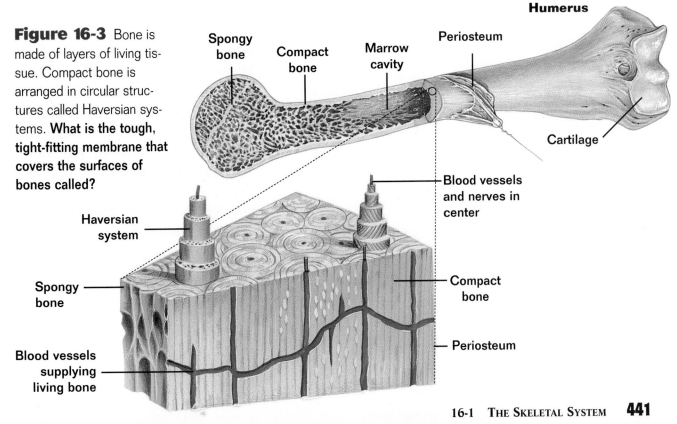

Figure 16-3 Bone is made of layers of living tissue. Compact bone is arranged in circular structures called Haversian systems. **What is the tough, tight-fitting membrane that covers the surfaces of bones called?**

protein base or scaffolding with deposits of calcium and phosphorus. The flexible protein base keeps bone from being too rigid and brittle or easily broken.

Spongy bone is found toward the ends of long bones like the humerus, as seen in **Figure 16-3.** Spongy bone is much less compact and has many small, open spaces that make bone lightweight. If all your bones were completely solid, you'd have a much greater mass. Long bones have large openings, or cavities. The cavities in the center of long bones and the spaces in spongy bone are filled with marrow. Marrow produces red blood cells at an incredible rate of more than 2 million cells per second. White blood cells also are produced in bone marrow, but in lesser amounts.

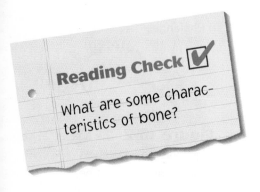

Reading Check ✔

What are some characteristics of bone?

Cartilage

Notice in **Figure 16-3** that the ends of the bone are covered with a thick, slippery, smooth layer of tissue called **cartilage.** Cartilage does not contain blood vessels or minerals. It is flexible and is important at joints, where it absorbs shock and makes movement easier by reducing friction. In some athletes and in older people, cartilage sometimes wears away, resulting in a condition called arthritis. People with arthritis feel pain when they move.

Figure 16-4 Bone formation starts with cartilage. Starting in the middle of the bone, the cartilage is replaced by hard bone. The solid tissue grows outward until the entire bone has hardened. **What type of bone cell builds up bone?**

Bone Development

Months before you were born, your skeleton was first made of cartilage. Gradually, the cartilage was broken down and replaced by bone-forming cells called osteoblasts (AHS tee oh blasts). These cells deposit calcium and phosphorus that make bone tissue hard. At birth, your skeleton was made up of more than 300 bones. As you developed, some bones fused, or grew together, so that now you have only 206 bones.

Healthy bone tissue is dynamic. **Figure 16-4** shows that it is always being formed and re-formed. Osteoblasts are bone cells that build up bone. A second type of bone cell, called an osteoclast, breaks down bone tissue in other areas. This is a normal process in a healthy person.

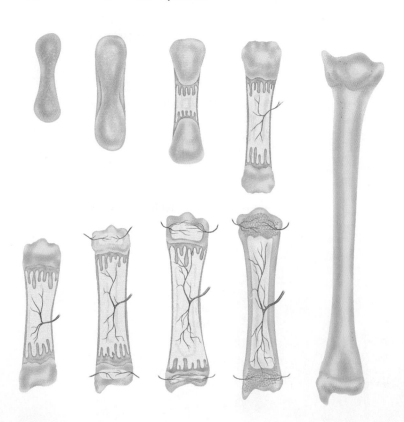

When osteoclasts break down bone, they release calcium and phosphorus into the bloodstream. This process keeps the calcium and phosphorus in your blood at about the same levels.

Where Bones Meet

Think of the different actions you performed this morning. You opened your mouth to yawn, chewed your breakfast, reached for a toothbrush, and stretched out your arm to turn the doorknob as you walked out the door. All these motions were possible because your skeleton has joints.

Any place where two or more bones meet is a **joint.** A joint keeps the bones far enough apart that they do not rub against each other as they move. At the same time, a joint holds the bones in place. A **ligament** is a tough band of tissue that holds bones together at joints. Many joints, such as your knee, are held together by more than one ligament.

*inter*NET
CONNECTION

Visit the Glencoe Science Web Site at **www.glencoe.com/ sec/science/ca** for more information about bone development.

Problem Solving

Shape Affects Strength

When designing a building, architects know that certain shapes provide more support. Look closely at the shapes of the Haversian systems found in the cross section of a bone. Does this system's design add to the overall strength of a bone? To find out, build two different support structures and see which is stronger.

Solve the Problem

1. Determine what geometric design is formed by Haversian systems.

2. Use two flat disks of modeling clay, plastic drinking straws, and two wooden boards to build the two different support structures.

3. Insert the straws, in random order, in one clay disk. Lay a board on top. Put pressure on the board until the structure collapses.

4. Repeat step 3, but arrange the straws in the same design as the Haversian systems.

Think Critically

1. Which structure withstood more pressure? How does this relate to the strength of your bones?

2. What geometric shape provides strength for your bones?

3. Compact bone is made of a series of Haversian systems. What impact do several of these structures have on the strength of the whole bone?

4. Suppose paper were wrapped around the straws in the second structure. What impact would this have on the strength of the structure? What part of an actual bone does the paper represent?

Types of Joints

Joints are classified as immovable or movable. Refer to **Figure 16-5** as you learn about different types of joints. An **immovable joint** allows little or no movement. The joints of the bones in your skull and pelvis are classified as immovable. A **movable joint** allows the body to make a wide range of movements. Gymnastics and working the controls of a video game require movable joints. There are several types of movable joints: pivot, ball-and-socket, hinge, and gliding. In a pivot joint, one bone rotates in a ring of another stationary bone. Turning your head is an example of a pivot movement. In a ball-and-socket joint, one bone has a rounded end that fits into a cuplike cavity on another bone. This provides a wider range of movement. Thus, your hips and shoulders can swing in almost any direction.

A third type of joint is a hinge joint. This joint has a back-and-forth movement like hinges on a door. Elbows, knees, and fingers have hinge joints. While hinge joints are less flexible than the ball-and-socket, they are more stable. They are not as easily dislocated, or put out of joint, as a ball-and-socket joint. A fourth type of joint is a gliding joint, where one part of a bone slides over another bone. Gliding joints move in a back-and-forth motion and are found in your

Figure 16-5 When a soccer player kicks a ball, several types of joints are in action. **Which type of joint permits the widest range of movement?**

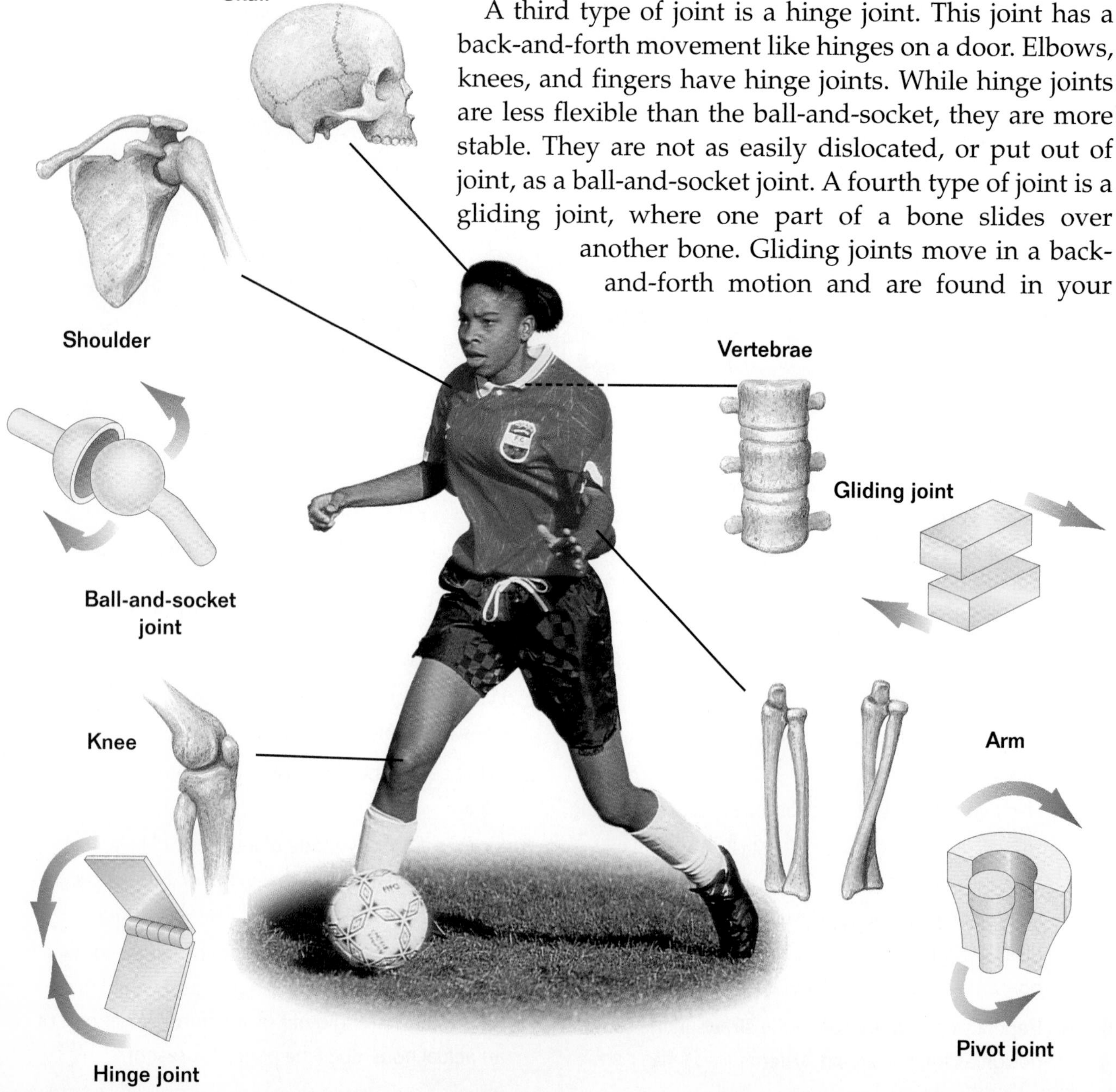

Skull

Shoulder

Ball-and-socket joint

Knee

Hinge joint

Vertebrae

Gliding joint

Arm

Pivot joint

wrists and ankles and between vertebrae. Gliding joints are the most frequently used joints in your body. You can't write a word, pick up a sock, or take a step without using a gliding joint.

Making a Smooth Move

Think about what happens when you rub two pieces of chalk together. Their surfaces begin to wear away. Without protection, your bones also wear away at the joints. Recall that cartilage is found at the ends of bones. Cartilage helps make joint movements easier. It reduces friction and allows the bones to slide over each other more easily. The joint also is lubricated by a fluid that comes from nearby capillaries. Pads of cartilage called disks are found between the vertebrae. Here, cartilage acts as a cushion and prevents injury to your spinal cord. **Figure 16-6** shows how a damaged hip joint can be replaced.

Your skeleton is a living framework in the form of bones. Bones not only support the body but also supply it with minerals and blood cells. Joints are places between bones that enable the framework to be flexible and to be more than just a storehouse for minerals.

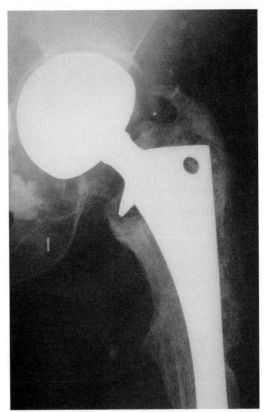

Figure 16-6 Some joints damaged by arthritis can be replaced with artificial joints. **How would this kind of surgery help a person stay active?**

Section Assessment

1. What are the five major functions of a skeleton?

2. Name and give an example of a movable joint and an immovable joint.

3. What are the functions of cartilage?

4. **Think Critically:** A thick band of bone forms around a healing broken bone. In time, the thickened band disappears. Explain how this extra bone can disappear.

5. **Skill Builder**
   Interpreting Scientific Illustrations You can learn a lot about bones when you see their internal structure. Do the **Chapter 16 Skill Activity** on page 721 to interpret sectional views of bones.

Using Computers

Database Use different references to find the names and shapes of the major bones in the human body. Classify the bones as long, short, flat, and irregular. Use your computer to make a database. Then, graph the different classifications of bones. If you need help, refer to page 697.

Observing Bones

Materials

- Beef bones (cut in half lengthwise)
- Chicken leg bone (cut in half lengthwise)
- Hand lens
- Paper towels

To move, animals must overcome the force of gravity. A skeleton aids in this movement. Land animals need skeletons that provide support against gravity. A flying animal needs a skeleton that provides support yet also allows it to overcome the pull of gravity and fly. Bones are adapted to the functions they perform. Find out if there is a difference between the bones of a land animal and those of a flying animal.

What You'll Investigate

What are the differences in the bone structures of land animals and flying animals?

Goals

- **Learn** the parts of a bone.
- **Observe** the differences between the bones of land animals and those of flying animals.

Procedure

1. Copy the data table and use it to **record** your observations.

2. **Obtain** a beef bone and a chicken leg bone that have been cut in half along the length from your teacher.

3. **Observe** the bones with a hand lens.

4. **Identify** the periosteum, compact bone, spongy bone, and the remains of any marrow that may be present.

5. In your Science Journal, **draw** a diagram of the bones and label their parts.

6. In the data table, **write** down any observations that you make.

7. Try to bend the bones to determine their flexibility.

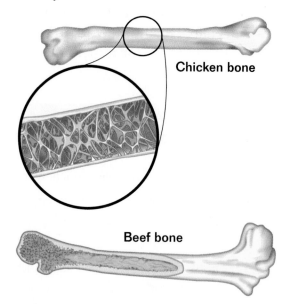

Chicken bone

Beef bone

Conclude and Apply

1. Do your data indicate any adaptations for flight in the bones?

2. **Infer** which type of bone would require more force to move? Explain why.

3. How do the structures of the two types of bone tissue aid in their function?

4. Which type of bone tissue is more flexible?

Bone Features		
Part	Description of Beef Bone	Description of Chicken Bone
Periosteum		
Compact bone		
Spongy bone		
Marrow		

The Muscular System

Moving the Human Body

A driver uses a road map to find out what highway connects two cities within a state. You can use the picture in **Figure 16-7** to find out which muscles connect some of the bones in your body. A **muscle** is an organ that can relax and contract to allow movement. This contraction, or pull, within the muscle provides the force to move your body parts. In the process, energy is used and work is done. Imagine how much energy is used by the more than 600 muscles in your body each day. No matter how still you might try to be, some muscles are always moving in your body. ☑

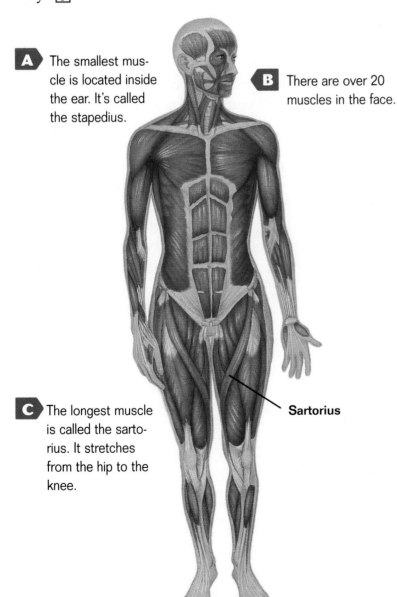

A The smallest muscle is located inside the ear. It's called the stapedius.

B There are over 20 muscles in the face.

C The longest muscle is called the sartorius. It stretches from the hip to the knee.

Sartorius

What You'll Learn

► The major function of muscles
► How to compare and contrast three types of muscles
► How muscle action results in movement of body parts

Vocabulary
muscle
voluntary muscle
involuntary muscle
skeletal muscle
tendon
smooth muscle
cardiac muscle

Why It's Important

► The muscular system is responsible for how you move and the production of heat in your body. Muscles also give your body its shape.

Reading Check ☑
What is a muscle?

Figure 16-7 Your muscles come in many shapes and sizes. Even simple movements require the coordinated use of several muscles. **Do you think most of your muscles are voluntary or involuntary? Why?**

Muscle Control

Muscles that you are able to control are called **voluntary muscles.** Your arm and leg muscles are voluntary. So are the muscles of your hands and face. You can choose to move them or not to move them. In contrast, **involuntary muscles** are muscles you can't consciously control. You don't have to decide to make these muscles work. They just go on working all day long, all your life. Blood gets pumped through blood vessels, and food is moved through your digestive system by the action of involuntary muscles. You can sleep at night without having to think about how to keep these muscles working.

**PHYSICS
INTEGRATION ➤**

Levers—Your Body's Simple Machines

Your skeletal system and muscular system work together to move your body like machine parts move. A machine is a device that makes work easier. A simple machine does work with only one movement. The action of muscles on bones and joints often works like one type of simple machine called a lever. A lever is defined as a rigid bar that moves on a fixed point, called a fulcrum. **Figure 16-8** shows a common lever being used to cut a piece of paper. In your body, bones are the bar, a joint is the fulcrum, and contraction and relaxation of muscles provide the effort force to move the body part.

Levers are classified into three types. Examples of the three types of levers are shown in **Figure 16-9.**

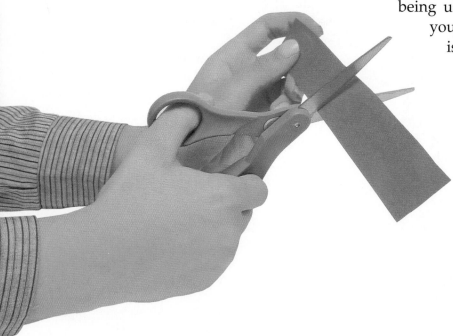

Figure 16-8 Scissors are used as a lever to cut paper. Your fingers push down on the handle of the scissors, providing the force. The blades of the scissors cut the paper. **What is the fulcrum in this lever?**

VISUALIZING
Human Body Levers

Figure 16-9 Your body uses all three types of levers for various movements.

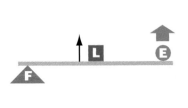

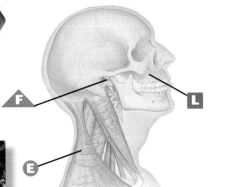

- **E** Effort force
- **L** Load
- **F** Fulcrum

A First-Class Lever

A first-class lever has the fulcrum between the load and the effort force. In your body, the skull pivots on the top vertebra as neck muscles raise your head up and down.

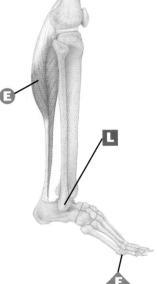

B Second-Class Lever

A second-class lever has the load between the fulcrum and the effort force. Raising the body up on your toes occurs when the leg muscles pull on the leg and foot.

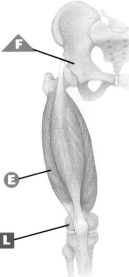

C Third-Class Lever

A third-class lever has the effort force between the fulcrum and the load. Your leg works like a lever when you move. The contracting muscle is the force that moves the bones of your leg at the knee.

16-2 THE MUSCULAR SYSTEM **449**

Types of Muscle Tissue

Three types of muscle tissue are found in your body: skeletal, smooth, and cardiac. **Skeletal muscles** are the muscles that move bones. They are attached to bones by thick bands of tissue called **tendons.** Skeletal muscles are the most numerous muscles in the body. When viewed under a microscope, skeletal muscle cells look striped, or striated (STRI ayt ud). You can see the striations in **Figure 16-10A.** Skeletal muscles are voluntary muscles, which means you can control their use. You choose when to walk or not to walk. Skeletal muscles tend to contract quickly and tire easily.

The remaining two types of muscles, shown in **Figure 16-10B** and **C,** are involuntary. **Smooth muscles** are nonstriated, involuntary muscles that move many of your internal organs. Your intestines, bladder, and blood vessels are made of one or more layers of smooth muscles. These muscles contract and relax slowly.

Figure 16-10 There are three types of muscle tissue—skeletal muscle, cardiac muscle, and smooth muscle.

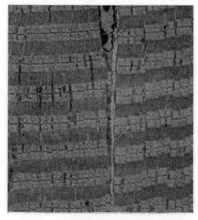

A Skeletal muscles move bones. The muscle tissue appears striped, or striated.

Magnification: 400×

B Cardiac muscle is found only in the heart. The muscle tissue has striations.

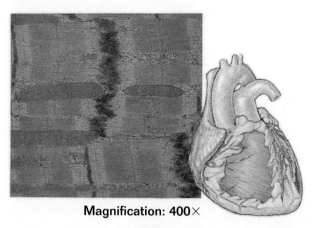

Magnification: 400×

C Smooth muscle is found in many of your internal organs, such as the intestines. The muscle tissue is nonstriated.

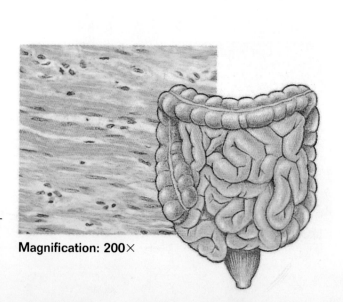

Magnification: 200×

Cardiac muscle is found only in the heart. Like smooth muscle, cardiac muscle also is involuntary. As you can see from **Figure 16-10B,** cardiac muscle has striations like skeletal muscle. Cardiac muscle contracts about 70 times per minute every day of your life.

Muscles at Work

Skeletal muscle movements are the result of pairs of muscles working together. When one muscle of a pair contracts, the other muscle relaxes, or returns to its original length. For example, when the muscles on the back of your upper leg contract, they pull your lower leg back and up. Muscles always pull. They never push. When you straighten your leg, the back muscles relax and the muscles on the front of your upper leg contract. Compare how the muscles of your legs work with how the muscles of your arms work, as shown in **Figure 16-11.**

Muscle Action and Energy

When you straightened your leg, your muscles used energy. Muscles use chemical energy in glucose. As the bonds in glucose break, chemical energy changes to mechanical energy and the muscle contracts.

Try at Home

Mini Lab

Observing Muscle Pairs at Work

Procedure

1. Find out which muscles are used to move your arm.
2. Stretch your arm out straight. Bring your hand to your shoulder, then down again.
3. Use the muscles shown in **Figure 16-11** to determine which skeletal muscles in your upper arm enable you to perform this action.

Analysis

1. How many muscles were involved in this action?
2. Which muscle contracted to bring the forearm closer to the shoulder?

Figure 16-11 When the biceps of the upper arm contract, the lower arm moves upward. When the triceps muscles on the back of the upper arm contract, the lower arm moves down. **What class of lever is shown here?**

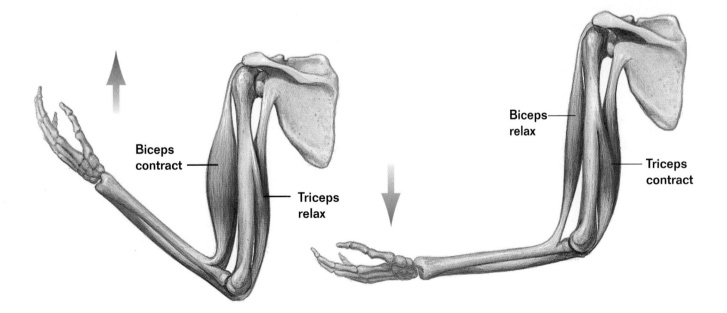

Biceps contract — Triceps relax

Biceps relax — Triceps contract

When the supply of glucose in a muscle is used up, the muscle becomes tired and needs to rest. During the resting period, the muscle is resupplied with glucose via the bloodstream. Muscles also produce thermal energy when they contract. The heat produced by muscle contraction helps to keep your body temperature constant.

Over a period of time, muscles can become larger or smaller, depending on whether or not they are used. You can see in **Figure 16-12** that skeletal muscles that do a lot of work, such as those in your writing hand or in the arms of a person on crutches, become larger and stronger. In contrast, if you watch TV all day, your muscles will become soft and flabby and will lack strength. Muscles that aren't exercised become smaller in size.

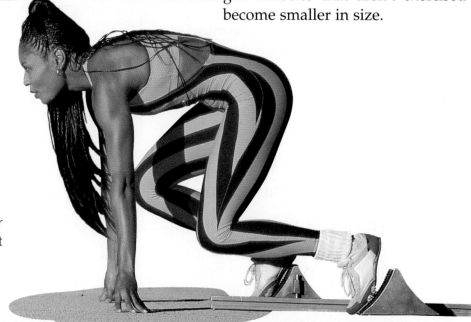

Figure 16-12 The number of muscles in an adult does not increase with exercise and body building. The cells simply get larger.

Section Assessment

1. What is the function of the muscular system?
2. Compare and contrast the three types of muscle.
3. What type of muscle tissue is found in your heart?
4. Describe how a muscle attaches to a bone.
5. **Think Critically:** What happens to your upper arm muscles when you bend your arm at the elbow?
6. **Skill Builder**
   Sequencing Sequence the activities that take place when you bend your leg at the knee. If you need help, refer to Sequencing in the **Skill Handbook** on page 678.

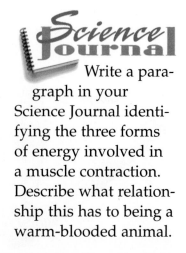

Science Journal
Write a paragraph in your Science Journal identifying the three forms of energy involved in a muscle contraction. Describe what relationship this has to being a warm-blooded animal.

Observing Muscle

Muscles can be identified by their appearance. In this activity, you will make observations to distinguish among the three types of muscle tissue.

What You'll Investigate

You will learn how to distinguish among the three types of muscle tissue. What do different types of muscles look like?

Goals

- **Examine** three types of muscle tissue.
- **Examine** muscle fibers.

Procedure

1. **Copy** the data table and use it to **record** your observations.

2. Using the microscope, first on low power and then on high power, **observe** prepared slides of three different types of muscle.

3. In the data table, **draw** each type of muscle that you **observe.**

4. **Obtain** a piece of cooked turkey leg from your teacher. Muscle tissue is made up of groups of cells held together in fibers, usually by a transparent covering called connective tissue.

5. **Place** the turkey leg in the dissecting pan. Use the forceps to remove the skin. **Locate** and **tease apart** the muscle fibers.

6. **Use** a hand lens to examine the muscle fibers and any connective tissue you see in the turkey leg.

7. **Draw** and **measure** five turkey leg fibers and describe the shape of these muscle fibers.

Materials

- Prepared slides of smooth, skeletal, and cardiac muscles
  - *detailed posters of the three types of muscle
- Microscope
- Cooked turkey leg or chicken leg
- Dissecting pan or cutting board
- Dissecting probes (2)
- Hand lens
  - *Alternate Materials

Muscle Types			
Types of Muscle	**Diagram of Muscle**	**Length of Fibers**	**Description of Fibers**
Skeletal			
Cardiac			
Smooth			

Conclude and Apply

1. How are muscle fibers arranged in the prepared slides?

2. **Predict** how the shape of a muscle fiber relates to its function.

3. Can you **conclude** that striations have anything to do with whether a muscle is voluntary or involuntary? **Explain.**

Frankenstein
by Mary Shelley

In this chapter, you've studied the structure of the bones and muscles of your own body. Many authors have written about the beauty and complexity of the human form. In the classic book *Frankenstein*, author Mary Shelley (inset) pays tribute to the science of anatomy in the story about a scientist, Dr. Frankenstein, who creates life from lifeless body parts. The 1931 movie, based on the book, portrayed the Frankenstein "monster" as seen in the photo, right. In the following excerpt from the book, Shelley details how Dr. Frankenstein slowly pieces together his creation.

As the minuteness of the parts formed a great hindrance to my speed, I resolved, contrary to my first intention, to make a being of a gigantic stature, that is to say, about eight feet in height, and proportionately large. After having formed this determination and having spent some months in successfully collecting and arranging my materials, I began....

His limbs were in proportion, and I had selected his features as beautiful. Beautiful!...His yellow skin scarcely covered the work of muscles and arteries beneath; his hair was of a lustrous black, and flowing; his teeth of a pearly whiteness; but these luxuriances only formed a more horrid contrast with his watery eyes that seemed almost of the same colour as the dun white sockets in which they were set, [with] his shriveled complexion and straight black lips.

Many people agree that the human body is a sort of living machine. The creation of the monster's face is like the story of a technician piecing together a complex machine. Mary Shelley's vivid descriptions have been compared to scientific writing. Which parts of this excerpt do you think would be similar to the writing of someone detailing the structure of the human body?

Science JOURNAL

Choose a living organism. Imagine you are a scientist trying to describe your organism to other scientists. Try to paint a vivid picture of the organism by describing its features in detail in your Science Journal.

Skin

The Body's Largest Organ

Your skin is the largest organ of your body. Much of the information you receive about your environment comes through your skin. You can think of your skin as your largest sense organ.

Skin Structures

Skin is made up of two layers of tissue, the epidermis and the dermis. You can see in **Figure 16-13** that the **epidermis** is the surface layer of your skin. The cells on the top of the epidermis are dead. Thousands of these cells rub off every time you take a shower, shake hands, blow your nose, or scratch your elbow. New cells are constantly produced at the bottom of the epidermis. These new cells are moved up and eventually replace the ones that are rubbed off. Cells in the epidermis produce the chemical melanin. **Melanin** (MEL uh nun) is a pigment that gives your skin color. The more melanin, the darker the color of the skin. Melanin increases when your skin is exposed to the ultraviolet rays of the sun. If someone has few melanin-producing cells, little color gets deposited. These people have less protection from the sun. They burn more easily and may develop skin cancer more easily. ☑

What **You'll Learn**

► The differences between the epidermis and dermis of the skin
► The functions of the skin
► How skin protects the body from disease and how it heals itself

Vocabulary
epidermis
melanin
dermis

Why **It's Important**

► Skin plays a vital role in protecting your body against injury and disease.

Reading Check ☑

What is melanin?

Figure 16-13 Hair, nails, and sweat and oil glands are all part of your body's largest organ. **What two layers of tissue make up your skin?**

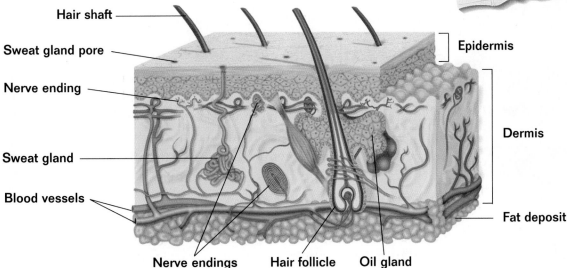

Hair shaft

Sweat gland pore

Nerve ending

Sweat gland

Blood vessels

Nerve endings

Hair follicle

Oil gland

Epidermis

Dermis

Fat deposit

The **dermis** is the layer of tissue under the epidermis. This layer is thicker than the epidermis and contains many blood vessels, nerves, and oil and sweat glands. Notice in **Figure 16-13** that fat cells are located under the dermis. This fatty tissue insulates the body. When a person gains too much weight, this is where much of the extra fat is deposited.

Functions of the Skin

Your skin is not only the largest organ of your body, it also carries out several major functions, including protection, sensory response, formation of vitamin D, regulation of body temperature, and the excretion of wastes. Of these functions, the most important is that skin forms a protective covering over the body. As a covering, it prevents both physical and chemical injury, as well as disease. Glands in the skin secrete fluids that damage or destroy some bacteria. Skin also prevents excess water loss from body tissues.

The skin also serves as a sensory organ. Specialized nerve cells in the skin detect and relay information about temperature, pressure, and pain. Some of the sensors are shown in **Figure 16-13.** Because of these sensors, you are able to detect the softness of a cat, the sharp point of a pin, or the heat of a frying pan.

A third vital function of skin is the formation of vitamin D. Vitamin D is essential for your good health because it helps your body to absorb calcium from the food you eat. Small amounts of this vitamin are produced in the epidermis in the presence of ultraviolet light from the sun.

Heat and Waste Exchange

Your skin plays an important role in helping to regulate your body temperature. Humans, unlike the fur-bearing animal in **Figure 16-14,** have very little hair to help them regulate body temperature. Hair is an adaptation that usually helps control body temperature. In humans, blood vessels in the skin can help release or hold heat. If the blood vessels expand or dilate, blood flow increases and heat is released. Less heat is released when the blood vessels constrict.

The dermis has about 3 million sweat glands. These glands also help regulate the body's temperature.

Figure 16-14 All animals must be able to control body temperature. Insulation of an animal's body occurs when the fur is raised. **What happens to fur when the animal's body temperature is high?**

When the blood vessels dilate, pores leading to the sweat glands in the skin open. Perspiration, or sweat, moves out onto the skin. Heat moves from inside the body to the sweat on the body's surface. The body then cools as the sweat evaporates. This system balances heat that has been produced by muscle contractions.

The fifth function of the skin is to excrete wastes. Sweat glands release water, salt, and a protein product called urea. If too much water and salt are released during periods of extreme heat or physical exertion, you might faint.

Injury to the Skin

Despite its daily dose of scratching, burning, ripping and exposure to harsh conditions, the skin still continues to produce new cells in its outer layer, the epidermis, and repair tears in its inner layer, the dermis. When an injury occurs in the skin, as shown in **Figure 16-15,** disease-causing organisms can enter the body rapidly. An infection may result.

However, if there is injury to large areas of the skin, such as burning or rubbing away of the epidermis, there are no longer any cells left that can divide to replace this lost layer. In severe cases of skin loss or damage, nerve endings and blood vessels in the dermis are exposed. Water is lost rapidly from the dermis and muscle tissues. Body tissues are exposed to bacteria and to potential infection, shock, and death.

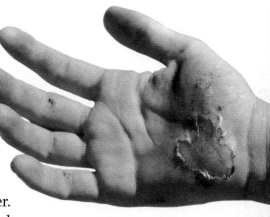

Figure 16-15 Injuries to your skin make it easier for bacteria and viruses to infect the body.

Section Assessment

1. Compare and contrast the epidermis and dermis.
2. List the five functions of skin.
3. How does skin help prevent disease in the body?
4. **Think Critically:** Why is a person who has been severely burned in danger of dying from loss of water?
5. **Skill Builder**
   Concept Mapping Make an events chain concept map to show how skin helps keep body temperature constant. If you need help, refer to Concept Mapping in the **Skill Handbook** on page 678.

Using Computers

Database Use references to research common skin lesions. Include warts, psoriasis, burns, acne, scrape wounds, insect bites, freckles, athlete's foot, and other lesions. Use your computer to make a database. Classify the lesions as flat, depressed, or elevated. If you need help, refer to page 697.

For a **preview** of this chapter, study this Reviewing Main Ideas before you read the chapter. After you have studied this chapter, you can use the Reviewing Main Ideas to **review** the chapter.

The Glencoe MindJogger, Audiocassettes, and CD-ROM provide additional opportunities for review.

16-1 BONES AND MUSCLES

Bodies have a great range of movement, from picking up a feather to kicking a soccer ball, because of coordinated activities of the bones and muscles. In addition, these organs give shape to bodies, which are wrapped with a remarkable membrane, the skin. *What two systems work together to allow body movement?*

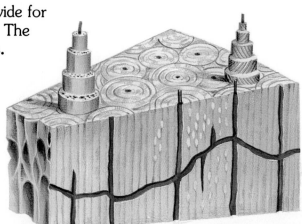

SKELETAL SYSTEM

Bones are complex, living structures that have a variety of functions. They protect other organs, give support, make blood cells, store minerals, and provide for muscle attachment that allows movement. The places where bones meet are called **joints.** Some joints are **immovable,** other joints can move slightly, and others can move a lot. Consider the difference between the movement of the toes and the movement of the wrist. *How do the shapes of bones often relate to their function?*

Reading Check ✓

• Review the levers in **Figure 16-9.** Then, identify another example that could have been used to illustrate each class of lever.

Section

16-2 MUSCLES

Muscles can only contract and relax to produce movement of bones and body parts. Muscles do not stretch. **Skeletal muscle** movements are voluntary and move bones. **Smooth muscle** movements are involuntary and control internal organs. **Cardiac muscles** control the involuntary contractions of the heart. *How are skeletal muscles attached to the bones they move?*

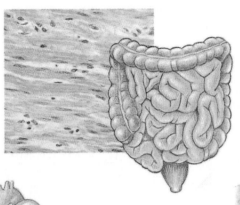

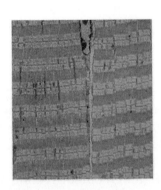

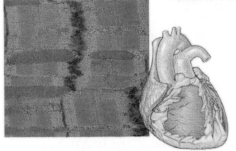

Section

16-3 SKIN

The skin is the largest organ of the body and is in direct contact with the environment. This body covering gives protection, helps retain moisture, aids in the formation of vitamin D, and assists in regulating the body's temperature. *How do sweat glands and blood vessels in the skin help the body maintain an even temperature?*

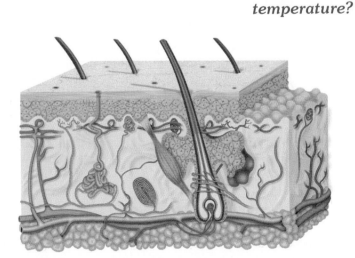

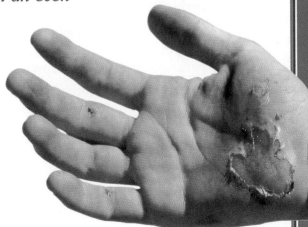

Using Vocabulary

a. cardiac muscle
b. cartilage
c. dermis
d. epidermis
e. immovable joint
f. involuntary muscle
g. joint
h. ligament
i. marrow
j. melanin
k. movable joint
l. muscle
m. periosteum
n. skeletal muscle
o. skeletal system
p. smooth muscle
q. tendon
r. voluntary muscle

Each phrase below describes a science term from the list. Write the term that matches the phrase describing it.

1. tough outer covering of bone
2. internal body framework
3. outer layer of skin
4. skin pigment
5. attaches muscle to bone

Checking Concepts

Choose the word or phrase that best answers the question.

6. Which of the following is the most solid form of bone?
   A) compact
   B) periosteum
   C) spongy
   D) marrow

7. Where are blood cells made?
   A) compact bone
   B) periosteum
   C) cartilage
   D) marrow

8. Where are minerals stored?
   A) bone
   B) skin
   C) muscle
   D) blood

9. What are the ends of bones covered with?
   A) cartilage
   B) tendons
   C) ligaments
   D) muscle

10. Where are immovable joints found?
    A) at the elbow
    B) at the neck
    C) in the wrist
    D) in the skull

11. What kind of joints are the knees and fingers?
    A) pivot
    B) hinge
    C) gliding
    D) ball-and-socket

12. Which vitamin is made in the skin?
    A) A
    B) B
    C) D
    D) K

13. Where are dead cells found?
    A) dermis
    B) marrow
    C) epidermis
    D) periosteum

14. What is a nutrient found in bone?
    A) iron
    B) calcium
    C) vitamin D
    D) vitamin K

15. What helps retain fluids in the body?
    A) bone
    B) muscle
    C) skin
    D) a joint

Thinking Critically

16. When might skin not be able to produce enough vitamin D?

17. What effects do sunblocks have on melanin?

18. What would lack of calcium do to bones?

19. Using a microscope, how could you distinguish among the three muscle types?

20. What function of skin in your lower lip changes when a dentist gives you novocaine for a filling in your bottom teeth? Why?

Developing Skills

If you need help, refer to the Skill Handbook.

21. **Observing and Inferring:** The joints in the skull of a newborn baby are flexible, whereas those of a 17 year old have grown together tightly. Infer why the infant's skull joints are flexible.

22. **Designing an Experiment:** Design an experiment to compare the heartbeat rates of athletes and nonathletes in your class.

23. **Hypothesizing:** Make a hypothesis about the distribution of sweat glands throughout the body. Are they evenly distributed?

24. **Concept Mapping:** Construct an events chain concept map to describe how a bone heals.

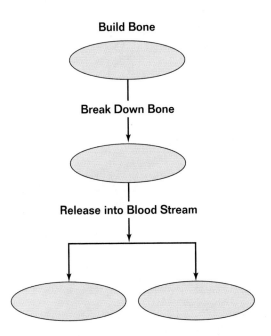

Build Bone

Break Down Bone

Release into Blood Stream

25. **Hypothesizing:** When exposed to direct sunlight, dark-colored hair absorbs more energy than light-colored hair. Given this information, make a hypothesis as to the most adaptive colors for desert animals.

Test-Taking Tip

Work Weak Muscles, Maintain Strong Ones It's sometimes difficult to focus on all the concepts needed for a test. So, ask yourself "What's my strongest area?" "What's my weakest area?" Focus most of your energy on your weak areas. But, also put in some upkeep time in your best areas.

Test Practice

Use these questions to test your Science Proficiency.

1. The skin has specialized sensory cells that detect and pass on information from the external environment to the body. To which group of stimuli can the skin respond?
   A) touch, temperature, time
   B) pressure, pain, sound
   C) pressure, temperature, pain
   D) hunger, odor, temperature

2. Cartilage is a specialized tissue that covers the ends of some bones. Which group of characteristics is correctly associated with this tissue?
   A) nerves and blood vessels
   B) muscles and tendons
   C) fat cells and blood vessels
   D) none of the above

3. The skeletal and muscular systems work together to move body parts like one of the simple machines called a lever. Which body movement is an example of a first-class lever?
   A) picking up an object with your hand
   B) raising the body up on your toes
   C) waving your hand up and down
   D) moving your head up and down

Chapter Preview

Skills Preview

Skill Builders
- Compare and Contrast
- Observe and Infer

Activities
- Experiment
- Collect Data

MiniLabs
- Measure in SI
- Make a Model

Reading Check ✓

As you skim this chapter, choose five illustrations. Without reading the captions, write what they tell you about nutrients or digestion.

Explore Activity

What does a paper fan have in common with your stomach? Both the fan and the wall of your stomach, as shown in the photograph, are made of folds. Because of the folds and its elastic wall, the stomach can expand to hold about 2 L of food or liquid. In the stomach, one part of the process that releases energy from food occurs. How long do you think it takes for the food to go through this process?

Model the Digestive Tract

1. Use index cards to make labels for all of the organs listed below. Each card should include the name of the structure, its length, and the time it takes for food to pass through that structure. Mouth (8 cm, 5–30 s), Pharynx and Esophagus (26 cm, 10 s), Stomach (16 cm, 2–3 h), Small Intestine (4.75 m, 3 h), and Large Intestine (1.25 m, 2 days).

2. Working with a partner, place a piece of masking tape 6.5 m long on the classroom floor.

3. Beginning at one end of the tape, measure off and mark the lengths for each section of the digestive tract. Place each label next to its proper section.

Science Journal

In your Science Journal, record what factors might alter the amount of time digestion takes. Suggest reasons why there is such variation in the time food spends in each of the structures.

17•1 Nutrition

Why do you eat?

WhatYou'll Learn

▶ The six classes of nutrients
▶ The importance of each type of nutrient
▶ The relationship between diet and health

Vocabulary

nutrient	fat
carbohydrate	vitamin
protein	mineral
amino acid	food group

WhyIt's Important

▶ Learning about nutrients will help you plan well-balanced meals and ensure good health.

What to have for breakfast? You may base your decision on taste and amount of time available. A better factor might be the nutritional value of the food you choose. A chocolate-iced donut might be tasty and quick to eat, but it provides few of the nutrients your body needs to carry out your morning activities. **Nutrients** (NEW tree unts) are substances in foods that provide energy and materials for cell development, growth, and repair, as shown in **Figure 17-1**.

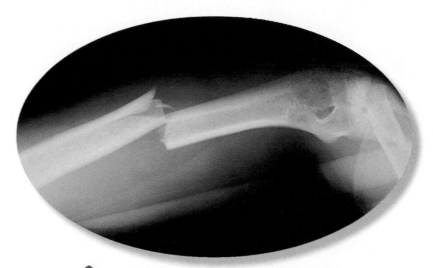

Figure 17-1 Just as a race car runs best with high-grade fuel, your body can best grow, maintain, and heal when you provide it with proper nutrients.

A To repair an injury, your body requires certain nutrients. **What nutrients do you think are needed to repair a broken bone?**

B Your body gets the nutrients it needs to grow from the food you eat.

Classes of Nutrients

Six kinds of nutrients are available in food: carbohydrates, proteins, fats, vitamins, minerals, and water. Carbohydrates, proteins, vitamins, and fats all contain carbon. Nutrients that contain carbon are called organic nutrients. In contrast, minerals and water are inorganic. These nutrients do not contain carbon. Foods containing carbohydrates, fats, and proteins are usually too complex to be absorbed right away by your body. These substances need to be broken down into simpler molecules before the body can use them. In contrast, minerals and water can be absorbed directly into your bloodstream. They don't require digestion or need to be broken down.

Carbohydrates

Study the panels on several boxes of cereal. You'll notice that the number of grams of carbohydrates found in a typical serving is usually higher than the amounts of the other nutrients. That means that the major nutrient in the cereal is in the form of carbohydrates. **Carbohydrates** (kar boh HI drayts) are the main sources of energy for your body. They contain carbon, hydrogen, and oxygen atoms. During cellular respiration, energy is released when molecules of carbohydrates break down in your cells.

CHEMISTRY
◄ INTEGRATION

Types of Carbohydrates

The three types of carbohydrates—sugar, starch, and cellulose—are shown in **Figure 17-2.** Sugars are simple carbohydrates. There are many types of sugars. You're probably most familiar with one called table sugar. Fruits, honey, and milk also are sources of sugar. Your cells use sugar in the form of glucose. Starch and cellulose are complex carbohydrates. Starch is in foods such as potatoes and those made from grains such as pasta. Cellulose occurs in plant cell walls.

VISUALIZING Carbohydrates

Glucose Molecule

Figure 17-2 Carbohydrates are found in three forms: sugar, starch, and cellulose. While all three are made of carbon, hydrogen, and oxygen, their molecules have different kinds of chemical bonds and structures.

A A simple sugar called glucose is the basic fuel that provides the energy to carry out life's processes.

Starch Molecule

B Starch is stored in plant cells. During the digestive process, your body breaks down the complex starch molecules into the simple sugar glucose.

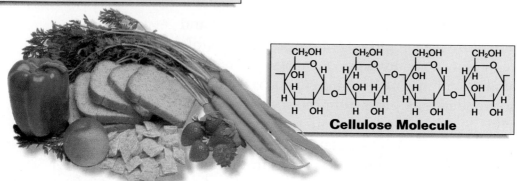

Cellulose Molecule

C Cellulose is a complex carbohydrate that is a major part of the strong cell walls in a plant. While your body cannot break down cellulose, its fiber is important in maintaining a smooth-running digestive system. Sources of cellulose include fresh fruits, vegetables, and grains.

Proteins

Your body uses proteins for growth. As enzymes, they affect the rate of chemical reactions in your body. They also are involved in the replacement and repair of body cells. **Proteins** are large molecules that contain carbon, hydrogen, oxygen, and nitrogen. A molecule of protein is made up of a large number of subunits, or building blocks, called **amino acids.** Some sources of proteins are shown in **Figure 17-3.**

Essential Amino Acids

Proteins are made according to directions supplied by genes that you inherit. Your body needs 20 different amino acids to be able to construct the proteins needed in your cells.

Twelve of these amino acids can be made in your cells. The eight remaining amino acids are called essential amino acids. Your body doesn't have genetic instructions to construct these. They must be supplied through the food you eat. Eggs, milk, and cheese contain all the essential amino acids. Beef, pork, fish, and chicken supply most of them. You might be surprised to know that whole grains such as wheat, rice, and soybeans supply many needed amino acids in addition to supplying carbohydrates. In order to get their full complement of amino acids, vegetarians need to eat a wide variety of vegetables that are good sources of protein.

Figure 17-3 Meats, poultry, eggs, fish, peas, beans, and nuts are all rich in protein. **Which of these protein-rich foods do you think a vegetarian would choose?**

Problem Solving

Analyzing a Menu

Blanca is a long-distance runner. She plans to run in the Boston Marathon on Patriot's Day. This world-famous race is more than 42 km long. Like most runners, Blanca is conscious about eating food that will provide the nutrients needed for endurance. The night before the marathon, Blanca must choose what to eat for dinner. She wants a meal with lots of carbohydrates.

Study the menu. Then, select a suitable dinner for Blanca. Keep in mind that Blanca will run in a marathon the next morning and needs foods rich in carbohydrates.

Think Critically

1. List all the foods on this menu that contain carbohydrates.

2. Why does Blanca want to eat carbohydrates before the marathon?

3. What foods on this menu are rich in complex carbohydrates?

Menu

APPETIZER

Potato Skins..............$4
Caesar Salad..............$3
Sizzling Rice Soup..............$2
Vegetable Salad..............$3

ENTREE

Baked Chicken..............$6
Shrimp with Lobster Sauce..............$8
Grilled Pork Chop..............$7
Grilled Steak..............$9

VEGETABLES

Mashed Potatoes..............$2
Baked Potato..............$2
Boiled Rice..............$2
Green Beans..............$2

DESSERT

Fresh Fruit..............$3
Ice Cream..............$2
Chocolate Cake..............$3

DRINKS

Milk..............$1
Water..............$1
Orange Juice..............$1

Fats

You may not think of fat as being a necessary part of your diet. In today's health-conscious society, the term *fat* has a negative meaning. However, **fats** are necessary because they provide energy and help your body absorb some vitamins. Fats are stored in your body in the form of fat tissue as shown in **Figure 17-4.** This tissue cushions your internal organs. You learned that carbohydrates are the main source of energy for your body. This is because people eat a large amount of carbohydrates. However, a gram of fat can release twice as much energy as a gram of carbohydrate. During this process, fat breaks down into smaller molecules called fatty acids and glycerol. Because fat is such a good storage unit for energy, any excess energy we eat is converted to fat until the body needs it. ☑

Reading Check ☑

Why are fats a necessary part of your diet?

Types of Fat

Fats are classified as unsaturated and saturated. Unsaturated fats, which come from plants, are usually liquid at room temperature. Corn, sunflower, and soybean oils are all unsaturated fats. Some unsaturated fats also are found in poultry, fish, and nuts. Saturated fats are found in red meats and are usually solid at room temperature. Saturated fats have been associated with high levels of blood cholesterol. Cholesterol occurs normally in all your cell membranes. However, too much of it in your diet causes excess fat deposits to form on the inside walls of blood vessels. The deposits cut off the blood supply to organs and increase blood pressure. Heart disease and strokes may result if blood is cut off to the heart and brain.

Figure 17-4 Fat is stored in certain cells in your body.

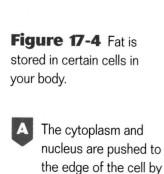

A The cytoplasm and nucleus are pushed to the edge of the cell by the fat deposits.

Nucleus   Cytoplasm

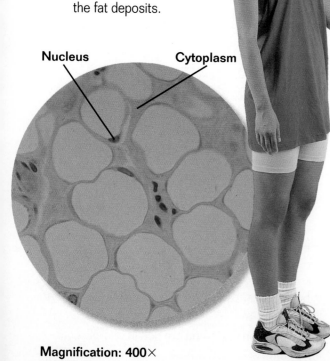

B The first source of energy for your body comes from the sugars in carbohydrates. When the supply of sugars runs low, your body begins to use the reservoir of energy stored in body fat.

Magnification: 400×

Vitamins

Those essential, organic nutrients needed in small quantities to help your body use other nutrients are called **vitamins.** For instance, bone cells need vitamin D to use calcium. In general, vitamins promote growth and regulate body functions.

Most foods, like those in **Figure 17-5,** supply some vitamins, but no one food has them all. Although some people feel that taking extra vitamins is helpful, eating a well-balanced diet is usually good enough to give your body all the vitamins it needs.

Vitamins are placed into the two groups. Some vitamins dissolve easily in water and are called water-soluble vitamins. Others dissolve only in fat and are called fat-soluble vitamins. While you get most vitamins from outside sources, your body makes vitamin D when your skin is exposed to sunlight. Some vitamin K is made with the help of bacteria that live in your large intestine. **Table 17-1** lists some major vitamins, their effects on your health, and some of the foods that provide them.

Figure 17-5 Fruits and vegetables are especially good sources of vitamins. However, to get all of the vitamins that your body needs, you must eat a balanced diet that includes a variety of foods.

Table 17-1

Vitamins		
Vitamin	**Body Function**	**Food Sources**
Water Soluble		
B (thiamine, riboflavin, niacin, B_6, B_{12})	growth, healthy nervous system, use of carbohydrates, red blood cell production	meat, eggs, milk, cereal grains, green vegetables
C	growth, healthy bones and teeth, wound recovery	citrus fruits, tomatoes, green leafy vegetables
Fat Soluble		
A	growth, good eyesight, healthy skin	green/yellow vegetables, liver and fish, liver oils, milk, yellow fruit
D	absorption of calcium and phosphorus by bones and teeth	milk, eggs, fish
E	formation of cell membranes	vegetable oils, eggs, grains
K	blood clotting, wound recovery	green leafy vegetables, egg yolks, tomatoes

Figure 17-6 Calcium and phosphorus are used in the formation and maintenance of your bones. In this x-ray, you can see that the lack of these minerals has caused the bones in this woman's spine to become less dense and, as a result, to bend.

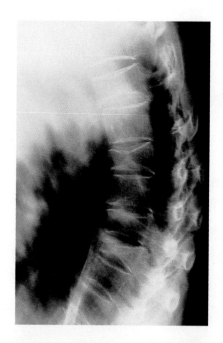

Minerals

Inorganic nutrients that regulate many chemical reactions in your body are **minerals.** They are chemical elements such as phosphorus. About 14 minerals are used by your body to build cells, take part in chemical reactions in cells, send nerve impulses throughout your body, and carry oxygen to body cells. Minerals used in the largest amounts in your body are presented in **Table 17-2.** Of the 14 minerals, calcium and phosphorus are used in the largest amounts for

Table 17-2

Minerals		
Mineral	Health Effect	Food Sources
Calcium	strong bones and teeth, blood clotting, muscle and nerve activity	milk, eggs, green leafy vegetables
Phosphorus	strong bones and teeth, muscle contraction, stores energy	cheese, meat, cereal
Potassium	balance of water in cells, nerve impulse conduction	bananas, potatoes, nuts, meat
Sodium	fluid balance in tissues, nerve impulse conduction	meat, milk, cheese, salt, beets, carrots
Iron	oxygen is transported in hemoglobin by red blood cells	raisins, beans, spinach, eggs
Iodine (trace)	thyroid activity, metabolic stimulation	seafood, iodized salt

a variety of body functions. One of these functions is the formation and maintenance of bone, as shown in **Figure 17-6**. Some minerals, called trace minerals, are required in only small amounts. Copper and iodine are usually listed as trace minerals.

Water

You don't have to be lost in a desert to know how important water is for your body. Next to oxygen, water is the most vital factor for survival. You could live a few weeks without food, but only a few days without water. Most of the nutrients you have studied in this chapter can't be used by your body unless they are carried in a solution. This means that they have to be dissolved in water. Water enables chemical reactions to take place in cells.

Water in Your Body

As shown in **Figure 17-7,** different organisms require different amounts of water to survive. The human body is about 60 percent water by weight. This water is found in and around cells and in plasma and lymph. Water removes waste products from cells. Wastes dissolved in water leave your body as urine or perspiration. To balance water lost each day, you need to drink about 2 L of liquids. But, don't think that you have to drink just water to

*inter*NET
CONNECTION

Visit the Glencoe Science Web Site at **www.glencoe.com/ sec/science/ca** for more information about water in the human body.

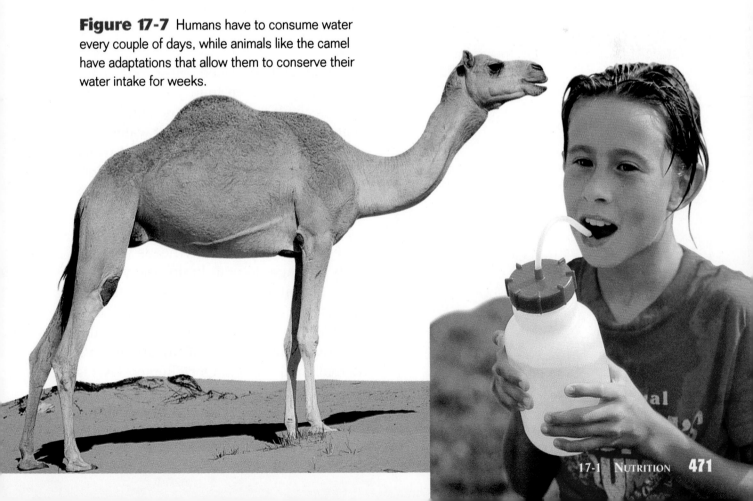

Figure 17-7 Humans have to consume water every couple of days, while animals like the camel have adaptations that allow them to conserve their water intake for weeks.

Table 17-3

Water Loss	
Through	Amount (mL/day)
Exhaled air	350
Feces	150
Skin (mostly as sweat)	500
Urine	1800

Figure 17-8 About two-thirds of your body water is located within your body cells. Water helps maintain the cells' shapes and sizes. During exercise, the water that is lost through perspiration and respiration must be replaced.

Mini Lab

Measuring the Water Content of Food

Procedure

1. Use a pan balance to find the mass of an empty 250-mL beaker.
2. Fill the beaker with sliced celery and find the mass of the filled beaker.
3. Estimate the amount of water you think is in the celery.
4. Put the celery on a flat tray. Leave the celery out to dry for one to two days.
5. Determine the mass of the celery.

Analysis

1. How much water was in the fresh celery?
2. Infer how much water might be in other fresh fruits and vegetables.

keep your cells supplied. Most foods have more water in them than you realize. An apple is about 80 percent water, and many meats are as much as 90 percent water.

Your body also loses about 2 L of water every day through excretion, perspiration, and respiration. **Table 17-3** shows how water is lost from the body. The body is equipped to maintain its fluid content, however. When your body needs water, it sends messages to your brain, and you feel thirsty. Drinking a glass of water usually restores the body's homeostasis (hoh mee oh STAY sus). Homeostasis is the regulation and maintenance of an organism's internal environment. Once homeostasis is restored, the signal to the brain stops.

Food Groups

Because no one food has every nutrient, you need to eat a variety of foods. Nutritionists have developed a simple system to help people plan meals that include all the nutrients required for good health.

Foods that contain the same nutrients belong to a **food group.** The food pyramid in **Figure 17-9** presents the basic food groups and serving suggestions. Eating a certain amount from each food group each day will supply your body with the nutrients it needs for energy and growth. Of course, most people eat foods in combined forms. Combinations of food contain ingredients from more than one food group and supply the same nutrients as the foods they contain. Chili and macaroni and cheese are both food group combinations.

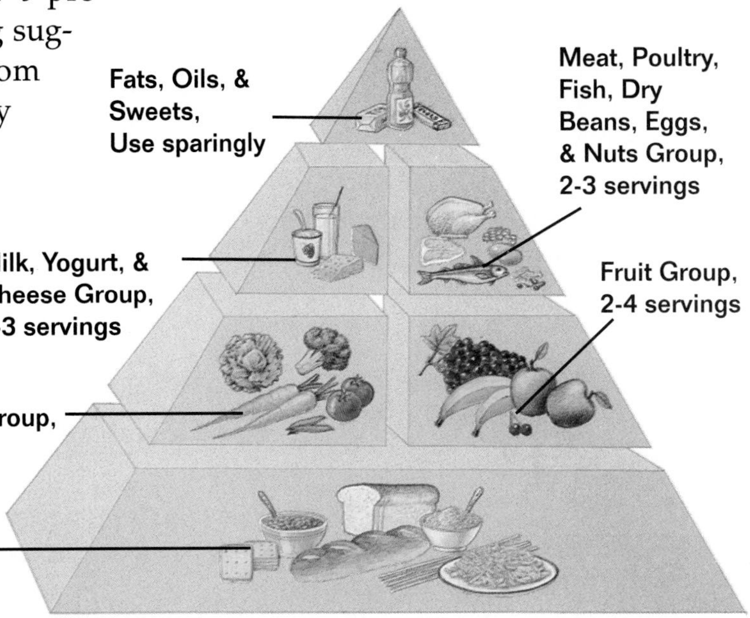

Figure 17-9 The pyramid shape reminds you that you should consume more servings from the bread and cereal group than from the meat and milk group. **Where should the least number of servings come from?**

Fats, Oils, & Sweets, Use sparingly

Meat, Poultry, Fish, Dry Beans, Eggs, & Nuts Group, 2-3 servings

Milk, Yogurt, & Cheese Group, 2-3 servings

Fruit Group, 2-4 servings

Vegetable Group, 3-5 servings

Bread, Cereal, Rice, & Pasta Group, 6-11 servings

Section Assessment

1. List six classes of nutrients and give one example of a food source for each.
2. Describe a major function of each class of nutrient.
3. Discuss the relationship between your diet and your health.
4. Explain the importance of water in the body.
5. **Think Critically:** What foods from each food group would provide a balanced breakfast? Explain why.
6. **Skill Builder**
   Interpreting Data Nutritional information can be found on the labels of most foods. Do the **Chapter 17 Skill Activity** on page 722 to interpret the information found on different food-product labels.

Using Computers

Spreadsheet Use the format of **Table 17-2** and prepare a spreadsheet for a data table of the minerals. Use reference books to gather information about the following minerals and add them to the table: sulfur, magnesium, copper, manganese, cobalt, and zinc. If you need help, refer to page 702.

Materials

- Indophenol solution
- Graduated cylinder (10 mL)
  *graduated container
- Glass-marking pencil
  *tape
- Test tubes (10)
  *paper cups
- Test-tube rack
- Dropper
- Dropping bottles (10)
- Test substances: water, orange juice, pineapple juice, apple juice, lemon juice, tomato juice, cranberry juice, carrot juice, lime juice, mixed vegetable juice
  *Alternate Materials

Identifying Vitamin C Content

Vitamin C is found in a variety of fruits and vegetables. In some plants, the concentration is high; in others, it is low. Try this activity to test various juices and find out which contains the most vitamin C.

What You'll Investigate

Which juices contain vitamin C?

Goals

- **Observe** differences in the vitamin C content of juices.

Test Results for Vitamin C

Test Tube	Juice	Prediction (yes or no)	Number of drops
1	water		
2	orange		
3	pineapple		
4	apple		
5	lemon		
6	tomato		
7	cranberry		
8	carrot		
9	lime		
10	vegetable		

Procedure

1. **Make** a data table like the example shown to record your observations.
2. **Label** the test tubes 1 through 10.
3. **Predict** which juices contain vitamin C. **Record** your predictions in your table.
4. **Measure** 5 mL of indophenol into each of the ten test tubes. **CAUTION:** *Wear your goggles and apron. Do not taste any of the juices.* Indophenol is a blue liquid that turns colorless when vitamin C is present. The more vitamin C in a juice, the less juice it takes to turn indophenol colorless.
5. **Add** 20 drops of water to test tube 1. **Record** your observations.
6. Begin adding orange juice, one drop at a time, to test tube 2.

7. **Record** the number of drops needed to turn indophenol colorless.
8. **Repeat** steps 6 and 7 to test the other juices.

Conclude and Apply

1. What is the purpose of testing water for the presence of vitamin C?
2. Does the amount of vitamin C vary in fruit juices?
3. Which juice did not contain vitamin C?

Antioxidants

In the 1990s, food scientists learned that certain nutrients help lower the risk of getting various diseases. Animal studies show that some cancers may be prevented—possibly cured—by chemicals in certain nutrients. Many of these cancer-combating chemicals are being tested to find out how they enhance cellular defenses against disease.

Fighting Cancer

Scientists are closely studying one group of chemicals called anti-oxidants. Antioxidants are subatances that prevent other chemicals from reacting with oxygen. Chemicals that enter the body from smoking or from pollutants in the air may cause cancer when combined with oxygen. By preventing this reaction, antioxidants help fight cancer. Antioxidants also can prevent cancer cells from repairing their damaged DNA. Carotenoids—the yellow-orange pigments in carrots (far left), squashes, and other produce—are antioxidants. Vitamin C (see crystals in inset) is also an antioxidant, as is vitamin D. Two unusually good sources of antioxidants are tomato sauce and green tea.

Taking antioxidants along with anticancer drugs used to fight cancer seems to make these drugs more effective. Some doctors are prescribing antioxidants for their patients, either to try to prevent cancer or to help fight an existing cancer condition. However, researchers have cautioned that the use of antioxidants may not successfully eliminate all the cancer cells in a person's body. Furthermore, some antioxidants can have harmful side effects, may disrupt certain bodily functions, and may interfere with the effectiveness of radiation treatments. But, if laboratory tests show conclusively that antioxidants are successful fighters of some diseases, you may one day hear, "Eat your antioxidants. They're good for you!"

interNET CONNECTION

Visit the Glencoe Science Web Site at **www.glencoe.com/ sec/science/ca** for more information about antioxidants. Look for the most recent information on how antioxidants are used to prevent disease.

Your Digestive System

What You'll Learn

▶ How to distinguish between mechanical and chemical digestion

▶ The organs of the digestive system and what takes place in each

▶ How homeostasis is maintained in digestion

Vocabulary
digestion
enzyme
mechanical digestion
chemical digestion
saliva
peristalsis
chyme
villi

Why It's Important

▶ Through the processes of the digestive system, the food you eat is made available to your cells.

Processing Food

Like other animals, you are a consumer. The energy you need for life comes from food sources outside yourself. To keep the cells in your body alive, you take in food every day. Food is processed in your body in four phases: ingestion, digestion, absorption, and elimination. Whether it is a fast-food burger or a home-cooked meal, all the food you eat is treated to the same processes in your body. As soon as it enters your mouth, or is ingested, food begins to be broken down. **Digestion** is the process that breaks down food into small molecules so they can move into the blood. From the

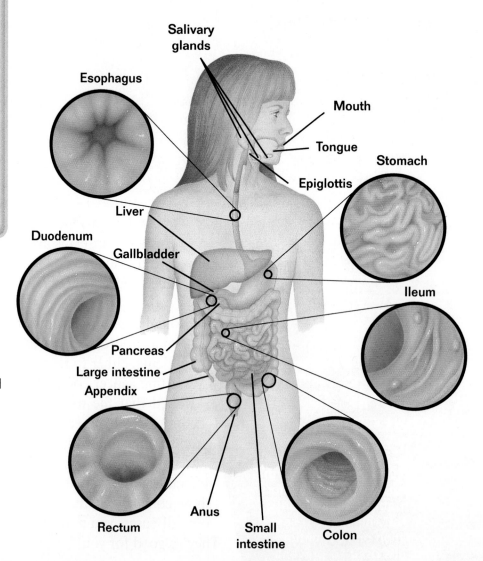

Figure 17-10 The human digestive system can be described as a tube divided into several specialized sections. If stretched out, an adult's digestive system is 6 m to 9 m long. **Where in the digestive tract does digestion begin?**

Salivary glands

Esophagus

Mouth

Tongue

Stomach

Epiglottis

Liver

Duodenum

Gallbladder

Ileum

Pancreas

Large intestine

Appendix

Anus

Rectum

Small intestine

Colon

blood, food molecules are transported across the cell membrane to be used by the cell. Molecules that aren't absorbed are eliminated and pass out of your body as wastes.

The major organs of your digestive tract—mouth, esophagus (ih SAH fuh guhs), stomach, small intestine, large intestine, rectum, and anus—are shown in **Figure 17-10.** Food passes through all of these organs. However, food doesn't pass through your liver, pancreas, or gallbladder. These three organs produce or store enzymes and chemicals that help break down food as it passes through the digestive tract.

Enzymes

Chemical digestion is possible only because of the actions of certain kinds of proteins. These proteins are called enzymes. **Enzymes** (EN zimez) are molecules that speed up the rate of chemical reactions in all living organisms. You can see in **Figure 17-11** that they speed up reactions without themselves being changed or used up. One way enzymes speed up reactions is by reducing the amount of energy necessary for a chemical reaction to begin. ☑

Enzymes in Digestion

A variety of enzymes are involved with the digestion of carbohydrates, proteins, and fats. Amylase (AM uh lays) is an enzyme produced by the salivary glands in the mouth. This enzyme begins the process of breaking down the complex carbohydrate into simpler sugars. In the stomach, the enzyme pepsin causes complex proteins to break down into less complex proteins. In the small intestine, a number of other enzymes continue the process by breaking down the proteins into amino acids. The pancreas, an organ on the back side of

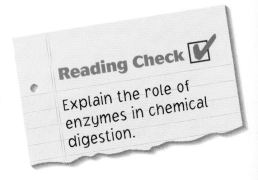
Reading Check ☑
Explain the role of enzymes in chemical digestion.

Figure 17-11 Enzymes speed up the rate of certain body reactions. During these reactions, the enzymes are not used up or changed in any way. **What happens to the enzyme after it is released?**

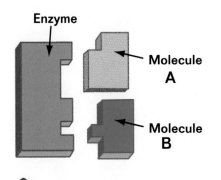

Enzyme

Molecule **A**

Molecule **B**

A The surface shape of an enzyme fits the shape of specific molecules that need to be broken down.

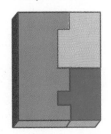

Temporary complex forms

B The enzyme and the molecules join and the reaction occurs.

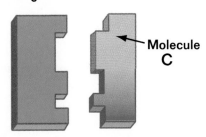

Enzyme is unchanged

Molecule **C**

C Following the reaction, the enzyme and the molecule separate. The enzyme is not changed by the reaction. The resulting new molecule has a new chemical structure.

the stomach, secretes several enzymes through a tube into the small intestine. Some continue the process of starch breakdown that started in the mouth. The resulting sugars are turned into glucose and used by the body's cells. Other enzymes are involved in the breakdown of fats.

Other Enzyme Actions

Enzyme reactions are not only involved in the digestive process. Enzymes also are responsible for building your body. They are involved in the energy production activities of muscle and nerve cells. They also are involved in the blood-clotting process. Without enzymes, the chemical reactions of your body would not happen. You would not exist.

Where and How Digestion Occurs

Digestion is both mechanical and chemical. **Mechanical digestion** takes place when food is chewed and mixed in the mouth and churned in your stomach. **Chemical digestion** breaks down large molecules of food into different, smaller molecules that can be absorbed by cells. Chemical digestion takes place in your mouth, stomach, and small intestine. Some digestive processes are both physical and chemical such as when bile acts on food.

Figure 17-12 About 1.5 L of saliva are produced each day by salivary glands in your mouth. **What happens in your mouth when you think about a food you like?**

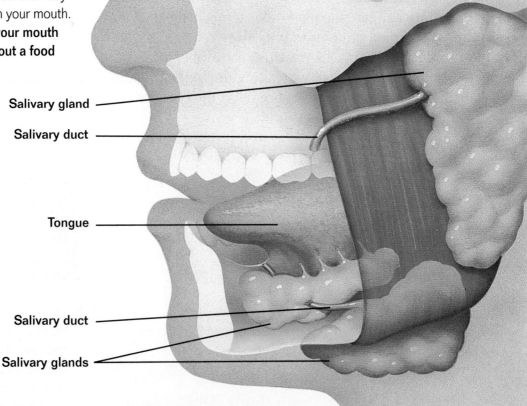

Salivary gland

Salivary duct

Tongue

Salivary duct

Salivary glands

In Your Mouth

Mechanical digestion begins in your mouth. There, your tongue and teeth break food up into small pieces. Humans are adapted with several kinds of teeth for cutting, grinding, tearing, and crushing.

Some chemical digestion also starts in your mouth. As you chew, your tongue moves food around and mixes it with a watery substance called saliva. Saliva is produced by three sets of glands near your mouth that are shown in **Figure 17-12. Saliva** (suh LI vuh) is made up mostly of water, but it also contains mucus and the enzyme salivary amylase. You learned that salivary amylase starts the breakdown of starch to sugar. Food that is mixed with saliva becomes a soft mass. The food mass is moved to the back of your tongue where it is swallowed and passes into your esophagus. Now the process of ingestion is complete, and the process of digestion has begun.

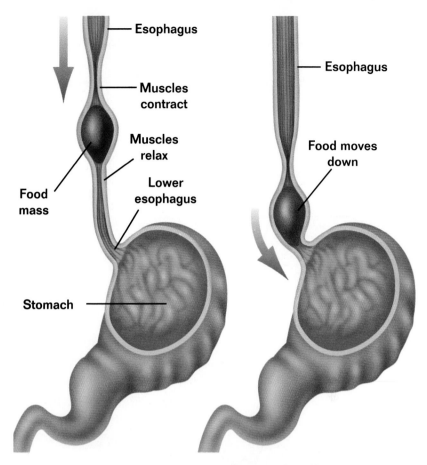

Figure 17-13 During peristalsis, muscles behind the food contract and push the food forward. Muscles in front of the food relax.

Passing Through the Esophagus

Your esophagus is a muscular tube about 25 cm long. Through it, food passes to your stomach in about 4 s to 10 s. No digestion takes place in the esophagus. Smooth muscles in the walls of the esophagus move food downward by a squeezing action. These waves, or contractions, called **peristalsis** (per uh STAHL sus), move food along throughout the digestive system. **Figure 17-13** shows how peristalsis works.

In Your Stomach

The stomach, shown in **Figure 17-13,** is a muscular bag. When empty, it is somewhat sausage shaped, with folds on the inside. As food enters from the esophagus, the stomach expands, and the folds smooth out. Both mechanical and chemical digestion take place in the stomach. Mechanically, food is mixed by the muscular walls of the stomach and by peristalsis. Food also is mixed with strong digestive juices,

PHYSICS
INTEGRATION

Surface Area
Besides mixing food and saliva, chewing food breaks it up into smaller pieces. This gives the food a larger surface area, exposing it to more digestive enzymes. Compare the surface area of two toy blocks when they are separate and when they are put together.

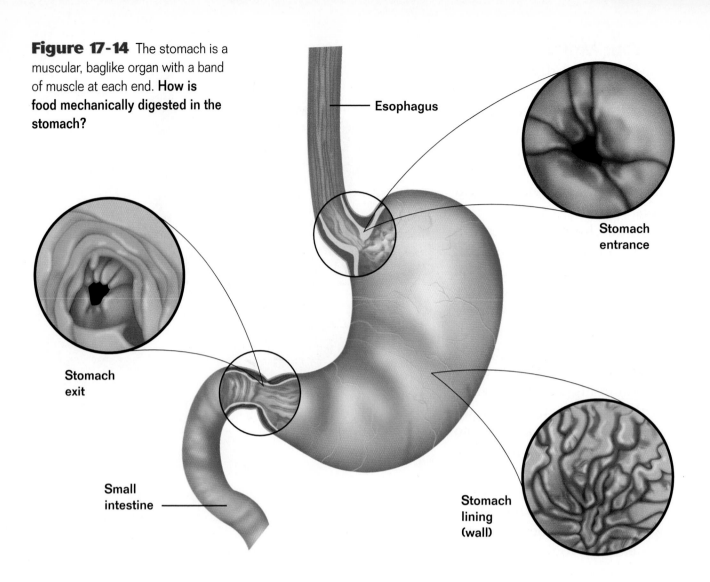

Figure 17-14 The stomach is a muscular, baglike organ with a band of muscle at each end. **How is food mechanically digested in the stomach?**

Esophagus

Stomach entrance

Stomach exit

Small intestine

Stomach lining (wall)

interNET

C O N N E C T I O N

Visit the Glencoe Science Web Site at **www.glencoe.com/ sec/science/ca** for more information about the stomach's role in digestion.

which include hydrochloric acid and enzymes. The acid is made by cells in the walls of the stomach. The stomach, shown in **Figure 17-14,** also produces a mucus that lubricates the food, making it more slick. The mucus protects the stomach from the strong digestive juices. Food moves through your stomach in about four hours. At the end of this time, the food has been changed to a thin, watery liquid called **chyme** (KIME). Little by little, chyme moves out of your stomach and into your small intestine.

In Your Small Intestine

Your small intestine may be small in diameter, but it is 4 m to 7 m in length. As chyme leaves your stomach, it enters the first part of your small intestine, called the duodenum (doo AUD un um). The major portion of all digestion takes place in your duodenum. Digestive juices from the liver and pancreas are added to the mixture. Your liver, shown in **Figure 17-15,** produces a greenish fluid called bile. Bile is stored in a small sac called the gallbladder. The acid from the stomach makes large fat particles float to the top of the liquid. Bile physically breaks up these particles into smaller pieces, the way detergent acts on grease on dishes. This process is called emulsification (ih mul suh fuh KAY shun). Although the bile physically breaks apart the fat into smaller droplets, the fat molecules are not changed chemically. Chemical digestion of carbohydrates, proteins, and fats occurs when the digestive juices from the pancreas are added.

You learned that the pancreas produces enzymes that help break down carbohydrates, fats, and proteins. Your pancreas also makes insulin. Insulin is a hormone that allows glucose to pass from the bloodstream into your body's cells. Without a supply of glucose, your body's cells must use proteins and fats for energy.

In addition to insulin, the pancreas produces another solution. This solution contains bicarbonate. Bicarbonate helps neutralize the stomach acid that is mixed with chyme.

Mini Lab

Determining How Fats Are Emulsified

Procedure

1. Fill two glasses with warm water. Add a large spoonful of cooking oil to each glass.
2. Add a small spoonful of liquid dish-washing detergent to one glass. Stir both glasses.

Analysis

1. Compare what happens to the oil in each glass.
2. How does emulsification change the surface area of the oil drops?
3. How does emulsification speed up digestion?
4. Where in the digestive system does emulsification take place?
5. What is the emulsifier in the digestive system?

Reading Check ✓

What digestive process occurs in the duodenum?

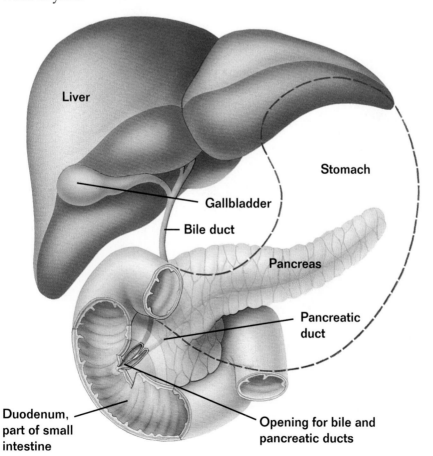

Figure 17-15 The liver, gallbladder, and pancreas are at the beginning of the small intestine. **If your gallbladder had to be removed, what nutrient would your doctor advise you to eat less of?**

Surface Area of the Small Intestine

Look at the wall of the small intestine in **Figure 17-16.** The walls of your small intestine are not smooth like the inside of a garden hose. Rather, they have many ridges and folds. These folds are covered with tiny, fingerlike projections called **villi.** Villi make the surface of the small intestine greater so that food has more places to be absorbed.

Food Absorption

After the chyme leaves the duodenum, it has become a soup of molecules that is ready to be absorbed through the cells on the surface of the villi. Peristalsis continues to move and mix the chyme. In addition, the villi themselves move and are bathed in the soupy liquid. Molecules of nutrients pass by diffusion, osmosis, or active transport into blood vessels in each villus. From there, blood transports the nutrients to all the cells of the body. Peristalsis continues to force the remaining materials that have not been digested or absorbed slowly into the large intestine.

Figure 17-16 Hundreds of thousands of densely packed villi give the impression of a velvet cloth surface. If the surface area of your villi could be stretched out, it would cover an area the size of a baseball diamond. **What would happen to a person's weight if the number of villi were drastically reduced? Why?**

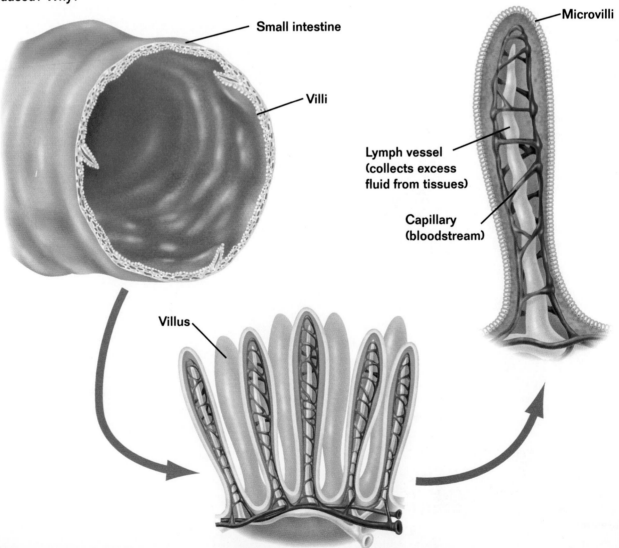

Small intestine

Villi

Microvilli

Lymph vessel (collects excess fluid from tissues)

Capillary (bloodstream)

Villus

In Your Large Intestine

As chyme enters the large intestine, it is still a thin, watery mixture. The main job of the large intestine, shown in **Figure 17-17,** is to absorb this water from the undigested mass. In doing so, large amounts of water are returned to the body, and homeostasis is maintained. Peristalsis slows down somewhat in the large intestine. As a result, chyme may stay in the large intestine for as long as three days. After the excess water is absorbed, the remaining undigested materials become more solid.

The Role of Bacteria

Bacteria that live in your large intestine feed on undigested materials like cellulose. This is a symbiotic relationship. The bacteria feed on cellulose, and in return they produce several vitamins that you need. Muscles in the rectum and anus control the release of solidified wastes from the body in the form of feces.

Food is processed in your digestive system for the purpose of supplying your body with raw materials for metabolism. These raw materials are in the form of nutrients. What is not digested is eliminated.

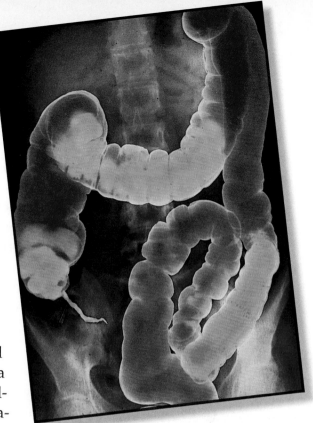

Figure 17-17 The large, twisting tube in this X ray is the large intestine. **What do you think the thinner tube connected to the left end of the intestine is?**

Section Assessment

1. Compare mechanical and chemical digestion.
2. Name, in order, the organs through which food passes as it moves through the digestive system.
3. How do activities in the large intestine help maintain homeostasis?
4. **Think Critically:** Crackers contain starch. Explain why a cracker held in your mouth for five minutes begins to taste sweet.
5. **Skill Builder**
   Observing and Inferring What would happen to food if the pancreas did not secrete its juices into the small intestine? If you need help, refer to Observing and Inferring in the **Skill Handbook** on page 684.

Science Journal Write a paragraph in your Science Journal explaining what would happen to the mechanical and chemical digestion process of foods if a person had a major portion of the stomach removed due to a disease.

Protein Digestion

Possible Materials

- Test tubes with gelled, unflavored gelatin (3)
- Dropper
- Test-tube rack
- Pepsin powder
- Glass-marking pen
- Cold water
- Dilute hydrochloric acid
- Beaker
- Watch or clock

You learned that proteins are large, complex, organic compounds necessary for living things to carry out their life processes. To be useful for cell functions, proteins must be broken down into their individual amino acids. The process of chemically breaking apart protein molecules involves several different factors, one of which is the presence of the enzyme pepsin in your stomach.

Recognize the Problem

Under what conditions will the enzyme pepsin begin the digestion of protein?

Form a Hypothesis

Formulate a hypothesis about what conditions are necessary for protein digestion to occur. When making your hypothesis, consider the various contents of the digestive juices that are found in your stomach.

Goals

- **Design** an experiment that tests the effect of a variable, such as the presence or absence of acid, on the activity of the enzyme pepsin.
- **Observe** the effects of pepsin on gelatin.

Safety Precautions

Always use care when working with acid and wear goggles and an apron. Avoid contact with skin and eyes. Wash your hands thoroughly after pouring the acid.

Test Your Hypothesis

Plan

1. **Decide** how your group will test your hypothesis.

2. Your teacher will supply you with three test tubes containing gelled, unflavored gelatin. Pepsin powder will liquefy the gelatin if the enzyme is active.

3. As a group, list the steps you will need to take to test your hypothesis. Consider the following factors as you plan your experiment. Based on information provided by your teacher, how will you use the pepsin and the acid? How often will you make observations?

Be specific, describing exactly what you will do at each step.

4. **List** your materials.

5. **Prepare** a data table and **record** it in your Science Journal so that it is ready to use as your group collects data.

6. **Read** over your entire experiment to make sure that all steps are in logical order.

7. **Identify** any constants, variables, and controls of the experiment.

Do

1. Make sure your teacher approves your plan before you proceed.

2. **Carry** out the experiment as planned.

3. While the experiment is going on, **write** down any observations that you make and complete the data table in your Science Journal.

Analyze Your Data

1. **Compare** your results with those of other groups.

2. Did you **observe** a difference in the test tubes?

3. **Identify** the constants in this experiment.

Draw Conclusions

1. Did the acid have any effect on the activity of the pepsin? How does this relate to the activity of this enzyme in the stomach?

2. **Predict** the effects of the pepsin on the gelatin if you increased or

decreased the concentration of the acid.

3. Is time a factor in the effectiveness of the pepsin on the gelatin? **Explain.**

For a **preview** of this chapter, study this Reviewing Main Ideas before you read the chapter. After you have studied this chapter, you can use the Reviewing Main Ideas to **review** the chapter.

The Glencoe MindJogger, Audiocassettes, and CD-ROM provide additional opportunities for review.

Section 17-1 NUTRIENTS

All foods can be grouped into six kinds of **nutrients: carbohydrates, fats, proteins, minerals, vitamins,** and water. Nutrients are the parts of food your body can use. Each kind of nutrient has a function in maintaining the health of the body. *How can your diet affect your health?*

FUNCTIONS OF NUTRIENTS

Carbohydrates provide energy. **Proteins** are needed for growth and repair. **Fats** store energy and cushion organs. **Vitamins** and **minerals** regulate body functions. Water is used for a variety of homeostatic functions. To keep your body strong and healthy, you must eat a balanced diet. A balanced diet contains food from the five **food groups.** *How can an apple provide energy?*

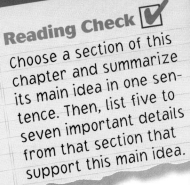

Reading Check ☑

Choose a section of this chapter and summarize its main idea in one sentence. Then, list five to seven important details from that section that support this main idea.

Section 17-2 THE DIGESTIVE SYSTEM

The digestive system breaks down food mechanically by chewing and churning, and chemically with the help of enzymes. Food passes into the mouth and then through the esophagus. A wavelike motion called **peristalsis** pushes the food downward toward the stomach. In the stomach, gastric juices and **enzymes** break down some of the food. As food enters the small intestine, the digestive process continues. Bile produced by the liver helps emulsify fat. The pancreas also produces enzymes that help digest the food in the small intestine. The large intestine absorbs water, and waste is eliminated through the anus. *Where does mechanical digestion occur?*

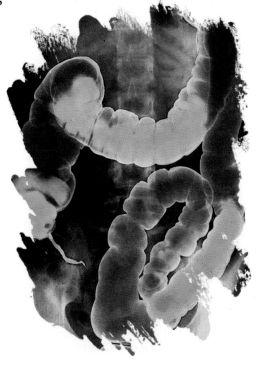

ABSORPTION OF FOOD

Nutrients are absorbed through the **villi** into the bloodstream in the small intestine. Water is absorbed in the large intestine. Bacteria that live in your large intestine produce several vitamins that are absorbed into the bloodstream at this stage. Undigested food or feces is eliminated from the body through the anus. *How do the useful substances from the nutrients reach the cells?*

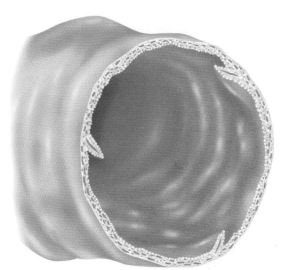

Chapter 17 Assessment

Using Vocabulary

a. amino acid
b. carbohydrate
c. chemical digestion
d. chyme
e. digestion
f. enzyme
g. fat
h. food group
i. mechanical digestion
j. mineral
k. nutrient
l. peristalsis
m. protein
n. saliva
o. villi
p. vitamin

Each phrase below describes a science term from the list. Write the term that matches the phrase describing it.

1. muscular contractions that move food
2. enzyme-containing fluid in the mouth
3. fingerlike projections in small intestine
4. subunit of protein
5. liquid product that is the result of digestion

Checking Concepts

Choose the word or phrase that best answers the question.

6. Where does most digestion occur?
   A) duodenum   C) liver
   B) stomach   D) large intestine

7. Which organ makes bile?
   A) gallbladder   C) stomach
   B) liver   D) small intestine

8. In which organ is water absorbed?
   A) liver   C) esophagus
   B) small intestine D) large intestine

9. Which organ does food **NOT** pass through?
   A) mouth   C) small intestine
   B) stomach   D) liver

10. What is produced by bacteria in the large intestine?
    A) fats   C) vitamins
    B) minerals   D) proteins

11. Which vitamin is not used for growth?
    A) A   C) C
    B) B   D) K

12. Where is hydrochloric acid added to the food mass?
    A) mouth   C) small intestine
    B) stomach   D) large intestine

13. Which organ produces enzymes that digest proteins, fats, and carbohydrates?
    A) mouth   C) large intestine
    B) pancreas   D) gallbladder

14. Which food group contains yogurt and cheese?
    A) dairy   C) meat
    B) grain   D) fruit

15. From which food group are carbohydrates **BEST** obtained?
    A) milk   C) meat
    B) grains   D) eggs

16. From which food group should the largest number of servings in your diet come?
    A) fruit   C) vegetable
    B) milk, yogurt, and cheese   D) bread, cereal, rice, and pasta

Thinking Critically

17. Food does not really enter your body until it is absorbed into the blood. Explain why.

18. In what part of the digestive system do antacids work? Explain your choice.

19. Bile's action is similar to soap. Use this information to explain bile working on fats.

20. Vitamins are in two groups: water soluble and fat soluble. Which of these might your body retain? Explain your answer.

21. Based on your knowledge of food groups and nutrients, discuss the meaning of the familiar statement: "You are what you eat."

Developing Skills

If you need help, refer to the **Skill Handbook.**

22. Making and Using Graphs:
Recommended Dietary Allowances (RDA) are made for the amounts of nutrients people should take in to maintain health. Prepare a bar graph of the percent of RDA of each nutrient from the product information listed below.

Recommended Dietary Allowances	
Nutrient	**Percent U.S. RDA**
Protein	2
Vitamin A	20
Vitamin C	25
Vitamin D	15
Calcium (Ca)	less than 2
Iron (Fe)	25
Zinc (Zn)	15
Total Fat 3.0 g	5
Saturated Fat 0.5 g	3
Cholesterol 0 mg	0
Sodium 60 mg	3

Which nutrients are given the greatest percent of the Recommended Dietary Allowance? Could a person on a fat-restricted diet eat this product? Explain.

23. Sequencing: In a table, sequence the order of organs through which food passes in the digestive system. Indicate whether ingestion, digestion, absorption, or elimination takes place in the individual organs.

24. Comparing and Contrasting: Compare and contrast the location, size, and functions of the esophagus, stomach, small intestine, and large intestine.

25. Concept Mapping: Make a concept map showing the process of fat digestion.

THE PRINCETON REVIEW

Test-Taking Tip

Don't Use Outside Knowledge When answering questions for a reading passage, do not use anything you already know about the subject of the passage, or any opinions you have about it. Always return to the passage to reread and get the details from there.

Test Practice

Use these questions to test your Science Proficiency.

1. The villi are tiny, fingerlike projections that cover the wall of the small intestine. Which statement **BEST** relates their structure with their function?
   A) They are able to contract and expand more rapidly.
   B) They offer the best protection against stomach acid.
   C) They greatly increase the surface area for digestion.
   D) They strain food passing through the intestine.

2. Certain nutrients are needed for growth and repair. Which menu is the **BEST** source of foods for this function?
   A) milk, ham, eggs, whole wheat bread
   B) cereal, milk, orange juice, donut
   C) waffles, honey, margarine, milk
   D) toast, jelly, butter, apple juice

3. Everyone depends on water to survive. Which statement **BEST** emphasizes that need?
   A) We wash our bodies with water.
   B) Many foods contain lots of water.
   C) We add water to many foods that we eat.
   D) Body nutrients are in solution.

CHAPTER 18

The Circulatory System

Chapter Preview

Skills Preview

Skill Builders
- Make and Use a Table
- Compare and Contrast

Activities
- Observe
- Experiment

MiniLabs
- Compare
- Interpret Data

Reading Check ✔

Find out how a different culture views the heart. Do people in this culture draw the heart in a valentine shape? Do they think of the heart as the center of people's emotions?

Explore Activity

If you live in a big city or have ever visited one, you may have noticed a beltway that circles the city. Most big cities also have one or more interstate highways that cross through them. The human circulatory system can be compared to a city's highway system. Goods are transported to individual homes and factories. Completed products and wastes are collected and removed. In a similar way, substances are transported throughout your body.

Map a Route in the City

1. Obtain a map that shows the streets, interstate roads, and a beltway around a large city.

2. Study the map to find the center, or heart, of the city. Use the map key to identify roads that are interstates and roads that are state and country routes.

3. Plan a route from the center of the city to a street in the suburbs.

Science Journal

In your Science Journal, compare the different types of streets you could take. If the city represented a human body, what would the center of town represent? What would the suburbs represent?

18•1 Circulation

Your Cardiovascular System

What You'll Learn

▶ How to compare arteries, veins, and capillaries
▶ The pathway of blood through the chambers of the heart
▶ The pulmonary and systemic circulation systems

Vocabulary

atria
ventricle
pulmonary circulation
systemic circulation
coronary circulation
artery
vein
capillary
blood pressure
atherosclerosis
hypertension

Why It's Important

▶ Blood plays a vital role as the transport system of the body.

With a body made up of trillions of cells, you may seem quite different from a one-celled amoeba living in a puddle of water. But, are you really that different? Even though your body is larger and made up of complex systems, the cells in your body have the same needs as a single-celled organism, the amoeba. You both need a continuous supply of oxygen and nutrients and a way to remove cell wastes.

An amoeba takes oxygen directly from its watery environment. Nutrients are distributed throughout its single cell by moving through the cytoplasm. In your body, a cardiovascular system distributes materials. Your cardiovascular system includes your heart, blood, and kilometers of vessels that carry blood to every part of your body and then back to the heart as shown in **Figure 18-1A.** It is a closed system

Figure 18-1 Humans have a closed circulatory system.

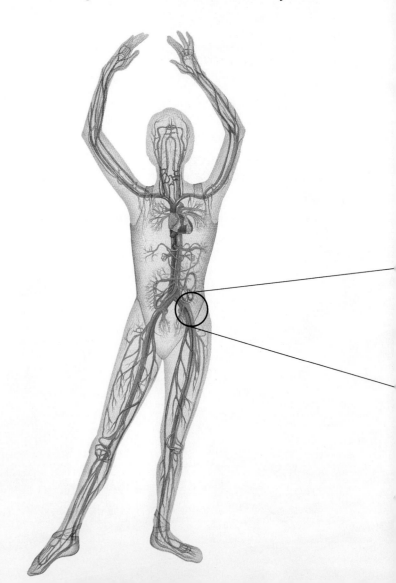

A The blood is pumped by a heart to all the cells of the body and back to the heart through a closed network of blood vessels.

because blood moves within vessels. The system moves oxygen and nutrients to cells and removes carbon dioxide and other wastes from the cells. Movement of materials into and out of your cells happens by diffusion. Diffusion, shown in **Figure 18-1B,** is when a material moves from an area of high concentration to an area of lower concentration.

Your Heart

Your heart is an organ made of cardiac muscle. It is located behind your sternum, which is the breastbone, and between your lungs. Your heart has four cavities called chambers. The two upper chambers are the right and left **atria** (AY tree uh). The two lower chambers are the right and left **ventricles** (VEN trih kulz). During a single heartbeat, both atria contract at the same time. Then, both ventricles contract at the same time. A valve separates each atrium from the ventricle below it so that blood flows only from an atrium to a ventricle. A wall prevents blood from flowing between the two atria or the two ventricles. It is important to separate blood rich in oxygen from blood low in oxygen to ensure that all cells get an oxygen supply.

Try at Home

Mini Lab

Inferring How Hard the Heart Works

Procedure

1. Take a racquetball and hold it in your out-stretched arm.
2. Squeeze the racquetball again and again for one minute.

Analysis

1. How many times did you squeeze the racquetball in one minute? A resting heart beats at approximately 70 beats per minute.
2. What can you do when the muscles of your arm get tired? Explain why cardiac muscle in your heart cannot do the same.

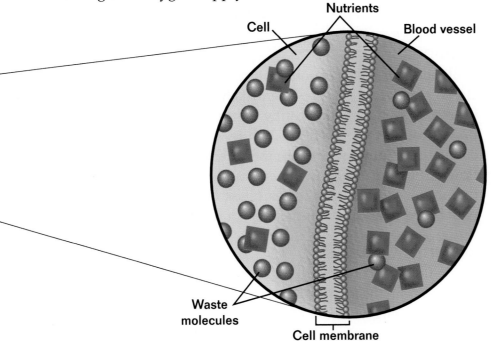

Nutrients

Cell

Blood vessel

Waste molecules

Cell membrane

B In a closed circulatory system, blood remains in blood vessels. Nutrients move from the blood into cells by diffusion or active transport. Waste products produced by the cell move out into the circulatory system to be carried away.

Figure 18-2 Pulmonary circulation moves blood between the heart and lungs.

C Oxygen-rich blood travels through the pulmonary vein and into the left atrium. The pulmonary veins are the only veins that carry oxygen-rich blood.

A Blood, high in carbon dioxide and low in oxygen, returns from the body to the heart. It enters the right atrium through the superior and inferior vena cavae.

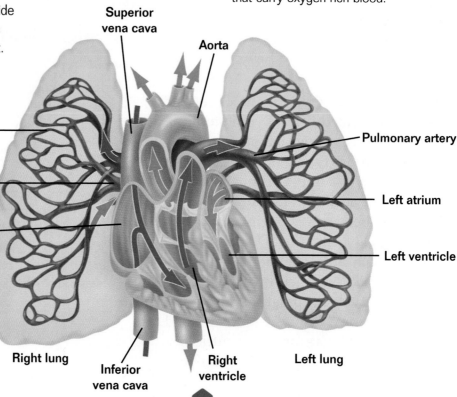

Superior vena cava

Aorta

Capillaries

Pulmonary artery

Pulmonary vein

Left atrium

Right atrium

Left ventricle

Right lung

Inferior vena cava

Right ventricle

Left lung

B The right atrium contracts, forcing the blood into the right ventricle. When the right ventricle contracts, the blood leaves the heart and goes through the pulmonary artery to the lungs, where it picks up oxygen.

D The left atrium contracts and forces the blood into the left ventricle. The left ventricle contracts, forcing the blood out of the heart and into the aorta.

Pulmonary Circulation

Blood moves continuously throughout your body in a closed circulatory system. Scientists have divided the system into three sections. The beating of your heart controls blood flow through these sections. **Figure 18-2** shows pulmonary circulation. **Pulmonary** (PUL muh ner ee) **circulation** is the flow of blood through the heart, to the lungs where it picks up oxygen, and back to the heart. Use **Figure 18-2** to trace the path blood takes through this part of the circulatory system.

Systemic Circulation

The final step of pulmonary circulation occurs when blood is forced from the left ventricle into the aorta (ay ORT uh). The aorta is the largest artery of your body. It carries blood away from the heart. **Systemic circulation** moves oxygen-rich blood to all of your organs and body tissues except for the heart and lungs. It is the most extensive of the three sections of your circulatory system. **Figure 18-3** shows the major arteries and veins involved in systemic circulation. Once nutrients and oxygen are delivered by blood to your body cells and exchanged for carbon dioxide and wastes, the blood returns to the heart in veins. From the head and neck areas, blood returns through the superior vena cava. From your abdomen and the lower parts of your body, blood returns through the inferior vena cava. More information about arteries and veins will be presented later in this chapter.

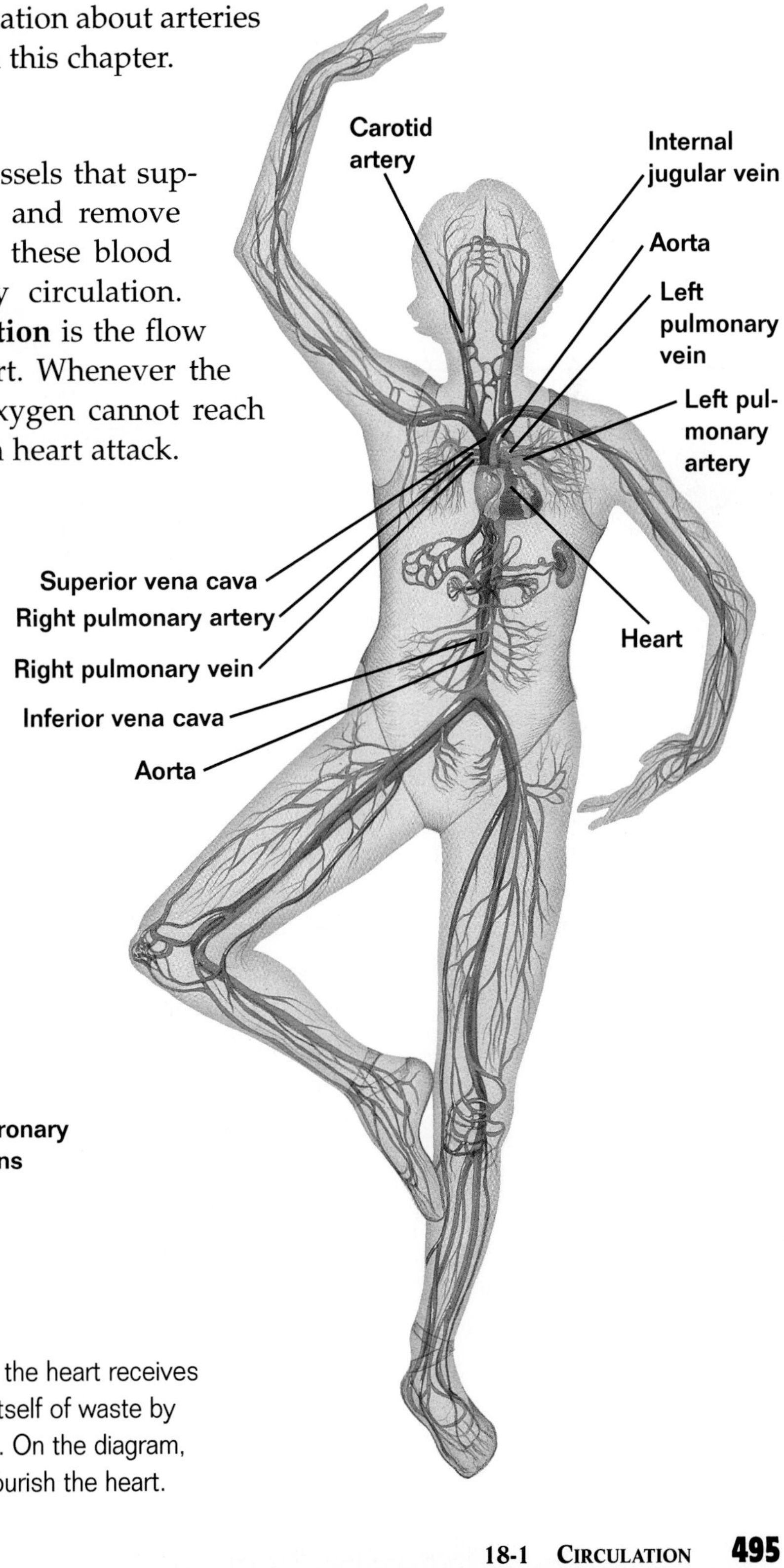

Coronary Circulation

Your heart has its own blood vessels that supply it with nutrients and oxygen and remove wastes. As shown in **Figure 18-4,** these blood vessels are involved in coronary circulation. **Coronary** (KOR uh ner ee) **circulation** is the flow of blood to the tissues of the heart. Whenever the coronary circulation is blocked, oxygen cannot reach the cells of the heart. The result is a heart attack.

Figure 18-3 The rate at which blood flows through the systemic system depends on how quickly the left ventricle contracts. **How does the rate change when a person has completed a race?**

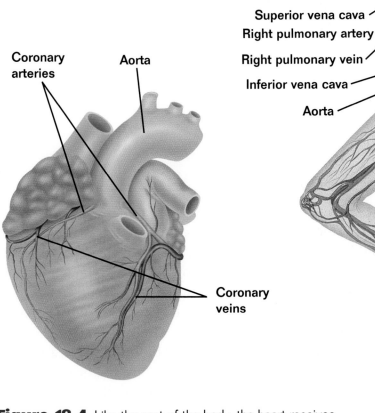

Figure 18-4 Like the rest of the body, the heart receives the oxygen and nutrients it needs and rids itself of waste by way of blood flowing through blood vessels. On the diagram, you can see the coronary arteries, which nourish the heart.

Blood Vessels

It wasn't until the middle 1600s that scientists confirmed that blood circulates only in one direction and that it is moved by the pumping action of the heart. They found that blood flows from arteries to veins. What they couldn't figure out is *how* blood gets from the arteries to the veins. With the invention of the microscope, capillaries were seen.

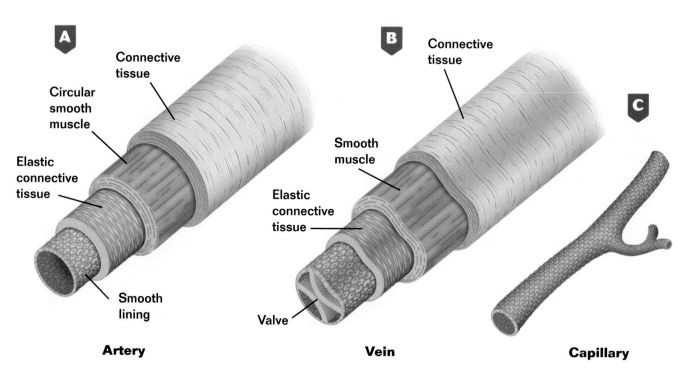

Figure 18-5 The structures of arteries (A), veins (B), and capillaries (C) are different. Valves in veins help blood flow back toward the heart. Capillaries are much smaller and only one cell thick.

Types of Blood Vessels

As blood moves out of the heart, it begins a journey through arteries, capillaries, and veins. **Arteries** are blood vessels that move blood away from the heart. Arteries, shown in **Figure 18-5,** have thick elastic walls made of smooth muscle. Each ventricle of the heart is connected to an artery. With each contraction of the heart, blood is moved from the heart into arteries.

Veins are blood vessels that move blood to the heart. Veins have valves to keep blood moving toward the heart. If blood flows backward, the pressure of the blood closes the valves. Veins that are near skeletal muscles are squeezed when these muscles contract. This action helps blood move toward the heart. Blood in veins carries waste materials, such as carbon dioxide, from cells and is therefore low in oxygen. ☑

Reading Check ☑

Compare and contrast arteries and veins.

Capillaries are microscopic blood vessels that connect arteries and veins. The walls of capillaries are only one cell thick. You can see the capillaries when you have a bloodshot eye. They are the tiny red lines visible in the white area of the eye. Nutrients and oxygen diffuse to body cells through thin capillary walls. Waste materials and carbon dioxide move from body cells into the capillaries to be carried back to the heart.

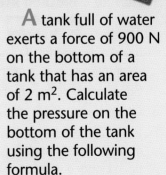

Figure 18-6 Blood pressure is measured in large arteries using a blood-pressure cuff and stethoscope.

Blood Pressure

When you pump up a bicycle tire, you can feel the pressure of the air on the walls of the tire. In the same way, when the heart pumps blood through the cardiovascular system, blood exerts a force called **blood pressure** on the walls of the vessels. This pressure is highest in arteries. Blood pressure is lower in capillaries and even lower in veins. As the wave of pressure rises and falls in your arteries, it is felt as your pulse. Normal pulse rates are between 65 and 80 beats per minute.

Blood pressure is measured in large arteries and is expressed by two numbers, such as 120 over 80. The first number is a measure of the pressure caused when the ventricles contract and blood is pushed out of the heart. Then, blood pressure suddenly drops as the ventricles relax. The lower number is a measure of the pressure when the ventricles are filling up, just before they contract again. **Figure 18-6** shows the instruments used to measure blood pressure.

Using Math

A tank full of water exerts a force of 900 N on the bottom of a tank that has an area of 2 m². Calculate the pressure on the bottom of the tank using the following formula.

$$P = \frac{F}{A}$$

How does calculating pressure in a water tank relate to blood pressure in humans?

Figure 18-7 When pressure is exerted on a fluid in a closed container, the pressure is transmitted through the liquid in all directions. A balloon filled with water has the same amount of pressure pushing on all the inner surfaces of the balloon. Your circulatory system is like a closed container.

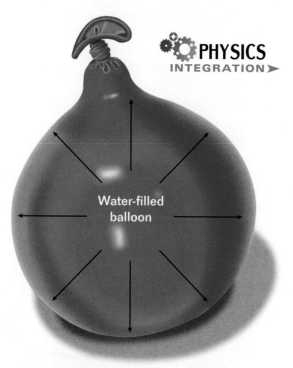

PHYSICS
INTEGRATION

Water-filled
balloon

Mini Lab

Modeling a Blocked Artery

Procedure

1. Insert a dropperful of mineral oil into a piece of clear, narrow, plastic tubing.
2. Squeeze the oil through the tube.
3. Observe how much oil comes out the tube.
4. Next, refill the dropper and squeeze mineral oil through a piece of clear plastic tubing that has been clogged with cotton.

Analysis

1. How much oil comes out of the clogged tube?
2. Explain how the addition of the cotton to the tube changed the way the oil flowed through the tube.
3. How does this activity demonstrate what takes place when arteries become clogged?

The Big Push

You learned that a force is exerted on the inner walls of your blood vessels. The force is the result of blood being pumped through your body by the heart. Blood pressure is a measure of this force.

The total amount of force exerted by a fluid, such as blood or the gases in the atmosphere, depends on the area on which it acts. This is called pressure. In other words, as shown in **Figure 18-7,** pressure is the amount of force exerted per unit of area. This is written with the following formula.

$$\text{Pressure} = \frac{\text{Force}}{\text{Area}}$$

For example, a force of 400 N (F = 400 N) on a container with an area of 50 m² (A = 50 m²) would result in a pressure of 8 N/m².

$$P = \frac{F}{A} = \frac{400 \text{ N}}{50 \text{ m}^2} = 8 \text{ N/m}^2$$

Pressure Measurement

Scientists measure atmospheric pressure with a mercury barometer. At sea level, normal atmospheric pressure is 760 mm mercury. This means that the force of the atmosphere will raise a column of mercury (Hg) 760 mm in the barometer. Compare this to a normal blood pressure reading of 120 over 80 for a young adult. The first number is the systolic pressure (the pressure produced when the ventricles force blood from the heart). In this reading, the systolic pressure would raise a column of mercury 120 mm in a barometer. The second number is the diastolic pressure (the pressure at the end of the cardiac cycle). This pressure would raise a column of mercury 80 mm in a barometer.

Magnification: 10×

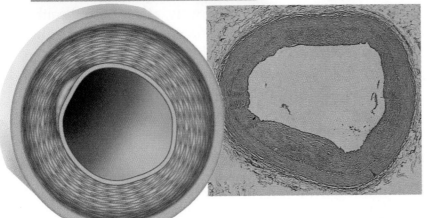

Figure 18-8 Atherosclerosis interferes with blood flow by blocking blood vessels with fatty substances. Each of these photos is paired with an illustration showing the build up of fatty deposits. **What happens if an artery in the heart is blocked?**

A This cross section of a healthy coronary artery shows a clear, wide-open pathway through which blood easily flows.

B Here, the blood-flow pathway has been narrowed by a buildup of fatty deposits. Blood flow is slowed. The heart muscle does not get enough oxygen and nutrients to do its work. The muscle begins to die.

Magnification: 10×

Fatty deposit

Magnification: 10×

C If the deposit continues to build, blood flow through the artery becomes limited and may stop. The person will suffer a heart attack.

Control of Blood Pressure

Special nerve cells in the walls of some arteries sense changes in blood pressure. Messages are sent to the brain, and the amount of blood pumped by the heart is regulated. This provides for a regular, normal pressure within the arteries.

*inter*NET
CONNECTION

Visit the Glencoe Science Web Site at **www.glencoe.com/sec/science/ca** for more information about cardiovascular disease.

Cardiovascular Disease

Any disease or disorder that affects the cardiovascular system can seriously affect your health. Heart disease is the major cause of death in the United States. One leading cause of heart disease is **atherosclerosis** (ah thur oh skluh ROH sus), a condition, shown in **Figure 18-8,** of fatty deposits on arterial walls. Eating foods high in cholesterol and saturated fats may cause these deposits to form. The fat builds up and forms a hard mass that clogs the inside of the vessel. As a result, less blood flows through the artery. If the artery is clogged completely, blood is not able to flow through.

Another disorder is high blood pressure, or **hypertension.** Atherosclerosis can cause hypertension. A clogged artery can cause the pressure within the vessel to increase. This causes the walls to lose their ability to contract and dilate. Extra strain is placed on the heart as it works harder to keep blood flowing. Being overweight as well as eating foods with too much salt and fat may contribute to hypertension. Smoking and stress also can increase blood pressure. Regular checkups, as shown in **Figure 18-9,** a careful diet, and exercise are important to the health of your cardiovascular system.

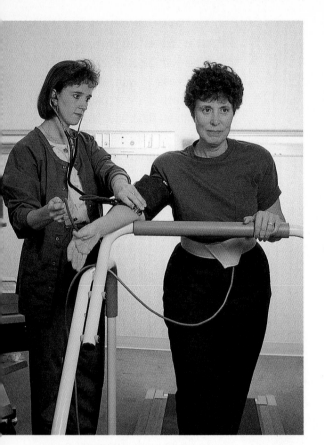

Figure 18-9 A stress test is used to determine the amount of strain placed on the heart.

Section Assessment

1. Compare and contrast the three types of blood vessels.

2. Explain the pathway of blood through the heart.

3. Contrast pulmonary and systemic circulations.

4. **Think Critically:** What waste product builds up in blood and cells when the heart is unable to pump blood efficiently?

5. **Skill Builder**
   Concept Mapping Make an events chain concept map to show pulmonary circulation beginning at the right atrium and ending at the aorta. If you need help, refer to Concept Mapping in the **Skill Handbook** on page 678.

Using Computers

Database Use different references to research diseases and disorders of the circulatory system. Make a database showing what part of the circulatory system is affected by each disease or disorder. Categories should include the organs, vessels, and cells of the circulatory system. If you need help, refer to page 697.

Activity 18·1

The Heart as a Pump

Materials

- Stopwatch, watch, or a clock with a second hand

The heart is a pumping organ. Blood is forced through the arteries and causes the muscles of the walls to contract and then relax. This creates a series of waves as the blood flows through the arteries. We call this the pulse. Try this activity to learn about the pulse and the pumping of the heart.

What You'll Investigate

How can you measure heartbeat rate?

Goals

- **Observe** pulse rate.

Procedure

1. **Make** a table like the one shown. Use it to **record** your data.

2. Your partner should sit down and take his or her pulse. You will serve as the recorder.

3. **Find** the pulse rate by placing the middle and index fingers over one of the carotid arteries in the neck as shown in the photo.
   CAUTION: *Do not press too hard.*

4. **Calculate** the resulting heart rate. Your partner should count each beat of the carotid pulse rate silently for 15 s. Multiply the number of beats by four and **record** the number in the data table.

5. Your partner should then jog in place for one minute and take his or her pulse again.

6. **Calculate** this new pulse rate and **record** it in the data table.

7. Reverse roles with your partner. You are now the pulse taker.

8. **Collect and record** the new data.

Conclude and Apply

1. How does the pulse rate change?

2. What causes the pulse rate to change?

3. What can you **infer** about the heart as a pumping organ?

Pulse Rate		
Pulse Rate	**Partner's**	**Yours**
At rest		
After jogging		

18·2 Blood

Functions of Blood

Blood is a tissue consisting of cells, cell fragments, and liquid. Blood has many important functions. It plays a part in every major activity of your body. First, blood carries oxygen from your lungs to all body cells. It also removes carbon dioxide from your body cells and carries it to the lungs to be exhaled. Second, it carries waste products of cell activity to your kidneys to be removed. Third, blood transports nutrients from the digestive system to body cells. Fourth, materials in blood fight infections and help heal wounds. Anything that disrupts or changes any of these functions affects all the tissues of the body.

Blood makes up about eight percent of your body's total mass. If you weigh 45 kg, you have about 3.6 kg of blood moving through your body. The amount of blood in an adult would fill five 1-L bottles. If this volume falls, the body goes into shock because blood pressure falls rapidly.

Parts of Blood

If you've ever taken a ride on a water slide at an amusement park, you have some idea of the twists and turns a blood cell travels inside a blood vessel. On the ride, surrounded by water, you travel rapidly through a narrow, watery passageway, much like a red blood cell moves in the liquid part of blood, as shown in **Figure 18-10.**

What You'll Learn

▶ The characteristics and functions of the blood
▶ The importance of checking blood types before a transfusion
▶ Diseases and disorders of blood

Vocabulary
plasma
hemoglobin
platelet

Why It's Important

▶ Blood has many important functions and plays a part in every major activity of your body.

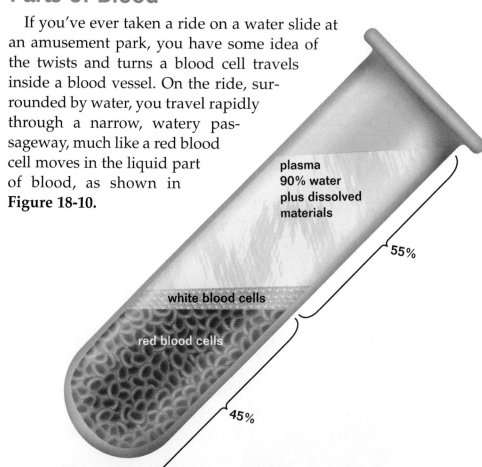

plasma
90% water
plus dissolved
materials

55%

white blood cells

red blood cells

45%

Figure 18-10 The blood in this test tube has been separated into its parts. Each part plays a key role in body functions. **What part of blood is the most dense?**

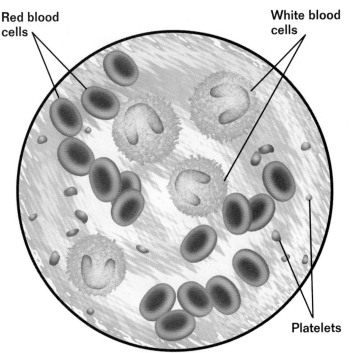

Blood smear

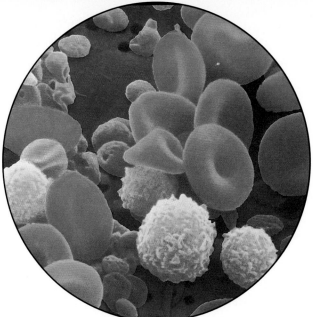

Magnification: 1000×

Figure 18-11 Blood consists of a liquid portion called plasma and a solid portion that includes red blood cells, white blood cells, and platelets. **What type of cells are most numerous in the human circulatory system?**

Plasma

If you examine blood closely, as in **Figure 18-11,** you see that it is not just a red-colored liquid. Blood is a tissue made of red and white blood cells, platelets, and plasma. **Plasma** is the liquid part of blood and consists mostly of water. It makes up more than half the volume of blood. Nutrients, minerals, and oxygen are dissolved in plasma.

Blood Cells

A cubic millimeter of blood has more than 5 million red blood cells. In these disk-shaped blood cells is **hemoglobin,** a chemical that can carry oxygen and carbon dioxide. Hemoglobin carries oxygen from your lungs to your body cells. Red blood cells also carry carbon dioxide from body

CHEMISTRY
INTEGRATION

Artificial Blood
Artificial blood substances have been developed to use in blood transfusions. They can carry oxygen and carbon dioxide. Predict what other properties they must have to be safe.

Magnification: 2000×

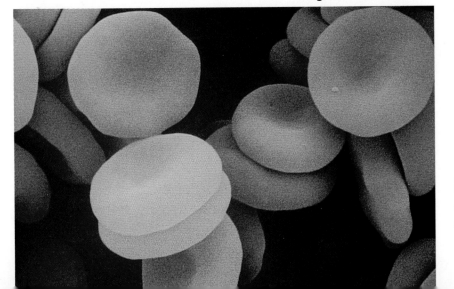

Figure 18-12 Red blood cells carry oxygen and carbon dioxide and are disk shaped.

Figure 18-13 While red blood cells supply your body with oxygen, white blood cells and platelets have more protective roles.

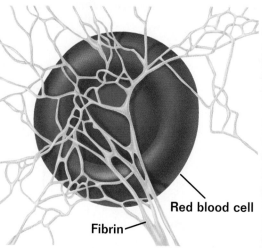

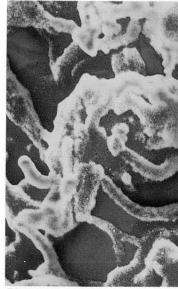

A Platelets help stop bleeding. Platelets not only plug holes in small vessels, but they also release chemicals that help form filaments of fibrin.

B Several types, sizes, and shapes of white blood cells exist. These cells destroy bacteria, viruses, and foreign substances.

Red blood cell

Fibrin

Platelets

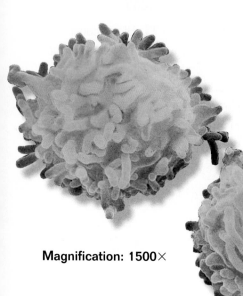

Magnification: 1500×

*inter***NET**
CONNECTION

Visit the Glencoe Science Web Site at **www.glencoe.com/ sec/science/ca** for more information about blood clotting.

cells to your lungs. Red blood cells have a life span of about 120 days. They are formed in the marrow of long bones such as the femur and humerus at a rate of 2 to 3 million per second and contain no nuclei. About an equal number of old ones wear out and are destroyed in the same time period.

In contrast to red blood cells, there are only about 5000 to 10 000 white blood cells in a cubic millimeter of blood. White blood cells fight bacteria, viruses, and other foreign substances that constantly try to invade your body. Your body reacts to infection by increasing its number of white blood cells. White blood cells slip between the cells of capillary walls and out around the tissues that have been invaded. Here, they absorb foreign substances and dead cells. The life span of white blood cells varies from a few days to many months.

Circulating with the red and white blood cells are platelets. **Platelets** are irregularly shaped cell fragments that help clot blood. A cubic millimeter of blood may contain as many as 400 000 platelets. Platelets have a life span of five to nine days. **Figure 18-13** summarizes the solid parts of blood and their functions.

Blood Clotting

Everyone has had a cut, scrape, or other minor wound at some time. The initial bleeding is usually stopped quickly, and the wounded area begins to heal. Most people will not bleed to death from a minor wound. The bleeding stops because platelets in your blood make a blood clot that helps prevent blood loss. A blood clot is somewhat like a bandage. When you cut yourself, a series of chemical reactions causes threadlike fibers called fibrin to form a sticky net that traps escaping blood cells and plasma. This forms a clot and helps prevent further loss of blood. **Figure 18-14** shows the blood-clotting process that occurs after a cut. Some people have the genetic disease hemophilia. Their blood lacks one of the clotting factors that begins the clotting process.

Figure 18-14 A sticky blood clot seals the leaking blood vessel. Eventually, a scab forms, protecting the wound from further damage and allowing it to heal.

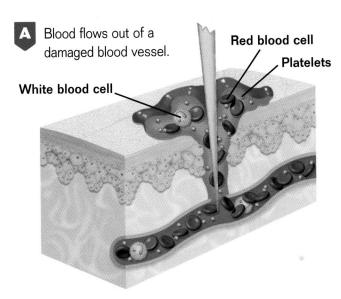

A Blood flows out of a damaged blood vessel.

White blood cell

Red blood cell

Platelets

B Platelets stick to the area of the wound and release chemicals. The chemicals make other nearby platelets sticky and cause threads of fibrin to form. More and more platelets and blood cells become trapped and seal the wound.

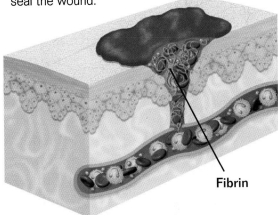

Fibrin

C The clot becomes harder. White blood cells destroy invading bacteria. Skin cells begin the repair process.

Scab

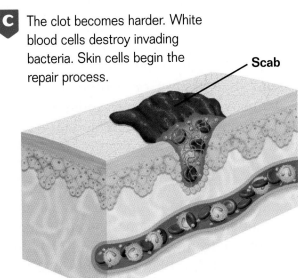

D The wound continues to heal. Eventually the scab will fall off.

Blood Types

Sometimes, a person loses a lot of blood. This person may receive blood through a blood transfusion. During a blood transfusion, a person receives blood or parts of blood. Doctors must be sure that the right type of blood is given.

Table 18-1

Blood Types

Blood Type	Antigen	Antibody
A — Red blood cell	A	Anti-B
B	B	Anti-A
AB	A B	None
O	None	Anti-A Anti-B

If it is the wrong type, the red blood cells of the person clump together. Clots form in the blood vessels, and the person dies.

The ABO Identification System

Doctors know that humans can have one of four types of blood: A, B, AB, and O. Each type has a chemical identification tag called an antigen on its red blood cells. As shown in **Table 18-1,** type A blood has A antigens. Type B blood has B antigens. Type AB blood has both A and B antigens on each blood cell. Type O blood has no A or B antigens.

Each blood type also has specific antibodies in its plasma. Antibodies are proteins that destroy or neutralize foreign substances, such as pathogens, in your body. Antibodies prevent certain blood types from mixing. Type A blood has antibodies against type B blood. If you mix type A blood with type B blood, type A red blood cells react to type B blood as if it were a foreign substance. The antibodies in type A blood respond by clumping the type B blood. Type B blood has antibodies against type A blood. Type AB blood has no antibodies, so it can receive blood from A, B, AB, and O types. Type O blood has both A and B antibodies. **Table 18-2** lists the four blood types, what they can receive, and what blood types they can donate to. ☑

The Rh Factor

Just as antigens are one chemical identification tag for blood, the Rh marker is another. Rh blood type also is inherited. If the Rh marker is present, the person has Rh-positive (Rh+) blood. If it is not present, the person is said to be

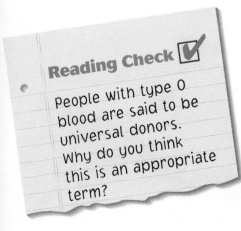

Reading Check ☑

People with type O blood are said to be universal donors. Why do you think this is an appropriate term?

Table 18-2

Blood Transfusion Possibilities		
Type	Can receive	Can donate to
A	O, A	A, AB
B	O, B	B, AB
AB	all	AB
O	O	all

Rh-negative (Rh−). Any Rh− person receiving blood from an Rh+ person will produce antibodies against the Rh+ factor.

A problem also occurs when an Rh− mother carries an Rh+ baby. Close to the time when the baby is about to be born, antibodies from the mother can pass from her blood vessels into the baby's blood vessels and destroy the baby's red blood cells. If this happens, the baby must receive a blood transfusion before or right after birth. At 28 weeks of pregnancy and immediately after the birth, the mother can receive an injection that prevents the production of antibodies to the Rh factor. To prevent deadly consequences, blood groups and Rh factor are checked before transfusions and during pregnancies.

Problem Solving

The Baby Exchange

Two mothers took their new babies home from the hospital on the same day. On the first day home, when mother number one was removing the hospital name tag from her baby, she discovered that the other mother's name was on the tag. The other mother was contacted, but she was sure that she had the right baby. She did not want to give up the baby she had brought home from the hospital. Because the identity of the babies was disputed, the issue had to be decided in court. Analyze the data provided in the table and apply the laws of inheritance to solve the problem.

Think Critically: What is the only blood type the baby from family one could have? Should the babies be exchanged? Because A and B blood types are always dominant to blood type O, what other blood type could babies from family two have?

Blood Test Results	
Person	Blood Type
Mother #1	O
Father #1	O
Baby taken home by parents #1	B
Mother #2	O
Father #2	AB
Baby taken home by parents #2	O

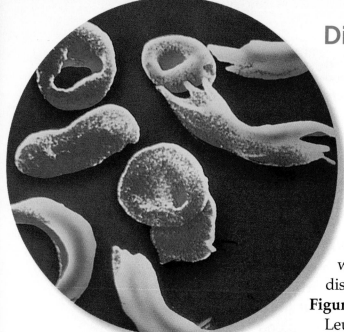

Diseases and Disorders of Blood

Blood, like other body tissues, is subject to disease. Because blood circulates to all parts of the body and performs so many vital functions, any disease of this tissue is cause for concern. Anemia is a disorder in which there are too few red blood cells or there is too little hemoglobin in the red blood cells. Because of this, body tissues can't get enough oxygen. They are unable to carry on their usual activities. Sometimes, the loss of great amounts of blood or improper diet will cause anemia. Anemia also can result from disease or as a side effect of treatment for a disease. **Figure 18-15** illustrates another blood disease.

Leukemia (lew KEE mee uh) is a disease in which one or more types of white blood cells are produced in increased numbers. However, these cells are immature and do not effectively fight infections. Blood transfusions and bone marrow transplants are used to treat this disease, but they are not always successful, and death can occur.

Blood transports oxygen and nutrients to body cells and takes wastes from these cells to organs for removal. Cells in blood help fight infection and heal wounds. You can understand why blood is sometimes called the tissue of life.

Figure 18-15 Persons with sickle-cell anemia have deformed red blood cells. The sickle-shaped cells clog the capillaries of the person with this disease. Oxygen cannot reach tissues served by the capillaries, and wastes cannot be removed. **How does this damage the affected tissues?**

Section Assessment

1. What are the four functions of blood in the body?
2. Compare blood cells, plasma, and platelets.
3. Why is blood type checked before a transfusion?
4. Describe a disease and a disorder of blood.
5. **Think Critically:** Think about the main job of your red blood cells. If red blood cells couldn't pick up carbon dioxide and wastes from your cells, what would be the condition of your tissues?
6. **Skill Builder**
   Making and Using Tables Look at the data in **Table 18-2** about blood group interactions. To which group(s) can type AB donate blood? If you need help, refer to Making and Using Tables in the **Skill Handbook** on page 680.

Using Math

Calculate the ratio of the number of red blood cells to the number of white blood cells and to the number of platelets in a cubic millimeter of blood. What are the percentages of each kind of solid?

Comparing Blood Cells

Blood is an important tissue for all vertebrates. How do human blood cells compare with those of other vertebrates?

What You'll Investigate

How does human blood compare with the blood of other vertebrates?

Goals

- **Observe** the characteristics of red blood cells, white blood cells, and platelets.
- **Compare** human blood cells with those of other vertebrates.

Procedures

1. Under low power, **examine** the prepared slide of human blood. **Locate** the red blood cells.

2. **Examine** the red blood cells under high power.

3. Make a data table. Draw, count, and **describe** the red blood cells.

4. Move the slide to another position. Find one or two white blood cells. They will be blue or purple due to the stain.

5. Draw, count, and **describe** the white cells in a data table.

Materials

- Prepared slides of human blood
  *photos of human blood
- Prepared slides of two other vertebrates' (fish, frog, reptile, bird) blood
  *photos of two other vertebrates' blood
- Microscope

  *Alternate Materials

6. **Examine** the slide for small fragments that appear blue. These are platelets.

7. Draw, count, and **describe** the platelets on your data table.

8. Follow steps 1 to 7 for each of the other vertebrate cells.

Conclude and Apply

1. Does each vertebrate studied have all three cell types?

2. What might you infer about the ability of the different red blood cells to carry oxygen?

3. What is the function of each of the three types of blood cells?

Human blood

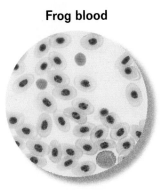

Frog blood

Snake blood

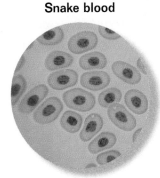

Bird blood

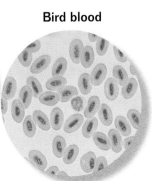

Fantastic Voyage
by Isaac Asimov

In the science fiction novel *Fantastic Voyage*, later made into a movie (see scene below), a scientist defecting from his native country develops a blood clot in his brain and lapses into a coma. Valuable information that governments are competing for is now beyond reach. A traditional operation won't work, but luckily for science fiction fans, an alternative is available. This new method uses miniaturization to operate on the blood clot from inside the body. A small submarine, *Proteus*, and its five passengers—one of whom is a brain surgeon—are reduced to one millionth their former size. They make their way through the patient's circulatory system (see blood vessel at right) to the blood clot. The operation must be done quickly because the ship and its crew will return to their normal size in 60 minutes. Here is Asimov's description of their fantastic voyage in the bloodstream:

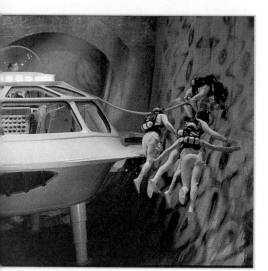

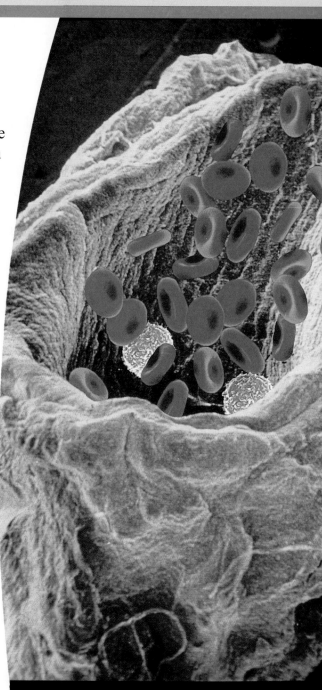

It was a vast, exotic aquarium they faced, one in which not fish but far stranger objects filled their vision. Large rubber tires, the centers depressed but not pierced through, were the most numerous objects. Each was twice the diameter of the ship, each an orange-straw color, each sparkling and blazing intermittently, as though faceted with slivers of diamonds.

What are the objects described in the paragraph above? What color did you expect these objects to be?

Science
JOURNAL

In your Science Journal, describe the inside of your mouth as it might have looked to the crew of the *Proteus*. If you could undergo miniaturization, what part of your body would you most like to see and explore? Why?

Your Lymphatic System

Functions of Your Lymphatic System

You have learned that blood carries nutrients and oxygen to cells. Molecules of these substances pass through capillary walls to be absorbed by nearby cells. Some of the water and dissolved substances that move out of your blood become part of a tissue fluid that is found between cells. Your **lymphatic** (lihm FAT ihk) **system,** shown in **Figure 18-16,** collects this fluid from body tissue spaces and returns it to the blood through a system of lymph capillaries and larger lymph vessels. This system also contains cells that help your body defend itself against disease-causing organisms.

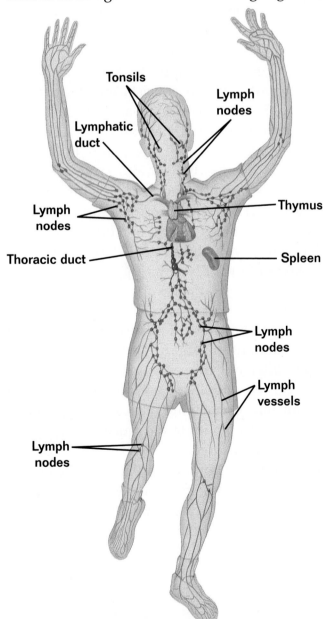

Tonsils

Lymph nodes

Lymphatic duct

Lymph nodes

Thoracic duct

Thymus

Spleen

Lymph nodes

Lymph vessels

Lymph nodes

What You'll Learn

► The functions of the lymphatic system
► Where lymph comes from
► The role of lymph organs in fighting infections

Vocabulary
lymphatic system
lymph
lymphocyte
lymph node

Why It's Important

► The lymphatic system plays a vital role in protecting the body against infections and diseases.

Figure 18-16 Like the circulatory system, the lymphatic system is connected by a vast network of vessels, but does not have a pump or heart. **How do muscles help move lymph?**

Figure 18-17 Lymph is fluid that has moved from around cells into lymph vessels.

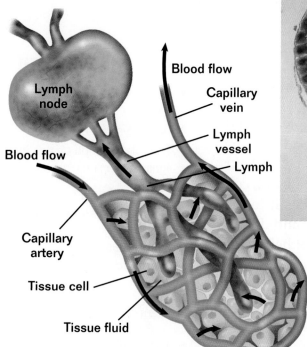

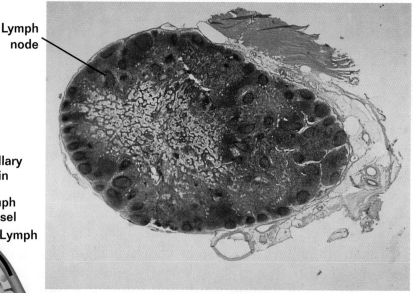

Lymph node

Blood flow

Capillary vein

Lymph vessel

Lymph

Lymph node

Blood flow

Capillary artery

Tissue cell

Tissue fluid

Reading Check ✓

What makes up lymph?

Lymphatic Organs

Once tissue fluid moves from around body tissues and into lymphatic capillaries, shown in **Figure 18-17,** it is known as lymph. It enters the capillaries by absorption and diffusion. **Lymph** consists mostly of water, dissolved substances such as nutrients and small proteins, and **lymphocytes** (LIHM fuh sites), a type of white blood cell. The lymphatic capillaries join with larger vessels that eventually drain the lymph into large veins near the heart. No heartlike structure pumps the lymph through the lymphatic system. The movement of lymph is due to contraction of skeletal muscles and the smooth muscles in lymph vessels. Like veins, lymphatic vessels have valves that prevent the backward flow of lymph. ✓

Lymph Nodes

Before lymph enters blood, it passes through bean-shaped structures throughout the body known as lymph nodes. **Lymph nodes** filter out microorganisms and foreign materials that have been engulfed by lymphocytes. When your body fights an infection, lymphocytes fill the nodes. They become inflamed and tender to the touch.

Tonsils are lymphatic organs in the back of the throat. They provide protection to the mouth and nose against pathogens. The thymus is a soft mass of tissue located behind the sternum. It produces lymphocytes that travel to other lymph organs. The spleen is the largest organ of the lymphatic system and is located behind the upper-left part of the stomach. Blood flowing through the spleen gets filtered. Here, worn out and damaged red blood cells are broken down. Specialized cells in the spleen engulf and destroy bacteria and other foreign substances.

A Disease of the Lymphatic System

As you have probably learned, HIV is a deadly virus. As shown in **Figure 18-18,** when HIV enters a person's body, it attacks and destroys a particular kind of lymphocyte called helper T cells. Normally, helper T cells help produce antibodies to fight infections. With fewer helper T cells, a person infected with HIV is less able to fight pathogens. The infections become difficult to treat and often lead to death.

The lymphatic system collects extra fluid from body tissue spaces. It also produces lymphocytes that fight infections and foreign materials that enter your body. This system works to keep your body healthy. This system is critical in defending your body against disease. Through a network of vessels, lymph nodes, and other organs, your lymphatic system is a strong defense against invasion. However, if the system is not working properly, even a common cold can become a serious threat.

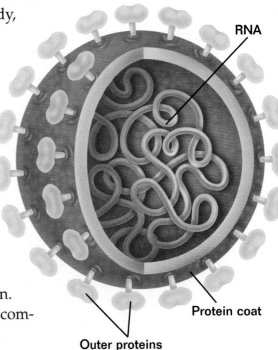

Figure 18-18 HIV, shown below, is a virus that attacks helper T cells. This makes it harder for the body to fight infections.

RNA

Protein coat

Outer proteins

Section Assessment

1. Describe the role of your lymphatic system.

2. Where does lymph come from and how does it get into the lymphatic capillaries?

3. List the major organs of the lymphatic system.

4. What happens when HIV enters the body?

5. **Think Critically:** When the amount of fluid in the spaces between cells increases, so does the pressure in these spaces. What do you infer will happen?

6. **Skill Builder**
   Concept Mapping The circulatory system and the lymphatic system are separate systems, yet they work together in several ways. Do the **Chapter 18 Skill Activity** on page 723 to make a concept map comparing the two systems.

Science Journal An infectious microorganism gains entrance into your body. In your Science Journal, describe how the lymphatic system provides the body with protection against the microorganism.

For a **preview** of this chapter, study this Reviewing Main Ideas before you read the chapter. After you have studied this chapter, you can use the Reviewing Main Ideas to **review** the chapter.

The Glencoe MindJogger, Audiocassettes, and CD-ROM provide additional opportunities for review.

Section

18-1 TRANSPORTATION SYSTEM

The main function of the circulatory system is to transport materials through the body. It carries food, oxygen, carbon dioxide, and a variety of other chemicals. The blood circulates in a closed system. The heart is a four-chambered pump that circulates the blood throughout the body. Through a series of coordinated muscular contractions, the heart provides the pressure that pushes blood through the vessels. *What component of blood carries oxygen to the cells of the body?*

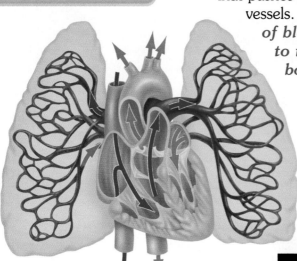

CIRCULATION

Arteries carry blood from the heart. **Capillaries** exchange food, oxygen, and wastes in cells. **Veins** return blood to the heart. Blood enters the heart through the right **atrium,** moves to the right **ventricle,** and goes to the lungs through the pulmonary artery. Blood rich in oxygen returns to the left atrium of the heart and passes through a valve into the left ventricle. Blood leaves the heart through the aorta and travels to all parts of the body. *What is the pathway of blood in the pulmonary circulation system?*

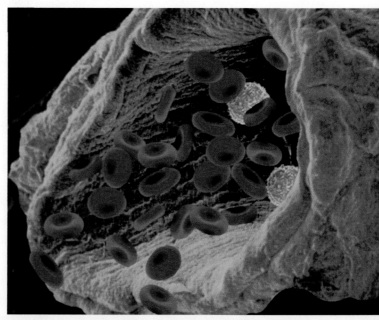

Reading Check ✔

Compare and contrast the three types of vessels. Explain why all three are necessary for circulation.

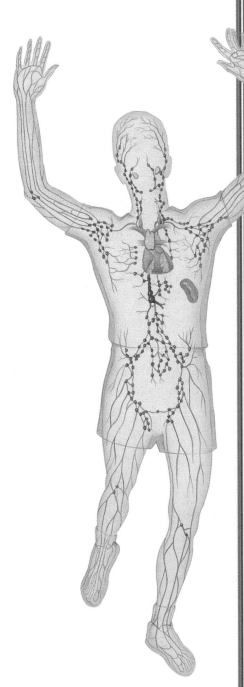

Section

18-2 BLOOD

Blood is a tissue consisting of cells, cell fragments, and liquid. Each of the solid components of blood has a specific function: the red blood cells carry oxygen and carbon dioxide, **platelets** form clots, and white blood cells fight infection. Blood also contains a liquid portion called **plasma.** The plasma consists mostly of water plus some dissolved materials. Blood types A, B, AB, and O are determined by the presence or absence of antigens. *How do sickle-shaped red blood cells cause anemia?*

Section

18-3 THE LYMPHATIC SYSTEM

Fluid found in body tissue is collected by the vessels in the **lymphatic system** and returned to the blood system. Structures in the lymphatic system filter the blood and produce white blood cells that destroy microorganisms and foreign materials. *How is an inflamed lymph node a sign that the body is fighting an infection?*

Chapter 18 Assessment

Using Vocabulary

a. artery
b. atherosclerosis
c. atria
d. blood pressure
e. capillary
f. coronary circulation
g. hemoglobin
h. hypertension
i. lymph
j. lymph node

k. lymphatic system
l. lymphocyte
m. plasma
n. platelet
o. pulmonary circulation
p. systemic circulation
q. vein
r. ventricle

Each phrase below describes a science term from the list. Write the term that matches the phrase describing it.

1. filters microorganisms
2. upper heart chambers
3. vessel connected to the heart ventricle
4. fatty deposit on artery walls
5. blood vessel that connects arteries to veins

Checking Concepts

Choose the word or phrase that best answers the question.

6. Where does the exchange of food, oxygen, and wastes occur?
   A) arteries   C) veins
   B) capillaries   D) lymph vessels

7. Where does oxygen-rich blood enter first?
   A) right atrium   C) left ventricle
   B) left atrium   D) right ventricle

8. What is circulation to all body organs?
   A) coronary   C) systemic
   B) pulmonary   D) organic

9. Where is blood under great pressure?
   A) arteries   C) veins
   B) capillaries   D) lymph vessels

10. What is blood's function?
    A) digest food   C) dissolve bone
    B) produce CO_2 D) carry oxygen

11. Which cells fight off infection?
    A) red blood   C) white blood
    B) bone   D) nerve

12. In blood, what carries oxygen?
    A) red blood cells   C) white blood cells
    B) platelets   D) lymph

13. To clot blood, what is required?
    A) plasma   C) platelets
    B) oxygen   D) carbon dioxide

14. What kind of antigen does type O blood have?
    A) A   C) A and B
    B) B   D) no antigen

15. What is the largest filtering lymph organ?
    A) spleen   C) tonsil
    B) thymus   D) node

Thinking Critically

16. Identify the following as having oxygen-rich or carbon dioxide-full blood: *aorta, coronary arteries, coronary veins, inferior vena cava, left atrium, left ventricle, right atrium, right ventricle,* and *superior vena cava.*

17. Compare and contrast the three types of blood vessels.

18. Explain how the lymphatic system works with the cardiovascular system.

19. Why is cancer of the blood or lymph hard to control?

20. Arteries are distributed throughout the body, yet a pulse is usually taken at the neck or wrist. Why do you think this is so?

Developing Skills

If you need help, refer to the **Skill Handbook.**

21. **Concept Mapping:** Complete the events chain concept map showing how lymph moves in your body.

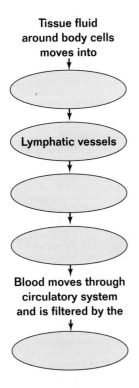

Tissue fluid around body cells moves into

Lymphatic vessels

Blood moves through circulatory system and is filtered by the

22. **Comparing and Contrasting:** Compare the life span of the different types of blood cells.

23. **Interpreting Data:** Interpret the data listed below. Find the average heartbeat rate of four males and four females and compare the two averages.
    Males: 72, 64, 65, 72
    Females: 67, 84, 74, 67

24. **Designing an Experiment:** Design an experiment to compare the heartbeat rate at rest and after exercising.

25. **Hypothesizing:** Make a hypothesis to suggest the effects of smoking on heartbeat rate.

THE PRINCETON REVIEW

Test-Taking Tip

Investigate Ask what kinds of questions to expect on the test. Ask for practice tests so that you can become familiar with the test-taking materials.

Test Practice

Use these questions to test your Science Proficiency.

1. The veins in the blood circulatory system and the vessels of the lymphatic system have valves. What is the major function of these structures?
   A) Valves help filter out microorganisms and foreign matter.
   B) Valves keep the fluids from moving too rapidly in the vessels.
   C) Valves permit the fluids to flow in only one direction.
   D) Valves connect arteries, veins, and lymphatic vessels.

2. Veins never carry oxygen-rich blood. Which statement below **BEST** defends or refutes the above statement?
   A) The pulmonary vein carries blood to the left atrium.
   B) The vena cava carries blood to the right atrium.
   C) The pulmonary artery carries blood to the lungs.
   D) The aorta carries blood from the heart to the body.

Respiration and Excretion

Chapter Preview

Skills Preview

Skill Builder

- Sequence
- Map Concepts

Activities

- Design an Experiment
- Observe and Infer

MiniLabs

- Measure
- Model

Reading Check ✓

As you read this chapter, look for clues that can help you understand unfamiliar terms. These clues can include nearby words and sentences, as well as illustrations.

Explore Activity

Have you ever played basketball or run so hard that it felt like your lungs would burst? How long did it take your breathing rate to return to normal? You can live more than a week without food. You might live several days without water. But, you can live only several minutes without oxygen. Your body has the ability to store food and water. It cannot store much oxygen. It needs a continuous supply to keep your body cells functioning. Sometimes, your body needs a lot of oxygen. In the following activity, find out about one factor that can change your breathing rate.

Observe Breathing Rate

1. Put your hand on your chest. Take a deep breath. Feel your chest move up and down slightly. Notice how your rib cage moves out and upward when you inhale.

2. Count your breathing rate for 15 s. Multiply this number by four to figure your breathing rate for one minute. Repeat this activity and calculate your average breathing rate.

3. Jog in place for one minute and count your breathing rate again.

4. How long does it take for your breathing rate to return to normal?

Science Journal

In your Science Journal, record your breathing rate before and after physical activity. Also, write down how long it took for your breathing rate to return to normal. Describe any changes you observed. Write an explanation of how breathing rate appears to be related to physical activity.

19•1 The Respiratory System

Functions of the Respiratory System

People have always known that air and food are needed for life. However, until about 225 years ago, no one knew why air was so important. At that time, a British chemist discovered that a mouse couldn't live in a container in which a candle had previously been burned. He reasoned that a gas in the air of the container had been destroyed when the candle burned. He also discovered that if he put a plant into the container, whatever was necessary for life returned in eight or nine days, and a mouse again could live in the container. What do you think the plant produced when it was in the container? Think about photosynthesis. It had produced the gas needed for life that was later named oxygen.

Breathing and Respiration

People often get the terms *breathing* and *respiration* confused. Breathing is the process whereby fresh air moves into and stale air moves out of lungs. Fresh air contains oxygen, which passes from the lungs into your circulatory system. Blood then carries the oxygen to your individual cells. At the same time, your digestive system has prepared a supply of glucose in

Figure 19-1 Several processes are involved in how the body obtains, transports, and utilizes oxygen.

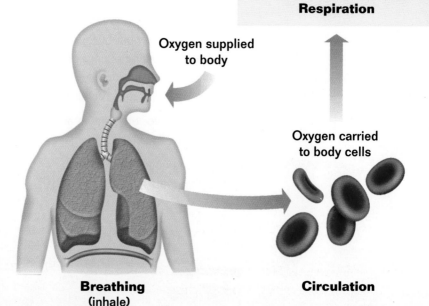

Oxygen used in chemical reaction to release energy from glucose

Respiration

Oxygen supplied to body

Oxygen carried to body cells

Breathing
(inhale)

Circulation

your cells from digested food. Now, oxygen is used in a series of chemical reactions to release the energy in glucose. These reactions, shown in the equation in **Figure 19-1,** are called respiration and occur in the mitochondria of cells. Carbon dioxide and water molecules are waste products of respiration. These molecules are carried in your blood to your lungs. When you exhale, you get rid of respiration's waste product. ☑

Figure 19-2 shows a place where there is decreased air pressure. The air is less dense at extreme heights, so there are fewer oxygen molecules in every breath you take. Why would it be harder to breathe on top of mountains?

Figure 19-2 Mount Everest is the highest place on Earth. Mountain climbers experience headaches, nausea, and shortness of breath while ascending to the top of high mountains.

Reading Check ☑

What is the difference between breathing and respiration?

$$C_6H_{12}O_6 + 6O_2 \rightarrow 6CO_2 + 6H_2O + Energy$$

(Glucose) + (Oxygen) → (Carbon dioxide) + (Water) + (Energy)

Respiration

Carbon dioxide
exhaled

Carbon dioxide
waste expelled

Carbon dioxide
removed from
cells to lungs

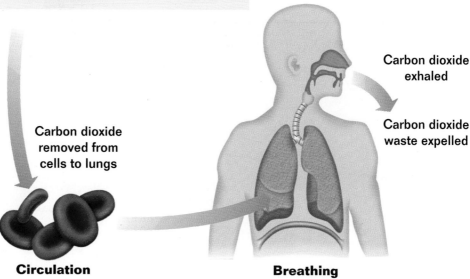

Circulation

Breathing
(exhale)

Compare the composition of the air you inhale and the air you exhale by making two circle graphs. Inhaled air is made up of 78.62 percent nitrogen, 0.5 percent water vapor, 0.04 percent carbon dioxide, and 20.84 percent oxygen. Exhaled air is made up of 74.5 percent nitrogen, 6.2 percent water vapor, 3.6 percent carbon dioxide, and 15.7 percent oxygen.

Organs of the Respiratory System

Your respiratory system is made up of body parts that help move oxygen into your body and carbon dioxide out of your body. The major structures and organs of your respiratory system are shown in **Figure 19-3.** These include your nasal cavity, pharynx (FER ingks), larynx (LER ingks), trachea (TRAY kee uh), bronchi (BRAHN ki), bronchioles (BRAHN kee ohlz), lungs, and alveoli. Air enters your body through two openings in your nose called nostrils or through your mouth. Once inside the nostrils, hair traps dust from the air. From your nostrils, air passes through your nasal cavity, where it gets moistened and warmed. Glands that produce sticky mucus line the nasal cavity. The mucus traps dust, pollen, and other materials that were not trapped by the nasal hair. This helps filter and clean the air you breathe. Tiny hair-like structures, called cilia, move mucus and trapped material to the back of the throat where it can be swallowed.

Figure 19-3 Air can enter the body through both the nostrils and the mouth. **What is the advantage of having air enter through the nostrils?**

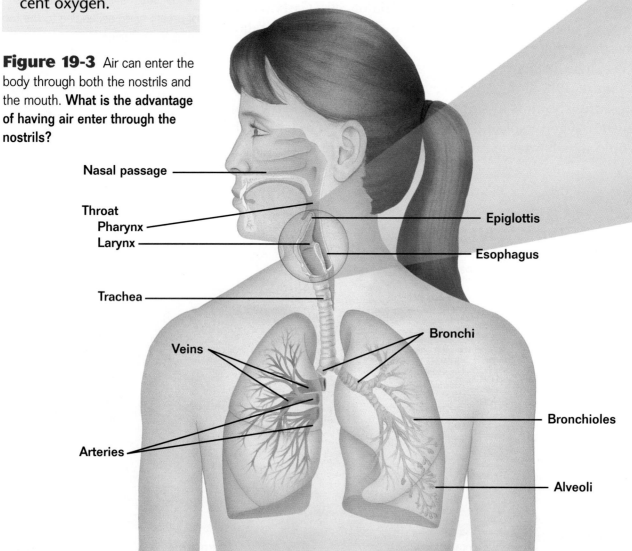

Nasal passage

Throat
Pharynx
Larynx

Trachea

Veins

Arteries

Epiglottis

Esophagus

Bronchi

Bronchioles

Alveoli

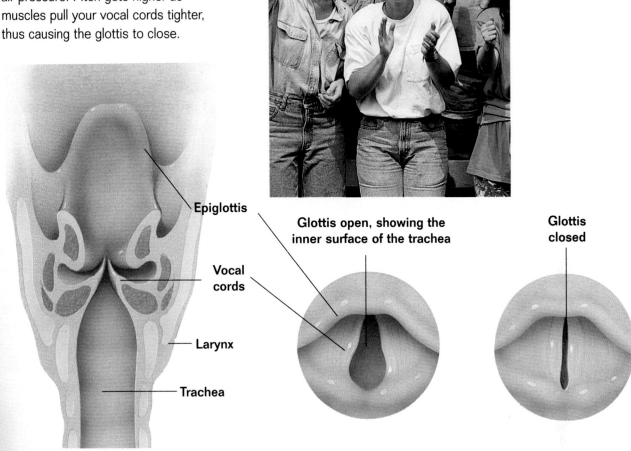

Figure 19-4 Sound made by your vocal cords gets louder with increased air pressure. Pitch gets higher as muscles pull your vocal cords tighter, thus causing the glottis to close.

Epiglottis

Vocal cords

Larynx

Trachea

Glottis open, showing the inner surface of the trachea

Glottis closed

Pharynx, Larynx, and Trachea

Warm, moist air now moves to the **pharynx,** a tubelike passageway for both food and air. At the lower end of the pharynx is a flap of tissue called the epiglottis. When you swallow, the epiglottis folds down over the glottis, the opening between your vocal cords. By doing this, food or liquid is prevented from entering your larynx. The food goes into your esophagus instead. What do you think could happen if you talk or laugh while eating?

The **larynx** is the airway to which your vocal cords are attached. Look at **Figure 19-4.** When you speak, muscles tighten or loosen your vocal cords. Sound is produced when air moves past, causing them to vibrate.

Below the larynx is the **trachea,** a tube about 12 cm in length. C-shaped rings of cartilage keep the trachea open and prevent it from collapsing. The trachea is lined with mucous membranes and cilia to trap dust, bacteria, and pollen. Why is it necessary for the trachea to stay open all the time?

Mini Lab

Measuring Surface Area

Procedure

1. Make a cylinder out of a large sheet of paper. Tape it together.
2. Make cylinders out of small sheets of paper. Place as many as will fit inside the large cylinder without crushing the cylinders.
3. Unroll each cylinder. Place the small sheets next to each other in a rectangle. Lay the large sheet on top.

Analysis

1. Compare the surface area of the large sheet with all the small sheets put together.
2. What do the large sheet and small sheets represent?
3. How does this make gas exchange more efficient?

Figure 19-5 About 300 million alveoli are in each lung. The exchange of oxygen and carbon dioxide with the environment takes place between the alveoli and the surrounding capillaries. **What is the name for the energy-releasing process that is fueled by oxygen?**

The Bronchi and the Lungs

At the lower end of the trachea are two short branches, called **bronchi** (singular, *bronchus*), that carry air into the lungs. Your lungs take up most of the space in your chest cavity. Within the lungs, the bronchi branch into smaller and smaller tubes. The smallest tubes are the bronchioles. At the end of each bronchiole are clusters of tiny, thin-walled sacs called **alveoli** (al VE uh li). As shown in **Figure 19-5,** lungs are actually masses of alveoli arranged in grapelike clusters. Capillaries surround the alveoli. The exchange of oxygen and carbon dioxide takes place between the alveoli and capillaries. This happens easily because the walls of the alveoli and the walls of the capillaries are only one cell thick. Oxygen diffuses through the walls of the alveoli and then through the walls of the capillaries into the blood. There the oxygen is picked up by hemoglobin in red blood cells and carried to all body cells. Hemoglobin is a chemical that can carry oxygen and carbon dioxide. As this takes place, carbon dioxide is transported back from body cells in the blood. It diffuses through the walls of the capillaries and through the walls of the alveoli. Carbon dioxide then leaves your body when you breathe out, or exhale.

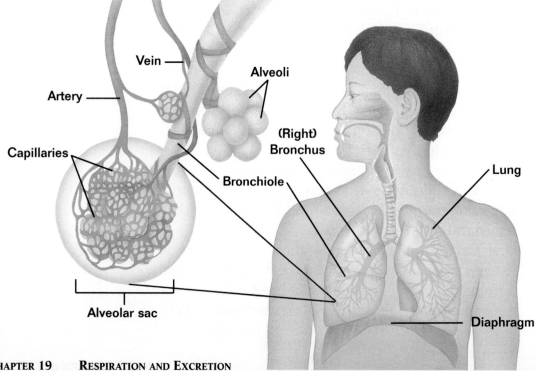

Vein — Alveoli

Artery —

Capillaries

(Right) Bronchus

Bronchiole

Lung

Alveolar sac

Diaphragm

How You Breathe

Breathing is partly the result of changes in air pressure. Under normal conditions, a gas moves from an area of high pressure to an area of low pressure. When you squeeze an empty plastic bottle, air rushes out. This happens because pressure outside the top of the bottle is less than inside the bottle while your hand is gripping it. As you release your grip on the bottle, the pressure inside the bottle becomes less than outside the bottle. Air rushes back in, and the bottle resumes its shape.

PHYSICS
◀**INTEGRATION**

Inhale and Exhale

Your lungs work in a similar way to the squeezed bottle. Your **diaphragm** (DI uh fram) is a muscle beneath your lungs that helps move air in and out of your body. It contracts and relaxes when you breathe. Like your hands on the plastic bottle, the diaphragm exerts pressure or relieves pressure on your lungs. **Figure 19-6** illustrates breathing.

Figure 19-6 Your lungs inhale and exhale about 500 mL of air with an average breath. This may increase to 2000 mL of air per breath when you do strenuous physical activity.

VISUALIZING
Breathing

Inhale

Exhale

A When you inhale, your diaphragm contracts and moves down. The upward movement of your rib cage and the downward movement of your diaphragm cause the volume of your chest cavity to increase. Air pressure is reduced in your chest cavity. Air under pressure outside the body pushes into your air passageways and lungs. Your lungs expand as the air rushes into them.

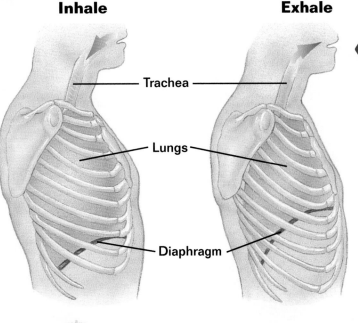

Trachea

Lungs

Diaphragm

B When you exhale, your diaphragm relaxes and moves up to return to its dome shape. Your rib cage moves downward. These two actions reduce the size of your chest cavity. Your lungs also return to their original position. Pressure on your lungs is increased by these two actions. The gases inside your lungs are pushed out through the air passages.

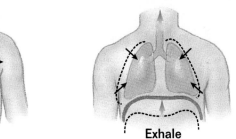

Inhale

Exhale

A Life-Saving Maneuver

The epiglottis closes over your larynx to stop food from entering the trachea. Sometimes, this process does not happen quickly enough. Each year, thousands of people die because food or other objects become lodged in the trachea. Air flow between the lungs and the mouth and nasal cavity is blocked. Death can occur in a matter of minutes.

Pressure Dislodges the Food

Rescuers use abdominal thrusts (also called the Heimlich maneuver), **Figure 19-7,** to save the life of a choking victim. **CAUTION:** *This maneuver can cause harm and should be done only if necessary.* The theory behind this maneuver is to use pressure to force out the food or object. When the diaphragm is forced up, the volume of the chest cavity quickly decreases. Pressure is suddenly increased. Air is forced up in the trachea. There may be enough force to dislodge food or an object. The victim is able to breathe again.

Figure 19-7 Abdominal thrusts are used to save a person from choking.

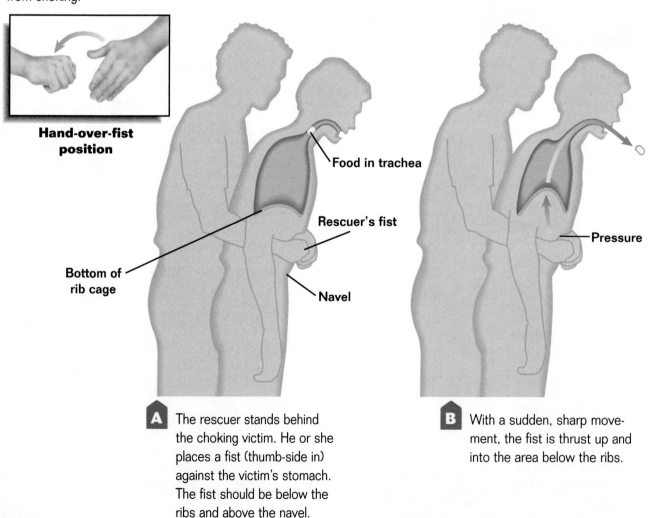

Hand-over-fist position

Food in trachea

Rescuer's fist

Bottom of rib cage

Navel

Pressure

A The rescuer stands behind the choking victim. He or she places a fist (thumb-side in) against the victim's stomach. The fist should be below the ribs and above the navel.

B With a sudden, sharp movement, the fist is thrust up and into the area below the ribs.

Diseases and Disorders

If you were asked to list some of the things that can harm your respiratory system, you would probably put smoking at the top. Many serious diseases are related to smoking. Being around others who smoke also can harm your respiratory system. Smoking, polluted air, and coal dust have been related to respiratory problems such as bronchitis, emphysema, cancer, and asthma.

Chronic Bronchitis

Bronchitis is a disease in which the bronchial tubes are irritated and too much mucus is produced. Many cases of bronchitis clear up within a few weeks, but sometimes the disease will last for a long time. When bronchitis persists for a long time, it is called **chronic bronchitis.** Many cases of chronic bronchitis result from smoking. People who have chronic bronchitis cough often to try to clear the mucus from the airway, as **Figure 19-8** shows. However, the more a person coughs, the more the cilia and bronchial tubes can be harmed. When cilia are damaged, their ability to move mucus, bacteria, and dirt particles out of the lungs is impaired. If this happens, harmful substances, such as sticky tar from burning tobacco, build up in the airways. Sometimes, scar tissue forms, impairing the ability of the respiratory system to function.

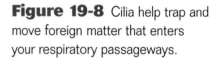

*inter*NET
CONNECTION

Visit the Glencoe Science Web Site at **www.glencoe.com/ sec/science/ca** for more information about lung disease.

Figure 19-8 Cilia help trap and move foreign matter that enters your respiratory passageways.

A Coughing is a reflex that moves unwanted matter from respiratory passages.

B Hairlike cilia in the respiratory passage are shown here. **How do damaged cilia weaken your body's defense against disease?**

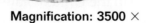
Magnification: 3500 ✕

Figure 19-9 Lung diseases can have major effects on breathing.

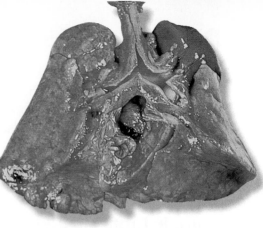

A A normal, healthy lung can exchange oxygen and carbon dioxide effectively.

B A diseased lung cuts down on the amount of oxygen that can be delivered to body cells.

C Emphysema may take 20 to 30 years to develop.

Using Computers

At the beginning of this chapter, you determined your breathing rate for one minute. Use that number to calculate how many breaths you take in a day. If every two breaths filled a liter bottle, how many bottles would you fill in a day?

Emphysema

A disease in which the alveoli in the lungs lose their ability to expand and contract is called **emphysema** (em fuh SEE muh). Most cases of emphysema result from smoking. In fact, many smokers who are afflicted with chronic bronchitis eventually progress to emphysema. When a person has emphysema, cells in the bronchi become inflamed. An enzyme released by the cells causes the alveoli to stretch and lose their elasticity. As a result, alveoli can't push air out of the lungs. Less oxygen moves into the bloodstream from the alveoli. Blood becomes low in oxygen and high in carbon dioxide. This condition results in shortness of breath. As shown in **Figure 19-9,** some people with emphysema can't blow out a match or walk up a flight of stairs. Because the heart works harder to supply oxygen to body cells, people who have emphysema often develop heart problems, as well.

Lung Cancer

Lung cancer is the third leading cause of death in men and women in the United States. Inhaling the tar in cigarette smoke is the greatest contributing factor to lung cancer. Once in the body, tar and other ingredients found in smoke are changed into carcinogens (kar SIHN uh junz). These carcinogens trigger lung cancer by causing uncontrolled growth of cells in lung tissue. Smoking also is believed to be a factor in the development of cancer of the mouth, esophagus, larynx, and pancreas. **Figure 19-10** shows one way people are encouraged not to smoke.

Asthma

Some lung disorders are common in nonsmokers. **Asthma** (AZ muh) is a disorder of the lungs in which there may be shortness of breath, wheezing, or coughing. When a person has an asthma attack, the bronchial tubes contract quickly. Asthma attacks are generally treated by inhaling drugs that enlarge the bronchial tubes. Asthma is often an allergic reaction. An asthma attack can result from a reaction to breathing certain substances, such as cigarette smoke or plant pollen. Eating certain foods or stress also have been related to the onset of asthma attacks.

Figure 19-10 More than 85 percent of all lung cancer is related to smoking.

Except for certain bacteria, all living things would die without oxygen. Your respiratory system takes in oxygen and gets rid of carbon dioxide. This system also helps get rid of some pathogens. You can help keep your respiratory system healthy by avoiding smoking and breathing polluted air. Regular exercise helps increase your body's ability to use oxygen.

Section Assessment

1. What is the main function of the respiratory system?
2. How are oxygen and carbon dioxide gases exchanged in the lungs and in body tissues?
3. What causes air to move in and out of the lungs?
4. How does emphysema affect a person's alveoli?
5. **Think Critically:** How is the work of the digestive and circulatory systems related to the respiratory system?
6. **Skill Builder**
   Making Models Lungs are important organs used in the process of respiration. Do the **Chapter 19 Skill Activity** on page 724 and make a model of how lungs function.

Science Journal Use library references to find out about a lung disease common among coal miners, stonecutters, and sandblasters. In your Science Journal, write a paragraph about the symptoms of this disease. Research what safety measures are now required when working with coal and rock.

The Effects of Exercise on Respiration

Possible Materials

- Clock or watch with second hand
- Drinking straws
- Bromothymol blue solution (200 mL)
- Glass cups (12 oz) (2)
  * *beakers (400 mL) (2)*
- Metric measuring cup
  * *graduated cylinder (100 mL)*
  * *Alternate Materials*

Breathing rate increases with an increase in physical activity. A bromothymol blue solution changes color when carbon dioxide is bubbled into it. Can you predict whether there will be a difference in the time it takes for the solution to change color before and after exercise?

Recognize the Problem

How will an increase in physical activity affect the amount of carbon dioxide exhaled?

Form a Hypothesis

State a hypothesis about how exercise will affect the amount of carbon dioxide exhaled by the lungs.

Goals

- **Observe** the effects of the amount of carbon dioxide on the bromothymol blue solution.

- **Design an experiment** that tests the effects of a variable, such as the amount of carbon dioxide exhaled before and after exercise, on the rate at which the solution changes color.

Safety Precautions

Protect clothing from the solution. Wash hands after using the solution. **CAUTION:** *Do not inhale the solution through the straw.*

Test Your Hypothesis

Plan

1. As a group, agree upon and **write out** the hypothesis statement.

2. As a group, **list** the steps that you will need to take to test your hypothesis. Consider each of the following factors. How will you introduce the exhaled air into the bromothymol blue solution? How will you collect data on exhaled air before and after physical activity? What kind of activity is involved? How long will it go?

3. **List** your materials. Your teacher will provide instruction on safe procedures for using bromothymol blue.

4. **Design** a data table and **record** it in your Science Journal so that it is ready to use as your group collects data.

5. **Read** over your entire experiment to make sure that all the steps are in logical order.

6. **Identify** any constants, variables, and controls of the experiment.

Do

1. Make sure your teacher approves your plan before you proceed.

2. Carry out the experiment as planned.

3. While the experiment is going on, write down any observations that you make and complete the data table in your Science Journal.

Analyze Your Data

1. What caused the bromothymol blue solution to change color? What color was it at the conclusion of each test?

2. What was the control? What was the constant(s)? What was the variable(s)?

3. **Compare** the time it took the bromothymol blue solution to change color before exercise and after exercise. Explain any difference.

4. Prepare a table of your data and **graph** the results.

Draw Conclusions

1. Did exercise affect your rate of respiration? Explain your answer using data from your experiment.

2. Using your graph, **estimate** the time of color change if the time of your physical activity were twice as long.

How it Works

Scuba

For humans, having a constant supply of oxygen is a matter of life or death. People get the oxygen they need from the air they breathe. This means swimmers can stay underwater only for as long as they can hold their breath. Those who want to dive deeper and stay underwater longer must use scuba equipment. Scuba stands for Self-Contained Underwater Breathing Apparatus.

GEARED FOR THE DEPTHS

Three pieces of equipment (on the diver, right) enable divers to spend a longer period of time underwater: (1) a buoyancy-control device, or BCD, (2) a scuba tank, and (3) a regulator.

1 **BCD** Before the dive, the BCD—an inflatable vest or jacket—is partially filled with air. The diver descends by letting air out of the BCD. The diver maintains his or her position at different depths by controlling the amount of air in the BCD.

2 **Scuba tank** Worn on the diver's back, the tank holds a large amount of compressed air—air that has been squeezed into a smaller space under high pressure. The diver breathes the air in this tank while underwater. The compressed air in the scuba tank also is used to add air to the BCD to increase a diver's buoyancy (make a diver rise in the water).

3 **Regulator** On the water's surface, air pressure in the lungs is equal to outside air pressure, measured as atmospheres (atm). Pressure increases at a rate of 1 atm for each 10 m underwater. As a diver descends, the regulator automatically compensates for the increase in depth (and thus, pressure). So, the regulator supplies air from the tank to the diver at the same pressure as the surrounding water. The diver never feels squeezed by the increased pressure of the deeper water.

Think Critically

1. The volume of air increases as pressure decreases. Relate this to the fact that divers should never hold their breath as they ascend.
2. Why does a diver use a weight belt in addition to a BCD when diving?

Career CONNECTION

Professional scuba divers are paid to dive for specific purposes. Professional divers work for the military, the government, and commercial agencies. A military diver may look for a hidden bomb under the sea. A commercial diver may work on an oil platform. Law enforcement agencies often hire divers to look for missing bodies or weapons.

The Excretory System

Functions of the Excretory System

Just as wastes, in the form of sewage or garbage, are removed from your home, your body also eliminates wastes by means of your excretory system. Undigested material is eliminated by your digestive system. The waste gas, carbon dioxide, is eliminated through the combined efforts of your circulatory and respiratory systems. Some salts are eliminated when you sweat. Together, these systems function as a part of your excretory system. If wastes aren't eliminated, you can become sick. Toxic substances build up and damage organs. If not corrected, serious illness or death occurs.

Figure 19-11 shows how the urinary system functions as a part of the excretory system. The organs of your urinary system are excretory organs. Your **urinary system** is made up of organs that rid your blood of wastes produced by the metabolism of nutrients. This system also controls blood volume by removing excess water produced by body cells. A specific amount of water in blood is important to maintain normal blood pressure, the movement of gases, and excretion of solid wastes. Your urinary system also balances specific concentrations of certain salts and water that must be present for cell activities to take place.

Figure 19-11 The urinary system is linked with the digestive, circulatory, and respiratory systems, as well as skin to make up the excretory system.

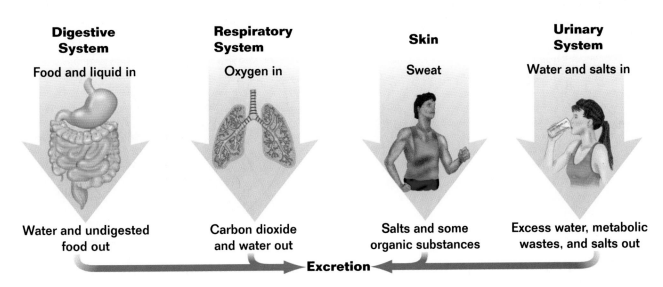

Organs of the Urinary System

The major organs of your urinary system, as shown in **Figure 19-12,** are two bean-shaped kidneys. Kidneys are located on the back wall of the abdomen at about waist level. The **kidneys** filter blood that has collected wastes from cells. All of your blood passes through your kidneys many times a day. In **Figure 19-12,** you can see that blood enters the kidneys through a large artery and leaves through a large vein.

The Filtering Unit

Each kidney is made up of about 1 million **nephrons** (NEF rahnz), the tiny filtering units of the kidney. Each nephron has a cuplike structure and a duct. Blood moves from the renal artery to capillaries in the cuplike structure. Water, sugar, salt, and wastes from your blood pass into the cuplike structure. From there, the liquid is squeezed into a narrow tubule. Capillaries that surround the tubule reabsorb most of the water, sugar, and salt and return it to the blood. These capillaries merge to form small veins. The small veins merge to form the renal veins, which return purified blood to your main circulatory system. The liquid left behind flows into collecting tubules in each kidney. This waste liquid, or **urine,** contains excess water, salts, and other wastes not reabsorbed by the body. The average adult produces about 1 L of urine per day.

*inter***NET**
CONNECTION

Visit the Glencoe Science Web Site at **www.glencoe.com/ sec/science/ca** for more information about how kidneys work.

Figure 19-12 The urinary system (A) is made of your kidneys, bladder, and the connecting tubes. The kidneys (B) are made up of many nephrons (C). A single nephron is shown in detail. **What is the main function of the nephron?**

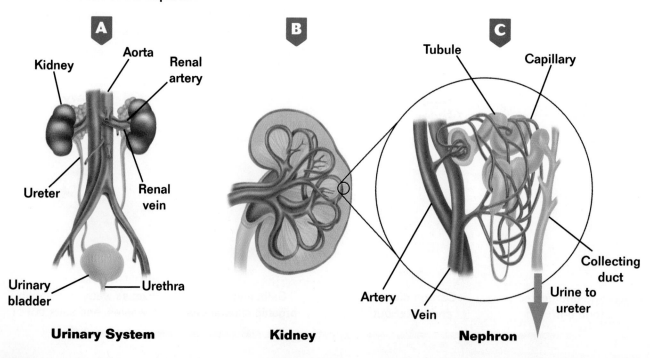

A

Kidney · Aorta · Renal artery

Ureter · Renal vein

Urinary bladder · Urethra

Urinary System

B

Kidney

C

Tubule · Capillary

Artery · Vein

Collecting duct

Urine to ureter

Nephron

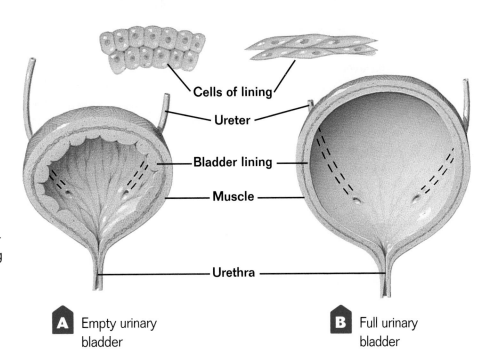

Figure 19-13 The elastic walls of the bladder can stretch to hold up to 500 mL of urine. When empty, the bladder looks wrinkled (A). The cells of the lining are thick. When full, the bladder looks similar to an inflated balloon (B). The cells of the lining are stretched and thin.

Cells of lining

Ureter

Bladder lining

Muscle

Urethra

A Empty urinary bladder

B Full urinary bladder

Urine Collection and Release

The urine in each collecting tubule drains into a funnel-shaped area of each kidney that leads to the ureters (YER ut urz). **Ureters** are tubes that lead from each kidney to the bladder. The **bladder** is an elastic, muscular organ that holds urine until it leaves the body. **Figure 19-13** shows how the shape of the cells that make up the lining of the bladder changes with the amount of urine stored in it. A tube called the **urethra** (yoo REE thruh) carries urine from the bladder to the outside of the body.

Other Water Loss

Other parts of the excretory system also help your body maintain proper fluid levels. In addition to losing salt, an adult loses about 0.5 L of water each day through perspiration. When air is exhaled, you also lose water. When you see your breath on a cold day or breathe on a cold windowpane and notice water vapor, you see this moisture. Each day, about 350 mL of water are removed from your body through your respiratory system. A small amount of water also is expelled with the undigested material that passes out of your digestive system.

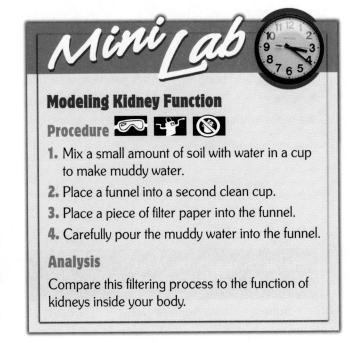

Mini Lab

Modeling Kidney Function

Procedure

1. Mix a small amount of soil with water in a cup to make muddy water.
2. Place a funnel into a second clean cup.
3. Place a piece of filter paper into the funnel.
4. Carefully pour the muddy water into the funnel.

Analysis

Compare this filtering process to the function of kidneys inside your body.

Figure 19-14 The amount of urine that you eliminate each day is determined by the level of a hormone. This hormone is produced by your hypothalamus.

Balancing Fluid Levels

To maintain good health, the fluid levels within your body must be balanced and your blood pressure must be maintained. This happens because an area of your brain, the hypothalamus, is involved in controlling your body's homeostasis (hoh mee oh STAY sus). The hypothalamus produces a hormone that regulates how much urine is produced. **Figure 19-14** shows what happens when there is too much water in your blood.

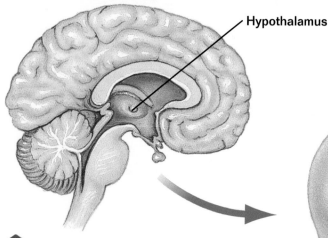

Increased level of liquid in blood

Hypothalamus

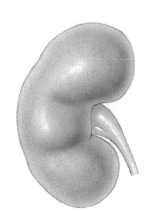

B This release signals the kidneys to return less water to the blood and increase the amount of urine excreted.

A Your brain detects too much water in your blood. Your hypothalamus then releases a lesser amount of hormone.

Problem Solving

Analyzing Water Gain and Loss

Cell activity and body functions depend on water. The balance of water must be maintained. Table A shows the major sources by which body water is gained.

Table B lists the major sources by which body water is lost.

Construct tables and calculate the percentages of sources of gain and loss of water. Complete your table with these data.

Think Critically

1. What is the greatest source of liquids gained by your body?

2. How would the percentages of water gained and lost change in a person who was working in extremely warm temperatures? What organ of the body would be the greatest contributor to water loss?

Table A

Major Sources by Which Body Water Is Gained		
Source	Amount (mL)	Percent
Oxidation of nutrients	250	
Foods	750	
Liquids	1500	
Total	**2500**	

Table B

Major Sources by Which Body Water Is Lost		
Source	Amount (mL)	Percent
Urine	1500	
Skin	500	
Lungs	350	
Feces	150	
Total	**2500**	

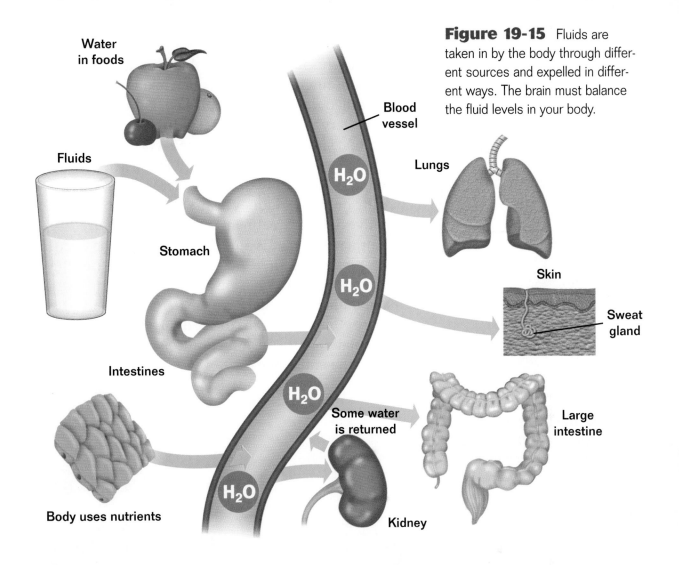

Figure 19-15 Fluids are taken in by the body through different sources and expelled in different ways. The brain must balance the fluid levels in your body.

Water in foods

Fluids

Blood vessel

Lungs

Skin

Sweat gland

Stomach

Intestines

H_2O

H_2O

H_2O

Some water is returned

Large intestine

H_2O

Body uses nutrients

Kidney

If too little water is in the blood, more of the hormone is released by your hypothalamus and more water is returned to the blood. The amount of urine excreted decreases. At the same time, your brain sends a signal that causes you to feel thirsty. You drink liquids to quench this thirst. **Figure 19-15** illustrates the different sources of fluid intake and output within your body.

Diseases and Disorders

What happens when someone's urinary organs don't work properly? Waste products that are not removed build up and act as poisons in body cells. Water that normally is removed from body tissues accumulates and causes swelling of the ankles and feet. Sometimes, fluids also can build up around the heart. The heart must work harder to move less blood to the lungs. Without excretion, an imbalance of salts may occur. The body responds by trying to restore this balance. If the balance is not restored, the kidneys and other organs can be damaged.

PHYSICS
INTEGRATION

Kidney Stones
Small, solid particles may form in the kidneys. If these stones pass into the ureter, severe pain results. One method of kidney stone removal involves the use of a lithotripter. This machine produces sound waves that cause the stones to break into small pieces. These pieces are carried out of the body in urine.

Dialysis

Persons who have damaged kidneys may need to have their blood filtered by an artificial kidney machine in a process called dialysis (di AL uh sus). During dialysis, blood from an artery is pumped through tubing that is bathed in a salt solution similar to blood plasma. Waste materials diffuse from the tube containing blood and are washed away by the salt solution. The cleaned blood is returned to a vein. A person with only one kidney can still function normally. An alternative dialysis treatment is pictured in **Figure 19-16**.

The urinary system is a purifying unit for the circulatory system. Wastes are filtered from blood as it passes through the kidneys. Some water, salts, and nutrients are reabsorbed to maintain homeostasis. Waste materials, dissolved in water, are eliminated from the body. This system helps to maintain the health of cells and, therefore, the entire body.

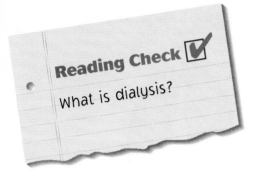

Reading Check

What is dialysis?

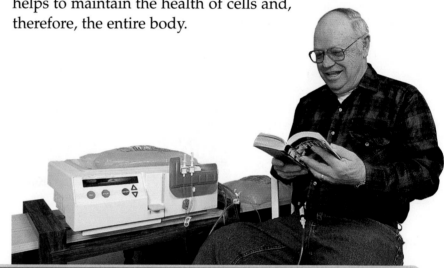

Figure 19-16 Peritoneal hemodialysis is a procedure that can be done at home for many dialysis patients. Dialysis fluid is pumped into the stomach cavity. Waste products then move from the blood vessels into the fluid, which is then drained from the patient.

Section Assessment

1. Describe the functions of the urinary system.
2. Explain how the kidneys remove wastes and keep fluids and salts in balance.
3. Compare the excretory and urinary systems.
4. **Think Critically:** Explain why reabsorption of certain materials in the kidneys is important.
5. **Skill Builder**
   Concept Mapping Using a network tree concept map, compare the excretory functions of the kidneys and the lungs. If you need help, refer to Concept Mapping in the **Skill Handbook** on page 678.

Using Computers

All 5 L of blood in the body pass through the kidneys in approximately five minutes. Calculate the average rate of flow through the kidneys in liters per minute.

Activity 19•2

Kidney Structure

As your body uses nutrients, wastes are created. One role of kidneys is to filter waste products out of the bloodstream and excrete this waste outside the body.

Materials
- Large animal kidney
- Scalpel
- Hand lens

What You'll Investigate

How does the structure of the kidney relate to its function?

Goals

- **Observe** the external and internal structures of a kidney.

Procedure

1. **Examine** the kidney supplied by your teacher.

2. If the kidney is still encased in fat, **peel** the fat off carefully.

3. Using a scalpel, carefully **cut** the tissue lengthwise in half around the outline of the kidney. This cut should result in a section similar to the illustration on this page.

4. **Observe** the internal features of the kidney using a hand lens, or view the features in a model.

5. **Compare** the specimen or model with the kidneys in the illustration.

6. **Draw** the kidney in your Science Journal and **label** the structures.

Conclude and Apply

1. What part makes up the cortex of the kidney? Why is this part red?

2. What is the main function of nephrons?

3. The medulla of the kidney is made up of a network of tubules that come together to form the ureter. What is the function of this network of tubules?

4. How can the kidney be compared to a portable water-purifying system?

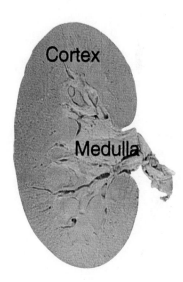

Cortex

Medulla

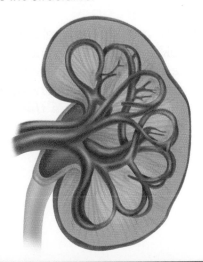

For a **preview** of this chapter, study this Reviewing Main Ideas before you read the chapter. After you have studied this chapter, you can use the Reviewing Main Ideas to **review** the chapter.

The Glencoe MindJogger, Audiocassettes, and CD-ROM provide additional opportunities for review.

Section
19-1 THE RESPIRATORY SYSTEM

Your respiratory system helps take oxygen into your lungs and body cells and helps you remove carbon dioxide. Inhaled air passes through the nasal cavity, **pharynx, larynx, trachea, bronchi,** and bronchioles and into the **alveoli** of the lungs. The mechanism of breathing results in part from the **diaphragm's** movement, which changes the pressure within the lungs. *Why does the trachea have cartilage but the esophagus does not?*

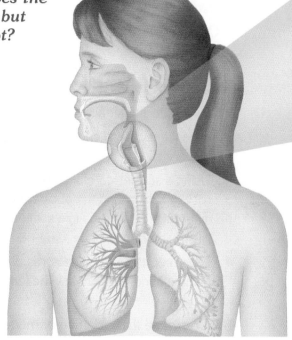

DISEASES AND DISORDERS

Many serious respiratory problems are related to smoking. In addition to smoking, polluted air and coal dust also have been associated with diseases such as **chronic bronchitis, emphysema,** lung cancer, and **asthma.** *Which respiratory disease is the third leading cause of death in men and women in the United States?*

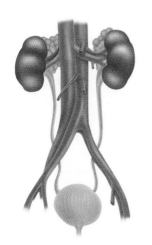

Reading Check ✔

What probable outcome could you predict for a young person who begins smoking? What is the basis for your prediction?

Section
19-2 THE EXCRETORY SYSTEM

Your **urinary system** is made up of organs that rid your blood of wastes produced by the metabolism of nutrients. It also controls blood volume by removing excess water produced by body cells. **Kidneys** are the major organs of the urinary system. They filter wastes from your body and keep sodium, water, and other chemicals in balance. When kidneys fail to work, dialysis may be used. In addition to the urinary system, parts of the digestive, circulatory, and respiratory systems work together as the excretory system. *How do the kidneys maintain homeostasis?*

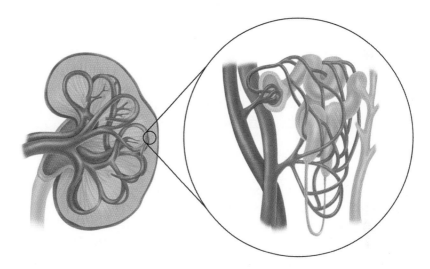

Career
CONNECTION
DR. BENJAMIN CARSON, SURGEON

Dr. Benjamin Carson is a surgeon at Johns Hopkins Hospital. Dr. Carson says that operating on a patient is like if you were a tightrope walker: If you are experienced, walking the rope isn't frightening, but if you haven't done it before, it can be scary. Dr. Carson admits that operating is sometimes taxing—especially when you do it for 16 hours at a stretch. Dr. Carson encourages young people to ask themselves, "What have I always been good at?" and to ask other people what they see that you're good at. *What problems of the respiratory system and excretory system could require surgery?*

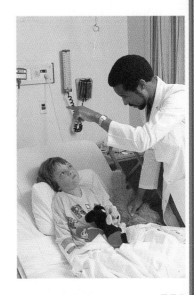

Using Vocabulary

a. alveoli
b. asthma
c. bladder
d. bronchi
e. chronic bronchitis
f. diaphragm
g. emphysema
h. kidney
i. larynx
j. nephron
k. pharynx
l. trachea
m. ureter
n. urethra
o. urinary system
p. urine

Using the list above, replace the underlined words with the correct Vocabulary term.

1. At the lower end of the <u>tubelike passageway for both food and air</u> is a flap of tissue called the epiglottis.
2. At the lower end of the trachea are two <u>short branches that carry air into the lungs.</u>
3. Each kidney is made up of about 1 million <u>tiny filtering units.</u>
4. <u>An elastic, muscular organ</u> holds urine until it leaves the body.
5. <u>A tube</u> carries urine from the bladder to the outside of the body.

Checking Concepts

Choose the word or phrase that best answers the question.

6. When you inhale, which of the following contracts and moves down?
   A) bronchioles
   B) diaphragm
   C) nephrons
   D) kidneys

7. Air is moistened, filtered, and warmed in which of the following structures?
   A) larynx
   B) pharynx
   C) nasal cavity
   D) trachea

8. Exchange of gases occurs between capillaries and which of the following structures?
   A) alveoli
   B) bronchi
   C) bronchioles
   D) trachea

9. When you exhale, which way does the rib cage move?
   A) It moves up.
   B) It moves down.
   C) It moves out.
   D) It stays the same.

10. Which of the following is a lung disorder that may occur as an allergic reaction?
   A) asthma
   B) chronic bronchitis
   C) emphysema
   D) cancer

11. Which of the following conditions does smoking worsen?
   A) arthritis
   B) respiration
   C) excretion
   D) emphysema

12. Which of the following are filtering units of the kidneys?
   A) nephrons
   B) ureters
   C) neurons
   D) alveoli

13. Urine is temporarily held in which of the following structures?
   A) kidneys
   B) bladder
   C) ureter
   D) urethra

14. Through which of the following is approximately 1 L of water lost per day?
   A) sweat
   B) lungs
   C) urine
   D) none of these

15. Which of the following substances is **NOT** reabsorbed by blood after it passes through the kidneys?
   A) salt
   B) sugar
   C) wastes
   D) water

Thinking Critically

16. Compare air pressure in the lungs during inhalation and exhalation.

17. What is the advantage of the lungs having many air sacs instead of being just two large sacs, like balloons?

18. Explain the damage smoking does to cilia, alveoli, and lungs.

19. What would happen to the blood if the kidneys stopped working?

20. Explain why a large kidney stone is often painful.

Developing Skills

If you need help, refer to the **Skill Handbook**.

21. **Making and Using Graphs:** Make a circle graph of total lung capacity.
    - Tidal volume (inhaled or exhaled during a normal breath) = 500 mL
    - Inspiratory reserve volume (air that can be inhaled forcefully after a normal inhalation) = 3000 mL
    - Expiratory reserve volume (air that can be exhaled forcefully after a normal expiration) = 1100 mL
    - Residual volume (air left in the lungs after forceful exhalation) = 1200 mL

22. **Interpreting Data:** Interpret the data below. How much of each substance is reabsorbed into the blood in the kidneys? What substance is totally excreted in the urine?

Materials Filtered by the Kidneys		
Substance	Amount moving through kidney to be filtered	Amount excreted in urine
water	125 L	1 L
salt	350 g	10 g
urea	1 g	1 g
glucose	50 g	0 g

23. **Recognizing Cause and Effect:** Discuss how lack of oxygen is related to lack of energy.

24. **Hypothesizing:** Hypothesize the number of breaths you would expect a person to take per minute in each situation and give a reason for each hypothesis.
    - while sleeping
    - while exercising
    - while on top of Mount Everest

THE PRINCETON REVIEW

Test-Taking Tip

Survey the Surroundings Find out what the conditions will be for taking the test. Will the test be timed? Will you be allowed to take a break? Know these things in advance so that you can practice taking tests under the same conditions.

Test Practice

Use these questions to test your Science Proficiency.

1. Air inhaled through the nose is filtered, warmed, and moistened. What are some benefits of these actions?
    A) The process prevents nitrogen and carbon dioxide from reaching the lungs.
    B) The process prevents bad odors from reaching the trachea and bronchi.
    C) The process prevents drying out of passageways and traps foreign materials.
    D) The process prevents the formation of mucus and cilia in the nasal cavity.

2. Blood flowing through the kidneys is filtered to remove excess materials and wastes. Which of the following are the major substances removed?
    A) salts, sugar, water, and wastes
    B) water, salt, sugar, and urine
    C) carbon dioxide, salt, sugar, and wastes
    D) water, salts, oxygen, and wastes

Chapter Preview

Section 20-1
The Nervous System

Section 20-2
The Senses

Section 20-3
The Endocrine System

Skills Preview

Skill Builders
- Map Concepts
- Make and Use a Table

Activities
- Compare and Contrast
- Design an Experiment

MiniLabs
- Interpret Data

Reading Check ✔

Before beginning Section 20-1, make a chart that will allow you to compare and contrast the central nervous system and the peripheral nervous system. Fill it in as you read.

Explore Activity

Who's in front of you? What note do we start on? Where's the conductor? Am I marching in rhythm? There's a lot to be aware of when you're part of a marching band. You must be sensitive to your surroundings and aware when changes take place. All organisms must be able to detect what is happening around them. Sights or sounds can warn of danger. Odors can help find food. Sensations of hot and cold can protect from fire or extreme temperatures. In this chapter, you will learn how your body's nervous system interprets all of the sensations it receives to produce a picture of its surroundings. In the following activity, find out whether your eyes can interpret objects correctly.

Observe Objects

1. Look at the figure at the right of the page.

2. Estimate the difference in heights between pole A and pole C.

3. Use a metric ruler to measure the heights of poles A, B, and C.

Science Journal

In your Science Journal, record what you found out about the height of the lines. Were your estimates correct? What did your eyes tell you?

The Nervous System at Work

After doing the dishes and finishing your homework, you settle down in your favorite chair and pick up that mystery novel you've been trying to finish. Only three pages to go . . . Who did it? Why did she do it? Then, "CRASH!" You scream and throw your book in the air. What made that unearthly noise? You turn around to find that your dog's wagging tail just swept the lamp off the table beside you. Suddenly, you're aware that your heart is racing and your hands are shaking. But, then, after a few minutes, your breathing returns to normal and your heartbeat is back to its regular rate. What's going on?

Response to Stimuli

The scene described above is an example of how your body responds to changes in its environment and adjusts itself. Your body makes these adjustments with the help of your nervous system. Any change inside or outside your body that brings about a response is called a stimulus. Each day, you're bombarded by thousands of stimuli. Noise, light, the smell of food, and the temperature of the air are all stimuli from outside your body. A growling stomach is an example of an internal stimulus.

How can your body handle all these stimuli? Your body has internal control systems that maintain steady conditions, no matter what's going on outside the body. This is called homeostasis. Breathing rate, heartbeat rate, and digestion are just a few of the activities that are constantly checked and regulated. Your nervous system and the endocrine system, a chemical control system described later in this chapter, are the main ways your body maintains homeostasis.

Figure 20-1 A neuron is made up of a cell body, dendrites, and an axon. **How does the branching of the dendrites allow for more impulses to be picked up by the neuron?**

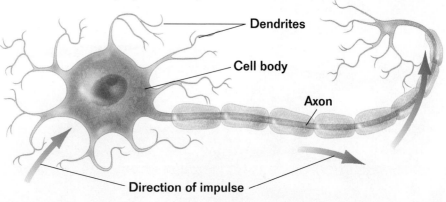

Dendrites

Cell body

Axon

Direction of impulse

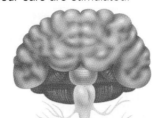

A When you hear the lamp break, sensory receptors in your ears are stimulated.

Figure 20-2 In your nervous system, impulses travel a pathway. Together, the three types of neurons act like a relay team, moving impulses through your body from stimulus to response.

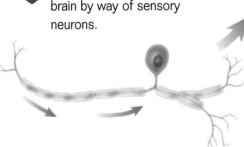

B A message is sent to your brain by way of sensory neurons.

C Your brain sorts the information and determines a response.

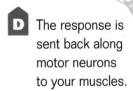

D The response is sent back along motor neurons to your muscles.

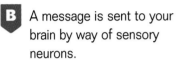

Neurons

The working unit of the nervous system is the nerve cell, or **neuron** (NOO rahn). The single neuron in **Figure 20-1** is made up of a cell body and branches called dendrites and axons. **Dendrites** receive messages and send them to the cell body. An **axon** (AK sahn) carries messages away from the cell body. Any message carried by a neuron is called an impulse. Notice that the end of the axon branches. This allows the impulses to move to many other muscles, neurons, or glands.

Types of Neurons

Your skin and other sense organs are equipped with structures called receptors that respond to various stimuli. Three types of neurons—sensory neurons, motor neurons, and interneurons—then become involved with transporting impulses about the stimuli. As illustrated in **Figure 20-2,** sensory neurons (B) receive information and send impulses to the brain or spinal cord. Once the impulses reach your brain or spinal cord, interneurons relay the impulses from the sensory to motor neurons. You have more interneurons in your body than either of the other two types of neurons. Motor neurons (D) then conduct impulses from the brain or spinal cord to muscles or glands throughout your body.

E Your heart immediately starts to pound and your breathing rate increases. You throw the book.

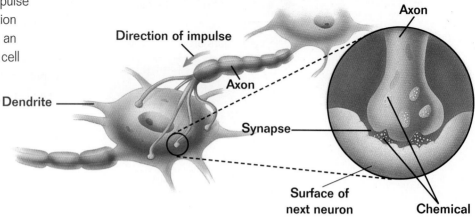

Figure 20-3 An impulse moves in only one direction across a synapse—from an axon to the dendrites or cell body of another neuron.

Direction of impulse

Dendrite

Axon

Synapse

Axon

Surface of next neuron

Chemical

Synapse

Neurons don't touch each other. How does an impulse move from one neuron to another? To get from one neuron to the next, an impulse moves across a small space called a **synapse** (SIHN aps). In **Figure 20-3,** you can see that when an impulse reaches the end of an axon, a chemical is released by the axon. This chemical diffuses across the synapse and starts an impulse in the dendrite or cell body of the next neuron. In this way, an impulse moves from one neuron to another.

The Central Nervous System

Figure 20-4 shows how organs of the nervous system are grouped into two major divisions: the central nervous system (CNS) and the peripheral nervous system (PNS). The **central nervous system** is made up of the brain and spinal cord. The **peripheral** (puh RIHF rul) **nervous system** is made up of all the nerves outside the CNS, including cranial nerves and spinal nerves. These nerves connect the brain and spinal cord to other body parts.

The brain coordinates all your body activities. If someone pokes you in the ribs, your whole body reacts. Your neurons are adapted in such a way that impulses move in only one direction. Sensory neurons send impulses that move from a receptor to the brain or spinal cord.

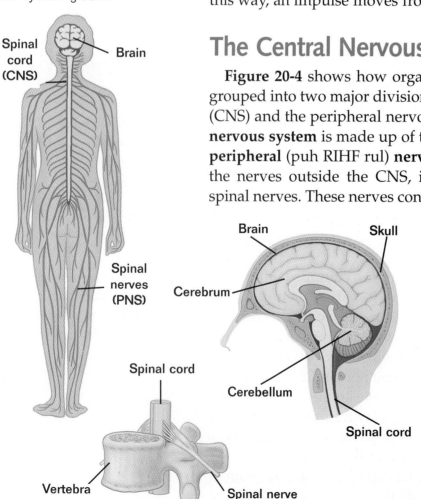

Figure 20-4 The brain and spinal cord (yellow) form the central nervous system, which sorts and interprets information from stimuli. All other nerves are part of the peripheral nervous system (green).

Spinal cord (CNS)

Brain

Spinal nerves (PNS)

Brain

Skull

Cerebrum

Cerebellum

Spinal cord

Spinal cord

Vertebra

Spinal nerve

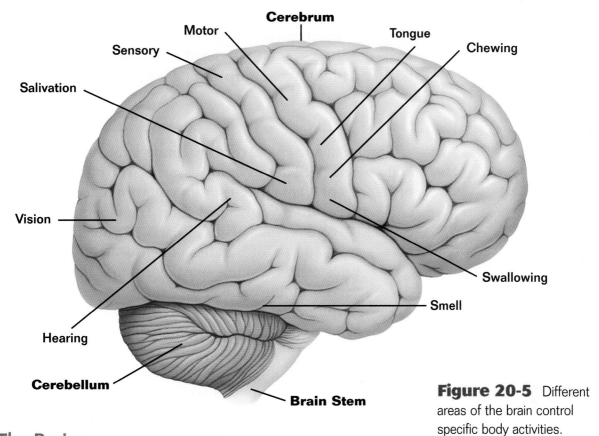

Motor
Cerebrum
Sensory
Tongue
Chewing
Salivation
Vision
Swallowing
Smell
Hearing
Cerebellum
Brain Stem

Figure 20-5 Different areas of the brain control specific body activities.

The Brain

The brain is made up of approximately 100 billion neurons. You can see in **Figure 20-5** that the brain is divided into three major parts: cerebrum, cerebellum, and brain stem. The largest part of the brain, the **cerebrum** (suh REE brum), is divided into two large sections called hemispheres. Here, impulses from the senses are interpreted, memory is stored, and the work of voluntary muscles is controlled. The outer layer of the cerebrum, the cortex, is marked by many ridges and grooves. The diagram also shows some of the tasks that sections of the cortex control.

A second part of the brain, the **cerebellum** (ser uh BEL um), is behind and under the cerebrum. It coordinates voluntary muscle movements and maintains balance and muscle tone.

The **brain stem** extends from the cerebrum and connects the brain to the spinal cord. It is made up of the midbrain, the pons, and the medulla. The brain stem controls your heartbeat, breathing, and blood pressure by coordinating the involuntary muscle movements of these functions.

The Spinal Cord

Your spinal cord is an extension of the brain stem. It is made up of bundles of neurons that carry impulses from all parts of the body to the brain and from the brain to all parts of your body. The spinal cord, illustrated in **Figure 20-4,** is about as big around as an adult thumb and it is about 43 cm long.

PHYSICS
INTEGRATION

Watching the Brain
Scientists use positron emission tomography (PET) to learn more about the brain. Brain cells that are active take up radioactive glucose, which causes an image to appear on a color monitor. Different colors indicate which areas of the brain are being stimulated. By comparing different PET images, researchers have located the areas of the brain used for seeing, reading, hearing, speaking, and thinking.

The CNS is protected by a bony cap called the skull, by vertebrae, and by three layers of membranes. Between some of these membranes is a fluid called cerebrospinal (suh ree broh SPINE ul) fluid. What purpose might this fluid serve?

The Peripheral Nervous System

Your brain and spinal cord are connected to the rest of your body by the peripheral nervous system. The PNS is made up of 12 pairs of cranial nerves from your brain and 31 pairs of spinal nerves from your spinal cord. These nerves link your central nervous system with all parts of your body. Spinal nerves are made up of bundles of sensory and motor neurons. For this reason, a single spinal nerve may have impulses going to and from the brain at the same time.

The peripheral nervous system has two divisions. The *somatic system* consists of the cranial and spinal nerves that go from the central nervous system to your skeletal muscles. The second division, the *autonomic system*, controls your heartbeat rate, breathing, digestion, and gland functions. When your salivary glands release saliva, your autonomic system is at work. Use **Figure 20-6** to help you remember these two divisions.

Using Math

One of the longest spinal nerves extends from the spinal cord to muscles in the foot. Estimate the length of this nerve. If the rate of travel of a nerve pulse is approximately 120 m per second, what is the length of time for an impulse to travel from the spinal cord to the foot?

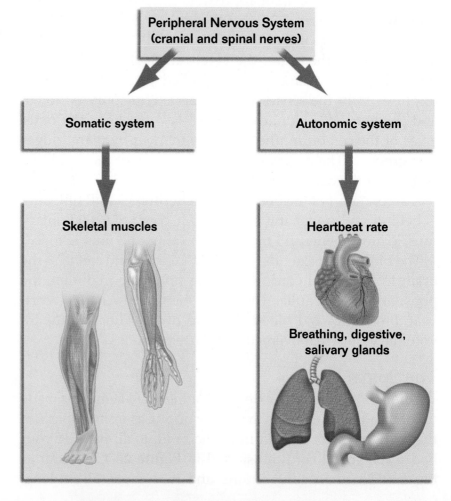

Figure 20-6 The divisions of the peripheral nervous system are shown. **What part of the PNS controls your breathing while you sleep?**

Figure 20-7 Your response in a reflex is controlled in your spinal cord, not in your brain.

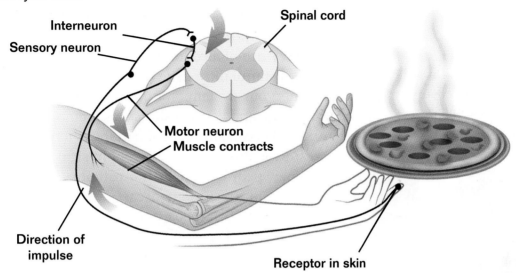

Interneuron

Sensory neuron

Spinal cord

Motor neuron
Muscle contracts

Direction of impulse

Receptor in skin

Reflexes

Have you ever moved quickly from something hot or sharp? Then you've experienced a reflex. A **reflex** is an involuntary and automatic response to a stimulus. Usually, you can't control reflexes because they occur before you know what has happened. A reflex involves a simple nerve pathway called a reflex arc. **Figure 20-7** shows a reflex arc. As you reach for the pizza, some hot cheese falls on your finger. Sensory receptors in your finger respond to the hot cheese, and an impulse is sent to the spinal cord. The impulse passes to an interneuron in the spinal cord that immediately relays the impulse to motor neurons. Motor neurons transmit the impulse to muscles in your arm. Instantly, without thinking, you pull your arm back in response to the burning food. This is a withdrawal reflex. A reflex allows the body to respond without having to think about what action to take. Reflex responses are controlled in your spinal cord, not in your brain. Your brain acts after the reflex to help you figure out what to do to make the pain stop. ☑

Remember in **Figure 20-2** how the girl was frightened after the lamp was broken? What would have happened if her breathing and heartbeat rate didn't calm down within a few minutes? Your body system can't be kept in a state of continual excitement. The organs of your nervous system control and coordinate responses to maintain homeostasis within your body.

*inter***NET**
CONNECTION

Visit the Glencoe Science Web Site at **www.glencoe.com/ sec/science/ca** for more information about the nervous system.

Reading Check ☑

Why are reflexes important?

Drugs and the Nervous System

Many drugs, such as alcohol and caffeine, have a direct effect on your nervous system. When swallowed, alcohol passes directly through the walls of the stomach and small intestine into the circulatory system. Alcohol is classified as a depressant drug. A depressant slows down the activities of the central nervous system. Judgment, reasoning, memory, and concentration are impaired. Muscle functions also are affected. Heavy use of alcohol destroys brain and liver cells.

Caffeine is a stimulant, a drug that speeds up the activity of the central nervous system. Too much caffeine can increase heartbeat rate and cause restlessness, tremors, and insomnia. It also can stimulate the kidneys to produce more urine. Caffeine can cause physical dependence. When people stop taking caffeine, they can have headaches and nausea. Caffeine is found in coffee, tea, cocoa, and many soft drinks, as seen in **Figure 20-8.**

Think again about a scare from the loud noise. The organs of your nervous system control and coordinate responses to maintain homeostasis within your body. This task is more difficult when your body must cope with the effects of drugs.

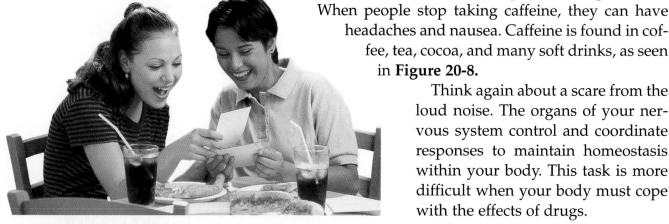

Figure 20-8 Caffeine, a substance found in cola, coffee, and other types of food and drink, can cause excitability and sleeplessness.

Section Assessment

1. Draw and label the parts of a neuron.
2. Compare the central and peripheral nervous systems.
3. Compare sensory and motor neurons.
4. **Think Critically:** During a cold winter evening, you have several cups of hot cocoa. Explain why you have trouble falling asleep.
5. **Skill Builder**
   Concept Mapping Prepare an events chain concept map of the different kinds of neurons an impulse moves along from a stimulus to a response. If you need help, refer to Concept Mapping in the **Skill Handbook** on page 678.

Using Computers

Word Processing Create a flowchart showing the reflex pathway of a nerve impulse when you step on a sharp object. Label the body parts involved in each step of the process. If you need help, refer to page 696.

Reaction Time

Materials

• Metric ruler

Your body responds quickly to some kinds of stimuli, and reflexes allow you to react quickly without even thinking. Sometimes you can improve how quickly you react. Complete this activity to see if you can improve your reaction time.

What You'll Investigate

How can reaction time be improved?

Goals

• **Observe** reflexes.
• **Identify** stimuli and responses.

Procedure

1. Make a data table in your Science Journal to record where the ruler is caught during this activity. Possible column heads are *Trial*, *Right Hand*, and *Left Hand*.

2. Have a partner hold the ruler at the top end.

3. Hold the thumb and finger of your right hand apart at the bottom of the ruler. Do not touch the ruler.

4. Your partner must let go of the ruler without warning you.

5. Try to catch the ruler by bringing your thumb and finger together quickly.

6. Repeat this activity several times and **record** where the ruler was caught in a data table.

7. Repeat this activity with your left hand. **Record** your results.

Conclude and Apply

1. **Identify** the stimulus in this activity.
2. **Identify** the response in this activity.
3. **Identify** the variable in this activity.
4. Use the table on this page to find your reaction time.
5. What was your average reaction time for your right hand? For your left hand?
6. **Compare** the response of your writing hand and your other hand for this activity.
7. **Draw a conclusion** about how practice relates to stimulus-response time.

Reaction Time	
Where Caught (cm)	**Reaction Time (s)**
5	0.10
10	0.14
15	0.17
20	0.20
25	0.23
30	0.25

In Touch with Your Environment

Science fiction stories about space often describe energy force fields around spaceships. When some form of energy tries to enter the ship's force field, the ship is put on alert. Your body has an alert system as well, in the form of sense organs. Your senses enable you to see, hear, smell, taste, touch, and feel whatever comes into your personal territory. The energy that stimulates your sense organs may be in the form of light rays, heat, sound waves, chemicals, or pressure. Sense organs are adapted for capturing and transmitting these different forms of energy.

Hearing

Sound energy is to hearing as light energy is to vision. As illustrated in **Figure 20-9,** when an object vibrates, it causes the air around it to vibrate, thus producing energy in the form of sound waves. When sound waves reach your ears, they stimulate nerve cells deep in your ear. Impulses are sent to the brain. The brain responds, and you hear a sound.

What You'll Learn

▶ The sensory receptors in each sense organ
▶ What type of stimulus each sense organ responds to and how
▶ Why healthy senses are needed

Vocabulary

cochlea   olfactory cell
retina   taste bud

Why It's Important

▶ Your senses make you aware of your environment, which helps keep you safe.

Figure 20-9 A vibrating object produces sound waves that are heard by your ears.

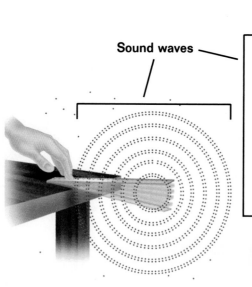

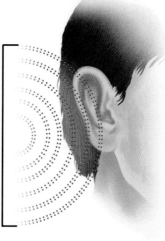

A When the ruler vibrates upward or downward, it pushes the particles of air in front of its movement closer together.

Sound waves

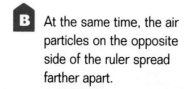

B At the same time, the air particles on the opposite side of the ruler spread farther apart.

C As the ruler vibrates up and down, it creates a wave-pattern of alternating particles of air that are compressed and spread out. This wave of sound travels to your eardrum, where the sound is received.

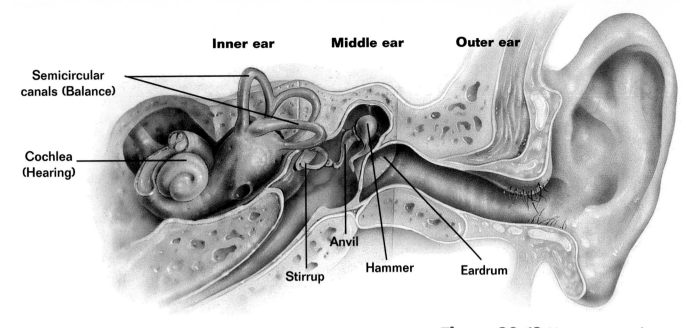

Inner ear   Middle ear   Outer ear

Semicircular
canals (Balance)

Cochlea
(Hearing)

Anvil

Stirrup

Hammer

Eardrum

Figure 20-10 Your ear responds to sound waves and to changes in the position of your head. **Why does spinning around make you dizzy?**

Figure 20-10 shows that your ear is divided into three sections: the outer, middle, and inner ear. Your outer ear traps sound waves and funnels them down the ear canal to the middle ear. The sound waves cause the eardrum to vibrate much like the membrane on a drum. These vibrations then move through three little bones called the hammer, anvil, and stirrup. The stirrup bone rests against a second membrane on an opening to the inner ear.

The Inner Ear

The **cochlea** (KOH klee uh) is a fluid-filled structure shaped like a snail's shell, in the inner ear. When the stirrup vibrates, fluids in the cochlea also begin to vibrate. These vibrations stimulate nerve endings in the cochlea, and impulses are sent to the brain by the auditory nerve. Depending on how the nerve endings are stimulated, you hear a different type of sound. High-pitched sounds make the endings move differently than lower, deeper sounds.

Balance also is controlled in the inner ear. Special structures and fluids in the inner ear constantly adjust to the position of your head. This stimulates impulses to the brain, which interprets the impulses and helps you make the necessary adjustments to maintain your balance.

Try at Home

Mini Lab

Observing Balance Control

Procedure

1. Place two narrow strips of paper on the wall to form two parallel vertical lines. Have a student stand between them, as still and straight as possible without leaning on the wall, for three minutes.

2. Observe how well balance is maintained.

3. Have the student close his or her eyes and repeat standing within the lines for three minutes.

Analysis

1. When was balance more difficult to maintain? Why?

2. What other factors might cause a person to lose the sense of balance?

Vision

Think about the different kinds of objects you look at every day. It's amazing that, at one glance, you can see the words on this page, the color illustrations, and your classmate sitting next to you.

Light travels in a straight line unless something bends or refracts it. Your eyes are equipped with structures that bend light. As light enters the eye, its waves are first bent by the cornea and then a lens, as illustrated in **Figure 20-11.** The lens directs the rays onto the retina (RET nuh). The **retina** is a tissue at the back of the eye that is sensitive to light energy. Two types of cells called rods and cones are found in the retina. Cones respond to bright light and color. Rods respond to dim light. They are used to help you detect shape and movement. Light energy stimulates impulses in these cells. The impulses pass to the optic nerve, which carries them to the brain. There, the impulses are interpreted, and you see what you are looking at.

Figure 20-11 Light moves through several structures—the cornea and the lens—before striking the retina.

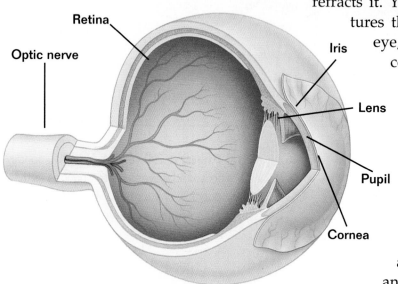

Retina

Optic nerve

Iris

Lens

Pupil

Cornea

PHYSICS
INTEGRATION ➤

Lenses—Refraction and Focus

Light is refracted, or bent, when it passes through a lens. Just how it bends depends on the type of lens it passes through. A lens that is thicker in the middle and thinner on the edges is called a convex lens. The lens in your eye is convex. If you follow the light rays in **Figure 20-12,** you'll see that the lens causes parallel light rays to come together at a focus point. Convex lenses can be used to magnify objects. The light rays enter the eyes in such a way through a convex lens that the object appears enlarged. Magnifying lenses, hand lenses, microscopes, and telescopes all have convex lenses.

A lens that has thicker edges than the middle is called a concave lens. Follow the light rays in **Figure 20-12** as they pass through a concave lens. You'll see that this kind of lens causes the parallel light to spread out. A concave lens is used along with convex lenses in telescopes to allow distant objects to be seen clearly.

Using Math

At four years of age, a young child can see clearly at a distance as close as 6.3 cm away. As the eye's lens hardens with age, this distance increases. At 30 years old, the distance is 15 cm. At 50 years old, the distance has become 40 cm. Estimate how many times longer the distance at 30 and 50 years old is compared to the distance clearly seen at four years old.

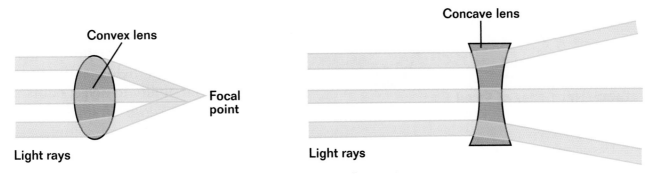

Figure 20-12 Light rays passing through a convex lens are bent toward the center and meet at a focal point. Light rays that pass through a concave lens are bent outward. They do not meet.

Correcting Vision

In an eye with normal vision, light rays are focused by the cornea and lens onto the retina. A sharp image is formed on the retina, and the brain interprets the signal as being clear. However, if the eyeball is too long from front to back, light from distant objects is focused in front of the retina. A blurred image is formed. This condition is called nearsightedness because near objects are seen clearly. To correct nearsightedness, eyeglasses with concave lenses are used. Concave lenses focus these images sharply on the retina. If the eyeball is too short from front to back, light from nearby objects is focused behind the retina. Again, the image appears blurred. Convex lenses correct this condition known as farsightedness. **Figure 20-13** shows how lenses are used to correct these vision problems. ☑

Reading Check ☑

What causes nearsightedness?

Figure 20-13 Glasses and contact lenses use concave or convex lenses to sharpen your vision.

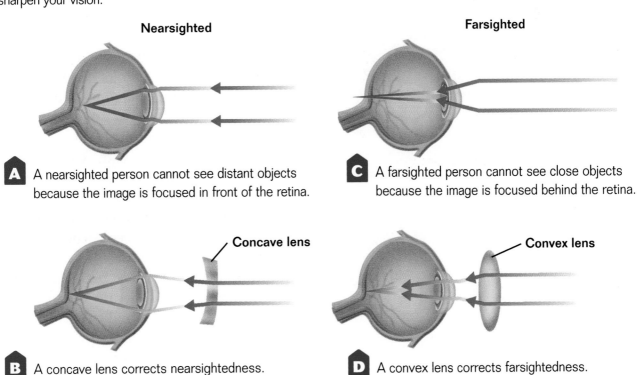

Nearsighted

A A nearsighted person cannot see distant objects because the image is focused in front of the retina.

B A concave lens corrects nearsightedness.

Farsighted

C A farsighted person cannot see close objects because the image is focused behind the retina.

D A convex lens corrects farsightedness.

Mini Lab

Comparing Sense of Smell

Procedure

1. Design an experiment to test your classmates' abilities to recognize the odors of different foods, colognes, or household products.
2. Record their responses in a data table according to the gender of the individuals tested.

Analysis

1. Compare the numbers of correctly identified odors for both males and females.
2. What can you conclude about the differences between males and females in their ability to recognize odors?

Figure 20-14 Although your taste buds distinguish four separate taste sensations (A), scientists cannot determine differences among individual taste buds (B).

B

A

Bitter

Sour

Sour/salty

Salty

Sweet

Smell

A bloodhound is able to track a particular scent through fields and forest. Even though your ability to detect odors is not as sharp, your sense of smell is still important.

You can smell food because it gives off molecules into the air. Nasal passages contain sensitive nerve cells called **olfactory cells** that are stimulated by gas molecules. The cells are kept moist by mucous glands. When gas molecules in the air dissolve in this moisture, the cells become stimulated. If enough gas molecules are present, an impulse starts in these cells and travels to the brain. The brain interprets the stimulus. If it is recognized from previous experience, you can identify the odor. If you can't recognize a particular odor, it is remembered and can be identified the next time, especially if it's a bad one.

Taste

Have you ever tasted a new food with the tip of your tongue and found that it tasted sweet? Then when you swallowed it, you were surprised to find that it tasted bitter. **Taste buds** on your tongue are the major sensory receptors for taste. About 10 000 taste buds are found all over your tongue, enabling you to tell one taste from another.

Taste buds respond to chemical stimuli. When you think of food, your mouth begins to water with saliva. This adaptation is helpful because in order to taste something, it has to be dissolved in water. Saliva begins this process. The solution washes over the taste buds, and an impulse is sent to your brain. The brain interprets the impulse, and you identify the taste.

Most taste buds respond to several taste sensations. However, certain areas of the tongue seem more receptive to one taste than another. The four basic taste sensations are sweet, salty, sour, and bitter. **Figure 20-14** shows where these tastes are commonly stimulated on your tongue.

Smell and taste are related. When you have a head cold with a stuffy nose, food seems tasteless because it is blocked from contacting the moist membranes in your nasal passages.

Touch, Pressure, Pain, and Temperature

How important is it to be able to feel pain inside your body? Several kinds of sensory receptors in your internal organs, as well as throughout your skin, respond to touch, pressure, pain, and temperature, as illustrated in **Figure 20-15.** These receptors pick up changes in touch, pressure, and temperature and transmit impulses to the brain or spinal cord. The body responds to protect itself or maintain homeostasis.

Your fingertips have many different types of receptors for touch. As a result, you can tell whether an object is rough or smooth, hot or cold, light or heavy. Your lips are sensitive to heat and prevent you from drinking something so hot that it would burn you. Pressure-sensitive cells in the skin give warning of danger to a body part and enable you to move to avoid injury.

Your senses are adaptations that help you enjoy or avoid things around you. You constantly react to your environment because of information received by your senses.

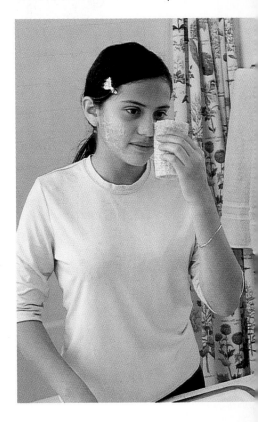

Figure 20-15 Many of the sensations picked up by receptors in the skin are stimulated by mechanical energy. Pressure, motion, and touch are examples.

Section Assessment

1. What type of stimulus do your ears respond to?
2. What are the sensory receptors for the eyes and nose?
3. Why is it important to have receptors for pain and pressure in your internal organs?
4. **Think Critically:** The brain is insensitive to pain. What is the advantage of this?
5. **Skill Builder**
   Observing and Inferring How can you tell the direction of a sound? Do the **Chapter 20 Skill Activity** on page 725 to explore how your ears detect sound.

Science Journal
Write a paragraph in your Science Journal to describe what each of the following objects would feel like.

1. coarse sand from a beach
2. ice cube
3. silk blouse
4. snake
5. smooth rock

Investigating Skin Sensitivity

Possible Materials

- Index card
  (3 inches × 5 inches)
- Toothpicks
- Tape or glue
- Metric ruler

Your body responds to touch, pressure, and temperature. Not all parts of your body are equally sensitive to stimuli. Some areas are more sensitive than others. For example, your lips are sensitive to heat. This protects you from burning your mouth. Now think about touch. How sensitive is the skin on various parts of your body to touch? Which areas can distinguish the smallest amount of distance between stimuli?

Recognize the Problem

What areas of the body are most sensitive to touch?

Form a Hypothesis

Based on your experiences, state a hypothesis about which of the following five areas of the body you believe to be most sensitive—fingertip, forearm, back of the neck, palm, and back of the hand. Rank the areas from 5 (the most sensitive) to 1 (the least sensitive).

Goals

- **Observe** the sensitivity to touch on specific areas of the body.

- **Design an experiment** that tests the effects of a variable, such as the closeness of contact points, to determine which body areas can distinguish between the closest stimuli.

Safety Precautions

 Do not apply heavy pressure when using the toothpicks.

Test Your Hypothesis

Plan

1. As a group, agree upon and write out the hypothesis statement.

2. As a group, **list** the steps you need to take to test your hypothesis. Be specific, describing exactly what you will do at each step. Consider the following factors as you list the steps. How will you know that sight is not a factor? How will you use the card shown on the right to **determine** sensitivity to touch? How will you **determine** and **record** that one or both points of touch are felt? List your materials.

3. Design a data table to use in your Science Journal.

4. Read over your entire experiment to make sure that all steps are in order.

5. Identify any constants, variables, and controls of the experiment.

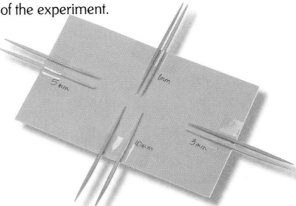

Do

1. Make sure your teacher approves your plan and your data table before you proceed.

2. **Carry out** the experiment as planned.

3. While the experiment is going on, **write down** any observations that you make and complete the data table in your Science Journal.

Analyze Your Data

1. **Compare** your results with those of other groups.

2. **Identify** which part of the body tested can distinguish between the closest stimuli.

3. **Identify** which part of the body is least sensitive.

4. **Rank** body parts tested from most to least sensitive. How did your results **compare** with your hypothesis?

Draw Conclusions

1. Based on the results of your investigation, what can you **infer** about the distribution of touch receptors on the skin?

2. What other parts of your body would you **predict** to be less sensitive? Explain your predictions.

The Endocrine System

Functions of the Endocrine System

"The tallest man in the world!" and "the shortest woman on Earth!" used to be common attractions in circuses. These people became attractions because of their extraordinary and unusual height. In most cases, their sizes were the result of a malfunction in their endocrine systems.

The endocrine system is the second control system of your body. Whereas impulses are control mechanisms of your nervous system, chemicals are the control mechanisms of your endocrine system. Endocrine chemicals called **hormones** are produced in several tissues called glands throughout your body. As the hormones are produced, they move directly into your bloodstream. Hormones affect specific tissues called **target tissues**. Target tissues are frequently located in another part of the body at a distance from the gland that affects them. Thus, the endocrine system doesn't react as quickly as the nervous system. **Table 20-1** shows the position of eight endocrine glands and what they regulate.

Table 20-1

Endocrine Glands		
	Gland	**Regulates**
	Pituitary	Endocrine glands, which produce hormones; milk production; growth
	Thyroid	Carbohydrate use
	Parathyroids	Calcium
	Adrenal	Blood sugar; salt and water balance; metabolism
	Pancreas	Blood sugar
	Ovaries	Egg production; sex organ development in females
	Testes	Sperm production; sex organ development in males

The Pancreas—Playing Two Roles

The pancreas produces a digestive enzyme. This enzyme is released into the small intestine through tubelike vessels called ducts. The pancreas is also part of your endocrine system because other groups of cells in the pancreas secrete hormones. One of these hormones, insulin, enables cells to take in glucose. Recall that glucose is the main source of energy for respiration in cells. Normally, insulin enables glucose to pass from the bloodstream through cell membranes. Persons who can't make insulin are diabetic because insulin isn't there to enable glucose to get into cells.

A Negative-Feedback System

To control the amount of hormone an endocrine gland produces, the endocrine system sends chemical information back and forth to itself. This is a negative-feedback system. It works much the way a thermostat works. When the temperature in a room drops below a certain level, a thermostat signals the furnace to turn on. Once the furnace has raised the temperature to the level set on the thermostat, the furnace shuts off. It will stay off until the thermostat signals again. In your body, once a target tissue responds to its

*inter*NET
CONNECTION

Visit the Glencoe Science Web Site at www.glencoe.com/ sec/science/ca for more information about endocrine diseases.

Problem Solving

Interpreting Blood Sugar Levels

Diabetes results when the pancreas does not produce enough insulin. Insulin is a hormone that enables cells to take in glucose. Glucose is a sugar needed for energy. Extra glucose is not stored, so the glucose is carried in the blood unless insulin enables the cells to take it in. Patients with diabetes have high amounts of sugar in the blood. Normal levels of sugar in the morning are between 60 and 100 milligrams per deciliter (mg/dL). Eating a meal increases glucose in the blood.

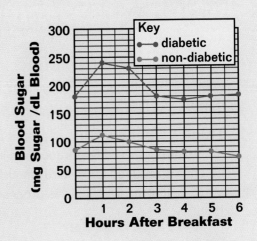

The graph shows the sugar in the blood from morning to afternoon. Notice the difference in blood sugars between a diabetic and a nondiabetic person.

Think Critically: Approximately how much difference is there in blood sugar levels between the two persons first thing in the morning? What might the diabetic person do to prevent such high readings one and two hours after breakfast? What might account for the increased level in blood sugar after the fourth hour?

hormone, the tissue sends a chemical signal back to the gland. This signal causes the gland to stop or slow down production of the hormone. When the level of the hormone in the bloodstream drops below a certain level, the endocrine gland is signaled to begin secreting the hormone again. In this way, the concentration of the hormone in the bloodstream is kept at the needed level. **Figure 20-16** illustrates how a negative-feedback system works.

Hormones produced by endocrine glands go directly into the bloodstream and affect target tissues. The level of the hormone is controlled by a negative-feedback system. In this way, many chemicals in the blood and body functions are controlled.

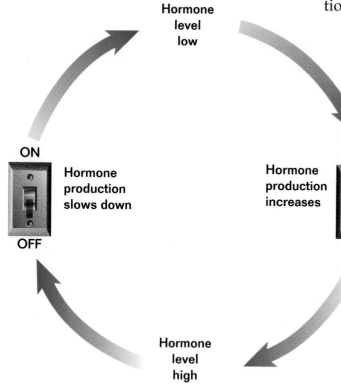

Hormone level low

ON
Hormone production slows down
OFF

ON
Hormone production increases
OFF

Hormone level high

Figure 20-16 Many internal body conditions, such as hormone level and body temperature, are controlled by negative-feedback systems.

Section Assessment

1. What is the function of hormones?

2. What is a negative-feedback system?

3. Choose one hormone and explain how it works.

4. **Think Critically:** Glucose passes from the bloodstream through cell membranes and into the cells. Glucose is required for respiration within cells. How would lack of insulin affect this process?

5. **Skill Builder**
   Comparing and Contrasting In what ways are the nervous system and endocrine system alike? If you need help, refer to Comparing and Contrasting in the **Skill Handbook** on page 684.

Science Journal
Pretend you are a doctor and have to explain to a young patient about diabetes. What would you say to him?

How it Works

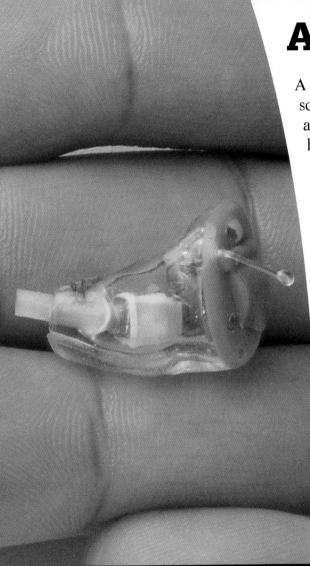

A Hearing Aid

A hearing aid is a small, electronic instrument (left) that makes sounds louder and easier to understand. A hearing aid fits around the outside of the ear or inside the ear canal. Some hearing aids are so small that they are hardly noticeable.

PARTS OF A HEARING AID

1 The tiny **microphone** built into the hearing aid picks up sounds. It changes sound waves into electrical signals.

2 The **amplifier** makes the electrical signals stronger. A hearing aid user can control the degree to which sounds are amplified, or made stronger.

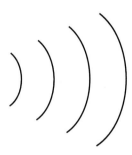
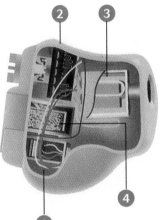

3 The **receiver** changes the amplified electrical signals back into sound signals and sends them to the eardrum.

4 The **battery** is the power source that makes the hearing aid work. Like batteries in portable tape or CD players, batteries in a hearing aid must be changed when they lose power.

Think Critically
1. Why must a person be able to hear at some level in order for a hearing aid to work?
2. How might background noise cause problems for people with hearing aids?

For a **preview** of this chapter, study this Reviewing Main Ideas before you read the chapter. After you have studied this chapter, you can use the Reviewing Main Ideas to **review** the chapter.

The Glencoe MindJogger, Audiocassettes, and CD-ROM provide additional opportunities for review.

Section 20-1 BODY REGULATION

Your body is constantly receiving a variety of stimuli from inside and outside the body. The nervous and endocrine systems respond to these stimuli to maintain homeostasis. *What are some body functions that are constantly being checked and regulated?*

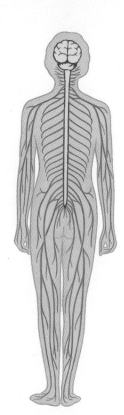

NERVOUS SYSTEM

The basic unit of the nervous system is the **neuron.** Stimuli are detected by sensory neurons, and the impulse is carried to an interneuron and then transmitted to a motor neuron. The result is the movement of a body part. Some responses are automatic and are called **reflexes.** *What are the two major divisions of the nervous system?*

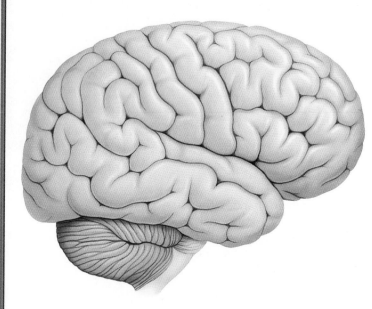

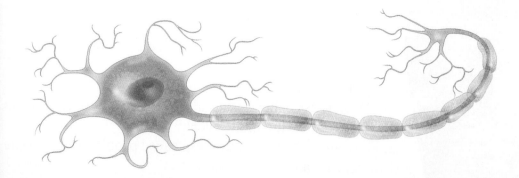

Reading Check ☑

• List two or three generalizations about the nervous and endocrine systems. Exchange lists and determine if they are accurate.

^{Section}
20-2 THE SENSES

Your senses respond to energy. The eyes respond to light, and the ears respond to sound waves. The **olfactory cells** of the nose and the **taste buds** of the tongue are stimulated by chemicals. *What senses are involved as you pick up and eat a freshly baked chocolate chip cookie?*

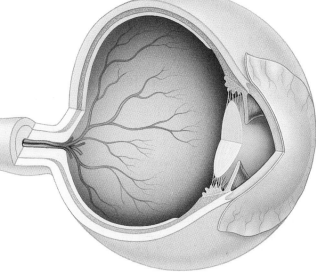

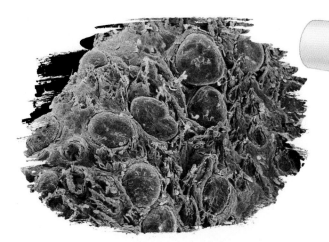

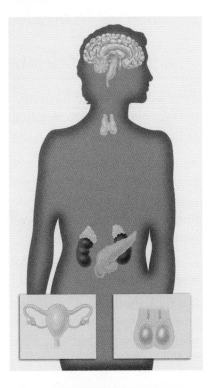

^{Section}
20-3 THE ENDOCRINE SYSTEM

Endocrine glands secrete **hormones** directly into your bloodstream. Hormones affect specific tissues throughout the body and regulate their activities. A feedback system regulates the hormone levels in your blood. *How can a gland that is near your head control the rate of chemical activities throughout your entire body?*

Using Vocabulary

a. axon
b. brain stem
c. central nervous system
d. cerebellum
e. cerebrum
f. cochlea
g. dendrite
h. hormone
i. neuron
j. olfactory cell
k. peripheral nervous system
l. reflex
m. retina
n. synapse
o. target tissue
p. taste bud

Match each phrase with the correct term from the list of Vocabulary words.

1. a small space between neurons
2. basic unit of nervous system
3. division containing brain and spinal cord
4. an automatic response to stimuli
5. center for coordination of voluntary muscle action

Checking Concepts

Choose the word or phrase that best answers the question.

6. How do impulses cross synapses?
   A) by osmosis
   B) through interneurons
   C) through a cell body
   D) by a chemical

7. What are the neuron structures that carry impulses to the cell body?
   A) axons   C) synapses
   B) dendrites   D) nuclei

8. What are neurons detecting stimuli in the skin and eyes called?
   A) interneurons   C) sensory neurons
   B) motor neurons D) synapses

9. What is the largest part of the brain?
   A) cerebellum   C) cerebrum
   B) brain stem   D) pons

10. What part of the brain controls voluntary muscle?
    A) cerebellum   C) cerebrum
    B) brain stem   D) pons

11. What is the part of the brain that is divided into two hemispheres?
    A) pons   C) cerebrum
    B) brain stem   D) spinal cord

12. What is controlled by the somatic division of the PNS?
    A) skeletal muscles
    B) heart
    C) glands
    D) salivary glands

13. Which of the following are endocrine chemicals produced in glands?
    A) enzymes   C) hormones
    B) target tissues D) saliva

14. Which gland controls many other endocrine glands throughout the body?
    A) adrenal   C) pituitary
    B) thyroid   D) pancreas

15. Which of the following does the inner ear contain?
    A) anvil   C) eardrum
    B) hammer   D) cochlea

Thinking Critically

16. Why is it helpful to have impulses move in only one direction in a neuron?

17. How are reflexes protective?

18. You have had your blood tested for sugar, and the doctor says you have a problem. How might your doctor determine which gland is responsible for this regulation problem?

19. Describe an example of a problem that results from improper gland functioning.

20. If a fly were to land on your face and another one on your back, which might you feel first? Explain how you would test your choice.

Developing Skills

If you need help, refer to the Skill Handbook.

21. **Classifying:** Classify the types of neurons as to their location and direction of impulse.

22. **Comparing and Contrasting:** Compare and contrast the structures and functions of the cerebrum, cerebellum, and brain stem. Include in your discussion the following functions: balance, involuntary muscle movements, muscle tone, memory, voluntary muscles, thinking, and senses.

23. **Concept Mapping:** Prepare a concept map showing the correct sequence of the structures through which light passes in the eye.

24. **Interpreting Scientific Illustrations:** Using the following diagram of the synapse, explain how an impulse moves from one neuron to another.

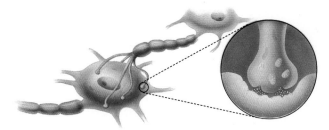

25. **Observing and Inferring:** If an impulse traveled down one neuron, but failed to move on to the next neuron, what might you infer about the first neuron?

26. **Predicting:** Refer to the Try at Home MiniLab in Section 20-2 and predict ways to improve your balance. Test your prediction.

THE PRINCETON REVIEW

Test-Taking Tip

What does the test expect of me? Find out what concepts, objectives, or standards are being tested before the test. Keep those concepts in mind as you answer the questions.

Test Practice

Use these questions to test your Science Proficiency.

1. What happens to an endocrine gland when the blood level of its hormone is increased?
   A) The gland stops producing hormones until the hormone level in the blood falls below a certain point.
   B) The gland continues producing hormones until the blood can't hold any more hormones.
   C) All endocrine glands keep producing their hormones until all hormone levels in the blood are equal.
   D) All endocrine glands stop producing hormones until all hormone levels in the blood are balanced.

2. Which statement below is the correct pathway from the stimulus to the response in a reflex response?
   A) receptor—interneuron—brain—motor neuron—muscle
   B) sensory neuron—brain—spinal cord—motor neuron
   C) muscle—receptor—sensory neuron—interneuron—motor neuron
   D) receptor—sensory neuron—interneuron—motor neuron—muscle

Reproduction and Growth

Chapter Preview

Skills Preview

Skill Builders
• Sequence and
  Outline Data

Activities
• Interpret and
  Graph Data

MiniLabs
• Interpret Data

Reading Check ✓

As you meet new vocabulary terms, help yourself remember their meanings by identifying related words. One example would be menopause and menstruation.

Explore Activity

You or some of your friends may come from families with both brothers and sisters. Some may come from families that have only boys or only girls. What do you think are the odds of a small family having all boys or all girls? Do the odds change as the family grows larger? What do you think is the proportion of boys to girls among children born in the general population?

Observe the Proportion of Boys to Girls

1. Take a penny and toss it in the air. The chance is equal that it will land heads or tails.

2. Toss the penny a hundred times.

3. Keep a record of the number of times it lands heads up and the number of times it lands tails up.

4. Keep a record of the order in which the penny lands.

Science Journal

In your Science Journal, record the results of your trials. Analyze your record for any patterns that occurred. Write your observations about sequences of five or more heads before a tails fell. Relate this to families that have five girls or five boys. Infer the chances that a girl would be born if there were a sixth child.

21·1 Human Reproduction

What You'll Learn

- The function of the reproductive system
- The major structures of the male and female reproductive system
- The stages of the menstrual cycle

Vocabulary

reproduction   uterus
testis   vagina
sperm   menstrual
semen   cycle
ovary   menstruation
ovulation   menopause

Why It's Important

- The unique process that creates new life takes place in the reproductive system.

The Reproductive System

Reproduction is the process that continues life on Earth. Organisms that carry out sexual reproduction form eggs and sperm that transfer genetic information from one generation to the next. The number of offspring an organism has varies with the species. Humans and other mammals have fewer offspring than most other animals. If you baby-sit, you know that babies and young children require almost constant attention. For this reason, most humans have only one or two babies at a time. However, in rare cases, mothers have given birth to as many as eight babies. Organisms such as spiders can lay thousands of eggs, which results in thousands of offspring at one time, as shown in **Figure 21-1.**

Figure 21-1

Animals such as spiders that produce large numbers of eggs have young that are usually able to take care of themselves from birth. Compare this to the ability of a human baby to care for itself. Imagine trying to care for these septuplets.

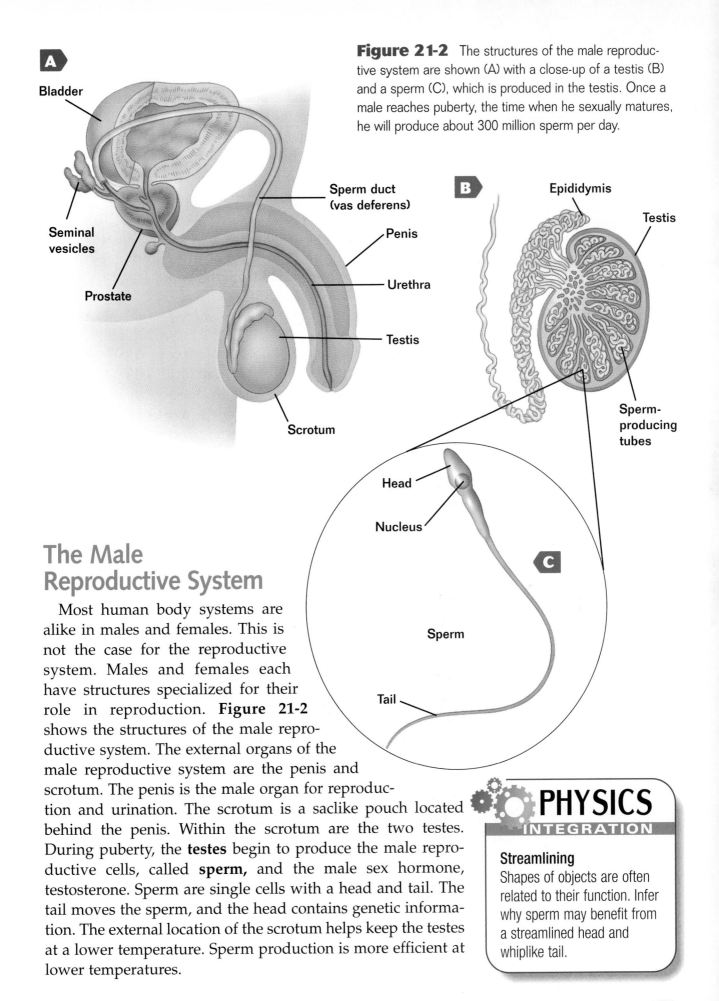

A

Bladder

Seminal vesicles

Prostate

Sperm duct (vas deferens)

Penis

Urethra

Testis

Scrotum

Figure 21-2 The structures of the male reproductive system are shown (A) with a close-up of a testis (B) and a sperm (C), which is produced in the testis. Once a male reaches puberty, the time when he sexually matures, he will produce about 300 million sperm per day.

B

Epididymis

Testis

Sperm-producing tubes

C

Head

Nucleus

Sperm

Tail

The Male Reproductive System

Most human body systems are alike in males and females. This is not the case for the reproductive system. Males and females each have structures specialized for their role in reproduction. **Figure 21-2** shows the structures of the male reproductive system. The external organs of the male reproductive system are the penis and scrotum. The penis is the male organ for reproduction and urination. The scrotum is a saclike pouch located behind the penis. Within the scrotum are the two testes. During puberty, the **testes** begin to produce the male reproductive cells, called **sperm,** and the male sex hormone, testosterone. Sperm are single cells with a head and tail. The tail moves the sperm, and the head contains genetic information. The external location of the scrotum helps keep the testes at a lower temperature. Sperm production is more efficient at lower temperatures.

PHYSICS INTEGRATION

Streamlining
Shapes of objects are often related to their function. Infer why sperm may benefit from a streamlined head and whiplike tail.

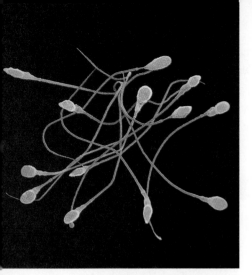

Magnification: 4500×

Figure 21-3 The photograph shows sperm swimming in fluid. A mixture of sperm and fluid is called semen.

Figure 21-4 The structures of the female reproductive system are shown from the side. **Where in the female reproductive system do the eggs develop?**

Sperm Movement

Many organs help in the production, transport, and storage of sperm inside the male body. After sperm are produced, they travel from the testes through tubes that circle the bladder. Behind the bladder, a gland called the seminal vesicle provides sperm with a fluid that gives them energy and helps them move as shown in **Figure 21-3.** This mixture of sperm and fluid is called **semen.** Semen leaves the body through the urethra, the same tube that at other times carries urine from the body. Semen and urine never mix. A muscle at the back of the bladder contracts to prevent urine from entering the urethra as sperm are ejected from the body.

The Female Reproductive System

Eggs are the female reproductive cells. A female baby already has her total supply of eggs at birth. When the female reaches puberty, her eggs start to develop in **ovaries,** the female sex organs. Unlike the male's, most of the reproductive organs of the female are internal. The ovaries are located in the lower part of the body cavity. Each of the two ovaries is about the size and shape of an almond. **Figure 21-4** shows the structures of the female reproductive system.

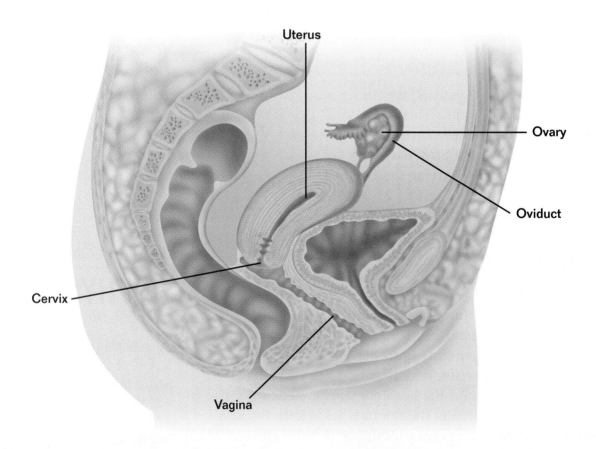

Uterus

Ovary

Oviduct

Cervix

Vagina

Egg Movement

About once a month, an egg is released from an ovary, as in **Figure 21-5.** This process is called **ovulation** (ahv yuh LAY shun). The two ovaries take turns releasing an egg. One month, the first ovary releases an egg. Next month, the other ovary releases an egg and so on. When the egg is released, it enters the oviduct, as shown in **Figure 21-6.** Sometimes, the egg is fertilized by a sperm. If fertilization occurs, it will happen in an oviduct. Short, hairlike structures called cilia help sweep the egg through the oviduct to the uterus. The **uterus** is a hollow, pear-shaped, muscular organ with thick walls in which a fertilized egg develops. The lower end of the uterus is connected to the outside of the body by a muscular tube called the **vagina.** The vagina also is called the birth canal because a baby travels through this passageway during birth.

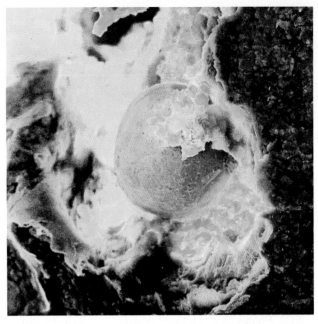

Magnification: 1850×

Figure 21-5 The egg in the photograph has just been released from the ovary.

The Menstrual Cycle

The **menstrual cycle** is the monthly cycle of changes in the female reproductive system. Before and after an egg is released from an ovary, the uterus undergoes certain changes. The menstrual cycle of a human female averages 28 days. However, the cycle can vary in some individuals from 20 to 40 days. The changes include the maturing of an egg,

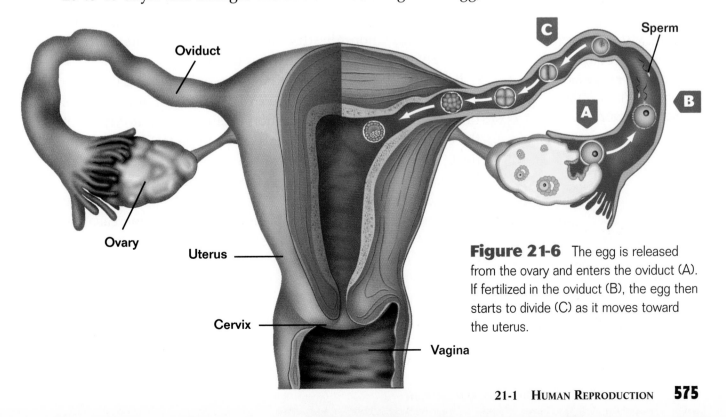

Figure 21-6 The egg is released from the ovary and enters the oviduct (A). If fertilized in the oviduct (B), the egg then starts to divide (C) as it moves toward the uterus.

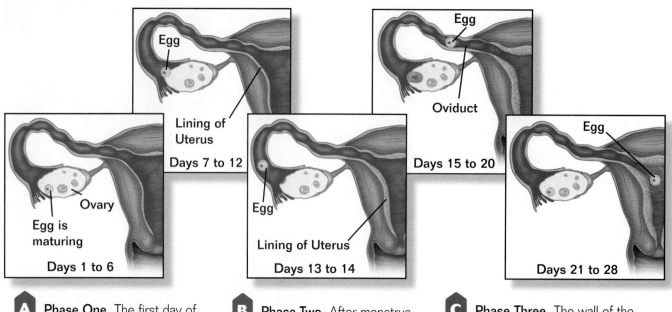

Days 7 to 12 — Egg, Lining of Uterus

Days 1 to 6 — Ovary, Egg is maturing

Days 13 to 14 — Egg, Lining of Uterus

Days 15 to 20 — Egg, Oviduct

Days 21 to 28 — Egg

A **Phase One** The first day of the cycle starts when the menstrual flow begins.

B **Phase Two** After menstruation, the wall of the uterus begins to thicken again. Ovulation occurs on about day 14.

C **Phase Three** The wall of the uterus continues to thicken due to the action of hormones. If a fertilized egg arrives, the uterus is ready to support it.

Figure 21-7 A regular menstrual cycle is approximately 28 days long. Notice how the thickness of the uterine lining changes during the cycle. **On what day does ovulation occur?**

*inter*NET
CONNECTION

Visit the Glencoe Science Web Site at **www.glencoe.com/sec/science/ca** for more information about the menstrual cycle.

Reading Check

What causes the uterine wall to thicken again after menstruation?

the secretion of female sex hormones, and the preparation of the uterus to receive a fertilized egg, as shown in **Figure 21-7.** When an egg inside an ovary matures, the lining of the uterus thickens and prepares to receive a fertilized egg.

Three Phases

You can see in **Figure 21-7** that the first day of phase one starts when menstrual flow begins. Menstrual flow consists of blood and tissue cells from the thickened lining of the uterus. This monthly discharge is called **menstruation.** Menstruation usually lasts from four to six days.

In the second phase, hormones cause the uterine lining to thicken again. One egg in the ovary develops and matures until ovulation occurs. Ovulation occurs on about day 14 of the cycle. Once the egg is released, it can be fertilized for the next 24 to 48 hours as it moves through the oviduct. Pregnancy can occur if live sperm are in the oviduct 48 hours before or after ovulation.

During the third phase, hormones continue to increase the thickness of the uterine lining. In this way, the uterus is prepared for the arrival of a fertilized egg. If a fertilized egg does arrive, the uterus is ready to help support and nourish the developing embryo. If the egg is not fertilized, hormone levels decrease and the uterine lining deteriorates. Menstruation begins again. Another egg begins to mature and the cycle repeats itself.

Menopause

Menstruation begins when a girl reaches puberty and her reproductive organs have matured. For most females, the first menstrual period happens between ages eight and 13 and continues until age 45 to 55. Then, there is a gradual reduction of ovulation and menstruation. **Menopause** occurs when the menstrual cycle becomes irregular and eventually stops.

When the reproductive systems of males and females mature, sperm are produced in the male testes, while eggs mature in the female ovaries. The reproductive process allows for the species to continue.

Figure 21-8 For most women, the menstrual cycle continues normally until around age 45 to 55. After that, the cycle becomes irregular and finally stops.

Section Assessment

1. What is the major function of a reproductive system?
2. Explain the movement of sperm through the male reproductive system.
3. List the organs of the female reproductive system and describe their functions.
4. Explain the cause of menstrual flow.
5. **Think Critically:** Adolescent females often require additional amounts of iron in their diet. Explain why.
6. **Skill Builder**
   Sequencing Sequence the movement of an egg through the female reproductive system and the movement of a sperm through the male reproductive system. If you need help, refer to Sequencing in the **Skill Handbook** on page 678.

Using Math

Usually, one egg is released each month during the reproductive years of a female. For a woman whose first menstruation starts at age 12 and ends at age 50, calculate the number of eggs released. In males, about 300 million sperm are produced in a day. Relate this number to the number of eggs released by a woman during her entire life.

Materials

• Paper and pencil

Interpreting Diagrams

Starting in adolescence, the hormone estrogen causes changes in the uterus. These changes prepare the uterus to accept a fertilized egg that may embed itself in the uterine wall.

What You'll Investigate

What happens to the uterus during a female's monthly cycle?

Goals

• **Observe** the stages in a diagram of the menstrual cycle.

• **Relate** the process of ovulation to the cycle.

Procedure

1. The diagram below shows what is explained in Section 21-1 on the menstrual cycle.

2. **Study** the diagram and labels.

3. **Use** the information in Section 21-1 and the diagram below to complete a table like the one shown.

4. How are the diagrams different?

5. On approximately what day in a 28-day cycle is the egg released from the ovary?

Conclude and Apply

1. How long is the average menstrual cycle?

2. How many days does menstruation usually last?

3. On what days does the lining of the uterus build up?

4. **Infer** why this process is called a cycle.

5. **Calculate** how many days before menstruation ovulation usually occurs.

6. **Interpret** the diagram to explain the menstrual cycle.

Menstruation Cycle		
Days	**Condition of Uterus**	**What Happens**
1–6		
7–12		
13–14		
15–28		

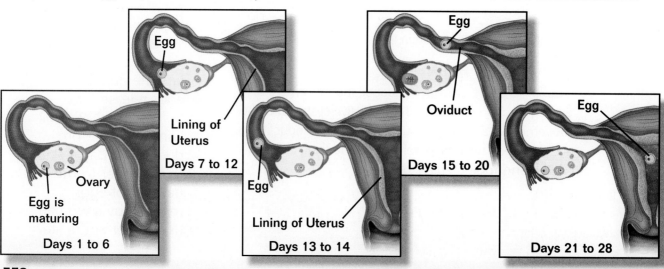

Egg

Egg

Lining of Uterus

Days 7 to 12

Oviduct

Days 15 to 20

Egg

Ovary

Egg is maturing

Days 1 to 6

Egg

Lining of Uterus

Days 13 to 14

Egg

Days 21 to 28

Fertilization to Birth

Fertilization

Before the invention of powerful microscopes, some people imagined a sperm to be a miniature person that grew in the uterus of a female. Others thought the egg contained a miniature individual that started to grow when stimulated by semen. In the latter part of the 1700s, experiments using amphibians showed that contact between an egg and sperm is necessary for life to begin development. With the development of the cell theory in 1839, scientists recognized that a human develops from a single egg that has been fertilized by a sperm. The uniting of a sperm with an egg is known as fertilization.

As you see in **Figure 21-9,** the process begins when sperm, deposited into the vagina, move through the uterus into the oviducts. Whereas only one egg is usually present, nearly 200 to 300 million sperm are deposited. Of that number, only one sperm will fertilize the egg. The nucleus of the sperm and the nucleus of the egg have 23 chromosomes each. When the egg and sperm unite, a zygote with 46 chromosomes is formed. Most fertilization occurs in an oviduct.

What **You'll Learn**

► How an egg becomes fertilized
► The major events in the stages of development of an embryo and fetus
► The difference between fraternal and identical twins

Vocabulary
pregnancy   amniotic sac
embryo   fetus

Why **It's Important**

► Fertilization begins the entire process of human growth and development.

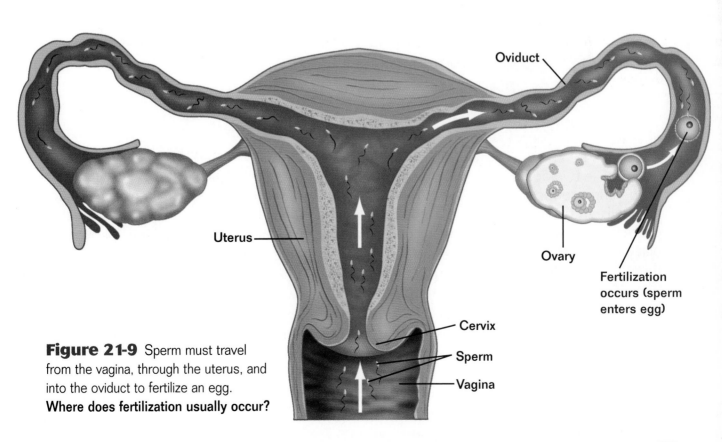

Figure 21-9 Sperm must travel from the vagina, through the uterus, and into the oviduct to fertilize an egg. **Where does fertilization usually occur?**

Labels: Oviduct, Uterus, Ovary, Fertilization occurs (sperm enters egg), Cervix, Sperm, Vagina

Figure 21-10 The sperm releases enzymes that disrupt the membrane on the surface of the egg. The sperm head can now penetrate the egg.

Magnification: 2700×

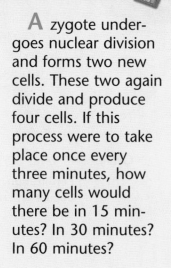

Using Math

A zygote undergoes nuclear division and forms two new cells. These two again divide and produce four cells. If this process were to take place once every three minutes, how many cells would there be in 15 minutes? In 30 minutes? In 60 minutes?

A Biochemical Event

Several hundred million sperm may be deposited in the vagina, but only several thousand actually reach the egg in the oviduct. During their travels, the sperm come in contact with chemical secretions in the vagina. It appears that this contact causes a change in the membrane of the sperm. The sperm then become capable of fertilizing eggs.

Although many sperm may actually reach the egg, only one will fertilize it, as shown in **Figure 21-10.** The one sperm that makes successful contact with the egg releases an enzyme from the saclike structure on its head. Enzymes help speed up chemical reactions. The enzyme has a direct effect on the protective egg-surface membranes. The structure of the membrane is disrupted, and the sperm head is now able to penetrate the egg.

Response of the Egg

Once a sperm has penetrated the egg, another series of chemical actions take place. These actions prevent further penetration by other sperm. Special chemical secretions are released onto the egg's surface. These secretions prevent other sperm from binding. Other chemicals cause changes on the surface of the egg itself that prevent penetration. At this point, the nucleus of the successful sperm fuses with the nucleus of the egg. This fusion creates a new cell, called a zygote, that undergoes mitosis, as shown in **Figure 21-11.**

CHEMISTRY
◄ INTEGRATION

Figure 21-11 Fertilization results from the fusion of an egg nucleus and a sperm (A). The resulting zygote undergoes mitosis as shown in (B) and (C) to form a hollow ball of cells (D).

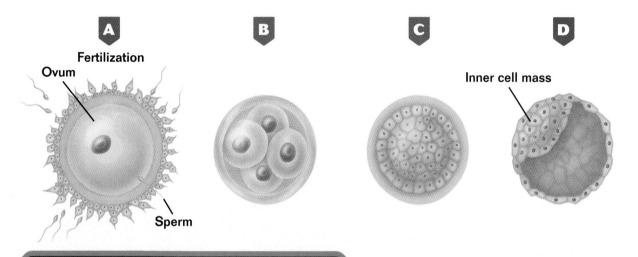

A **B** **C** **D**

Fertilization
Ovum
Sperm
Inner cell mass

Problem Solving

When to Test?

Expectant mothers want to know, "Will my baby be healthy?" Several tests to check for birth defects can be done before a baby is born. One test is known as amniocentesis (am nee oh sen TEE sus). In this test, the doctor extracts a small amount of fluid from the amniotic sac that surrounds the fetus. Examination of the fluid can reveal certain abnormalities. A similar test takes a tissue sample of the placenta, the tissue that connects mother and child. Analysis of the tissue can show evidence of certain diseases.

One of the most frequently used tests is an ultrasound. A device generates sound waves that are transmitted through the mother's body. The sound waves produce photographic images of the fetus. Doctors observe the images to detect not only deformities, but also the size, sex, and rate of development of the fetus.

While each procedure has a benefit, each also has a

risk. Some risks are to the mother, and some are to the unborn fetus. Some doctors also think that too many tests may have an adverse effect on the development of the fetus.

Think Critically: Under what conditions might parents want to know the sex of their unborn child? Study the ultrasound photo and infer what information could be obtained from these types of photos and how a doctor might make use of that information.

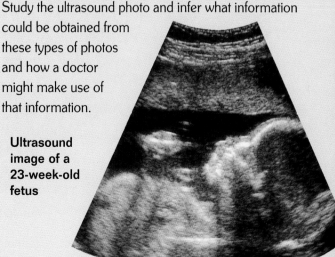

Ultrasound image of a 23-week-old fetus

Development Before Birth

The zygote moves along the oviduct to the uterus. During this time, the zygote is dividing and forming a ball of cells. After about seven days, the ball of cells is implanted in the wall of the uterus. The uterine wall has been thickening in preparation to receive a fertilized egg. Here the fertilized egg will develop for nine months until the birth of the baby. This period of time is known as **pregnancy.**

The Embryo

During the first two months of pregnancy, the unborn child is known as an **embryo.** In **Figure 21-12,** you can see how the embryo receives nutrients and removes wastes. Nutrients from the wall of the uterus are received by the embryo through villi. Blood vessels develop from the villi and form the placenta. The umbilical cord is attached to the embryo's navel and connects with the placenta. The umbilical cord transports nutrients and oxygen from the mother to the baby through a vein. Carbon dioxide and other wastes are carried through arteries in the umbilical cord back to the mother's blood. Other substances in the mother's blood can pass to the embryo, as well. These include drugs, toxins, and

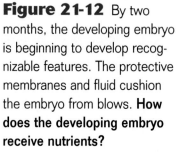

interNET CONNECTION

Visit the Glencoe Science Web Site at **www.glencoe.com/ sec/science/ca** for more information about development before birth.

Figure 21-12 By two months, the developing embryo is beginning to develop recognizable features. The protective membranes and fluid cushion the embryo from blows. **How does the developing embryo receive nutrients?**

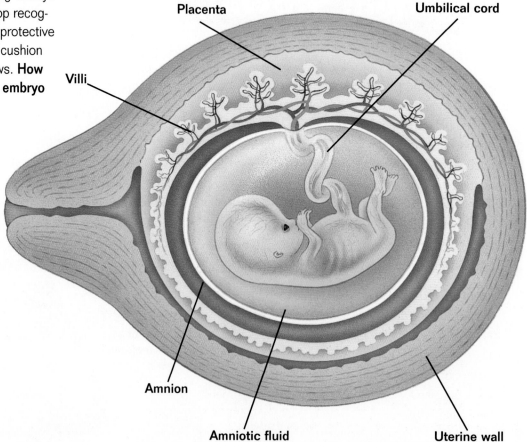

Placenta

Umbilical cord

Villi

Amnion

Amniotic fluid

Uterine wall

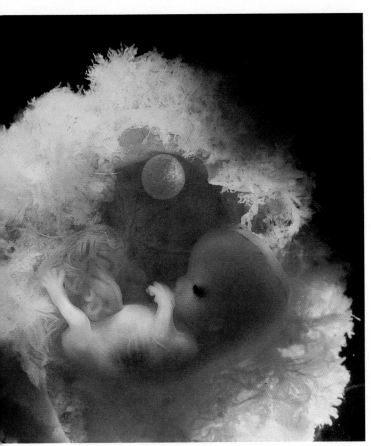

Magnification: 3×

Figure 21-13 The photograph shows an enlarged view of a two-month-old embryo. The actual size is approximately 2 cm. You can see the head with eyes and nose. Tiny arms, legs, and toes are developing. The soft looking tissue behind the embryo is the placenta.

Figure 21-13 The photograph shows an enlarged view of a two-month-old embryo. The actual size is approximately 2 cm. You can see the head with eyes and nose. Tiny arms, legs, and toes are developing. The soft looking tissue behind the embryo is the placenta.

disease organisms. Because these substances can harm the embryo, a mother needs to avoid harmful drugs, alcohol, and tobacco during pregnancy.

During the third week of pregnancy, a thin membrane begins to form around the embryo. This is called the amnion or the **amniotic** (am nee AH tihk) **sac.** It is filled with a clear liquid called amniotic fluid. The amniotic fluid in the amniotic sac helps cushion the embryo against blows and can store nutrients and wastes. This sac attaches to the placenta.

During the first three months of development, as shown in **Figure 21-13,** all of an embryo's major organs form. A heart structure begins to beat and move blood through the embryo's blood vessels. At five weeks, the embryo is only as large as a single grain of rice, but there is a head with recognizable eye, nose, and mouth features. During the sixth and seventh weeks, tiny arms and legs develop fingers and toes.

Try at Home

Mini Lab

Interpreting Embryo Development

Procedure

1. Interpret this data table of embryo development.

End of month	Length
3	8 cm
4	15 cm
5	25 cm
6	30 cm
7	35 cm
8	40 cm
9	51 cm

2. On a piece of paper, draw a line the length of the unborn baby at each date.

3. Using reference materials, find out what developmental events happen at each month.

Analysis

1. During which month does the greatest increase in length occur?

2. What size is the unborn baby when movement can be felt by the mother?

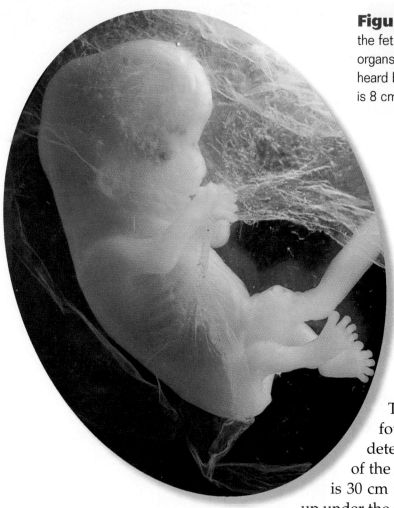

Figure 21-14 The photograph shows the fetus at about three months. The body organs are present, and the heart can be heard beating using a stethoscope. The fetus is 8 cm to 10 cm long.

The Fetus

After the first two months of pregnancy, as shown in **Figure 21-14,** the developing baby is called a **fetus.** At this time, body organs are present. Around the third month, the fetus is 8 cm to 10 cm long, the heart can be heard beating using a stethoscope, and the mother may feel the baby's movements within her uterus. The fetus may suck its thumb. By the fourth month, an ultrasound test can determine the sex of the fetus. By the end of the seventh month of pregnancy, the fetus is 30 cm to 38 cm in length. Fatty tissue builds up under the skin, and the fetus looks less wrinkled. By the ninth month, the fetus usually has shifted to a head-down position within the uterus. The head usually is in contact with the opening of the uterus to the vagina. The fetus is about 50 cm in length and weighs from 2.5 kg to 3.5 kg. The baby is ready for birth. ✔

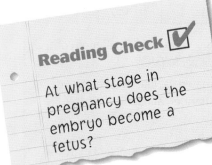

Reading Check ✔

At what stage in pregnancy does the embryo become a fetus?

Multiple Births

Sometimes, two eggs leave the ovary at the same time. If both eggs are fertilized and both develop, fraternal twins are born. Fraternal twins may be two girls, two boys, or a boy and a girl. Fraternal twins do not always look alike. Not all twins are fraternal. Sometimes, a single egg splits apart shortly after it is fertilized. Each part of the egg then develops and forms an embryo. Because both children developed from the same egg and sperm, they are identical twins. Each has the same set of genes. Identical twins must be either two girls or two boys. **Figure 21-15** illustrates both identical and fraternal twin development. Triplets and other multiple births may occur when either three or more eggs are produced at one time or an egg splits into three or more parts.

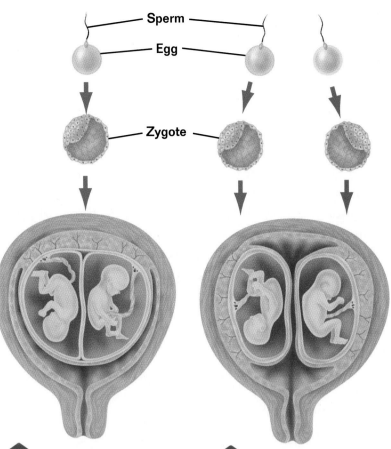

Sperm

Egg

Zygote

Figure 21-15 The development of fraternal and identical twins is quite different.

A Identical twins develop from a single egg that has been fertilized by a single sperm. The resulting zygote later splits.

B Fraternal twins develop from two different eggs that have been fertilized by two different sperm.

Section Assessment

1. What happens when an egg is fertilized?

2. What is one major event that occurs during the embryo and fetal stages?

3. At what stage in the pregnancy does the embryo become a fetus?

4. **Think Critically:** If a mother is taking drugs during pregnancy, how can these harmful substances pass into the blood system of the embryo?

5. **Skill Builder**
   Interpreting Data A human fetus grows at different rates during its development. Do the **Chapter 21 Skill Activity** on page 726 in the **Skill Handbook** and interpret data about fetal development.

Science Journal Use different references to look up information on multiple births. In your Science Journal, describe how twins and triplets develop. Describe the differences in origin and appearance of fraternal and identical twins.

21•3 Development After Birth

What You'll Learn

▶ The sequence of events of childbirth

▶ The stages of infancy and childhood

▶ Adolescent development and preparation for adulthood

Vocabulary

infancy   adolescence
childhood   adulthood

Why It's Important

▶ During adolescence, your body and mind change from a child to an adult.

Childbirth

After developing for nine months within the mother, the baby is ready to be born. Like all newborn, living things, the baby finds itself suddenly pushed out into the world. Within the uterus and amniotic sac, the baby was in a warm, watery, dark, and protected environment. In contrast, the new environment is cooler, drier, brighter, and not as protective.

Labor

The process of childbirth as shown in **Figure 21-16** begins with labor, which is the muscular contractions of the uterus. As the contractions increase in strength and frequency, the amniotic sac usually breaks and releases its fluid. Over a period of hours, the contractions cause the opening of the uterus to widen to allow the baby to pass through. More powerful and frequent contractions push the baby out through the vagina into its new environment.

VISUALIZING Childbirth

Figure 21-16 Childbirth begins with labor. The opening to the uterus widens, and the baby passes through.

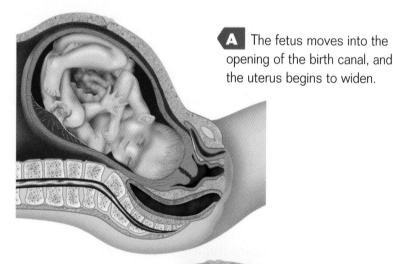

A The fetus moves into the opening of the birth canal, and the uterus begins to widen.

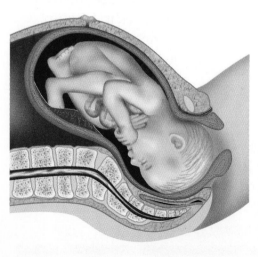

B The base of the uterus is completely dilated.

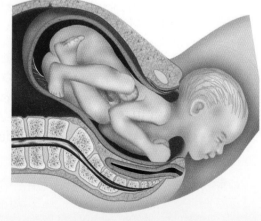

C The fetus is pushed out through the birth canal.

Figure 21-17 Infancy is a period of rapid growth and development. An early skill is the ability to smile. **What are some of the developments that occur during infancy?**

Sometimes, the mother's pelvis is too small for the baby to fit through or the baby is in the wrong position for birth. In cases like this, the baby is delivered through an incision in the mother's uterus and abdomen. This surgery is called cesarean section.

Post Labor

At birth, the baby is still attached to the umbilical cord and placenta. The person assisting with the birth of the baby ties the cord and then cuts it. The baby may cry. Crying forces air into its lungs. The scar that later forms where the cord was attached is the navel. Soon after the baby's delivery, contractions expel the placenta from the mother's body.

Infancy and Childhood

The first four weeks after birth are known as the neonatal period. *Neonatal* means "newborn." During this time, the baby adjusts to life outside of the uterus. Body functions such as respiration, digestion, and excretion are now performed by the baby rather than through the placenta. Unlike some other living things, the human baby depends on others to survive. The human baby needs to be fed and have its diaper changed. In contrast, a newborn colt begins walking a few hours after its birth.

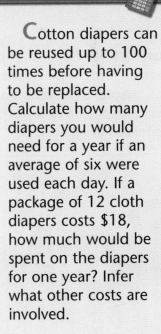

Using Math

Cotton diapers can be reused up to 100 times before having to be replaced. Calculate how many diapers you would need for a year if an average of six were used each day. If a package of 12 cloth diapers costs $18, how much would be spent on the diapers for one year? Infer what other costs are involved.

Mini Lab

Investigate Immunizations

Procedure

1. Find out what immunizations are usually given to babies and young children.

2. Compare these to what vaccines are required for children to enter your school.

Analysis

1. What booster shots are given to school children?

2. Investigate what immunizations are required for travel to foreign countries.

Figure 21-18 Childhood begins around the age of one and continues until age 12. Muscular coordination and mental abilities develop. Children also learn how to interact socially with others.

Infancy

The next stage of development is **infancy,** the period from the neonatal stage to one year. It is a period of rapid growth and development for both mental and physical skills. At around six weeks of age, babies are able to smile. At four months, most babies can laugh, sit up when propped, and recognize their mother's face. At eight months, the infant is usually able to say a few simple words. One of the major events within the first year is the ability to stand unsupported for a few seconds. Some children walk before age one.

Childhood

After infancy is **childhood,** which lasts until age 12. The physical growth rate for height and weight is not as rapid as in infancy. However, muscular coordination and mental abilities develop. By 18 months, the child is able to walk without help. Between two and three years, the child learns to control his or her bladder and bowel. At age three, the child can speak in simple sentences. By age five, many children can read a limited number of words. Throughout this stage, children develop their abilities to speak, read, write, and reason. At the same time, children also mature emotionally and learn how to get along with other people, as shown in **Figure 21-18.** Find out how old you were when you began to talk. What were your first words?

Adolescence

The next stage of development is adolescence. You are in this stage. **Adolescence** begins around ages 12 to 13. A part of adolescence is puberty. As you read earlier, puberty is the time of development when a person becomes physically able to reproduce. For girls, puberty occurs between ages eight and 13. For boys, puberty occurs between ages 13 and 15.

Figure 21-19 During puberty, hormones cause changes in the bodies of adolescents.

During puberty, hormones that cause changes in the body are produced by the pituitary gland. The hormone FSH helps produce reproductive cells. LH helps with the production of sex hormones. As a result of the secretion of these hormones, secondary sex characteristics, some of which are evident in **Figure 21-19,** result. In females, the breasts develop, pubic and underarm hair appears, and fatty tissue is added to the buttocks and thighs. In males, the hormones cause the growth of facial, pubic, and underarm hair; a deepened voice; and an increase in muscle size. Many young adults begin to feel sexual attraction, as well. ☑

Reading Check ☑

List three changes that occur in the female body during puberty.

The Growth Spurt

Adolescence is the time of your final growth spurt. Are you shorter or taller than your classmates? Because of differences in the time hormones begin functioning among individuals

Figure 21-20 You can compare body proportions of newborns, young children, and adults with this chart. **How does the proportion of the head compared to the rest of the body change from baby to adult?**

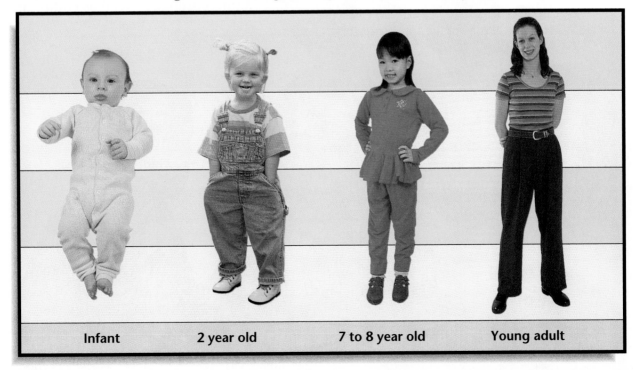

| Infant | 2 year old | 7 to 8 year old | Young adult |

At birth, the head of a newborn is about one-quarter of the total body length. Measure the head length and height of at least ten classmates and ten adults. Calculate the ratio of the head length to body length for the adolescents and the adults. Graph your data and compare the results.

and between males and females, boys' and girls' growth rates differ. Girls often begin their final growth phase between the ages of 11 and 13 and end at ages 15 to 16. Boys usually start their growth spurt at ages 13 to 15 and end at 17 to 18 years of age. Hormonal changes also cause underarm sweating and acne, requiring extra cleanliness and care. All of these physical changes can cause you to feel different or uncomfortable. This is normal. As you move through the period of adolescence, you will find that you will become more coordinated, be better able to handle problems, and gain improved reasoning abilities.

Adulthood

The final stage of development is that of **adulthood**. It begins with the end of adolescence and extends to old age. Young adults are people in their twenties. Many young adults are completing an education, finding employment, and possibly marrying and beginning a family. This is when the growth of the muscular and skeletal system stops. You can see in **Figure 21-20** how body proportions change as you grow from infancy to adulthood.

People from age 30 to age 60 are in the stage of middle adulthood. During these years, physical strength begins to decline. Blood circulation and respiration become less efficient. Bones become more brittle, and the skin's elastic tissues are lost, causing the skin to become wrinkled. People in this group are busy with family and work commitments. They often care for aging parents, as well as children.

Figure 21-21 Adulthood is the final stage of development. This is when the growth of the muscular and skeletal system stops. **What is the approximate age range for a person in middle adulthood?**

Senior Citizens

Think about someone you know over age 60. How is that person like or different from you? Around this age, many people retire. They take up hobbies, travel, or volunteer at hospitals and community organizations. Many continue to work. They are an active part of society. People over 75 years are placed in the oldest age group. While many in this group are mentally and physically active, others may need assistance in meeting their needs.

Figure 21-22 In 1998, former astronaut and senator John Glenn, a senior citizen, took part in a space shuttle mission. This helped to change people's views of what many senior citizens are capable of.

After birth, the stages of development of the human body begin with a baby making adjustments to a new environment. From infancy to adolescence, the body's systems mature, enabling the person to be physically and mentally ready for adulthood. During the next 50 years or longer, people live their lives making contributions to family, community, and society. Throughout the life cycle, people who care for their health enjoy a higher quality of life.

Section Assessment

1. What are major events during childbirth?
2. Compare infancy with childhood.
3. How does the period of adolescence prepare you for the stage of adulthood?
4. **Think Critically:** Why is it hard to compare the growth and development of different adolescents?
5. **Skill Builder**
   Concept Mapping Prepare a concept map of the various life stages of human development from the neonatal period to adulthood. If you need help, refer to Concept Mapping in the **Skill Handbook** on page 678.

Using Computers

Spreadsheet Using your text and other resources, make a spreadsheet for the stages of human development from a zygote to a fetus. Title one column *zygote,* another *embryo,* and a third *fetus.* Complete the information for all three columns. If you need help, refer to page 702.

New View of the Old

Imagine that you are 90 years old. How would you describe yourself? Some young people think that the elderly are forgetful and physically impaired. They associate certain conditions with aging—loss of hearing and sight, arthritis, osteoporosis, diabetes, and Alzheimer's disease, for example. They assume that older people have less physical energy and mental ability than younger people.

New Findings

The traditional view of the elderly has changed in light of recent studies. Researchers who studied people over age 90 discovered that the majority were mentally alert and physically active. Those over 90 suffered fewer health problems than those in their 70s and 80s. Centenarians, people 100 years old and over, participated in golf, tennis, bowling, swimming, and other physical activities. Some also were active in writing, art, reading, and business.

Longevity Genes

Why do some people remain in good health to an advanced age? Researchers think that certain genes control the aging process. Genes also may be responsible for a person's physical and mental ability to deal with disease or injury. Scientists think that genes also may determine how much functional reserve a person's organs have. For example, a centenarian may have extensive areas of damaged brain cells, but healthy cells in reserve allow these people to function normally. Obviously, good health habits also contribute to a long, healthy life.

A New View

This new image of the physical and mental wellness of the very old has had an effect on health care. Traditionally, health care programs have assumed that more and more resources would be needed as a person grows older. However, the overall good health of people over 90 may keep their health maintenance costs lower than predicted.

*inter*NET
CONNECTION

The American Association of Retired Persons is a nonprofit organization dedicated to helping older Americans. Visit the Glencoe Science Web Site at **www.glencoe.com/sec/science/ca** to learn more about AARP and its activities.

Average Growth Rate in Humans

Materials
- Graph paper
- Red and blue pencils

A n individual's growth is dependent upon both the effects of hormones and his or her genetic makeup.

What You'll Investigate

Is average growth rate the same in males and females?

Goals

- **Analyze** the average growth rate of young males and females.
- **Compare and contrast** their growth rates.

Procedure

1. **Construct** a graph. **Label** mass on the vertical axis and age on the horizontal axis.

2. **Plot** the data in the table below for the average female growth in mass from ages eight to 18. **Connect** the points with a red line.

3. On the same graph, **plot** the data for the average male growth in mass from ages eight to 18. **Connect** the points with a blue line.

4. **Construct** a separate graph. **Label** height on the vertical axis and age on the horizontal axis.

5. **Plot** the data for the average female growth in height from ages eight to 18. **Connect** the points with a red line. **Plot** the data for the average male growth in height from ages eight to 18. **Connect** the points with a blue line.

Conclude and Apply

1. Up to what age is average growth rate in mass similar in males and females?

2. Up to what age is average growth rate in height similar in males and females?

3. When does the mass of females generally change the most?

4. How can you explain the differences in growth between males and females?

5. **Interpret** the data to determine whether the average growth rate is the same in males and females.

Average Growth and Mass in Humans

Averages for Growth in Humans

Age	Mass (kg)		Height (cm)	
	Female	Male	Female	Male
8	25	25	123	124
9	28	28	129	130
10	31	31	135	135
11	35	37	140	140
12	40	38	147	145
13	47	43	155	152
14	50	50	159	161
15	54	57	160	167
16	57	62	163	172
17	58	65	163	174
18	58	68	163	178

Chapter 21 Reviewing Main Ideas

For a **preview** of this chapter, study this Reviewing Main Ideas before you read the chapter. After you have studied this chapter, you can use the Reviewing Main Ideas to **review** the chapter.

The Glencoe MindJogger, Audiocassettes, and CD-ROM provide additional opportunities for review.

Section
21-1 HUMAN REPRODUCTION

Reproduction is a means to continue life. The union of an egg and **sperm** starts the process of development from a zygote to a complete human being. The reproductive system allows new organisms to be created. **Testes** in males produce sperm. Sperm are single cells with a head and a tail. The tail allows the sperm to move as it travels through the uterus and along the oviduct to the egg. Eggs are produced by the **ovaries** in females. An egg is released from one of the ovaries on about the fourteenth day of the menstrual cycle. The egg is drawn into the oviduct, where fertilization can occur. The fertilization of an egg by a sperm forms new life. Eggs that are not fertilized disintegrate, and the lining of the **uterus** is shed. *What are the differences in the structure of the egg and sperm?*

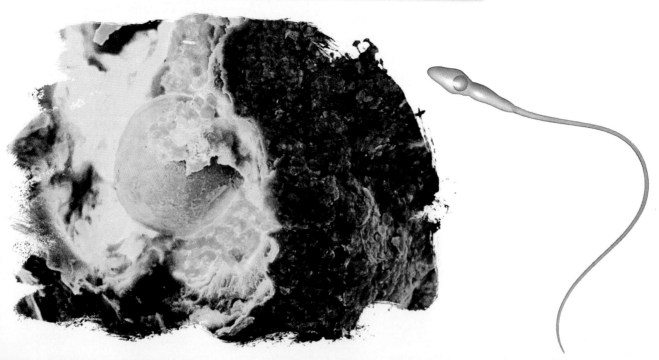

Reading Check ✓

Review a child's development. What signal words indicate the sequence of development? (An example includes words such as *next*.)

Section
21-2 FERTILIZATION TO BIRTH

When fertilized, the egg forms a zygote. The zygote moves through the oviduct and implants in the wall of the uterus. During the first two months of pregnancy, the unborn child is known as an **embryo.** A placenta forms, and the umbilical cord supplies nutrients and oxygen from the mother to the baby. Wastes are carried away through the umbilical cord. After two months, the body organs have formed and the developing baby is called a **fetus.** After nine months, the developed baby is pushed out of the mother by contractions of the uterus. Twins occur when two eggs are fertilized or when a single egg splits after fertilization. *Why are so many sperm released if only one is needed to fertilize the egg?*

Section
21-3 DEVELOPMENT AFTER BIRTH

Infancy is the stage of development from the neonatal period to one year. This stage is followed by **childhood,** which lasts to age 12 and is marked by development of muscular coordination and mental abilities. **Adolescence** is when a person becomes physically able to reproduce. The final stage of development is **adulthood.** A number of conditions are associated with aging. Certain genes are believed to be responsible for aging and for a person's adaptive ability and functional reserve. *How are the characteristics of the stages of infancy and childhood alike?*

Chapter 21 Assessment

Using Vocabulary

a. adolescence
b. adulthood
c. amniotic sac
d. childhood
e. embryo
f. fetus
g. infancy
h. menopause
i. menstrual cycle
j. menstruation
k. ovary
l. ovulation
m. pregnancy
n. reproduction
o. semen
p. sperm
q. testis
r. uterus
s. vagina

Which science term describes each of the following?

1. birth canal
2. egg-producing organ
3. release of egg from the ovary
4. place where a fertilized egg develops into a baby
5. membrane that protects the unborn baby

Checking Concepts

Choose the word or phrase that best answers the question.

6. Where does the embryo develop?
   A) oviduct
   B) ovary
   C) uterus
   D) vagina

7. What is the monthly process of egg release called?
   A) fertilization
   B) ovulation
   C) menstruation
   D) puberty

8. What is the union of an egg and sperm?
   A) fertilization
   B) ovulation
   C) menstruation
   D) puberty

9. Where is the egg fertilized?
   A) oviduct
   B) uterus
   C) vagina
   D) ovary

10. During which period do mental and physical skills rapidly develop?
    A) the neonatal period
    B) infancy
    C) adulthood
    D) adolescence

11. During which period does puberty occur?
    A) childhood
    B) adulthood
    C) adolescence
    D) infancy

12. What are sex characteristics common to both males and females?
    A) breasts
    B) increased muscles
    C) increased fat
    D) pubic hair

13. During which period does growth stop?
    A) childhood
    B) adolescence
    C) adulthood
    D) infancy

14. What is the period of development with three stages?
    A) infancy
    B) adulthood
    C) adolescence
    D) childhood

15. During which period does the ability to reproduce begin?
    A) adolescence
    B) adulthood
    C) childhood
    D) infancy

Thinking Critically

16. Explain the similar functions of the ovaries and testes.

17. Identify the structure in which each process occurs: ovulation, fertilization, and implantation.

18. When does menopause occur?

19. What kind of cell division occurs as the zygote develops?

20. Describe one major change in each stage of human development.

Developing Skills

If you need help, refer to the **Skill Handbook.**

21. **Classifying:** Classify each of the following structures of the male and female reproductive systems as female or male and internal or external: ovary, penis, scrotum, testes, uterus, and vagina.

22. **Concept Map:** Construct a concept map of egg release using the following terms: *ovary, ovulation, oviduct, uterus,* and *zygote.*

23. **Hypothesizing:** Make a hypothesis about the effects of raising identical twins apart from each other.

24. **Making and Using Graphs:** The growth of an embryo does not occur at the same rate throught development. Use the data below to make a graph showing the week of development versus size of the embryo. When is the fastest period of growth?

Embryo Size During Development

Week After Fertilization	Size
3	3 mm
4	6 mm
6	12 mm
7	2 cm
8	4 cm
9	5 cm

25. **Sequencing:** Sequence the steps involved in the birth process.

THE PRINCETON REVIEW

Test-Taking Tip

Maximize Your Score Ask how your test will be scored. In order to do your best, you need to know if there is a penalty for guessing, and if so, how much of one. If there is no penalty at all, you should always fill in what you think is the best answer.

Test Practice

Use these questions to test your Science Proficiency.

1. During the menstrual cycle, the lining of the uterus thickens. Which statement **BEST** explains the need for this phase?
   A) to prepare the uterus for sperm to fertilize an egg
   B) to prepare the uterus for discharging excess eggs from the body
   C) to prepare the uterus for supporting and nourishing the developing embryo
   D) to prepare the uterus for hormones that fight infections

2. Sperm travel a long pathway before being discharged from the body. Which statement is the correct sequence of structures through which the sperm pass?
   A) testis—sperm duct—prostate—urethra
   B) testis—sperm duct—ureter—prostate
   C) testis—seminal vesicles—sperm duct—urethra
   D) testis—urethra—prostate—sperm duct

Chapter Preview

Skills Preview

Skill Builders
- Compare and Contrast

Activities
- Experiment and Analyze

MiniLabs
- Test and Observe
- Calculate and Graph

Reading Check ✔

As you read this chapter, complete a chart with three columns: the name of the disease, its cause, and its effects.

Explore Activity

Even though you can't see them, there are disease-causing bacteria and viruses lurking in every corner, waiting for the opportunity to invade your body. They may not look that impressive, but the white blood cells shown in the photograph are an important part of your body's defense against disease. A simple cold or flu could prove deadly if your body lacks this critical defense. To find out how these cells protect your body from invasion, it's helpful to know how diseases are spread. You can begin to answer this question by doing the following activity.

Determine How Disease-Causing Organisms Spread

1. Wash your hands before and after this activity.

2. Work with a partner. Place a drop of peppermint food flavoring on a cotton ball. Pretend that the flavoring is a mass of cold viruses.

3. Use the cotton ball to rub an X over the palm of your right hand. Let it dry.

4. Shake hands with a classmate.

5. Have your classmate shake hands with another student.

In your Science Journal, describe some ways diseases are spread. Infer how many persons could be infected by your "virus."

22•1 Communicable Diseases

What You'll Learn

▶ The work of Pasteur, Koch, and Lister in the discovery and prevention of disease
▶ Diseases caused by viruses and bacteria
▶ Sexually transmitted diseases (STDs), their causes, and treatments

Vocabulary
pasteurization
disinfectant
antiseptic
communicable disease
sexually transmitted disease (STD)

Why It's Important

▶ You can help prevent certain illnesses if you know what causes disease and how disease spreads.

Discovering Disease

"Ring around the rosie, A pocket full of posies,
Ashes, Ashes, We all fall down."

You may not know that this rhyme is more than 600 years old. Some think this rhyme is about a disease called the Black Death, or the Plague. As shown in **Figure 22-1,** several times during the fourteenth century, the Plague spread through Europe. "Ring around the rosie" was a symptom of the disease—a ring around a red spot on the skin. People carried a pocket full of flower petals, "posies," and spices to keep away the stench of dead bodies. In spite of these efforts, 25 million people "all fell down" and died from this terrible disease.

Causes of Disease

No one knew what caused the Plague or how to stop it as it swept through Europe. It wasn't until about 150 years ago that scientists began to find out how some diseases are caused. Today, we know that diseases are caused by viruses, protozoans, and harmful bacteria. These are known as pathogens.

The French chemist Louis Pasteur proved that harmful bacteria could cause disease. He developed a method of using heat to kill pathogens. **Pasteurization** (pas chuh ruh ZAY shun), named for him, is the process of heating food to a temperature that kills most bacteria. Pasteur's work began the science of bacteriology.

Figure 22-1 Plague is caused by a bacterium that reproduces in fleas that live on rats. **What conditions in the towns of the fourteenth century encouraged the spread of this disease?**

Figure 22-2 The steps used to identify an organism as the cause of a specific disease are known as Koch's rules.

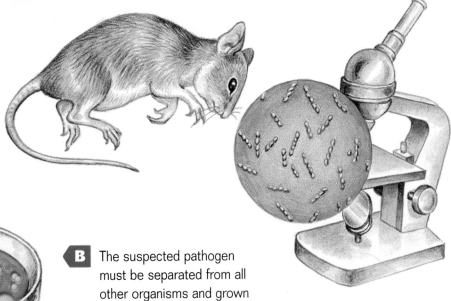

A In every case of a particular disease, the organism thought to cause the disease must be present.

B The suspected pathogen must be separated from all other organisms and grown in a culture with no other organisms present.

C When the suspected pathogen from the pure culture is placed in a healthy host, it must become sick with the original disease.

D Finally, when the suspected pathogen is removed from the host and grown on agar gel again, it must be compared with the original organism to see whether they are the same. When they match, that organism is the pathogen that causes that disease.

Koch's Rules

Pasteur may have shown that bacteria caused disease, but he didn't know how to tell which specific organism caused a specific disease. It was a German doctor, Robert Koch, who first developed a way to isolate and grow, or culture, one type of bacterium at a time. Koch developed a set of rules to figure out which organism caused a particular disease. These rules are illustrated in **Figure 22-2.**

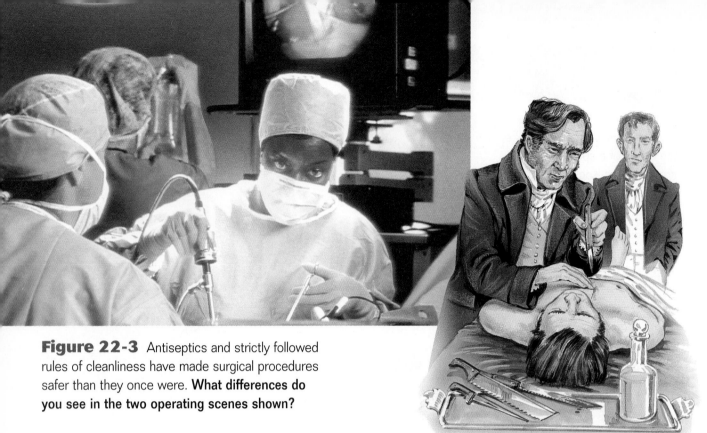

Figure 22-3 Antiseptics and strictly followed rules of cleanliness have made surgical procedures safer than they once were. **What differences do you see in the two operating scenes shown?**

Reading Check

Outline the work done by Pasteur, Koch, and Lister in the discovery and prevention of disease.

PHYSICS
INTEGRATION

Surface Tension
Many chemical disinfectants lower the surface tension of bacteria, allowing the chemical to be more easily absorbed. Find out what surface tension is. Infer what makes a disinfectant effective.

Keeping Clean

Washing your hands before or after certain activities is an accepted part of your daily routine. This was not always true, even for doctors. Into the late 1800s, doctors, such as those in **Figure 22-3,** regularly operated in their street clothes and with bare hands. More patients died in surgery than survived surgery. Joseph Lister, an English surgeon, was horrified. He recognized the relationship between the infection rate and cleanliness in surgery. Lister dramatically reduced deaths among his surgical patients by washing their skin and his hands before surgery.

Disinfectants and Antiseptics

Lister used a disinfectant to reduce surgical infections. A **disinfectant** kills pathogens on objects such as instruments, floors, and bathtubs. Today, antiseptics also are used. An **antiseptic** kills pathogens on skin and continues to prevent them from growing for some time after. Doctors now wash their hands often with antiseptic soaps. They also wear sterile gloves to keep from spreading pathogens from person to person.

While the role of bacteria in causing disease was better understood and the use of disinfectants and antiseptics reduced the spread of disease, doctors did not understand why some diseases could not be controlled. Not until the late 1800s and early 1900s did scientists make a connection between viruses and disease transmission.

How Diseases Are Spread

A disease that is spread to an organism from an infected organism or the environment is a **communicable disease.** Communicable diseases are caused by agents such as viruses, some bacteria, protists, and fungi. Some diseases caused by these agents are listed in **Table 22-1.**

Communicable diseases are spread through water and air, on food, by contact with contaminated objects, and by biological vectors. A biological vector is a carrier of a disease. Examples of vectors that spread disease are rats, flies, birds, cats, dogs, and mosquitos as in **Figure 22-4.** To prevent the spread of disease, city water systems add chlorine to drinking water and swimming pools. When you have influenza and sneeze, you hurl thousands of virus particles through the air. Colds and many other diseases are spread through contact. Each time you turn a doorknob or press the button on a water fountain at school, your skin comes in contact with bacteria and viruses. Some dangerous communicable diseases are transmitted by sexual contact.

In the United States, the Centers for Disease Control and Prevention (CDC) in Atlanta, Georgia, monitors the spread of diseases throughout the country. The CDC also watches for diseases brought into the country.

Mini Lab

Detecting Bacteria

Procedure

1. Methylene blue is used to detect bacteria. The faster the color fades, the more bacteria are present.
2. Use the food samples provided by your teacher. Label four test tubes 1, 2, 3, and 4.
3. Fill three test tubes half full of the food samples.
4. Fill all four tubes with water.
5. Add 20 drops of methylene blue and 2 drops of mineral oil to each tube.
6. Place the tubes into a warm-water bath for 20 minutes.
7. Record the time and your observations.

Analysis

1. Compare how long it takes each tube to lose its color.
2. What was the purpose of tube 4?
3. Why is it important to eat and drink only the freshest food?

Table 22-1

Diseases and Their Agents				
	Bacteria	**Protists**	**Fungi**	**Viruses**
Diseases	Tetanus	Malaria	Athlete's foot	Colds
	Tuberculosis	Sleeping sickness		Influenza
	Typhoid fever		Ringworm	AIDS
	Strep throat			Measles
	Bacterial pneumonia			Mumps
		Mosquito		Polio
	Plague			Smallpox

Figure 22-4

Pathogenic organisms include bacteria, protists, fungi, and viruses. **How does the mosquito transport pathogens from infected people or objects to new hosts?**

Virus

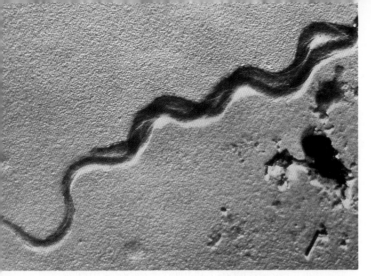

Magnification: 19 000×

Figure 22-5 The bacterium that causes syphilis can be seen in this electron micrograph.

Try at Home

Mini Lab

Determining Reproduction Rates

Procedure

1. Make a chart like the one below.
2. Complete the chart up to the fifth hour. Assume that this bacteria divides every 20 minutes if conditions are favorable.
3. Graph your data.

Analysis

1. How many bacteria are present after five hours?
2. Why is it important to take antibiotics promptly if you have an infection?

Time	Number of bacteria
0 hours 0 minutes	1
20 minutes	2
40 minutes	4
1 hour 0 minutes	8
20 minutes	
40 minutes	

Sexually Transmitted Diseases

Diseases transmitted from person to person during sexual contact are called **sexually transmitted diseases (STDs).** You can become infected with an STD by engaging in sexual activity with an infected person. STDs are caused by both viruses and bacteria.

Genital herpes causes painful blisters on the sex organs. Herpes can be transmitted during sexual contact or by an infected mother to her child during birth. The herpes virus hides in the body for long periods and then reappears suddenly. Herpes has no cure, and no vaccine can prevent it.

Gonorrhea and chlamydial infections are STDs caused by bacteria that may not produce any symptoms. When symptoms do appear, they can include painful urination, genital discharge, and sores. Antibiotics are used to treat these diseases. If left untreated, both diseases can cause sterility, which is the inability to reproduce.

The strangely shaped bacterium that causes syphilis is seen in **Figure 22-5.** Syphilis has several stages. In stage 1, a sore that lasts ten to 14 days appears on the mouth or genitals. Stage 2 may involve a rash, a fever, and swollen lymph glands. Within weeks to a year, these symptoms usually disappear. The victim often believes that the disease has gone away, but it hasn't. In Stage 3, syphilis may infect the cardiovascular and nervous systems. Syphilis is treated in all stages with antibiotics. However, the damage to body organs in the third stage cannot be reversed and death may result.

HIV and AIDS

HIV, shown in **Figure 22-6,** is a latent virus that can exist in blood and body fluids. A latent virus is one that hides in body cells. You can contract HIV by having sex with an HIV-infected person, or by sharing an HIV-contaminated needle used to inject drugs. The risk of contracting HIV through blood transfusion is small. Donated blood is tested for the presence of HIV. A pregnant female with HIV may infect her child when the virus passes through the placenta, when blood contacts the child during birth, or when nursing after birth. An HIV infection can lead to AIDS, a disease that attacks the body's immune system and eventually kills its victims. AIDS stands for Acquired Immune Deficiency Syndrome. No vaccine prevents AIDS, and no medication cures it. In the next section, more information will be given on how HIV breaks down the immune system.

Some communicable diseases are chronic. A chronic disease lasts a long time. AIDS is a chronic disease that, as yet, cannot be cured. Some chronic diseases can be cured. Lyme disease, carried by ticks, is a bacterial infection that can become chronic if not treated. The bacteria can affect the nervous system, heart, and joints for weeks to years. Antibiotics will kill the bacteria, but any permanent damage cannot be reversed. In Section 22-3, you will learn about chronic diseases that are not caused by pathogens.

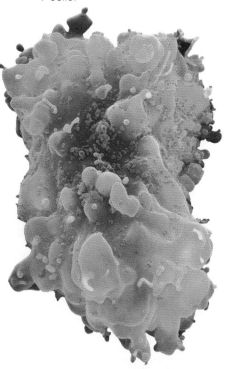

Figure 22-6 HIV is a latent virus that can exist in blood and body fluids. It attacks the helper T cells.

Section Assessment

1. How did the discoveries of Pasteur, Koch, and Lister help in the battle against disease?

2. List a communicable disease caused by a virus, a bacterium, a protist, and a fungus.

3. What are STDs? How are they contracted and treated?

4. **Think Critically:** In what ways does Koch's procedure reflect the use of scientific methods?

5.  **Skill Builder**
   Recognizing Cause and Effect How is not washing your hands related to the spread of disease? Do the **Chapter 22 Skill Activity** on page 727 to analyze the effects of certain health habits.

Science Journal Research the history of the building of the Panama Canal. Write a report in your Science Journal about the relationship between the diseases of malaria and yellow fever and the building of the canal.

Microorganisms and Disease

Materials

- Fresh apples (6)
- Rotting apple
- Alcohol (5 mL)
- Self-sealing plastic bags (6)
- Labels and pencil
- Paper towels
- Sandpaper
- Cotton ball
- Soap and water

Microorganisms are all around us. They are on the surfaces of everything we touch. Try this experiment to see how microorganisms are involved in spreading infections.

What You'll Investigate

How do microorganisms cause infection?

Goals

- **Observe** the transmission of microorganisms.
- **Relate** microorganisms to infections.

Procedure

1. **Label** the plastic bags 1 through 6. **Put** a fresh apple in bag 1 and **seal** it.

2. **Rub** the rotting apple over the entire surface of the remaining five apples. This is your source of microorganisms. **CAUTION:** *Always wash your hands after handling microorganisms.* **Put** one apple in bag 2.

3. **Hold** one apple 1.5 m above the floor and drop it. **Put** this apple into bag number 3.

4. **Rub** one apple with sandpaper. **Place** this apple in bag number 4.

5. **Wash** one apple with soap and water. **Dry** it well. **Put** this apple in bag number 5.

6. **Use** a cotton ball to spread alcohol over the last apple. Let it air dry. **Place** it in bag 6.

7. **Place** all of the apples in a dark place for three days. Then, **wash** your hands.

8. **Write a hypothesis** to explain what you think will happen to each apple.

9. At the end of day 3 and again on day 7, **compare** all of the apples. **Record** your observations in a data table like the one shown. **CAUTION:** *Give all apples to your teacher for proper disposal.*

Conclude and Apply

1. Did you **observe** changes in apple numbers 5 and 6?

2. Why is it important to clean a wound?

3. Were your hypotheses supported?

4. **Relate** microorganisms to infections on your skin.

Apple Data			
	Condition	Observations	
Apple	of the apple	Day 3	Day 7
1	Fresh apple		
2	Untreated apple		
3	Dropped apple		
4	Apple rubbed with sandpaper		
5	Apple washed with soap and water		
6	Apple covered with alcohol		

Your Immune System

Lines of Defense

Most microorganisms do not cause disease. Your body has many ways to defend itself against the ones that do. First-line defenses are general and work against all types of pathogens. Second-line defenses are specific and work against particular pathogens.

Your **immune system** is a complex group of defenses that your body has to fight disease. It is made up of cells, tissues, organs, and body systems that fight pathogens, harmful chemicals, and cancer cells.

General Defenses

Several body systems are involved in defending your body from pathogens. Your skin is a barrier that prevents many pathogens from entering your body. Your respiratory system contains cilia and mucus that trap pathogens. When you cough, you expel trapped bacteria. In the digestive system, enzymes in the stomach, pancreas, and liver destroy pathogens. Pathogens are disease-causing organisms. Hydrochloric acid in your stomach kills bacteria that enter your body on food.

Your circulatory system contains white blood cells that engulf and digest foreign organisms and chemicals. These white blood cells constantly patrol the body, sweeping up and digesting bacteria that manage to get into the body. As you see in **Figure 22-7,** they slip between cells in the walls of capillaries to destroy bacteria. When the white blood cells cannot destroy the bacteria fast enough, a fever may develop. A fever helps fight pathogens by slowing their growth and speeding up your body's reactions.

All of these processes are general defenses that work to keep you disease-free. If pathogens get past these general defenses, your body has another line of defense in the form of specific immunity.

Figure 22-7 White blood cells leave capillaries (A) and engulf harmful bacteria (B) in surrounding tissues. **What are harmful bacteria called?**

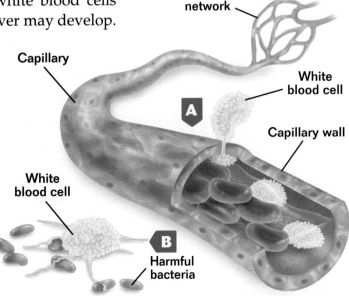

Capillary network

Capillary

White blood cell

Capillary wall

A

White blood cell

B

Harmful bacteria

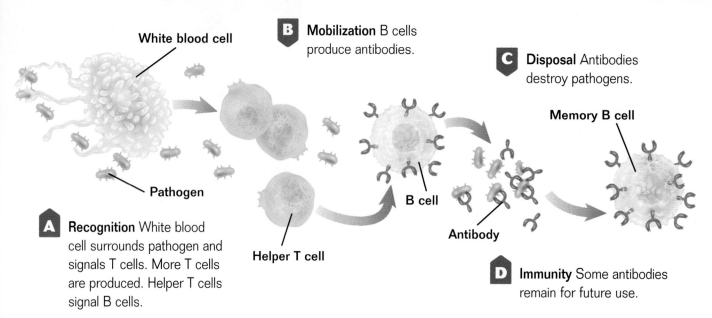

A **Recognition** White blood cell surrounds pathogen and signals T cells. More T cells are produced. Helper T cells signal B cells.

B **Mobilization** B cells produce antibodies.

C **Disposal** Antibodies destroy pathogens.

D **Immunity** Some antibodies remain for future use.

White blood cell

Pathogen

Helper T cell

B cell

Antibody

Memory B cell

Figure 22-8 The response of your immune system to disease-causing organisms can be divided into four steps: recognition, mobilization, disposal, and immunity. **What is the function of B cells?**

Visit the Glencoe Science Web Site at **www.glencoe.com/ sec/science/ca** for more information about your lines of defense.

Reading Check ☑️ What are the body's major lines of defense against invading organisms?

Specific Defenses

When your body fights disease, it is really battling proteins or chemicals that don't belong there. Proteins and chemicals that are foreign to your body are called **antigens** (AN tih junz). Antigens are located on the surfaces of pathogens. When your immune system recognizes a foreign protein or chemical, as in **Figure 22-8,** it forms specific antibodies. An **antibody** is a protein made by an animal in response to a specific antigen. The antibody binds up the antigen, making it harmless. Antibodies help your body build defenses in two ways, actively and passively. **Active immunity** occurs when your body makes its own antibodies in response to an antigen. **Passive immunity** occurs when antibodies that have been produced in another animal are introduced into the body.

Active Immunity

When your body is invaded by a pathogen, it immediately starts to make antibodies to inactivate the antigen. Once enough antibodies form, you get better. Some antibodies stay on duty in your blood, and more are rapidly produced if the pathogen enters your body again. This is why you do not get some diseases more than once. ☑️

Another way to develop active immunity to a particular disease is to be inoculated with a vaccine. The process of giving a vaccine by injection or orally is called **vaccination.** A vaccine is a noninfectious form of the antigen and gives you active immunity against a disease without you actually getting the disease first. For example, suppose a vaccine for measles is injected into your body. Your body forms antibodies against the measles antigen. If you later encounter the virus, antibodies necessary to fight that virus are already in your bloodstream ready to destroy the pathogen. Antibodies that immunize you against one virus may not guard against a different virus. As you grow older, you will be exposed to many more types of pathogens and will build a separate immunity to each one.

Passive Immunity

How is passive immunity different from active immunity? Recall that passive immunity is the transfer of antibodies into your body. For example, you were born with all the antibodies that your mother had in her blood. However, these antibodies stayed with you for only a few months. Passive immunity does not last as long as active immunity. Because newborn babies lose their passive immunity in a few months, they need to be vaccinated to develop their own immunity.

Tetanus is a toxin produced by a bacterium in soil. The toxin paralyzes muscles. As a child, you received active vaccines that stimulated antibody production to tetanus toxin. As shown in **Figure 22-9,** you should continue to get active vaccines or "boosters" every ten years to maintain active protection. Suppose a person who has never been vaccinated against tetanus toxin gets a puncture wound. The person would be given passive immunity—antibodies to the toxin. These antibodies usually are from humans but can be from horses or cattle if human antibodies are not available.

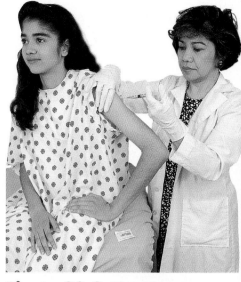

Figure 22-9 Tetanus is a toxin produced by a bacterium that lives in the soil. An active vaccine or "booster" every ten years will maintain active protection against the toxin.

Problem Solving

Interpreting Data

Each year, many people die from diseases. Medical science has found many ways to treat and cure disease. New drugs, improved surgery techniques, and healthier lifestyles have contributed to the decrease in deaths from disease. The chart shown here indicates the percent of total deaths due to six major diseases for a 45-year span. Study the statistics for each disease.

Think Critically: Which diseases have had a steady decline in deaths through the 45 years? Have any diseases shown an increase in deaths? What factors may have contributed to this increase?

Percentage of Deaths Due to Major Diseases

Disease	Year			
	1950	1980	1990	1995
Heart	37.1	38.3	33.5	32.0
Cancer	14.6	20.9	23.5	23.3
Stroke	10.8	8.6	6.7	6.8
Diabetes	1.7	1.8	2.2	2.6
Pneumonia and Flu	3.3	2.7	3.7	3.6
Tuberculosis	2.3	0.10	0.08	0.06

HIV and Your Immune System

HIV, as shown in **Figure 22-10,** is different from other viruses. It attacks cells in the immune system called helper T cells. A **helper T cell** is a type of white blood cell that helps other types of white blood cells produce antibodies.

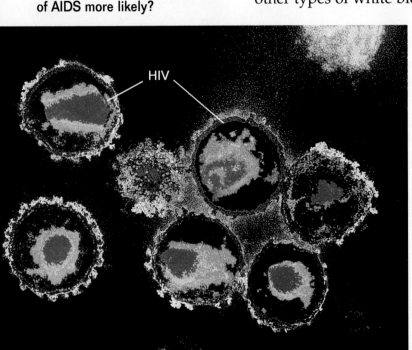

HIV

Magnification: 130 000×

Because HIV destroys helper T cells, the body is left with no way to fight invading antigens. The immune system breaks down. The body is unable to fight HIV, many other pathogens, and certain types of cancer. For this reason, people with AIDS die from other diseases such as pneumonia, cancer, or tuberculosis. The victim's body becomes defenseless.

When a microbe enters your body, it must get past all of your general defenses. If it gets past these defenses, it encounters your specific defenses—your second line of defense.

Section Assessment

1. List natural defenses your body has against disease.

2. How does an active vaccine work in the human body?

3. Explain how HIV attacks your immune system.

4. **Think Critically:** Several diseases have the same symptoms as measles. Why doesn't the measles vaccine protect you from all of these diseases?

5.  **Skill Builder**
   Developing Multimedia
   Presentations Prepare a presentation for the class on the history of immunization for a specific disease. If you need help, refer to Developing Multimedia Presentations in the **Technology Skills Handbook** on page 700.

Using Computers

Graphics Use the information in this section to create a flowchart that compares active and passive immunity. If you need help, refer to page 698.

AIDS Vaccine

Moving Target

One of the most intensive efforts in the history of medicine is currently under way—to develop a vaccine against the human immunodeficiency virus, or HIV (round virus particles, inset). Because HIV mutates, or changes, rapidly, it is difficult to develop a single vaccine that can stimulate the human immune system to mount a successful attack on the virus and its many variations. Researchers are trying different vaccine strategies to try to solve this problem. The HIV researcher, left, is working in sterile clothing, his hands placed under a protective hood. Some of the vaccine strategies being tested are discussed below.

Subunit

The subunit method involves using a piece of the HIV's outer surface that contains certain proteins. The human immune system produces antibodies that recognize this subunit on complete HIV viruses.

Viruslike Particles

Another experimental vaccine uses a noninfectious HIV look-alike. The look-alike causes the body to produce antibodies against actual HIV.

Live Attenuated Virus

The live attenuated virus method uses actual HIV virus particles that have been weakened by the removal of one or more of their disease-causing genes. This type of vaccine seems to offer the broadest protection of all the experimental HIV vaccines tested so far.

Whole Inactivated Virus

Another strategy involves using an HIV virus that is inactivated by chemicals, irradiation, or other means. The resulting virus is not infectious, and it can cause the immune system to produce antibodies against HIV.

Only with thorough research will scientists find a vaccine powerful enough to solve the unique problems that HIV presents.

CONNECTION

AIDS research is such a massive effort that information is updated constantly. Visit the Glencoe Science Web Site at **www.glencoe.com/sec/science/ca** to find links that will help you locate the latest information available. Prepare and present a report on the progress of AIDS vaccine research.

Design Your Own Experiment

Microorganism Growth

Possible Materials

- Sterile petri dishes with agar (5)
- Filter paper (2-cm squares)
- Test chemicals (disinfectant, hydrogen peroxide, mouthwash, alcohol)
- Transparent tape
- Pencil and labels
- Scissors
- Metric ruler
- Forceps
- Small jars for chemicals (4)
- Cotton balls

Infections are caused by microorganisms. Without cleanliness, the risk of getting an infection from a wound is high. Disinfectants are chemicals that kill or remove disease organisms from objects. Antiseptics are chemicals that kill or prevent growth of disease organisms on living tissues. You will test the effect of these chemicals by growing microorganisms in petri dishes filled with agar. Agar is a gel that provides the ideal nutrients for growing microorganisms.

Recognize the Problem

What conditions do microorganisms need to grow? How can they be prevented from growing?

Form a Hypothesis

Based on your knowledge of disinfectants and antiseptics, **state a hypothesis** about methods that will prevent the growth of microorganisms.

Goals

- **Observe** the effects of antiseptics and disinfectants on microorganism growth in petri dishes.
- **Design** an experiment that will test the effects of chemicals on microorganisms growing in contaminated petri dishes.

Safety Precautions

Handle the forceps carefully. When you complete the experiment, give your sealed petri dishes to your teacher for proper disposal.

Test Your Hypothesis

Plan

1. As a group, agree upon and write out a hypothesis statement.

2. To test disinfectants, first introduce microorganisms to the agar by rubbing your finger gently over each dish. Then, soak a different square of filter paper in each of the disinfectants. Place each square on the agar and seal the dishes with tape. Never break the seal. Look for bacteria growth under and around each square.

3. As a group, list the steps that you will need to take to test your

hypothesis. Consider what you learned about how infections are stopped. **List** your materials.

4. **Design** a data table and record it in your Science Journal so that it is ready to use as your group collects data.

5. Read over your entire experiment to make sure that all steps are in logical order.

6. **Identify** any **constants, variables,** and the **control** of the experiment.

Do

1. Make sure your teacher approves your plan before you proceed.

2. Carry out the experiment as planned.

3. While the experiment is going on, write down any **observations** that you make and complete the **data table** in your Science Journal.

Analyze Your Data

1. **Compare** your results with those of other groups.

2. How did you **compare** growth beneath and around each chemical-soaked square in the petri dishes?

3. **Interpret the data** to determine what substances appeared to be most effective in preventing microorganism growth and what substances appeared to be least effective.

Draw Conclusions

1. What methods prevented the growth of microorganisms?

2. How does the growth of microorganisms on the control compare with their growth on the variables?

Noncommunicable Disease

What **You'll Learn**

▶ Causes of noncommunicable diseases
▶ The basic characteristics of cancer
▶ What happens during an allergic reaction

Vocabulary
noncommunicable disease
cancer
chemotherapy
allergy
allergen

Why **It's Important**

▶ The causes of noncommunicable diseases can help you understand their prevention and treatment.

Chronic Disease

Diseases and disorders such as diabetes, allergies, asthma, cancer, and heart disease are noncommunicable diseases. These diseases are called **noncommunicable diseases** because they are not spread from one person to another. You can't "catch" them. Allergies, genetic disorders, lifestyle diseases, or chemical imbalances such as diabetes are not spread by sneezes or handshakes.

Some communicable diseases can be chronic (KRAH nihk). Some noncommunicable diseases also are chronic. A chronic disease is one that lingers. Some chronic diseases can be cured. Others cannot. These diseases may result from improperly functioning organs, contact with harmful chemicals, or an unhealthy lifestyle. For example, your pancreas produces the hormone insulin. Diabetes is a chronic disease in which the pancreas cannot produce the amount of insulin the body needs.

Rheumatoid arthritis is a chronic disease that results from a faulty immune system. The immune system begins to treat the body's own normal proteins as if they were antigens. The faulty immune system forms antibodies against the normal proteins in joints. You can see in **Figure 22-11** that the joints become distorted and movement becomes difficult and painful.

Figure 22-11 Rheumatoid arthritis turns the body's immune system against itself. Healthy joints (A) may become severely deformed (B) as these X rays show.

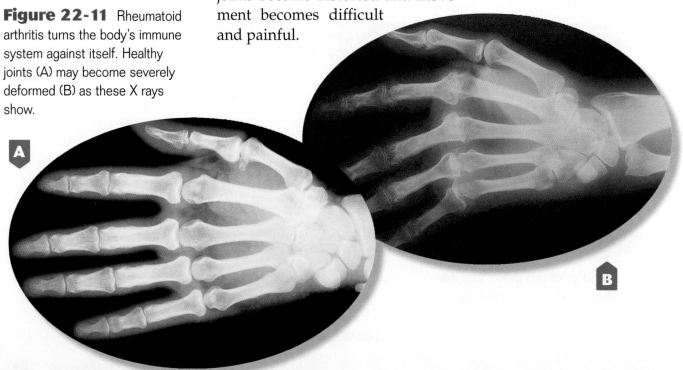

Figure 22-12 These scientists (A) are testing the contents of barrels found in a dump. Asbestos, if inhaled into the lungs over a long period of time, can cause chronic diseases of the lungs. Protective clothing must be worn when removing asbestos (B).

Chemicals and Disease

We are surrounded by chemicals. They are found in foods, cosmetics, cleaning products, pesticides, fertilizers, and building materials. Of the thousands of chemical substances used by consumers, less than two percent are harmful. Those chemicals that are harmful to living things are called toxins. Some chronic diseases are caused by toxins.

CHEMISTRY
◄ INTEGRATION

The Effects

The effects of a chemical toxin are determined by the amount that is taken into the body and how long the body is in contact with it. For example, a toxin taken into the body at low levels might cause cardiac or respiratory problems. Higher levels might even cause death. Some chemicals, such as asbestos shown in **Figure 22-12B,** may be inhaled into the lungs over a long period of time. Eventually, the asbestos can cause chronic diseases of the lungs. Lead-based paints are chemical toxins. If ingested, they can cause damage to the central nervous system. ✓

Manufacturing, mining, transportation, and farming produce waste products. These chemical substances may adversely affect the ability of the soil, water, and air to support life. Pollution, such as that caused by harmful chemicals, sometimes produces chronic diseases in humans. For example, the long-time exposure to carbon monoxide, sulfur oxides, and nitrogen oxides in the air may cause a number of diseases, including bronchitis, emphysema, and lung cancer.

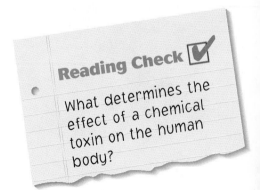

Reading Check ✓

What determines the effect of a chemical toxin on the human body?

Cancer

Cancer is a major chronic disease. **Cancer** results from uncontrolled cell growth. There are many different types of cancer, but most of them have the characteristics shown in **Table 22-2.**

interNET
CONNECTION

Visit the Glencoe Science Web Site at **www.glencoe.com/ sec/science/ca** for more information about cancer.

Table 22-2

Characteristics of Cancer Cells
• Cell growth is uncontrolled.
• These cells do not function as part of the body.
• The cells take up space and interfere with normal bodily functions.
• The cells travel throughout the body.
• The cells produce tumors and abnormal growths anywhere in the body.

Treatment

Treatment for cancer includes surgery to remove cancerous tissue, radiation with X rays to kill cancer cells, and chemotherapy. **Chemotherapy** (kee moh THAYR uh pee) is the use of chemicals to destroy cancer cells.

Cancers are complicated, and no one fully understands how cancers form. Some scientists hypothesize that cancer cells form regularly in the body. However, the immune system destroys them. Only if the immune system fails or becomes overwhelmed does the cancer begin to expand. Still, warnings, such as that in **Figure 22-13,** emphasize that tobacco products and exposure to harmful chemicals stimulate some cancers to form.

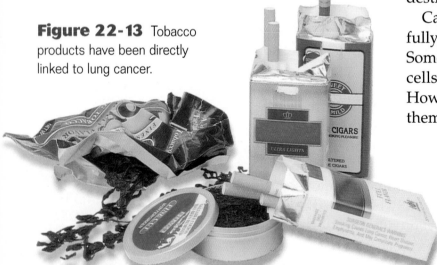

Figure 22-13 Tobacco products have been directly linked to lung cancer.

Allergies

Have you ever broken out in an itchy rash after eating a certain food? An **allergy** is an overly strong reaction of the immune system to a foreign substance. Many people have allergic reactions to cosmetics, shrimp, strawberries, peanuts, and bee stings. Allergic reactions to some things such as antibiotics can even be fatal.

Allergens

Substances that cause the allergic response are called **allergens.** These are substances that the body would normally respond to as a mild antigen. Chemicals, dust, food, pollen, molds, and some antibiotics are allergens for some sensitive people. When you come in contact with an allergen, your immune system forms antibodies and your body may react. When the body responds to an allergen, chemicals called histamines are released. Histamines promote red, swollen tissues. Allergic reactions are sometimes treated with antihistamines. Pollen is an allergen that causes a stuffy nose, breathing difficulties, watery eyes, and a tired feeling in some people. Some foods cause blotchy rashes such as hives, shown in **Figure 22-14,** or stomach cramps and diarrhea. Most allergic reactions are minor. But, severe allergic reactions can occur, causing shock and even death if not treated promptly. Some severe allergies are treated with repeated injections of small doses of the allergen. This allows the body to become less sensitive to the allergen.

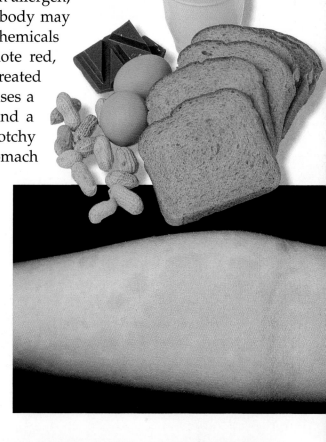

Figure 22-14 Some common substances (A) such as cosmetics, foods, dust mites, and wool stimulate allergic responses in people. Hives (B) are one kind of allergic reaction.

Section Assessment

1. What are two noncommunicable diseases?
2. What are the basic characteristics of cancer cells?
3. **Think Critically:** Joel has an ear infection. The doctor prescribes an antibiotic. After taking the antibiotic, Joel breaks out in a rash and has difficulty breathing. What is happening to him? What should he do immediately?
4. 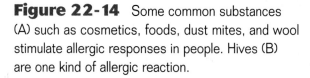 **Skill Builder**
   Making and Using Tables Make a table that lists some chronic diseases and their treatments. Use the information in this section. If you need help, refer to Making and Using Tables in the **Skill Handbook** on page 680.

Using Computers

Database Use references to find information on different allergens. Group the allergens into chemical, food, mold, pollen, and antibiotic. Use your computer to make a database. Note which group has the most allergens. If you need help, refer to page 697.

FIELD GUIDE

to First Aid

Have you ever found yourself in an emergency situation and wondered if you were the person who needed to help? Emergencies happen every day and everywhere. At the moment an emergency starts, you may not know how to react, but it is good to be well prepared. Learning ahead of time how to react can prevent disaster.

When and Where?

Emergencies come in all sorts of situations. It may be an auto accident or a fire. Maybe someone has slipped and twisted an ankle or perhaps cut a finger. Such things can happen at school, in the grocery store, at the movies, or at home. Regardless of where it happens or how big or small it is, what kinds of things might call your attention to an emergency situation?

Noises
- screaming or calls for help
- breaking glass
- sudden or loud noises made by things or a person falling
- screeching tires

Sights
- a stalled vehicle or a vehicle off the road
- spilled medicine or an opened, empty medicine container
- smoke or fire
- a person lying on the ground

FIELD *ACTIVITY*

In the cafeteria at school, or in a place permitted by your principal, set up a display of first-aid information pamphlets and different types of first-aid kits. From the local Red Cross, find out the five most frequent types of emergencies that occur and set up posters at school showing how to treat each of these emergencies.

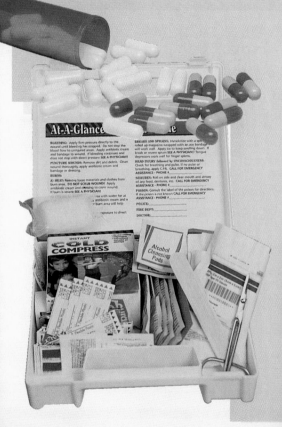

Odors
- different or strange odors
- odors that are stronger than usual

Appearance or Behavior of Another Person
- difficulty breathing
- grabbing his or her own throat
- unexplained confusion or drowsiness
- sudden change in skin color

To Act or Not to Act?

Someone must act in an emergency. Why not you? What things should you consider if you see an emergency? There are three basic steps to follow in an emergency. The steps are: Check, Call, and Care.

CHECK

Examine the scene
- Is it safe for you and any victims?
- Is there traffic, a chemical spill, extreme weather, or odors?
- If it's a dangerous situation, get help. **Remember, if you become injured, you can't help.**

Find out what happened
- Look for clues that may help to explain what caused the emergency.

Find all the victims
- Carefully account for everyone involved. Sometimes, a quiet victim may be overlooked if another is screaming.
- **Do not move victims unless they are in danger** from an explosion, fire, or poisonous gas.

Get help from others
- Anyone nearby may be able to provide more information about what happened, know where the nearest phone is, help with first aid, or comfort victims.

CALL

The most effective first-aid tool at your disposal is the telephone. In an emergency, call 911 or your local emergency number. Take the time now to find out your local emergency number. It will be valuable information if you find yourself in an emergency. Most importantly, don't hesitate to call for help, especially if you find yourself in the situations listed below. Emergency operators are trained to help you through emergency situations.

If the victim is:
- unconscious
- bleeding severely
- vomiting or passing blood

or has:
- chest pains or pressure
- trouble breathing or is making unusual noises as he or she breathes
- unexplained abdominal pressure or pain
- seizures, a severe headache, or slurred speech
- injuries to the head, neck, or back
- possible broken bones

Situations that require an immediate call are fire or explosion, downed electrical wires, flood conditions, presence of a poisonous gas, vehicle collisions, and victims who cannot be moved easily.

When calling the emergency service, **remember not to hang up first.** The emergency operator asks many questions, so it's important that you stay on the line until he or she has all the required information.

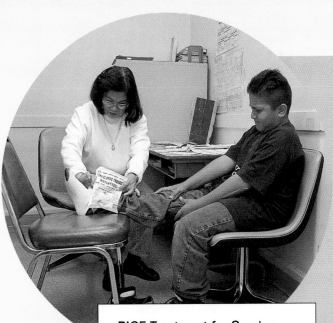

CARE

Before helping an ill or injured person, get his or her permission. Tell who you are, what training you have, and what you plan to do. If the person refuses permission, do not insist. Only a child's parent or guardian can give permission for that child. General guidelines for care are as follows:

- treat life-threatening emergencies first
- keep victims comfortable, talk to them, and be reassuring
- prevent the victim from becoming chilled or overheated
- talk with victims to identify location, type, and duration of pain
- if trained in first aid, follow standard procedures
- stay with victims until help arrives

If you remember and follow the 3 Cs, someone who is injured or ill may have a better chance to recover.

At some time in your life, you may be part of an emergency. What can you do to prepare should anything ever happen?

RICE Treatment for Sprains

The basic treatment for all types of sprains is the same. Use the term *RICE* to remember how to treat a sprain.

Rest—Rest the joint when there is swelling.

Ice—Apply ice for five to 15 minutes every hour.

Compression—Use an elastic bandage to gently wrap the entire sprained joint.

Elevation—Try to keep the joint straight and higher than the heart.

Emergency Checklist

- Learn first aid techniques.
- Learn when and how to use CPR (cardiopulmonary resuscitation) and the abdominal thrust for choking victims.
- Post emergency numbers by all phones and tape them to the first-aid kit. Teach young children how to telephone for help. Find out if your city has a 911 system.
- Place first-aid kits in your home, car, garage, and recreation areas.
- Put easy-to-read street numbers on your home or apartment. Numerals are easier to read than numbers that have been written out.
- If you have special medical needs, wear a medical alert tag.

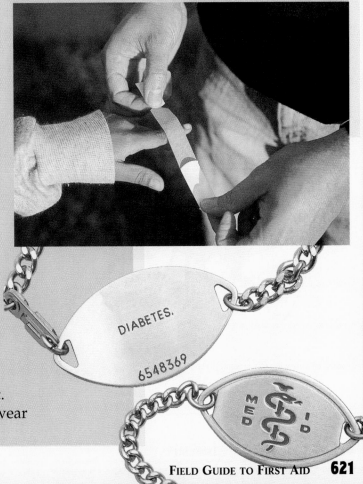

For a **preview** of this chapter, study this Reviewing Main Ideas before you read the chapter. After you have studied this chapter, you can use the Reviewing Main Ideas to **review** the chapter.

The Glencoe MindJogger, Audiocassettes, and CD-ROM provide additional opportunities for review.

Section 22-1 COMMUNICABLE DISEASES

Medical researchers Pasteur and Koch discovered that diseases are caused by microbes. **Communicable diseases** are caused by pathogenic bacteria, viruses, fungi, and protists and can be passed on through human contact, air, water, food, and animal contact. *How did people in the past believe diseases were spread?*

ANTISEPTICS AND DISINFECTANTS

One way to reduce the spread of disease is through the use of **antiseptics** and **disinfectants.** These kill pathogens on surfaces where they can be spread, such as skin, medical instruments, floors, and bathtubs. Doctors are careful to make sure their equipment is sterile and to prevent the spread of pathogens. *Why is washing your hands an effective way to lower your chances of getting a communicable disease?*

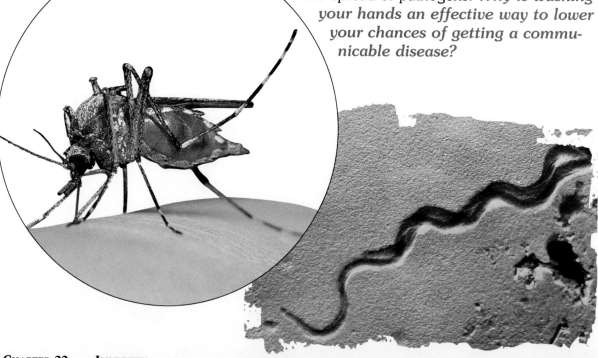

Section
22-2 YOUR IMMUNE SYSTEM

One of the body's defenses against disease is the **immune system. Antibodies** are produced by the lymphocytes. These react with **antigens** and make them harmless. Vaccines can provide immunity. **Active immunity** is long lasting. **Passive immunity** does not last. As people grow and develop from childhood to adulthood, their bodies are usually more successful in fighting diseases. The immune system becomes better adapted. It can recognize foreign proteins and chemicals and destroy them. The body's naturally acquired immunity can be aided by vaccines. *How can diseases be prevented from spreading?*

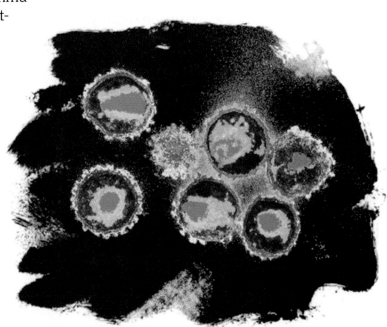

Section
22-3 NONCOMMUNICABLE DISEASES

Causes of **noncommunicable disease** include genetics, chemicals, poor diet, and uncontrolled cell growth. Chronic noncommunicable diseases include diabetes, cancer, arthritis, and allergies. *How do cancer cells move from one part of the body to another?*

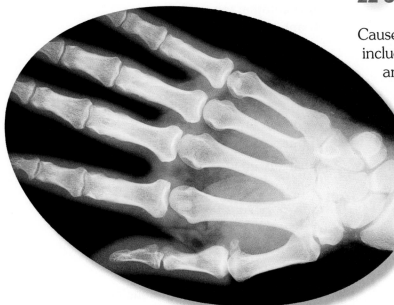

Chapter 22 Assessment

Using Vocabulary

a. active immunity
b. allergen
c. allergy
d. antibody
e. antigen
f. antiseptic
g. cancer
h. chemotherapy
i. communicable disease
j. disinfectant
k. helper T cell
l. immune system
m. noncommunicable disease
n. passive immunity
o. pasteurization
p. sexually transmitted disease (STD)
q. vaccination

Each phrase below describes a science term from the list. Write the term that matches the phrase describing it.

1. causes an allergic reaction
2. foreign protein attacked by the body
3. chemicals used to destroy cancer cells
4. uncontrolled cell division
5. introduces antigens for long-term immunity

Checking Concepts

Choose the word or phrase that best answers the question.

6. How do scientists know if a pathogen causes a specific disease?
   A) It is present in all cases of the disease.
   B) It does not infect other animals.
   C) It causes other diseases.
   D) It is treated with heat.

7. How can communicable diseases be caused?
   A) heredity   C) chemicals
   B) allergies   D) organisms

8. What organism carries the bacterium that causes Lyme disease?
   A) bird   C) rabbit
   B) tick   D) worm

9. Which of the following does a virus cause?
   A) AIDS   C) chlamydia
   B) gonorrhea   D) syphilis

10. Which of the following is **NOT** one of your body's defenses against pathogens?
    A) stomach enzymes   C) white blood cells
    B) skin   D) hormones

11. Which of the following is a communicable disease?
    A) allergies   C) asthma
    B) syphilis   D) diabetes

12. White blood cells are attacked by the virus that causes what?
    A) AIDS   C) flu
    B) chlamydia   D) polio

13. Which of the following is a chronic joint disease?
    A) asthma   C) diabetes
    B) arthritis   D) muscular dystrophy

14. What is formed in the blood to fight invading antigens?
    A) hormones   C) pathogens
    B) allergens   D) antibodies

15. How are cancer cells destroyed?
    A) chemotherapy   C) vaccines
    B) antigens   D) viruses

Thinking Critically

16. Which is better—to vaccinate people or to wait until they build their own immunity?

17. What advantage might a breast-fed baby have compared to a bottle-fed baby?

18. How does your body protect itself from antigens?

19. How do helper T cells eliminate antigens?

20. Describe the differences among antibodies, antigens, and antibiotics.

Developing Skills

If you need help, refer to the **Skill Handbook.**

21. **Making and Using Tables:** Make a chart comparing the following diseases and their prevention: cancer, diabetes, tetanus, and measles.

22. **Concept Mapping:** Make a network tree concept map comparing the defenses your body has against disease. Compare general defenses, active immunity, and passive immunity.

23. **Classifying:** Classify the following diseases as communicable or noncommunicable: diabetes, gonorrhea, herpes, strep throat, syphilis, cancer, and flu.

24. **Recognizing Cause and Effect:** Use a library reference to identify the cause of each disease as bacteria, virus, fungus, or protist: athlete's foot, AIDS, cold, dysentery, flu, pinkeye, pneumonia, strep throat, and ringworm.

25. **Making and Using Graphs:** Interpret the graph below showing the rate of polio cases. Explain the rate of cases between 1950 and 1965. What conclusions can you draw about the effectiveness of the polio vaccines?

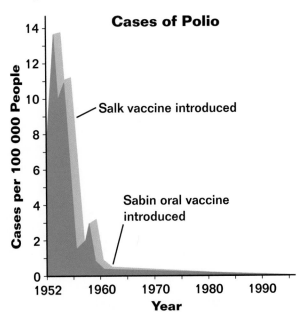

Cases of Polio

Salk vaccine introduced

Sabin oral vaccine introduced

Cases per 100 000 People

Year

THE PRINCETON REVIEW

Test-Taking Tip

Ignore Everyone While you take a test, pay no attention to anyone else in the room. Don't worry if friends finish a test before you do. If someone tries to talk with you during a test, don't answer. You run the risk of the teacher thinking you are cheating—even if you aren't.

Test Practice

Use these questions to test your Science Proficiency.

1. Communicable diseases are spread from one organism to another. Which statement is **NOT** true about these types of diseases?
   A) Communicable diseases can be transmitted by flies and mosquitoes.
   B) Communicable diseases can be transmitted by unclean food utensils.
   C) Communicable diseases can be transmitted by genes.
   D) Communicable diseases can be transmitted by fungi.

2. The human body has a complex group of defenses to fight disease organisms. Which statement describes a general body defense against infection?
   A) A natural body defense is the use of herbs.
   B) A natural body defense is getting a vaccination.
   C) A natural body defense is taking an antibiotic medicine.
   D) A natural body defense is the action of stomach acid.

California
Science Standards
and Case Studies

GLENCOE
California Edition

SCIENCE VOYAGES
LIFE
SCIENCE

Mc Graw Hill **Glencoe McGraw-Hill**

CALIFORNIA REPUBLIC

Level Green

California
The Golden State

State Tree:
The California
Red Wood

State Bird:
The California
Quail

State Flower:
The Golden Poppy

Cell Biology

Content Standard 1
All living organisms are composed of cells, from just one to many trillions, whose details usually are visible only through a microscope.

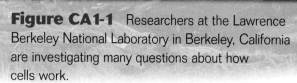

Figure CA1-1 Researchers at the Lawrence Berkeley National Laboratory in Berkeley, California are investigating many questions about how cells work.

1a. Function of Cells

Most cells respire, grow, reproduce, and release and transfer energy. Cells in plants and animals may do these things differently, but most cells share these characteristics of life.

1b. Plant Cells and Animal Cells

Plant and animal cells have many distinguishing features. The most outstanding difference between plant and animal cells is that plant cells have a cell wall made up of a tough material called cellulose. The cell wall supports and protects the plant cell. Plant cells also contain organelles called chloroplasts, which are necessary for the process of photosynthesis. The chloroplast is the organelle where photosynthesis takes place. Chloroplasts contain a green pigment called chlorophyll that traps light energy. This means that sunlight is the ultimate source of energy for most living things and converts it to usable chemical energy in the form of food.

Investigation & Experimentation

Standards 7a, 7e
Use a microscope to examine prepared slides of plant cells and animal cells. Draw a diagram of each and label the structures that you can see. Use the labeled diagrams in **Figures CA1-2** and **CA1-3**.

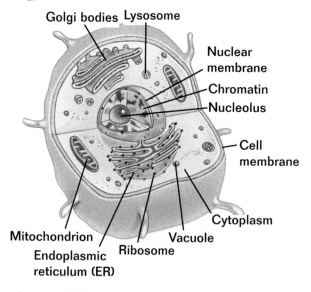

Golgi bodies Lysosome
Nuclear membrane
Chromatin
Nucleolus
Cell membrane
Cytoplasm
Mitochondrion Vacuole
Endoplasmic Ribosome
reticulum (ER)

Figure CA1-2 Animal cells are made up of a cell membrane, cytoplasm, a nucleus, and several other organelles.

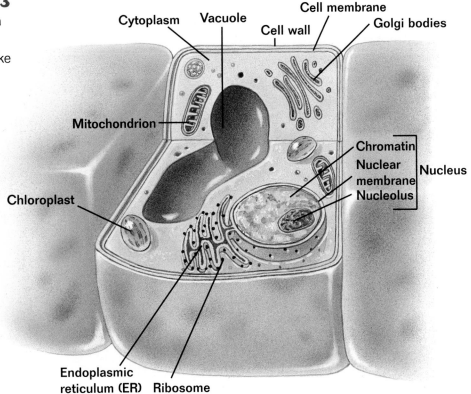

Figure CA1-3
Plant cells have a rigid cell wall and chloroplasts, unlike animal cells.

Cytoplasm Vacuole Cell membrane Cell wall Golgi bodies

Mitochondrion

Chromatin
Nuclear membrane — Nucleus
Nucleolus

Chloroplast

Endoplasmic reticulum (ER) Ribosome

1c. The Cell's Information Storehouse

The largest organelle in the cytoplasm of a eukaryotic cell is the nucleus. It contains the genetic blueprint for the cell's operations and directs all activity in the cell. Long strands of chromatin, a form of hereditary material, are located inside the nucleus. They contain genetic information and, at a certain point in the life cycle of the cell, take the form of chromosomes.

Standard 7f
Think about what you would need to have with you for a weekend camping trip to Yosemite National Park. Write a report, including an itinerary, about what you would need and why. Compare the function of your suitcase or backpack to the function of a cell's nucleus.

Figure CA1-4 The nucleus directs all the activities of the cell.

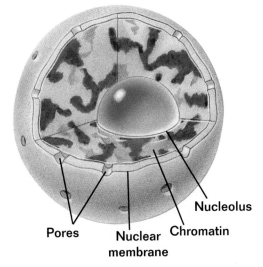

Nucleolus

Pores Nuclear membrane Chromatin

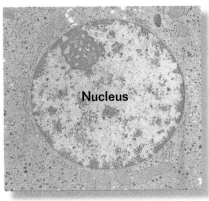

Nucleus

1d. The Energy Source of Cells

Cells, whether plant or animal, require a continuous supply of energy. Mitochondria are organelles where food is broken down and energy is released. Active cells, like those in muscles, contain many mitochondria. Why do you think muscle cells generally have more mitochondria?

It's easy to think of animals using energy, but what about plants? Plants need a source of energy as well. How does a plant get the energy it needs? Plant cells contain organelles called chloroplasts. Chloroplasts are responsible for transforming light energy for the plant. Through photosynthesis, they convert light energy into chemical energy.

Investigation & Experimentation

Standards 7b, 7c
Use the Internet and library to research cells and their organelles. Compare plant and animal cells. Share your findings with the class.

1e. Cell Reproduction

For most organisms to survive and grow, their cells must reproduce. Mitosis is the process in which plant and animal cells divide. Cell division is a continuous process. Most of a cell's life cycle is spent growing and preparing for division. Then, through a series of stages, the chromosomes duplicate and the nucleus divides. Both of the nuclei contain identical sets of chromosomes. Once the nucleus has divided, the cytoplasm separates, and two new cells are formed. Each of the new cells then continues into another cycle of cell reproduction. Some cells, such as those that make up your skin, don't live long. Mitosis continually replaces the dead cells with new ones.

Investigation & Experimentation

Standards 7b, 7d
Look up the stages of mitosis. Hypothesize at what point a cell divides into two identical cells. What do you think happens that makes a cell begin to divide? What evidence supports your hypothesis?

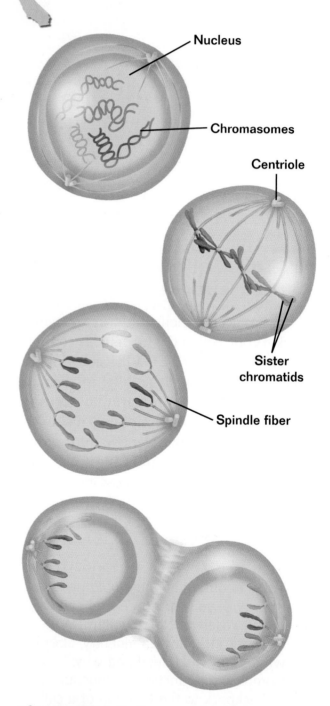

Nucleus

Chromasomes

Centriole

Sister chromatids

Spindle fiber

Figure CA1-5 During mitosis, a cell divides, resulting in two cells with identical sets of chromosomes.

1f. Cell Specialization

If you ever compare the parts of your hand to the parts of your eye, you will quickly realize that they are quite different. They have different functions and the parts have different characteristics. Remember that life starts as a single egg fertilized by a single sperm. As an organism develops, its cells specialize, or differentiate. This means they start to acquire characteristics that suit them to their function. For example, muscle cells become different than blood cells, allowing them to contract and attach to bones. Blood cells differentiate to a rounded shape that allows them to slide through small blood vessels and to transport oxygen.

Figure 1-6 As humans develop, our cells differentiate, allowing them to do specialized functions.

During development, human cells change to account for the variety of cells that make up the different systems of the body. The same is true for plants and fungi, too.

Investigation & Experimentation

Standard 7d
Think about the differences between a nerve cell and a cell in your cheek. How does each cell's structure allow it to do what it does? Construct models of the two types of cells that show how they are different. How do the materials that you use in your model reflect the structure and function of the cell?

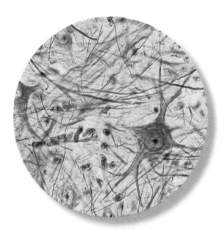

Nerve cells

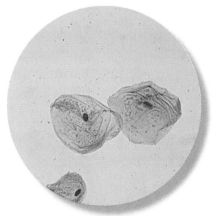

Cheek cells

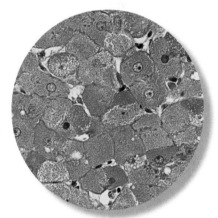

Liver cells

Going Further

To learn more about the biology of cells, see:

Powerhouses of the Cell

SCIENCE FOCUS

Read this case study to learn about research being done in California to help people who have a rare kind of disease that affects their cells.

Correlates with Content Standard 1

Inside cells, tiny power houses—called mitochondria—release energy from food. This energy is then used by cells to carry out life activities. But, what happens when mitochondria can't do their jobs correctly? Researchers at the University of California at San Diego have formed a special research center to find out.

What are mitochondria?

Mitochondria are organelles within cells. Almost every cell in your body has between five and 2000 mitochondria. Using as much as 80 percent of the oxygen you breathe in, mitochondria are the sites where more than 90 percent of the energy your body uses is released. Your body needs energy to run, play, think—even to sleep.

Mitochondria That Malfunction

Think about what would happen if your cells couldn't get the energy they needed. People with a mitochondrial disease have this problem. Their cells can't get enough energy. The cells that use the most energy are in the brain, the heart, and the muscles. Without enough energy, these parts of the body don't work well.

Mitochondrial diseases are rare. In the United States, about one in every 4000 babies is born with a mitochondrial disease. Because these diseases are rare, it sometimes takes a long time to find out what is wrong, and many doctors don't know how to treat them.

Figure CA1-7 Your body depends on mitochondria to release the energy cells need to function properly.

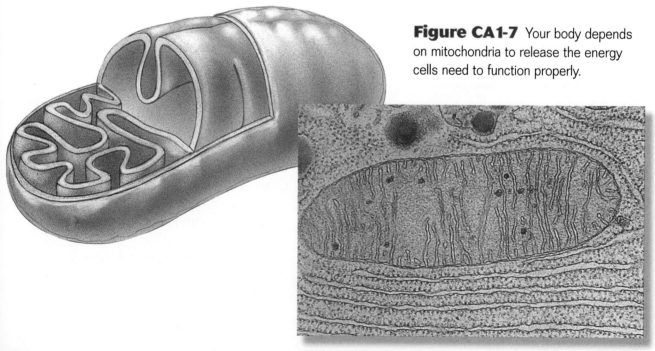

Figure CA1-8 At the Mitochondrial and Metabolic Disease Center at the University of California at San Diego, researchers explore ways to treat patients with mitochondrial diseases.

Meeting the Medical Needs

In 1994, Dr. Richard Haas opened Leigh's Center at the University of California at San Diego. This center specializes in studying one kind of mitochondrial disease called Leigh's syndrome. During the first two years, more than 150 people came to the center to be treated. Only 14 of them had Leigh's syndrome. However, all of these patients had a mitochondrial disease.

So, in 1996, Dr. Robert Naviaux opened the Mitochondrial and Metabolic Disease Center at the University of California at San Diego. This center treats children with all different kinds of mitochondrial diseases.

Finding a Cure

There is no cure for mitochondrial diseases. As scientists and doctors try to help patients with mitochondrial diseases, they also study the diseases and explore possible cures. They have discovered several different possible ways to fight the diseases.

Gene Therapy

You know that your cells have DNA. The DNA tells every cell what its job is. Even though mitochondria are inside cells, they have their own DNA. Mitochondrial diseases are inherited. They are caused by problems in the individual's DNA. One possible cure that scientists at the center are studying is called gene therapy. Gene therapy involves replacing a part of DNA that is unhealthy with a healthy piece of DNA.

Helping the Young and Old

Mitochondrial diseases that affect children are similar to many diseases that occur as people age, such as cancer, Alzheimer's disease, and Parkinson's disease. Scientists hope that a cure for mitochondrial diseases in children will lead to cures for many other diseases.

Investigation & Experimentation

Standard 7e
Search for different pictures of cells. Then, plan a three-dimensional model of a cell. Be sure to include at least five mitochondria in the cell. Working as a group, construct your cell model and label its cell membrane, cytoplasm, mitochondria, and nucleus.

Genetics

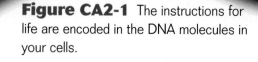

Figure CA2-1 The instructions for life are encoded in the DNA molecules in your cells.

2a. and 2b. Sexual and Asexual Reproduction

Most organisms share common traits of life. They grow, develop, reproduce, and die. Reproduction is the process by which organisms produce others of the same kind. There are two forms of reproduction.

In asexual reproduction, all the genetic material comes from one parent organism. Asexual reproduction includes budding, vegetative propagation, regeneration, and cloning. For example, strawberry plants can reproduce by vegetative propagation.

In sexual reproduction, the new organism that is produced is the result of two parents. The new organism is a combination of half of the genetic material from the mother and half from the father.

Investigation & Experimentation

Standards 7b, 7f
How has plant cloning helped the agricultural industry? Utilize resources in your classroom and the library to research plant cloning and agricultural industry. Write a report on your findings and present it to the class.

2c. Genes—Trait Identifiers

Genes are made up of DNA, which controls all the traits that show up in an organism. Some traits, like hairline, only have one gene. Other traits, like eye color, have multiple genes. The way genes are combined determines what color your eyes will be or what color your hair will be, or whether you will be able to digest milk easily.

2d. Dominant and Recessive Genes

Most plant and animal cells have two copies of every gene. The copies are called alleles for that trait. If the alleles for a trait are exactly the same, they are called homozygous. If the alleles for the trait are different, they are called heterozygous. Some alleles show dominance. They mask the effect of the other alleles, which is called recessive. Visible traits, traits you can actually see in an organism, are called phenotypes. The environment can modify a phenotype. For example, a lack of water during a drought in California could modify the growth of grapes in Napa Valley.

Investigation & Experimentation

Standards 7c, 7d
Research the Human Genome Project. Describe to the class why scientists are conducting the project, what data they have collected, and why they think it is important information.

2e. DNA

Have you ever tried to send a message using a special code? Codes are helpful when you have a lot of information to convey. Your cells contain so much information and they have a code in the form of DNA.

DNA is a ladder-like nucleic acid that forms the basis of genetic inheritance in all living organisms. It is located in the chromosomes of each cell.

Investigation & Experimentation

Standard 7e
Construct a model of DNA. Then, list some traits. Use a three-unit code combination of DNA bases for each trait. They may include eye color, hair color, and type of hairline. Or, choose traits that a plant or a pet might show. Provide a key to your code and ask another student from your class to describe the person, pet, or plant by looking at its DNA model.

Figure CA2-2 The DNA molecule looks like a twisted ladder with rungs made of nitrogen bases.

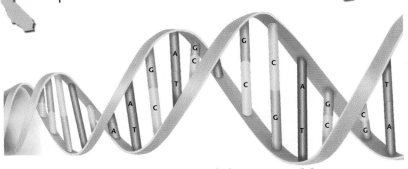

| G | Guanine | T | Thymine |
| C | Cytosine | A | Adenine |

Going Further

To learn more about genetics, see:

2a. and 2b. Chapter 4, Section 1, Cell Growth and Division
    Chapter 4, Section 2, Sexual Reproduction and Meiosis
2c. Chapter 4, Section 3, DNA
    Chapter 6, Section 1, What is genetics?

Chapter 6, Section 2, Genetics Since Mendel
2d. Chapter 6, Section 1, What is genetics?
2e. Chapter 4, Section 3, DNA

Breast Cancer Genes

SCIENCE FOCUS

Read this case study to learn about how mutations to certain genes can increase a woman's risk of breast cancer.

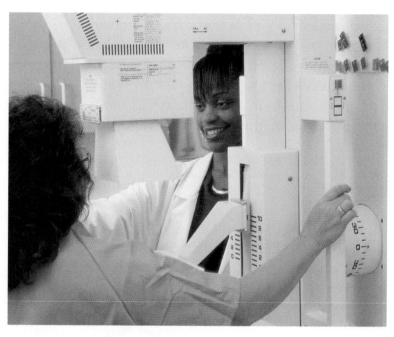

Figure CA2-3 Regular testing for breast cancer is important for women over 40.

There are many different types of cancer. One type of cancer that you have probably heard about is breast cancer. Breast cancer is a disease that most often affects women, although some men also get it. It has been estimated that over the course of her entire lifetime, an average woman has a one-in-eight chance of getting breast cancer. However, the risk of getting the disease is not the same for every woman. Some women are at higher risk, while others have a lower risk.

What factors influence how high the risk of getting breast cancer is? A woman's risk of breast cancer depends in part on her age, her race or ethnicity, whether or not she has family members with the disease, and her genes. Overall, about five percent to ten percent of cases of breast cancer are related to inherited genes with certain types of mutations. Inherited genes are more often the cause (about 20 percent of cases) for women who get breast cancer before age 45.

What causes breast cancer?

Diseases can be caused by several different factors. Some diseases, such as Huntington's disease, are caused by a single gene. Other diseases are caused by a combination of multiple genes. Diseases also can be caused by things in the environment, such as skin cancers due to exposure to the sun. Lifestyle factors, such as smoking cigarettes or cigars, eating a high-fat diet, or doing little or no exercise, can also lead people to get diseases such as heart disease or some types of cancer.

Which of these factors are related to breast cancer? For a long time, it was assumed that breast cancer was caused by a combination of several genes, as well as environmental and lifestyle factors. Although breast cancer has many different causes, there is a type that runs in families. This type of breast cancer is caused by a mutation to a single gene.

Breast Cancer Genes

Recent research has identified two specific genes, called BRCA1 and BRCA2 (BRCA stands for BReast CAncer), each of which is related to breast cancer. Together, mutations to these two genes may account for 40 percent to 50 perent of all inherited breast cancers. It has been estimated that about one in 500 people have a mutation to the BRCA1 gene (mutations to the BRCA2 gene are less common). The researcher who discovered the breast cancer gene BRCA1 is Mary-Claire King. She discovered the gene while working at the University of California at Berkeley.

How did Dr. King and her colleagues identify BRCA1 as a breast cancer gene? They studied families in which several members had been diagnosed with breast cancer. By looking at the genes of these families, the researchers located a gene marker (on part of chromosome 17) that the families had in common. Once the researchers studied this gene more closely, they identified more than 100 different mutations to BRCA1. The risk of breast cancer varies depending on the type of mutation.

How is BRCA1 related to the development of breast cancer? BRCA1 is considered a tumor suppressor gene. It is a gene that slows down or stops the growth of cancer cells. In some cases, a healthy BRCA1 gene might even be able to reverse the progress of cancer. When the BRCA1 gene is damaged or undergoes a mutation, it no longer works to prevent the growth of cancer. A person with the mutated gene is more likely to develop a cancerous tumor.

How can identifying breast cancer genes help?

How can information about these breast cancer genes be used? Once researchers better understand how these genes work normally and after mutations, it may be possible to prevent breast cancers from

Figure CA2-4 Dr. Mary-Claire King is one of the country's foremost breast cancer researchers.

developing in women who have these mutated genes. If a tumor has already developed, knowing how the genes are supposed to function may be useful for treating the cancers. It is also possible that knowing more about how these genes work will help in the prevention or treatment of other cancers. For example, ovarian cancers are sometimes related to mutations of the BRCA1 and BRCA2 genes.

Investigation & Experimentation

Activity: Standards 7b, 7c, 7f
In the library or with other resources, find out how researchers have come to understand the genes involved in Huntington's disease, sickle-cell anemia, or cystic fibrosis (or another disease with a clear genetic component). How is studying diseases with a fairly simple genetic cause useful for leading to an understanding of diseases with more complex causes (such as breast cancer)?

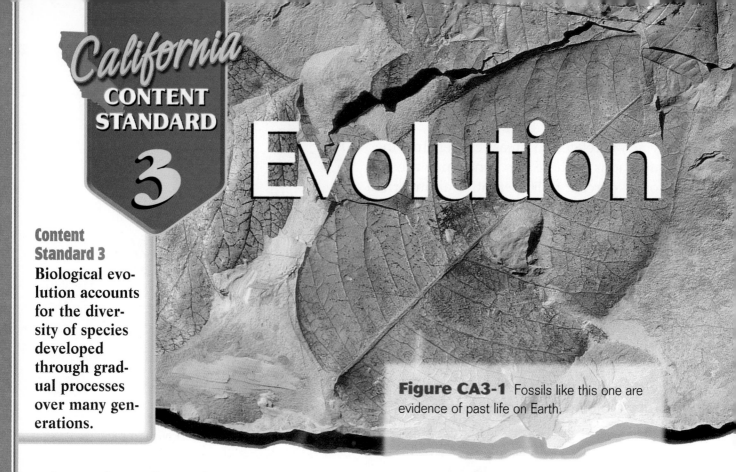

Evolution

Content Standard 3
Biological evolution accounts for the diversity of species developed through gradual processes over many generations.

Figure CA3-1 Fossils like this one are evidence of past life on Earth.

3a. Diversity of Organisms

Variations are found among individuals of a species. A variation is the appearance of an inherited trait that makes an individual different from other members of the same species. Some examples of variations are human hairline, albinism, and camouflage.

What do you think would happen if a shift of Earth's continents forced you to be isolated from everyone else? Environmental forces also cause diversity among organisms. The isolation of some organisms and changes in climate also can result in changes to the species over many generations.

Investigation & Experimentation

Standards 7c, 7f
On a map, locate Death Valley National Monument and Redwood National Park. Research both areas using library resources. Select an organism common to both areas. Then, explain what variations may occur in that organism that would live in both areas. Share your ideas with the class.

Figure CA3-2 Although all of these squirrels can be found in California, they are quite different.

Figure CA3-3 The bones in this brown pelican's wing have similarities to the bones in your arm.

3b. Darwin's Natural Selection Theory

Why do some species survive longer in a certain place than others? Darwin suggested that natural selection was the reason why certain species did well or died out. Natural selection means that organisms with traits best suited to their environment are more likely to survive. Therefore, the species must be well suited to its environment, or it is at risk of becoming extinct.

The evidence Darwin used to support his theory of natural selection was based on his observations and experiments. The factors that he identified that govern natural selection are:

1. Organisms produce more offspring than can survive.
2. Variations are found among individuals of a species.
3. Some variations enable members of a population to survive and reproduce better than others.
4. Over time, offspring of individuals with helpful variations make up more and more of a population.

The last factor, Darwin reasoned, could lead to a radical change in a population over many generations. In this way, natural selection could be the mechanism for evolution.

Investigation & Experimentation

Standards 7a, 7b, 7d
Read about Darwin's research after his trip as a ship's naturalist. Determine whether Darwin followed a scientific method while conducting his research. Give specific evidence to support your conclusion. Present your results to the class.

3c. Evidence for the Theory of Evolution

Have you ever picked up a rock and seen the imprint of a shell or leaf imbedded in it? If you have, you were looking at a fossil. Fossils provide a lot of evidence for the theory of evolution. They tell us about the history of life on Earth and allow us to compare how life has changed over time.

Rocks also give us a clue about the nature of evolution. By understanding the history of rock layers, we can determine how old a fossil is. Relative dating is used to determine the approximate age of a rock layer by examining the position of the rock layers in a sequence. Radiometric dating measures ratios of isotopes in the rock to determine how old the rock is. By using this type of data, geologists can build a history of what happened in a particular location over time. Oceans, glaciers, earthquakes, volcanoes, and plate movements can all be pieced together. Knowing this information has helped scientists better understand how evolution may have worked.

Finally, comparing the anatomy of similar species supports evolution. A brown pelican's wing, a human arm, and a dolphin's flipper all contain similar bones. They give evidence that two or more species may share common ancestors.

Figure CA3-4 This sloth fossil, found in the La Brea Tar Pits in California, shows that life was once quite different in the Los Angeles area.

Investigation & Experimentation

Standards 7b, 7c, 7d

Find out what the state of California and the federal government did to prevent the extinction of the California condor. Write down the steps they used and present a similar plan for another endangered animal.

3d. Branching Diagrams

Branching diagrams are used to classify several groups of organisms by shared characteristics. It is set up like a tree with each branch of the tree representing a group of organisms with a certain characteristic. Branching diagrams can be used for comparisons as well and expanded to include fossil organisms. This is especially useful when illustrating that a species evolved from a common ancestor.

3e. Extinction

Extinction is the dying out of a species. It is a natural event that occurs when a species' environment changes and the species can't adapt. Today, we are trying to prevent the extinction of some threatened species by federally protecting them.

Figure CA3-5 This California condor hatchling is being raised in captivity in an effort to save the species from extinction. Handlers use an artificial mother to reduce contact with humans.

Going Further

To learn more about the diversity of organisms and evolution, see:

The Stewart Valley Insect Fossils

SCIENCE FOCUS

Read this case study to learn about the fossil insect collection at Golden Gate Park in San Francisco.

Correlates with Content Standard 3

If you visit the California Academy of Sciences museum at Golden Gate Park in San Francisco, you will see many interesting things. One thing you might not see is the collection of fossil insects that scientists there are studying.

Scientists who study insects have collected 4000 fossils of insects from one area. The fossils were found in Stewart Valley, a region rich in fossils not far from the California border in Nevada. Scientists hope to find tens of thousands more fossils in Stewart Valley. If they are correct, Stewart Valley could be the best glimpse of ancient life in North America.

Figure CA3-7 Fossils like this are commonly found in the Santa Margarita sandstone in the Santa Cruz, California, area.

Figure CA3-6 The California Academy of Sciences Museum in San Francisco has an extensive fossil insect collection.

What's so special about fossils?

Fossils are the remains of ancient life-forms. You may have seen fossilized shells or bones. Other fossils are prints left in rocks from the bodies of ancient plants or animals. Sometimes, the whole body of an insect is preserved in ancient tree sap or some other substance. Whatever form a fossil takes, it gives us a window into the past.

Most fossilized ancient organisms had some body parts that were hard enough to leave an impression or to become a cast. Because insects lack teeth and bones, and have few hard body parts, they rarely formed fossils. Even organisms that are made of hard parts require special circumstances to form fossils. As you might expect, we have few fossils for most ancient

Figure CA3-8 Stewart Valley is rich in insect fossils like these.

plants and animals. Fossil insects are even more rare. In fact, all the fossils ever discovered are thought to represent less than 15 percent of the species that once lived.

How old are the fossil insects?

The insect fossils found at Stewart Valley are thought to be about 16 million years old. These ancient insects lived 50 million years *after* dinosaurs became extinct. That actually makes them fairly recent. Because the Stewart Valley insects lived relatively recently, many of them have close relatives alive today.

What can we learn from the fossils?

By studying the Stewart Valley area and the layers of fossils embedded there, scientists have pieced together part of the history of Earth and the life-forms that once lived there. Over many millions of years, volcanoes, movements in Earth's crust, and flowing water shaped Stewart Valley. At one time, fine material and mud accumulated in Stewart Valley Lake. These materials sank to the bottom of the lake preserving leaves, insects, feathers, and fish skeletons. These items became the fossils that scientists now study. No other place in the world provides so many different and well-preserved fossils from this time period.

By examining the insect fossils, scientists hope to learn about ancient forms of life. As you can see in the photographs on these pages, some of the fossilized insects are similar to insects alive today. These similarities allow scientists to trace the evolution of species over time.

Learning about Earth's past also may help scientists improve life in the future. Knowing how ancient Earth and its organisms interacted in the past could help us prevent or prepare for changes in the future.

Investigation & Experimentation

Standard 7b
Two important sites of fossils in California from the same time period as the Stewart Valley fossils are the Santa Margarita Sandstone and the Monterey Formation. Use library and Internet sources to find out what kinds of fossils have been found at these sites. Then, working as a group, compare the fossil finds of the three areas. Discuss what kinds of information the three different sites provide. Present your findings and conclusions to the class.

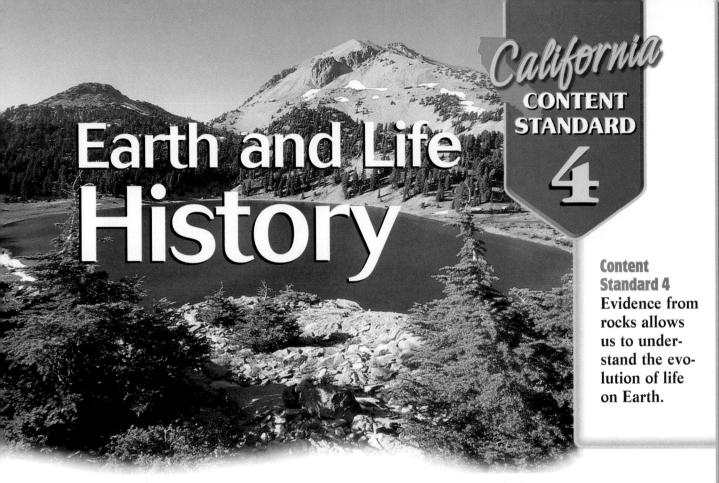

Earth and Life History

Content Standard 4
Evidence from rocks allows us to understand the evolution of life on Earth.

4a. Earth Processes

When trying to interpret the geological history of an area, geologists assume that the same Earth processes that occur today also were at work in the past. That means things like earthquakes, volcanoes, erosion, deposition, and plate movements have occurred throughout the history of Earth. Many of these processes, although slow, can have a large effect over a long time.

4b. Events That Alter Life

Natural events have a huge impact on Earth and the life that exists on it. If they alter the land and its climate in a short period of time, they are considered catastrophic. Species usually have little time to adapt. They must leave or be destroyed. Asteroid impact, volcanic eruption, and earthquakes are examples of events that can quickly alter life.

Lassen Volcanic Park in California is an area that changed dramatically as a result

Figure CA4-1 When the Lassen volcano erupted, it had a dramatic effect on the surrounding area.

of a volcanic eruption. Large eruptions can destroy forests in a matter of seconds and leave the land covered in ash. It takes many years for the environment to recover.

Investigation & Experimentation

Standard 7d
Earthquakes cannot be prevented, but steps can be taken to prevent catastrophic damage. Discover what California is doing to lessen the devastation of earthquakes.

4c. The Rock Cycle

Sandstone, limestone, granite, and obsidian are various types of rocks that are formed by environmental forces. Rocks

Figure CA4-2 The rock layers in Death Valley, California, have been rearranged by various geological processes.

undergo changes due to weathering, erosion, compaction, cementation, melting, and cooling. The rock cycle is the continuous transformation of rock materials.

Sedimentary rocks often form as layers. The older layers are on the bottom because they were deposited first. Then, as more sediments pile up, other layers are formed. The only time these layers are not ordered in this way is when a natural force, like an earthquake, disturbs them.

Investigation & Experimentation

Standards 7b, 7f
The rock layers in Death Valley, California comprise a nearly complete record of Earth's past. However, the record has been jumbled out of sequence due to natural events. Use a variety of resources to research the geology of Death Valley. Document any current work that is being done and prepare a presentation for the class.

4d. The Existence of Life

How can scientists tell the age of Earth by looking at rocks? They know that the oldest layer of rock is located on the bottom. They also know that the radioactive isotopes of certain elements decay at a measurable rate. Half-life is the time it takes for half of the atoms in an isotope to decay. By measuring the amounts of materials in an igneous rock and knowing the half-life of isotopes in that rock, a geologist can calculate the age of the rock. This process is called radiometric dating.

Through radiometric dating, geologists have evidence indicating that Earth is 4.6 billion years old. They also have discovered evidence of life that is 3.5 billion years old.

4e. Fossils

Fossils are the remains of an organism that has been preserved by natural processes. One thing geologists have learned by studying fossils is that species are constantly changing. Some species inhabit Earth for long periods of time without changing. Other species remain unchanged for only a short period of time. By examining the type of fossils in a sedimentary rock layer, geologists can determine the age of the rock layer.

Figure CA4-3 This dolphin fossil was found far inland in California, giving evidence that the area was once underwater.

Fossils also can be used to determine what the environment of an area was like long ago. California did not always have the land and climate it does today. This is known because fossil evidence suggests that sea organisms once lived where dry land exists today.

Figure CA4-4 The San Andreas Fault runs most of the length of California. The fault is where two plates meet and are sliding past each other.

Investigation & Experimentation

Standard 7b

Using the library of a local museum, see if you can determine whether your area or an area elsewhere in your state was once under water. Draw a diagram of the area as it was then and now.

4f. Plate Tectonics

If you live in California, you probably have witnessed what can happen when the plates in Earth's crust move. Throughout Earth's history, this movement has caused lakes to be drained, seas to deepen, and mountains to appear where none were before. This rearranging of land and sea causes climate changes. If species adapt to the changes, or evolve, they survive. If they don't adapt, they become extinct. Many of the organisms that exist today have adapted, over a period of time, to their environment. A significant change in the climate could cause extinction of any organism that couldn't adapt.

4g. The Geologic Time Scale

The appearance and disappearance of types of organisms throughout Earth's history provide scientists with markers in time. The geologic time scale divides Earth's past into smaller units. Each unit marks a specific event like a mass extinction or appearance of new species.

Going Further

CASE STUDY

A Blast from the Past

SCIENCE FOCUS

Read this case study to learn about the ancient volcanic crater that makes up Long Valley.

If you have been to Yosemite National Park, you may have stopped at Long Valley. Long Valley is a giant crater that formed about 700 000 years ago during a volcanic eruption. During that eruption, a mountain collapsed forming the crater. Several lakes lie within the ancient crater. Beneath the crater is a huge cavity of molten rock, called a magma chamber.

Recent History of Long Valley Caldera

The last time the volcano at Long Valley erupted was 550 years ago. Then, it was silent until 1980. In 1980, Long Valley was shaken by several earthquakes. Scientists concluded that the earthquakes signaled the filling of the magma chamber four miles under the valley floor with magma. When this happened, instruments were set up in Long Valley to help monitor the volcano's activity.

Since 1980, many earthquakes have occurred in the area. Gas bubbles rise to the top of the magma chamber just as bubbles rise to the top of a bottle of cola. The lid on the cola bottle keeps all the liquid and gas inside, but cracks in the rocks around the magma chamber allow some gas to seep out. This causes small earthquakes in the region.

Could the volcano erupt?

There are signs that the volcano could erupt. In 1990, scientists noticed that carbon dioxide and radon gas were escaping from vents. Trees in the area started dying in 1993 as larger quantities of carbon dioxide seeped out of the magma chamber. In 1998, 170 acres of trees had been killed by the leaking carbon dioxide. Some people have even died because the carbon dioxide accumulated in their cabins in the area. And, snow camping has been banned in certain areas of the park because the snow holds in the gas and could kill sleeping campers.

Figure CA4-5 With the help of glaciers, several lakes like this one have formed in the Long Valley volcanic crater.

Figure CA4-6 Steaming volcanic vents are evidence that there is some volcanic activity deep beneath Long Valley.

Earthquake activities continue in the area as well. During parts of 1998, 20 or more earthquakes were observed per day. However, most of the earthquakes were too weak for people to feel. In addition, the level of magma has grown about one inch each year since 1990. If the growth continues, there is a good chance that the volcano at Long Valley will erupt.

Despite these signs, there seems to be no immediate danger. The United States Geological Survey (USGS) has ranked the volcano a code green throughout the 1990s. The volcano activity system includes green, yellow, orange, and red. Green is the safest rating for a volcano and red is the most dangerous.

What if it does erupt?

Most volcanoes show warning signs before they erupt. It is possible that the volcano could erupt with no advance warning, but it's likely that scientists will be forewarned of the eruption. People living in the area may detect earthquakes and see steam rising from the ground. The most important sources of warning signs are the instruments scientists have in place to monitor rising levels of magma in the magma chamber and other signs that precede an eruption.

Because volcanic eruptions cannot be stopped, people will be evacuated from the area if an eruption is likely. Emergency procedures, such as evacuation routes, emergency communication systems, and the distribution of educational materials about the emergency procedures, should be in place. These plans would limit the loss of life and property caused by the volcanic eruption.

Investigation & Experimentation

Standard 7e

There are more than 500 volcanoes in California. Seventy-six of these are known to have erupted within the past 10 000 years. Find out which areas of California are likely to be affected by future volcanic eruptions. Mark these areas on a map of California and present it to your class.

Structure and Function in Living Systems

Content Standard 5
The anatomy and physiology of plants and animals illustrate the complementary nature of structure and function.

Figure CA5-1 Even though they are different, the Pacific dogwood and acorn woodpecker both have organized structures.

5a. Organization of Plants and Animals

What do an acorn woodpecker and a Pacific dogwood have in common? They both have specific levels of organization for structure and function.

The cell is the basic unit of function, but it can't do everything by itself. Therefore, in many-celled organisms, cells are organized into tissues. Tissues are groups of cells that do the same job. Tissues are further organized into organs. Organs are different types of tissue that work together to perform a job. A group of organs working together to do a certain job make up an organ system. All of these put together make up the entire organism.

Investigation *&* **Experimentation**

Standard 7f
Choose a common houseplant and observe how it is organized. Write a report describing how the plant is organized into tissues and systems. If you need help, refer to your text or library resource.

5b. Teamwork Within Organ Systems

Organ systems like your cardiovascular system function because individual organs, tissues, and cells contribute vital work. If one or more of these contributors can no longer perform their duties, the entire system can be affected. For example, the cardiovascular system cannot function if the heart stops pumping blood. This is true in plants as well as animals. If a tree's roots are damaged, eventually the tree will not be able to get enough water and nutrients needed to survive.

Investigation & Experimentation

Standard 7b
Heart disease kills thousands of people in California every year. Luckily, great strides have been made in treating many diseases of the heart. Research the procedure of balloon angioplasty. What are the pros and cons of the procedure? How is it done? Diagram and label what takes place during angioplasty.

Figure CA5-3
The circulatory system is a collection of cells, tissues, and organs that work together to transport oxygen, nutrients, and wastes through your body.

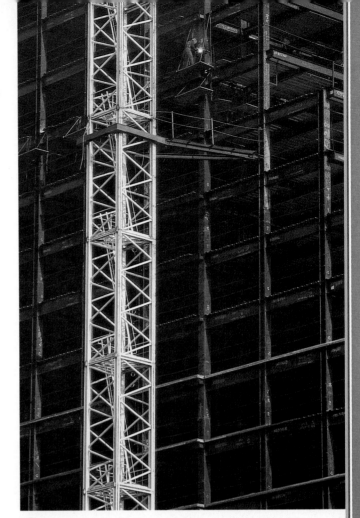

Figure CA5-2 Your skeletal system supports your body much like the steel beams support this building in San Francisco.

5c. Bones and Muscles

Have you ever wondered why the skyscrapers in cities like San Francisco don't collapse under the weight of everything inside them? A strong framework of steel girders supports them. A framework also supports your body. It is called the skeletal system. It provides support, gives shape to your body, and protects internal organs. Bones are the hard structures that make up the skeletal system.

Muscles are organs that contract and get shorter. They are attached to your bones and are responsible for moving them. Without muscles, you would be stuck in one place just like a skyscraper.

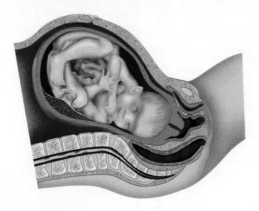

Figure CA5-4 The fetus develops within the mother's uterus. Both nutrients and wastes are transported through the umbilical cord.

5d. Human Reproduction

Reproduction is the process that continues life on Earth. Many systems in males and females are alike, but that is not the case for the reproductive system. The male reproductive system consists of the external organs of the penis and scrotum. Inside the scrotum are the testes. The testes produce the male reproductive cells called sperm.

The female reproductive system consists of the ovaries where the eggs develop. Eggs are the female reproductive cells. When sperm is deposited into the vagina, the possibility exists for one sperm to reach the egg. If this happens, fertilization occurs and the eggs and sperm combine to form a new cell or zygote.

5e. Pregnancy

During pregnancy, the unborn child is helpless and must depend on the mother to survive. It can not feed itself so it receives nutrients from the mother. Nutrients from the wall of the uterus are received by the embryo through villi. Blood vessels develop from the villi and form the placenta. The placenta stores the nutrients for the child and transports them through the umbilical cord. The umbilical cord is attached to the embryo's naval. It also carries the waste products like carbon dioxide back to the mother's blood to be released.

Standard 7c

How big is an embryo? Use textbooks and other print resources to investigate the size of the embryo at various stages of pregnancy.

5f. Flowering Plant Reproduction

The flowers of some plants, like the California poppy, are brightly colored while others like wheat are hardly noticeable. If you look closely at the flower, you will see the reproductive organs of the plant.

The stamen is the male reproductive organ, and it is where the pollen grains form. The pistil is the female reproductive

Figure CA5-5 The California poppy, along with many other wildflowers, blossoms in the spring in California.

organ, and it is where the pollen grains land. It also contains the style and ovary. The ovary is where ovules are formed. As the ovule develops, eggs are produced. The process is referred to as pollination. As the new cell develops, it becomes enclosed in a seed, which protects it and helps keep it alive. Soon after fertilization, changes take place in the flower. The ovary, where the eggs are, swells and develops into a fruit, which contains the seeds.

Investigation & Experimentation

Standard 7e
Draw and label the parts of a flower. Be sure to include the stamen, pistil, stigma, style, and ovary.

5g. The Senses

How would a mule deer in the Sierra Nevadas know that it was in danger? It would rely on its senses to warn it that danger was near. Your senses include seeing, hearing, smelling, tasting, and touching. The structures that make up your senses are specific to the sense being performed.

The eye allows us to see what is around us. It contains structures that bend light. The cornea and lens bend the light and direct it to the retina. The retina has tissues and cells that help detect shape and movement. The information is uncoded by the brain and you see what you are looking at.

The ear is divided into three sections. The outer ear traps waves and funnels them down the ear canal to the middle ear. The middle ear has a series of bones and an eardrum that vibrate with the sound waves. The inner ear contains the cochlea, which has nerve endings. Depending on how the nerve endings are stimulated, you hear a different sound.

Olfactory cells that are stimulated by gas molecules control the sense of smell. Taste buds on your tongue are receptors for taste.

Investigation & Experimentation

Standard 7f
At home, try sampling a substance like lemon juice on the tip of your tongue. Rinse your mouth with water and sample again, placing the lemon juice at the back of your tongue. Did you notice a difference? Did it taste the same both times? Suggest why or why not.

Going Further

To learn more about structure and function in living systems, see:

The Case of the Poisonous Fish

SCIENCE FOCUS

Read this case study to learn about the effects of a toxin on the human body.

Correlates with Content Standard 5

Would you put your life in the hands of a chef? That's exactly what many do when they eat fugu, or pufferfish. The fish contains a lethal dose of tetrodotoxin, a chemical that blocks nerves from transmitting signals throughout the body. If not prepared properly, the tetrodotoxin in the fish can cause the muscles that control breathing to stop working. To serve fugu, chefs must be licensed by passing a series of courses and written exams, and by working with experienced chefs.

What is tetrodotoxin?

Tetrodotoxin is a chemical that is deadly to the human nervous system. In fact, it is one of the strongest poisons known.

Tetrodotoxin gets its name from the family name of the pufferfish: Tetraodontidae. Several organs of the pufferfish contain high concentrations of the toxin. Other animals in this family also contain the toxin. These include porcupinefish, globefish, ocean sunfish, and triggerfish.

Three species of newts found in California also contain high doses of tetrodotoxin. One species, the rough-skinned newt, contains enough tetrodotoxin to kill several adults. Most other newts found in the United States contain the toxin, but in much lower concentrations than the newts in California.

How do people accidentally eat the toxin?

The main way that people eat tetrodotoxin is by eating prepared pufferfish. Pufferfish, which live off the coast of Japan, are a Japanese delicacy. When cleaned and cooked properly, pufferfish can be safe to eat.

Only certain restaurants with chefs who know how to remove the toxin when they prepare the Japanese dish are allowed to serve pufferfish in the United States. In Japan, a chef must be licensed to prepare pufferfish. Still, about 100 to 200 people are thought to become ill from eating pufferfish every year. Half of these people die.

Figure CA5-6 Although poisonous, the pufferfish can be safely eaten if prepared properly.

Figure CA5-7 Rough-skinned newts carry lethal levels of tetrodotoxin.

Eating just a tiny bit of poisonous pufferfish can make you sick. One California chef ate a piece about the size of a quarter and became seriously ill.

The chef was lucky. He ate very little of the toxin and was quickly treated at a nearby hospital. The pufferfish he had eaten had been brought into the United States illegally.

How does tetrodotoxin affect the body?

Within as little as three minutes after taking in the poison, it begins to affect the body. The person usually first feels tingling in the mouth. Then the person becomes dizzy, has a tight chest, and feels weak.

What does the toxin do to the body? Tetrodotoxin blocks communication between nerves in muscles. People often fall down after eating the poison because their muscles become weak. Then they become paralyzed. Death usually occurs because the muscles in the chest cavity that carry out breathing

become paralyzed. Without these muscles to breathe oxygen into the body and to expel carbon dioxide, the person can die quickly.

The body's organ systems work together. When one or more organs fail, the whole system breaks down. This is what happens when a person eats tetrodotoxin.

Investigation & Experimentation

Standard 7b

The United States Food and Drug Administration (FDA) allows certain Japanese restaurants to serve pufferfish. Use library resources to find out what precautions the FDA requires for restaurants to serve the pufferfish. Also find out what procedures the Japanese Ministry of Health and Welfare follows to ensure that the pufferfish imported into the United States are safe to eat.

Figure CA5-8 Pufferfish are abundant off the coast of Japan.

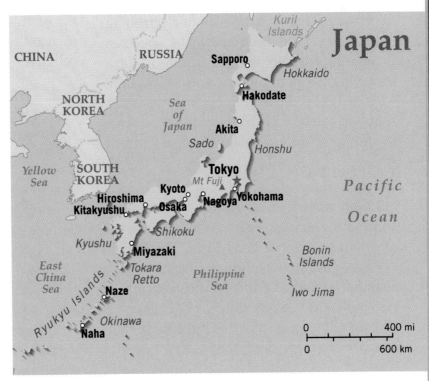

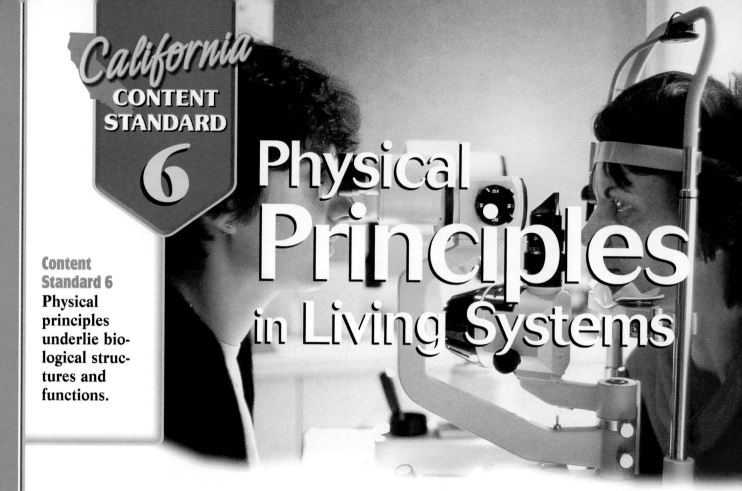

California
CONTENT
STANDARD
6

Content
Standard 6
Physical
principles
underlie bio-
logical struc-
tures and
functions.

Physical Principles in Living Systems

Figure CA6-1 We see things by sensing light that the objects give off or reflect from another source.

6a. Visible Light and the Electromagnetic Spectrum

Did you use a microwave to heat your food today? Light, radio waves, and microwaves are all examples of electromagnetic waves. The electromagnetic spectrum is made of radio waves, infrared, ultraviolet, X rays, gamma rays, and visible light. Visible light is the only light in the spectrum that you can see. Visible light is only a small portion of the electromagnetic spectrum.

6b. and 6c. Light and the Eye

Light travels in a straight line unless something bends or refracts it. The cornea and lens of the eye bend light. The lens in your eye is convex, allowing light to come together at a focal point. In the case of people who are nearsighted, light passes through the lens, but the light isn't bent sharply enough, and the light does not focus on the retina.

For an object to be seen, light must either be emitted by an object, or light must reflect off of it. The light then enters the eye, is focused by the lens, and is sensed by nerve cells on the retina.

6d. Instruments to Aid the Eye

The human eye is a great tool but it is limited in what it can see. For this reason, instruments to aid the eyes have been developed. They use simple lenses to allow the eye to see objects that are small, like a cell, or objects that are great distances away, like the moon. Magnifying glasses and eyeglasses are important examples of visual aids, as are telescopes and microscopes.

Telescopes use convex lenses and mirrors to gather and focus light from distant objects. Microscopes and magnifying glasses allow us to see objects that are too small to be seen clearly with the eye. A microscope uses two convex lenses with short focal lengths to magnify small, close objects. Cameras use lenses to focus light and an image onto light-sensitive film. Depending on the type of photograph you want, different lenses are used.

Investigation & Experimentation

Standard 7a
Examine several pairs of glasses. Can you tell by looking at the lens whether the person is nearsighted or farsighted? If you need help, refer to your text for reference.

6e. White Light

When light enters your eye, it is focused on the retina. The retina is made of two types of nerve cells that act as photoreceptors. One type of photoreceptor is called the cone. It allows you to see color and distinguish shapes. There are three types of cones. Red cones absorb red and yellow, green cones absorb yellow and green, and blue cones absorb blue and violet.

Investigation & Experimentation

Standard 7b
Use a variety of resources to research color blindness. What causes it? Who is at risk? Write a report and share your results in a verbal presentation.

6f. Transmission of Light

When light encounters an object, three things may happen depending on the material that the object is made of. The light may be completely or partially absorbed, making the object appear black or a particular color. Or, the light may be bent, or refracted. This can make the object appear distorted. This can be seen when you stick a pencil partially in water. The pencil will appear to be bent, even though it isn't. Finally, light can be scattered, or reflected, off the object. What happens depends on the material. Water, for example, may reflect some light, while some light is refracted and the rest is absorbed. A piece of charcoal will absorb almost all of the light that encounters it.

Figure CA6-2 Eyeglasses must be made specifically for the person using them to make sure light is focused on the right spot in the eye.

Figure CA6-3 The pencil appears to be bent because the light coming from the pencil refracts as it leaves the water.

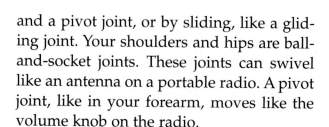

Standard 7e
Draw a picture of a person casting a fishing rod. Label all the joints that are being used and what type of joint each one is.

and a pivot joint, or by sliding, like a gliding joint. Your shoulders and hips are ball-and-socket joints. These joints can swivel like an antenna on a portable radio. A pivot joint, like in your forearm, moves like the volume knob on the radio.

6i. Levers and the Skeletal System

A lever is a bar that is free to pivot, or turn, about a fixed point. It consists of a fulcrum, the fixed point; an effort arm, the part of the lever where force is applied; and the resistance arm, the part that exerts the resistance. The length of the arms of a lever can be used to find the ideal mechanical advantage of the lever. To find the mechanical advantage of the lever, you divide the length of the effort arm by the length of the resistance arm.

In your body, bones are the lever, joints are the fulcrum, and muscles provide the effort force. Depending on the way the bones and muscles are attached, your body uses the mechanical advantage of levers in different ways. When you lift a glass of water to take a drink, your arm muscles don't have to move very far because the muscles are exerting a force over a small distance to move the end of your hand a greater distance. When you stand on your toes, you are doing the opposite. Mechanical advantage is allowing your calf muscles to lift most of your weight off of the ground. They are able to exert a smaller force over a longer distance to accomplish this.

6g. The Law of Reflection

When light hits a reflective surface, the angle at which the light hits the surface is the same as the angle at which it is reflected off the surface. So, if the light approaches an object at a 30-degree angle, it will reflect off of the object at a 30-degree angle.

6h. Joints—Simple Machines at Work

A joint is a place where two or more bones meet. Together with muscles, movable joints allow your bones to move. Some joints work similarly to things you can find at home. Your knee joint, for example, moves much like a door hinge. Other joints move by rotating, like a ball-and-socket

6j. Blood—How do we handle the pressure?

The total amount of force exerted by a fluid is called its pressure. When the heart contracts, it pumps the blood through the cardiovascular system. Blood exerts pressure on the walls of the vessels as it travels. This pressure is called blood pressure. It is highest in the arteries and lowest in the veins.

During a heartbeat, both atria contract at the same time. Then, both ventricles contract at the same time. A valve separates each atrium from the ventricle to prevent blood from flowing back into the atrium.

Investigation & Experimentation

Standards 7c, 7f

Use your library to research the heart. What happens if the heart valves malfunction? Investigate how heart valve problems can be corrected and present your findings to the class.

Figure CA6-4 Blood pressure can easily be checked using a blood pressure cuff and a stethoscope.

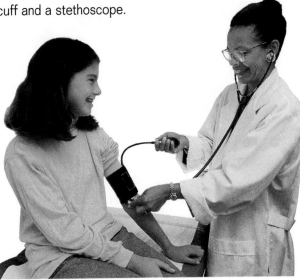

Photo Credits

Going Further

To learn more about physical principles in living systems, see:

California CASE STUDY

Mapping the Skin Using Space Technology

SCIENCE FOCUS

Read this case study to learn how space research applies to health care in California.

Correlates with Content Standard 6

What do Venus and skin cancer have in common? Ask scientists at the Jet Propulsion Lab (JPL) in Pasadena, California. If you've ever seen videos or photographs of another planet, then you have probably seen the work of scientists at the Jet Propulsion Lab. Scientists at JPL lead the world in designing robots to explore space.

The Jet Propulsion Lab is a research center for the National Aeronautics and Space Administration (NASA). Caltech and NASA run the center together. Spacecraft from this lab have visited all the planets in our solar system, except Pluto.

One of the jobs of space exploration is to transmit pictures of other planets back to Earth. In 1990, after 20 years of preparation, scientists at the Jet Propulsion Lab began to map the surface of Venus and construct a three-dimensional map of Venus's surface. To make three-dimensional images, scientists compared images of the same area taken at different angles.

How is the skin like the surface of Venus?

Melanoma is a deadly form of skin cancer that can start out looking like a mole. Melanoma is caused by sun damage to the skin. It is detected by closely monitoring a person's moles. For example, if a mole has an irregular shape or color, or it changes over time, it may be a melanoma.

Melanoma skin cancer spreads throughout the body and can kill a person. The best

Figure CA6-5 This computer-generated image of a volcano on Venus was made using radar images taken by the *Magellan* space probe.

way to survive a melanoma is to detect it early and have it removed. For people who have one or two moles, this is an easy task. Some people, however, have hundreds of moles. Scientists realized that the surface of the skin is similar to the surface of a planet. Dotted with moles and bumps, the skin is a landscape that can be charted just like the surface of a planet can be mapped.

Using Space Technology to Fight Skin Cancer

The Jet Propulsion Lab has found a way to use its space imaging technology to track moles over time. When a person goes to the doctor, a photograph of his or her moles can be taken and compared to photographs taken in the past. The system categorizes the moles and codes them with different colors. Just as they can compare photographs of a planet's surface, they can also compare photographs of a person's skin taken over time. This way, they can monitor any changes that occur in moles that are likely to become melanomas.

P/N G86499.11

Appendices

Appendix A

Safety in the Science Classroom

1. Always obtain your teacher's permission to begin an investigation.

2. Study the procedure. If you have questions, ask your teacher. Be sure you understand any safety symbols shown on the page.

3. Use the safety equipment provided for you. Goggles and a safety apron should be worn during an investigation.

4. Always slant test tubes away from yourself and others when heating them.

5. Never eat or drink in the lab, and never use lab glassware as food or drink containers. Never inhale chemicals. Do not taste any substances or draw any material into a tube with your mouth.

6. If you spill any chemical, wash it off immediately with water. Report the spill immediately to your teacher.

7. Know the location and proper use of the fire extinguisher, safety shower, fire blanket, first aid kit, and fire alarm.

8. Keep all materials away from open flames. Tie back long hair and loose clothing.

9. If a fire should break out in the classroom, or if your clothing should catch fire, smother it with the fire blanket or a coat, or get under a safety shower. NEVER RUN.

10. Report any accident or injury, no matter how small, to your teacher.

Follow these procedures as you clean up your work area.

1. Turn off the water and gas. Disconnect electrical devices.

2. Return all materials to their proper places.

3. Dispose of chemicals and other materials as directed by your teacher. Place broken glass and solid substances in the proper containers. Never discard materials in the sink.

4. Clean your work area.

5. Wash your hands thoroughly after working in the laboratory.

Table A-1

First Aid	
Injury	**Safe Response**
Burns	Apply cold water. Call your teacher immediately.
Cuts and bruises	Stop any bleeding by applying direct pressure. Cover cuts with a clean dressing. Apply cold compresses to bruises. Call your teacher immediately.
Fainting	Leave the person lying down. Loosen any tight clothing and keep crowds away. Call your teacher immediately.
Foreign matter in eye	Flush with plenty of water. Use eyewash bottle or fountain.
Poisoning	Note the suspected poisoning agent and call your teacher immediately.
Any spills on skin	Flush with large amounts of water or use safety shower. Call your teacher immediately.

Appendix B

SI/Metric to English Conversions

	When you want to convert:	To:	Multiply by:
Length	inches	centimeters	2.54
	centimeters	inches	0.39
	feet	meters	0.30
	meters	feet	3.28
	yards	meters	0.91
	meters	yards	1.09
	miles	kilometers	1.61
	kilometers	miles	0.62
Mass and Weight*	ounces	grams	28.35
	grams	ounces	0.04
	pounds	kilograms	0.45
	kilograms	pounds	2.2
	tons (short)	tonnes (metric tons)	0.91
	tonnes (metric tons)	tons (short)	1.10
	pounds	newtons	4.45
	newtons	pounds	0.23
Volume	cubic inches	cubic centimeters	16.39
	cubic centimeters	cubic inches	0.06
	cubic feet	cubic meters	0.03
	cubic meters	cubic feet	35.30
	liters	quarts	1.06
	liters	gallons	0.26
	gallons	liters	3.78
Area	square inches	square centimeters	6.45
	square centimeters	square inches	0.16
	square feet	square meters	0.09
	square meters	square feet	10.76
	square miles	square kilometers	2.59
	square kilometers	square miles	0.39
	hectares	acres	2.47
	acres	hectares	0.40
Temperature	Fahrenheit	$5/9 (°F - 32) =$	Celsius
	Celsius	$9/5 (°C) + 32 =$	Fahrenheit

*Weight as measured in standard Earth gravity

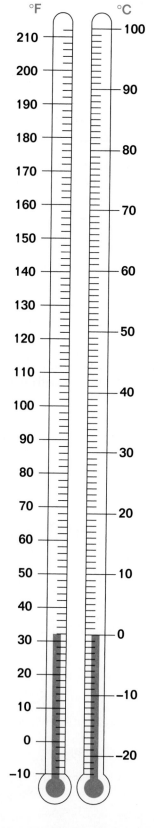

Appendix C

SI Units of Measurement

Table C-1

SI Base Units					
Measurement	**Unit**	**Symbol**	**Measurement**	**Unit**	**Symbol**
length	meter	m	temperature	kelvin	K
mass	kilogram	kg	amount of substance	mole	mol
time	second	s			

Table C-2

Units Derived from SI Base Units		
Measurement	**Unit**	**Symbol**
energy	joule	J
force	newton	N
frequency	hertz	Hz
potential difference	volt	V
power	watt	W
pressure	pascal	Pa

Table C-3

Common SI Prefixes					
Prefix	**Symbol**	**Multiplier**	**Prefix**	**Symbol**	**Multiplier**
Greater than 1			Less than 1		
mega-	M	1 000 000	*deci-*	d	0.1
kilo-	k	1 000	*centi-*	c	0.01
hecto-	h	100	*milli-*	m	0.001
deca-	da	10	*micro-*	μ	0.000 001

Care and Use of a Microscope

Eyepiece Contains a magnifying lens you look through

Arm Supports the body tube

Low-power objective Contains the lens with low-power magnification

Stage clips Hold the microscope slide in place

Coarse adjustment Focuses the image under low power

Fine adjustment Sharpens the image under high and low magnification

Body tube Connects the eyepiece to the revolving nosepiece

Revolving nosepiece Holds and turns the objectives into viewing position

High-power objective Contains the lens with the highest magnification

Stage Supports the microscope slide

Light source Allows light to reflect upward through the diaphragm, the specimen, and the lenses

Base Provides support for the microscope

Care of a Microscope

1. Always carry the microscope holding the arm with one hand and supporting the base with the other hand.

2. Don't touch the lenses with your fingers.

3. Never lower the coarse adjustment knob when looking through the eyepiece lens.

4. Always focus first with the low-power objective.

5. Don't use the coarse adjustment knob when the high-power objective is in place.

6. Store the microscope covered.

Using a Microscope

1. Place the microscope on a flat surface that is clear of objects. The arm should be toward you.

2. Look through the eyepiece. Adjust the diaphragm so that light comes through the opening in the stage.

3. Place a slide on the stage so that the specimen is in the field of view. Hold it firmly in place by using the stage clips.

4. Always focus first with the coarse adjustment and the low-power objective lens. Once the object is in focus on low power, turn the nosepiece until the high-power objective is in place. Use ONLY the fine adjustment to focus with the high-power objective lens.

Making a Wet-Mount Slide

1. Carefully place the item you want to look at in the center of a clean, glass slide. Make sure the sample is thin enough for light to pass through.

2. Use a dropper to place one or two drops of water on the sample.

3. Hold a clean coverslip by the edges and place it at one edge of the drop of water. Slowly lower the coverslip onto the drop of water until it lies flat.

4. If you have too much water or a lot of air bubbles, touch the edge of a paper towel to the edge of the coverslip to draw off extra water and force out air.

Appendix E

Diversity of Life: Classification of Living Organisms

Scientists use a six-kingdom system of classification of organisms. In this system, there are two kingdoms of organisms, Kingdoms Archaebacteria and Eubacteria, which contain organisms that do not have a nucleus and lack membrane-bound structures in the cytoplasm of their cells. The members of the other four kingdoms have cells which contain a nucleus and structures in the cytoplasm that are surrounded by membranes. These kingdoms are Kingdom Protista, Kingdom Fungi, the Kingdom Plantae, and the Kingdom Animalia.

Kingdom Archaebacteria

One-celled prokaryotes; absorb food from surroundings or make their own food by chemosynthesis; found in extremely harsh environments including salt ponds, hot springs, swamps, and deep-sea hydrothermal vents.

Kingdom Eubacteria

Cyanobacteria one-celled prokaryotes; make their own food; contain chlorophyll; some species form colonies; most are blue-green

Bacteria one-celled prokaryotes; most absorb food from their surroundings; some are photosynthetic; many are parasites; round, spiral, or rod-shaped

Kingdom Protista

Phylum Euglenophyta one-celled; can photosynthesize or take in food; most have one flagellum; euglenoids

Phylum Bacillariophyta one-celled; make their own food through photosynthesis; have unique double shells made of silica; diatoms

Phylum Dinoflagellata one-celled; make their own food through photosynthesis; contain red pigments; have two flagella; dinoflagellates

Phylum Chlorophyta one-celled, many-celled, or colonies; contain chlorophyll; make their own food; live on land, in fresh water, or salt water; green algae

Phylum Rhodophyta most are many-celled; photosynthetic; contain red pigments; most live in deep saltwater environments; red algae

Phylum Phaeophyta most are many-celled; photosynthetic; contain brown pigments; most live in saltwater environments; brown algae

Phylum Foraminifera many-celled; take in food; primarily marine; shells constructed of calcium carbonate, or made from grains of sand; forams

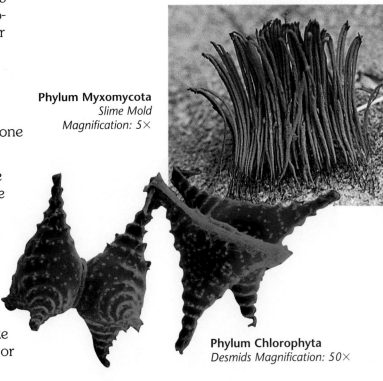

Phylum Myxomycota
Slime Mold
Magnification: 5×

Phylum Chlorophyta
Desmids Magnification: 50×

Appendix E

Phylum Rhizopoda one-celled; take in food; move by means of pseudopods; free-living or parasitic; amoebas

Phylum Zoomastigina one-celled; take in food; have one or more flagella; free-living or parasitic; zoomastigotes

Phylum Ciliophora one-celled; take in food; have large numbers of cilia; ciliates

Phylum Sporozoa one-celled; take in food; no means of movement; parasites in animals; sporozoans

Phylum Myxomycota and Acrasiomycota: one- or many-celled; absorb food; change form during life cycle; cellular and plasmodial slime molds

Phylum Oomycota many-celled; live in fresh or salt water; are either parasites or decomposers; water molds, rusts and downy mildews

Kingdom Fungi

Phylum Zygomycota many-celled; absorb food; spores are produced in sporangia; zygote fungi; bread mold

Phylum Ascomycota one- and many-celled; absorb food; spores produced in asci; sac fungi; yeast

Phylum Basidiomycota many-celled; absorb food; spores produced in basidia; club fungi; mushrooms

Phylum Deuteromycota: members with unknown reproductive structures; imperfect fungi; penicillin

Lichens organisms formed by symbiotic relationship between an ascomycote or a basidiomycote and green alga or cyanobacterium

Kingdom Plantae

Non-seed Plants

Division Bryophyta nonvascular plants; reproduce by spores produced in capsules; many-celled; green; grow in moist land environments; mosses and liverworts

Division Lycophyta many-celled vascular plants; spores produced in conelike structures; live on land; are photosynthetic; club mosses

Division Sphenophyta vascular plants; ribbed and jointed stems; scalelike leaves; spores produced in conelike structures; horsetails

Division Pterophyta vascular plants; leaves called fronds; spores produced in clusters of sporangia called sori; live on land or in water; ferns

Division Bryophyta
Liverwort

Lichens
British soldier lichen × 3

Appendix E

Seed Plants

Division Ginkgophyta: deciduous gymnosperms; only one living species; fan-shaped leaves with branching veins; reproduces with seeds; ginkgos

Division Cycadophyta: palmlike gymnosperms; large featherlike leaves; produce seeds in cones; cycads

Division Coniferophyta: deciduous or evergreen gymnosperms; trees or shrubs; needlelike or scalelike leaves; seeds produced in cones; conifers

Division Gnetophyta: shrubs or woody vines; seeds produced in cones; division contains only three genera; gnetum

Division Anthophyta: dominant group of plants; ovules protected in an ovary; sperm carried to ovules by pollen tube; produce flowers and seeds in fruits; flowering plants

Kingdom Animalia

Phylum Porifera: aquatic organisms that lack true tissues and organs; they are asymmetrical and sessile; sponges

Phylum Cnidaria: radially symmetrical organisms; have a digestive cavity with one opening; most have tentacles armed with stinging cells; live in aquatic environments singly or in colonies; includes jellyfish, corals, hydra, and sea anemones

Phylum Platyhelminthes: bilaterally symmetrical worms; have flattened bodies; digestive system has one opening; parasitic and free-living species; flatworms

Phylum Cnidaria
Jellyfish

Phylum Arthopoda
Orb Weaver Spider

Phylum Arthropoda
Hermit Crab

Division Coniferophyta
Pine cone

Division Anthophyta
Strawberry Blossoms

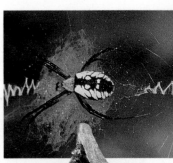

Phylum Mollusca
Florida Fighting Conch

Division Anthophyta
Strawberries

Phylum Annelida
Sabellid Worms Feather Duster

Appendix E

Phylum Nematoda: round, bilaterally symmetrical body; digestive system with two openings; many parasitic forms but mostly free-living; roundworms

Phylum Mollusca: soft-bodied animals, many with a hard shell; a mantle covers the soft body; aquatic and terrestrial species; includes clams, snails, squid, and octopuses

Phylum Annelida: bilaterally symmetrical worms; have round, segmented bodies; terrestrial and aquatic species; includes earthworms, leeches, and marine polychaetes

Phylum Arthropoda: largest phylum of organisms; have segmented bodies; pairs of jointed appendages; have hard exoskeletons; terrestrial and aquatic species; includes insects, crustaceans, spiders, and horseshoe crabs

Phylum Echinodermata: marine organisms; have spiny or leathery skin; water-vascular system with tube feet; radial symmetry; includes sea stars, sand dollars, and sea urchins

Phylum Chordata: organisms with internal skeletons; specialized body systems; paired appendages; all at some time have a notochord, dorsal nerve cord, gill slits, and a tail; include fish, amphibians, reptiles, birds, and mammals

Phylum Arthropoda
Giant Swallowtail Butterfly

Phylum Echinodermata
Blood Sea Star and Red Sea Urchin

Phylum Chordata
Eastern Box Turtle

Phylum Chordata
Lemon Butterfly fish

Phylum Chordata
Great Horned Owl

Appendix
F

Minerals

Mineral (formula)	Color	Streak	Hardness	Breakage pattern	Uses and other properties
graphite (C)	black to gray	black to gray	1–1.5	basal cleavage (scales)	pencil lead, lubricants for locks, rods to control some small nuclear reactions, battery poles
galena (PbS)	gray	gray to black	2.5	cubic cleavage perfect	source of lead, used in pipes, shields for X rays, fishing equipment sinkers
hematite (Fe_2O_3)	black or reddish brown	reddish brown	5.5–6.5	irregular fracture	source of iron; converted to "pig" iron, made into steel
magnetite (Fe_3O_4)	black	black	6	conchoidal fracture	source of iron, naturally magnetic, called lodestone
pyrite (FeS_2)	light, brassy, yellow	greenish black	6–6.5	uneven fracture	source of iron, "fool's gold"
talc ($Mg_3Si_4O_{10}(OH)_2$)	white greenish	white	1	cleavage in one direction	used for talcum powder, sculptures, paper, and tabletops
gypsum ($CaSO_4 \cdot 2H_2O$)	colorless, gray, white brown	white	2	basal cleavage	used in plaster of paris and dry wall for building construction
sphalerite (ZnS)	brown, reddish brown, greenish	light to dark brown	3.5–4	cleavage in six directions	main ore of zinc; used in paints, dyes and medicine
muscovite ($KAl_3Si_3O_{10}(OH)_2$)	white, light gray, yellow, rose, green	colorless	2–2.5	basal cleavage	occurs in large flexible plates; used as an insulator in electrical equipment, lubricant
biotite ($K(Mg, Fe)_3(AlSi_3O_{10})(OH)_2$)	black to dark brown	colorless	2.5–3	basal cleavage	occurs in large flexible plates
halite (NaCl)	colorless, red, white, blue	colorless	2.5	cubic cleavage	salt; soluble in water; a preservative

Appendix F

Minerals

Mineral (formula)	Color	Streak	Hardness	Breakage pattern	Uses and other properties
calcite ($CaCO_3$)	colorless, white, pale blue	colorless, white	3	cleavage in three directions	fizzes when HCl is added; used in cements and other building materials
dolomite ($CaMg$ $(CO_3)_2$)	colorless, white, pink green, gray black	white	3.5–4	cleavage in three directions	concrete and cement; used as an ornamental building stone
fluorite (CaF_2)	colorless, white, blue green, red yellow, purple	colorless	4	cleavage in four directions	used in the manufacture of optical equipment; glows under ultraviolet light
hornblende ($(CaNa)_{2-3}(Mg, Al,Fe)_5(Al,Si)_2$ $Si_6O_{22}(OH)_2$)	green to black	gray to white	5–6	cleavage in two directions	will transmit light on thin edges; 6-sided cross section
feldspar ($KAlSi_3O_8$) ($NaAlSi_3O_8$) ($CaAl_2Si_2O_8$)	colorless, white to gray, green	colorless	6	two cleavage planes meet at ~90° angle	used in the manufacture of ceramics
augite $((Ca, Na)$ (Mg, Fe, Al) $(Al, Si)_2O_6)$	black	colorless	6	cleavage in two directions	square or 8-sided cross section
olivine $((Mg, Fe)_2$ $SiO_4)$	olive, green	none	6.5–7	conchoidal fracture	gemstones, refractory sand
quartz (SiO_2)	colorless, various colors	none	7	conchoidal fracture	used in glass manufacture, electronic equipment, radios, computers, watches, gemstones

Rocks

Rock Type	Rock Name	Characteristics
Igneous (intrusive)	Granite	Large mineral grains of quartz, feldspar, hornblende, and mica. Usually light in color.
	Diorite	Large mineral grains of feldspar, hornblende, mica. Less quartz than granite. Intermediate in color.
	Gabbro	Large mineral grains of feldspar, hornblende, augite, olivine, and mica. No quartz. Dark in color.
Igneous (extrusive)	Rhyolite	Small mineral grains of quartz, feldspar, hornblende, and mica or no visible grains. Light in color.
	Andesite	Small mineral grains of feldspar, hornblende, mica or no visible grains. Less quartz than rhyolite. Intermediate in color.
	Basalt	Small mineral grains of feldspar, hornblende, augite, olivine, mica or no visible grains. No quartz. Dark in color.
	Obsidian	Glassy texture. No visible grains. Volcanic glass. Fracture looks like broken glass.
	Pumice	Frothy texture. Floats. Usually light in color.
Sedimentary (detrital)	Conglomerate	Coarse-grained. Gravel or pebble-sized grains.
	Sandstone	Sand-sized grains 1/16 to 2 mm in size.
	Siltstone	Grains are smaller than sand but larger than clay.
	Shale	Smallest grains. Usually dark in color.
Sedimentary (chemical or biochemical)	Limestone	Major mineral is calcite. Usually forms in oceans, lakes, rivers, and caves. Often contains fossils.
	Coal	Occurs in swampy. low-lying areas. Compacted layers of organic material, mainly plant remains.
Sedimentary (chemical)	Rock Salt	Commonly forms by the evaporation of seawater.
Metamorphic (foliated)	Gneiss	Well-developed banding because of alternating layers of different minerals, usually of different colors. Common parent rock is granite.
	Schist	Well-defined parallel arrangement of flat, sheet-like minerals, mainly micas. Common parent rocks are shale, phyllite.
	Phyllite	Shiny or silky appearance. May look wrinkled. Common parent rocks are shale, slate.
	Slate	Harder, denser, and shinier than shale. Common parent rock is shale.
Metamorphic (non-foliated)	Marble	Interlocking calcite or dolomite crystals. Common parent rock is limestone.
	Soapstone	Composed mainly of the mineral talc. Soft with a greasy feel.
	Quartzite	Hard and well cemented with interlocking quartz crystals. Common parent rock is sandstone.

Appendix H

Topographic Map Symbols

Primary highway, hard surface

Secondary highway, hard surface

Light-duty road, hard or
Improved surface

Unimproved road

Railroad: single track and
multiple track

Railroads in juxtaposition

Buildings

Schools, church, and cemetery

Buildings (barn, warehouse, etc)

Wells other than water
(labeled as to type)

Tanks: oil, water, etc.
(labeled only if water)

Located or landmark object;
windmill

Open pit, mine, or quarry;
prospect

Marsh (swamp)

Wooded marsh

Woods or brushwood

Vineyard
Land subject to controlled
inundation

Submerged marsh

Mangrove

Orchard

Scrub

Urban area

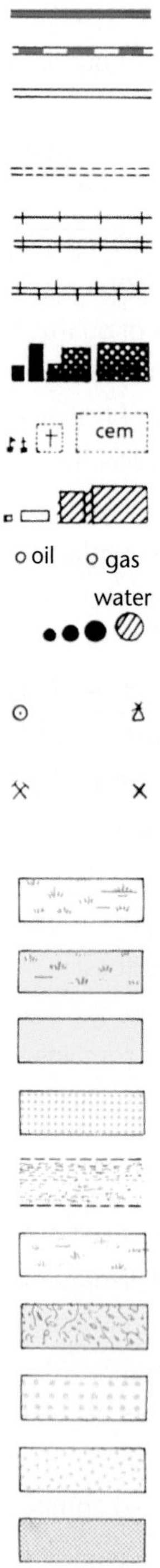

Spot elevation ×7369

Water elevation 670

Index contour

Supplementary contour

Intermediate contour

Depression contours

Boundaries: National
    State
    County, parish, municipal
    Civil township, precinct,
    town, barrio
    Incorporated city, village,
    town, hamlet
    Reservation, National or State
    Small park, cemetery,
    airport, etc.
    Land grant

Township or range line,
United States land survey

Township or range line,
approximate location

Perennial streams

Elevated aqueduct

Water well and spring

Small rapids

Large rapids

Intermittent lake

Intermittent streams

Aqueduct tunnel

Glacier

Small falls

Large falls

Dry lake bed

Appendix

I

Weather Map Symbols

Sample Plotted Report at Each Station

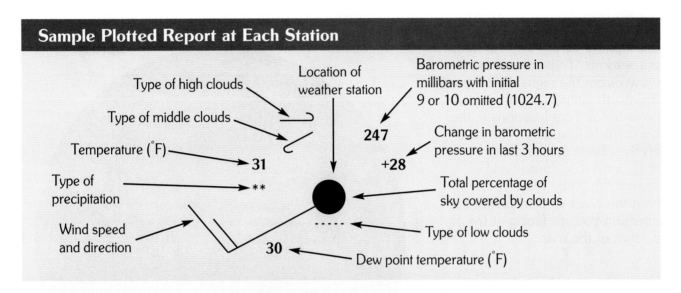

Type of high clouds
Type of middle clouds
Temperature (°F)
Type of precipitation
Wind speed and direction

Location of weather station
Barometric pressure in millibars with initial 9 or 10 omitted (1024.7)
Change in barometric pressure in last 3 hours
Total percentage of sky covered by clouds
Type of low clouds
Dew point temperature (°F)

247
+28
31
**
30

Sample Plotted Report at Each Station

Precipitation		Wind Speed and direction		Sky coverage		Some types of high clouds	
≡	Fog	◯	0 knots; calm	◯	No cover	⌐⊃	Scattered cirrus
★	Snow	╱	1-2 knots	◐	1/10 or less	⊃⊃	Dense cirrus in patches
●	Rain	╲	3-7 knots	◗	2/10 to 3/10	⊃⌐	Veil of cirrus covering entire sky
⊺⊱	Thunder-storm	╲	8-12 knots	◑	4/10		
		╲	18-17 knots	◖	1/2		
		╲	18-22 knots	◕	6/10	⌐⌐	Cirrus not covering entire sky
,	Drizzle	╲	23-27 knots	◕	7/10		
		◣	48-52 knots	◒	Overcast with openings		
▽	Showers	1 knot = 1.852 km/h		●	Complete overcast		

Some types of middle clouds		Some types of low clouds		Fronts and pressure systems	
╱	Thin altostratus layer	⌓	Cumulus of fair weather	(H) or High	Center of high-or
╱╱	Thick altostratus layer	⌣	Stratocumulus	(L) or Low	low-pressure system
╱⌣	Thin altostratus in patches	-----	Fractocumulus of bad weather	▲▲▲▲	Cold front
╱⌣	Thin altostratus in bands	—	Stratus of fair weather	●●●●	Warm Front
				▲●▲●	Occluded front
				●▲●▽	Stationary front

Star Charts

Shown here are star charts for viewing stars in the northern hemisphere during the four different seasons. These charts are drawn from the night sky at about 35° north latitude, but they can be used for most locations in the northern hemisphere. The lines on the charts outline major constellations. The dense band of stars is the Milky Way. To use, hold the chart vertically, with the direction you are facing at the bottom of the map.

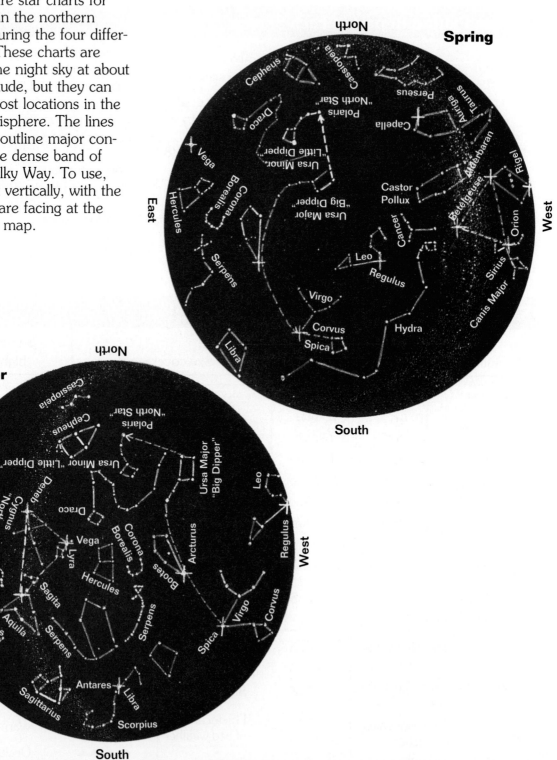

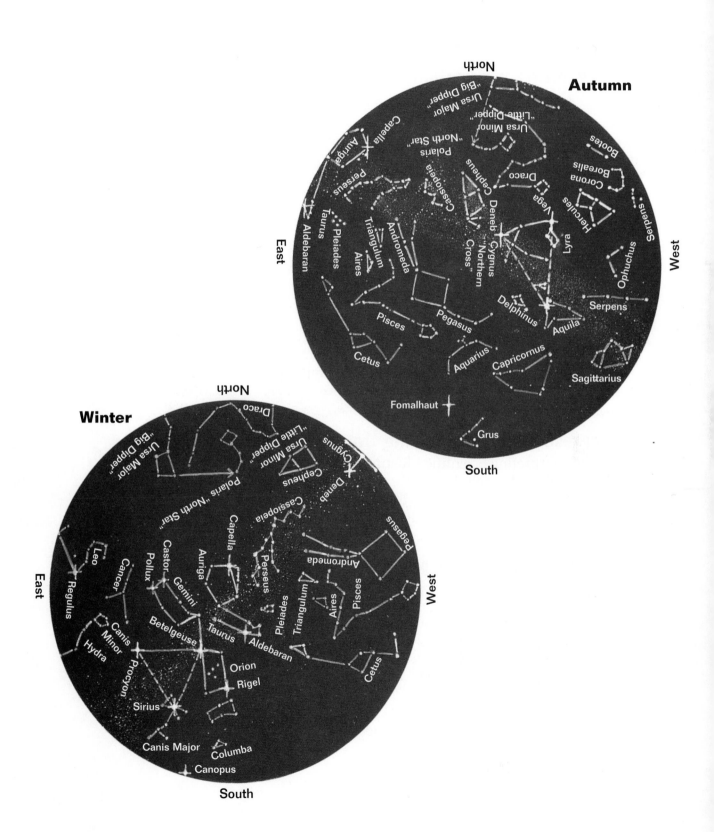

Skill Handbook

Table of Contents

Science Skill Handbook

Organizing Information

Communicating

The communication of ideas is an important part of our everyday lives. Whether reading a book, writing a letter, or watching a television program, people everywhere are expressing opinions and sharing information with one another. Writing in your Science Journal allows you to express your opinions and demonstrate your knowledge of the information presented on a subject. When writing, keep in mind the purpose of the assignment and the audience with which you are communicating.

Examples Science Journal assignments vary greatly. They may ask you to take a viewpoint other than your own; perhaps you will be a scientist, a TV reporter, or a committee member of a local environmental group. Maybe you will be expressing your opinions to a member of Congress, a doctor, or to the editor of your local newspaper, as shown in **Figure 1.** Sometimes, Science Journal writing may allow you to summarize information in the form of an outline, a letter, or in a paragraph.

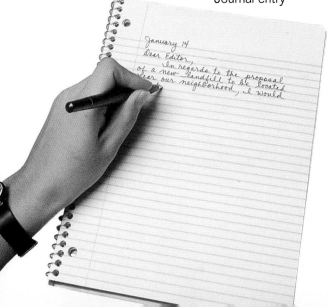

Figure 1 A Science Journal entry

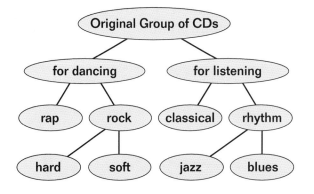

Figure 2 Classifying CDs

Classifying

You may not realize it, but you make things orderly in the world around you. If you hang your shirts together in the closet or if your favorite CDs are stacked together, you have used the skill of classifying.

Classifying is the process of sorting objects or events into groups based on common features. When classifying, first observe the objects or events to be classified. Then, select one feature that is shared by some members in the group, but not by all. Place those members that share that feature into a subgroup. You can classify members into smaller and smaller subgroups based on characteristics.

Remember, when you classify, you are grouping objects or events for a purpose. Keep your purpose in mind as you select the features to form groups and subgroups.

Example How would you classify a collection of CDs? As shown in **Figure 2,** you might classify those you like to dance to in one subgroup and CDs you like to listen to in the next subgroup. The CDs you like to dance to could be subdivided into a rap subgroup and a rock subgroup. Note that for each feature selected, each CD fits into only one subgroup. You would keep selecting features until all the CDs are classified. **Figure 2** shows one possible classification.

Figure 3 A recipe for bread contains sequenced instructions

Sequencing

A sequence is an arrangement of things or events in a particular order. When you are asked to sequence objects or events within a group, figure out what comes first, then think about what should come second. Continue to choose objects or events until all of the objects you started out with are in order. Then, go back over the sequence to make sure each thing or event in your sequence logically leads to the next.

Example A sequence with which you are most familiar is the use of alphabetical order. Another example of sequence would be the steps in a recipe, as shown in **Figure 3.** Think about baking bread. Steps in the recipe have to be followed in order for the bread to turn out right.

Concept Mapping

If you were taking an automobile trip, you would probably take along a road map. The road map shows your location, your destination, and other places along the way. By looking at the map and finding where you are, you can begin to understand where you are in relation to other locations on the map.

A concept map is similar to a road map. But, a concept map shows relationships among ideas (or concepts) rather than places. A concept map is a diagram that visually shows how concepts are related. Because the concept map shows relationships among ideas, it can make the meanings of ideas and terms clear, and help you understand better what you are studying.

There is usually not one correct way to create a concept map. As you construct one type of map, you may discover other ways to construct the map that show the

Figure 4 Network tree describing U.S. currency

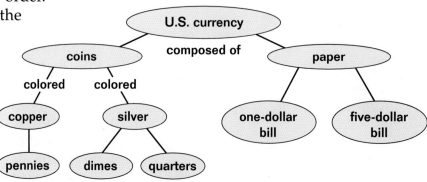

relationships between concepts in a better way. If you do discover what you think is a better way to create a concept map, go ahead and use the new one. Overall, concept maps are useful for breaking a big concept down into smaller parts, making learning easier.

Examples

Network Tree Look at the concept map about U.S. currency in **Figure 4.** This is called a network tree. Notice how some words are in ovals while others are written across connecting lines. The words inside the ovals are science concepts. The lines in the map show related concepts. The words written on the lines describe the relationships between concepts.

When you are asked to construct a network tree, write down the topic and list the major concepts related to that topic on a piece of paper. Then look at your list and begin to put them in order from general to specific. Branch the related concepts from the major concept and describe the relationships on the lines. Continue to write the more specific concepts. Write the relationships between the concepts on the lines until all concepts are mapped. Examine the concept map for relationships that cross branches, and add them to the concept map.

Events Chain An events chain is another type of concept map. An events chain map, such as the one describing a typical morning routine in **Figure 5,** is used to describe ideas in order. In science, an events chain can be used to describe a sequence of events, the steps in a procedure, or the stages of a process.

When making an events chain, first find the one event that starts the chain. This

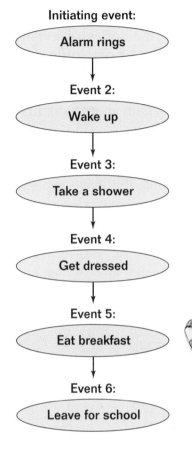

Initiating event:

Alarm rings

Event 2:

Wake up

Event 3:

Take a shower

Event 4:

Get dressed

Event 5:

Eat breakfast

Event 6:

Leave for school

Figure 5 Events chain of a typical morning routine

event is called the initiating event. Then, find the next event in the chain and continue until you reach an outcome. Suppose you are asked to describe what happens when your alarm rings. An events chain map describing the steps might look like **Figure 5.** Notice that connecting words are not necessary in an events chain.

Cycle Map A cycle concept map is a special type of events chain map. In a cycle concept map, the series of events does not produce a final outcome. Instead, the last event in the chain relates back to the initiating event.

As in the events chain map, you first decide on an initiating event and then list each event in order. Because there is no outcome and the last event relates back to the initiating event, the cycle repeats itself. Look at the cycle map describing the relationship between day and night in **Figure 6.**

Figure 6 Cycle map of day and night.

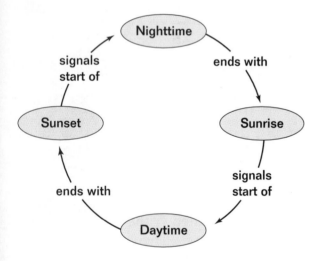

Spider Map A fourth type of concept map is the spider map. This is a map that you can use for brainstorming. Once you have a central idea, you may find you have a jumble of ideas that relate to it, but are not necessarily clearly related to each other. As illustrated by the homework spider map in **Figure 7,** by writing these ideas outside the main concept, you may begin to separate and group unrelated terms so that they become more useful.

Figure 7 Spider map about homework.

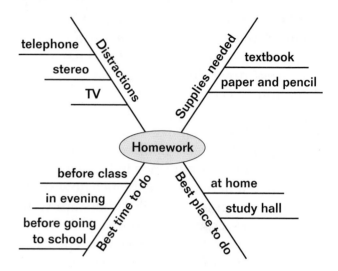

Making and Using Tables

Browse through your textbook and you will notice tables in the text and in the activities. In a table, data or information is arranged in a way that makes it easier for you to understand. Activity tables help organize the data you collect during an activity so that results can be interpreted.

Examples Most tables have a title. At a glance, the title tells you what the table is about. A table is divided into columns and rows. The first column lists items to be compared. In **Figure 8,** the collection of recyclable materials is being compared in a table. The row across the top lists the specific characteristics being compared. Within the grid of the table, the collected data are recorded.

What is the title of the table in **Figure 8?** The title is "Recycled Materials." What is being compared? The different materials being recycled and on which days they are recycled.

Making Tables To make a table, list the items to be compared down in columns and the characteristics to be compared across in rows. The table in

Science Skill Handbook

Figure 8 Table of recycled materials

Recycled Materials			
Day of Week	Paper (kg)	Aluminum (kg)	Plastic (kg)
Mon.	4.0	2.0	0.5
Wed.	3.5	1.5	0.5
Fri.	3.0	1.0	1.5

Figure 8 compares the mass of recycled materials collected by a class. On Monday, students turned in 4.0 kg of paper, 2.0 kg of aluminum, and 0.5 kg of plastic. On Wednesday, they turned in 3.5 kg of paper, 1.5 kg of aluminum, and 0.5 kg of plastic. On Friday, the totals were 3.0 kg of paper, 1.0 kg of aluminum, and 1.5 kg of plastic.

Using Tables How much plastic, in kilograms, is being recycled on Wednesday? Locate the column labeled "Plastic (kg)" and the row "Wed." The data in the box where the column and row intersect is the answer. Did you answer "0.5"? How much aluminum, in kilograms, is being recycled on Friday? If you answered "1.0," you understand how to use the parts of the table.

Making and Using Graphs

After scientists organize data in tables, they may display the data in a graph. A graph is a diagram that shows the relationship of one variable to another. A graph makes interpretation and analysis of data easier. There are three basic types of graphs used in science—the line graph, the bar graph, and the circle graph.

Examples

Line Graphs A line graph is used to show the relationship between two variables. The variables being compared go on two axes of the graph. The independent variable always goes on the horizontal axis, called the x-axis. The dependent variable always goes on the vertical axis, called the y-axis.

Suppose your class started to record the amount of materials they collected in one week for their school to recycle. The collected information is shown in **Figure 9**.

You could make a graph of the materials collected over the three days of the school week. The three weekdays are the independent variables and are placed on the x-axis of your graph. The amount of materials collected is the dependent variable and would go on the y-axis.

After drawing your axes, label each with a scale. The x-axis lists the three weekdays. To make a scale of the amount of materials collected on the y-axis, look at the data values. Because the lowest amount collected was 1.0 and the highest was 5.0, you will have to start numbering at least at 1.0 and go through 5.0. You decide to start numbering at 0 and number by ones through 6.0, as shown in **Figure 10**.

Next, plot the data points for collected paper. The first pair of data you want to plot is Monday and 5.0 kg of paper.

Figure 9 Amount of recyclable materials collected during one week

Materials Collected During Week		
Day of Week	Paper (kg)	Aluminum (kg)
Mon.	5.0	4.0
Wed.	4.0	1.0
Fri.	2.5	2.0

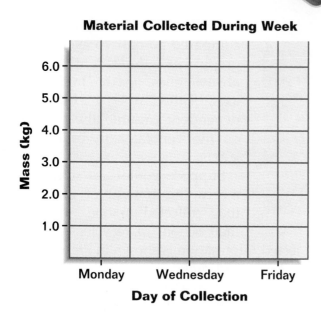

Figure 10 Graph outline for material collected during week

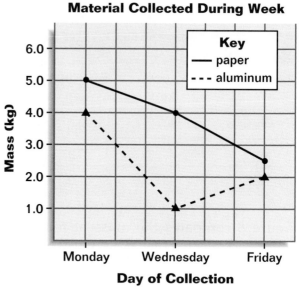

Figure 11 Line graph of materials collected during week

Locate "Monday" on the *x*-axis and locate "5.0" on the *y*-axis. Where an imaginary vertical line from the *x*-axis and an imaginary horizontal line from the *y*-axis would meet, place the first data point. Place the other data points the same way. After all the points are plotted, connect them with the best smooth curve. Repeat this procedure for the data points for aluminum. Use continuous and dashed lines to distinguish the two line graphs. The resulting graph should look like **Figure 11.**

Bar Graphs Bar graphs are similar to line graphs. They compare data that do not continuously change. In a bar graph, vertical bars show the relationships among data.

To make a bar graph, set up the *x*-axis and *y*-axis as you did for the line graph. The data is plotted by drawing vertical bars from the *x*-axis up to a point where the *y*-axis would meet the bar if it were extended.

Look at the bar graph in **Figure 12** comparing the mass of aluminum collected

over three weekdays. The *x*-axis is the days on which the aluminum was collected. The *y*-axis is the mass of aluminum collected, in kilograms.

Circle Graphs A circle graph uses a circle divided into sections to display data. Each section represents part of the whole. All the sections together equal 100 percent.

Suppose you wanted to make a circle graph to show the number of seeds that germinated in a package. You would count the total number of seeds. You find that there are 143 seeds in the package. This represents 100 percent, the whole circle.

You plant the seeds, and 129 seeds germinate. The seeds that germinated will make up one section of the circle graph, and the seeds that did not germinate will make up the remaining section.

To find out how much of the circle each section should take, divide the number of seeds in each section by the total number of seeds. Then, multiply your answer by 360, the number of degrees in a circle, and round to the nearest whole number. The

Science Skill Handbook

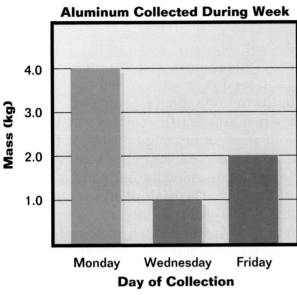

Aluminum Collected During Week

(Mass (kg) vs. Day of Collection: Monday 4.0, Wednesday 1.0, Friday 2.0)

Figure 12 Bar graph of aluminum collected during week

section of the circle graph in degrees that represents the seeds germinated is figured below.

$$\frac{129}{143} \times 360 = 324.75 \text{ or } 325 \text{ degrees (or } 325°)$$

Plot this group on the circle graph using a compass and a protractor. Use the compass to draw a circle. It will be easier to

measure the part of the circle representing the non-germinating seeds, so subtract 325° from 360° to get 35°. Draw a straight line from the center to the edge of the circle. Place your protractor on this line and use it to mark a point at 325°. Use this point to draw a straight line from the center of the circle to the edge. This is the section for the group of seeds that did not germinate. The other section represents the group of 129 seeds that did germinate. Label the sections of your graph and title the graph as shown in **Figure 13**.

Figure 13 Circle graph of germinated seeds

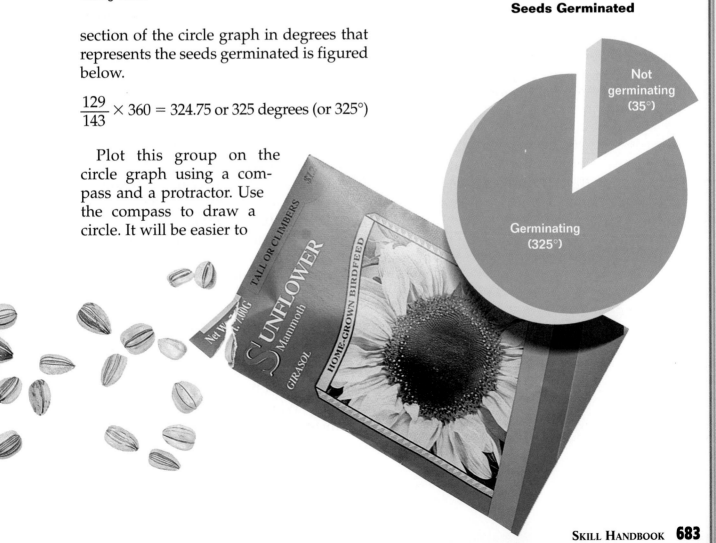

Seeds Germinated

Not germinating (35°)

Germinating (325°)

Thinking Critically

Observing and Inferring

Observing Scientists try to make careful and accurate observations. When possible, they use instruments such as microscopes, thermometers, and balances to make observations. Measurements with a balance or thermometer provide numerical data that can be checked and repeated.

When you make observations in science, you'll find it helpful to examine the entire object or situation first. Then, look carefully for details. Write down everything you observe.

Example Imagine that you have just finished a volleyball game. At home, you open the refrigerator and see a jug of orange juice on the back of the top shelf. The jug, shown in **Figure 14,** feels cold as you grasp it. Then, you drink the juice, smell the oranges, and enjoy the tart taste in your mouth.

Figure 14 Why is this jug of orange juice cold?

As you imagined yourself in the story, you used your senses to make observations. You used your sense of sight to find the jug in the refrigerator, your sense of touch when you felt the coldness of the jug, your sense of hearing to listen as the liquid filled the glass, and your senses of smell and taste to enjoy the odor and tartness of the juice. The basis of all scientific investigation is observation.

Inferring Scientists often make inferences based on their observations. An inference is an attempt to explain or interpret observations or to say what caused what you observed.

When making an inference, be certain to use accurate data and observations. Analyze all of the data that you've collected. Then, based on everything you know, explain or interpret what you've observed.

Example When you drank a glass of orange juice after the volleyball game, you observed that the orange juice was cold as well as refreshing. You might infer that the juice was cold because it had been made much earlier in the day and had been kept in the refrigerator, or you might infer that it had just been made, using both cold water and ice. The only way to be sure which inference is correct is to investigate further.

Comparing and Contrasting

Observations can be analyzed by noting the similarities and differences between two or more objects or events that you observe. When you look at objects or events to see how they are similar, you are comparing them. Contrasting is looking for differences in similar objects or events.

Figure 15 Table comparing the nutritional value of *Cereal A* and *Cereal B*

Nutritional Value		
	Cereal A	**Cereal B**
Serving size	103 g	105 g
Calories	220	160
Total Fat	10 g	10 g
Protein	2.5 g	2.6 g
Total Carbohydrate	30 g	15 g

Example Suppose you were asked to compare and contrast the nutritional value of two kinds of cereal, *Cereal A* and *Cereal B.* You would start by looking at what is known about these cereals. Arrange this information in a table, like the one in **Figure 15.**

Similarities you might point out are that both cereals have similar serving sizes, amounts of total fat, and protein. Differences include *Cereal A* having a higher calorie value and containing more total carbohydrates than *Cereal B.*

Recognizing Cause and Effect

Have you ever watched something happen and then made suggestions about why it happened? If so, you have observed an effect and inferred a cause. The event is an effect, and the reason for the event is the cause.

Example Suppose that every time your teacher fed the fish in a classroom aquarium, she or he tapped the food container on the edge of the aquarium. Then, one day your teacher just happened to tap the edge of the aquarium with a pencil while making a point. You observed the fish swim to the surface of the aquarium to feed, as shown in **Figure 16.** What is the effect, and what would you infer to be the cause? The effect is the fish swimming to the surface of the aquarium. You might infer the cause to be the teacher tapping on the edge of the aquarium. In determining cause and effect, you have made a logical inference based on your observations.

Perhaps the fish swam to the surface because they reacted to the teacher's waving hand or for some other reason. When scientists are unsure of the cause of a certain event, they design controlled experiments to determine what causes the event. Although you have made a logical conclusion about the behavior of the fish, you would have to perform an experiment to be certain that it was the tapping that caused the effect you observed.

Figure 16 What cause-and-effect situations are occurring in this aquarium?

Practicing Scientific Processes

You might say that the work of a scientist is to solve problems. But when you decide how to dress on a particular day, you are doing problem solving, too. You may observe what the weather looks like through a window. You may go outside and see whether what you are wearing is heavy or light enough.

Scientists use an orderly approach to learn new information and to solve problems. The methods scientists may use include observing to form a hypothesis, designing an experiment to test a hypothesis, separating and controlling variables, and interpreting data.

Forming Operational Definitions

Operational definitions define an object by showing how it functions, works, or behaves. Such definitions are written in terms of how an object works or how it can be used; that is, what is its job or purpose?

Example Some operational defini-

Figure 17 What observations can be made about this dog?

tions explain how an object can be used.
- A ruler is a tool that measures the size of an object.
- An automobile can move things from one place to another.

Or such a definition may explain how an object works.
- A ruler contains a series of marks that can be used as a standard when measuring.
- An automobile is a vehicle that can move from place to place.

Forming a Hypothesis

Observations You observe all the time. Scientists try to observe as much as possible about the things and events they study so they know that what they say about their observations is reliable.

Some observations describe something using only words. These observations are called qualitative observations. Other observations describe how much of something there is. These are quantitative observations and use numbers, as well as words, in the description. Tools or equipment are used to measure the characteristic being described.

Example If you were making qualitative observations of the dog in **Figure 17,** you might use words such as *furry, yellow,* and *short-haired.* Quantitative observations of this dog might include a mass of 14 kg, a height of 46 cm, ear length of 10 cm, and an age of 150 days.

Hypotheses Hypotheses are tested to help explain observations that have been made. They are often stated as *if* and *then* statements.

Examples Suppose you want to make a perfect score on a spelling test. Begin by thinking of several ways to accomplish this. Base these possibilities on past observations. If you put each of these possibilities into sentence form, using the words *if* and *then*, you can form a hypothesis. All of the following are hypotheses you might consider to explain how you could score 100 percent on your test:

If the test is easy, then I will get a perfect score.

If I am intelligent, then I will get a perfect score.

If I study hard, then I will get a perfect score.

Perhaps a scientist has observed that plants that receive fertilizer grow taller than plants that do not. A scientist may form a hypothesis that says: If plants are fertilized, then their growth will increase.

Designing an Experiment to Test a Hypothesis

In order to test a hypothesis, it's best to write out a procedure. A procedure is the plan that you follow in your experiment. A procedure tells you what materials to use and how to use them. After following the procedure, data are generated. From this generated data, you can then draw a conclusion and make a statement about your results.

If the conclusion you draw from the data supports your hypothesis, then you can say that your hypothesis is reliable. *Reliable* means that you can trust your conclusion. If it did not support your hypothesis, then you would have to make new observations and state a new hypothesis—just make sure that it is one that you can test.

Example Super premium gasoline costs more than regular gasoline. Does super premium gasoline increase the efficiency or fuel mileage of your family car? Let's figure out how to conduct an experiment to test the hypothesis, "*if* premium gas is more efficient, *then* it should increase the fuel mileage of our family car." Then a procedure similar to **Figure 18** must be written to generate data presented in **Figure 19** on the next page.

These data show that premium gasoline is less efficient than regular gasoline. It took more gasoline to travel one mile (0.064) using premium gasoline than it does to travel one mile using regular gasoline (0.059). This conclusion does not support the original hypothesis made.

PROCEDURE

1. Use regular gasoline for two weeks.

2. Record the number of miles between fill-ups and the amount of gasoline used.

3. Switch to premium gasoline for two weeks.

4. Record the number of miles between fill-ups and the amount of gasoline used.

Figure 18 Possible procedural steps

Figure 19 Data generated from procedure steps

Gasoline Data

	Miles traveled	Gallons used	Gallons per mile
Regular gasoline	762	45.34	0.059
Premium gasoline	661	42.30	0.064

Separating and Controlling Variables

In any experiment, it is important to keep everything the same except for the item you are testing. The one factor that you change is called the *independent variable.* The factor that changes as a result of the independent variable is called the *dependent variable.* Always make sure that there is only one independent variable. If you allow more than one, you will not know what causes the changes you observe in the independent variable. Many experiments have *controls*—a treatment or an experiment that you can compare with the results of your test groups.

Example In the experiment with the gasoline, you made everything the same except the type of gasoline being used. The driver, the type of automobile, and the weather conditions should remain the same throughout. The gasoline should also be purchased from the same service station. By doing so, you made sure that at the end of the experiment, any differences were the result of the type of fuel being used—regular or premium. The type of gasoline was the *independent factor* and the gas mileage achieved was the *dependent factor.* The use of regular gasoline was the *control.*

Interpreting Data

The word *interpret* means "to explain the meaning of something." Look at the problem originally being explored in the gasoline experiment and find out what the data show. Identify the control group and the test group so you can see whether or not the variable has had an effect. Then, you need to check differences between the control and test groups.

Figure 20 Which gasoline type is most efficient?

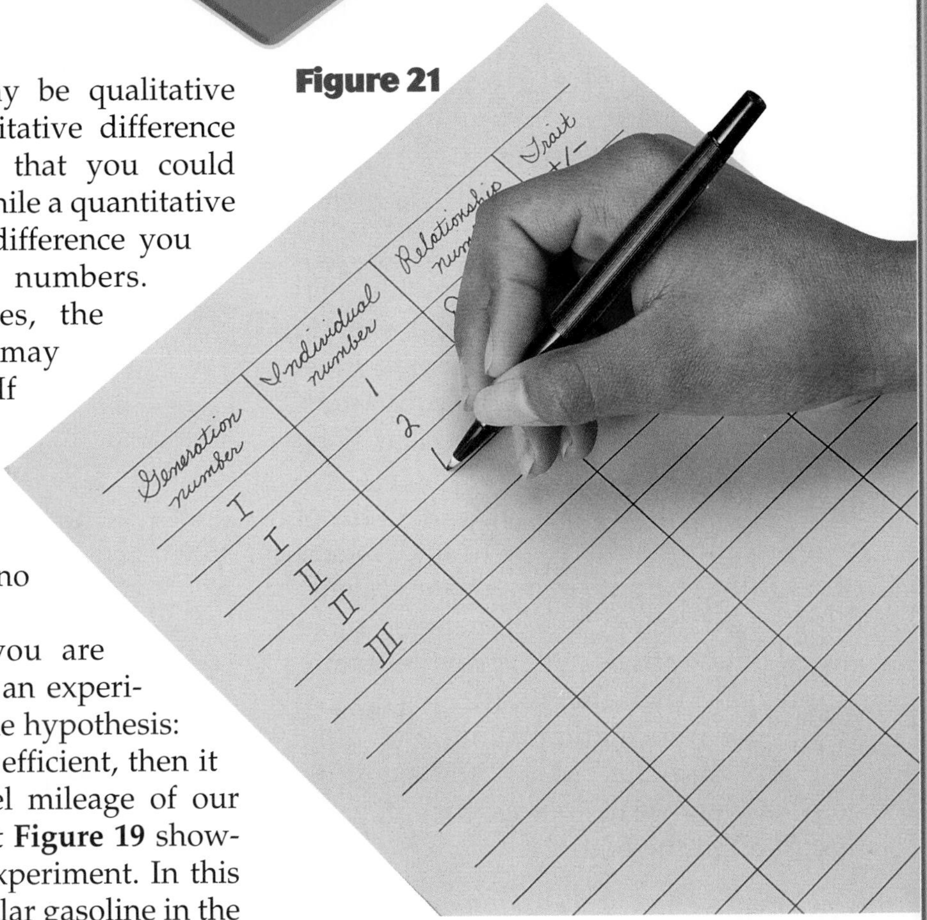

These differences may be qualitative or quantitative. A qualitative difference would be a difference that you could observe and describe, while a quantitative difference would be a difference you can measure using numbers. If there are differences, the variable being tested may have had an effect. If there is no difference between the control and the test groups, the variable being tested apparently has had no effect.

Example Perhaps you are looking at a table from an experiment designed to test the hypothesis: If premium gas is more efficient, then it should increase the fuel mileage of our family car. Look back at **Figure 19** showing the results of this experiment. In this example, the use of regular gasoline in the family car was the control, while the car being fueled by premium gasoline was the test group.

Data showed a quantitative difference in efficiency for gasoline consumption. It took 0.059 gallons of regular gasoline to travel one mile, while it took 0.064 gallons of the premium gasoline to travel the same distance. The regular gasoline was more efficient; it increased the fuel mileage of the family car.

What are data? In the experiment described on these pages, measurements were taken so that at the end of the experiment, you had something concrete to interpret. You had numbers to work with. Not every experiment that you do will give you data in the form of numbers. Sometimes, data will be in the form of a description. At the end of a chemistry experiment, you might have noted that

Figure 21

one solution turned yellow when treated with a particular chemical, and another remained colorless, as water, when treated with the same chemical. Data, therefore, are stated in different forms for different types of scientific experiments.

Are all experiments alike? Keep in mind as you perform experiments in science that not every experiment makes use of all of the parts that have been described on these pages. For some, it may be difficult to design an experiment that will always have a control. Other experiments are complex enough that it may be hard to have only one dependent variable. Real scientists encounter many variations in the methods that they use when they perform experiments. The skills in this handbook are here for you to use and practice. In real situations, their uses will vary.

Science Skill Handbook

Representing and Applying Data

Interpreting Scientific Illustrations

As you read a science textbook, you will see many drawings, diagrams, and photographs. Illustrations help you to understand what you read. Some illustrations are included to help you understand an idea that you can't see easily by yourself. For instance, we can't see atoms, but we can look at a diagram of an atom and that helps us to understand some things about atoms. Seeing something often helps you remember more easily. Illustrations also provide examples that clarify difficult concepts or give additional information about the topic you are studying. Maps, for example, help you to locate places that may be described in the text.

Examples

Captions and Labels Most illustrations have captions. A caption is a comment that identifies or explains the illustration. Diagrams, such as **Figure 22,** often have

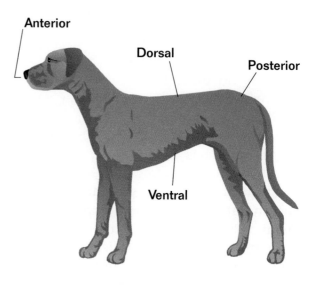

Figure 23 The orientation of a dog is shown here.

labels that identify parts of the organism or the order of steps in a process.

Learning with Illustrations An illustration of an organism shows that organism from a particular view or orientation. In order to understand the illustration, you may need to identify the front (anterior) end, tail (posterior) end, the underside (ventral), and the back (dorsal) side, as shown in **Figure 23.**

You might also check for symmetry. A shark in **Figure 24** has bilateral symmetry. This means that drawing an imaginary line through the center of the animal from the anterior to posterior end forms two mirror images.

Radial symmetry is the arrangement of similar parts around a central point. An object or organism, such as a hydra, can be divided anywhere through the center into similar parts.

Some organisms and objects cannot be divided into two similar parts. If an

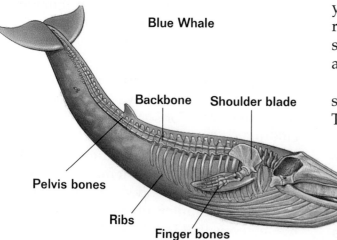

Figure 22 A labeled diagram of a blue whale

Figure 24 A shark (A) illustrating bilateral symmetry and a pear (B) illustrating a longitudinal section and a cross section

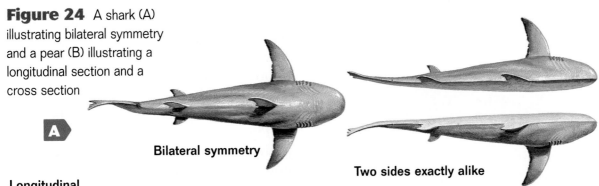

A

Bilateral symmetry

Two sides exactly alike

Longitudinal section

B

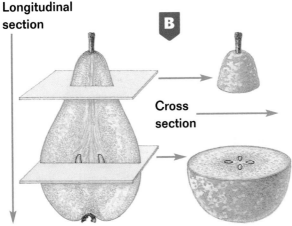

Cross section

organism or object cannot be divided, it is asymmetrical. Regardless of how you try to divide a natural sponge, you cannot divide it into two parts that look alike.

Some illustrations enable you to see the inside of an organism or object. These illustrations are called sections. **Figure 24** also illustrates some common sections.

Look at all illustrations carefully. Read captions and labels so that you understand exactly what the illustration is showing you.

Making Models

Have you ever worked on a model car, plane, or rocket? These models look, and sometimes work, much like the real thing, but they are often on a different scale than the real thing. In science, models are used to help simplify large or small processes or structures that otherwise would be dif-

ficult to see and understand. Your understanding of a structure or process is enhanced when you work with materials to make a model that shows the basic features of the structure or process.

Example In order to make a model, you first have to get a basic idea about the structure or process involved. You decide to make a model to show the differences in size of arteries, veins, and capillaries. First, read about these structures. All three are hollow tubes. Arteries are round and thick. Veins are flat and have thinner walls than arteries. Capillaries are small.

Now, decide what you can use for your model. Common materials are often most useful and cheapest to work with when making models. As illustrated in **Figure 25** on the next page, different kinds and sizes of pasta might work for these models. Different sizes of rubber tubing might do just as well. Cut and glue the different noodles or tubing onto thick paper so the openings can be seen. Then label each. Now you have a simple, easy-to-understand model showing the differences in size of arteries, veins, and capillaries.

What other scientific ideas might a model help you to understand? A model of a molecule can be made from balls of modeling clay (using different colors for the different elements present) and toothpicks (to show different chemical bonds).

Figure 25 Different types of pasta may be used to model blood vessels

A working model of a volcano can be made from clay, a small amount of baking soda, vinegar, and a bottle cap. Other models can be devised on a computer. Some models are mathematical and are represented by equations.

Measuring in SI

The metric system is a system of measurement developed by a group of scientists in 1795. It helps scientists avoid problems by providing standard measurements that all scientists around the world can understand. A modern form of the metric system, called the International System, or SI, was adopted for worldwide use in 1960.

The metric system is convenient because unit sizes vary by multiples of 10. When changing from smaller units to larger units, divide by 10. When changing from larger units to smaller, multiply by 10. For example, to convert millimeters to centimeters, divide the millimeters by 10. To convert 30 millimeters to centimeters, divide 30 by 10 (30 millimeters equal 3 centimeters).

Prefixes are used to name units. Look at **Figure 26** for some common metric prefixes and their meanings. Do you see how the prefix *kilo-* attached to the unit *gram* is *kilogram*, or 1000 grams? The prefix *deci-* attached to the unit *meter* is *decimeter*, or one-tenth (0.1) of a meter.

Examples

Length You have probably measured lengths or distances many times. The meter is the SI unit used to measure length. A baseball bat is about one meter long. When measuring smaller lengths, the meter is divided into smaller units called centimeters and millimeters. A centimeter is one-hundredth (0.01) of a meter, which is about the size of the width of the fingernail on your ring finger. A millimeter is one-thousandth of a meter (0.001), about the thickness of a dime.

Most metric rulers have lines indicating centimeters and millimeters, as shown in

Figure 26 Common metric prefixes

Metric Prefixes			
Prefix	Symbol	Meaning	
kilo-	k	1000	thousand
hecto-	h	200	hundred
deca-	da	10	ten
deci-	d	0.1	tenth
centi-	c	0.01	hundredth
milli-	m	0.001	thousandth

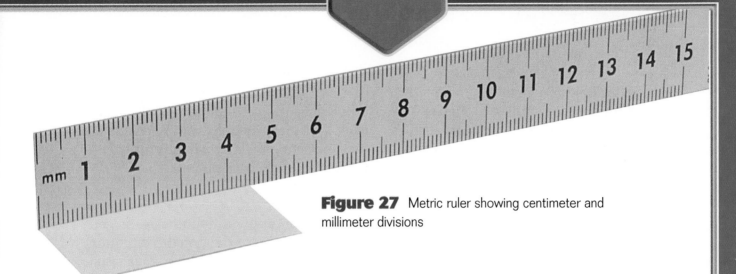

Figure 27 Metric ruler showing centimeter and millimeter divisions

Figure 27. The centimeter lines are the longer, numbered lines; the shorter lines are millimeter lines. When using a metric ruler, line up the 0-centimeter mark with the end of the object being measured, and read the number of the unit where the object ends, in this instance 4.5 cm.

Surface Area Units of length are also used to measure surface area. The standard unit of area is the square meter (m²). A square that's one meter long on each side has a surface area of one square meter. Similarly, a square centimeter, (cm²), shown in **Figure 28,** is one centimeter long on each side. The surface area of an object is determined by multiplying the length times the width.

Volume The volume of a rectangular solid is also calculated using units of length. The cubic meter (m³) is the standard SI unit of volume. A cubic meter is a cube one meter on each side. You can determine the volume of rectangular solids by multiplying length times width times height.

Liquid Volume During science activities, you will measure liquids using beakers and graduated cylinders marked in milliliters, as illustrated in **Figure 29.** A graduated cylinder is a cylindrical container marked with lines from bottom to top.

Liquid volume is measured using a unit called a liter. A liter has the volume of 1000 cubic centimeters. Because the prefix *milli-* means thousandth (0.001), a milliliter equals one cubic centimeter. One milliliter of liquid would completely fill a cube measuring one centimeter on each side.

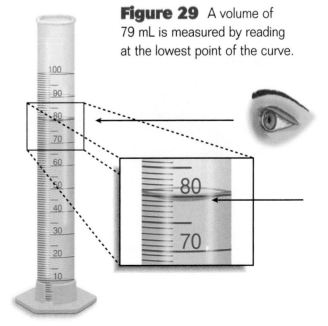

Figure 29 A volume of 79 mL is measured by reading at the lowest point of the curve.

Figure 28 A square centimeter

1 cm

1 cm

Mass Scientists use balances to find the mass of objects in grams. You might use a beam balance similar to **Figure 30.** Notice that on one side of the balance is a pan and on the other side is a set of beams. Each beam has an object of a known mass called a *rider* that slides on the beam.

Before you find the mass of an object, set the balance to zero by sliding all the riders back to the zero point. Check the pointer on the right to make sure it swings an equal distance above and below the zero point on the scale. If the swing is unequal, find and turn the adjusting screw until you have an equal swing.

Place an object on the pan. Slide the rider with the largest mass along its beam until the pointer drops below zero. Then move it back one notch. Repeat the process on each beam until the pointer swings an equal distance above and below the zero point. Add the masses on each beam to find the mass of the object.

You should never place a hot object or pour chemicals directly onto the pan. Instead, find the mass of a clean beaker or a glass jar. Place the dry or liquid chemicals in the container. Then find the combined mass of the container and the chemicals. Calculate the mass of the chemicals by subtracting the mass of the empty container from the combined mass.

Predicting

When you apply a hypothesis, or general explanation, to a specific situation, you predict something about that situation. First, you must identify which hypothesis fits the situation you are considering.

Examples People use prediction to make everyday decisions. Based on previous observations and experiences, you may form a hypothesis that if it is wintertime, then temperatures will be lower. From past experience in your area, temperatures are lowest in February. You may then use this hypothesis to predict specific temperatures and weather for the month of February in advance. Someone could use these predictions to plan to set aside more money for heating bills during that month.

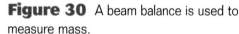

Figure 30 A beam balance is used to measure mass.

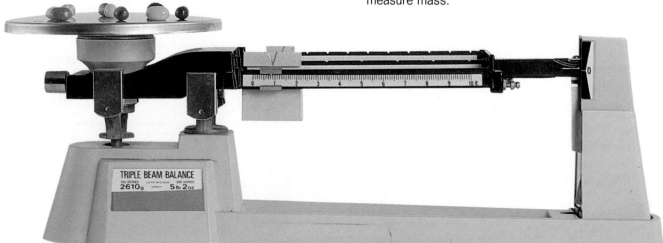

Using Numbers

When working with large populations of organisms, scientists usually cannot observe or study every organism in the population. Instead, they use a sample or a portion of the population. To sample is to take a small representative portion of organisms of a population for research. By making careful observations or manipulating variables within a portion of a group, information is discovered and conclusions are drawn that might then be applied to the whole population.

Scientific work also involves estimating. To estimate is to make a judgment about the size of something or the number of something without actually measuring or counting every member of a population.

Examples Suppose you are trying to determine the effect of a specific nutrient on the growth of black-eyed Susans. It would be impossible to test the entire population of black-eyed Susans, so you would select part of the population for your experiment. Through careful experimentation and observation on a sample of the population, you could generalize the effect of the chemical on the entire population.

Here is a more familiar example. Have you ever tried to guess how many beans were in a sealed jar? If you did, you were estimating.

What if you knew the jar of beans held one liter (1000 mL)? If you knew that 30 beans would fit in a 100-milliliter jar, how many beans would you estimate to be in the one-liter jar? If you said about 300 beans, your estimate would be close to the actual number of beans. Can you estimate how many jelly beans are on the cookie sheet in **Figure 31?**

Scientists use a similar process to estimate populations of organisms from bacteria to buffalo. Scientists count the actual number of organisms in a small sample and then estimate the number of organisms in a larger area. For example, if a scientist wanted to count the number of bacterial colonies in a petri dish, a microscope could be used to count the number of organisms in a one-square-centimeter sample. To determine the total population of the culture, the number of organisms in the square-centimeter sample is multiplied by the total number of square centimeters in the culture.

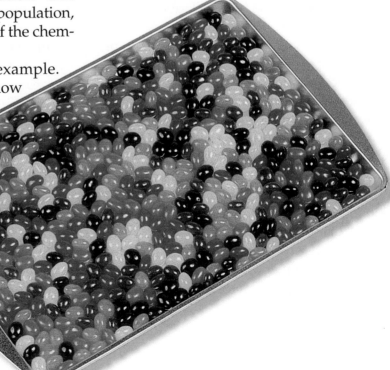

Figure 31

Sampling a group of jelly beans allows for an estimation of the total number of jelly beans in the group.

Technology Skill Handbook

Using a Word Processor

Suppose your teacher has assigned you to write a report. After you've done your research and decided how you want to write the information, you need to put all that information on paper. The easiest way to do this is with a word processor.

A word processor is a computer program in which you can write your information, change it as many times as you need to, and then print it out so that it looks neat and clean. You can also use a word processor to create tables and columns, add bullets or cartoon art, include page numbers, and even check your spelling.

Example Last week in Science class, your teacher assigned a report on the history of the atom. It has to be double spaced and include at least one table. You've collected all the facts, and you're ready to write your report. Sitting down at your computer, you decide you want to begin by explaining early scientific ideas about the atom and then talk about what scientists think about the atom now.

After you've written the two parts of your report, you decide to put a heading or subtitle above each part and add a title to the paper. To make each of these look different from the rest of your report, you can use a word processor to make the words bigger and bolder. The word processor also can double space your entire report, so that you don't have to add an extra space between each line.

You decide to include a table that lists each scientist that contributed to the theory of the atom along with his or her contribution. Using your word processor, you can create a table with as many rows and columns as you need. And, if you forget to include a scientist in the middle, you can go back and insert a row in the middle of your table without redoing the entire table.

When you've finished with your report, you can tell the word processor to check your spelling. If it finds misspelled words, it often will suggest a word you can use to replace the misspelled word. But, remember that the word processor may not know how to spell all the words in your report. Scan your report and double check your spelling with a dictionary if you're not sure if a word is spelled correctly.

After you've made sure that your report looks just the way you want it on the screen, the word processor will print your report on a printer. With a word processor, your report can look like it was written by a real scientist.

Helpful Hints

- If you aren't sure how to do something using your word processor, look under the help menu. You can look up how to do something, and the word processor will tell you how to do it. Just follow the instructions that the word processor puts on your screen.

- Just because you've spelled checked your report doesn't mean that the spelling is perfect. The spell check can't catch misspelled words that look like other words. So, if you've accidentally typed *mind* instead of *mine*, the spell checker won't know the difference. Always reread your report to make sure you didn't miss any mistakes.

Technology Skill Handbook

Using a Database

Imagine you're in the middle of research project. You are busily gathering facts and information. But, soon you realize that its becoming harder and harder to organize and keep track of all the information. The tool to solve "information overload" is a database. A database is exactly what it sounds like—a base on which to organize data. Similar to how a file cabinet organizes records, a database also organizes records. However, a database is more powerful than a simple file cabinet because at the click of a mouse, the entire contents can be reshuffled and reorganized. At computer-quick speeds, databases can sort information by any characteristic and filter data into multiple categories. Once you use a database, you will be amazed at how quickly all those facts and bits of information become manageable.

Example For the past few weeks, you have been gathering information on living and extinct primates. A database would be ideal to organize your information. An entry for gorillas might contain fields (categories) for fossil locations, brain size, average height, earliest fossil, and so on. Later on, if you wanted to know which primates have been found in Asia, you could quickly filter all entries using Asia in the field that listed locations. The database will scan all the entries and select the entries containing Asia. If you wanted to rank all the primates by arm length, you would sort all the entries by arm length. By using different combinations of sorting and filtering, you can discover relationships between the data that otherwise might remain hidden.

Helpful Hints

- Before setting up your own database, it's easier to learn the features of your database software by practicing with an established database.
- Entering the data into a database can be time consuming. Learn shortcuts such as tabbing between entry fields and automatic formatting of data that your software may provide.
- Get in the habit of periodically saving your database as you are entering data. That way, if something happens and your computer locks up or the power goes out, you won't lose all of your work.

Most databases have specific words you can use to narrow your search.

- AND: If you place an AND between two words in your search, the database will look for any entries that have both the words. For example, "blood AND cell" would give you information about both blood and cells.
- OR: If you place an OR between two words, the database will show entries that have at least one of the words. For example, "bird OR fish" would show you information on either birds or fish.
- NOT: If you place a NOT between two words, the database will look for entries that have the first word but do not have the second word. For example, "reproduction NOT plant" would show you information about reproduction but not about plant reproduction.

Technology Skill Handbook

Using Graphics Software

Having trouble finding that exact piece of art you're looking for? Do you have a picture in your mind of what you want but can't seem to find the right graphic to represent your ideas? To solve these problems, you can use graphics software. Graphics software allows you to change and create images and diagrams in almost unlimited ways. Typical uses for graphics software include arranging clip-art, changing scanned images, and constructing pictures from scratch. Most graphics-software applications work in similar ways. They use the same basic tools and functions. Once you master one graphics application, you can use any other graphics application relatively easily.

Example For your report on bird adaptations, you want to make a poster displaying a variety of beak and foot types. You have acquired many photos of birds, scanned from magazines and downloaded off the Internet. Using graphics software, you separate the beaks and feet from the birds and enlarge them. Then, you use arrows and text to diagram the particular features that you want to highlight. You also highlight the key features in color, keeping the rest of the graphic in black and white. With graphics software, the possibilities are endless. For the final layout, you place the picture of the bird next to enlarged graphics of the feet and beak. Graphics software allows you to integrate text into your diagrams, which makes your bird poster look clean and professional.

Helpful Hints
- As with any method of drawing, the more you practice using the graphic software, the better your results.
- Start by using the software to manipulate existing drawings. Once you master this, making your own illustrations will be easier.
- Clip art is available on CD-ROMs, and on the Internet. With these resources, finding a piece of clip art to suit your purposes is simple.
- As you work on a drawing, save it often.
- Often you can learn a lot from studying other people's art. Look at other computer illustrations and try to figure out how the artist created it.

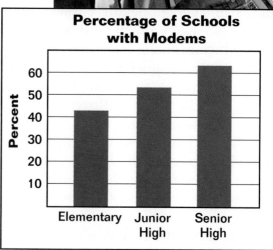

Percentage of Schools with Modems

Using a Computerized Card Catalog

When you have a report or paper to research, you go to the library. To find the information, skill is needed in using a computerized card catalog. You use the computerized card catalog by typing in a subject, the title of a book, or an author's name. The computer will list on the screen all the holdings the library has on the subject, title, or author requested.

A library's holdings include books, magazines, databases, videos, and audio materials. When you have chosen something from this list, the computer will show whether an item is available and where in the library to find it.

Example You have a report due on dinosaurs, and you need to find three books on the subject. In the library, follow the instructions on the computer screen to select the "Subject" heading. You could start by typing in the word *dinosaurs*. This will give you a list of books on that subject. Now you need to narrow your search to the kind of dinosaur you are interested in, for example, *Tyrannosaurus rex*. You can type in *Tyrannosaurus rex* or just look through the list to find titles that you think would have information you need. Once you have selected a short list of books, click on each selection to find out if the library has the books. Then, check on where they are located in the library.

Helpful Hints

- Remember that you can use the computer to search by subject, author, or title. If you know a book's author, but not the title, you can search for all the books the library has by that author.
- When searching by subject, it's often most helpful to narrow your search by using specific search terms. If you don't find enough, you can then broaden your search.
- Pay attention to the type of materials found in your search. If you need a book, you can eliminate any videos or other resources that come up in your search.
- Knowing how your library is arranged can save a lot of time. The librarian will show you where certain types of material are kept and how to find something.

Technology Skill Handbook

Developing Multimedia Presentations

It's your turn—you have to present your science report to the entire class. How do you do it? You can use many different sources of information to get the class excited about your presentation. Posters, videos, photographs, sound, computers, and the Internet can help show our ideas. First, decide the most important points you want your presentation to make. Then, sketch out what materials and types of media would be best to illustrate those points. Maybe you could start with an outline on an overhead projector, then show a video, followed by something from the Internet or a slide show accompanied by music or recorded voices. Make sure you don't make the presentation too complicated, or you will confuse yourself and the class. Practice your presentation a few times for your parents or brothers and sisters before you present it to the class.

Example Your assignment is to give a presentation on bird-watching. You could have a poster that shows what features you use to identify birds, with a sketch of your favorite bird. A tape of the calls of your favorite bird or a video of birds in your area would work well with the poster. If possible, include an Internet site with illustrations of birds that the class can look at.

Helpful Hints

- Carefully consider what media will best communicate the point you are trying to make.
- Keep your topic and your presentation simple.
- Make sure you learn how to use any equipment you will be using in your presentation.
- Practice the presentation several times.
- If possible, set up all of the equipment ahead of time. Make sure everything is working correctly.

Technology Skill Handbook

Using E-Mail

It's science fair time and you want to ask a scientist a question about your project, but he or she lives far away. You could write a letter or make a phone call. But you can also use the computer to communicate. You can do this using electronic mail (E-mail). You will need a computer that is connected to an E-mail network. The computer is usually hooked up to the network by a device called a *modem*. A modem works through the telephone lines. Finally, you need an address for the person you want to talk with. The E-mail address works just like a street address to send mail to that person.

Example There are just a few steps needed to send a message to a friend on an E-mail network. First, select Message from the E-mail software menu. Then, enter the E-mail address of your friend. Next, type your message. Make sure you

check it for spelling and other errors. Finally, click the Send button to mail your message and off it goes! You will get a reply back in your electronic mailbox. To read your reply, just click on the message and the reply will appear on the screen.

Helpful Hints

- Make sure that you have entered the correct address of the person you're sending the message to.
- Reread your message to make sure it says what you want to say, and check for spelling and grammar.
- If you receive an E-mail message, respond to it as soon as possible.
- If you receive frequent email messages, keep them organized by either deleting them, or saving them in folders according to the subject or sender.

Technology Skill Handbook

Using an Electronic Spreadsheet

Your science fair experiment has produced lots of numbers. How do you keep track of all the data, and how can you easily work out all the calculations needed? You can use a computer program called a *spreadsheet* to keep track of data that involve numbers. A spreadsheet is an electronic worksheet. Type in your data in rows and columns, just as in a data table on a sheet of paper. A spreadsheet uses some simple math to do calculations on the data. For example, you could add, subtract, divide, or multiply any of the values in the spreadsheet by another number. Or you can set up a series of math steps you want to apply to the data. If you want to add 12 to all the numbers and then multiply all the numbers by 10, the computer does all the calculations for you in the spreadsheet. Below is an example of a spreadsheet that is a schedule.

Example Let's say that to complete your project, you need to calculate the speed of the model cars in your experiment. Enter the distance traveled by each car in the rows of the spreadsheet. Then enter the time you recorded for each car to travel the measured distance in the column across from each car. To make the formula, just type in the equation you want the computer to calculate; in this case, *speed = distance ÷ time*. You must make sure the computer knows what data are in the rows and what data are in the

	A	B	C	D
	Test Runs	Time	Distance	Speed
1				
2	Car 1	5 mins.	5 miles	60 mph
3	Car 2	10 mins.	4 miles	24 mph
4	Car 3	6 mins.	3 miles	30 mph
5				
6				
7				
8				
9				
10				
11				
12				
13				
14				

columns so the calculation will be correct. Once all the distance and time data and the formula have been entered into the spreadsheet program, the computer will calculate the speed for all the trials you ran. You can even make graphs of the results.

Helpful Hints

- Before you set up the spreadsheet, sketch out how you want to organize the data. Include any formulas you will need to use.
- Make sure you have entered the correct data into the correct rows and columns.
- As you experiment with your particular spreadsheet program you will learn more of its features.
- You can also display your results in a graph. Pick the style of graph that best represents the data you are working with.

Technology Skill Handbook

Using a CD-ROM

What's your favorite music? You probably listen to your favorite music on compact discs (CDs). But, there is another use for compact discs, called CD-ROM. CD-ROM means Compact Disc-Read Only Memory. CD-ROMs hold information. Whole encyclopedias and dictionaries can be stored on CD-ROM discs. This kind of CD-ROM and others are used to research information for reports and papers. The information is accessed by putting the disc in your computer's CD-ROM drive and following the computer's installation instructions. The CD-ROM will have words, pictures, photographs, and maybe even sound and video on a range of topics.

Example Load the CD-ROM into the computer. Find the topic you are interested in by clicking on the Search button. If there is no Search button, try the Help button. Most CD-ROMs are easy to use, but refer to the Help instructions if you have problems. Use the arrow keys to move down through the list of titles on your topic. When you double-click on a title, the article will appear on the screen. You can print the article by clicking on the Print button. Each CD-ROM is different. Click the Help menu to see how to find what you want.

Helpful Hints

- Always open and close the CD-ROM drive on your computer by pushing the button next to the drive. Pushing on the tray to close it will stress the opening mechanism over time.
- Place the disc in the tray so the side with no printing is facing down.
- Read through the installation instructions that come with the CD-ROM.
- Remember to remove the CD-ROM before you shut your computer down.

Using Probeware

Data collecting in an experiment sometimes requires that you take the same measurement over and over again. With probeware, you can hook a probe directly to a computer and have the computer collect the data about temperature, pressure, motion, or pH. Probeware is a combination sensor and software that makes the process of collecting data easier. With probes hooked to computers, you can make many measurements quickly, and you can collect data over a long period of time without needing to be present. Not only will the software record the data, most software will graph the data.

Example Suppose you want to monitor the health of an enclosed ecosystem. You might use an oxygen and a carbon dioxide sensor to monitor the gas concentrations or humidity or temperature. If the gas concentrations remain stable, you could predict that the ecosystem is healthy. After all the data is collected, you can use the software to graph the data and analyze it. With probeware, experimenting is made efficient and precise.

Helpful Hints

- Find out how to properly use each probe before using it.
- Make sure all cables are solidly connected. A loose cable can interrupt the data collection and give you inaccurate results.
- Because probeware makes data collection so easy, do as many trials as possible to strengthen your data.

Technology Skill Handbook

Using a Graphing Calculator

Science can be thought of as a means to predict the future and explain the past. In other language, if x happens, can we predict y? Can we explain the reason y happened? Simply, is there a relationship between x and y? In nature, a relationship between two events or two quantities, x and y, often occur. However, the relationship is often complicated and can only be readily seen by making a graph. To analyze a graph, there is no quicker tool than a graphing calculator. The graphing calculator shows the mathematical relationship between two quantities.

Example If you have collected data on the position and time for a migrating whale, you can use the calculator to graph the data. Using the linear regression function on the calculator, you can determine the average migration speed of the whale. The more you use the graphing calculator to solve problems, the more you will discover its power and efficiency.

Graphing calculators have some keys that other calculators do not have. The keys on the bottom half of the calculator are those found on all scientific calculators. The keys located just below the screen are the graphing keys. You will also notice the up, down, left, and right arrow keys. These allow you to move the cursor around on the screen, to "trace" graphs that have been plotted, and to choose items from the menus. The other keys located on the top of the calculator access the special features such as statistical computations and programming features.

A few of the keystrokes that can save you time when using the graphing calculator are listed below.

- The commands above the calculator keys are accessed with the [2nd] or [ALPHA] key. The [2nd] key and its commands are yellow and the [ALPHA] and its commands are green.
- [2nd] [ENTRY] copies the previous calculation so you can edit and use it again.
- Pressing [ON] while the calculator is graphing stops the calculator from completing the graph.
- [2nd] [QUIT] will return you to the home (or text) screen.
- [2nd] [A-LOCK] locks the [ALPHA] key, which is like pressing "shift lock" or "caps lock" on a typewriter or computer. The result is that all letters will be typed and you do not have to repeatedly press the [ALPHA] key. (This is handy for programming.) Stop typing letters by pressing [ALPHA] again.
- [2nd] [OFF] turns the calculator off.

Helpful Hints

- Mastering the graphing calculator takes practice. Don't expect to learn it all in an afternoon.
- Programming a graphing calculator takes a plan. Write out all of the steps before entering them.
- It's easiest to learn how to program the calculator by first using programs that have already been written. As you enter them, figure out what each step is telling the calculator to do.

Skill Activities

Table of Contents

Measuring Length

Background

We have many different units for measuring sizes and distances. It is important to know how to select the most useful unit for measuring the length of a particular object or distance. Units that are used for measuring the distance an animal can run would not be useful for measuring the length of the animal's tooth. Read this problem and answer the questions below.

What units are most useful for measuring various lengths?

Procedure 🥽

1. Using a meter stick or ruler, measure the length of your classroom in meters (m), centimeters (cm), and millimeters (mm). Record the measurements in a table like the one shown below.

2. Measure the length of this book and a pencil eraser in meters, centimeters, and millimeters. Record the measurements in your table.

3. Choose more items to measure. Record your measurements in your table.

Practicing the SKILL

1. What difficulties did you encounter while making your measurements?

2. Which unit would you select if you were to measure the length of the school parking lot?

3. Which unit would you select if you were to measure the length of an insect? Why?

For more skill practice, do the Chapter 1 Interactive Exploration on the **Science Voyages Level Green CD-ROM.**

GLENCOE TECHNOLOGY

Lengths of Items			
	Length in Meters	**Length in Centimeters**	**Length in Millimeters**
Classroom			
Textbook			
Pencil Eraser			

Interpreting Scientific Illustrations

Background

Every cell carries on the complex chemical processes required to survive as an organism or as part of an organism. Some chemical processes are the same for plant and animal cells. Because of this, plant and animal cells have similar parts but there are differences.

How does a scientific illustration help you understand what you read?

Use the illustrations to determine the similarities and differences between plant and animal cells.

Procedure

1. Observe the illustrations.

2. Carefully read the labels and follow the line(s) from each label to the cell part(s).

3. Record the location of each cell part as animal, plant, or both in a table like the one below.

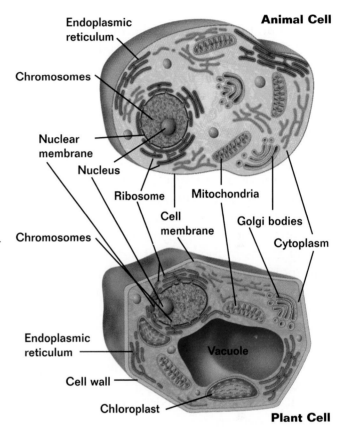

Animal Cell

Endoplasmic reticulum

Chromosomes

Nuclear membrane

Nucleus

Ribosome

Cell membrane

Mitochondria

Golgi bodies

Cytoplasm

Chromosomes

Endoplasmic reticulum

Vacuole

Cell wall

Chloroplast

Plant Cell

Cell Data	
Cell Part	**Location**
cell membrane	
nucleus	
cytoplasm	
cell wall	
endoplasmic reticulum	
ribosomes	
Golgi bodies	
mitochondria	
chloroplasts	
chromosomes	
vacuol	

Practicing the SKILL

1. Identify the cell parts found in both cells.

2. Identify the cell parts found only in an animal cell and those found only in a plant cell.

For more skill practice, do the Chapter 2 Interactive Exploration on the **Science Voyages Level Green CD-ROM.**

GLENCOE TECHNOLOGY

Skill Activity

Using Numbers

Background

H$_2$O and C$_6$H$_{12}$O$_6$ are chemical formulas for water and sugar, respectively. Each represents one molecule of the compound.

What do the numbers in chemical formulas tell us?

The letters are the symbols for elements. Each element symbol is written as one upper case letter or an upper case letter followed by a lower case letter. Numbers in formulas are called subscripts. A subscript is written below and after an element's symbol. It tells how many atoms of the element before it, are in the molecule. If there is no subscript, it means that there is just one atom of that element. Sometimes two or more elements are inside a set of parentheses followed by a subscript. This means that the number of atoms of each element inside the parentheses is multiplied by the subscript. For example, (H$_2$0)$_3$ is six atoms of hydrogen and three atoms of oxygen.

Procedure

Complete the table below. Look at the Periodic Table of Elements in the back of your book to identify the element symbols.

Practicing the SKILL

1. What do numbers as subscripts mean?

2. Which substance(s) have the most elements?

3. Which substance(s) have the most atoms?

For more skill practice, do the Chapter 3 Interactive Exploration on the **Science Voyages Level Green CD-ROM.**

Chemical Formulas					
Formula	Element/ number of atoms	Element/ number of atoms	Element/ number of atoms	Element/ number of atoms	Total number of atoms
CO$_2$					
CaCO$_3$					
NaC$_2$H$_3$O$_2$					
C$_3$H$_7$OH					
C$_{12}$H$_{22}$O$_{11}$					
Al(OH)$_3$					
Ba$_3$(PO$_4$)$_2$					

Designing an Experiment to Test a Hypothesis

Background

Sam's teacher has a sweet potato vine growing on a windowsill in the classroom. The sweet potato is submerged halfway in water in a glass jar. The sweet potato has toothpicks inserted around its middle to support it. Stems and leaves grow from the part of the sweet potato above the water. Roots grow from the part of the sweet potato that is under water. Sam's teacher tells the class that the sweet potato is a root. Sam thinks that if a root can grow a new plant, maybe other plant parts can grow new plants. He decides to test this idea. How does Sam begin? He may start by asking others about how to grow plants without using seeds. Then, he may read about different ways to grow new plants. Finally, Sam decides to do an experiment to see what plant parts can be used to grow new plants.

Do this activity to design an experiment that could test Sam's idea.

Procedure

1. Form a hypothesis about which parts of a plant might grow into a new plant when planted in soil.

2. Design an experiment to test your hypothesis. Be sure to include a control and identify the variable.

3. List the steps needed to complete the experiment. Be as specific as possible.

4. Make a list of materials needed to do the experiment.

5. Decide what data and observations will be taken and how they will be recorded.

6. Decide how results will be analyzed and presented.

7. Have your teacher check your design.

Practicing the SKILL

1. Compare your design to those of your classmates.

2. What is the variable in your experiment.

3. What could be sources of error?

For more skill practice, do the Chapter 4 Interactive Exploration on the **Science Voyages Level Green CD-ROM.**

GLENCOE TECHNOLOGY

Sequencing

Background

Sequence diagrams illustrate in a simple way series of events in the order in which they occur. The events in the life cycle of a plant are represented by a series of diagrams that show how the separate stages of the life cycle pass from one to the other.

What are the stages and events in the life cycle of a fern?

Each stage in the life cycle of a plant, such as a fern, occurs in a particular order. This order is indicated by the use of arrows that are placed between the stages. The drawings in a sequence diagram are labeled to identify each stage and the important structures of each drawing.

Procedure

1. Examine **Figure 5-6** in Chapter 5. This diagram shows drawings of the individual stages in the life cycle of a fern.

2. Observe the number and direction of the arrows that are drawn between each stage of the life cycle.

3. Copy the Fern Observations table on this page. Record three events in the fern gametophyte stage and three in the sporophyte stage on the table.

4. Examine **Figure 5-9** in Chapter 5. Copy the Pine Observations table on this page. Number the items listed in the correct order as they occur in a pine's life cycle.

Fern Observations	
Gametophyte Stage	**Sporophyte Stage**
1.	
2.	
3.	

Pine Observations	
Gametophyte Stage	**Sporophyte Stage**
pollen grains	
fertilization	
pollen cone	
embryo forms	
seed dispersal	

Practicing the SKILL

1. How many stages are there in the life cycle of a fern?

2. In which stage are spores formed?

3. In which stage are sex organs formed?

4. What structure begins the sporophyte stage?

For more skill practice, do the Chapter 5 Interactive Exploration on the **Science Voyages Level Green CD-ROM.**

GLENCOE TECHNOLOGY

Making and Using Graphs

Background

A graph is a diagram that shows the relationship of one variable to another. Graphs are a useful tool for scientists because they have many practical uses. Graphs can be used to organize a large amount of data into a more manageable format. When data is put into a graph, it is easier to see patterns that develop. This helps the scientist with the interpretation and analysis of the data. It also helps scientists determine if the original hypothesis is correct. Graphs are also helpful when presenting your conclusions to others. It presents the data in an already organized, easily understood format.

Procedure

1. Using a metric ruler, measure the length between the tip of your thumb and the tip of your little finger (excluding your fingernails) to the nearest centimeter. This is your handspan.

2. Record your handspan measurement and those of your classmates on the board.

3. Make a table like the one shown. Count the number of students with each handspan for the different measurements given. Record these numbers in your table.

4. Sets of variable data, such as handspan, can be plotted on a graph. Line graphs are used to show variation. Draw a graph on a sheet of paper. Label the horizontal (x) axis *Handspan Length*. Label the vertical (y) axis *Number of Students*.

5. Plot the number of students with each handspan measurement. Draw a curved line to connect the dots.

6. The *range* of a set of data is the difference between the greatest and the least number. The *median* is the middle number when the data are placed in order. The *mean* is the sum of the numbers divided by the number of measurements taken. The *mode* is the number that appears most often. Using the graph you have just made, find all of these numbers.

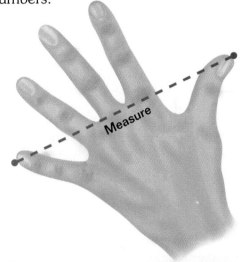

Measure

Handspan Measurements									
Handspan (cm)	12	13	14	15	16	17	18	19	20
Numbers									

Practicing the SKILL

1. What does the graph tell you about the amount of genetic variation in the population you sampled?

For more skill practice, do the Chapter 6 Interactive Exploration on the **Science Voyages Level Green CD-ROM.**

GLENCOE TECHNOLOGY

Making and Using Graphs

Background

A bar graph is used to compare similar things that show variations. The numbers of each group are normally plotted on the vertical y-axis. The horizontal x-axis is used for plotting each separate group. The data are graphed within separate bars.

Procedure

(1) Examine Table 7-1 of the Geologic Time Scale in Chapter 7. Observe the names listed under the heading *Period*.

(2) Calculate the length of time for each period. The first two have been done for you in the table shown here.

Geologic Time	
Period	**Length of Period in Millions of Years**
Quaternary	$1.6 - 0 = 1.6$
Tertiary	$66 - 1.6 = 64.4$

(3) Make a bar graph showing the length of time for each period.

(4) Mark the number of years up the vertical axis. (Each block on the graph paper should represent one million years.) Make the highest number on this line the highest number of years calculated in your table. The bottom of the vertical line is 0.

(5) List the periods along the horizontal axis starting with Cambrian on the left and going to Quaternary. Allow one block on the graph paper for each period.

(6) Complete the graph by drawing each bar the correct height for the number of years. Color in each bar.

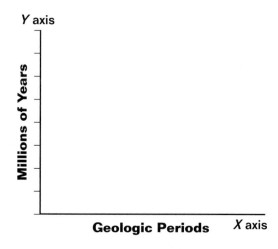

Y axis

Millions of Years

Geologic Periods   X axis

Practicing the SKILL

(1) Other than Precambrian, which period lasted the longest time?

(2) Which period is the shortest?

(3) What kind of pattern in the lengths of periods can be seen from the graph?

(4) Why is a graph more helpful than a table in comparing geologic time periods?

For more skill practice, do the Chapter 7 Interactive Exploration on the **Science Voyages Level Green CD-ROM.**

GLENCOE TECHNOLOGY

Observing and Inferring

Background

Scientists classify organisms because they are related in some way or several ways. One group of related animals is the Phylum Arthropoda. It has one of the largest groups of animals, the Class Insecta.

How can insects be classified?

The Class Insecta is divided into orders that are smaller groups with similar features. Below are the Latin names and wing descriptions for five orders of insects.

- *Hymenoptera* means "membrane wing" and both pair of wings are thin and transparent.

- *Coleoptera* means "sheath wing," and the front wings are hard coverings that protect a pair of membranous wings and the insect's abdomen.

- *Hemiptera* means "half wing." One half of the front wing is thick and leathery, and the other half is membranous.

- *Lepidoptera* means "scale wing," which describes the powdery scales on the wings.

- *Orthoptera* means "straight wing," and some members of this group have long straight wings.

Procedure

① Copy the Insect Observations table in your Science Journal.

② Examine the eight insects shown on this page.

③ From their appearance, decide which insects belong in which order and write their names in your Insect Observations table.

Insect Observations

Order	Insects
Hymenoptera	
Coleoptera	
Hemiptera	
Lepidoptera	
Orthoptera	

Practicing the SKILL

① How might this sort of classification be useful to people who study insects?

② Using the same eight insects, make another classification of them.

For more skill practice, do the Chapter 8 Interactive Exploration on the **Science Voyages Level Green CD-ROM.**

GLENCOE TECHNOLOGY

Interpreting Data

Background

Bacteriologists are people who study microorganisms, grow bacteria in dishes, and perform experiments on them. Although individual bacteria are too small to see with the naked eye, colonies that contain large numbers of bacteria are visible. The color and shape of the colony can help to identify the type of bacteria.

Scientists often use tables to organize data from experiments. Having data laid out in a logical way makes it easier to interpret. To interpret means to explain why something is the way it is. Interpreting data is determining why you got the results you did. Reading the following procedure and studying the data table will help you learn to interpret data.

Bacterial Growth		
Dish	Square	Observations
1	hydrogen peroxide	a few colonies are observed
	mouthwash	many colonies are observed
	alcohol	very little growth under square or in surrounding area
	disinfectant	no growth under square or in surrounding area
2	none	hundreds of colonies are present
3	none	no colonies are observed

Procedure

1. Imagine you are a bacteriologist trying to determine which household item is most effective in preventing the growth of bacteria. You design an experiment in which you have three sterile petri dishes that contain nutrient agar. You rub your finger over the entire surface of the agar in dishes 1 and 2 to introduce bacteria.

2. Next, you cut four small squares of filter paper, soaking them each in one of the following substances: hydrogen peroxide, mouthwash, alcohol, and disinfectant. They are labeled and placed in dish 1, without touching or overlapping. All three petri dishes are covered and placed in a warm, dark place for two days.

3. At the end of two days, you take out each dish to observe any growth. The Bacterial Growth table is a record of your observations.

Practicing the SKILL

1. According to the data above, which substance was most effective in preventing bacterial growth? Which was least effective?

2. In dish 2, bacteria were added but no substance was placed in the dish. What was the purpose of this?

3. Dish 3 contained neither bacteria nor a substance. What purpose did this dish serve?

For more skill practice, do the Chapter 9 Interactive Exploration on the **Science Voyages Level Blue CD-ROM.**

GLENCOE TECHNOLOGY

Making and Using Tables

Background

Tables are used to record information so that it can be understood easily. Tables help you find information quickly by summarizing information given in the text. A table is similar to a system of classification. Information is grouped in vertical columns so that similarities and differences can be recognized easily. A table has three main parts: a title, vertical columns, and column headings. Sometimes, horizontal lines are used to group the information further.

Procedure

1. Study **Table 10-1** in the Protists and Fungi chapter. Examine the title. Look down the four columns to see if the information is related to the title and to each of the column headings.

2. Examine the information in **Table 10-1.** Notice how all four columns contain information on plantlike protists.

3. Using **Table 10-1,** answer the questions under Practicing the Skill.

4. Make a table of your own, similar to **Table 10-1,** in which you compare the different types of fungi discussed in Section 10-2.

Practicing the SKILL

1. What is the purpose of **Table 10-1?**

2. Which plantlike protist is used to give food a creamy texture?

3. What two plantlike protists have flagella?

4. Which plantlike protist has an eye-spot?

5. What groups of protists contain one-celled organisms, and which contain many-celled organisms?

6. Which plantlike protist can cause red tide?

7. Which has cell walls that contain silica?

8. Which protist is an important food source?

9. Why are tables used?

For more skill practice, do the Chapter 10 Interactive Exploration on the **Science Voyages Level Blue CD-ROM.**

GLENCOE TECHNOLOGY

Classifying

Background

Keys are used to identify things that are already classified.

In this Skill Activity, you will learn about some trees and how they have been classified. For this activity you need to know that needlelike leaves are shaped like needles and scalelike leaves are like the scales on a fish or a lizard.

How can you use a key to classify plants?

Procedure

1. Look at illustrations or actual examples of gymnosperm leaves.

2. Make a data table and record the number of each leaf down one side.

3. Use the key below to identify the leaves. There may be differences among the leaves. Choose the statement that describes most of the leaves on the branch. By following the key, the numbered steps will lead you to the name of the plant.

Key to Classifying Leaves

1. All leaves are needlelike.
   a. yes, go to 2
   b. no, go to 8

2. Needles are in clusters.
   a. yes, go to 3
   b. no, go to 4

3. Clusters contain 2, 3, or 5 needles.
   a. yes, pine
   b. no, cedar

4. Needles grow on all sides of the stem.
   a. yes, go to 5
   b. no, go to 7

5. Needles grow from a woody peg.
   a. yes, spruce
   b. no, go to 6

6. Needles appear to grow from the branch.
   a. yes, Douglas fir
   b. no, hemlock

7. Most of the needles grow upward.
   a. yes, fir
   b. no, redwood

8. All needles are scalelike but not prickly.
   a. yes, arborvitae
   b. no, juniper

Practicing the SKILL

1. What trait was used to separate the gymnosperm leaves into two groups?

2. What are two traits of a hemlock?

3. What gymnosperms have scalelike leaves?

4. Describe a spruce leaf.

5. How are pine and cedar leaves alike?

For more skill practice, do the Chapter 11 Interactive Exploration on the **Science Voyages Level Green CD-ROM.**

Comparing and Contrasting

Background

Determining the type of symmetry an animal has will help you describe the animal, as well as to determine what other animals it might be related to. In this Skill Activity, you will make some decisions about the type of symmetry of several animals.

Procedure

1. Review the discussion of symmetry in Section 12-1 of your textbook. Observe the animals pictured on this page.

2. Decide if the animal has radial symmetry, bilateral symmetry, or no symmetry.

3. Make a copy of the table below and record your answers in this table. If you need additional help, read about the animal's structure in reference books.

4. Explain how you decided what type of symmetry the animal has. Write your explanation in the table column labeled "Reason."

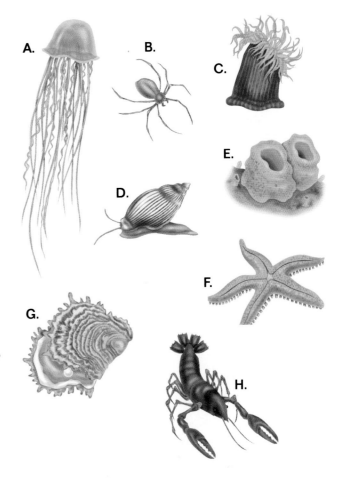

A. B. C. E. D. F. G. H.

Animal Symmetry		
Animal	**Symmetry**	**Reason**
jellyfish		
crayfish		
sponge		
spider		
sea star		
oyster		
snail		
sea anemone		

Practicing the SKILL

1. Which animals have radial symmetry? Bilateral symmetry? No symmetry?

2. What kind of symmetry do you think most animals have?

3. If an animal has a front and hind end, what kind of symmetry does it have?

For more skill practice, do the Chapter 12 Interactive Exploration on the **Science Voyages Level Green CD-ROM.**

GLENCOE TECHNOLOGY

Observing and Inferring

Background

Have you ever seen an animal track in the snow or mud? If you have, you probably tried to identify what animal left it there. You probably inferred what type of animal left it there based on observations you made about the area you were in.

Scientists also draw conclusions based on observations of the environment. In this activity, you will identify animal tracks and determine which animal made the tracks.

Procedure

1. Look at the figure below.

2. Decide which track belongs to which type of animal.

3. Copy the table in your Science Journal and record your answers.

4. Describe how each animal's foot is adapted to its environment.

Identifying Animal Tracks		
Animal	Track	Adaptation
Bear		
Beaver		
Cheetah		
Deer		
Horse		
Moose		
Raccoon		

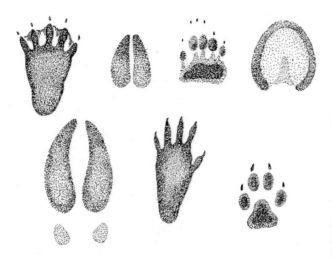

Practicing the SKILL

1. Could you expect to find a raccoon track in the same area you found a cheetah track? Explain.

2. What are the differences between track **b** and **e**? How does that help you identify the track?

For more skill practice, do the Chapter 13 Interactive Exploration on the **Science Voyages Level Green CD-ROM.**

GLENCOE TECHNOLOGY

Predicting

Background

Large populations of organisms need to be counted to determine the overall health of the species. However, counting each individual in a population can be time consuming and confusing. Therefore, scientists have developed methods of estimating the number of individuals in a population in order to save time. In this activity, you will predict the number of beetles by estimating the total number.

Ladybird Numbers		
Predicted number _____ Time _____		
Number in top left square	× Total number of squares	= Estimated total number
_____	_____	_____
Actual number _____ Time _____		

Procedure

1 Estimate the number of ladybird beetles in the figure to the right and record the number in a table like the one shown.

2 Place tracing paper over the diagram. Make a population count by placing a checkmark next to each ladybird beetle. Record the actual number of beetles in the table. Next to this number, record the amount of time it took to make the count.

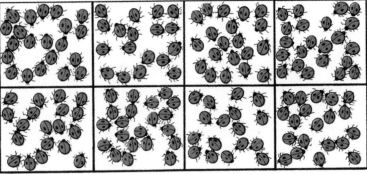

3 Count the ladybird beetle population a second time by sampling. A sample is made by selecting and counting only a portion of the population. Count the number of ladybird beetles in the top left square and record this number in the table.

4 Enter the total number of squares in the table. Multiply the number of ladybird beetles in the top left square by the total number of squares. Record this estimated total number in the table.

5 At the top of the table, record the amount of time it took to make the sample count.

Practicing the SKILL

1 How many ladybird beetles did you estimate were shown?

2 Which way was faster—making an actual count or sampling?

3 Were the results exactly the same?

For more skill practice, do the Chapter 14 Interactive Exploration on the **Science Voyages Level Green CD-ROM.**

Observing and Inferring

Background

Living things survive in their environments because they have behavioral and physical adaptations that allow them to live. For example, a jackrabbit will run when it sees a coyote. This is a behavioral adaptation. The jackrabbit also has strong legs. This is a physical adaptation. Both adaptations, working together, give the jackrabbit an advantage in escaping predators. In this activity, you will observe adaptations that help living things near your classroom survive.

Procedure

1. Read Section 2, Land Environments. Pay special attention to the Adaptations of Desert Plants and Animals.

2. In a table like the one shown below, record the names of five living things you find near your classroom.

3. Briefly describe two behavioral adaptations and two physical adaptations for each. Record these in your table.

4. Write how you think each of the adaptations might give each organism an advantage that allows it to survive in the wild.

Practicing the SKILL

1. Many birds, insects, and bats are able to fly. What are the advantages of this adaptation?

2. Many mammals in both hot and cold climates have thick fur. What might the advantages of this adaptation be?

For more skill practice, do the Chapter 15 Interactive Exploration on the **Science Voyages Level Green CD-ROM.**

 GLENCOE TECHNOLOGY

Organism Behavior			
Organism	**Physical adaptations**	**Behavioral adaptations**	**Advantages in the wild**

Interpreting Scientific Illustrations

Background

Using textbook illustrations is a helpful way to learn new information. Drawings in textbooks often have labeled, cutaway views of organs to show the internal structures of the organ. The cutaway view is called a sectional cut. A horizontal cut through an object is called a cross section. A vertical cut through an object is called a longitudinal, or long, section.

What does a sectional view of a bone show?

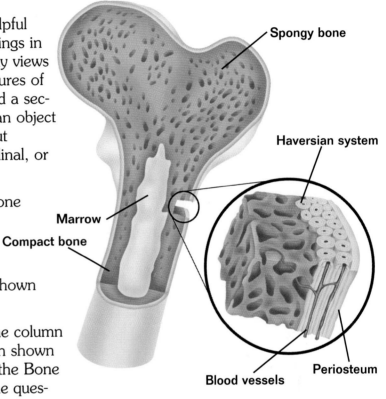

Spongy bone

Haversian system

Marrow

Compact bone

Periosteum

Blood vessels

Procedure

1. Make a data table like the one shown below.

2. Study the sections pictured in the column to the right. Use the information shown to complete the information in the Bone Parts table below and answer the questions in the Practicing the Skill box.

Bone Parts		
Bone Part	Description	Location in the Bone
periosteum		
compact bone		
spongy bone		
marrow		
blood supply		

Practicing the SKILL

1. How does the compact bone differ from the spongy bone in appearance?

2. What does a sectional view of a bone show that a solid uncut view does not show?

For more skill practice, do the Chapter 16 Interactive Exploration on the **Science Voyages Level Green CD-ROM.**

GLENCOE TECHNOLOGY

Interpreting Data

Background

Reading food labels can help a person make informed decisions about which product to buy. The United States Food and Drug Administration requires that all food labels list the name and net weight of the product. The name and address of the manufacturer, a list of ingredients, and the nutritional information per serving also are often listed. Nutrients must be listed in order of the amount by weight that the product contains. Often a column with the head RDA (recommended dietary allowance) is included on a label. The RDA is the amount of each vitamin and mineral a person needs each day for good health. RDAs listed on the labels are usually in percents and indicate what percentage of each vitamin or mineral that food provides.

How can the information on a food label be used?

Cereal A

Serving Size	2 oz.
Servings per container	2
Calories	100
Total Fat	1 g
Sodium	310 mg
Total Carbohydrates	0 g
Protein	12 g

Cereal B

Serving Size	2 oz.
Servings per container	2
Calories	230
Total Fat	8 g
Sodium	35 mg
Total Carbohydrates	28 g
Protein	15 g

Serving Size	2 oz.
Servings per container	2
Calories	140
Total Fat	4 g
Sodium	180 mg
Total Carbohydrates	32 g
Protein	7 g

Cereal C

Procedure

1. Read the food labels of Cereal A, B, and C.

2. Make a table like the Labels table below. Complete the table with the information from the food labels.

Labels			
2 oz serving	Cereal A	Cereal B	Cereal C
Calories			
Protein			
Carbohydrates			
Fat			
Sodium			

Practicing the SKILL

1. Which nutrient is in the largest amount in each of the products shown?

2. What are RDAs?

3. Bill must limit sodium intake. Which product should he buy? Why?

For more skill practice, do the Chapter 17 Interactive Exploration on the **Science Voyages Level Green CD-ROM.**

GLENCOE TECHNOLOGY

Concept Mapping

Background

The circulatory system consists of many parts with a wide variety of functions. Blood flows through the circulatory system. Some of the fluid from the blood moves into the body tissues and is returned to the circulatory system by the lymphatic system. Try the following activity to determine how concept maps help us organize information.

Procedure

1. Read Chapter 18. Pay special attention to the differences between and similarities of the cardiovascular and lymphatic systems.

2. Look at the concept map shown below. How is the information organized?

3. Using the concept map and the text, answer the questions in the Practicing the Skill box.

Practicing the SKILL

1. Compare and contrast the parts of the cardiovascular and lymphatic systems.

2. Compare the functions of the cardiovascular and lymphatic systems.

3. Compare the way blood and lymph are pumped through their vessels.

4. Lymph has little color. Blood is red. Explain the difference.

For more skill practice, do the Chapter 18 Interactive Exploration on the **Science Voyages Level Green CD-ROM.**

GLENCOE TECHNOLOGY

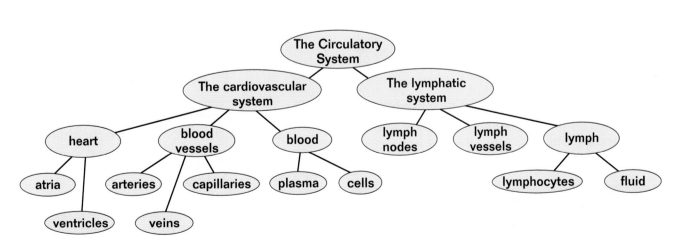

Making Models

Background

Sometimes it is useful to make a model of a system in order to understand it. It is difficult to see inside a human chest while a person is breathing, so you can make a model that works in a similar way.

How can you make a model of the human breathing mechanism?

Procedure

1. Look at the illustration on this page of a model of the lungs and diaphragm. This is a model on paper. In this skill, you will construct a physical model of the illustration.

2. Cut the bottom from a clear, 2-liter plastic bottle using scissors. **CAUTION:** *Always be careful when using scissors. Be careful of the sharp edges of the cut plastic as well.*

3. With your teacher's assistance, insert a y-shaped plastic tube upside down into the hole in a rubber stopper. Use a twist tie to fasten a balloon to each branch of the y-shaped tube.

4. Insert the rubber stopper into the top opening of the plastic bottle. The balloons should be inside the bottle.

5. Use a thick rubber band to tightly fasten the rubber sheet over the bottom opening of the bottle.

6. Push up gently on the rubber sheet. Observe the balloons inside the bottle. Record your observations in your Breathing Data table.

7. Pull down gently on the rubber sheet. Observe the balloons inside the bottle. Record your observations in your table.

Breathing Data		
Rubber Sheet	**Balloons Empty/Filled**	**Person Breathing Exhale/Inhale**
Pushed Up		
Pulled Down		

Practicing the SKILL

1. What happens when you push up and pull down on the rubber sheet?

2. When does air enter and leave the balloons? Why?

3. Draw the human respiratory system and compare it to the model. Label both.

For more skill practice, do the Chapter 19 Interactive Exploration on the **Science Voyages Level Green CD-ROM.**

GLENCOE TECHNOLOGY

Observing and Inferring

Background

People enjoy listening to music on a stereo that has multiple speakers placed in different areas. Dogs tilt their heads when they hear a strange sound. People turn their heads in various directions when they wonder where a sound is coming from. These actions occur while our brains are receiving information about the sounds. Two ears seem to be better than one. And, two ears on a moving head may be better than two held still.

Infer how humans can tell the direction of a sound.

Procedure

1. Put one person (the subject) in the center of the room with a blindfold on. Have eight people each sit in a circle three meters from the subject.

2. Have one of the eight people clap once. The subject is to point toward the source of the sound. If the subject points closer to the source of the sound than to any other person, count this as correct. Mark an X for each correct or incorrect response in a table like the one shown below.

3. Repeat the procedure until each of the eight people has clapped, in random order, two times.

4. Have the subject cover one ear with a small pillow or other sound-absorbing object. Repeat steps 1 through 3.

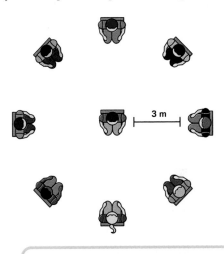

Practicing the SKILL

1. What differences in accuracy did you notice between listening with one ear and two?

2. Infer how this experiment helps you to understand the function of two ears.

3. Did the subject make any wrong guesses when listening with two ears? How do you explain this?

For more practice, do the Chapter 20 Interactive Exploration on the **Science Voyages Level Green CD-ROM.**

Hearing Chart																		
	Mark an X for Each Correct or Incorrect																	
Two Ears	Correct																	
	Incorrect																	
One Ear	Correct																	
	Incorrect																	

Interpreting Data

Background

Graphs present data in a way that is easier to interpret.

A human fetus grows at different rates during its development. In this activity, you will learn about rapid fetal growth and at which times during pregnancy it occurs.

When do the most changes in length and mass occur in a fetus?

Procedure

(1) Construct a graph similar to that shown in Graph A. Put time in weeks on the horizontal *x*-axis and length in millimeters on the vertical *y*-axis.

(2) On the graph, plot the data shown in the first two columns of the table. The first four points have been plotted for you.

(3) Construct a second graph similar to Graph B. Put time in weeks on the horizontal axis and mass in grams on the vertical axis.

(4) On the graph, plot the data shown in the first and third columns of the table. The first few points have been plotted for you.

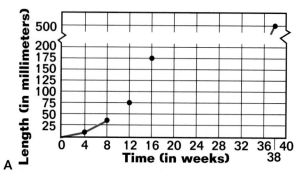

A

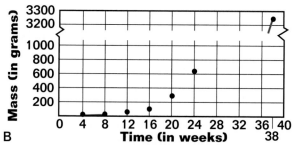

B

Change in Size of Average Developing Fetus

Time (weeks)	Length (mm)	Mass (g)
4	7	0.5
8	30	1
12	75	28
16	180	110
20	250	300
24	300	650
28	350	1200
32	410	2000
36	450	2200
38	500	3300

Practicing the SKILL

(1) How long is the average fetus at 15 weeks?

(2) How long is the average fetus at 34 weeks?

(3) At what week does the fetus reach half its full length?

(4) At what week does the fetus reach half its full mass?

For more skill practice, do the Chapter 21 Interactive Exploration on the **Science Voyages Level Green CD-ROM.**

GLENCOE TECHNOLOGY

Recognizing Cause and Effect

Background

As you have learned in this chapter, many diseases are caused by microorganisms. One way to prevent disease is through immunization. Another way to prevent disease is to monitor and evaluate our daily habits.

Personal Health		
	Health Habit	**✓ or —**
a	take a shower or bath each day	
b	wash hands before meals	
c	wash hands after going to bathroom	
d	wash hair three times each week	
e	brush hair each day	
f	brush teeth after meals	
g	floss teeth daily	
h	change socks and underclothes each day	
i	cut toenails each week	
j	trim fingernails each week	
k	exercise for 30 minutes three or four times each week	
l	eat three well-balanced meals each day	
m	eat breakfast each day	
n	eat high-fiber foods each day	
o	do not drink alcohol	
p	have a dental checkup twice a year	
q	have regular medical checkups	
r	sleep seven to eight hours each night	
s	maintain good posture at all times	
t	keep up to date with vaccinations	
u	wear a seat belt	

The following activity will help you recognize your responsibility.

Procedure

1. There are many steps you can follow to maintain personal health. Good habits can keep you healthy for many years. Examine the list of health habits in the chart.

2. Find those habits that you have developed.

3. From the list of health habits on the left, find the habits that you sometimes or never carry out and need to develop.

4. Make a table of habits like the one shown and make a checkmark next to those habits you have developed. Make a dash next to those habits that you need to develop.

Practicing the SKILL

1. Which habits involve exercise and diet?

2. Which habits are related to preventive health practices?

3. Which of the personal health habits do you need to improve?

4. What is one way to plan for good health?

5. How will having good health habits now benefit your future health?

For more skill practice, do the Chapter 22 Interactive Exploration on the **Science Voyages Level Green CD-ROM.**

English Glossary

This glossary defines each key term that appears in bold type in the text. It also shows the chapter and page number where you can find the word used.

Pronunciation Key

a...back (bak)	oh...go (goh)	sh...shelf (shelf)
ay...day (day)	aw...soft (sawft)	ch...nature (nay chur)
ah...father (fahth ur)	or...orbit (or but)	g...gift (gihft)
ow...flower (flow ur)	oy...coin (coyn)	j...gem (jem)
ar...car (car)	oo...foot (foot)	ing...sing (sing)
e...less (les)	ew...food (fewd)	zh...vision (vihzh un)
ee...leaf (leef)	yoo...pure (pyoor)	k...cake (kayk)
ih...trip (trihp)	yew...few (fyew)	s...seed, cent (seed, sent)
i (i + con + e)...idea	uh...comma (cahm uh)	z...zone, raise (zohn, rayz)
(i dee uh), life (life)	u (+ con)...flower (flo ur)	

A

abiotic factors: all the nonliving, physical features of the environment, including light, soil, water, and temperature, and that help determine which species can survive in an area. (ch. 14, p. 379)

active immunity: long-lasting immunity that occurs when the body makes its own antibodies to inactivate an antigen. (ch. 22, p. 608)

active transport: energy-requiring movement of substances through a cell membrane. (ch. 3, p. 80)

adolescence: stage of development when a person becomes physically able to reproduce, beginning around ages 12 to 13. (ch. 21, p. 588)

adulthood: final stage in a person's development, extending from the end of adolescence to old age. (ch. 21, p. 590)

aerobes: organisms that require oxygen to survive—for example, humans and most bacteria. (ch. 9, p. 240)

algae (AL gee): one- or many-celled plantlike protists, all of which contain chlorophyll and can make their own food; organized into six main phyla based on their structure, their pigments, and the way they store food. (ch. 10, p. 257)

alleles (uh LEELZ): different forms a gene may have for a trait. (ch. 6, p. 152)

allergen: substance that causes an allergic reaction. (ch. 22, p. 617)

allergy: overly strong reaction of the immune system to a foreign substance (an allergen). (ch. 22, p. 616)

alternation of generations: occurs when a plant's life cycle alternates between a sex-cell–producing stage and a spore-producing stage. (ch. 5, p. 125)

alveoli (al VE uh li): in the lungs, the tiny, thin-walled sacs arranged in grapelike clusters at the end of each bronchiole; oxygen and carbon dioxide exchange takes place between the alveoli and capillaries. (ch. 19, p. 524)

amino acid: building block of protein. (ch. 17, p. 466)

amniotic (am nee AH tihk) **sac:** thin membrane that begins to form around the embryo during the third week of pregnancy; helps cushion and protect the unborn baby and can store nutrients and wastes. (ch. 21, p. 583)

amphibian: ectothermic vertebrate that spends part of its life in water and part on land. (ch. 13, p. 348)

anaerobes: organisms that are able to live without oxygen—for example, methanogens and thermophiles. (ch. 9, p. 240)

angiosperms (AN jee uh spurmz): vascular plants that flower, have their seeds contained in a fruit, and are the most common form of plant life on Earth. (ch. 11, p. 301)

antibiotic: substance, such as penicillin, produced by one organism that inhibits or kills another organism. (ch. 9, p. 244)

antibody: protein made by the body in response to a specific antigen and that reacts with the antigen to make it harmless. (ch. 22, p. 608)

antigens: proteins and chemicals that are foreign to the body. (ch. 22, p. 608)

antiseptic: agent that is applied to the skin to kill pathogens and prevent their regrowth. (ch. 22, p. 602)

appendages: jointed structures, such as legs, claws, and antennae, that grow from a body. (ch. 12, p. 330)

artery: blood vessel with a thick elastic wall made of smooth muscle that moves blood away from the heart. (ch. 18, p. 496)

arthropod: animals that have jointed appendages, such as an insect or a crustacean, that is classified by the number of body segments and appendages, and that has a protective exoskeleton. (ch. 12, p. 330)

asexual reproduction: process by which a new organism is produced that has DNA identical to the DNA of the parent organism. (ch. 4, p. 101)

asthma (AZ muh): lung disorder in which there may be shortness of breath, wheezing, or coughing and that may occur as an allergic reaction. (ch. 19, p. 529)

atherosclerosis (ah thur oh skluh ROH sus): cardiovascular condition resulting from fatty deposits on arterial walls, which can clog blood vessels and interfere with blood flow. (ch. 18, p. 500)

atria (AY tree uh): two upper chambers of the heart. (ch. 18, p. 493)

axon (AK sahn): branch of neuron that carries messages, or impulses, away from the cell body. (ch. 20, p. 547)

B

binomial nomenclature (bi NOH mee ul NOH mun klay chur): Linnaeus's system of classification, which gives a two-word name to every organism—the first word of the name is the genus and the second word is the specific name. (ch. 8, p. 212)

biomes (BI ohmz): large geographic areas with similar climates and ecosystems; the six most common are tundra, taiga, temperate forest, tropical rain forest, grassland, and desert. (ch. 15, p. 415)

biosphere (BI uh sfihr): part of Earth that supports organisms, is the highest level of biological organization, and is made up of all Earth's ecosystems. (ch. 14, p. 378)

biotic factors: living or once-living organisms in the environment. (ch. 14, p. 381)

bird: endothermic vertebrate with feathers, two legs, two wings, and bills, or beaks, and that lays hard-shelled eggs. (ch. 13, p. 354)

bladder: muscular, elastic organ that holds urine until it leaves the body. (ch. 19, p. 535)

blood pressure: force exerted on vessel walls by blood when the heart pumps it through the cardiovascular system; normally 120 over 80 for a young adult. (ch. 18, p. 497)

brain stem: part of the brain that controls heartbeat, breathing, and blood pressure by coordinating the involuntary movements of these functions; extends from the cerebrum and connects the brain to the spinal cord. (ch. 20, p. 549)

bronchi: two short branches at the lower end of the trachea that carry air into the lungs. (ch. 19, p. 524)

budding: form of asexual reproduction in which a new organism grows off the side of the parent. (ch. 10, p. 270)

cambium (KAM bee um): vascular plant tissue that produces new xylem and phloem cells. (ch. 11, p. 297)

cancer: chronic, noncommunicable disease that results from uncontrolled cell division. (ch. 22, p. 616)

capillary: microscopic blood vessel that connects arteries and veins; nutrients, oxygen, waste materials, and carbon dioxide diffuse through its walls. (ch. 18, p. 497)

carbohydrates (kar boh HI drayts): class of organic nutrients that supplies the body with its major energy sources—sugar, starch, and cellulose; contain carbon, hydrogen, and oxygen atoms. (ch. 17, p. 465)

cardiac muscle: striated, involuntary muscle that is found only in the heart. (ch. 16, p. 451)

carnivore: flesh-eating animals. (ch. 13, p. 366)

carrying capacity: largest number of individuals an environment can support and maintain over a long period of time. (ch. 14, p. 386)

cartilage: thick, slippery tissue layer covering the ends of bones; absorbs shock and helps make joint movements easier by reducing friction. (ch. 16, p. 442); tough, flexible tissue that is similar to bone but is not as hard. (ch. 13, p. 346)

cell membrane: structure that allows only certain things to pass in and out of the cell and forms the outer boundary of the cell. (ch. 2, p. 50)

cell theory: major theory based on observations and conclusions by many scientists; states that the cell is the basic unit of life, organisms are composed of one or more cells, and all cells come from other cells. (ch. 2, p. 44)

cellulose (SEL yuh lohs): organic compound made of long chains of glucose molecules; forms the rigid cell walls of plants. (ch. 11, p. 284)

cell wall: rigid structure that supports and protects the plant cell and is made mostly of bundles of cellulose fibers. (ch. 2, p. 55)

central nervous system: division of the nervous system, containing the brain and spinal cord, which sorts and interprets information from stimuli. (ch. 20, p. 548)

cerebellum (ser uh BEL um): part of the brain that coordinates voluntary muscle movements and maintains balance and muscle tone; located behind and under the cerebrum. (ch. 20, p. 549)

cerebrum (suh REE brum): largest part of the brain; is divided into two hemispheres; controls the work of voluntary muscles, interprets impulses from the senses, and stores memory. (ch. 20, p. 549)

chemical digestion: process that breaks down large molecules of food into different, smaller molecules that can be absorbed by the body's cells; takes place in the mouth, stomach, and small intestine. (ch. 17, p. 478)

chemotherapy: use of chemicals to destroy cancer cells. (ch. 22, p. 616)

childhood: period from the end of infancy to age 12 that is marked by development of muscular coordination and mental abilities. (ch. 21, p. 588)

chloroplast: green, chlorophyll-containing organelle in the cytoplasm of many plant cells, where plants make their own food. (ch. 2, p. 55)

chordate: animal with a notochord, a dorsal hollow nerve cord, and gill slits. (ch. 13, p. 344)

chromatin: long strands of hereditary material within the cell nucleus that are made up of proteins and DNA. (ch. 2, p. 51)

chromosomes: structures in the cell nucleus that contain hereditary material. (ch. 4, p. 99)

chronic bronchitis: long-lasting respiratory disease in which the bronchial tubes are irritated and too much mucus is produced. (ch. 19, p. 527)

chyme (KIME): thin, watery product that is the result of digestion. (ch. 17, p. 480)

cilia (SIHL ee uh): short, threadlike structures that extend from the cell membrane of ciliates and are used for movement. (ch. 10, p. 263)

class: taxonomic group that is larger than an order but smaller than a phylum or division. (ch. 8, p. 216)

classify: to group information, objects, or ideas based on their similarities. (ch. 8, p. 210)

climax community: community that has reached the final stage of ecological succession. (ch. 15, p. 409)

closed circulatory system: type of blood-circulation system in which blood is carried through blood vessels. (ch. 12, p. 323)

cnidarians (NIH dar ee uns): phylum of hollow-bodied, water-dwelling animals with stinging cells, radial symmetry, a body two layers thick, and both sexual and asexual reproduction. (ch. 12, p. 317)

cochlea (KOH klee uh): structure of the inner ear that is shaped like a snail's shell and contains fluids that vibrate, sending impulses to the brain by the auditory nerve. (ch. 20, p. 555)

communicable disease: disease that spreads from an infected organism or the environment through agents such as viruses, fungi, protists, and some bacteria. (ch. 22, p. 603)

community: consists of groups of populations that interact with each other in a given area and depend on each other for food, shelter, and for other needs. (ch. 14, p. 382)

compound light microscope: magnifies by allowing light to pass through an object and then through two or more lenses. (ch. 2, p. 41)

constant: variable that stays the same in an experiment. (ch. 1, p. 19)

consumer: organism that can't make its own food. (ch. 3, p. 83)

contour feathers: strong, lightweight feathers that give birds their coloring and streamlined shape and that are used to fly and to steer. (ch. 13, p. 357)

control: sample that is treated like other experimental groups except that the variable is not applied. (ch. 1, p. 19)

coronary (KOR uh ner ee) **circulation:** flow of blood to the tissues of the heart. (ch. 18, p. 495)

cuticle (KYEWT ih kul): waxy, protective layer covering the stems, leaves, and flowers of some land plants; is secreted by the plant's cell walls and slows the evaporation of water. (ch. 11, p. 285)

cytoplasm: constantly moving, gelatin-like mixture inside the cell membrane; contains structures that carry out life processes of the cell. (ch. 2, p. 52)

D

dendrite: branch of neuron that receives messages and sends them to the cell body. (ch. 20, p. 547)

dependent variable: factor that is being measured in an experiment. (ch. 1, p. 19)

dermis: layer of tissue beneath the dermis; contains blood vessels, nerves, and oil and sweat glands. (ch. 16, p. 456)

desert: driest biome on Earth that receives less than 25 cm of rain each year and supports little plant life. (ch. 15, p. 420)

diaphragm (DI uh fram): muscle beneath the lungs that contracts and relaxes with breathing and that helps move air in and out of the body. (ch. 19, p. 525)

dichotomous (di KAH toh mus) **key:** detailed list of characteristics used to identify organisms and that includes scientific names. (ch. 8, p. 223)

dicot: class of angiosperm that has two seed leaves inside its seeds, vascular bundles that occur in rings, and flower parts in multiples of four or five. (ch. 11, p. 302)

diffusion: movement of molecules from areas where there are more of them to areas where there are fewer of them. (ch. 3, p. 77)

digestion: mechanical and chemical process that breaks down food into small molecules so they can be used by the body's cells. (ch. 17, p. 476)

disinfectant: agent that is used to kill disease-causing organisms on objects such as surgical instruments. (ch. 22, p. 602)

division: in the taxonomy of plants, the group smaller than a kingdom but larger than a class. (ch. 8, p. 216)

DNA (deoxyribonucleic [dee AHK sih ri boh noo klay ihk] acid): chemical that contains an organism's information code and is found in the cell nucleus; is made up of two twisted strands of sugar-phosphate molecules and nitrogen bases. (ch. 4, p. 110)

dominant (DAHM uh nunt): describes a trait that covers up, or dominates, another form of the trait. (ch. 6, p. 154)

down feathers: soft, fluffy feathers that provide an insulating layer next to theskin of adult birds and that cover the bodies of young birds. (ch. 13, p. 357)

E

ecological pyramid: model used to describe the transfer of energy from the producers of an ecosystem through successive levels of organisms in the food chain. (ch. 14, p. 394)

ecological succession: process of gradual change from one community of organisms to another. (ch. 15, p. 406)

ecology: study of the interactions that take place among organisms and between organisms and the physical features of the environment. (ch. 14, p. 379)

ecosystem: consists of a biotic community and the abiotic factors that affect it. (ch. 14, p. 382)

ectotherm: vertebrate whose body temperature changes with the temperature of its surroundings. (ch. 13, p. 344)

egg: sex cell that is formed in the reproductive organs of a female and has only half the number of chromosomes of a body cell. (ch. 4, p. 104)

electron microscope: bends beams of electrons in a magnetic field and can magnify images up to one million times or more. (ch. 2, p. 42)

embryo: unborn child during the first two months of pregnancy. (ch. 21, p. 582)

embryology (em bree AHL uh jee): study of development in organisms. (ch. 7, p. 194)

emphysema (em fuh SEE muh): respiratory disease in which the alveoli in the lungs lose their ability to expand and contract. (ch. 19, p. 528)

endocytosis: process in which substances too large to cross the cell membrane enter the cell; occurs when the cell membrane folds in on itself and encloses the large particles in a sphere, which pinches off, allowing the vacuole to enter the cytoplasm. (ch. 3, p. 81)

endoplasmic reticulum (ER): complex series of folded membranes in the cell cytoplasm that is involved in moving cellular products. (ch. 2, p. 52)

endoskeleton: internal system of bones that protects and supports an animal's internal organs and also provides a place for muscle attachment. (ch. 13, p. 344)

endospores: heat-resistant, thick-walled structures many bacteria can produce around themselves when conditions are unfavorable. (ch. 9, p. 245)

endotherm: vertebrate that maintains a constant body temperature. (ch. 13, p. 344)

enzymes: specific proteins that regulate almost all chemical reactions in cells without being changed themselves (ch. 17, p. 477)

epidermis: outer layer of the skin; constantly produces new cells to replace those that are rubbed off. (ch. 16, p. 455)

equilibrium: state in which the molecules of a substance are evenly distributed throughout another substance. (ch. 3, p. 78)

estivation: behavioral adaptation for survival during hot, dry summer months, during which an animal becomes inactive; in amphibians, involves hiding in cooler, more humid ground. (ch. 13, p. 349)

estuary: area where a river meets the ocean that contains a mixture of freshwater and salt water and serves as nursery for many species of ocean fish. (ch. 15, p. 426)

evolution: changes in the inherited features of a species over time; can occur slowly (gradualism) or rapidly (punctuated equilibrium). (ch. 7, p. 178)

exocytosis: process in which large particles leave the cell; occurs when vesicles and vacuoles fuse with the cell membrane and release their contents outside the cell. (ch. 3, p. 81)

exoskeleton: lightweight body covering that protects and supports an arthropod's body, prevents it from drying out, and is shed by molting. (ch. 12, p. 330)

F

family: taxonomic group that is smaller than an order but larger than a genus. (ch. 8, p. 216)

fats: class of organic nutrients that provides energy and helps the body absorb some vitamins; may be saturated or unsaturated. (ch. 17, p. 468)

fermentation: form of respiration without oxygen; releases only part of the energy in food. (ch. 3, p. 84)

fertilization: joining of an egg and a sperm, generally from two different organisms. (ch. 4, p. 104)

fetus: developing baby after the first two months of pregnancy until birth. (ch. 21, p. 584)

fins: fanlike structures of most fish that are used for balancing, steering, and moving, and usually are paired. (ch. 13, p. 345)

fish: ectotherm that lives in water and uses gills to get oxygen; usually has fins and scales. (ch. 13, p. 345)

fission: simplest form of asexual reproduction in which two cells are produced with genetic material identical to that of the parent cell; the method by which bacteria reproduce. (ch. 9, p. 240)

flagella: whiplike tails that help many types of bacteria move around in moist environments. (ch. 9, p. 237)

food chain: model that describes the feeding relationships in a community, usually has three or four links, and shows how energy in the form of food passes from one organism to another. (ch. 14, p. 393)

food group: foods that contain the same nutrients; for example, the milk, yogurt, and cheese group. (ch. 17, p. 473)

food web: model used to describe a series of overlapping food chains and that shows the many organisms that feed on more than one level in an ecosystem. (ch. 14, p. 394)

free-living: organism, such as a planarian, that doesn't depend on one particular organism for food or a place to live. (ch. 12, p. 319)

frond: leaf of a fern that grows from a rhizome. (ch. 5, p. 126)

G

gametophyte (guh MEET uh fite) **stage:** plant life cycle stage in which all plant structures are made of cells with a haploid number (n) of chromosomes. (ch. 5, p. 124)

gene: section of DNA on a chromosome that directs the making of a specific protein. (ch. 4, p. 112)

genetic engineering: changing of a gene's DNA sequence by biological and chemical methods. (ch. 6, p. 170)

genetics (juh NET ihks): study of how traits are inherited through the actions of alleles. (ch. 6, p. 153)

genotype (JEE nuh tipe): genetic makeup of an organism. (ch. 6, p. 156)

genus (JEE nus): taxonomic group of different organisms with similar characteristics; can have one or more species. (ch. 8, p. 212)

gills: organs that exchange oxygen and carbon dioxide with water. (ch. 12, p. 321)

Golgi bodies: stacks of membrane-covered sacs that package materials and move them to the outside of the cell. (ch. 2, p. 53)

gradualism: model of evolution that shows a slow change of one species to another, new species through continued mutations and variations over time. (ch. 7, p. 184)

grasslands: temperate and tropical regions that receive between 25 cm and 75 cm of precipitation each year and are dominated by climax communities of grasses. (ch. 15, p. 420)

guard cells: in a plant leaf, the cells that surround the stomata and that open and close them. (ch. 11, p. 299)

gymnosperms (JIHM nuh spurmz): vascular plants that produce seeds on the surface of the female reproductive structures, do not have flowers, and generally have needlelike or scalelike leaves. (ch. 11, p.300)

H

habitat: physical location where an organism lives. (ch. 14, p. 389)

helper T cell: type of white blood cell that helps other types of white blood cells produce antibodies. (ch. 22, p. 610)

hemoglobin: chemical in red blood cells that can carry oxygen and carbon dioxide. (ch. 18, p. 503)

herbivore: grazing animal that eats only plants. (ch. 15, p. 366)

heredity (huh RED ut ee): passing of traits from parent to offspring. (ch. 6, p. 152)

heterozygous (het uh roh ZI gus): organism that has two different alleles for a single trait. (ch. 6, p. 156)

hibernation: behavioral adaptation for survival during cold, winter months, where an animal becomes inactive and its metabolic needs are lowered; in amphibians, involves burying themselves in mud or leaves until temperatures become warmer. (ch. 13, p. 349)

hominids: humanlike primates that walked upright on two feet and ate both meat and vegetables. (ch. 7, p. 199)

Homo sapiens: human species thought to have evolved about 400 000 years ago. (ch. 7, p. 200)

homologous (huh MAHL uh gus): body structures that are similar in origin and show that two or more species may share common ancestors. (ch. 7, p. 193)

homozygous (hoh muh ZI gus): organism that has two identical alleles for a single trait. (ch. 20, p. 562)

hormones: endocrine chemicals that are produced from glands directly into the bloodstream and that affect target tissues. (ch. 20, p. 562)

host cell: cell in which a virus reproduces. (ch. 2, p. 60)

hypertension: cardiovascular disorder, also called high blood pressure, that can be caused by atherosclerosis. (ch. 18, p. 500)

hyphae (HI fee): mass of many-celled, threadlike tubes that usually make up the body of a fungus. (ch. 10, p. 268)

hypothesis: prediction or statement that can be tested; may be formed by using prior knowledge, new information, and previous observations. (ch. 1, p. 18)

I

immovable joint: type of joint that allows little or no movement. (ch. 16, p. 444)

immune system: complex group of defenses that work to fight disease in the body. (ch. 22, p. 607)

incomplete dominance: production of a phenotype that is intermediate to those of the two homozygous parents. (ch. 6, p. 160)

independent variable: factor that is changed in an experiment. (ch. 1, p. 19)

infancy: period of rapid growth and development of both mental and physical skills that extends from the neonatal period to one year. (ch. 21, p. 588)

inorganic compounds: most compounds made from elements other than carbon; for example, water, which makes up a large part of living matter. (ch. 3, p. 76)

invertebrates (ihn VURT uh brayts): animals lacking a backbone; about 97 percent of animals are invertebrates. (ch. 12, p. 313)

involuntary muscles: muscles, such as cardiac muscles, that can't be consciously controlled. (ch. 16, p. 448)

J

joint: place where two or more bones meet; may be immovable, such as in the skull, or movable, such as in the hip. (ch. 16, p. 443)

K

kidney: bean-shaped organ of the urinary system that is made up of about one million nephrons and that filters blood to produce waste liquid (urine). (ch. 19, p. 534)

kingdom: the first taxonomic category and the group that has the most members. (ch. 8, p. 211)

L

larynx: airway to which the vocal chords are attached. (ch. 19, p. 523)

lichen (LI kun): organism that is made up of a fungus and a green alga or a cyanobacterium; an important food source for many animals; used by scientists to monitor pollution levels. (ch. 10, p. 271)

ligament: tough band of tissue that holds bones together at joints. (ch. 16, p. 443)

limiting factor: any biotic or abiotic factor that restricts the number of individuals in a population. (ch. 14, p. 385)

lymph: tissue fluid that has moved from around cells and into lymph vessels; consists mostly of water, dissolved substances, and lymphocytes. (ch. 18, p. 512)

lymph nodes: bean-shaped structures found throughout the body that filter out microorganisms and foreign materials engulfed by lymphocytes. (ch. 18, p. 512)

lymphatic (lihm FAT ihk) **system:** collects fluid from body tissue spaces and returns it to the blood through lymph capillaries and lymph vessels; plays a vital role in protecting against infection. (ch. 18, p. 511)

lymphocyte (LIHM fuh site): type of white blood cell produced by the lymphatic system that fights infections and foreign materials that enter the body. (ch. 18, p. 512)

lysosome: eukaryotic cell organelle that contains digestive chemicals that break down food molecules, cell wastes, and worn-out cell parts. (ch. 2, p. 54)

M

mammal: endothermic vertebrate that has hair and produces milk to feed its young. (ch. 13, p. 360)

mantle: thin tissue layer covering a mollusk's soft body; secretes the protective shell of those mollusks having a shell. (ch. 12, p. 321)

marrow: fatty, soft tissue in the center of long bones and the spaces of spongy bones; produces red blood cells and white blood cells. (ch. 16, p. 440)

marsupial: mammal that gives birth to immature offspring and that has a pouch in which its young complete their development. (ch. 13, p. 362)

mechanical digestion: process that occurs when food is chewed and mixed in the mouth and churned in the stomach. (ch.17, p. 478)

medusa: free-swimming, bell-shaped body plan of a cnidarian, such as a jellyfish, that allows it to drift with the ocean currents. (ch. 12, p. 317)

meiosis (my OH sus): process by which sex cells are created in the reproductive organs, producing four haploid sex cells from one diploid cell. (ch. 4, p. 104)

melanin (MEL uh nun): pigment that gives skin its color. (ch. 16, p. 455)

menopause: occurs for most women between the ages of 45 and 60 when the menstrual cycle becomes irregular and eventually stops. (ch. 21, p. 577)

menstrual cycle: monthly cycle of changes in the female reproductive system. (ch. 21, p. 575)

menstruation: monthly discharge of blood and tissue cells from the thickened lining of the uterus that begins when a girl reaches puberty and her reproductive organs have matured. (ch. 21, p. 576)

metabolism: total of all chemical reactions in a living thing. (ch. 3, p. 83)

metamorphosis (met uh MOR fuh sus): process in which insects change their body form as they mature; can be complete (egg, larva, pupa, and adult) or incomplete (egg, nymph, and adult). (ch. 12, p. 332)

minerals: inorganic nutrients that regulate many chemical reactions in the body. (ch. 17, p. 470)

mitochondria: eukaryotic cell organelles where food molecules are broken down and energy is released. (ch. 2, p. 53)

mitosis (mi TOH sus): series of continuous steps (prophase, metaphase, anaphase, and telophase) in which the cell nucleus divides to form two identical nuclei. (ch. 4, p. 98)

mixture: combination of substances in which each substance retains its own properties. (ch. 3, p. 73)

model: mathematical equation or object that saves time and money by testing ideas that may be too large or too small, take too long to build, happen too quickly, or are too dangerous to observe directly. (ch. 1, p. 16)

mollusk: soft-bodied invertebrate that has a mantle, a large muscular foot, a complete digestive system with two openings, and usually has a protective shell. (ch. 12, p. 321)

monocot: class of angiosperm that has one seed leaf inside its seeds, vascular tissues arranged as bundles scattered throughout the stem, and flower parts in multiples of three. (ch. 11, p. 302)

monotreme: mammal that lays eggs with tough, leathery shells; the duckbilled platypus and two species of spiny anteaters. (ch. 13, p. 362)

movable joint: type of joint (pivot, ball-and-socket, hinge, gliding) that allows a wide range of movements. (ch. 16, p. 444)

multiple alleles: term used when a trait is controlled by more than two alleles. (ch. 6, p. 160)

muscle: organ that relaxes and contracts to allow movement of bones and body parts. (ch. 16, p. 447)

mutation: any permanent change in a gene or chromosome of a cell. (ch. 4, p. 114)

N

natural selection: Darwin's theory of evolution, which says that organisms with traits best suited to their environments are more likely to survive and reproduce. (ch. 7, p. 181)

nephron: tiny filtering unit of the kidney. (ch. 19, p. 534)

neuron (NOO rahn): working unit of the nervous system, made up of a cell body and branches called dendrites and axons. (ch. 20, p. 547)

niche: role of an organism in the ecosystem, including what it eats, how it interacts with other organisms, and how it gets its food. (ch. 14, p. 389)

nitrogen cycle: transfer of nitrogen from the atmosphere to plants and back to the atmosphere or directly into plants again. (ch. 14, p. 398)

nitrogen-fixing bacteria: bacteria that live in the root nodules of certain kinds of plants and change nitrogen from the air into forms useful for animals and plants. (ch. 9, p. 244)

noncommunicable disease: disease that is not spread from one person to another but may result from factors such as poor diet or uncontrolled cell growth. (ch. 22, p. 614)

nonvascular plant: plant lacking vascular tissue and that absorbs water and other dissolved substances directly through its cell walls. (ch. 11, p. 286)

nucleus: eukaryotic organelle that directs all the activities of the cell and is surrounded by a double membrane. (ch. 2, p. 51)

nutrients (NEW tree unts): substances in foods that provide energy and materials for cell development, growth, and repair; carbohydrates, proteins, fats, vitamins, minerals, and water. (ch. 17, p. 464)

O

olfactory cells: nerve cells in the nasal passages that respond to gas molecules in the air and send impulses to the brain for the interpretation of odors. (ch. 20, p. 558)

omnivore: animals that eat both plants and animals. (ch. 13, p. 366)

open circulatory system: type of blood-circulation system in which the blood is not contained in vessels but instead surrounds the organs. (ch. 12, p. 322)

order: taxonomic group that is larger than a family but smaller than a class. (ch. 8, p. 216)

organ: structure made up of different types of tissues that work together to do a certain job. (ch. 2, p. 56)

organelle: structure within the cytoplasm of a eukaryotic cell having a specific function or functions. (ch. 2, p. 52)

organic compounds: most compounds that contain carbon; four groups make up living things: carbohydrates, lipids, proteins, and nucleic acids. (ch. 3, p. 74)

osmosis: diffusion of water through a cell membrane. (ch. 3, p. 79)

ovary: in angiosperms, the swollen base of the pistil where ovules are formed (ch. 21, p. 574)

ovulation (AHV yuh LAY shun): process in which an egg is released about once a month from an ovary. (ch. 21, p. 575)

ovule: in a seed plant, the structure that contains an egg cell, food-storage tissue, and a sticky fluid. (ch. 5, p. 130)

P

parasite: organism, such as a tapeworm, that depends on its host for food and a place to live. (ch. 12, p. 319)

passive immunity: shorter-term immunity that occurs when antibodies produced in another animal are transferred into the body. (ch. 22, p. 608)

passive transport: movement of substances through a cell membrane without the use of cellular energy. (ch. 3, p. 80)

pasteurization: process of heating food to a temperature that kills most bacteria. (ch. 22, p. 600)

pathogen: any organism that produces disease. (ch. 9, p. 244)

pedigree: tool that shows the occurrence of a trait in a family. (ch. 6, p. 169)

periosteum (per ee AHS tee um): tough, tight-fitting membrane that covers the surface of bones. (ch. 16, p. 441)

peripheral (puh RIHF rul) **nervous system:** division of the nervous system, made up of all the nerves outside the central nervous system; connects the brain and spinal cord to other parts of the body. (ch. 20, p. 548)

peristalsis (per uh STAHL sus): wavelike, muscular contractions that move food through the digestive system. (ch. 19, p. 479)

pharynx: tubelike passageway for both food and air through which inhaled air passes after it is warmed and moistened in the nasal cavity. (ch. 18, p. 523)

phenotype (FEE nuh tipe): physical expression of a particular genotype. (ch. 6, p. 156)

phloem (FLOH em): vascular plant tissue made up of tubular cells that transport food from where it is made to other parts of the plant where it is used or stored. (ch. 11, p. 297)

phylogeny (fi LAH jon nee): evolutionary history of an organism. (ch. 8, p. 215)

phylum (FI lum): taxonomic group that is smaller than a kingdom but larger than a class. (ch. 8, p. 216)

pioneer community: first community of organisms to move into a new environment. (ch. 15, p. 407)

pioneer species: first plants to grow in new or disturbed environments and that change environmental conditions so that other plant species can grow there. (ch. 11, p. 289)

pistil: female reproductive organ inside the flower of an angiosperm; consists of a sticky stigma, a style, and an ovary. (ch. 5, p. 133)

placental mammal: mammal whose embryo develops in the uterus of the female. (ch. 13, p. 363)

plankton: microscopic algae, plants, and other organisms that float in warm, sunlit waters near the surface of freshwater lakes and ponds. (ch. 15, p. 425)

plasma: liquid part of blood, consisting mostly of water plus dissolved nutrients, minerals, and oxygen; makes up more than half the volume of blood. (ch. 18, p. 503)

platelet: irregularly shaped cell fragment that circulates with red and white blood cells and helps to clot blood. (ch. 18, p. 504)

pollen grains: produced by the male reproductive organs of seed plants; two sperm develop in each pollen grain. (ch. 5, p. 130)

pollination: transfer of pollen grains from the stamen to the stigma. (ch. 5, p. 134)

polygenic (pahl ih JEHN ihk) **inheritance:** occurs when a group of gene pairs acts together to produce a single trait. (ch. 6, p. 161)

polyp (PAHL up): vase-shaped body plan of a cnidarian, such as a hydra, that allows it to twist to capture prey and to somersault to a new location. (ch. 12, p. 317)

population: all the individuals of one species that live in the same area at the same time and compete with each other for food, water, mates, and space. (ch. 14, p. 382)

population density: size of a population that occupies an area of limited size. (ch. 14, p. 385)

pregnancy: nine-month period of development during which the fertilized egg grows into a baby within the uterus. (ch. 21, p. 582)

primary succession: ecological succession that begins in a place that does not have soil. (ch. 15, p. 407)

primates: group of mammals that includes monkeys, apes, and humans and that shares several characteristics, such as opposable thumbs and binocular vision. (ch. 7, p. 198)

producer: organism, such as a green plant, that makes its own food. (ch. 3, p. 83)

proteins: large, organic molecules that are made up of amino acids and that are needed for growth and repair of body cells. (ch. 17, p. 466)

prothallus: fern gametophyte, which can make its own food, absorb water and nutrients, and has both male and female reproductive structures. (ch. 5, p. 126)

protist: single- or many-celled eukaryotic organism that lives in a moist or wet environment; can be plantlike, animal-like, or funguslike. (ch. 10, p. 256)

protozoans: complex, one-celled, animal-like protists that contain special vacuoles for digesting food and eliminating excess water; classified by their method of movement. (ch. 10, p. 261)

pseudopods (SEWD uh pahdz): temporary, footlike extensions of cytoplasm used by rhizopods for movement and for trapping food. (ch. 10, p. 262)

pulmonary (PUL muh ner ee) **circulation:** flow of blood through the heart, to the lungs, and back to the heart. (ch. 18, p. 494)

punctuated equilibrium: model of evolution that shows the rapid change of a species caused by the mutation of just a few genes, resulting in the appearance of a new species. (ch. 7, p. 184)

Punnett square: tool used to predict results in Mendelian genetics; shows all the ways in which alleles can combine. (ch. 6, p. 156)

R

radioactive element: element that gives off radiation due to an unstable nucleus. (ch. 7, p. 190)

radula (RAJ uh luh): scratchy, tongue-like organ in many mollusks that acts like a file with rows of teeth to break up food into smaller pieces. (ch. 12, p. 321)

recessive (rih SES ihv): describes a trait that is covered up, or dominated, by another form of the trait. (ch. 6, p. 154)

reflex: involuntary and automatic response to a stimulus that allows the body to respond without having to think about what action to take. (ch. 20, p.551)

reproduction: the process through which organisms produce more individuals. (ch. 21, p. 572)

reptile: ectothermic vertebrate that has thick, dry, scaly skin, and does not depend on water for reproduction. (ch. 13, p. 351)

retina: light-sensitive tissue at the back of the eye; contains rods and cones; impulses stimulated here pass to the optic nerve, which carries them to the brain. (ch. 20, p. 556)

rhizoids: threadlike roots that are only a few cells in length and that anchor liverworts and mosses in place. (ch. 11, p. 288)

rhizome: underground stem of a fern, from which fronds and roots grow. (ch. 5, p. 126)

ribosomes: small, two-part organelles on which cells make their own proteins. (ch. 2, p. 53)

RNA (ribonucleic acid): nucleic acid that carries codes for making proteins from the nucleus to the ribosomes. (ch. 4, p. 113)

saliva (suh LI vuh): watery, enzyme-containing fluid in the mouth that is mixed with food during digestion. (ch. 17, p. 479)

saprophyte: any organism that uses dead material as a food and energy source; sprophytes decompose dead organisms and recycles nutrients so that they are available for use by other organisms; saprophytic bacteria keep dead material from building up over all of Earth. (ch. 9, p. 243)

science: process used to solve problems or answer questions about what is happening in the world; can provide information that people use to make decisions. (ch. 1, p. 6)

Scientific Methods: approaches taken to solve a problem in science; steps can include recognize the problem, form a hypothesis, test the hypothesis, do the experiment, analyze the data, and draw conclusions. (ch. 1, p. 14)

secondary succession: ecological succession that begins in a place that already has soil and was once the home of living organisms. (ch. 15, p. 408)

sedimentary rock: rock formed by compaction and cementation of sediments or when minerals precipitate out of solution or are left behind when a solution evaporates (ch. 7, p. 189)

semen: mixture of sperm and fluid that leaves the body through the urethra. (ch. 21, p. 574)

sex-linked gene: allele inherited on a sex chromosome. (ch. 6, p. 168)

sexual reproduction: process by which a new, unique organism is created when two sex cells, an egg and a sperm, come together. (ch. 4, p. 104)

sexually transmitted diseases (STDs): diseases that are transmitted from one person to another during sexual contact and that are caused by both viruses and bacteria. (ch. 22, p. 604)

skeletal muscles: striated, voluntary muscles that move bones. (ch. 16, p. 450)

skeletal system: all the bones in the body; gives the body shape and support, protects internal organs, forms blood cells, stores minerals for later use, and provides for muscle attachment. (ch. 16, p. 440)

smooth muscles: nonstriated, involuntary muscles that move many internal organs. (ch. 16, p. 450)

sori: spore-producing structures on the undersides of fern fronds. (ch. 5, p. 126)

species (SPEE sheez): smallest, most precise taxonomic classification. (ch. 8, p. 212); group of similar organisms that can successfully reproduce among themselves in their natural environment. (ch. 7, p. 178)

sperm: sex cell produced in the reproductive organs of a male and that has only half the number of chromosomes of a body cell; has a whiplike tail that provides motion and a head that contains genetic information. (ch. 21, p. 573)

spore: reproductive cell that forms new organisms without fertilization. (ch. 10, p. 269)

sporophyte (SPOR uh fite) **stage:** plant life-cycle stage in which all plant structures are made of cells with a diploid number ($2n$) of chromosomes. (ch. 5, p. 124)

stamen: male reproductive organ inside the flower of an angiosperm; consists of a filament and an anther. (ch. 5, p. 133)

stomata: small pores in the leaf surfaces surrounded by guard cells; allow carbon dioxide, oxygen, and water to enter and leave a leaf. (ch. 11, p. 299)

symbiosis (sihm bee OH sus): any close relationship between two or more different species. (ch. 14, p. 387)

symmetry: arrangement of the individual parts of an object; animals with bilateral symmetry have mirror image body parts; animals with radial symmetry have body parts arranged in a circle around a central point; asymmetrical animals have no definite shape. (ch. 12, p. 313)

synapse (SIHN aps): small space between neurons, across which an impulse moves by means of a chemical released by the axon. (ch. 20, p. 548)

systemic circulation: most extensive part of the circulatory system in which blood moves to and from all body organs and tissues except the heart and lungs. (ch. 18, p. 495)

T

taiga (TI guh): cold region of cone-bearing evergreen trees that lies just below the tundra and is the world's largest terrestrial biome. (ch. 15, p. 416)

target tissue: specific tissue affected by hormones; often is located in a part of the body distant from the gland that affects it. (ch. 20, p. 562)

taste buds: major sensory receptors for taste that are located on the tongue and respond to chemical stimuli. (ch. 20, p. 558)

taxonomy (tak SAHN uh mee): the science of classification. (ch. 8, p. 210)

technology: application of science to make products or tools. (ch. 1, p. 10)

temperate deciduous forest: biome that lies at latitudes below about 50° in both the northern and southern hemispheres, usually has four distinct seasons, and supports a wide variety of plants and animals. (ch. 15, p. 417)

tendon: thick band of tissue that attaches muscle to bone. (ch. 16, p. 450)

testes: male reproductive organs that produce sperm and the male sex hormone, testosterone. (ch. 21, p. 573)

tissue: group of similar cells that work together to do one job. (ch. 2, p. 56)

toxin: poison produced by a bacterial pathogen. (ch. 9, p. 245)

trachea: cartilage-reinforced tube that remains open and connects with the bronchi; is lined with mucous membranes and cilia to trap dust, bacteria, and pollen. (ch. 19, p. 523)

tropical rain forest: hot, wet, equatorial biome that contains the largest number of species. (ch. 15, p. 419)

tundra (TUN dra): cold, dry, treeless biome located at latitudes surrounding the north pole and that has winters six to nine months long. (ch. 15, p. 415)

U

ureter: tube that leads from the kidney to the bladder. (ch. 19, p. 535)

urethra (yoo REE thruh): tube that carries urine from the bladder to the outside of the body. (ch. 19, p. 535)

urinary system: system of excretory organs that rids the blood of wastes produced by the metabolism of nutrients, controls blood volume by removing excess water produced by body cells, and balances concentrations of certain salts and water. (ch. 19, p.533)

urine: waste liquid of the urinary system, containing excess water, salts, and other wastes. (ch. 19, p. 534)

uterus: hollow, pear-shaped, thick-walled muscular organ where a fertilized egg develops into a baby. (ch. 21, p. 575)

V

vaccination: process of giving a vaccine either orally or by injection. (ch. 22, p. 608)

vaccine: preparation made from damaged virus particles that are no longer able to cause disease and that can prevent some viral disease such as polio and measles. (ch. 2, p. 62); substance that is made from killed bacteria or damaged bacterial particles and can prevent, but not cure, many bacterial diseases. (ch. 9, p. 244)

vagina: female muscular tube connecting the lower end of the uterus with the outside of the body; also called the birth canal. (ch. 21, p. 575)

variation: an inherited trait that makes an individual different from other members of the same species; can be beneficial, harmful, or neutral in a population. (ch. 7, p. 182)

vascular plant: plant with vascular tissue, a "pipeline" that moves water, food, and dissolved substances to cells throughout the plant. (ch. 11, p. 286)

vein: blood vessel that moves blood to the heart and has valves to prevent backward movement of the blood. (ch. 18, p. 496)

ventricles (VEN trih kulz): two lower chambers of the heart. (ch. 18, p. 493)

vertebrates (VURT uh brayts): animals with a backbone; only about 3 percent of animals are vertebrates. (ch. 12, p. 313)

vestigial (veh STIHJ ee ul) **structure:** body structure with no obvious use, which may once have functioned in an ancestor. (ch. 7, p. 194)

villi: fingerlike projections in the small intestine where nutrients are absorbed into the bloodstream. (ch. 17, p. 482)

virus: nonliving structure that consists of a core of hereditary material surrounded by a protein coat. (ch. 2, p. 58)

vitamins: water-soluble or fat-soluble essential, organic nutrients that are needed in small quantities to help regulate body functions. (ch. 17, p. 469)

voluntary muscles: muscles, such as face muscles, that can be consciously controlled. (ch. 16, p. 448)

W

water cycle: constant journey of water molecules on Earth as they rise into the atmosphere, fall to land or the ocean as rain or snow, and flow into rivers and oceans through the processes of evaporation, condensation, and precipitation. (ch. 14, p. 396)

X

xylem (ZI lum): vascular plant tissue made up of tubular vessels that transport water and dissolved substances up from the roots throughout the plant. (ch. 11, p. 297)

Z

zygote: new diploid cell that is formed when a sperm fertilizes an egg. (ch. 4, p. 105)

Glossary/Glosario

Este glossario define cada término clave que aparece en **negrillas** en el texto. También muestra el número de página donde se usa dicho término.

A

abiotic factors/factores abióticos: Características físicas inanimadas que a menudo determinan los organismos que pueden sobrevivir en cierto ambiente. (Cap. 14, pág. 379)

active immunity/inmunidad activa: Ocurre cuando el cuerpo, por sí solo, produce anticuerpos en respuesta a un patógeno. (Cap. 22, pág. 608)

active transport/transporte activo: Movimiento de sustancias a través de la membrana celular que requiere energía. (Cap. 3, pág. 80)

adolescence/adolescencia: Etapa de desarrollo que comienza alrededor de los 12 a 13 años, cuando una persona es capaz de producir progenie. (Cap. 21, pág. 588)

adulthood/edad adulta: Etapa final de desarrollo; comienza al terminar la adolescencia y se extiende hasta la vejez. (Cap. 21, pág. 590)

aerobes/aerobios: Organismos que requieren oxígeno para sobrevivir, por ejemplo, los seres humanos y la mayoría de las bacterias. (Cap. 9, pág. 240)

algae/algas: Protistas unicelulares o multicelulares que parecen plantas, contienen clorofila y pueden fabricar su propio alimento; organizadas en seis filos principales con base en sus estructuras, sus pigmentos y la manera en que fabrican alimento. (Cap. 10, pág. 257)

alleles/alelos: Diferentes formas que puede tener un gene para cierto rasgo. (Cap. 6, pág. 152)

allergen/alérgeno: Sustancia que causa una respuesta alérgica. (Cap. 22, pág. 617)

allergy/alergia: Reacción potente del sistema inmunológico a una sustancia extraña. (Cap. 22, pág. 616)

alternation of generations/alternación de generaciones: Ciclo vital de las plantas en la cual se alternan las etapas de producción de esporas y de producción de células sexuales. (Cap. 5, pág. 125)

alveoli/alvéolos: Manojos de sacos pequeños de paredes delgadas ubicados en el extremo de cada bronquiolo; el intercambio de oxígeno y dióxido de carbono se lleva a cabo entre los alvéolos y los capilares. (Cap. 19, pág. 524)

amino acid/aminoácido: Subunidad de la cual están compuestas las proteínas. (Cap. 17, pág. 466)

amniotic sac/bolsa amniótica: Bolsa pegada a la placenta que contiene el fluido amniótico; ayuda a proteger al embrión contra golpes y puede almacenar nutrientes y desperdicios. (Cap. 21, pág. 583)

amphibian/anfibio: Vertebrado de sangre fría que pasa parte de su vida en agua y parte sobre tierra. (Cap. 13, pág. 348)

anaerobes/anaerobios: Organismos con variaciones que les permiten vivir sin oxígeno, por ejemplo los metanógenos y los termófilos. (Cap. 9, pág. 240)

angiosperms/angiospermas: Plantas vasculares que florecen y producen frutos que contienen semillas. Son la forma más común de vida vegetal sobre la Tierra. (Cap. 11, pág. 301)

antibiotic/antibiótico: Sustancia producida por un organismo que inhibe o destruye otro organismo. La penicilina es un antibiótico muy conocido, el cual impide que las bacterias produzcan nuevas paredes celulares. (Cap. 9, pág. 244)

antibody/anticuerpo: Proteína que fabrica un animal en respuesta a un antígeno específico. (Cap. 22, pág. 608)

antigens/antígenos: Proteínas y químicos extraños para el cuerpo. (Cap. 22, pág. 608)

antiseptic/antiséptico: Sustancia química que destruye los patógenos sobre la piel y previene su crecimiento. (Cap. 22, pág. 602)

appendages/apéndices: Estructuras, tales como garras, patas o incluso antenas que crecen del cuerpo. (Cap. 12, pág. 330)

artery/arteria: Vaso sanguíneo de paredes gruesas y elásticas, hechas de músculo liso, que transporta sangre fuera del corazón. (Cap. 18, pág. 496)

arthropod/artrópodo: Animal de patas articuladas, tal como un insecto o un crustáceo, que se clasifica de acuerdo con el número de segmentos corporales y apéndices y el cual tiene un exoesqueleto protector. El término artrópodo proviene de la palabra arthros que significa "unido" y de la palabra poda que significa "pata". (Cap. 12, pág. 330)

asexual reproduction/reproducción asexual: Tipo de reproducción en que se produce un nuevo organismo con DNA idéntico al del organismo progenitor. (Cap. 4, pág. 101)

asthma/asma: Trastorno pulmonar en que la persona puede sentirse corta de aliento, sufrir resollos asmáticos o tos; puede ocurrir como una reacción alérgica. (Cap. 19, pág. 529)

atherosclerosis/aterosclerosis: Acumulación de depósitos grasos en las paredes arteriales, la cual puede obstruir vasos sanguíneos e interferir con el flujo de sangre. (Cap. 18, pág. 500)

atria/aurículas: Las dos cavidades superiores del corazón. (Cap. 18, pág. 493)

axon/axón: Parte de la neurona que transmite mensajes, llamados impulsos, desde el cuerpo celular. (Cap. 20, pág. 547)

binomial nomenclature/nomenclatura binaria: Sistema de clasificación de Linneo que usa dos términos, o nombre científico, para nombrar cada organismo. (Cap. 8, pág. 212)

biomes/biomas: Áreas geográficas extensas que poseen climas y ecosistemas similares. (Cap. 15, pág. 415)

biosphere/biosfera: La parte de la Tierra que sostiene organismos vivos. (Cap. 14, pág. 378)

biotic factors/factores bióticos: Cualquier organismo vivo o que alguna vez estuvo vivo, en un ambiente. (Cap. 14, pág. 381)

bird/ave: Vertebrado de sangre caliente con plumas, dos patas, dos alas y un pico, que pone huevos con cáscara dura. (Cap. 13, pág. 354)

bladder/vejiga: Órgano muscular elástico que almacena la orina hasta que sale del cuerpo. (Cap. 19, pág. 535)

blood pressure/presión sanguínea: Fuerza que ejerce la sangre sobre las paredes de los vasos sanguíneos a medida que el corazón la bombea a través del sistema cardiovascular. (Cap. 18, pág. 497)

brain stem/bulbo raquídeo: Parte del encéfalo que se extiende desde el cerebro y conecta el encéfalo con la médula espinal; controla los latidos del corazón, la respiración y la presión sanguínea, al coordinar los movimientos involuntarios de estas funciones. (Cap. 20, pág. 549)

bronchi/bronquios: Dos ramificaciones cortas en el extremo bajo de la tráquea que llevan aire a los pulmones. (Cap. 19, pág. 524)

budding/gemación: Es una forma de reproducción asexual en que un nuevo organismo crece de un lado del organismo progenitor. (Cap. 10, pág. 270)

cambium/cambium: Tejido que produce nuevas células de xilema y de floema. (Cap. 11, pág. 297)

cancer/cáncer: Enfermedad crónica grave que resulta del crecimiento celular descontrolado. (Cap. 22, pág. 616)

capillary/capilar: Vaso sanguíneo microscópico, con paredes de una sola célula, que conecta las arterias y las venas. (Cap. 18, pág. 497)

carbohydrates/carbohidratos: Nutrientes orgánicos que le proveen al cuerpo sus principales fuentes de energía: azúcares, almidones y celulosa; contienen átomos de carbono, hidrógeno y oxígeno. (Cap. 17, pág. 465)

cardiac muscle/músculo cardíaco: Músculo involuntario estriado que solo se encuentra en el corazón. (Cap. 16, pág. 451)

carnivore/carnívoro: Animal que se alimenta de la carne de otros animales. (Cap. 13, pág. 366)

carrying capacity/capacidad de carga: El mayor número de individuos que un ambiente puede soportar y mantener durante un largo período de tiempo. (Cap. 14, pág. 386)

cartilage/cartílago: Capa gruesa de tejido suave y resbaloso que cubre los extremos de los huesos; absorbe choques y facilita el movimiento al reducir la fricción. (Cap. 16, pág. 442); Tejido flexible fuerte que se parece al hueso, pero que no es tan duro como el hueso. (Cap. 13, pág. 346)

cell membrane/membrana celular: Estructura que forma el límite exterior de la célula y permite que solo ciertos materiales se muevan dentro y fuera de la célula. (Cap. 2, pág. 50)

cell theory/teoría celular: Teoría principal basada en las observaciones y conclusiones de muchos científicos; enuncia que la célula es la unidad constitutiva de la vida, que los organismos están compuestos de una o más células y que todas las células provienen de otras células. (Cap. 2, pág. 44)

cell wall/pared celular: Estructura rígida que brinda apoyo y protección a la célula vegetal. Está formada por manojos de fibras celulosas fuertes. (Cap. 2, pág. 55)

cellulose / celulosa: Compuesto orgánico hecho de cadenas largas de moléculas de glucosa, del cual están formadas las paredes celulares de las plantas. (Cap. 11, pág. 284)

central nervous system/sistema nervioso central: Uno de los dos sistemas principales en que se divide el sistema nervioso. Está compuesto por el encéfalo y la médula espinal. (Cap. 20, pág. 548)

cerebellum/cerebelo: Parte del encéfalo ubicada detrás y debajo del cerebro que coordina los movimientos de los músculos voluntarios y mantiene el equilibrio y el tono muscular. (Cap. 20, pág. 549)

cerebrum/cerebro: La parte más grande del encéfalo; está dividida en dos hemisferios; controla el trabajo de los músculos voluntarios, interpreta los impulsos provenientes de los sentidos y almacena la memoria. (Cap. 20, pág. 549)

chemical digestion/digestión química: Proceso que rompe las moléculas grandes de alimentos en diferentes moléculas más pequeñas que pueden ser absorbidas por las células; tiene lugar en la boca, el estómago y el intestino delgado. (Cap. 17, pág. 478)

chemotherapy/quimioterapia: Uso de sustancias químicas para destruir células cancerosas. (Cap. 22, pág. 616)

childhood/niñez: Etapa que le sigue a la lactancia y que dura hasta los 12 años. (Cap. 21, pág. 588)

chloroplast/cloroplasto: Organelo verde que contiene clorofila en el citoplasma de muchas células vegetales; donde las plantas fabrican su propio alimento. (Cap. 2, pág. 55)

chordate / cordado: Animal con notocordio, cordón nervioso dorsal hueco en sus espaldas y hendiduras branquiales. (Cap. 13, pág. 344)

chromatin/cromatina: Tipo de material hereditario que se encuentra en el núcleo en forma de hebras largas, las cuales contienen las instrucciones genéticas para las operaciones de la célula. (Cap. 2, pág. 51)

chromosomes/cromosomas: Estructuras dentro del núcleo que contienen el material hereditario. (Cap. 4, pág. 99)

chronic bronchitis/bronquitis crónica: Tipo de bronquitis que persiste por un largo período de tiempo, la cual puede ser el resultado de fumar. (Cap. 19, pág. 527)

chyme/quimo: Producto acuoso y delgado que resultada de la digestión. (Cap. 17, pág. 480)

cilia / cilios: Estructuras cortas que parecen hilos y se extienden desde la membrana celular de los ciliados. (Cap. 10, pág. 263)

class / clase: Grupo taxonómico en el cual se divide el filo o división. (Cap. 8, pág. 216)

classify / clasificar: Significa agrupar ideas, información u objetos basándose en sus semejanzas. (Cap. 8, pág. 210)

climax community / comunidad clímax: Comunidad que ha alcanzado la etapa final de sucesión ecológica. (Cap. 15, pág. 409)

closed circulatory system / sistema circulatorio cerrado: Sistema circulatorio en que la sangre se transporta por el cuerpo a través de vasos sanguíneos. (Cap. 12, pág. 323)

cnidarians / cnidarios: Filo de animales acuáticos de cuerpo hueco que poseen células urticantes que usan para aturdir o atrapar presas de alimento; también poseen simetría radial. (Cap. 12, pág. 317)

cochlea/cóclea: Estructura en forma de caracol llena de líquido, ubicada dentro del oído interno. (Cap. 20, pág. 555)

communicable disease/enfermedad comunicable: La causada por agentes tales como virus, bacterias patógenas, protistas y hongos; se puede difundir de una persona a otra. (Cap. 22, pág. 603)

community / comunidad: Grupo de poblaciones que interactúan entre sí en un área. (Cap. 14, pág. 382)

compound light microscope/microscopio de luz compuesto: Microscopio en que la luz pasa a través de un objeto y luego pasa a través de dos o más lentes. (Cap. 2, pág. 41)

constant/constante: Variable que permanece igual. (Cap. 1, pág. 19)

consumer/consumidor: Organismo que no puede elaborar su propio alimento. (Cap. 3, pág. 83)

contour feathers / plumas de contorno: Plumas fuertes y livianas que les dan a las aves sus bellos coloridos y sus perfiles aerodinámicos y las cuales usan para volar y para navegar. (Cap. 13, pág. 357)

control/control: Muestra que se trata exactamente como los otros grupos experimentales, excepto que no se le aplica la variable. (Cap. 1, pág. 19)

coronary circulation/circulación coronaria: Flujo de sangre hacia los tejidos del corazón. (Cap. 18, pág. 495)

cuticle / cutícula: Capa cerosa protectora que cubre los tallos, hojas y flores de algunas plantas terrestres; es secretada por las paredes celulares de la planta y disminuye la evaporación de agua. (Cap. 11, pág. 285)

cytoplasm/citoplasma: Mezcla que parece gelatina dentro de la membrana celular; contiene estructuras que llevan a cabo las funciones vitales de la célula. (Cap. 2, pág. 52)

dendrite/dendrita: Parte de la neurona que recibe mensajes y los transmite al cuerpo celular. (Cap. 20, pág. 547)

dependent variable/variable dependiente: Es el factor que se mide. (Cap. 1, pág. 19)

dermis/dermis: Capa de tejido debajo de la epidermis; contiene vasos sanguíneos, nervios y glándulas sebáceas y sudoríparas. (Cap. 16, pág. 456)

desert / desierto: El bioma más seco de la Tierra. Recibe menos de 25 cm de lluvia al año y sostiene poca vegetación. (Cap. 15, pág. 420)

diaphragm/diafragma: Músculo ubicado debajo de los pulmones, el cual se contrae y relaja y, además, ayuda a mover el aire dentro y fuera del cuerpo. (Cap. 19, pág. 525)

dichotomous key / clave dicotómica: Lista detallada de características que se usan para identificar organismos y la cual incluye el nombre científico. (Cap. 8, pág. 223)

dicot / dicotiledónea: Tipo de angiosperma que contiene dos cotiledones dentro de sus semillas. (Cap. 11, pág. 302)

diffusion/difusión: Movimiento de moléculas desde un área donde hay más moléculas hasta un área con menos moléculas. (Cap. 3, pág. 77)

digestion/digestión: Proceso químico y mecánico que descompone los alimentos en moléculas más pequeñas, de modo que puedan ser utilizadas por las células corporales. (Cap. 17, pág. 476)

disinfectant/desinfectante: Sustancia química que destruye los patógenos en objetos como los instrumentos quirúrgicos. (Cap. 22, pág. 602)

division / división: Reemplaza el filo en los reinos de las plantas; es el grupo taxonómico más pequeño que el reino, pero más grande que una clase. (Cap. 8, pág. 216)

DNA/DNA: Código de la información de un organismo, o ácido desoxirribonucleico, que contienen los cromosomas dentro del núcleo celular. (Cap. 4, pág. 110)

dominant/dominante: Factor que domina o cubre un rasgo recesivo en la progenie. (Cap. 6, pág. 154)

ecological pyramid / pirámide ecológica: Modelo que representa la transferencia de energía en la biosfera. (Cap. 14, pág. 394)

ecological succession / sucesión ecológica: Proceso de cambio gradual de una comunidad de organismos a otra. (Cap. 15, pág. 406)

ecology / ecología: Ciencia que estudia las interacciones entre los organismos y entre los organismos y los rasgos físicos del ambiente. (Cap. 14, pág. 379)

ecosystem / ecosistema: Consiste en una comunidad biótica y de los factores abióticos que la afectan. (Cap. 14, pág. 382)

ectotherm / de sangre fría: Animal vertebrado cuya temperatura corporal cambia con la del ambiente. (Cap. 13, pág. 344)

egg/óvulo: Célula sexual que se forma en los órganos reproductores de la hembra y la cual contiene solo la mitad de los cromosomas de una célula corporal. (Cap. 4, pág. 104)

electron microscope/microscopio electrónico: Usa un campo magnético para doblar los haces de electrones y que puede magnificar las imágenes hasta 1 000 000 de veces. (Cap. 2, pág. 42)

embryo/embrión: Bebé nonato durante los dos primeros meses de embarazo. (Cap. 21, pág. 582)

embryology/embriología: Estudio del desarrollo de los organismos. (Cap. 7, pág. 194)

emphysema/enfisema: Enfermedad en la cual los alvéolos pulmonares pierden su capacidad de expandirse y contraerse. (Cap. 19, pág. 528)

endocytosis/endocitosis: Proceso mediante el cual las moléculas grandes de proteínas y bacterias pueden entrar a una célula cuando se encuentran rodeadas por la membrana celular. La membrana celular se dobla sobre sí misma y encierra la sustancia en una esfera, la cual se desprende resultando en una vacuola que entra al citoplasma. (Cap. 3, pág. 81)

endoplasmic reticulum (ER)/retículo endoplasmático (RE): Serie compleja de membranas dobladas en el citoplasma celular, la cual está involucrada en el movimiento de productos celulares. (Cap. 2, pág. 52)

endoskeleton / endoesqueleto: Sistema óseo interno de los vertebrados que apoya y protege los órganos internos del animal y al cual se adhieren los músculos. (Cap. 13, pág. 344)

endospores / endoesporas: Estructuras con paredes gruesas que rodean a muchas bacterias que producen toxinas, cuando las condiciones son desfavorables. (Cap. 9, pág. 245)

endotherm / de sangre caliente: Animal que mantiene una temperatura corporal constante. (Cap. 13, pág. 344)

enzymes/enzimas: Proteínas específicas que regulan casi todas las reacciones químicas celulares, sin ser alteradas ellas mismas (Cap. 3, pág. 75); moléculas que aceleran el ritmo de las reacciones químicas en el cuerpo. (Cap. 17, pág. 477)

epidermis/epidermis: Capa superficial de la piel cuyas células más externas están muertas. (Cap. 16, pág. 455)

equilibrium/equilibrio: Estado en que las moléculas de una sustancia se encuentran esparcidas equitativamente en otra sustancia. (Cap. 3, pág. 78)

estivation / estivación: Período de inactividad durante los meses calurosos y secos del verano. (Cap. 13, pág. 349)

estuary / estuario: Área en donde un río desemboca en el océano y la cual contiene una mezcla de agua dulce y salada. Sirve de vivero para muchas especies de peces oceánicos. (Cap. 15, pág. 426)

evolution/evolución: Cambio en los rasgos hereditarios de una especie a lo largo del tiempo; puede ocurrir lentamente (gradualismo) o rápidamente (equilibrio puntuado). (Cap. 7, pág. 178)

exocytosis/exocitosis: Proceso en que las moléculas grandes abandonan la célula; ocurre cuando las vesículas o vacuolas se fusionan con la membrana celular y liberan su contenido fuera de la célula. (Cap. 3, pág. 81)

exoskeleton / exoesqueleto: Cubierta corporal externa que protege y apoya el cuerpo de los artrópodos y que también impide que se seque el animal. (Cap. 12, pág. 330)

F

family / familia: Grupo taxonómico más pequeño que el orden, pero más grande que el género. (Cap. 8, pág. 216)

fats/grasas: Sustancias orgánicas que proveen energía al cuerpo y que le ayudan a absorber ciertas vitaminas, además de amortiguar los órganos internos; pueden ser saturadas y no saturadas. (Cap. 17, pág. 468)

fermentation/fermentación: Forma de respiración sin oxígeno que libera solo parte de la energía de los alimentos. (Cap. 3, pág. 84)

fertilization/fecundación: La unión de un óvulo y un espermatozoide. (Cap. 4, pág. 104)

fetus/feto: Bebé nonato después de los dos primeros meses de embarazo y hasta el nacimiento. (Cap. 21, pág. 584)

fins / aletas: Estructuras en forma de abanico que usan los peces para cambiar de dirección, equilibrarse y moverse. (Cap. 13, pág. 345)

fish / pez: Animal de sangre fría que usa sus branquias para obtener oxígeno. (Cap. 13, pág. 345)

fission / fisión: La forma más simple de reproducción asexual, en la que se producen dos células con material genético idéntico al de la célula progenitora; es el método de reproducción más común de las bacterias. (Cap. 9, pág. 240)

flagella / flagelos: Estructuras en forma de látigo que poseen algunas bacterias para poder moverse en condiciones húmedas. (Cap. 9, pág. 237)

food chain / cadena alimenticia: Manera simple de mostrar cómo la energía de los alimentos pasa de un organismo a otro. (Cap. 14, pág. 393)

food group/grupo de alimentos: Alimentos que contienen los mismos nutrientes; por ejemplo, el grupo de la leche, el queso y el yogur. (Cap. 17, pág. 473)

food web / red alimenticia: Serie de cadenas alimenticias sobrepuestas. (Cap. 14, pág. 394)

free-living / de vida libre: Organismo que no depende de otro organismo en particular para su alimentación o morada. (Cap. 12, pág. 319)

frond/fronda: La hoja de un helecho. (Cap. 5, pág. 126)

G

gametophyte stage/etapa de gametofito: Etapa en que todas las estructuras de la planta están compuestas de células con un número haploide (*n*) de cromosomas. (Cap. 5, pág. 124)

gene/gene: Segmento del DNA en un cromosoma que dirige la fabricación de cierta proteína. (Cap. 4, pág. 112)

genetic engineering/ingeniería genética: Cambio de la secuencia del DNA de un gene mediante métodos biológicos y químicos. (Cap. 6, pág. 170)

genetics/genética: El estudio de cómo se heredan los rasgos a través de las acciones de los alelos. (Cap. 6, pág. 153)

genotype/genotipo: Composición genética de un organismo. (Cap. 6, pág. 156)

genus / género: Grupo de diferentes organismos que poseen características parecidas. (Cap. 8, pág. 212)

gills / branquias: Órganos de los moluscos que intercambian oxígeno y dióxido de carbono con el agua. (Cap. 12, pág. 321)

Golgi bodies/cuerpos de Golgi: Pilas de sacos cubiertos por una membrana que empaquetan los materiales y los mueven fuera de la célula. (Cap. 2, pág. 53)

gradualism/gradualismo: Modelo que describe la evolución como un cambio lento de una especie en otra especie nueva. (Cap. 7, pág. 184)

grasslands / praderas: Regiones tropicales y templadas que reciben de 25 a 75 cm de precipitación anual y en la cual dominan la comunidad clímax de hierbas. (Cap. 15, pág. 420)

guard cells / células guardianas: Células alrededor del estoma que lo abren y lo cierran. Junto con la cutícula y los estomas, son adaptaciones que ayudan a las plantas a sobrevivir sobre tierra. (Cap. 11, pág. 299)

gymnosperms / gimnospermas: Plantas vasculares que producen semillas en la superficie de las estructuras reproductoras femeninas. (Cap. 11, pág. 300)

H

habitat / hábitat: Ubicación física en donde vive un organismo (Cap. 14, pág. 389)

helper T cell/célula T ayudante: Tipo de glóbulo blanco que ayuda a otros tipos de glóbulos blancos a producir anticuerpos. (Cap. 22, pág. 610)

hemoglobin/hemoglobina: Sustancia química que contienen los glóbulos rojos, la cual puede transportar oxígeno y dióxido de carbono. (Cap. 18, pág. 503)

herbivore / herbívoro: Animal de pastoreo que come plantas. (Cap. 13, pág. 366)

heredity/herencia: Transferencia de rasgos del progenitor a la progenie. (Cap. 6, pág. 152)

heterozygous/heterocigoto: Organismo que posee dos alelos diferentes para cierto rasgo. (Cap. 6, pág. 156)

hibernation / hibernación: Período de inactividad y bajas necesidades metabólicas durante el invierno. (Cap. 13, pág. 349)

hominids/homínidos: Primates que parecían humanos y que comían tanto plantas como animales y caminaban erguidos. (Cap. 7, pág. 199)

Homo sapiens/Homo sapiens: El nombre de nuestra especie, la cual evolucionó hace unos 400 000 años. (Cap. 7, pág. 200)

homologous/homólogo: Estructuras corporales similares en origen y estructura que indican que dos o más especies pueden haber tenido antepasados comunes. (Cap. 7, pág. 193)

homozygous/homocigoto: Organismo con dos alelos exactamente iguales para cierto rasgo. (Cap. 6, pág. 156)

hormones/hormonas: Sustancias químicas endocrinas producidas en varias glándulas sin conductos a través de todo el cuerpo. (Cap. 20, pág. 562)

host cell/célula huésped: Célula dentro de la cual se reproduce un virus. (Cap. 2, pág. 60)

hypertension/hipertensión: Trastorno cardiovascular que puede ser causado por la aterosclerosis. (Cap. 18, pág. 500)

hyphae / hifas: Masas filamentosas multicelulares que, por lo general, componen el cuerpo de los hongos. (Cap. 10, pág. 268)

hypothesis/hipótesis: Predicción o enunciado que se puede probar. (Cap. 1, pág. 18)

I

immovable joint/articulación fija: Tipo de articulación que permite poco o ningún movimiento. (Cap. 16, pág. 444)

immune system/sistema inmunológico: Complejo de defensas que posee el cuerpo para combatir enfermedades. (Cap. 22, pág. 607)

incomplete dominance/dominancia incompleta: Producción de un fenotipo intermedio a los de dos progenitores homocigotos. (Cap. 6, pág. 160)

independent variable/variable independiente: Es la variable o factor que se cambia. (Cap. 1, pág. 19)

infancy/lactancia: Período de rápido crecimiento y desarrollo mental y físico del bebé desde el nacimiento hasta que cumple un año. (Cap. 21, pág. 588)

inorganic compounds/compuestos inorgánicos: Compuestos hechos de otros elementos menos el carbono; por ejemplo, el agua, la cual compone la mayor parte de la materia viva. (Cap. 3, pág. 76)

intertidal zone / zona entre la marea baja y la alta: Porción de la costa cubierta de agua durante la marea alta y expuesta al aire durante la marea baja. (Cap. 15, pág. 426)

invertebrates / invertebrados: Animal sin columna vertebral. (Cap. 12, pág. 313)

involuntary muscles/músculos involuntarios: Músculos que no se pueden controlar conscientemente. (Cap. 16, pág. 448)

J

joint/articulación: Cualquier lugar en donde se unen dos o más huesos. (Cap. 16, pág. 443)

K

kidney/riñón: Órgano que filtra la sangre y la limpia de los desperdicios que esta ha recogido de las células. (Cap. 19, pág. 534)

kingdom / reino: La primera categoría taxonómica y la más grande. (Cap. 8, pág. 211)

L

larynx/laringe: Vía aérea a la cual están adheridas las cuerdas vocales (Cap. 19, pág. 523)

lichen / liquen: Organismo compuesto de un hongo y un alga verde o una cianobacteria. (Cap. 10, pág. 271)

ligament/ligamento: Banda dura de tejido que mantiene unidos los huesos en las articulaciones. (Cap. 16, pág. 443)

limiting factor / factor limitante: Cualquier factor biótico o abiótico que limita el número de individuos en una población. (Cap. 14, pág. 385)

lymph/linfa: Fluido corporal que consiste principalmente en agua, sustancias disueltas, tales como nutrientes y pequeñas cantidades de proteínas y linfocitos. (Cap. 18, pág. 512)

lymph nodes/ganglios linfáticos: Estructuras, a través del cuerpo, que filtran los microorganismos y los materiales extraños que han sido engullidos por los linfocitos. (Cap. 18, pág. 512)

lymphatic system/sistema linfático: Sistema que recoge el fluido entre los tejidos corporales y lo devuelve a la sangre a través de un sistema de capilares y vasos linfáticos más grandes; juega un papel vital en la protección contra enfermedades. (Cap. 18, pág. 511)

lymphocyte/linfocito: Un tipo de glóbulo blanco. (Cap. 18, pág. 512)

lysosome/lisosoma: Organelo celular eucariótico que contiene los químicos digestivos necesarios para descomponer las moléculas alimenticias, los residuos celulares y las células desgastadas. (Cap. 2, pág. 54)

M

mammal / mamífero: Vertebrado de sangre caliente que tiene pelo y produce leche para amamantar a las crías. (Cap. 13, pág. 360)

mantle / manto: Capa fina de tejido que cubre el cuerpo blando de los moluscos y secreta la concha protectora de los moluscos que poseen concha. (Cap. 12, pág. 321)

marrow/médula: Tejido grasoso suave que se halla en el centro de huesos largos y en los espacios de huesos esponjosos; produce glóbulos rojos y glóbulos blancos. (Cap. 16, pág. 440)

marsupial / marsupio: Mamífero con bolsa que tiene crías inmaduras, las cuales completan su desarrollo en dicha bolsa. (Cap. 13, pág. 362)

mechanical digestion/digestión mecánica: Proceso que ocurre cuando los alimentos se mastican y se mezclan en la boca y se revuelven en el estómago. (Cap. 17, pág. 478)

medusa / medusa: Animal de vida libre, con cuerpo en forma de campana. (Cap. 12, pág. 317)

meiosis/meiosis: Proceso de creación de células sexuales en los órganos reproductores, y en el cual se producen cuatro células sexuales haploides a partir de dos células diploides. (Cap. 4, pág. 104)

melanin/melanina: Pigmento que da color a la piel y el cual aumenta con la exposición a los rayos ultravioleta del sol. Entre más melanina posea una persona, más oscuro es el color de su piel. (Cap. 16, pág. 455)

menopause/menopausia: Ocurre cuando el ciclo menstrual se vuelve irregular y, a la larga, cesa. (Cap. 21, pág. 577)

menstrual cycle/ciclo menstrual: Ciclo mensual de cambios en el sistema reproductor femenino. (Cap. 21, pág. 575)

menstruation/menstruación: Descarga mensual que consiste en células sanguíneas y tejidos de la cubierta interior gruesa del útero. (Cap. 21, pág. 576)

metabolism/metabolismo: La suma total de todas las reacciones químicas de un organismo. (Cap. 3, pág. 83)

metamorphosis / metamorfosis: Cambios por los que pasan muchos insectos y otros animales. Existen dos tipos de metamorfosis: completa e incompleta. (Cap. 12, pág. 332)

minerals/minerales: Nutrientes inorgánicos que regulan muchas reacciones químicas en el cuerpo. (Cap. 17, pág. 470)

mitochondria/mitocondrias: Organelos celulares eucarióticos en donde se descomponen las moléculas alimenticias y se libera energía. (Cap. 2, pág. 53)

mitosis/mitosis: Proceso mediante el cual el núcleo se divide para formar dos núcleos idénticos, que son también idénticos al núcleo original. Consta de cuatro fases o pasos: profase, metafase, anafase y telofase. (Cap. 4, pág. 98)

mixture/mezcla: Combinación de sustancias en la cual las sustancias individuales retienen sus propiedades. (Cap. 3, pág. 73)

model/modelo: Algo que se usa para pensar acerca de cosas que suceden muy lenta o muy rápidamente, que son muy grandes o muy pequeñas, o que son muy peligrosas o costosas para ser observadas directamente. (Cap. 1, pág. 16)

mollusk / molusco: Invertebrado de cuerpo blando, generalmente, con concha; posee un manto y una pata muscular grande. (Cap. 12, pág. 321)

monocot / monocotiledónea: Tipo de angiosperma que contiene un cotiledón dentro de sus semillas. (Cap. 11, pág. 302)

monotreme / monotrema: Mamífero que pone huevos con cáscara fuerte y correosa. (Cap. 13, pág. 362)

movable joint/articulación móvil: Tipo de articulación que permite que el cuerpo realice una amplia gama de movimientos. Existen varios tipos de articulaciones móviles: de charnela, de bola y receptáculo, en bisagra y deslizante. (Cap. 16, pág. 444)

multiple alleles/alelos múltiples: Dos o más alelos que controlan un rasgo específico en un organismo. (Cap. 6, pág. 160)

muscle/músculo: Órgano que puede relajarse y contraerse para permitir el movimiento de los huesos y de las partes corporales. (Cap. 16, pág. 447)

mutation/mutación: Cualquier cambio permanente en un gene o cromosoma celular. Las mutaciones añaden variedad a una especie, cuando el organismo afectado se reproduce, pero muchas son dañinas para los organismos. (Cap. 4, pág. 114)

natural selection/selección natural: Teoría que establece que los organismos cuyos rasgos los hacen más aptos para sus ambientes son los que sobreviven y pasan esos rasgos a la progenie. (Cap. 7, pág. 181)

nephron/nefrón: Unidad diminuta de filtración de los riñones. (Cap. 19, pág. 534)

neuron/neurona: Elemento estructural del sistema nervioso, compuesto de un cuerpo celular y ramificaciones llamadas dendritas y axones. (Cap. 20, pág. 547)

niche / nicho: Papel de un organismo en el ecosistema. (Cap. 14, pág. 389)

nitrogen cycle / ciclo del nitrógeno: Transferencia de nitrógeno de la atmósfera a las plantas y de regreso a la atmósfera o directamente a las plantas nuevamente. (Cap. 14, pág. 398)

nitrogen-fixing bacteria / bacterias nitrificantes: Bacterias que convierten el nitrógeno del aire en una forma útil para ciertas clases de plantas y animales. (Cap. 9, pág. 244)

noncommunicable disease/enfermedad no comunicable: Enfermedad o trastorno que no se disemina de una persona a otra, que puede resultar de factores tales como una dieta deficiente o el crecimiento descontrolado de las células. (Cap. 22, pág. 614)

nonvascular plant / planta no vascular: Planta que carece de tejido vascular y que usa otros medios para mover agua y sustancias a través de la planta. (Cap. 11, pág. 286)

nucleus/núcleo: El organelo más grande en una célula eucariota, el cual dirige todas las actividades de la célula. (Cap. 2, pág. 51)

nutrients/nutrientes: Sustancias provenientes de los alimentos que proveen energía y materiales para el desarrollo, el crecimiento y la reparación de las células; carbohidratos, proteínas, grasas, vitaminas, minerales y agua. (Cap. 17, pág. 464)

O

olfactory cells/células olfativas: Células nerviosas nasales las cuales son estimuladas por las moléculas de gas. (Cap. 20, pág. 558)

omnivore / omnívoro: Animal que come plantas y también come otros animales. (Cap. 13, pág. 366)

open circulatory system / sistema circulatorio abierto: Sistema circulatorio que no posee vasos sanguíneos y en el cual la sangre rodea los órganos. (Cap. 12, pág. 322)

order / orden: Grupo taxonómico más grande que la familia, pero más pequeño que la clase. (Cap. 8, pág. 216)

organ/órgano: Estructura compuesta de diferentes tipos de tejidos que funcionan juntos para realizar una tarea específica; por ejemplo, tu corazón es un órgano compuesto de tejidos musculares, nerviosos y sanguíneos. (Cap. 2, pág. 56)

organelle/organelo: Estructura dentro del citoplasma de células eucariotas cuyas funciones incluyen la desintegración de moléculas alimenticias, la eliminación de residuos y el almacenamiento de materiales. (Cap. 2, pág. 52)

organic compound/compuesto orgánico: Compuesto que contiene carbono. Existen cuatro grupos de compuestos orgánicos que componen a todos los seres vivos: carbohidratos, lípidos, proteínas y ácidos nucleicos. (Cap. 3, pág. 74)

osmosis/osmosis: Difusión de agua a través de la membrana celular. Es importante para las células porque estas contienen moléculas de agua y la mayoría está rodeada de moléculas de agua. (Cap. 3, pág. 79)

ovary/ovario: Base hinchada del pistilo donde se forman los óvulos en las angiospermas (Cap. 5, pág. 133); en los seres humanos, es el órgano sexual femenino donde se producen los óvulos. (Cap. 21, pág. 574)

ovulation/ovulación: Proceso en que se libera un óvulo cada mes de uno de los ovarios. (Cap. 21, pág. 575)

ovule/óvulo: Parte reproductora femenina de una planta de semillas. (Cap. 5, pág. 130)

P

parasite / parásito: Organismo que depende de su huésped para obtener alimento y morada. (Cap. 12, pág. 319)

passive immunity/inmunidad pasiva: La que ocurre cuando se introducen en el cuerpo los anticuerpos producidos en otros animales. (Cap. 22, pág. 608)

passive transport/transporte pasivo: Movimiento de sustancias a través de la membrana celular y que no usa energía celular. (Cap. 3, pág. 80)

pasteurization/pasteurización: Proceso que consiste en calentar los alimentos hasta una temperatura que destruye la mayoría de las bacterias. (Cap. 22, pág. 600)

pathogen / patógeno: Cualquier organismo causante de enfermedades. (Cap. 9, pág. 244)

pedigree/árbol genealógico: Herramienta para rastrear la ocurrencia de un rasgo en cierta familia, en la cual los varones se representan con cuadrados y las mujeres con círculos. (Cap. 6, pág. 169)

periosteum/periósteo: Membrana dura que cubre ajustadamente la superficie de los huesos. (Cap. 16, pág. 441)

peripheral nervous system/sistema nervioso periférico: Uno de los dos sistemas principales en que se divide el sistema nervioso. Está compuesto de todos los nervios por fuera del sistema nervioso central, incluyendo los nervios craneales y los nervios espinales. (Cap. 20, pág. 548)

peristalsis/peristalsis: Ondas o contracciones que mueven los alimentos a lo largo del sistema digestivo. (Cap. 17, pág. 479)

pharynx/faringe: Pasaje en forma de tubo por donde pasan el aire húmedo y cálido y los alimentos (Cap. 19, pág. 523)

phenotype/fenotipo: Expresión física de un genotipo en particular. (Cap. 6, pág. 156)

phloem / floema: Tejido vegetal compuesto de células tubulares. Transporta alimentos desde el lugar en donde se fabrican hasta otras partes de la planta, en donde es usado o almacenado. (Cap. 11, pág. 297)

phylogeny / filogenia: Historia de la evolución de un organismo. (Cap. 8, pág. 215)

phylum / filo: El grupo taxonómico más pequeño después del reino. (Cap. 8, pág. 216)

pioneer community / comunidad pionera: Primera comunidad de organismos que se mudan a un nuevo ambiente. (Cap. 15, pág. 407)

pioneer species / especie pionera: Organismos que son los primeros en crecer en áreas nuevas o que han sido alteradas. (Cap. 11, pág. 289)

pistil/pistilo: Organo reproductor femenino de la flor que consiste en un estigma, un estilo alargado en forma de tallo y un ovario. (Cap. 5, pág. 133)

placental mammal / mamífero placentario: Animal cuyos embriones se desarrollan dentro del útero de la hembra. (Cap. 13, pág. 363)

plankton / plancton: Algas, plantas y otros organismos microscópicos que flotan cerca de la superficie en las aguas cálidas y soleadas de lagos y lagunas de agua dulce. (Cap. 15, pág. 425)

plasma/plasma: Parte líquida de la sangre, la cual consiste principalmente en agua y comprende más de la mitad del volumen de la sangre. (Cap. 18, pág. 503)

platelet/plaqueta: Fragmento celular de forma irregular que ayuda en la coagulación de la sangre. (Cap. 18, pág. 504)

pollen grains/granos de polen: Partes reproductoras masculinas de las plantas de semillas; dos espermatozoides se desarrollan en cada grano de polen. (Cap. 5, pág. 130)

pollination/polinización: Proceso de transferencia de granos de polen desde el estambre hasta el estigma. (Cap. 5, pág. 134)

polygenic inheritance/herencia polígena: Mecanismo hereditario que ocurre cuando un grupo de pares de genes actúa en conjunto para producir un solo rasgo. (Cap. 6, pág. 161)

polyp / pólipo: Animal que tiene forma de jarrón y que generalmente es sésil. (Cap. 12, pág. 317)

population / población: Organismos individuales de la misma especie que viven en el mismo lugar y que pueden producir crías. (Cap. 14, pág. 382)

population density / densidad demográfica: El tamaño de una población que ocupa un área de tamaño limitado. (Cap. 14, pág. 385)

pregnancy/embarazo: Período de nueve meses de desarrollo, en el útero, del óvulo fecundado hasta el nacimiento del bebé. (Cap. 21, pág. 582)

primary succession / sucesión primaria: Sucesión ecológica que comienza en un lugar que no tiene suelo. (Cap. 15, pág. 407)

primates/primates: Grupo de mamíferos que incluye los monos, los simios y a los seres humanos, los cuales comparten varias características como pulgares oponibles, visión binocular y hombros flexibles. Los científicos consideran que todos los primates evolucionaron de un antepasado común. (Cap. 7, pág. 198)

producer/productor: Organismo que elabora su propio alimento. (Cap. 3, pág. 83)

proteins/proteínas: Moléculas orgánicas grandes compuestas principalmente de aminoácidos y las cuales se necesitan para el crecimiento y reparación de las células corporales. (Cap. 17, pág. 466)

prothallus/prótalo: Gametofito del helecho que produce células sexuales que se unen para formar el cigoto. (Cap. 5, pág. 126)

protist / protista: Organismo unicelular o multicelular que vive en ambientes húmedos o lluviosos. (Cap. 10, pág. 256)

protozoans / protozoarios: Protistas unicelulares que parecen animales; son complejos y viven en agua, tierra y tanto en organismos vivos como muertos. (Cap. 10, pág. 261)

pseudopods / seudopodios: Extensiones temporales del citoplasma, o patas falsas, de los Rhizopoda, que usan para moverse y alimentarse. (Cap. 10, pág. 262)

pulmonary circulation/circulación pulmonar: Flujo de sangre a través del corazón, hasta los pulmones y de regreso al corazón. (Cap. 18, pág. 494)

punctuated equilibrium/equilibrio puntuado: Modelo que muestra que la evolución rápida de una especie puede resultar debido a la mutación de unos cuantos genes, resultando en una nueva especie. (Cap. 7, pág. 184)

Punnett square/cuadrado de Punnett: Instrumento que se utiliza para predecir resultados en la genética mendeliana; muestra todas las formas en que se pueden combinar los alelos. (Cap. 6, pág. 156)

radioactive element/elemento radiactivo: Elemento que despide radiación debido a un núcleo inestable. Al despedir radiación, los elementos radiactivos se convierten en productos más estables. (Cap. 7, pág. 190)

radula / rádula: Órgano de los moluscos que parece una lengua y que actúa como una lima con hileras de dientes para romper los alimentos en pedazos más pequeños. (Cap. 12, pág. 321)

recessive/recesivo: Factor que parece desaparecer debido a un rasgo dominante en la progenie. (Cap. 6, pág. 154)

reflex/reflejo: Respuesta involuntaria y automática a un estímulo. (Cap. 20, pág. 551)

reproduction/reproducción: Proceso mediante el cual los organismos producen más individuos. (Cap. 21, pág. 572)

reptile / reptil: Vertebrado de sangre fría con piel seca y escamosa y el cual no depende del agua para su reproducción. (Cap. 13, pág. 351)

retina/retina: Tejido sensible a la energía luminosa ubicado en la parte posterior del ojo. (Cap. 20, pág. 556)

rhizoids / rizoides: Raíces filamentosas con solo unas cuantas células de grosor que anclan las hepáticas y los musgos en su lugar. (Cap. 11, pág. 288)

rhizome/risoma: Tallo subterráneo de donde crecen las hojas y las raíces de los helechos. (Cap. 5, pág. 126)

ribosomes/ribosomas: Estructuras pequeñas de dos partes dentro del citoplasma que fabrican sus propias proteínas. Reciben instrucciones del material hereditario en el núcleo sobre cómo y cuándo fabricar ciertas proteínas. (Cap. 2, pág. 53)

RNA/RNA: Segundo tipo de ácido nucleico, llamado ácido ribonucleico, que transporta los códigos para la fabricación de proteínas desde el núcleo hasta los ribosomas. (Cap. 4, pág. 113)

saliva/saliva: Sustancia producida por tres grupos de glándulas cerca de la boca. Contiene principalmente agua, pero también contiene mucosidad y la enzima salival amilasa. (Cap. 17, pág. 479)

saprophyte / saprofito: Cualquier organismo que usa materia muerta como su fuente alimenticia y energética; las bacterias saprofitas evitan la acumulación de materias muertas, por todo el mundo. (Cap. 9, pág. 243)

science/ciencia: Manera o proceso que se usa para investigar lo que sucede a nuestro alrededor y que nos provee algunas posibles respuestas. (Cap. 1, pág. 6)

scientific methods/métodos científicos: Pasos usados para resolver problemas en ciencia; involucran reconocer el problema, formular una hipótesis, probar la hipótesis, realizar el experimento, analizar los datos y sacar conclusiones. (Cap. 1, pág. 14)

secondary succession / sucesión secundaria: Sucesión que comienza en un lugar que ya tiene suelo y el cual fue la morada de organismos vivos. (Cap. 15, pág. 408)

sedimentary rock/roca sedimentaria: Tipo de roca que contiene la mayor cantidad de fósiles. (Cap. 7, pág. 189)

semen/semen: Mezcla de espermatozoides y fluido producida en la vesícula seminal, la cual sale del cuerpo a través de la uretra. (Cap. 21, pág. 574)

sex-linked gene/gene ligado al sexo: Alelo heredado en un cromosoma que determina el sexo. (Cap. 6, pág. 168)

sexual reproduction/reproducción sexual: Manera de crear un nuevo organismo de la unión de dos células sexuales—un óvulo y un espermatozoide—que por lo general provienen de diferentes organismos. (Cap. 4, pág. 104)

sexually transmitted disease (STD)/enfermedad transmitida sexualmente (ETS): enfermedad transmitida de una persona a otra mediante el contacto sexual. Causada por virus o bacterias. (Cap. 22, pág. 604)

skeletal muscles/músculos esqueléticos: Músculos que mueven los huesos y que cuando se observan bajo el microscopio se ven estriados. (Cap. 16, pág. 450)

skeletal system/sistema esquelético: Sistema compuesto de todos los huesos del cuerpo, el cual forma el marco que da apoyo y forma al cuerpo, protege los órganos internos y provee el lugar para que se adhieran los músculos. (Cap. 16, pág. 440)

smooth muscles/músculos lisos: Músculos involuntarios no estriados que mueven muchos de los órganos internos. Los intestinos, la vejiga y los vasos sanguíneos están hechos de una o más capas de músculo liso. (Cap. 16, pág. 440)

sori/soros: Estructuras productoras de esporas que se encuentran en los lados inferiores de las frondas maduras de los helechos. (Cap. 5, pág. 126)

species/especie: Grupo de organismos cuyos miembros pueden aparearse entre sí en su ambiente natural. (Cap. 7, pág. 178); La categoría de clasificación más pequeña y la más precisa. Los organismos pertenecientes a la misma especie pueden aparearse y producir progenie fértil. (Cap. 8, pág. 212)

sperm/espermatozoide: Célula masculina producida en los órganos reproductores de los hombres y la cual contiene solo la mitad del número de cromosomas de las células corporales; posee una cola que parece un latigo que provee movimiento y una cabeza que contiene información genética. (Cap. 4, pág. 104; Cap. 21, pág. 573)

spore / espora: Célula reproductora que forma nuevos organismos sin ayuda de la fecundación. (Cap. 10, pág. 269)

sporophyte stage/etapa de esporofito: Etapa en que todas las estructuras de la planta están compuestas de células con un número diploide de cromosomas. (Cap. 5, pág. 124)

stamen/estambre: Órgano reproductor masculino de la flor que consiste en un filamento y una antera. (Cap. 5, pág. 133)

stomata / estomas: Pequeños poros en la superficie de las hojas de las plantas, que permiten que el dióxido de carbono, el agua y el oxígeno entren y salgan de la hoja. (Cap. 11, pág. 299)

symbiosis / simbiosis: Cualquier relación estrecha entre dos o más especies diferentes. (Cap. 14, pág. 387)

symmetry / simetría: Se refiere al arreglo de las partes individuales de un objeto; los animales con simetría bilateral tienen partes corporales que son imágenes especulares una de la otra; los animales con simetría radiada poseen partes corporales arregladas en forma de círculo alrededor de un punto central y los animales asimétricos no tienen una forma corporal definitiva. (Cap. 12, pág. 313)

synapse/sinapsis: Espacio pequeño a través del cual se mueven los impulsos al ser transmitidos de una neurona a la siguiente. (Cap. 20, pág. 548)

systemic circulation/circulación sistémica: Flujo de sangre rica en oxígeno a todos los órganos y tejidos del cuerpo, excepto el corazón y los pulmones . (Cap. 18, pág. 495)

T

taiga / taiga: Región fría de árboles coníferos siempre verdes. (Cap. 15, pág. 416)

target tissue/tejido asignado: Tipo de tejido específico que se ve afectado por las hormonas. (Cap. 20, pág. 562)

taste buds/papilas gustativas: Receptores principales en la lengua para el sentido del gusto. (Cap. 20, pág. 558)

taxonomy / taxonomía: La ciencia que se encarga de clasificar. (Cap. 8, pág. 210)

technology/tecnología: La aplicación de la ciencia para fabricar productos o instrumentos que la gente puede usar. (Cap. 1, pág. 10)

temperate deciduous forest / bosque deciduo de zonas templadas: Comunidad clímax de árboles deciduos, los cuales pierden sus hojas en el otoño. (Cap. 15, pág. 417)

tendon/tendón: Bandas gruesas de tejido que unen los músculos esqueléticos a los huesos. (Cap. 16, pág. 450)

testes/testículos: Órganos sexuales masculinos donde se empiezan a producir las células reproductoras masculinas, los espermatozoides, y la hormona sexual masculina, testosterona, durante la pubertad. (Cap. 21, pág. 573)

tissue/tejido: En organismos multicelulares, es un grupo de células similares que trabajan juntas para realizar una función. (Cap. 2, pág. 56)

toxin / toxina: Veneno que producen los patógenos bacteriales. (Cap. 9, pág. 245)

trachea/tráquea: Tubo de unos 12 cm de largo ubicado debajo de la laringe y forrado con membranas mucosas y cilios para atrapar el polvo, las bacterias y el polen. (Cap. 19, pág. 523)

tropical rain forest / bosque pluvial tropical: La comunidad clímax más importante en las regiones ecuatoriales del mundo y que posee una vegetación frondosa. (Cap. 15, pág. 419)

tundra / tundra: Región fría, seca y sin árboles, que a veces se denomina desierto gélido porque tiene inviernos que duran de seis a nueve meses. (Cap. 15, pág. 415)

ureter/uréter: Conducto que une cada riñón con la vejiga. (Cap. 19, pág. 535)

urethra/uretra: Conducto por donde sale la orina de la vejiga. (Cap. 19, pág. 535)

urinary system/sistema urinario: Compuesto por los órganos que limpian la sangre de los desechos producidos por el metabolismo de los nutrientes. También controla el volumen sanguíneo eliminando el exceso de agua que producen las células. (Cap. 19, pág. 533)

urine/orina: Desecho líquido que contiene exceso de agua, sales y otros residuos que no fueron absorbidos por el cuerpo. (Cap. 19, pág. 534)

uterus/útero: Órgano muscular hueco con forma de pera y paredes gruesas en donde se desarrolla el óvulo fecundado. (Cap. 21, pág. 575)

vaccination/vacunación: Proceso de administrar una vacuna por inyección o por vía oral. (Cap. 22, pág. 608)

vaccine / vacuna: Sustancia que se produce a partir de partículas dañadas de las paredes celulares de bacterias o de bacterias muertas; puede prevenir, pero no curar muchas enfermedades causadas por bacterias. (Cap. 9, pág. 244); Sustancia hecha de partículas de virus dañados, los cuales ya no pueden causar enfermedades. (Cap. 2, pág. 62)

vagina/vagina: Tubo muscular en el extremo inferior del útero que lo conecta al exterior del cuerpo. También se le denomina canal de nacimiento. (Cap. 21, pág. 575)

variation/variación: Rasgo heredado que diferencia a un individuo de otros miembros de la misma especie; puede ser beneficiosa, dañina o no tener influencia en una población. (Cap. 7, pág. 182)

vascular plant / planta vascular: Planta con tejidos que forman un sistema que transporta agua, nutrientes y otras sustancias a lo largo de la planta. (Cap. 11, pág. 286)

vein/vena: Vaso sanguíneo que transporta sangre hacia el corazón y que tiene válvulas que facilitan el regreso de la sangre al corazón. (Cap. 18, pág. 496)

ventricles/ventrículos: Las dos cavidades inferiores del corazón. (Cap. 18, pág. 493)

vertebrates / vertebrados: Animal con columna vertebral; solo un 3 por ciento de todos los animales son vertebrados. (Cap. 12, pág. 313)

vestigial structure/estructura vestigial: Parte corporal que parece no tener función alguna. (Cap. 7, pág. 194)

villi/microvellosidades: Proyecciones pequeñísimas en forma de dedos que cubren los pliegues del intestino delgado. (Cap. 17, pág. 482)

virus/virus: Partícula no viva que consiste en un núcleo de material hereditario rodeado por una capa de proteínas. Es algo que no crece, no responde al ambiente ni come y sin embargo se reproduce dentro de las células. (Cap. 2, pág. 58)

vitamins/vitaminas: Nutrientes orgánicos esenciales necesarios en pequeñas cantidades para que el cuerpo pueda utilizar otros nutrientes. (Cap. 17, pág. 469)

voluntary muscles/músculos voluntarios: Músculos que se pueden controlar conscientemente. (Cap. 16, pág. 448)

water cycle / ciclo del agua: Viaje continuo del agua entre la atmósfera y la Tierra; involucra los procesos de evaporación, condensación y precipitación. (Cap. 14, pág. 396)

xylem / xilema: Tejido compuesto de vasos tubulares que transportan agua y sustancias disueltas desde las raíces, a través de toda la planta. (Cap. 11, pág. 297)

zygote/cigoto: La nueva célula que se forma a raíz de la fecundación. (Cap. 4, pág. 105)

Index

The index for *Science Voyages* will help you locate major topics in the book quickly and easily. Each entry in the index is followed by the numbers of the pages on which the entry is discussed. A page number given in **boldface type** indicates the page on which that entry is defined. A page number given in *italic type* indicates a page on which the entry is used in an illustration or photograph. The abbreviation *act.* indicates a page on which the entry is used in an activity.

A

Abdominal thrusts, 526, *526*
Abiotic factors, **379**–380, *379*, 400
ABO identification system, 506
Absorption, 476, 482, 487
Active immunity, **608,** 608–609, 619
Active transport, **80,** 91
Active virus, 60
   life cycle of, 60, *60*
Adaptation, 182–185
   of amphibians, 348–349, *349*
   of birds, 356, *356*
   to climate, 421, *421*
   of desert plants and animals, 421, *421*
   for flight, 356, *356*
   of reptiles, 352, *352*
Adenine, 111
Adolescence, **588,** 595
Adulthood, **590,** 595
Aerobe, **240,** 250
African sleeping sickness, *262*
Aging, 592
AIDS, *58,* 605
   HIV and, 605
   increase of, 60
   vaccine for, 611
Air pollution, lichens and, 272

Airplanes, 359, *359*
Alcohol, effect on nervous system, 552
Algae, **257**–261, *257, 258, 259, 260,* 380, 388, 392
   brown, 260, *260,* 261
   diatoms, 257–258, *257,* 261
   dinoflagellates, 258–259, *258,* 261
   euglena, 257, *257,* 261
   green, *258–259,* 259, 261, 283, 284, *284*
   lichens and, 271
   protozoa compared to, *act.* 267
   red, 260, *260,* 261
Alleles, **152,** 172
   multiple, 160–161, 173
   separation in meiosis, *152*
   and traits, 156
Allergens, **617**
Allergies, **616**
Alternation of generations, **125**
Alveoli, **524,** 540
Amino acids, **466**–467
Amniocentesis, 581
Amnion, *582,* **583**
Amniotic egg, 352, *352*
Amniotic fluid, *582*
Amniotic sac, **583**
Amoeba, *261,* 262
Amphibians, **348**–350, *348, 349, 350,* 370

adaptations of, 348–349, *349*
Amylase, 477
Anaerobe, **240,** *240,* 241, 250
Anaphase, 98, *99*
Anaphase I, 106–107
Anaphase II, 107
Anemia, 508
   Angiosperms, *287,* 296, **301**–302, *301, 302,* 304, *304,* 307
   reproduction of, 132–135, 147
   seed formation, *134*
Animal cells, 50–54
Animal cloning, 109
Animal–like protists, 261–263, *261, 262, 263*
Animals
   adaptation of, 421, *421*
   characteristics of, 312–314
   classification of, 213, *213,* 217
   classifying, *act.* 311, 313–314, 344, *344,* 361–367
   endangered and threatened species of, *act.* 410–411
   in forests, 214, *215,* 419
   in grasslands, 420
   invertebrate, 310–341, *312,* **313,** *338, 339*
   symmetry in, 313–314, *314*

O

P

Art Credits

Photo Credits

Researchers, (b)Zefa/The Stock Market; **173** (t)Matt Meadows, (b)Suzanne Szasz/Photo Researchers.

Chapter 7 - 176-7 Stan Wayman/Photo Researchers; **177** Aaron Haupt; **178** Tony Ward/FPG; **180** (tl)Christian Grzimek /Okapia/Photo Researchers, (tr)Kevin Schafer/Peter Arnold Inc., (c)Ron Sanford/The Stock Market, (b)Kenneth W. Fink/Photo Researchers; **181** Brian Parker/Tom Stack & Assoc.; **182** (l)John Gerlach/Visuals Unlimited, (r)Gregory K. Scott/Photo Researchers; **183** (l)Joe McDonald/Tom Stack & Assoc., (r)Mark Boulton/Photo Researchers; **186** Jeremy Woodhouse/DRK Photo; **187** Matt Meadows; **188** Patrick Aventurier/Liaison International; **189** (t)John Cancalosi/Tom Stack & Assoc., (bl)David M. Dennis/Tom Stack & Assoc., (br)Breck P. Kent/Earth Scenes; **191** D. Long/Visuals Unlimited; **195** Tim Davis/Photo Researchers; **196** (l)Bob Campbell, (r)John Reader; **198** M. Loup/Jacana/Photo Researchers; **199** Frans Lanting/Minden Pictures; **200** (t)Tom McHugh/Photo Researchers, (bl)RIA-Novosti/Sovfoto, (br)E.R. Degginger/Color-Pic; **201** E.R. Degginger/Color-Pic; **202** (t)John Gerlach/Visuals Unlimited, (b)Brian Parker/Tom Stack & Assoc.; **203** (tl)Patrick Aventurier/Liaison International, (tr)John Cancalosi/Tom Stack & Assoc., (bl)Frans Lanting/Minden Pictures, (br)E.R. Degginger/Color-Pic.

UNIT 2

Opener - 206-7 ©Chris Newbert; **207** ©David Young/Tom Stack & Associates.

Chapter 8 - 208-9 Aaron Haupt; **209** Mark Steinmetz; **211** Ken Cole/Animals Animals; **212** Wally Eberhart/Visuals Unlimited; **213** (l)Ruth Dixon, (c)Stephen J. Krasemann/DRK Photo, (r)Renee Lynn/Photo Researchers; **214** James P. Blair; **215** (l)David M. Dennis, (c)Mark Steinmetz, (r)Mark Steinmetz; **216** Doug Perrine/Innerspace Visions; **218 219** Geoff Butler; **220** (l)Stephan J. Krasemann/DRK Photo, (tr)Robert Maier/Animals Animals, (br)John Cancalosi/DRK Photo; **221** (l)Doug Perrine/Innerspace Visions, (c)Denise Tackett/Tom Stack & Assoc., (r)Don Enger/Animals Animals; **223** Aaron Haupt; **225** (l)Stephan J. Krasemann/DRK Photo, (r)Jeff Lepore/Photo Researchers; **226** Roy Morsch/The Stock Market; **226-9** (bkgd)file photo; **227** (tl)Donald Specker/Animals Animals, (tr)Photo Researchers, (cr)David M. Dennis, (bl)Harry Rogers/Photo Researchers, (br)Patti Murray/Animals Animals; **228** (tr)Donald Specker/Animals Animals, (cl)Harry Rogers/Photo Researchers, (cr)Tom McHugh/Photo Researchers, (bl)Patti Murray/Animals Animals, (bc)Carroll W. Perkins/Animals Animals, (br)Donald Specker/Animals Animals; **229** (tl)Linda Bailey/Animals Animals, (tr)Ken Brate/Photo Researchers, (cr)Harry Rogers/Photo Researchers, (bl)James H. Robinson/Photo Researchers, (br)Ed Reschke/Peter Arnold, Inc.; **230** (tl)Ruth Dixon, (bl)Renee Lynn/Photo Researchers, (r)Stephen J. Krasemann/DRK Photo; **231** (t)Doug Perrine/Innerspace Visions, (bl)Stephen Krasemann/DRK Photo, (br)Jeff Lepore/Photo Researchers; **233** (t)Victoria Hurst/Tom Stack & Assoc., (c)Ken Cole/Animals Animals, (b)Peter Weimann/Animals Animals.

Chapter 9 - 234-235 Manfred Kage/Peter Arnold, Inc.; **235** Michael Abbey/Photo Researchers; **236** R. Calentine/Vissuals Unlimited; **239** Matt Meadows; **240** (t)Tom E. Adams/Peter Arnold, Inc., (b)Visuals Unlimited, **241** D. Foster/Visuals Unlimited; **242** (tl)Michael Abbey/Photo Researchers, (tr)Michael Abbey/Photo Researchers, (bl)Winston Pathnode/photo Researchers, (br) Michael Abbey/Photo Researchers; **243** (t)David R. Frazier/Photo Researchers, (b)Charles Gold/The Stock Market; **246** Alfred Pasieka/Science Photo Library/Photo Researchers; **247** Bryan Hodgson; **248 249** KS Studio; **250** (t) R. Calentine/Visuals Unlimited, (b)Visuals Unlimited **251** (1)Alfred Pasieka/Science Photo Library/Photo Researchers, (r)Charles Gold/The Stock Market; (b)Daniel Schaefer.

Chapter 10 - 254-5 Amanita Pictures; **255** Mark Burnett; **257** Jan Hinsch/Science Photo Library/Photo Researchers; **258** (t)Dr. David M. Phillips/Photo Researchers, (b)Biophoto Associates /Photo Researchers; **259** (tl)Runk/Schoenberger from Grant Heilman, (tr)Runk/Schoenberger from Grant Heilman, (b)Michael Abbey/Photo Researchers; **260** (t)Walter H. Hodge/Peter Arnold, Inc., (b)Gregory Ochoki/Photo Researchers; **262** (tl)Ronald Gorbutt/Britstock, (tr)Alfred Pasieka/Science Photo Library /Photo Researchers, (b)Oliver Meckes/Photo Researchers; **263** (t)M.I.Walker/Photo Researchers, (b)Sinclair Stammers/Science Photo Library/Photo Researchers; **264** (l)Scott Camazine/Photo Researchers, (c)Amanita Pictures, (r)Matt Meadows; **265** David M. Dennis/Tom Stack & Associates; **266** (l)Nigel Cattlin/Holt Studios International/Photo Reasearchers, Inc., (r)Noble Proctor/Photo Researchers; **267** Paul Johnson/BPS/Tony Stone Images; **268** Amanita Pictures; **269** Ed Reschke/Peter Arnold, Inc.; **270** J. Forsdyke, Gene Cox/Science Photo Library/Photo Researchers; **271** David M. Dennis/Tom Stack & Associates; **272** (l)Stephen J. Krasemann/DRK Photo, (c)Runk/Schoenberger from Grant Heilman, (r)L. West/Photo Researchers; **273** Emory Kristof, (inset)Manfred Kage/Peter Arnold, Inc.; **274** Matt Meadows; **275** Matt Meadows; **276** (t)Jan Hinsch/Science Photo Library/Photo Researchers, (l)Oliver Meckes/Photo Researchers, (r)Runk /Schoenberger from Grant Heilman; **277** The Birmingham News.

Chapter 11 - 280-1 Aaron Haupt; **281** file photo; **282** Michael P. Gadomski/Photo Researchers; **283** (t)Jan Hirsch/Science Photo Library/Photo Researchers, (b)Doug Sokell/Visuals Unlimited, (l)Pat O'Hara/DRK Photo, (r)John Shaw/Tom Stack & Associates; **285** (l)Runk/Schoenberger from Grant Heilman, (c)Harold Hofman/Photo Researchers, (r)Kevin Schafer/Peter Arnold, Inc.; **286** David Cavagnaro/DRK Photo; **288** (l)John Kaprielian/Photo Researchers, (r)Barry L. Runk from Grant Heilman; **289** Kevin Schafer/Peter Arnold, Inc.; **290** (tr)Jane Grushow from Grant Heilman, (c)Stephen J. Krasemann/Photo Researchers, (l)Rod Planck/Photo Researchers, (br)David S. Addison/Visuals Unlimited; **291** (t)Runk/Schoenberger from Grant Heilman, (c)Sydney Karp/Photos/NATS, (b)Richard L. Carton/Photo Researchers; **292** Walter H. Hodge/Peter Arnold, Inc.; **293** Ludek Pesek/Science Photo Library/Photo Researchers; **294** Aaron Haupt; **295** (l)John D. Cunningham/Visuals Unlimited, (r)Ira Block, Courtesy Silkeborg Museum, Denmark; **296** Jeff Greenberg/Visuals Unlimited; **298** Runk Schoenberger from Grant Heilman; **300** (l)Richard Shiel/Earth Scenes, (r)Kenneth W. Fink/Photo Researchers; **301** (l)Joyce Photographics/Photo Researchers, (r)M.A. Chappell/Earth Scenes; **302** (l)Photo/NATS, (r)George E. Jones III/Photo Researchers; **303** (t)Mark E. Gibson, (bl)Aaron Haupt, (br)Frank Siteman/Stock Boston; **304** (l)Aaron Haupt, (r)Angelina Lax/Photo Researchers; **305** Matt Meadows; **306** (t)Michael P. Gadomski/Photo Researchers, (b)Walter H. Hodge/Peter Arnold, Inc.; **307** (t)Richard Shiel/Earth Scenes, (b)Aaron Haupt.

Chapter 12 - 310-1 Roger K. Burnard; **311** KS Studio; **312** (l)Mitsuaki Iwago/Minden Pictures, (c)Lynn Stone, (r)Fred Bavendam/Minden Pictures; **315** Fred Bravendam/Minden Pictures; **318** Carolina Biological Supply/Phototake; **319** Breck P. Kent/Animals Animals; **320** James E. Hayden/Phototake; **321** (l)Zig Leszczynski/Animals Animals, (r)Andrew J. Martinez /Photo Researchers; **322** (l)William J. Weber, (r)Sharon M. Kurgis; **323** Flip Nicklin/Minden Pictures; **324** Runk/Schoenberger from Grant Heilman; **325** NMSB/Custom Medical Stock Photo; **326** (l)Geri Murphy, (r)Geri Murphy; **327** The New Zealand Herald; **328 329** KS Studio; **330** (l)David M. Dennis, (r)Mark Moffett/Minden Pictures; **331** (t)Frans Lanting/Minden Pictures, (c)Jack Wilburn/Animals Animals, (b)Sinclair Stammers/Animals Animals; **332** Lynn Stone; **333** (t)G.I. Bernard/Animals Animals,

Photo Credits

(c)E.R. Degginger/Animals Animals, (b)Fred Bravendam/Minden Pictures; **334** (tr)Ruth Dixon, (l)Fred Bavendam/Minden Pictures, (br)Fred Bavendam/Minden Pictures; **335** Fred Bavendam /Minden Pictures; **336** Dave Fleetham/Tom Stack & Associates; **337** KS Studio; **339** (tl)William J. Weber, (tr)Geri Murphy, (bl)Mark Moffett/Minden Pictures, (br)Frans Lanting/Minden Pictures.

Chapter 13 - 342-3 Roland Seitre/Peter Arnold, Inc.; **343** Dan Rest; **345** (t)Brian Parker/Tom Stack & Associates, (c)David R. Frazier, (b)Jesse Cancelmo; **347** (t)Breck P. Kent/Animals Animals, (b)Kelvin Aitken/Peter Arnold, Inc.; **348** David M. Dennis; **351** (t)Mark Moffett/Minden Pictures, (lc)Michael Collier, (rc)Alvin R. Staffan, (b)Lynn Stone; **353** Hans Pfletschinger/Peter Arnold, Inc.; **354** (l)Roger K. Burnard, (r)Lynn Stone; **355** (left-1)Don C. Nieman, (left-2)Alan Carey, (left-3)Roy Morsch/The Stock Market, (left-4)Alvin E. Staffan, (right-1)David R. Frazier, (right-2)William J. Weber, (right-3)Alan Nelson, (right-4)William J. Weber; **357** Michael Quinton/Minden Pictures; **359** (l)Mary Evans Picture Library/Photo Researchers, (r)Culver Pictures; **360** Johnny Johnson; **361** Tom McHugh/Photo Researchers; **362** Roger K. Burnard; **363** (t)Sharon Remmen, (b)CNRI/Phototake; **364** (left-1)Tom McHugh/Photo Researchers, (left-2)William J. Weber, (left-3)Stephen Dalton/Animals Animals, (left-4)Sharon M. Kurgis,(right-1)Sharon Remmen, (right-2)Alvin Staffan, (right-3)V. Berns; **365** (left-1)Tom Pantages, (left-2)Lynn Stone, (left-3)Alvin E. Staffan, (right-1)Alan Carey, (right-2)William J. Weber, (right-3)Frans Lanting/Minden Pictures; **366** (tr)Lynn M. Stone, (l)David R. Frazier, (br)Michael A. Keller/The Stock Market; **367** Gerard Lacz/Peter Arnold, Inc.; **368** Maslowski Photo; **370** (t)Kelvin Aitken/Peter Arnold, Inc., (c)Michael Collier, (b)David M. Dennis; **371** (t)Alan Nelson, (l)William J. Weber, (right-1)Don C. Nieman, (right-2)Stephen Dalton/Animals Animals, (right-3)V. Berns.

UNIT 3

Opener- 374-5 George F. Mobley.

Chapter 14 - 376-7 Breck P. Kent/Animals Animals; **377** Geoff Butler; **378** (l)ESA/TSADO/Tom Stack & Assoc., (r)Dan Guravich/Photo Researchers; **379** (l)Stephen J. Krasemann/DRK Photo, (c)Michael Gadomski/Earth Scenes, (r)John Gerlach/Animals Animals; **380** Larry Ulrich/Tony Stone Worldwide; **382** Mike Bacon/Tom Stack & Assoc.; **383** Matt Meadows; **385** Stephen J. Krasemann/DRK Photo; **387** Gunter Ziesler/Peter Arnold; **388** (l)Michael & Patricia Fogden/DRK Photo, (c)Stephen J. Krasemann/DRK Photo, (r)James H. Robinson /Animals Animals; **389** David M. Dennis/Tom Stack & Assoc.; **390 391** Matt Meadows; **399** Jeff Lepore/Photo Researchers; **400** Stephen J. Krasemann/DRK Photo; **401** courtesy Isidro Bosch.

Chapter 15 - 404-5 Carr Clifton/Minden Pictures; **405** file photo; **408** V. McMillan/Visuals Unlimited; **409** Larry Ulrich/DRK Photo; **410** Jesse Cancelmo; **413** Patti Murray/Earth Scenes; **416** (l)Johnny Johnson/Animals Animals, (r)Phil Degginger/Color-Pic; **417** Larry Lefever from Grant Heilman; **420** Jake Rajs/Tony Stone Images; **421** (t)Gary Braasch/Woodfin Camp & Assoc., (b)Zig Leszczynski/Animals Animals; **423** (l)Anna E. Zuckerman/Tom Stack & Assoc., (r)John Shaw/Tom Stack & Assoc.; **424** (l)Barbara Gerlach/DRK Photo, (r)Peter Weiman/Animals Animals; **425** (t)John Sohlden/Visuals Unlimited, (b)John Gerlach/Visuals Unlimited; **426** Mark Burnett; **427** (l)Sunstar/Photo Researchers, (r)Earl Scott/Photo Researchers; **428-431** (bkgd)Tom Van Sant, The Geosphere Project/The Stock Market; **429** (t)Greg Probst/Tony Stone Images, (b)Grant Heilman Photography; **430** (t)George Ranalli/Photo Researchers, (b)Tom Bean/Tony Stone Images; **431** (t)Tom Bean/DRK Photo, (b)Gary Braasch/Tony Stone Images; **433** (t)Johnny Johnson/Animals Animals, (b)Barbara Gerlach/DRK Photo.

UNIT 4

Opener - 436-7 David Madison/Tony Stone Images; **437** Lennart Nilsson/Albert Bonniers Förlag.

Chapter 16 - 438-9 Richard H. Smith/FPG; **439** Doug Martin; **440** Will & Deni McIntyre/Photo Researchers; **441** (t)J. Sekowski, (cl,b)James Stevenson/Science Photo Library/Photo Researchers, (cr)G.I. Bernard/Animals Animals; **443** Matt Meadows; **444** William Sallaz/Duomo; **445** Custom Medical Stock Photo; **448** Doug Martin; **449** (t)Michael Newman/PhotoEdit, (c)Tony Freeman/PNI, (b)David J. Sams/Stock Boston; **450** (t,c)D.W. Fawcett/Visuals Unlimited, (b)Custom Medical Stock Photo; **452** David Stoecklein/The Stock Market; **453** Doug Martin; **454** (l)Culver Pictures, (r)Photofest; **456** Johnny Johnson; **457** Peter Menzel/Stock Boston; **459** (tl,tr)D.W. Fawcett/Visuals Unlimited, (tc)Custom Medical Stock Photo, (b)Peter Menzel/Stock Boston.

Chapter 17 - 462-3 Boehringer Ingelheim International GmbH, photo Lennart Nilsson, The Incredible Machine, National Geographic Society; **463** Doug Martin; **464-5** Jerome Prevost /TempSport/Corbis Media; **464** (t)Matt Meadows/Peter Arnold, Inc., (b)Jeff Greenberg/Visuals Unlimited; **466** (t)Doug Martin, (c)Charles D. Winters/Photo Researchers, (b)Doug Martin; **467** (l)Don & Pat Valenti/DRK Photo, (r)Meinrad Faltner/The Stock Market; **468** (l)Cabisco/Visuals Unlimited, (r)Aaron Haupt/Photo Researchers; **469** Geoff Butler; **470** (l)Science Photo Library/Photo Researchers, (r)Larry Mulvehill/Photo Researchers; **471** (l)Mickey Gibson/Animals Animals, (r)Doug Martin; **472** Wolfgang Fischer/Peter Arnold, Inc.; **475** (l)Joseph Bailey, (r)M.I. Walker /Photo Researchers; **476** (tl)Dr. Harry Snady/Phototake NYC, (tr)Dr. R.K.F. Schiller/Science Photo Library/Photo Researchers, (cl)Dr. R.K.F. Schiller/Science Photo Library/Photo Researchers, (cr)Dr. Harry Snady/Phototake NYC, (b)CNRI/Science Photo Library/Photo Researchers; **483** CNRI/Science Photo Library /Photo Researchers; **484** (t)Elaine Shay, (b)Doug Martin; **485** Bob Mullenix; **486** (l)Cabisco/Visuals Unlimited, (r)Doug Martin; **487** CNRI/Science Photo Library/Photo Researchers.

Chapter 18 - 490-1 Alex S. MacLean/Peter Arnold, Inc.; **491** Aaron Haupt; **497** (t)Rod Joslin, (b)Matt Meadows; **499** (t)Cabisco/Visuals Unlimited, (c)W. Ober/Visuals Unlimited, (b)Sloop/Visuals Unlimited; **500** Charles Thatcher/Tony Stone Images; **501** Doug Martin; **503** (t)National Cancer Institute/Science Photo Library/Photo Researchers, (b)Dr. Tony Brain/Science Photo Library/Photo Researchers; **504** (t)Robert Becker/Custom Medical Stock Photo, (b)Biophoto Assoc./Photo Researchers, Inc.; **507** Laura Dwight/PhotoEdit; **508** Omikron/Photo Researchers; **509** (l)Fred Hossler/Visuals Unlimited, (lc)Biology Media/Photo Researchers, (rc)Michael Dalton/Fundamental Photographs, (r)Carolina Biological Supply; **510** (l)Ted Allan/MPTV/20th Century Fox, (r)Image Shop/Phototake NYC; **512** John Watney/Photo Researchers; **514** Image Shop/Phototake NYC; **515** (t)Dr. Tony Brain/Science Photo Library/Photo Researchers, (b)Robert Becker/Custom Medical Stock Photo.

Chapter 19 - 518-9 Bob Daemmrich/Stock Boston; **519** Aaron Haupt; **521** Chris Noble/Tony Stone Images; **523** Dick Luria/FPG; **527** (t)Boehringer Ingelheim International GmbH, photo Lennart Nilsson, THE INCREDIBLE MACHINE, National Geographic Society, (b)PhotoEdit; **528** (l)Aaron Haupt, (c)Custom Medical Stock Photo, (r)Custom Medical Stock Photo; **529** American Cancer Society/Mark Burnett; **530** Amanita Pictures; **531** PhotoEdit; **532** National Oceanic & Atmospheric Administration; **538** Aaron Haupt; **539** Matt Meadows; **540** American Cancer Society/Mark Burnett; **541** Peter Serling.

Chapter 20 - 544-5 David Young-Wolfe/PhotoEdit; **552** Jose L. Pelaez/The Stock Market; **553** Aaron Haupt; **558** Prof. P.

Motta/Dept. of Anatomy/University La Sapienza, Rome/Science Photo Library/Photo Researchers; **559** Michael Newman/PhotoEdit; **560 561** Amanita Pictures; **565** (l)National Geographic Society/Photo by Matt Muspratt/PhotoAssist Inc/Hearing aid courtesy Telex Communications, (r)Pat Moore/Starkey Laboratories Inc.; **567** Prof. P. Motta/Dept. of Anatomy/University La Sapienza, Rome/Science Photo Library/Photo Researchers.

Chapter 21 - 570-1 Jim Cummins/FPG; **571** Mark Burnett; **572** (t)Ray Coleman/Photo Researchers, (c)1998 SYGMA, (b)Brooks Kraft; **574** Dr. Tony Brain/Science Photo Library/Photo Researchers; **575** Prof. P. Motta/Dept. of Anatomy/Univ. La Sapienza, Rome/Science Photo Library/Photo Researchers; **577** John Henley/The Stock Market; **580** David M. Phillips/Science Source/Photo Researchers; **581** Russell D. Curtis/Photo Researchers; **583** Lennart Nilsson, THE INCREDIBLE MACHINE, National Geographic Society; **584** Joe Baker/FPG; **587** Penny Gentieu/Tony Stone Images; **588** James Levin/FPG; **589** (t)Arthur Tilley/FPG, (bl)Mark Burnett, (blc)Steve Smith/FPG, (brc)Mark Burnett, (br)Doug Martin; **590** Ariel Skelley/The Stock Market; **591** Paul S. Howell/Liaison International; **592** Phil Schofield/AllStock/PNI; **594** (t)Brooks Kraft/Sygma, (b)Prof. P. Motta/Dept. of Anatomy/University La Sapienza, Rome/Science Photo Library/Photo Researchers; **595** (t)Lennart Nilsson, THE INCREDIBLE MACHINE, National Geographic Society, (bl)James Levin/FPG, (br)Ariel Skelley/The Stock Market.

Chapter 22 - 598-9 Oliver Meckes/Photo Researchers; **599** Aaron Haupt; **602** Ted Horowitz/The Stock Market; **603** Dwight R. Kuhn/DRK Photo; **604** Science VU/Visuals Unlimited; **609** (t)Aaron Haupt, (b)Mary Kate Denny/PhotoEdit; **610** Oliver Meckes/E.O.S./Gelderblom/Photo Researchers; **611** (l)Will & Deni McIntyre/Photo Researchers, (r)Kairos, Latin Stock/Science Photo Library/Photo Researchers; **612** Geoff Butler; **613** Doug Martin; **614** (l)Erich Schrempp/Photo Researchers, (r)SIU/Visuals Unlimited; **615** (l)Mug Shots/The Stock Market, (r)J. Chiasson-Liats/Liaison International; **616** Amanita Pictures; **617** (t)Amanita Pictures, (b)Dr. P. Marazzi/Science Photo Library/Photo Researchers; **618** (tl)Myrleen Ferguson/PhotoEdit, (tr)Doug Martin, (b)Mak 1; **619** (t)Rob Crandall/The Image Works, (b)Jean-Marc Giboux/Liaison International; **620** (t)W. Hill Jr./The Image Works, (c)Marc Romanelli/The Image Bank, (b)Michal Heron/The Stock Market; **621** (t)Michael Newman/PhotoEdit, (bl)Jonathan Nourok/PhotoEdit, (br)Michael Newman/PhotoEdit; **622** (t)Dwight R. Kuhn/DRK Photo, (b)Science VU/Visuals Unlimited; **623** (t)Oliver Meckes/E.O.S./Gelderblom/Photo Researchers, (b)Erich Schrempp/Photo Researchers.

The Periodic Table

PERIODIC TABLE OF THE ELEMENTS

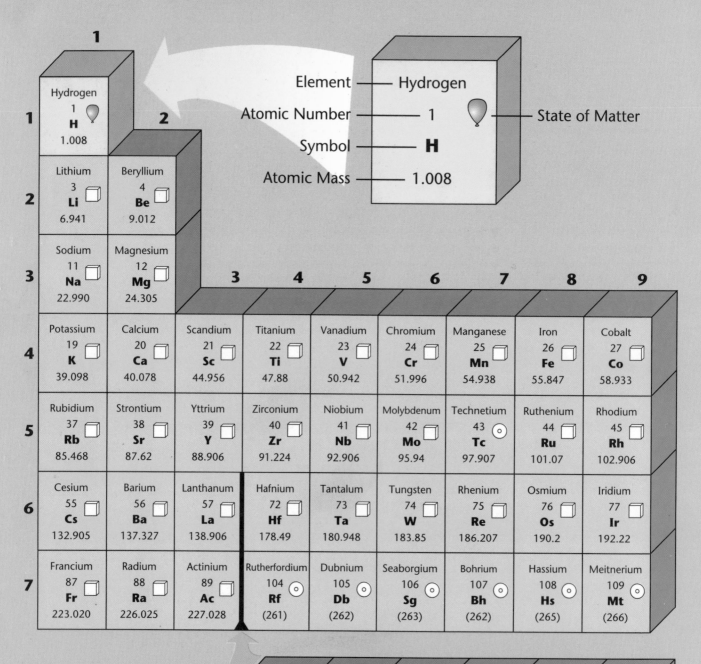